Cerneauism and American Freemasonry

Cerneauism and American Freemasonry

Westphalia Press
An imprint of Policy Studies Organization
1527 New Hampshire Ave NW
Washington, DC 20036
info@ipsonet.org

ISBN: 978-1-63391-943-3

Front cover design by Steve Adams:
EsotericEditions.com

Back cover design by Jeffrey Barnes
jbarnesbook.design

Daniel Gutierrez-Sandoval, Executive Director
Policy Studies Organization & Westphalia Press

Joseph Cerneau of Villeblevin, France, was a refugee to New York from Cuba. He established high-degree bodies in New York in 1807, and created his own Supreme Council of the Scottish Rite in 1813, which attracted many well-known and influential Masons, to the chagrin of the Supreme Council at Charleston. — Original portrait by Travis Simpkins, 32°

Also from Westphalia Press
westphaliapress.org

Brethren: Behold Your Supreme Council: Bio-Bibliographical Dictionary of the SGIG and Deputies of the Supreme Council, 33°

A Study in American Freemasonry

ESOTERIKA by Albert Pike: The Symbolism of the Blue Degrees of Freemasonry

Ancient Mysteries and Modern Masonry: The Collected Writings of Jewel P. Lightfoot

Essay on The Mysteries and the True Object of The Brotherhood of Freemasons

James Hoban's Secret Society

Female Emancipation and Masonic Membership: An Essential Collection

The Rosicrucian Philosophy in Questions and Answers

Freemasonry, Heir to the Enlightenment

Grand Crosses of the Court of Honour: Concise Scottish Rite Biographical Dictionary

Masonic Myths and Legends

A Radical In The East

Brought to Light: The Mysterious George Washington Masonic Cave

Worlds of Print: The Moral Imagination of an Informed Citizenry, 1734 to 1839

History of the Grand Orient of Italy

Why Thirty-Three?: Searching for Masonic Origins

A Place in the Lodge: Dr. Rob Morris, Freemasonry and the Order of the Eastern Star

The Great Transformation: Scottish Freemasonry 1725-1810

The 33 Principles Every Mason Should Live By: The True Meaning of Being a Mason

Masonic Regularity and Recognition: A Global Issue

Getting the Third Degree: Fraternalism, Freemasonry and History

Dudley Wright: Writer, Truthseeker & Freemason

Freemasonry: A French View

Cerneauism
and
American Freemasonry

Essays by
Alain Bernheim, 33°, Arturo de Hoyos, 33°, G∴C∴
S. Brent Morris, 33°, G∴C∴, and Michael R. Poll, 32°
from Heredom, *the Transactions of the*
Scottish Rite Research Society

Edited by

Arturo de Hoyos, 33°, G∴C∴ & S. Brent Morris, 33°, G∴C∴

WESTPHALIA PRESS
An imprint of
Policy Studies Organization

CONTENTS

ACKNOWLEDGEMENTS

"An Introduction to Cerneauism" is based on Arturo de Hoyos and S. Brent Morris, *Committed to the Flames: The History and Rituals of a Secret Masonic Rite* (Shepperton: Lewis Masonic, 2008).

"The Controversy of Joseph Cerneau: A Brief Examination" by Michael R. Poll was first published in *Heredom,* volume 4 (1995).

"An Introduction to Joseph Cerneau and His Biographers" by Alain Bernheim was first published in *Heredom,* volume 6 (1997).

"The Early Years of the Grand Consistory of Louisiana (1811–1815)" by Michael R. Poll was first published in *Heredom,* volume 8 (1999–2000).

"The Early Years of the Grand Consistory of Louisiana (1811–1815)—A Rejoinder" by Arturo de Hoyos was first published in *Heredom,* volume 9 (2001).

"A Few 'Rejoinder' Comments" by Michael R. Poll was first published in *Heredom,* volume 9 (2001).

"The Supreme Council of the 43rd Degree" by Arturo de Hoyos was first published in *Heredom,* volume 25 (2017).

"James Foulhouze: S.G.C. of the Supreme Council of Louisiana" by Michael R. Poll was first published in *Heredom,* volume 6 (1997).

"Joseph Cerneau, Part 1—His Grand Consistory's Minute Book" by Alain Bernheim was first published in *Heredom,* volume 18 (2010).

"Joseph Cerneau, Part 2—The Charleston Gr. Council P.R.S. & the Supreme Council of the U.S.A." by Alain Bernheim was first published in *Heredom,* volume 20 (2012).

"The Union of 1867" by Arturo deHoyos was first published in *Heredom,* volume 4 (1995).

An Introduction to Cerneauism

Arturo de Hoyos, 33°, G.·.C.·. &

S. Brent Morris, 33°, G.·.C.·.

The articles in this book focus on a type of Freemasonry that has long been a subject of controversy. Known as *Cerneauism,* it refers to Scottish Rite bodies which derived authority from Joseph Cerneau (1763–1840/45), a Frenchman who was the charter master of *La Temple des Vertus Theologalis* No. 103, a Pennsylvania lodge in Havana, Cuba. He fled to New York after being expelled from Cuba in 1806, after fleeing there from the slave rebellion in Haiti in 1802. The central issue with Cerneauism is the question of authority, i.e., the right to create and govern Masonic organizations. Masonic bodies worldwide maintain that the right and authority to create and preside over rites, orders, and systems must stem from a just and regular succession, with adherence to applicable constitutions, laws, and statutes. Cerneauism was a challenge to the concept of regularity because Joseph Cerneau did not personally possess any authority within the Scottish Rite, nor did he accept its governing constitutions. In spite of this, his self-created "supreme council" both flourished and claimed many prominent members who made valuable contributions to Freemasonry.

Although the full details of the Scottish Rite's origins are not known we do know that Col. John Mitchell and the Rev. Frederick Dalcho, acting under the *Constitutions of 1786,* opened "the Supreme Council of the 33d Degree for the United States of America" on May 31, 1801, in Charleston, South Carolina.[1] As the first supreme council in the world the Supreme Council at Charleston, now known as the Supreme Council, 33°, Southern Jurisdiction, is also affectionately known as the "Mother Supreme Council." The Scottish Rite, which has thirty-three degrees, has become the most widely practiced form of Masonry worldwide. Col. Mitchell and Rev. Dalcho were high officers in the "Order of the Royal Secret," an earlier Masonic system of twenty-five degrees, dating to the 1760s.[2] The Scottish Rite superseded that earlier system.[3] The *Constitutions of 1786* authorized two supreme councils in the United States but also mandated that no Scottish Rite Mason could exercise authority in any country where a supreme council existed without first obtaining its permission.[4] As the first supreme council in the world, and the only one in United States, the Supreme Council at Charleston possessed the sovereign Scottish Rite power and authority for the whole of the United States, and was content to wait until the right moment to create another supreme council and divide its territory. That moment, however, would come as the result of unexpected occurrences.

1. *Circular throughout the two Hemispheres* (Charleston, S.C., 1802). For a photo reproduction, see Ray Baker Harris, *History of the Supreme Council, 33°—1801–1861* (Washington, DC: The Supreme Council, 1964), 319–25.

2. See Arturo de Hoyos, *Freemasonry's Royal Secret* (Washington, DC: Scottish Rite Research Society, 2014).

3. For a brief history of the origins of the Scottish Rite, see Arturo de Hoyos, *Scottish Rite Ritual Monitor and Guide,* 3d ed. (Washington, DC: Supreme Council, 33°), 100–108.

4. Cerneau violated several of the statutes governing Supreme Councils: "9th. No Deputy Inspector can use his patent, in any Country, where a Supreme Council of Inspectors General is established — unless it shall be signed by the said Council.— 10th. No Deputy Inspector heretofore appointed, or who may hereafter be appointed, by virtue of this Constitution, shall have power to grant patents nor to give the degree of K.H. or the higher degrees— 11th. The Degree of K.H. and the Degrees of Prince of the Royal Secret <are> never to be given but in the presence of 3 Sovereign Grand Inspectors General. [...] 17th. No Inspector General possesses any Individual power in a Country where a Supreme Council is established, as a Majority of their Votes is necessary to give legality to their proceedings—. Except by Virtue of a patent granted for special purposes by the Council; & except the Sovn. Grand Comr. as is provided by in Art. 13." See Ray Baker Harris, *History of the Supreme Council, 33°—1801–1861* (Washington, DC: Supreme Council, 33°, S.J., 1964), 337–46.

Opportunists in New York

On February 21, 1802 the Supreme Council at Charleston created a Supreme Council of the "French West India Islands" with Alexandre François Auguste De Grasse-Tilly as grand commander.[5] A few years later, in August 1806, Antoine Bideaud, who was one of its members, visited New York City and found an opportunity to make a little extra money. He conferred the Scottish Rite degrees on J. J. J. Gourgas and four other Frenchmen for $46 each and then created a "Sublime Grand Consistory 30°; 31°; and 32°." Bideaud's Scottish Rite authority was for the islands only and did not extend into New York, which remained under the jurisdiction of the Charleston Supreme Council. In the words of J. J. J. Gourgas, who was one of the participants:

> This act of Bideaud's was completely irregular, unconstitutional. He had no right or power within any part of the United States of America, but then he was tempted and did succumb at the rate of five times $46, or $230. As to us, we were then new and raw in these matters, believing all was right....[6]

The principal officers of the Bideaud Grand Consistory were J. J. J. Gourgas, Daniel D. Tompkins, Sampson Simson, and Richard Riker. This act would eventually lead to the creation of another supreme council in the United States.[7]

After leaving Cuba Joseph Cerneau moved to New York City in 1807 with his family, and affiliated with Washington Lodge No. 21 in 1810.[8] In October 1807, Cerneau constituted a "Sovereign Grand Consistory of Sublime Princes of the Royal Secret." Cerneau had previously been made a "Deputy Grand Inspector, for the Northern part of the Island of Cuba" under the Order of the Royal Secret. His patent (preserved in the Archives of the Supreme Council, 33°, S.J.), reveals that his authority was limited to conferring the 4° through 24°

5. *Circular throughout the two Hemispheres* (Charleston, S.C., 1802), 5. The patent was transcribed in the register of Frederick Dalcho, folios 38v–41r (archives of the Supreme Council, 33°, SJ, Washington, DC), and reprinted in *Official Bulletin of the Supreme Council of the 33d Degree, for the Southern Jurisdiction of the United States* vol. 7 (1887), 726–27.

6. Manuscript of J. J. J. Gourgas, quoted in Robert Freke Gould, Adolphus Frederick Alexander Woodford, William James Hughan, et al., *A Library of Freemasonry: Comprising Its History, Antiquities, Symbols, Constitutions, Customs, Etc., and Concordant Orders of Royal Arch, Knights Templar, A. A. S. Rite, Mystic Shrine, with Other Important Masonic Information of Value to the Fraternity* [...] (John C. Yorston, 1911), vol. 5, 301.

7. *Abstract of Proceedings of the Supreme Council. United States* (Portland: Stephen Berry, 1876).

8. Robert W. Reid, *Washington Lodge No. 21, F. & A. M. and Some of its Members* (New York: Washington Lodge, 1911)

on lodge officers, and the 25° once a year.[9] Cerneau somehow learned that all twenty-five degrees of the Order of the Royal Secret had been subsumed by the Scottish Rite. With even less authority than Bideaud, Cerneau launched his foray into high-degree Masonry in New York when he created the "Grand Consistory of Supreme Chiefs of Exalted Masonry" in October 1807. Cerneau knew that the 25° of the Order of the Royal Secret had became the 32° of the Scottish Rite. This created a solution, since he might argue that his members held equivalent degrees. The primary officers of the Cerneau Grand Consistory included Cerneau, DeWitt Clinton, John W. Mulligan, and Cadwallader D. Colden.

Complicating the situation of the rival and equally illegitimate consistories were the personal, political, and Masonic rivalries of their principal officers.[10] Tompkins as governor of New York was succeeded by Clinton, his lieutenant governor; Clinton as grand master of New York was followed by Tompkins. Simson and Mulligan opposed each other in grand lodge; Mulligan defeated Simson as grand treasurer in 1814, but Simson regained the office in 1815. Colden was assistant attorney general in 1798 and replaced Riker as district attorney in 1811; Riker regained the position in 1812.

Clinton and Tompkins, essentially figureheads in Freemasonry, were shrewd politicians who allied themselves as needed to meet their political preferment. Mulligan and Simson were adversaries in the Grand Lodge of New York. The professional paths of Colden and Riker were continually crossing and soon we find their political reactions antagonistic.

LEGITIMACY IN THE NORTH

In 1809 Cerneau, who was not a Scottish Rite Mason, disregarded the Mother Supreme Council at Charleston, and published that his Sovereign Grand Consistory was the only authority within the United States with the right to confer the thirty-three degrees.[11] He did not explain how a grand consis-

9. See Appendix 1.

10. This Masonic and political rivalry is explored in Samuel Harrison Baynard, Jr., *History of the Supreme Council, 33°*, 2 vols. (Boston: The Supreme Council, 1938), vol. 1, 181–83.

11. "... the right of granting Constitutional patents for Masonic Institutions within the United States of America, their territories & dependencies, from the Secret Master, Fourth Degree, to that of Grand Inspector General, Thirty Third, both inclusive, exists only with the Sov. Gr. Consistory of Sup. Chiefs of Exalted Masonry." Extract from the Oct. 28, 1809, minutes of the "Most Potent

tory had authority over the Thirty-third Degree. Aware of his error, in 1813 he announced the formation of what he called a Supreme Council of Grand Inspectors General of the Thirty-third Degree for the United States of America. Cerneau's new organization similarly claimed sole authority over the whole of "United States of America, its Territories and Dependencies." In this body both Clinton and Colden were given high official posts. At one point it was limited to members of the schismatic St. John's Grand Lodge of New York (later healed by Killian Henry Van Rensselaer and Giles Fonda Yates[12]). Subsequently it contracted to only control New York State, encouraging the formation of independent supreme councils in each state, and then re-expanded to again cover the entire country. In 1853 it chartered two Blue Lodges in New York City, which may have sealed its fate as forever illegitimate.

In 1813 Emanuel de la Motta, 33°, Grand Treasurer of the Supreme Council at Charleston, traveled to New York City for his health. While there he found the two competing consistories, each created without authorization from Charleston. He examined the two groups and "healed" the Bideaud organization, making it legitimate. His actions were subsequently confirmed by the Mother Supreme Council.[13]

On May 1, 1813, De La Motta initiated J. J. J. Gourgas and Sampson Simson into the Thirty-third Degree.[14] Then, on August 5, De La Motta, acting as

Grand Consistory of the Sup. Chiefs of Exalted Masonry of the Ancient Constitutional Scottish Rite of Heredom for the United States of America, their Territories and Dependencies" as quoted in Robert B. Folger, *A History of the Ancient and Accepted Scottish Rite in the United States: More Especially as Connected with the Operations of the so-called Cerneau Supreme Council from its Organization in New York, in 1807 to its Final Absorption into the Supreme Council of the Northern Jurisdiction of the U.S. in 1867* (Unpublished Typescript prepared for E. T. Carson, Cincinnati, 1877), 74; emphasis added. Original in the archives of the Supreme Council, 33°, NMJ; copy in the Archives of the Supreme Council, 33°, S.J.

12. See the certificate of healing and regularization at Van Gordon-Williams Library and Archives Digital Collection, digital VGW, accessed July 28, 2020, *https://digitalvgw.omeka.net/items/show/442*

13. The "healing" instrument is transcribed in Samuel H. Baynard, Jr., *History of the Supreme Council, 33°* (Boston: Supreme Council, N.M.J., 1938), vol. 1, 170–74. In 1814 Emanuel De La Motta and the Supreme Council at Charleston issued a manifesto reiterating the action. For a photograph of the document, see digitalVGW, accessed July 28, 2020, *https://digitalvgw.omeka.net/items/show/228*

14. J. J. J. Gourgas, and others of his Council, may have irregularly received the 33° as early as 1809, and their initiation into the 33° by Emanuel De La Motta may have been an attempt to "heal" them. In a letter dated January 26, 1830, Gourgas admitted to Holbrook that he had received "The history of the 33d[,] Secret Consitns &c." from France and Kingston, Jamaica. The *Secret Constitutions*

grand commander in a "special sitting," initiated four others and "The Supreme Council of the Thirty-third Degree for the Northern Masonic District and Jurisdiction" was organized, with New York Governor (and later Vice President) Daniel D. Tompkins as grand commander. On May 21, 1814, this supreme council reopened and proceeded to "nominate, elect, appoint, install and proclaim, in due, legal and ample form" the elected officers "as forming the second Grand and Supreme Council...." Finally, the charter of the Northern Masonic Jurisdiction (written January 7, 1815, in Gourgas's hand) added, "We think the Ratification ought to be dated 21st day May 5815."[15]

As will be seen in the articles in this book, the two supreme councils continued side-by-side for years, usually as bitter rivals, each having their ups and downs, though the Cerneau faction had the more productive existence between about 1813 and 1832. There were splits, factions, and defections on both sides. Neither side was diplomatic in language, and each seemed to delight in bold, public condemnations of the other. Finally in 1867, after decades of feuding, the two sides peacefully united to form the current Supreme Council, 33°, for the Northern Masonic Jurisdiction of the United States. But, as we shall see, claims to Cerneau authority were far from dead.

Cerneauism in Louisiana

In early 1804 Jean-Baptiste Marie Delahogue, who was lieutenant grand commander of the Supreme Council of the French West Indies, and formerly a member of the Supreme Council at Charleston was granted a patent by Charleston, empowering him to initiate members and create lodges, chapters,

were a confidential document delivered *only* to people who had received the 33°. Each recipient of this document signed an oath swearing to keep it secret from anyone who had not received the 33°. This may explain why, years earlier, in a January 17, 1814, letter written by Gourgas, he asked De La Motta, "We should be glad to know what your ideas are *at present* respecting our Recognition in the 33d by your Supreme Council at Charleston, as it would be a very desirable thing to bring it about as soon as possible on account of the peculiar Situation at this Grand East of New York." The letter was signed by Sampson Simson, John G. Tardy, Richard Riker, and J. J. J. Gourgas, *none of them signing as a 33°*, but only as Knights Kadosh, Princes of the Royal Secret, and Deputy Inspectors General, *all titles of the Order of the Royal Secret.*

15. For the documents cited see Charles S. Lobingier, *The Supreme Council, 33°, Mother Council of the World, Ancient and Accepted Scottish Rite of Freemasonry, Southern Jurisdiction, U.S.A.* (Louisville, KY: Standard Printing Co., 1931), 60–68. The actual charter, with Gourgas's ratification note, is in the Archives of the Supreme Council, 33°, S.J.

and councils up to the 18th Degree in New Orleans.[16] He exercised his authority on several persons (including Pierre Chamau and Jean-Baptiste Modeste Lefebvre). On August 13, 1810, Gabriel Jastram, a member of the Supreme Council in Kingston, Jamaica, (created by de Grasse-Tilly, with authority from Charleston), chartered *La Bienfaisance Lodge*, and on December 20 of the same year he chartered a chapter of Rose Croix under the name *La Triple Bienfaisance*.[17] On March 28, 1811 Lusson and Lefebvre created a "Grand Consistory of Princes of the Royal Secret of Louisiana" submissive to the authority of the Supreme Council at Charleston.[18]

The precedence of Lusson's and Lefebvre's grand consistory notwithstanding, a Cerneau branch of the Scottish Rite body would soon be formed there which succeeded in luring some of the Charleston members away. As Alain Bernheim noted, "on 4 December 1812, Emanuel Gigaud … had formed a provisional Grand Council of Princes of the Royal Secret in New Orleans, which petitioned the New York Grand Consistory presided by Joseph Cerneau for a Charter on 8 February 1813."[19] Bernheim deduced that members of the Cerneau Scottish Rite would have been aware that there were two grand lodges in South Carolina, and that the members of the Charleston body belonged to the one which was not generally considered regular (although they later merged). This would have provided strong reasons for persons interested in the Scottish Rite to join the Cerneau bodies.

Over the next several years Cerneau's grand council in New Orleans enjoyed an active existence. During this time John H. Holland (grand master of Louisiana, and grand commander of the Cerneau Grand Council) corresponded with J. J. J. Gourgas (grand secretary of the Supreme Council, NMJ) and Moses Holbrook (grand commander of the Supreme Council at Charleston). In an 1828 letter to Gourgas, Holland explained that although his group had been

16. *Transactions of the Supreme Council of the 33d Degree, Ancient an Accepted Scottish Rite of Free-Masonry, for the Southern Jurisdiction of the United States of America. 1857 to 1866. Reprinted.* (Washington: Joseph L. Pearson, 1878), 18–19.

17. Gould, Woodford, Hughan, et al., *A Library of Freemasonry* […] (John C. Yorston, 1911), vol. 5, 299.

18. Gould, Woodford, Hughan, et al., *A Library of Freemasonry* […] (John C. Yorston, 1911), vol. 5, 299.

19. Alain Bernheim, Introduction to James B. Scot, *Outline of the Rise and Progress of Freemasonry in Louisiana* […] (New Orleans: Clarke and Hofelein, 1873; Reprint ed., Michael R. Poll, 1995), 13.

taught that the Supreme Council at Charleston was irregular, recent events required a reevaluation. Holland noted that he had sent many letters to the Cerneau Grand Consistory in New York, but that they had gone unanswered for three years.[20] The correspondence with Gourgas and Holbrook was cordial and fraternal. In a letter to Holbrook, written about a year and a half later, Holland proposed bringing his bodies under the authority of Charleston,[21] to which Holbrook cautiously responded. The terms under which the New Orleans Consistory could be healed and received by Charleston were discussed by Holbrook and Gourgas, with the latter summarizing them in a letter.[22] On February 21, 1831, the Louisiana Cerneau "Grand Consistory" (as it was now called) determined to come under the authority of Charleston.

THE SUPREME COUNCIL OF LOUISIANA

The relationship between the grand consistory and Charleston was to be short-lived. On November 16, 1827, the Italian-born Orazio Donato de Attellis Marquis de Santangelo received his Thirty-third Degree in New York from Joseph Cerneau,[23] and during the same year Cerneau's New York bodies ceased to function.[24] Five years later, in 1832, "an attempt was made … to gather together the fragments of the former Supreme Council and Consistory."[25] As a member of Cerneau's former supreme council, de Santangelo served on a committee "for the purpose of entering into and concluding a treaty of union and compact" between his own supreme council and the mysterious "Supreme Council for Terra Firma, South America, the Canary Islands, Porto Rico, etc.,"[26]

20. *John H. Holland, New Orleans, Louisiana, October 30, 1828, to J. J. J. Gourgas, New York, New York.* Copy in the archives of the Supreme Council, 33°, S.J., Washington, DC.

21. *John H. Holland, New Orleans, Louisiana, February 19, 1830, to Moses Holbrook, Charleston, South Carolina.* A copy of this letter was transcribed by Holbrook and sent to Gourgas on March 10, 1830. Copy in the archives of the Supreme Council, 33°, S.J., Washington, DC.

22. *J. J. J. Gourgas, New York, New York, March 27, 1830, to Moses Holbrook, Charleston, South Carolina.* Copy in the archives of the Supreme Council, 33°, S.J., Washington, DC.

23. Scot, *Outline of the Rise and Progress*, 53.

24. Robert B. Folger, *The Ancient and Accepted Scottish Rite in Thirty-three Degrees* 2d ed. (New York, 1862, 1881), 205.

25. Folger, *The Ancient and Accepted Scottish Rite in Thirty-three Degrees* 2d ed. (1881), 217.

26. Julius F. Sachse, *Ancient Documents Relating to the A. and A. Scottish Rite in the Archives of the R. W. Grand Lodge of Free and Accepted Masons of Pennsylvania* (Philadelphia, 1915), 232–46.

about which very little is known.[27] The two bodies joined and were known as the "United Supreme Council for the Western Hemisphere," sometimes also called the "Elias Hicks Supreme Council." This new council used the term "Scotch Rite" which would be adopted by other Cerneau supreme councils.[28]

In September 1832 de Santangelo visited the New Orleans consistory, as a representative of Elias Hicks, when he spoke on the history of the high degrees in America, and convinced the members of the consistory that the Cerneau bodies were regular. After some deliberation the members resolved to recognize the Hicks Supreme Council for the Western Hemisphere. After the Hicks council was said to be "slumbering," de Santangelo and four others formed a supreme council in New Orleans in 1839. It was initially called the "Supreme Council of the United States"[29] but was afterwards known as the Supreme Council of Louisiana. In 1846 the grand consistory placed itself under the jurisdiction of the Supreme Council of Louisiana.[30]

In February 1840 the Supreme Council of Louisiana addressed a baluster to the Supreme Council of France, in which they notified them of their adhesion to a "Treaty of Masonic, Alliance and Confederation," made in Paris in 1834. The Supreme Council of Louisiana demanded recognition and their admission to the treaty.[31] On July 25, 1845 the Supreme Council of France issued a decree in which it not only declined to admit the Supreme Council of Louisiana to

27. The grand commander of this supreme council, Count de St. Laurent (Maria-Anthonio-Alexandro-Roberto-de Jachim de Santa Rosa de Roume de St. Laurent), was made grand commander of this supreme council by Alexandre François Auguste De Grasse-Tilly on August 16, 1816. See Sachse, *Ancient Documents*, 218–20.

28. The term first appears in the "New Institutes Secret and Fundamental" (i.e., the Latin version of the *Grand Constitutions of 1786*) adopted by Hick's Supreme Council, and later re-translated as "Scottish Rite" in the version used in the Southern Jurisdiction. See Sachse, *Ancient Documents*, 213, 214, 215. This explains the unusual title of Jonathan Blanchard's exposure of Cerneau rituals in *Scotch Rite Masonry Illustrated*, 2 vols. (Chicago: Ezra A. Cook, 1888). For the names of the successive Cerneau councils see vol. 1, 124, 145, 303, 358, 419, 436; vol. 2, 137, 242, 287, 340, 388, 445, 462, 464, 470, 472, 475.

29. C. T. McClenachan, "Ancient Accepted Scottish Rite," in *Proceedings of the Supreme Council [...] for the Northern Masonic Jurisdiction* [...] (Binghamton, NY: George J. Reid, 1881), Appendix, 134; Claude P. Samory, "Address," in *Proceedings of the Annual Session of the Supreme Council of Sovereign Grand Inspectors General, 33d and Last Degree of the Ancient and Accepted Rite, for the Southern Jurisdiction of the U.S.A. Held in the Valley of New Orleans, on the 20th, 21st and 23d days of the month called "Sebat," A.·.M.·. 5617, corresponding to the 14th, 15th and 17th days of February, in the Vulgar Era, 1857* (New Orleans: Printed at the Bulletin Book and Job Office, 1857), 18.

30. Scot, *Outline of the Rise and Progress*, 59.

31. Samory, "Address," in *Proceedings* (1857), 19.

the Masonic Alliance of 1834, but declared "said Supreme Council to be spurious, clandestine, and illegal." In the words of Claude P. Samory,[32] who was lieutenant grand commander of the Supreme Council of Louisiana, "Thus, the so-called Supreme Council for the United States of America, otherwise, the late Supreme Council of New Orleans, has never been recognized by the Supreme Council of France, nor by the Masonic bodies who were parties to the Treaty of 1834."[33]

The Cerneau Supreme Council Revived

On October 27, 1846, the Cerneau Elias Hicks Supreme Council, which gave birth to the Cerneau Supreme Council of Louisiana, divided its funds among its four remaining members and disbanded.[34] Henry Atwood and others from St. John's Grand Lodge, a schismatic grand lodge in New York, stepped into this breach and revived the supreme council on May 15, 1849, on the theory that Scottish Rite authority reverted to the 33° Inspectors General with the dissolution of the Supreme Council. Atwood was elected grand commander. Robert B. Folger later claimed the revival was in 1846, but this could hardly be so as all except Atwood received their 33° the summer of 1848.[35]

The revolt of St. John's Grand Lodge had resulted in its members being shut out of most of the Masonic activities in New York State. Atwood tried to address this by using his position in the revived Cerneau Supreme Council to reward St. John's members with the 33°. Eventually the Grand Lodge of New York and St. John's Grand Lodge settled their differences, and Atwood was restored to Craft legitimacy. More than that, since he had served as grand master of St. John's Grand Lodge, he was given the rank of past grand master in the merged grand lodge.

32. Samory's father, Claude N. Samory, was treasurer the lodge *La Candeur, No. 12*, Charleston, SC, which was founded by Jean-Baptiste Marie Delahogue, whom I previously noted was lieutenant grand commander of the Supreme Council of the French West Indies, and formerly a member of the Supreme Council at Charleston.

33. Samory, "Address," in *Proceedings* (1857), 19.

34. Folger, *The Ancient and Accepted Scottish Rite,* 2d ed. (1881), 226–27.

35. Folger, "Recollections," part 16, *New York Dispatch,* Dec. 7, 1873, part 18, Jan. 4, 1874, and part 30, May 24, 1874.

The Fatal Step

On October 28, 1852, Atwood was grand commander of the Cerneau Supreme Council and reorganized again and created the "Supreme Council for the Sovereign, Free, and Independent State of New York." He was influenced in this change of territorial control by James Foulhouze, grand commander of the "Louisiana State Supreme Council, Scottish Rite." Foulhouze, who received his Thirty-third Degree from the Grand Orient of France in 1845,[36] had a goal to have a supreme council in every state in control of both the higher degrees and the Scottish Rite symbolic degrees, and New York was the first state to sign on to this program.[37]

It was at this point that the Cerneau Supreme Council took what would eventually be a fatal action: it chartered two Craft lodges in New York. Atwood's motivation was probably power—to have complete control over all of Masonry from 1° to 33°, but he genuinely may have been convinced by Foulhouze that the Scottish Rite had abdicated its responsibility to govern the Craft. In any event Atwood persuaded the Supreme Council to change its position against Craft lodges, and on March 8, 1853, the minutes clearly record the chartering of two Craft lodges, St. John the Forerunner and *La Sincérité*.[38] The Grand Lodge of New York vigorously responded, and soon condemnations came in from other grand lodges.[39]

The effect of this was to give additional ammunition to the Northern Masonic Jurisdiction, the descendants of Bideaud and Gourgas: not only was the Cerneau Supreme Council without a legitimate charter, but also they did not respect grand lodge sovereignty by chartering Craft lodges. Finally in 1867, after more than fifty years of feuding, the two sides peacefully united to form

36. Foulhouze related the incident of his reception of the thirty-third degree from the Grand Orient of France in 1845 in his *Historical Inquiry into the Origin of the Ancient and Accepted Scotch Rite (New Orleans: The True Delta Job Office, 1859), 60–61.*

37. Enoch T. Carson, "History of Ancient and Accepted Scottish Rite Masonry in the United States," in *The History of Freemasonry*, R. F. Gould et al., eds., 4 vols. (New York: John C. Yorston, 1889), 4:675.

38. Minutes of the Cerneau Supreme Council [Second Atwood Council], Mar. 8, 1853, Transcript in the hand of Robert B. Folger, Collection Number SC012, Archives, Supreme Council, A.A.S.R., N.M.J., USA, Lexington, Mass.

39. *Transaction of the Grand Lodge of New York, F. & A.M., from July 8th, A.L. 5852 to June 11th, AL. 5853* (New York: Robert Macoy, Printer, 1853), 65–66, 237; *Proceedings of the Grand Lodge of Alabama* (Montgomery, AL.: Masonic Signet Office, 1853), 19.

the current Supreme Council, 33°, for the Northern Masonic Jurisdiction of the United States.

THE CONCORDAT OF 1855

The grand commander of the Supreme Council of Louisiana during its most fateful period was James Foulhouze, In an effort to bring harmony to high grade Masonry Grand Master John Gedge contacted Albert G. Mackey in Charleston with the intent of organizing a new consistory in New Orleans. The new body was formed on December 24, 1851 and established on February 2, 1851.[40] In his own words Foulhouze resigned "both as Grand Commander and member of this Supreme Council" on July 30, 1853,[41] and would later be expelled by the Grand Orient of France in 1859.[42] He was succeeded in office by Charles Claiborne.

Weary of the conflicts and controversies surrounding the Scottish Rite the members of the new consistory sought reconciliation with their separated brethren. John Gedge initiated this action by making cordial overtures[43] to the members of the Supreme Council of Louisiana. In view of the resolution of grand lodge conflicts in the recent past, the new consistory established by Charleston in New Orleans, and the resignation of James Foulhouze only a few months earlier, the Supreme Council of Louisiana was willing to reconsider its position.

40. A copy of the warrant is in the Archives of the Supreme Council, 33°, S.J., Washington, DC.

41. A note appended to a copy of the 73d sitting of the Supreme Council of Louisiana (January 18, 1854), sent to Albert G. Mackey, states that Foulhouze submitted his demission on July 30, 1853, and Samory gives date of final resignation date as September 21, 1853. See his "Address," in *Proceedings* (1857), 21–22. For Foulhouze's resignation letter see Folger, *The Ancient and Accepted Scottish Rite,* 2d ed. (1881), 312.

42. On February 4, 1859 Foulhouze's name was "erased from its [i.e., the Grand Orient's] book of gold," and his patent was declared "void and of no effect." See "Action Taken by the Grand Orient of France and the Supreme Council of France in the Matter of the Foulhouze Supreme Council, 1858–9," in *Official Bulletin of the Supreme Council of the 33d Degree, for the Southern Jurisdiction of the United States,* Vol. VIII ([Washington, DC]: Grand Orient of Charleston, September, 1887), No. 1, 553–73. In particular, see the "Extrait du Ballustre des trav∴ 4 Février, 1859, (E∴ V∴)" which document is reprinted and translated.

43. "I would state for your information, that the first step which was taken towards effecting a reconciliation originated with our late & much lamented Th Ill∴ Bro John Gedge, and that he was met in his disposition by the opposite party with the utmost cordiality of sentiment...." —*Edward Barnett, New Orleans, July 26, 1854, to Albert G. Mackey, Charleston, South Carolina.* Unpublished letter in the Archives of the Supreme Council, 33°, S.J., Washington, DC.

A meaningful correspondence between the two supreme councils addressed concerns respecting constitutional authority. For example, in a letter to Albert G. Mackey, the officers of the Supreme Council of Louisiana initially reasoned that since the *Constitutions of 1786*, which governed the Scottish Rite, had ostensibly been prepared prior to the Louisiana Purchase of 1803, they were entitled to a Supreme Council. The notion was quickly dismissed. In a remarkable statement they even consented that they might be irregular, in which case they would have to come under the control of the Supreme Council at Charleston. The letter, written by Charles Claiborne, grand commander of the Supreme Council of Louisiana, and others, stated:

> In order to place the Ancient & Accepted Scotch Rite on a firm & solid basis in Louisiana, & to prevent any further difficulties or controversies, it is, we believe, necessary that our Sup∴ Council be recognized by the Southern & Northern Supreme Councils, & that the Consistory established in this East by the Sup∴ Council of Charleston be merged into our Sup∴ Council; and, in case the grounds on which are based our rights to a Sup∴ Council are proven erroneous & unfounded, then our Sup∴ Council must relinquish its claims, & be merged into the Consistory established in this city by your Supreme Council.[44]

Two months later, in July, Mackey responded in his "private capacity as an Inspector General and not officially as the Secretary General of the Supreme Council." He remarked that he had consulted with Grand Commander John H. Honour, and that he could assure them that "he is prepared to meet any propositions for reconciliation ... with the most fraternal feelings." In brief, Mackey explained that he thought it probable that if they merged, the officers of the Supreme Council of Louisiana would be elected honorary members of that Charleston, upon their taking an oath of allegiance.[45] The terms and conditions of the merger were submitted to the Supreme Council of Charleston in a letter dated August 12, 1854, which was to be amended and accepted by said Council. As the anticipated merger approached letters continued to

44. *Charles Claiborne, Charles Samory, J. L. Tissot, F. A. Lumsden, C. Laffon Ladébat, A. P. Lanaux, and A. R. Morel, New Orleans, May 23, 1854, to Albert G. Mackey, Charleston, South Carolina.* Unpublished letter in the handwriting of Charles Laffon de Ladébat, in the Archives of the Supreme Council, 33°, S.J., Washington, DC.

45. *Albert G. Mackey, Charleston, South Carolina, July 14, 1854 to Charles Claiborne, New Orleans, Louisiana.* Unpublished letter in the Archives of the Supreme Council, 33°, S.J., Washington, DC.

pass between Mackey and the Supreme Council of Louisiana clarifying constitutional matters and discussing the enumerated propositions of agreement.

The Supreme Council of Louisiana worked on the "articles of Concordat & agreement" and issued a "Preamble & Resolution," prepared during their meeting of November 18, 1854, which stated that it was "Resolved that a Committee of Three be appointed with full power & authority to adopt and accept, in the name of this Consistory, the articles of the agreement or Concordat" by which it would pass under the jurisdiction of Charleston. The committee of three consisted of Laffon de Ladébat, Samory, and Morel.[46] Extracts from the minutes of the same meeting relate the instances of the Concordat and agreement. Similarly, the Grand Consistory of New Orleans under Charleston's jurisdiction resolved, at their sitting of November 25, 1854, to sign and execute the agreement and Concordat.[47]

The Concordat was sent to Charleston on January 31, 1855, and signed on February 6, 1855, by Grand Commander John H. Honour, Lieutenant Grand Commander Charles M. Furman, and Grand Secretary General Albert G. Mackey. It was then taken back to New Orleans (likely by Mackey) and signed there on February 16–17, 1855, by Grand Commander Charles Claiborne, Lieutenant Grand Commander Claude Samory, and Grand Secretary General Charles Laffon de Ladébat.[48] On the same day the Supreme Council at Charleston issued a warrant to "our well-beloved, Princes and Knights" Charles Claiborne, Claude P. Samory, Charles Laffon de Ladébat, John H. Holland, and others, creating a Grand Consistory of Louisiana, and installing them as officers with all the powers relative thereto.[49]

The Cerneau Supreme Councils "Revived"

In spite of the regular succession and authorized action which ended the existence of the Supreme Council of Louisiana, an attempt was made to somehow

46. Untitled "Preamble & Resolution," dated November 18, 1854, in the handwriting of Charles Laffon-de Ladébat. Archives of the Supreme Council, 33°, S.J., Washington, DC.

47. Untitled resolution, signed by Edward Barnett, dated November 25, 1854, copied by Charles Laffon-de Ladébat. Archives of the Supreme Council, 33°, S.J., Washington, DC.

48. See photograph of the original Concordat in Carter and Harris, *History of the Supreme Council, 33° [...] 1801–1861* (1964), 353–56.

49. See photograph of the original warrant in Carter and Harris, *History of the Supreme Council, 33° [...] 1801–1861* (1964), 359.

revive it. On October 7, 1856, over a year after the Supreme Council of Louisiana had formed its concordat with Charleston, Foulhouze (who resigned in 1853), Thomas Wharton Collens (resigned December 19, 1853)[50] and J. J. E. Massicott (resigned December 3, 1853),[51] "declared the Sup∴ Coun∴ to be still in existence and continued its works."[52] None of these former members explained how they could appoint themselves as the heads of an organization from which they voluntarily resigned, and which had authorized its own dissolution. In spite of this they reorganized and assumed the name of the now-defunct Supreme Council of Louisiana and continued.

Foulhouze's new "Supreme Council of Louisiana" was not the only attempt to revive Cerneauism. Harry Seymour, expelled from the Cerneau Supreme Council in 1865, started the Ancient and Primitive Rite of Freemasonry, an outgrowth of the Rite of Memphis of about ninety degrees. In deference to actions by the Grand Orient of France, by 1872 Seymour had reduced the rite to thirty-three degrees and was claiming to confer Scottish Rite degrees as the only legitimate successor to Joseph Cerneau.

At its September 1881 session the Supreme Council, N.M.J., voted to publish a series of articles by Charles T. McClenachan. These were a condensed history of Scottish Rite Supreme Councils that contradicted much of Folger's writings. In particular McClenachan questioned Cerneau's possession of the 33°, the sine qua non of his authority to establish a Supreme Council. McClenachan said, "It has been asserted that prior to the year 1822, at least, Joseph Cerneau had not regularly received the 33d degree, and those whose greatest interest it was to prove the contrary have failed in response." On September 20 at the same session, Albert Pike, Grand Commander, S.J. addressed the Supreme Council. In Folger's words, Pike, for the "twenty-five years past, with all the polite bitterness he was capable of expressing, and all the malice he could politely bring to bear, Denounced, Defamed, & Spit at every man that loved the name of Joseph Cerneau, and every Masonic organization

50. Folger, *The Ancient and Accepted Scottish Rite,* 2d ed., 313.

51. Folger, *The Ancient and Accepted Scottish Rite,* 2d ed., 313; see also *Proceedings of the Annual Session of the Supreme Council of Sovereign Grand Inspectors General, 33d and Last Degree of the Ancient and Accepted Rite for the Southern Jurisdiction of the U.S.A.* (New Orleans: Bulletin Book and Job Office, 1857), 22.

52. Folger, *The Ancient and Accepted Scottish Rite,* 2d ed., p 322.

that manifested the least proclivity towards the doctrines taught by his bodies or himself."[53]

McClenachan's history of Scottish Rite Supreme Councils was an assault, albeit in polite, scholarly terms, on Folger's crowning achievement as a historian. Albert Pike's mere presence was an assault on any Cerneau Mason, and it is not known what Pike may have said about Cerneau when he addressed the Supreme Council.[54]

On September 27, 1881, Folger began his last fight against the Masonic status quo. He, Hopkins Thompson, and several other old Cerneau men resigned their honorary memberships in the Supreme Council, N.M.J., withdrew their Oaths of Fealty, and revived the Cerneau Supreme Council! All this came less than eight months after Folger had printed in his history that "he [disclaimed] any partiality for either of the parties, having long since withdrawn his connection with the 'High Degrees.'" Charges were preferred against the seceders on December 19, 1881, by the Supreme Council, N.M.J., and they were expelled at the September 1882 session.[55]

Both of the Seymour and Folger Supreme Councils proudly traced their origins to Joseph Cerneau, and about this time the term *Cerneauism* was coined to describe their movement.

Epilogue

In our 2008 book, *Committed to the Flames: The History and Rituals of a Secret Masonic Rite*,[56] we wrote that Cerneauism finally died when the corrosive rivalry of the groups spilled over into the activities of other Masonic organizations. Grand lodges began asserting their authority as the ultimate arbiters of Masonic regularity within their jurisdictions. Masons in state after state were forbidden to join a Cerneau body under pain of expulsion. Even today, visitors to any lodge in Pennsylvania must swear they do not belong to any Cerneau organization before they can be admitted. Several suits were brought

53. Charles T. McClenachan, "A Synoptical History of all of the Supreme Councils that have Ever Existed, and the manner of their Formation in Chronological Order," *Proceedings of the Supreme Council, 33°, N.M.J., 1881*, 128, 4; Folger to Carson, Nov. 17, 1881.

54. *Proceedings of the Supreme Council, 33°, N.M.J., 1881*, 8–84.

55. Robert B. Folger, *The Ancient and Accepted Scottish Rite*, 2nd ed., 324.

56. Arturo de Hoyos and S. Brent Morris, *Committed to the Flames: The History and Rituals of a Secret Masonic Rite* (Shepperton: Lewis Masonic, 2008).

by Cerneauists challenging the authority of grand lodges to declare them forbidden, but each case eventually was lost. The Cerneau movement ended in 1919 when M. W. Bayliss died; he was the head of Folger's revived Cerneau Supreme Council and probably the last national Cerneau officer.

In 2013, however, more light on Cerneauism appeared when the Scottish Rite Masonic Museum & Library of the NMJ received a small gift of material related to the Thompson-Folger Supreme Council. This material shows that the Supreme Council was active as late as 1951!

The material the NMJ museum received mostly consists of pamphlets published by this Supreme Council. In one, *A Brief History of the U.S. Jurisdiction,* the author lists the eleven Sovereign Grand Commanders from 1881 until 1951, including the starting year of their term after their names:

> Those serving as Sovereign Grand Commander since Ill. Bro. [Hopkins] Thompson have been Ill. Edward W. Atwood, 1883; Ill. John B. Harris, 1885, Ill. John Haigh, 1886; Ill. John J. Gorman, 1887; Ill. William A. Hershisher, 1895, Ill. Major W. Bayliss, 1897; Ill. Dr. Thomas G. Waller, 1916; Ill. Charles S. Webster, 1934; Ill. Leon W. Van Deusen, 1935, and Ill. Andrew F. Donnell, 1944, now serving.

One letter that came with the collection is dated March 12, 1949, and is addressed to Frank B. Spengler (1881–1957) from Andrew F. Donnell (1878–1967):

> Donnell, a newspaper reporter based in Melrose, Massachusetts, served as Sovereign Grand Commander of the group from 1944 until at least 1951. Spengler, a medical doctor based in Baldwinsville, New York, was his Lieutenant Grand Commander.
>
> Both men were active in their local lodges—Donnell with the Lodge of Eleusis and Fourth Estate Lodge, Spengler with Ark Lodge No. 33. These lodges were recognized subordinate lodges of the Grand Lodge of Massachusetts and the Grand Lodge of New York, respectively. Membership inquiries to both Grand Lodges show—perhaps surprisingly—that both men died as members in good standing. Donnell was even Master of his lodge (the Lodge of Eleusis) in 1942, just two years before taking over the helm for the Cerneau Supreme Council.
>
> American grand lodges often reminded their members not to participate in unrecognized appendant bodies and sometimes with expelled members who continued to participate. At this point there is not enough other evidence to know why both men continued to enjoy their Blue Lodge membership despite their participation in a clandestine Scottish Rite body. It is possible that, for example, some time between 1951 (the latest info we have on these two men's participation with this Supreme Council) and the death of Spengler in 1957,

> that they may have been asked to choose between maintaining their Blue Lodge membership or their participation in an unrecognized Scottish Rite organization and may have chosen the former. It is also possible that, with only two subordinate bodies, the much-diminished Supreme Council may have passed below the radar of both grand lodges. It is difficult to imagine a third possibility in which these two grand lodges would have simply tolerated Donnell's and Spengler's continued leadership of the Cerneau Council.[57]

And of course, there is always the possibility there is a secret supreme council today very privately maintaining the traditions of Joseph Cerneau!

57. Jeff Croteau, "The Persistence of 'Cerneauism': The 1950s," The official blog about the collections, exhibitions, and programs of the Scottish Rite Masonic Museum & Library, Dec. 3, 2013, accessed August 7, 2020, https://nationalheritagemuseum.typepad.com/library_and_archives/2013/12/the-persistence-of-cerneauism-the-1950s.html.

The Controversy of Joseph Cerneau: A Brief Examination

Michael R. Poll, 32°

Who was Joseph Cerneau? What was the "Cerneau" Supreme Council? Was Joseph Cerneau a "regular" or "irregular" Mason? Why did "Cerneau" Masonry cause such problems in the United States? These are a handful of the many questions asked by Masons concerning Joseph Cerneau, a figure at the center of a long-debated Masonic controversy. To assert that Joseph Cerneau was simply a misguided or troublesome individual does not fully explain his significant popularity in the 1800s. To assert that Cerneau's Supreme Council was simply a blatantly irregular body fails to explain the many prominent American Masons who were counted among the "Cerneau Masons."

The popularity of Cerneau Masonry had plagued the Supreme Councils for the Southern and Northern Jurisdiction throughout the 1800s. Albert Pike himself devoted a significant amount of time to the battle against Cerneau

Masonry. The "Cerneau problem" (for the Southern and Northern Councils) was amplified by the neutral position taken by many American Grand Lodges who presumably felt that aggressive and long term action was not needed on their part if Cerneau was not directly invading their territory with York Rite Bodies. The opinion likely held by many of these Grand Lodges was that "Scottish Rite problems" were of no concern to York Rite Grand Lodges. This attitude of non-involvement contributed to the confused state of Scottish Rite regularity and irregularity. For instance, DeWitt Clinton was not only Governor of the state of New York and long time Grand Master of the Grand Lodge of New York, he was also Cerneau's Deputy Grand Commander and later, in 1823, Grand Commander of Cerneau's Council.[1] In 1813 a Cerneau Grand Council of Princes of the Royal Secret, 32° was organized in New Orleans, and by the 1830s it began to exercise a dominant influence in the Grand Lodge of Louisiana.[2] By the 1820s, even the Grand Lodge of Ancient Free-Masons of South Carolina, whose home was in Charleston along with the Southern Jurisdiction, contained influential Cerneau Masons.[3] These Charleston Cerneau Masons certainly made things troublesome for the Southern Jurisdiction. During the 1800s, Cerneau Masonry was considered "regular" by many well educated and prominent Masons who held a spectrum of offices in quite a number of the American Grand Lodges. Albert Pike and those before him were not concerned without reason.

It became essential for the Supreme Councils of the Northern and Southern Jurisdictions to prove that Joseph Cerneau was either irregular or acted without authority when he organized his Sovereign Grand Consistory in New York in 1807. Establishing that Cerneau was completely irregular was not an easy task. It was confirmed that Cerneau was a regular Deputy Inspector General, 25° of the Order of the Royal Secret, also known as the Rite of Perfection.[4] The Order of the Royal Secret, however, was not the Ancient

x. Samuel H. Baynard, Jr., *History of the Supreme Council, 33° Ancient and Accepted Scottish Rite Northern Masonic Jurisdiction of the United States of America and its Antecedents* (Boston: The Supreme Council, 33°, N.M.J., 1938), vol. 1, 187–89.

2. James B. Scot, *Outline of the Rise and Progress of Freemasonry in Louisiana* (1873; reprint, Lafayette, La.: Michael Poll Pub., 1995), 90.

3. Ray Baker Harris and James D. Carter, *History of the Supreme Council, 33° (1801–1861)* (Washington, DC: The Supreme Council, 33°, S.J., 1964), 143–46.

4. Albert G. Mackey, *Encyclopedia of Freemasonry* (Chicago: The Masonic History Co., 1946),

and Accepted Scottish Rite consisting of thirty-three degrees.[5] Where, when, and from whom Cerneau received the 33° (and thereby his right to establish a Supreme Council) became a matter of great importance. Cerneau's 25° patent, empowering him to establish certain Scottish Rite Bodies in a portion of Cuba, certainly would not have been sufficient to establish a Supreme Council of the 33° in New York. If Cerneau possessed a valid patent for the 33° and was a legitimate Sovereign Grand Inspector General of the 33°, his claim of regularity would have been more difficult to disprove.

CERNEAU'S "RIGHT" TO ESTABLISH SCOTTISH RITE BODIES

To date, there is no convincing evidence that Cerneau received the 33° initiation. While it is impossible to enter into the mind of Joseph Cerneau and examine, from his point of view, the questions of his regularity or irregularity, we can, however, attempt to examine the possible motives behind his actions. Clearly, the only proof that Cerneau was not a 33° is the absence of proof that he received the degree. Still, it is only reasonable that he would have chosen to avoid controversy by producing a patent—if he had one. If Joseph Cerneau was not a 33° Mason then there seems to be only two reasonable explanations for the actions that he took: 1) He was a man of low moral character (or delusional) who sought to advance himself and capitalize on a new Masonic system; or 2) he *believed* that he was a 33° and *believed* that he was acting with proper authority.

If Cerneau acted out of ambition and blind hunger for power, then the story should end there. If, however, Cerneau truly believed he was a 33° and was acting with proper authority, then we must examine his actions from a different viewpoint. If there is validity to the hypothesis that Cerneau held an erroneous (or correct) belief that he possessed the 33° and possessed the right to organize a Supreme Council, then there must be a reason why he held this belief. Logic dictates that since Cerneau did organize a Supreme Council and did profess to hold the 33°, he must have learned of the thirty-three degree system from a member of the Charleston Council or someone else familiar

vol. 1, 187.

5. The name *Ancient and Accepted Scottish Rite* was not used by any Supreme Council in the USA until the 1832 Manifesto of the Hicks-St. Laurent Supreme Council (United Supreme Council of the Western Hemisphere). Harris and Carter, *History*, 216.

with the new arrangement. Cerneau obviously embraced this new system and organized his Council based on whatever knowledge he had of the Charleston Council or on what he viewed to be the new thirty-three degree rite.

The Pike-Drummond Affair

To examine the theory that Cerneau believed that he possessed a right to establish his Council, we must look at an event that took place between the Northern and Southern Jurisdictions, USA. In the 1860s the two Supreme Councils entered into a debate over territory. Josiah Drummond, the Grand Commander, N.M.J., and Albert Pike, Grand Commander, S.J., debated jurisdictional questions over certain states. Drummond wrote to Pike in 1868:

> I hold that under the Constitutions of 1786, the Northern Jurisdiction and the Southern Jurisdiction are, in every respect and for all purposes, as distinct as if they were separate nations: that we, as well as you, derive our rights of jurisdiction from those Constitutions; that those Constitutions create two separate Jurisdictions. On the other hand, I perceive, that you have held that your Supreme Council had jurisdiction throughout North America, and that we get our territory by *cession* from you; and if by cession, consequently we get only such territory *as you choose* to cede: and as necessary, that there could have been no Supreme Council in this Jurisdiction unless you had chosen to cede us territory.[6]

Albert Pike answered Drummond in his 1868 *Allocution* (emphasis added).

> I do not agree that the Constitutions *created* the two Jurisdictions. For the United States composed a single Jurisdiction until 1813 or 1815, and might have continued to be as such until today. The provision is restrictive,—that there shall not be *more* than two Supreme Councils established in the United States. That is the real meaning of it; not that there *shall* be two. But the point is of no practical importance, and I pass it.... If Illustrious Brother Drummond were right in holding that the Northern part of the United States did not belong to the Jurisdiction of the Southern Council, prior to 1813 or 1815, but was to vest, whether it willed it or not, in a Northern Council, whenever one should be created there, a consequence which he does not foresee might follow. That hypothesis would make the Northern states to have been unoccupied territory, in which any Inspector General could establish a Supreme Council; and it might thus make legitimate the Cerneau Council, and annihilate that created in 1813 or 1815, by De la Motta. It certainly would destroy the principal ground on which

6. *Transactions of the Supreme Council of the 33d for the Southern Jurisdiction of the United States.* (New York: Masonic Pub. Co., 1869), 9.

> the legitimacy of Cerneau's Council was always impeached; to-wit, that the Council at Charleston had jurisdiction over the whole United States, and that no other Council could be created any where in them, except with its consent.[7]

EXAMINING PIKE'S ARGUMENT

The first element of Pike's argument was based on his interpretation of Article Five of the French version of the *Grand Constitutions of 1786* (the version adhered to by the Northern Jurisdiction). While Pike debated the meaning of this portion of Article Five, he held that the French version was a forgery. Pike states in his 1872 *Grand Constitutions*:

> If I were satisfied that there never were any other Constitutions than those contained in the French version, I should not hesitate to admit that they were a clumsy forgery, and that there was nothing in the world to prove them authentic.[8]

Pike goes on to state that he was of the belief that the French version was forged by Comte de Grasse-Tilly. The point of disagreement between Drummond and Pike concerning the reading of the *Grand Constitutions* is from the portion of Article Five which, reads in the French and English:

> Il n'y aura qu'un Conseil de ce grade dans chaque nation ou royaume en Europe, deux dans les Etats-Unis de l'Amérique, aussi éloignés que possible l'un de l'autre....

> There shall be but one Council of this degree in each Nation or Realm in Europe, two in the United States of America, as far removed as possible one from another....[9]

In translating from one language to another, the original meaning of the author is of the utmost importance. Drummond interpreted the meaning of Article Five as to *provide* for two Councils in the US Pike argued in his *Grand Constitutions*, "Wherefore the provision to the United States simply is, that there shall be *only* two Councils in them; that there shall not be *more* than two; and it must be awfully twisted to make it read that there *shall be* two."[10]

7. *Transactions* (1869), 22–23.
8. Albert Pike, *The Grand Constitutions of Freemasonry* (New York: The Supreme Council, 33°, S.J., 1872), 282–83.
9. Pike, *Grand Constitutions*, 288.
10. Pike, *Grand Constitutions*, 289

The previous quotation is only a small portion of Pike's lengthy argument concerning French and English grammar and the reasons for his position concerning the meaning of Article Five. As was customary for Pike, he made a very persuasive argument for his point. Pike even changed a portion of the English translation in his *Grand Constitutions* to reflect his opinion of the meaning.[11] In his 1868 *Allocution*, Pike very skillfully debated this interpretation of Article Five at length and he did likewise in his *Grand Constitutions*—but why? Pike had already proclaimed the French version a "clumsy forgery" and the Latin version legitimate. Why should Pike bother to argue a point concerning a document that he claimed was historically worthless? Pike's entire argument concerning the French version was irrelevant and leads the reader into a misconception. By such a lengthy and grammatically technical argument concerning this portion of the French version of Article Five, the reader is easily inclined to forget that Pike labeled the subject of his argument a fraud. Pike should have, for the sake of clearly understanding his true position, debated the Latin version—which he claimed to be legitimate. So, why didn't he? Simply put, Pike could not debate this portion of the Latin version. The same portion of Article Five of the Latin version (the version Pike refers to as the "law of the Rite"[12]) reads:

> In each great nation of Europe, and in each Kingdom or Empire, there shall be but one single Supreme Council of this Degree. In all those States and Provinces, as well of the mainland as of the islands, whereof North America is composed, there shall be two Councils, one at as great a distance as may be from the other....[13]

11. Pike, *Grand Constitutions*, 289. Pike altered the English translation of Article five to, "... but two in the United States of America ..." in order to emphasize his point concerning his interpretation of the meaning of this phrase. (highlighting not in original text)

12. Pike, *Grand Constitutions*, 283.

13. Albert Pike, *The True Secret Institutes and Fundamental Bases of the Order of Ancient Free and Associated Masons and the Grand Constitutions of the Ancient Accepted Scottish Rite of the Year 1786*. (New Orleans: The Supreme Council, 33°, S.J., 1859), 163–65. In Pike's 1872 (A.M. 5632) *The Grand Constitutions of Freemasonry*, he altered the original translation to read as follows: "In each great nation of Europe, and in each Kingdom or Empire, there shall be a single Council of the said degree. In the States and Provinces, as well on the Continent as in the Islands, whereof North America consists, there will be two Councils, one at as great a distance from the other as may be possible." (emphasis added) Pike, the master linguist, replaced the word "shall" with "will" in his 1872 edition, which, while having the same meaning, was not such an obvious problem to inattentive readers. The edited edition carries the note, "Re-translated from the Latin by Albert Pike, 33°, Sov\Gr\Commander. A\M\, 5632," 213. Pike maintained the accuracy of his 1859 translation, at

Pike strongly contended that the meaning of Article Five was not that "there *shall be* two Councils," yet that is exactly what the Latin version, which Pike translated in *1859*, says. Pike based his argument on the French version of the Constitutions which was more open to interpretation as to the number of Councils in the US *being* two or *being limited* to two. Clearly, if Pike had argued that portion of Article Five using the Latin version, he would have been forced to agree with Drummond. Pike wisely used the French version of the Constitutions in this debate, for it gave him the benefit of a wording more open to interpretation. The "consequence" that Pike claimed would follow if Drummond's interpretation was accepted, is, clearly, present in the Latin version—Cerneau, it seems, might have had a reason, based on the *Grand Constitutions*, to believe that he possessed the right to establish his Council.

The position held by Drummond was not only based on his interpretation of Article Five of the French version of the Constitutions but also on the "birth certificate" of the Northern Council which reads in part:

> And whereas the Grand Constitutions of the 33° specifies particularly, that there shall be two Grand & Supreme Councils of the 33d Degree for the Jurisdiction of the United States of America, one for the South and the other for the North....[14]

Pike, in his response to Drummond, opened a Pandora's box for the Northern Jurisdiction—and also, although he may not have realized it, for the Southern Jurisdiction. If the Northern Jurisdiction did not submit to Pike's ruling on jurisdictional questions (which they ultimately did),[15] Pike would have, (if his subtle threat is to be taken seriously) made public that the Northern Jurisdiction had discovered and pronounced (according to Pike's conclusions) its own irregularity.

least, until 1868, as the questioned portion of Article Five is reproduced in the 1868 *Transactions* of the Supreme Council, S.J. exactly as they appeared in the 1859 translation, 28.

14. Baynard, 175–79. This quotation is taken from the facsimile reproduction of the 1813 "birth certificate" for the Northern Jurisdiction (reproduced on 176). In addition to the facsimile is a printed transcript of the "birth certificate" provided to us by Brother Baynard. Unfortunately, the printed transcription omits a number of words and phrases that appear in the facsimile. For example, the phrase, "one for the South and one for the North (line 26 in the facsimile) does not appear in the printed transcription." Many thanks to Alain Bernheim, 32° for this discovery.

15. Charles S. Lobingier, *The Supreme Council, 33°* (Louisville, Kentucky: The Supreme Council, 33° S.J., 1931) 77.

THE DALCHO VERSION OF THE *GRAND CONSTITUTIONS OF 1786*

At the time of the Pike and Drummond debate, Pike did not have in his possession the Dalcho version of the *Grand Constitutions*[16] and, clearly, he was unaware that the "birth certificate" of the Northern Jurisdiction supported Drummond's argument. Since, according to Ray Baker Harris, the Dalcho version of the Constitutions is the likely model from which the French version was made by translating Dalcho's English version,[17] it must follow that the early Charleston Council accepted the French or Dalcho version as legitimate. It must also follow that since the "birth certificate" of the Northern Jurisdiction, which was created by a member of and supported by the Charleston Council, states that the Constitutions provide for both a Southern and a Northern Council, then the meaning of Article Five of the French version to the early Southern and Northern Jurisdictions was that there should be *exactly* two (not one or more than two) Councils in the US. However, if the French or Dalcho version were a forgery, as Pike claimed, then it's meaning, however interpreted, did not matter and any ruling based on the French version must be reevaluated based on the Latin version.

Of course, the *Latin version* was not heard of before the 1834 treaty made at Paris between the Supreme Council of France, the United Supreme Council for the Western Hemisphere, and the Supreme Council of Brazil[18] (the last two being offspring of the Cerneau Council). Pike's argument concerning the French version of the *Grand Constitutions of 1786* painted Josiah Drummond (and also Pike) into something of a corner. On the one hand, Pike declared the French version was a forgery and the Latin version legitimate. On the other hand, Pike *used* the French version to support a point he made in his debate with Drummond.

The complication arose because if the French version were a forgery, then you became bound to the Latin version—which provided for two councils in North America and allowed any 33rd to establish a council in the Northern states prior to the establishment of the Northern Jurisdiction. If the French version were legitimate, then it became necessary to consider the original *meaning* of the French version, as understood by the Northern Jurisdiction

16. The Dalcho version was not discovered until this present century. *See:* Harris and Carter, 98.
17. Harris and Carter, 92.
18. Harris and Carter, 216.

and early Southern Jurisdiction. The French version provided for two councils in the United States and, like the Latin version, would allow any 33rd to establish a council in the Northern states prior to the establishment of the Northern Jurisdiction in 1813.

In Pike's debate with Drummond it was established that both versions of the *Grand Constitutions* provided for two Councils in the US (or North America, depending on the version). Of course, this is only true if the *Grand Constitutions*—any version—were approved in 1786 by Frederick the Great and are legitimate. This final conclusion could *not* have been what Pike intended. Pike's debate does, however, present us with an opportunity to consider that Cerneau *may* have had a valid reason to consider himself legitimate and justified in his actions. However, the problem that quickly comes to mind is the original question of where and when Cerneau received his 33°. Similarly, if Cerneau did not possess this degree, why did Pike say that, given the possibility of Drummond being correct, Cerneau "might" have had a right to establish a Supreme Council anywhere?

JOHN MITCHELL AND HIS 33°

In an attempt to make order out of chaos, the Cerneau situation can be further explored by looking at the Charleston situation. There is no proof of how or even if Cerneau received the 33°. A patent does exist establishing that on May 25, 1801, Frederick Dalcho received the 33° from John Mitchell, Charleston's first Grand Commander.[19] The question must now be asked, "Who gave John Mitchell his 33°?" On April 2, 1795, Barend Spitzer appointed Mitchell a Deputy Inspector General.[20] The problem is that Spitzer was a Deputy Inspector General (25°) of the Order of the Royal Secret (Rite of Perfection) tracing his authority in a line leading back to Stephen Morin (just like Cerneau). How could John Mitchell receive the 33° from a 25° Mason? Moses Holbrook, Grand Commander of the Southern Jurisdiction from 1826–1844, wrote to J. J. J. Gourgas of the Northern Jurisdiction in 1829 (strikeout in original text):

> I took the opportunity in mentioning it to Br. Dalcho, to ask how Mitchell got the 33rd. He replied that he could not ... recollect; but he [Mitchell] had

19. Harris and Carter, 96.

20. Harris and Carter, 32. This date, however, contradicts the 1802 Charleston Manifesto which states that Mitchell received this appointment on August 2, 1795. Harris and Carter, 323.

> signed some obligation in French for it. He thinks it came from some Prussian who was in Charleston, who was authorized to communicate it to him.[21]

Why would a "Prussian" give Mitchell (an Irishman in the United States) an obligation for the 33° *in French?* What did France have to do with Frederick the Great or the *Grand Constitutions*? (Could this statement support the French/Dalcho version of the *Grand Constitutions* being originally written in French?) Joseph Cerneau was accused of being everything negative that a man and Mason could be simply because he did not produce evidence that he received the 33°. Why would the Charleston Council (given their position on Cerneau) not know exactly where, when and by whom their first 33rd and first Grand Commander received the degree? Any objective examination must judge all parties by the same standards. There is no proof whatsoever that either Joseph Cerneau or John Mitchell ever received the 33° from anyone.

Samuel Baynard asserts that Stephen Morin and Henry Wilmans were the only two "known to us to be in possession of the Thirty-third Degree in the Western Hemisphere prior to 1801."[22] This statement contradicts a document Baynard published where the names of six more individuals are listed who reportedly signed the *Secret Grand Constitutions* as 33rds.[23] Morin is listed also as a 33° in these *Secret Grand Constitutions,* and it is from this that Baynard based his claim that Morin was a 33rd. The *Secret Grand Constitutions*, however, can not stand up under examination and be declared legitimate. Even Albert Pike knew this in 1872 and expressed his contempt for them when he published them and their accompanying 33° Ritual in his *Grand Constitutions* under the title of *The Pretended Secret Constitutions.*[24] As for Henry Wilmans, Baynard confesses, "We have no information as to when or where he received the Symbolic or other degrees of Freemasonry," and "... Wilmans is designated as a 'Grand Inspector,' and not a 'Deputy Inspector,' clearly indicating his higher rank, which prompts us to believe it possible that it was Wilmans who conferred the Thirty-third Degree on John Mitchell."[25]

21. Baynard, vol. 1, 89.
22. Baynard, vol. 1, 122.
23. Baynard, vol. 1, 40.
24. Pike, *Grand Constitutions*, 297–354.
25. Baynard, vol 1, 86–87.

Samuel Baynard was a learned man, but his work must be read with caution. He states that Wilmans held the 33° and possibly gave it to Mitchell. Yet he supports these statements only with his conjecture. The titles "Deputy Inspector General" and "Grand Inspector General" can no more be automatically associated with the 33° then can the degree name "Rose-Croix" be automatically assumed to be the Ancient and Accepted Scottish Rite. There is simply no reliable evidence whatsoever to validate a claim that Morin, Wilmans or anyone else possessed the Thirty-third Degree prior to 1801. Concerning this matter, *A Library of Freemasonry* determined,

> The thirty-third degree of the Masonic System of the Scottish Rite in thirty-three degrees was never heard of until after the organization of the Supreme Council in Charleston; there was no ceremonial or ritual in connection with the office of Deputy Inspector General prior to that time. It was simply an appointment and not a degree, given to Princes of the Royal Secret of the twenty-fifth degree, the highest known before 1801. No manuscript or printed paper has yet been found, of an earlier date than this, containing any reference whatever to a thirty-third degree.[26]

WHO CONFERRED THE FIRST 33°?

Cerneau and Mitchell were *both* regular and legitimate Masons who *both* claimed the 33°, and *both* established Supreme Councils. Since they *both* challenged the other's legitimacy (and honesty), then fairness dictates that before the word of either can be accepted, it must be supported by sound evidence. John Mitchell was made a Deputy Inspector General (25°) of the Order of the Royal Secret by Barend Spitzer in 1795. If Mitchell advanced himself to the 33° (is *that* possible ?) and organized the Charleston Council, then Cerneau, also a Deputy Inspector General of the 25°, could have felt very comfortable with acting in a similar manner in a portion of the United States that could be considered "unoccupied" and "distant" from Charleston. Both would have been giving up the older twenty-five degree Scottish Rite system for the new thirty-three degree rite.

Concerning the possibility of Mitchell and Cerneau advancing *themselves* to the 33°, *Coil's Masonic Encyclopedia* has this to say:

26. Robert F. Gould, et al., eds., *A Library of Freemasonry,* 4 vols. (Philadelphia: The John C. Yorston Pub. Co., 1911), 285.

> ... at Charleston, S.C., in 1801, the 32-degree system had been perfected and, in the process, the old 25th Degree, *Prince Mason*, or *Prince of the Royal Secret*, had been shifted to 32nd place. Since Cerneau held the *Prince Mason* Degree, he conceived that he should shift with it and as it went to the head of the list, so did he. Perhaps he was entitled to do that; perhaps others did so, especially, those who belonged to the Rite at Charleston.[27]

But wait—the old 25° became the 32°, not the 33°. If Mitchell and Cerneau advanced from the 25° to the 32° by adopting the new Scottish Rite system, how could they advance from the 32° to the 33°? If the 25° of the Order of the Royal Secret became the 32° of the new 1801 system, then evidence does exist that the senior 32° mason in any unoccupied area could advance himself to the 33°.

> Whenever, in a State there is neither a Grand Consistory nor a Grand Council of Sublime Princes of the Royal Secret, there are any Grand Inspectors General and Princes of the Royal Secret, the Grand Inspector General whose patent and recognition bear the oldest date, or, if there be no Inspectors General, then the oldest Prince of the Royal Secret, is invested with the administrative and dogmatic power of High Masonry, and takes accordingly the title Sovereign.[28]

Cerneau did not ask for Charleston's permission to form his Scottish Rite Bodies in New York as he obviously felt that it was unnecessary. As the Pike-Drummond debate establishes, the *Grand Constitutions do* provide for two Councils. If the French version of the Constitutions is to be accepted, then Cerneau's Council would have been the second Council in the United States. If the Latin version is to be accepted, then de Grasse's Council, established in the West Indies in 1802, would have been the second Council in North America. The Council in the West Indies, however, was short-lived, and by 1804 de Grasse was in France establishing the Supreme Council of France.[29] By 1807 when Cerneau arrived in New York and established his Sovereign Grand Consistory,[30] the Council in the West Indies was no longer an issue.

27. Henry Wilson Coil, *Coil's Masonic Encyclopedia* (New York: Macoy Pub. & Masonic Supply Co., 1961), 121.
28. Pike, *Grand Constitutions*, 117.
29. Baynard, vol. 1, 93.
30. Harris and Carter, 111.

THE BIDEAUD CONSISTORY

While the Supreme Council of the West Indies had ceased to exist by the time Cerneau arrived in New York in 1807, one element of that Body had survived. Antoine Bideaud, 33° was a member of de Grasse's Supreme Council in the West Indies.[31] Bideaud left the West Indies and made his way to New York City by way of New Orleans. In New York, Bideaud elevated five masons to the 32° and established a Grand Consistory of Princes of the Royal Secret, 32° on August 6, 1806.[32] Bideaud left New York for France soon after establishing his Grand Consistory. The establishment of the Bideaud Consistory would seem to nullify any claim that Cerneau might have had in establishing his Scottish Rite Bodies. Cerneau certainly would not have been the first 32° *or* the first 33° in New York.

An objective analysis of the situation, however, presents us with great problems and the situation (by attempting to see through the eyes of the participants) is anything but clear. The following points are known today:

- The Charleston Council has always held that Bideaud acted improperly and without authority when he established his Grand Consistory in New York.[33]
- Charges have been made that Bideaud was motivated to establish his Bodies simply for monetary gain.[34]
- The members of the Bideaud Consistory questioned their own authority and considered themselves as probably irregular.[35]
- DeWitt Clinton and other members of the Cerneau Bodies considered the members of the Bideaud Consistory as Masonic (and political) "opponents" in New York and clearly found their actions suspect.[36]

31. *1803 Register of Antoine Bideaud* located in the Scottish Rite Bodies of New Orleans, La.

32. John Gabriel Tardy, John Baptiste Desdoity, John James Joseph Gourgas, Lewis de Saulles and Pierre Adrien DePeyrat. Baynard, vol. 1, 153

33. Baynard, vol. 1, 153.

34. Baynard, vol. 1, 153.

35. Baynard, vol. 1, 157.

36. Baynard, vol. 1, 155, 181–83.

- The Bideaud Consistory was a descendent of the Charleston Council, and from 1809–1817 the members of the Charleston Council belonged to the then irregular Grand Lodge of South Carolina.[37]

Given these points, it is not difficult to conclude that the Bideaud Consistory was viewed as the irregular body by the Cerneau Masons (as it was, also, viewed by the Charleston Masons). This even may have been the catalyst for Cerneau to make the switch from the 25° Scottish Rite system to the 33° system. Cerneau's action may have been viewed, by himself and those in support of him, as a necessary response to bring regularity to the area (or maybe even simple jealously). The idea that they, *themselves*, might face charges of irregularity was likely far from their minds. The formation of the Northern Council by De La Motta not only was viewed as an intrusion by the Cerneau masons, but also conceivably reinforced the concept that the Charleston Council (and its descendants) were quite irregular.

More Objections to the Cerneau Bodies

In further exploring the objections made against the Cerneau Council, an interesting challenge initiated by Frederick Dalcho in the early 1800s should be examined. Writing from Charleston in an 1813 letter to De La Motta, Dalcho states that,

> It is well known to those who have lawfully received the 33rd degree, that there can be but one Council in a nation or kingdom; & that the Council for the U.S. was lawfully established in this City, May 31st, 1801....[38]

As incredible as it may seem, Dalcho made this statement on August 23, 1813. This was eighteen days *after* De La Motta had issued his "birth certificate" for the Supreme Council, N.M.J. The Supreme Council, S.J. did, of course, eventually sanction De La Motta's action, but Dalcho's letter must have caused a few anxious moments for De La Motta. In 1860 Pike echoed Dalcho's "one Council" interpretation of the *Grand Constitutions of 1786* (even after translating the *Latin* version in 1859).

37. Alain Bernheim, introduction, *Outline of the Rise and Progress of Freemasonry in Louisiana*, by James B. Scot, (1873; reprint, Lafayette, La.: Michael Poll Publishing, 1995), 7–8.

38. Bernheim, 118.

> Originally the Supreme Council at Charleston had jurisdiction over the whole of the United States; and it is greatly to be regretted, that, in order to put down the notorious *Joseph Cerneau* and his spurious Supreme Council, the Ill. Bro. De la Motta, as Plenipotentiary of his Supreme Council, was induced, in 1814 (sic), to violate the Constitutions of 1786, and organize a Supreme Council in New York; and still more, that this Supreme Council approved his action in the premises.[39]

According to the *Grand Constitutions of 1786*, Dalcho and Pike were clearly wrong in stating that the United States was limited to *one* Council. The fact that the Dalcho version of the *Grand Constitutions*, in Dalcho's own hand, exists today in the Archives of the Northern Jurisdiction makes his statement even more difficult to understand. John Mitchell corrected Dalcho's apparent error of interpretation by supporting, at some point, De La Motta's establishment of a Council in the Northern Jurisdiction.[40] Possibly, it was this act of support (permission?) for the creation of the Northern Jurisdiction that made them legitimate in the eyes of the Charleston Council. Pike's contention that De La Motta violated the Constitutions of 1786 is completely unfounded and unsupported by *any* version of the *Grand Constitutions*—unless, of course, Pike was suggesting that the Northern part of the United States was already occupied by Cerneau. It can only be assumed (giving Pike the benefit of the doubt) that he misread, or forgot, what he had translated one year earlier. In light of Pike's lengthy debates with Drummond, the contradiction of his 1860 and later statements become very significant. If such contradictory statements are published independently of each other, two very different conclusions are reached. The opportunity for confusion is enormous.

The battle to define American Scottish Rite regularity has been lengthy and often bitter. Cerneau masonry has long been the standard for "irregular" masonry, but why? Both Supreme Councils in the Southern and Northern Jurisdictions merged with Cerneau Councils.[41] Clearly this is a declaration that the Cerneau Councils could not have been *that* irregular. In the final analysis, it

39. *Transactions of the Supreme Council of the 33d Degree for the Southern Jurisdiction of the United States.* (New York: Macoy and Sickels, 1860), 23.

40. Harris and Carter, *History*, 119.

41. On February 16, 1855, a concordat was signed merging the Charleston Council, S.J., USA, with the Cerneau New Orleans Council. On May 17, 1867, a concordat took place merging the Van Rensselaer Council, N.M.J., USA, with the Cerneau Hays-Raymond Council. For a full treatment of the latter merger, *see* Art deHoyos, "The Union of 1867," *Heredom*, vol. 4, 1995, 7–45.

is clear that there is much still to be understood concerning Cerneau masonry. Possibly, with time and careful study we can discover more concerning this man who had such a powerful effect on American Scottish Rite Masonry.

REFERENCES

Baynard, Samuel H., Jr., *History of the Supreme Council, 33° Ancient and Accepted Scottish Rite Northern Masonic Jurisdiction of the United States of America and its Antecedents.* 2 vols. Boston: The Supreme Council, 33°, N.M.J., 1938.

Coil, Henry Wilson, et al. *Coil's Masonic Encyclopedia.* New York: Macoy Pub. & Masonic Supply Co., 1961.

deHoyos, Art. "The Union of 1867," *Heredom*, vol. 4, 1995, pp. 7–45.

Gould, Robert F., et al., eds. *A Library of Freemasonry.* 5 vols. Philadelphia: The John C. Yorston Pub. Co., 1911.

Harris, R. Baker and James D. Carter. *History of the Supreme Council, 33° (1801–1861).* Washington, DC: The Supreme Council, 33°, S.J., 1964.

Lobingier, Charles S. *The Supreme Council, 33°.* Louisville, Kentucky: The Supreme Council, 33°, S.J., 1931.

Mackey, Albert G. *Encyclopedia of Freemasonry.* 2 vols. Chicago: The Masonic History Co., 1946.

Pike, Albert. *The True Secret Institutes and Fundamental Bases of the Order of Ancient Free and Associated Masons and the Grand Constitutions of the Ancient Accepted Scottish Rite of the Year 1786.* New Orleans: Supreme Council, 33°, S.J., 1859.

Scot, James B. Scot. *Outline of the Rise and Progress of Freemasonry in Louisiana.* 1873. Reprint. Lafayette, La.: Michael Poll Pub., 1995.

Transactions of the Supreme Council of the 33d Degree for the Southern Jurisdiction of the United States. New York: Macoy and Sickels, 1860.

Transactions of the Supreme Council of the 33d for the Southern Jurisdiction of the United States. New York: Masonic Pub. Co., 1869.

EDITOR'S NOTE: This paper is adapted from Michael Poll's introduction to The 1886 Bulletin of the Supreme Council of France Concerning Joseph Cerneau, *reprinted in 1995 by Cornerstone Book Publishers.*

An Introduction to Joseph Cerneau and His Biographers

Alain Bernheim, 33°

Heredom HAS THE PLEASURE TO REPRODUCE IN THE PRESent issue a hitherto unknown document which was presented by the Sovereign Grand Consistory of the United States of America to Joseph Cerneau, November 10, 1827, on the occasion of his return to France. It was recently discovered in the shop window of an antiquarian in Paris by Pierre Mollier, Director of the Library, Archives, and Museum of the Grand Orient of France, who recognized immediately its unusual interest and was kind enough to put an excellent transparency at *Heredom*'s disposal.

Little is known about Joseph Cerneau's life and nothing definite about his death. In 1800, he was a member of *La Réunion Désirée*, a lodge warranted in 1784 by the Grand Orient of France in Port au Prince,[1] while he appears on the

1. Le Bihan 1967: 400.

June 1801 printed *Tableau* (List of Members) of *La Réunion des Coeurs* No. 47, warranted in 1789 by the Grand Lodge of Pennsylvania in the same town, as a goldsmith merchant (*marchand orfèvre*), "R.·. A.·., R.·. +.·." (Royal Arch and Rose Croix).[2] He was one of the first two Grand Secretaries of the Provincial Grand Lodge of Saint Domingue, founded with Antoine Mathieu-Dupotet as Provincial Grand Master at Port Républicain in January 1802 by the Grand Lodge of Pennsylvania. In December 1804, he petitioned that Grand Lodge to warrant Lodge *Le Temple des Vertus Théologales* in Havana of which he was then Worshipful Master. On July 15, 1806, at Baracoa, Cuba, he received a patent from Antoine Mathieu-Dupotet and arrived in New York in November. Various American historians have quoted from a minute book of the Consistory founded in New York by Cerneau, which is extant in the archives of the Northern Masonic Jurisdiction,[3] the full contents of which have never been published yet. Cerneau's patent together with his New York activities will be discussed in a future volume of *Heredom*.

In December 1827, Cerneau returned to his native village in France where he is said to have died some twenty years later.

Joseph Cerneau and Historians

The first public attack against Cerneau happened in an extremely rare pamphlet of eighteen pages, issued in 1810 at Philadelphia, a copy of which Kent Walgren kindly put at my disposal.[4] But as far as I am aware, the earliest-known sketch of Joseph Cerneau's life was included in a few paragraphs, altogether some 700 words, which appeared in the third edition (1844) of a four-hundred-page book, issued by Bègue-Clavel in 1843, *Histoire pittoresque de la Franc-Maçonnerie*.[5] Clavel's sources are discussed below. With a few words added, what he wrote about Cerneau was recopied in full as his own by J. M. Ragon.[6]

2. *OB* VIII: 677. In 1801, Germain Hacquet was Worshipful Master of the Lodge.

3. The minute-book quoted by various historians is likely the second one. It covers the period (Nov. 8) 1816 to (Mar. 30) 1826 (Stillson 1891: 814–15. Baynard 1938: i, 203–5). Also *see* Gardner 1864: 114 (quoted in Baynard 1938: i, 210) and Voorhis in the Sept. 1951 *Minutes of the History Committee*, NMJ: 18.

4. Walgren 1994: 75 under No. 27.

5. Bègue-Clavel 1844: 270–71. The 3d edition included (400–402) the first French translation of the Charleston 1802 *Report* (that is, the slightly modified version issued as an Appendix to Dalcho's *Oration* of 1803 as printed in Charleston, which was reproduced in the 1808 Dublin edition).

6. Ragon 1853: 328. Quoted in Folger 1862: 115.

Thirty years ago, Paul Naudon summarized both without any acknowledgment whatsoever.[7]

According to Ray Baker Harris, Albert Pike published during the 1880s thirty-four distinct pamphlets on the "Cerneau controversy."[8]

About 1884, William H. Peckham, one of Cerneau's successors as Grand Commander, thought fit to write to the *mairie* (Town Hall) of his birthplace in France. The answer Peckham received showed that Joseph Cerneau was born in Villeblevin near Sens, in the department Yonne, as "the legitimate son of Elme Etienne Cerneau, rector of the small schools [? likely *écoles primaires* or elementary schools] of Villeblevin, and of Félicité Perpétue Gateau, on the 14th day of November, 1765."[9] For the past century and a half, most historians stated that Cerneau was born in 1763.[10]

The *Report* issued in 1886 by the Supreme Council for France "In re Joseph Cerneau" showed the unfamiliarity of its Librarian with its own archives as well as his bias.[11] A series of articles by Emile Adrianyi-Pontet writing under the pseudonym of Br.·. Akim Haemeth appeared in 1929 in the *Wiener Freimaurer-Zeitung*, one of which was devoted to "Cerneauism." It was a fair compilation which brought no new information.[12]

Replying to comments made upon a remarkable paper he submitted before *Quatuor Coronati* Lodge on May 6, 1927, Bro. N.S.H. Sitwell wrote:

> ... when this paper was written, the collection of these West Indian manuscripts was but small. It now (October 1928) consists of over twenty of such documents.

7. Naudon 1984: 178.

8. Harris 1957: 84–86 under "Cerneau Controversy." Harris included there Pike's ***Historical Inquiry*** (1872) in which Cerneau's name doesn't appear once.

9. Peckham 1884: 124. On the cover-page of the book, the author is described as "Most Puissant Sovereign Grand Commander of the Supreme Grand Council of 1807." About Peckham, *see* Folger 1881 ***Supplement***: 99–100, and Baynard 1938: ii, 109.

10. Clavel 1844: 270. McClenachan 1905: 61. Baynard 1938: i, 185. Mellor 1971: 245. Naudon 1984: 178. Williams 1985: 10, and [Newbury and] Williams 1987: 87. Ligou 1987: 1,013. Gaudart de Soulages et Lamant 1995: 238. Charles Lobingier was wise enough to write that Cerneau was born "about 1764" (Lobingier 1931: 88).

11. A translation of the 1886 Supreme Council for France's *Report In re Joseph Cerneau* was issued the same year by the Southern Jurisdiction of the USA. It was reprinted in 1995, together with an index and an excellent Introduction by Michael R. Poll. Librarian Lebrun asserted (69) he could not find in his own archives the Cerneau protest mentioned by himself 53–55.

12. For his earlier denunciation of irregular masonry in Europe, Emile Adrianyi-Pontet (1865–1952) was awarded the 32° by the Southern Jurisdiction in 1907 (Carter 1971: 254. Bernheim 1987: 26). He introduced the A.&A.S.R. in Germany in 1926.

> ... We have new records about Cerneau, and new letters and documents about Morin and Martin [*sic*] de Pasquallis....[13]

The Cerneau records discovered by Sitwell were never mentioned again. In 1965, James Fairbairn Smith quoted the above reply but cut off the five words: "new records about Cerneau, and."[14]

In 1938, Samuel H. Baynard culled a few indications from Robert W. Reid's *Washington Lodge No. 21, F.&A.M., and Some of Its Members* (1911) and published the only-known portrait of Cerneau.[15] This was reproduced in *Heredom*, vol. 4, p. 15.

In a short paper issued in 1975, Jean Bossu mentioned that some Cerneau papers were extant at the Bibliothèque Nationale in Paris[16] and quoted the following sentence from a letter written to the Grand Orient of France on December 10, 1841, by Cerneau, then living at his birth-place and asking for financial help: "I believe I shall not bother you again much longer, then I am in my 77th year, the close of my existence cannot be far away, I experienced too many trials."[17] The Grand Orient granted him twenty francs after having granted him fifty in 1840.

Clavel and Leblanc De Marconnay

Like his contemporary fellow-historians, Clavel seldom mentioned his sources. However, in the Foreword of the third edition of his book, Clavel listed the names of five learned Brethren,[18] who furnished him with many important documents. One of them was Leblanc de Marconnay whose name seldom appears in masonic encyclopaedias, but which is familiar to students of the masonic history of Louisiana and is mentioned several times by Folger.

13. Sitwell 1927: 124–25. About Sitwell, the manuscripts he re-discovered and his 1927 paper, see Bernheim 1988: 98–104.

14. Smith 1965: 33.

15. Baynard 1938: i, 183–86.

16. Bossu 1975: 79 & 81. Bossu writes twice *Villeblain*, not *Villeblevin*.

17. "*Je pense que je ne vous importunerai pas longtemps encore car je suis dans ma 77e année, le terme de mon existence ne peut être éloigné, j'ai trop éprouvé de tribulations.*"

18. The other four were Charles Morison, Théodore Juge, Georg Kloss, and a Past Master of a Lodge in Mainz, named Foelix. About Doctor Charles Morison (of Greenfield), founder of the Supreme Council for Scotland, *see* Lindsay 1958: 61–64.

The story of the relations between Clavel, born in 1798, and Marconnay, his elder by four years, begins with that of their respective craft lodges in Paris. In 1822 Marconnay was Worshipful Master of *La Clémente Amitié*, warranted by the Grand Orient of France, March 8, 1805. Marconnay's Lodge decided in 1825 to "affiliate" with *Emeth* No. 12, a Lodge warranted July 12, 1822, by the Supreme Council for France, whose Worshipful Master was Clavel, 32°.

The Grand Orient considered the Craft lodges warranted by the Supreme Council for France since the latter's "re-organization" in May 1821[19] as "irregular associations" and forbade mutual contacts.[20] Accordingly on September 5, 1826, the Grand Orient of France erased Marconnay's *Clémente Amitié*. Together with its 18° Chapter, it was re-warranted as No. 24 and No. 25 by the Supreme Council for France on January 7, 1827. Four years later, following the denial of the Supreme Council to graft a 30° *Aréopage*[21] on *La Clémente Amitié*'s Chapter, Leblanc de Marconnay who was still Worshipful Master, decided to re-join the Grand Orient of France. Clavel's Lodge *Emeth* followed suit.

Leblanc de Marconnay received the 31° from the Supreme Council for France in June 1826. In 1832, he left for America and became a member of the United Supreme Council for the Western Hemisphere in New York which elevated him to the 33°.[22]

Marconnay appeared to have a considerable interest for masonic history. In May 1833, he wrote from New York to the Three Globes' Mother-Lodge in

19. A *Concordat* was signed in December 1804 between the Grand Orient and the Ancient and Accepted Scottish Rite organized in Paris by Grasse-Tilly. (The words *rit écossais ancien et accepté* appear—to my knowledge, for the first time in a masonic document—in art. 5 of the *Dispositions générales* of the *Concordat* [*Recueil des Actes* 1832: 74] and then in the Supreme Council Decretal dated Nov. 27, 1806, [*ibid.*: 91]). The *Concordat* was denounced one-sidedly Sep. 6, 1805. Most members of the Supreme Council for France emigrated in 1815 after the fall of Napoléon, but some of them remained in Paris and joined the Grand Orient of France's *Collège des Rites*, Supreme Council. Friendly contacts between both French Supreme Councils were cautiously restored from August 1830.

20. Bésuchet 1829: i, 285.

21. *Aréopage* was the usual European denomination for a Council of the 30°.

22. The United Supreme Council for the Western Hemisphere was the result of the union accomplished on April 5, 1832, between the Hicks (Cerneau) Supreme Council and that of the Comte de Saint Laurent. The latter was a Honorary Member of the Supreme Council for France since June 28, 1822.

Berlin about Frederic and his masonic activity in 1786.[23] He managed to find a copy of the *Annual Register* issued at Charleston toward the end of 1802.[24] In 1834, he wrote three letters to the Grand Consistory at New Orleans, stating that he was gathering material about masonic history and would appreciate receiving information about the establishment of Freemasonry in Louisiana and the number of Lodges presently in activity. At the same time, he suggested the establishment of "an active correspondence" between the three Louisiana Scottish Rite craft lodges and their respective grafted chapters with his own lodge and chapter in Paris, *La Clémente Amitié*, and the nomination of three Knights and of three Brethren on each side, one of whom should be entrusted with the correspondence.[25] He entered in relations with Celigny Ardouin in Haiti, who in 1836 published Marconnay's letter as a small pamphlet of forty-six pages under the title: *Rite Ecossais Ancien et Accepté*.[26]

I don't know whether Marconnay was already back in Paris in 1843 when his friend Clavel got into his first troubles with masonic authorities for having published his *Histoire pittoresque de la Franc-Maçonnerie* without having obtained permission first, as required by the Regulations of the Grand Orient of France. Summoned before a Masonic tribunal (*jury fraternel*), he decided not to appear and was suspended for two years by default in September 1843. One year later, he began issuing a masonic review, *L'Orient*, was again suspended, chose to demit, but was eventually excluded in November 1844.[27] Clavel's book was such a success that two further editions had to be printed within one year. The title-page of the third (1844) edition described it as "Carefully revised and augmented with new Facts and Documents." However it was castigated in the minutes of the Northern Masonic Jurisdiction of March 8, 1845, as

23. Folger 1862 *Appendix*, 60.

24. Folger 1862 *Appendix*, 62.

25. Original manuscript Minute-Book of the Grand Consistory of Louisiana, April 11, 1834, fo 127. Bro. Michael R. Poll, 32°, discovered the manuscript and was kind enough to furnish me with a full photocopy of its three hundred folios. See Bernheim 1995: 5–6. A few years ago, I found Marconnay's name on the 1843 *Tableau* of l'*Étoile Polaire* in New Orleans (Bibliothèque Nationale, FM2 560). I don't know whether this is the result of his letters to the Grand Consistory or if it implies that Marconnay spent some time in Louisiana.

26. Charassin's Report 1845: 122–23. Leblanc de Marconnay 1849: 209.

27. Rebold remarks that Clavel was still welcome in French Lodges after his exclusion (Rebold 1864: 187). During his judicial masonic strifes, *La Clémente Amitié* elected Clavel master of the lodge as a token of esteem.

> a great enemy and antagonist to the "Scottish Rite Ancient and Accepted," in thirty-three degrees, full of false assertions and of the most shameful calumnies relating to the two Grand and Supreme Councils of thirty-third degree at Charleston and New York, and their individual members.[28]

Marconnay obviously provided his friend with most of the new "elucidations" concerning American Freemasonry and "the creation of the Ancient and Accepted Scottish Rite in America" included in the revised 1844 edition and specified as such in its Foreword, but chose a different line for himself. He made a written report to the Grand Orient of France about the Masonic documents he found in America, which were summarized and quoted in the Charassin Report to the Correspondence Chamber, in which Marconnay's name appeared as "a member of the Supreme Council in New York." Once approved in January 1845, the Report was published the following April in the newly-created *Bulletin* of the Grand Orient of France.[29]

Shortly afterwards, James Foulhouze, a recently made Master Mason[30] and Grand Translator of the Grand Lodge of Louisiana founded in 1812, arrived in Paris. He received the 18° and the 30° in Marconnay's Chapter and Aréopage, La Clémente Amitié, and the 31° to 33° from the Supreme Council of the Grand Orient of France, September 27, 1845.

Keeping on with his masonic research, Marconnay sought the original of Dalcho's *Orations* and wrote to Albert Mackey in Charleston who answered, September 1, 1846:

> I have tried, but in vain, to procure for you a copy of the discourse of Dalcho: one single copy is still existing, but I could not find it in Charleston: it is in the Library of a gentleman. In fact, this work is not to be found in the Printing Offices.[31]

When the new Louisiana A.Y.M. Grand Lodge, founded in New Orleans in March 1848, wrote to the Grand Orient, Marconnay was logically asked to

28. NMJ 1876: 70. The quoted Minutes were signed by J. J. J. Gourgas, Sov∴ Gr∴ Commander, Edward A. Raymond, Chas. W. Moore, and Reuel Baker. Also *see ibid.* 74.

29. It included parts, translated in French by Marconnay, of the *Report... on the principles of the Sublime Degrees of Masonry, approved by the Charleston Council on December 4, 1802,* which were included in the third edition of Clavel's book.

30. Foulhouze, born October 1, 1800, in Riom, France, was made a Mason in New Orleans about 1843 by Antonio Costa in Lodge Los Amigos del Orden (Foulhouze 1858: 16, 87, 89, 193).

31. Leblanc de Marconnay 1853: 29.

translate the letter into French and write a report about the masonic situation in New Orleans. Published under Marconnay's name in the Grand Orient of France's *Bulletin* in 1848, his *Historical Report on the York Rite* was followed along the next two years with a series of articles about the history of Freemasonry in the island of Saint Domingue.

In 1852, Foulhouze returned to Paris in order to have the Supreme Council in New Orleans, of which he was Grand Commander since January 31, 1848, and Atwood's in New York recognized by the Grand Orient of France. He certainly met Marconnay who was in the process of issuing a second report on the Louisiana situation in his capacity of Orator of the Chambre de Conseil et d'Appel du Grand Orient of France, dated August 18, 1852. Marconnay concluded by suggesting that the Grand Orient of France ought to recognize the four Supreme Councils then existing in the United States, namely that at Charleston, Gourgas' in Boston, Atwood's in New York, and Foulhouze's in New Orleans. Foulhouze brought back Marconnay's Report to Louisiana where it was translated in English by Charles Laffon de Ladébat and published by Lamarre in New Orleans in 1853.

Clavel died in 1852. A few years later, Jouaust wrote that Clavel's book was "the most popular work printed in France about Masonry."[32]

BIBLIOGRAPHY

Baynard, Samuel Harrison. 1938. *History of the Supreme Council, 33° Ancient Accepted Rite of Freemasonry Northern Masonic Jurisdiction of the United States of America and its Antecedents.* 2 vols.

Bègue-Clavel, François-Timoléon (1798–1852). 1843. *Histoire pittoresque de la Franc-Maçonnerie et des Sociétés secrètes anciennes et modernes.* 3d ed. 1844. –1987. Facsimile reprint of the 1844 ed. Paris: Artefact.

Bernheim, Alain. 1987. "Further Light on the Masonic World of Joseph Glock," *AQC* 100: 33–60.

———. 1988. "The Fate of some French Masonic Archives," *AQC* 101: 98–104.

32. Jouaust 1865: 476.

———. 1995. Introduction and index to the reprint of *Outline on the Rise and Progress of Freemasonry in Louisiana* by James B. Scot. Lafayette, La.: Michael Poll Publishing.

Bésuchet, Jean-Claude (1790–1867). 1829. *Précis Historique de l'Ordre de la Franc-Maçonnerie....* 2 vol. Paris: Rapilly, Libraire.

Bossu, Jean (1911–1985). 1975. "Joseph Cerneau," *Renaissance Traditionnelle*, no. 21–22: 79–81.

Carter, James D. 1971. *History of The Supreme Council, 33° (Mother Council of the World) Ancient and Accepted Scottish Rite of Freemasonry Southern Jurisdiction, U.S.A.—1891–1921.*

Charassin. 1845. "Rapport fait au G∴O∴ en sa Ch∴ de Corresp∴ Sur des documents concernant le Rite Ecossais ancien et accepté," *Bulletin du Grand Orient de France*, 1845: 121–31.

Dalcho, Frederick. 1801. *An Oration Delivered in the Sublime Grand Lodge, in Charleston, South Carolina, On the 23d of September, 5801, Before the Members of that Lodge, the Symbolic Grand Lodge of Ancient York-Masons, and the Officers of the several Lodges in the City ; and Published at their Request. By Brother Frederick Dalcho, Member of the Supreme Council of the 33d. degree, and Grand Orator of the Sublime Lodge of Perfection.* Charleston, (South-Carolina) Printed by T. B. Bowen. No. 3 Broad-Street.

———. 1803. *An Oration Delivered in the Sublime Grand Lodge of South-Carolina, in Charleston, On the 21st of March, A.L. 5807, A.D. 1803, Before the Members of that Lodge, the Symbolic Grand Lodge of Free and Accepted Masons, and a considerable number of visiting Brethren And Published at their request, to which is added an Appendix Containing an historical inquiry into the origin of the difference of Ancient and Modern Masonry, usually so called ; &c. &c. by Brother Frederick Dalcho, Inspector General, and Grand Master of the Sublime Grand Lodge of South-Carolina.* Charleston, Printed by T. B. Bowen, No. 3, Bedon's-Alley.

———. 1808. *Orations of the Illustrious Brother Frederick Dalcho Esq.r M.D. Reprinted By Permission of the Author under the Sanction of the Ill. The College of Knights Of K.H. And the Original Chapter of Prince Masons of Ireland.* Dublin: Printed by John King, Westmoreland St.

Folger, Robert B. 1862. *The Ancient and Accepted Scottish Rite, in Thirty-three degrees... with an Appendix containing numerous authentic documents.* 1881. Second edition with a Supplement. New York: Published by the Author.

Foulhouze, James. 1858. *Mémoire à consulter sur l'Origine du Rite Ecossais Ancien Accepté, sur les Prétentions des Suprêmes Conseils Dalcho-Mackey de Charleston et Gourgas-Moore de Boston, sur les Droits du Suprême Conseil de l'Etat souverain et indépendant de la Louisiane et sur les Folies de Son Altesse Impériale et Royale, le Prince Lucien Murat, Prétendant à la Couronne de Naples, Grand-Maître pro tempore de l'Ordre Maçonnique en France.* Nouvelle-Orleans. L. Marchand & Cie, Imprimeurs, Rue Jefferson 35.

Gardner, W.S. "The spurious Supreme Councils in the Northern Jurisdiction," NMJ 1864: 109–73. (reprint from the *Freemason's Monthly Magazine*, vol. 23).

Gaudart de Soulages et Lamant. 1995. *Dictionnaire des Francs-Maçons.*

Haemeth, Br∴ Akim [pseudonym of Adrianyi-Pontet, Emile (1865–1952)]. "Irreguläre und betrügerische Riten," *Wiener Freimaurer-Zeitung*, Dec. 1928–Nov. 1929. "Der Cerneauismus" appeared in Mar. 1929: 8–13.

Harris, Ray Baker. 1957. *Bibliography of the Writings of Albert Pike.*

Homan, William. 1905. *The Ancient Accepted Scottish Rite of Freemasonry.*

Jouaust, Achille Godefroy (1825–1889). 1865. *Histoire du Grand Orient de France.* –1989. Facsimile reprint. Avant-Propos et Index par Alain Bernheim. Paris: Editions Télètes.

Le Bihan, Alain. 1967. *Loges et Chapitres de la Grande Loge et du Grand Orient de France (2e moitié du XVIIIe siècle).* Paris: Bibliothèque Nationale.

Leblanc de Marconnay. 1848. "Rapport Historique Sur le rite d'York professé par les GG∴ LL∴ d'Amérique," *Bulletin du Grand Orient de France* 1848: 178–86.

———. 1849. "Etat de la Maçonnerie dans l'ancienne Ile Saint-Domingue," *Bulletin du Grand Orient de France* 1849: 84–88, 151–57, 206–12, 323–27.

———. 1852. *Rapport sur des Différends élevés entre la Gr∴ Loge du Rite d'York pour l'Etat de la Louisiane et le Suprême Conseil du Rite Ecossais pour le même Etat, Ainsi que sur les Prétentions des divers Suprêmes Conseils existants en Amérique, et Preuves irrécusables que le Rite Ecossais Ancien et Accepté en 33 degrés appartenait originairement au G∴ O∴ de France.* Paris: Imprimerie Saintin, Dentan, Pinard. 9, Cour des Miracles.

———. 1853. *Report on the Difficulties which exist between the Grand Lodge of the York Rite for the State of Louisiana and the Supreme Council of the Scotch Rite for the same State, and on the Pretentions of the several Supreme Councils existing in America and Irrefutable Proofs that the Scotch Rite, Ancient and Accepted, in 33 Degrees, originally belonged to the Grand Orient of France. Translated from the French, by Br∴ Laffon-Ladébat, a M∴M∴ of the York Rite and a Member of the Supr∴ Council of the Scotch Rite, Ancient and Accepted.* New Orleans: Br∴ J. Lamarre's Printing Office, Exchange Alley, 102, between Conti and Bienville sts.

Ligou, Daniel (sous la direction de). 1987. *Dictionnaire de la Franc-Maçonnerie.*

Lindsay, R. S. 1958. *The Scottish Rite for Scotland.* Edinburgh: The Supreme Council for Scotland.

[Lobingier, Charles Sumner]. 1931. *The Supreme Council, 33°, Mother Council of the World.* Louisville, Ky.: The Standard Printing Co. Inc.

McClenachan. 1905. "Joseph Cerneau" in Homan 1905: 61–64.

Mellor, Alec. 1971. *Dictionnaire de la Franc-Maçonnerie et des Francs-Maçons.*

Minutes of the History Committee, Supreme Council, 33°, A.A.S.R., N.M.J., 1952–1955.

Naudon, Paul. 1966. *Histoire et Rituels des Hauts Grades Maçonniques Le Rite Ecossais Ancien et Accepté.* Reprinted since 1978 as: *Histoire, Rituels et Tuileur des Hauts Grades Maçonniques Le Rite Ecossais Ancien et Accepté.* [Four different editions 1966, 1972, 1978, 1984]. Paris: Dervy-Livres.

Newbury, George Adelbert, and Williams, Louis Lenway. 1987. *A History of the Supreme Council, 33° A.A.S.R., N.M.J., U.S.A.*

NMJ 1864. Abbreviation for *Proceedings of the Supreme Coucil of Sovereign Grand Inspectors-General of the Thirty-Third and last Degree, Ancient and Accepted Scottish Rite, for the Northern Masonic Jurisdiction of the United States of America.* Boston: Printed by John Wilson and Son, 5, Water Street. 1864.

NMJ 1876. *Abbreviation for Proceedings of the Supreme Council of Sov∴ Gr∴ Inspectors General, 33°, for the Northern Masonic Jurisdiction of the United States.* Portland: Stephen Berry, Printer. 1876.

OB. Abbreviation for *Official Bulletin* of the Supreme Council of the 33d Degree for the Southern Jurisdiction of the United States (vol. i, May 1870–vol. x, Jun. 1892).

Peckham, William H. 1884. *The Ancient and Accepted Scottish Rite in the United States of America from 1801 to 1883 inclusive.* New York.

Ragon, Jean-Marie (1781–1862). 1853. *Orthodoxie Maçonnique.* –1972. Facsimile reprint. Paris: Cercle des Amis de la Bibliothèque Initiatique.

Rebold, Emmanuel. 1864. *Histoire des Trois Grandes Loges.* Paris: Collignon, Libraire-Editeur.

Sitwell, N. S. H. 1927. "Some Mid-Eighteenth Century French Manuscripts," *AQC* 40: 91–125.

Smith, James Fairbairn. 1965. "The Rise of the Ecossais Degrees," *Proceedings of the Chapter of Research of the Grand Chapter of Royal Arch Masons of the State of Ohio,* vol. 10.

Stillson, Henry Leonard (Editor-in-Chief) and Hughan, William James (European Editor). 1891. *History of the Ancient and Honorable Fraternity of Free and Accepted Masons, and Concordant Orders.*

Sup∴ Council for France and its Dependencies, The. *[Report] In re Joseph Cerneau.* 1886. Published by the Supreme Council for the Southern Jurisdiction of the United States. Or∴ of Washington. –1995 Facsimile reprint. Introduction and Index by Michael R. Poll. Lafayette, La.: Michael Poll Pub.

Walgren, Kent. 1994. "A Bibliography of Pre-1851 American Scottish Rite Imprints (non-Louisiana)," In Heredom 3: 55–119.

Williams, Louis L. 1985. "Life and Legacy of Joseph Cerneau," *The Northern Light,* Apr. 1985: 10–13.

APPENDIX

Resolutions of respect to Joseph Cerneau on his return to France.

There are so few authentic documents directly pertaining to Joseph Cerneau that the discovery of a new one is a milestone in Masonic history. Until then, Cerneau was a person one spoke about. Badly.

A glibly hypocritical anonymous broadsheet published in French at Philadelphia in January 1810 under the pretence of calling him "Brother" accuses him of behaving in a most disgraceful way since he arrived in New York. In August 1813, Grand Commander John Mitchell mentions to La Motta "the man you say is called Mr. Joseph Cerneau," and for Frederick Dalcho, Cerneau is "a certain individual." One month later, Emanuel de la Motta meets "Mr. Joseph Cerneau" in New York but drops the "Mr." in the *Manifesto* he drafts shortly after that meeting for Charleston's approval, which will be made public in January, 1814. The expelled object, is therein reduced to the condition of "a certain individual of the name of Joseph Cerneau." A few days later, he and his Masonic body are described as "Joseph Cerneau and his company" in a joined letter addressed to Charleston by J. J. J. Gourgas, John G. Tardy, and Sampson Simson.

We never hear Cerneau speak for himself. We never hear his voice because we do not have a single letter he wrote nor a single document issued by him alone, in his own name. And we still don't.

But in this recently discovered document, we read—for the first time—about Bro. Joseph Cerneau as a completely different person. The document mentions "his zeal for the interests of the Order," his "perseverance and ability," and "his useful talents," We meet with brethren who wish to express their "highest esteem and regard for his person, virtues, and services."

Who was he actually ? What did he really do and why ? And what was his authority for acting the way he did, if any? The time may have come to ask such questions and to see if the previous answers we are all too well aware of were biased or not. At least, it may be worth a try.

Resolutions of respect to Joseph Cerneau on his return to France.

AD UNIVERSI TERRARUM ORBIS SUMMI ARCHITECTI GLORIAM

DEUS MEUMQUE JUS

ORDO AB CHAO

At the Orient of Most Potent Sov∴ Gd∴ Consistr∴ of Sup∴ Chiefs of Exalted Masonry according to the Ancient & Accepted Scottish Rite of Heredom for the United States Of America their Territories & Dependencies regularly constituted under the Cel∴ Can∴ near the B∴B∴ at the central point answering to the 40th∴ Deg∴ 41 M∴ N∴L∴

To all Regular Free and Accepted Masons
Stability, HEALTH, Power

——The M∴P∴ Sov∴ Gd∴ Consistory of the United States of America its Territories & Dependencies being informed that their M∴ Ill∴B∴ Joseph Cerneau aged 62 Years born at Villeblevin Dept∴ of Yonne France. M∴ P∴ Gd∴ Commander & Founder of the Sup∴Council of G∴ Insp∴ Genl∴ of the 33rd∴ Deg∴ Honorary Gd∴ Commander Ad Vitam of this Sov∴ Gd∴ Consistory is about to depart from this G∴O∴ for his native Country and desirous to testify as well to him than to all Mas∴ Bodies & Masons of whatever Degrees, the high sense this Gd∴ Consistr∴ entertain of the Masonic worth of their said Ill∴ B∴ of his zeal for the interests of the Order more especially in the Exalted and Perfect degrees which his zeal, perseverance and ability have led him to establish and contributed to maintain among us DO resolve that they view with emotions of sincere regret the Occurrence which is about to deprive the Gd∴ Consistr∴ of his useful talents, & that they entertain the highest esteem & regard for his person, virtues and services, and hope that he may receive the reward of his usefulness in the enjoyment of every comfort that can solace the course of his declining years.

——Resolved that a Copy of these resolves be engrossed on Parchment, Signed and Sealed in the most ample form and manner and presented to our

Ill.·. B.·. Joseph Cerneau, and that our Gd.·. Chancellor be charged with the execution thereof.

——We therefore request all regularly constituted M.·. Ill.·. Most Val.·. Knights Masonic Pces.·. and Gd.·. Insprs.·. Genl.·. of the 33rd.·. Degree to acknowledge and favourably receive our Most Ill.·. Br.·. Joseph Cerneau in the Sublime Dignity with which he is invested promising the same respect towards those who shall present themselves at the door of our Sacred Asylum clothed with like authentic Titles.

——Given under our hands and Mysterious Seal and the Gd.·. Seal of Pces.·. of Masonry at the City of New York in the United States of America near the B.·. B.·. at the point above mentioned a place where are deposited the greatest Treasures the sight of which fills us with Consolation Joy & Gratitude for all that is Great and Good this 10th day of the 9th.·. mas.·. month in the Year of T.·. L.·. 5827 & the Christian Era 1827.

Cadwallader D. Colden 1 Min. of State	**E. Hicks 33 Deg.·.** D.·. Gd.·. Comr.·.	George.·. Smith 33rd.·. Deg.·. 2nd Minister of State P.·. J.·.

Sealed by	Jonathan Schieffelin 1st Lieut.·. Gd.·. Commander	Francis Dubuar 2°.·. L.·. Gr.·. Com.·.	**By Order**

H^{n} Westiwell G.·. K.·. S.·. 32° degree	Orazio de Attelis Santangelo.·. 33rd.·. degree	Hampton Dunham 33 Deg.·. G.·. Secy.·..

The Early Years of the Grand Consistory of Louisiana (1811–1815)

Michael R. Poll, 32°

> For multiple reasons, I directed that the Grand Consistory of Louisiana be converted into a statutory consistory of the Valley of New Orleans. ... Grand Consistories were inaugurated when communications over long distances were difficult. Later they were found to be impediment to effective administration so became outmoded. All except Louisiana had been converted into statutory consistories. There is no longer any sanction under our Statutes for a Grand Consistory.
> — Henry C. Clausen, 33°, SGC, 1973[1]

A significant chapter in the colorful history of Louisiana Masonry was thus closed. While the "death" of the Southern Jurisdiction's last Grand Consistory is easily established, the events leading to and surrounding its birth are less apparent. The complex, elusive, and highly emotional history of Louisiana Scottish Rite

1. *Transactions of the Supreme Council, 33° for the Southern Jurisdiction, U.S.A.* (Washington, DC: Supreme Council, 33°, S.J., 1973), 46.

Masonry is often an enigmatic tale, which reads, more often than not, like a best-selling mystery novel. "Dry history" it is not.

The Beginning

The earliest known appearance of the Grand Consistory of Louisiana was in New Orleans in 1811. While research is ongoing, there are, unfortunately, no known surviving documents or minutes from this body. All the information that has been collected concerning the 1811 Grand Consistory is recorded in a few secondary sources. James Scot gave us, in his 1873 *Outline of the Rise and Progress of Freemasonry in Louisiana,* the first known published account concerning this body by reproducing a communication dated April 20, 1811, from the *Sov. Grand Consistory of Princes of the Royal Secret of Louisiana* to *Étoile Polaire* Lodge.[2] The communication sought to establish relations between the Grand Consistory and *Étoile Polaire* Lodge No. 1 and is issued under the name of "Des Bois, Grand Secretary." Scot explained, "The signature is that of Bro. Jean Baptiste Des Bois,[3] who was Grand Senior Warden of the Grand Lodge in 1818. He was Master of *Bienfaisance* Lodge No. 1 in 1811, and Master of Concord Lodge No. 3 in 1815." Scot also theorized that the members of the Consistory were likely "men of advanced age, and it may be that the Consistory of 1811 was formed more for the purpose of social reunion than propagating the Rite."[4]

However, Scot acknowledged, "This, however, is mere conjecture and it is not known how long the Consistory of 1811 maintained its organization."[5] and "Beyond the mere fact of its existence, nothing is known in regard to it."[6] Scot's report, in effect, only established that this consistory existed at the time that the communication was written. In addition to Scot being uncertain as

2. James Scot, *Outline of the Rise and Progress of Freemasonry in Louisiana* (1873; reprint, New Orleans: Michael Poll Publishing, 1995), 21–22. This communication no longer exists in the archives of the Grand Lodge of Louisiana.

3. Des Bois was a New Orleans schoolmaster turned attorney. His home still exists in the French Quarter at 631–633 Dauphine St. Des Bois decorated the balcony of his home with a wrought iron railing with an elaborate "J B D" monogram in the center. Above his monogram, and fashioned on the top rail iron-work, is a square and compass—a surprising public display considering the general disapproval of Masonry by many in New Orleans at that time.

4. Scot, 22.

5. Scot, 22.

6. Scot, 89.

to the length of time this body existed after the date of the communication, he, also, gave no clue as to its length of existence prior to the communication.

More information concerning the 1811 Grand Consistory is contributed by Albert Pike in his 1882 *Official Bulletin V.* Pike not only gave additional names of those who were associated with this body, but he also offers an explanation as to how this consistory was formed. Pike reports that Louis D'Huard,[7] Pierre Joseph Duhulquod, Christian Miltenberger, Jean Baptiste Des Bois, Nicolas Roche, Laurent Segui,[8] Jean Baptiste Labatut, Jean Soulié, Thomas Urquhart, and Pierre Francois Dubourg were members of this body. The consistory was granted a charter on March 28, 1811, by Louis Jean Lusson[9] and Jean Baptiste Modeste Lefebvre,[10] both S.G.I.G.s of the Supreme Council of Kingston, Jamaica, and the first meeting was held on Sunday April 7, 1811, at 5:00 PM in the hall of Perfect Union Lodge.[11]

Adding further to the information concerning the 1811 Grand Consistory is *A Library of Freemasonry,* which states:[12]

> There is a Manuscript Register in the Carson Collection[13] kept by one Jean Doszedardski, a Sovereign Grand Inspector General of the 33rd degree. This Register contains what purports to be a copy of Doszedardski's Patent, as a Prince of the Royal Secret, and Deputy Grand Inspector General and Member of the Sublime Council of the 33rd degree, dated May 5, 1813, signed by L. J. Lusson, S.G.I.G., 33rd degree, a member and representative of the Sovereign Senate sitting at Kingston, Island of Jamaica, in that Orient. ... A most important historical matter contained in this Register is an account of the

7. Misspelling for "Duhart."

8. Misspelling for "Sigur." Laurent Sigur was the first Master of Perfect Union Lodge in 1793. The lodge was organized under Sigur's Rose-Croix patent.

9. In 1811 Lusson was the Senior Warden of Réunion Désirie No. 112 and the owner a merchandise shop on St. Peter St. in New Orleans. He received his 33° from Gabriel Jastram in New Orleans on November 10, 1809.

10. In 1811 Lefebvre was a Past Master & Secretary of *Étoile Polaire* No. 129 and was a New Orleans merchant. Lefebvre received his 32° from Lusson on June 1, 1807. It is unknown how soon thereafter he received his 33°, but it is reasonable to suppose that he received it from Lusson.

11. Albert Pike, *Official Bulletin of the Supreme Council of the 33d Degree for the Southern Jurisdiction USA,* vol. v (Charleston: Supreme Council, 33°, S.J., 1882) 329–30. The hall of Perfect Union Lodge in 1811 was located right behind 333 St. Charles Ave. in New Orleans, which, until the sale of the Masonic Temple Building 1996, was the home of the Grand Lodge of Louisiana.

12. Charles T. McClenachan, *A Library of Freemasonry,* vol. IV, chapters XLI–XLIV (Philadelphia: John C. Yorston Publishing Co., 1889).

13. This collection resides in the Museum of our National Heritage, Lexington, Mass.

> organization of the first bodies of Sublime Masonry in New Orleans,[14] especially a Consistory of S.P.R.S.
>
> Under date August 13, 1810, Gabriel Jastram, 33°, "Member of the Supreme Council of the 33rd degree at Kingston, Island of Jamaica, organized by the Count de Grasse Tilley [*sic*],[15] Grand Inspector General of the 33rd degree, Grand Commander *ad vitam*, by authority and power of the Sovereign Grand Council sitting at *Charleston*, in *the State of South Carolina*," &c., granted a Patent to Pierre Joseph Duhalquod [*sic*],[16] P.R.S., Jean Baptiste Desbois,[17] Rose Croix, and others for a Symbolic Lodge in New Orleans, under the name La Bienfaisance, to confer the degrees of Entered Apprentice, Fellow Craft and Master Mason, of the Ancient Rite.
>
> Then, under date December 20, 1810, Gabriel Jastram, by the same authority and in addition, "Under the special protection of the said chiefs of Masonry (the Supreme Council at Kingston) representatives of the Grand and Sovereign Chapter Metropolitan d'Herodom of Kilwinning and Edinburgh in Scotland," granted a Patent to Duhalquod [*sic*],[18] Savary, Desbois [*sic*], and others for a Lodge of Perfection, Council of Elect, College of Scotland, Council of Knights of the East, Princes of Jerusalem, and Chapter of Scottish Rose-Croix, under the distinctive title of La Triple Bienfaisance, to be held in New Orleans, La., with powers to confer the degrees from the 4th to the 18th inclusive.[19]

What then follows is a near word for word duplication of what Pike reported in his *Official Bulletin* concerning the creation of the 1811 Grand Consistory. This would make the Doszedardski Register the likely source for the material that Pike published. At the conclusion of the report on the creation of the consistory is a most interesting line which reads: "They [the Grand Consistory] were required to report in the shortest time to the Sovereign Grand Councils of Charleston, South Carolina, and of Kingston, Jamaica."[20]

The communication from the 1811 Grand Consistory to *Étoile Polaire* Lodge establishes Des Bois as Grand Secretary, but we have no documents

14. This is an incorrect statement. The first known bodies of Sublime Masonry in New Orleans were organized on April 2, 1756, and connected to the 1752 Perfect Harmony Lodge in New Orleans. See: Sharp Document #102.

15. Misspelling for "Grasse-Tilly."

16. Misspelling for "Duhulquod."

17. Des Bois maintained the original spelling of his family name throughout his life. The family name, however, changed in later generations to "DesBois" and "Desbois" which accounts for the variations in its spelling.

18. Misspelling for "Duhulquod."

19. McClenachan, 652–653.

20. McClenachan, 299.

indicating the presiding officer of the Grand Consistory. Either Lusson or Lefebvre may have served in this capacity.[21] Given the practice of listing the members of a Masonic body by Masonic rank, it is also possible that Duhart, Miltenberger.[22] or Duhulquod[23] presided over the body. Without further documentation, we are left only with speculation.

An examination of the known data concerning this body does shed some more light than was previously known or understood. Clearly Scot's suggestion that the 1811 Grand Consistory might have been created by a group of old Masons "more for the purpose of social reunion than propagating the Rite" is not accurate. An assessment of the names offered in the Doszedardski Register reveals that the 1811 Grand Consistory contained some of the most active men in Louisiana Masonry and the community. In 1812 Pierre Francois Dubourg became the first Grand Master of the Grand Lodge of Louisiana, an office he held for three terms. Jean Soulié was the second Grand Master of the Grand Lodge also serving for three terms and was a successful merchant and a director of the Bank of Louisiana, an office also held by General Jean Baptiste Labatut who, in addition, held the position of City Treasurer. General Labatut (the Master of Perfect Union Lodge No. 29 in 1809) was also the Commander of the Corps of Veterans during the 1815 Battle of New Orleans and was a former attorney general of the Cabildo.[24] Louis Duhart would serve *La Triple Bienfaisance* No. 20 Rose-Croix Chapter as Venerable Master from 1820 until 1823 and again in 1825. In 1811, Thomas Urquhart was a Past Master and sitting Master of Perfect Union Lodge No. 29 (an office he would hold again in 1820) and President of the Bank of Louisiana. Christian Miltenberger[25] was a prominent physician who would serve the Grand Lodge as Grand Treasurer from 1825 to 1829.

21. While Lusson and Lefebvre were both living in New Orleans, there is no record in the City Directory nor available Masonic records to show that Gabriel Jastram was a resident of the city or held any Masonic position in any of the New Orleans Masonic Bodies.

22. Miltenberger received his 33° on October 21, 1809, from Jastrum, assisted by Lusson and Nicholas Tipaine. Albert Pike, *Official Bulletin of the Supreme Council of the 33d Degree for the Southern Jurisdiction USA*, vol. IX (Charleston: Supreme Council, 33°, S.J., 1889) 175.

23. Duhulquod received his 32° from Antoine Bideaud on April 16, 1803. *Register of Antoine Bideaud* located in the New Orleans Scottish Rite Library and Museum.

24. The Cabildo was the seat of government for the Louisiana Territory prior to its acquisition by the US.

25. The family name of "Miltenberger" was originally spelled "Milten-Berger."

The creation of the 1811 Grand Consistory followed the creation of two other subordinate Masonic Bodies in New Orleans by a thirty-third from the Kingston Supreme Council. The 1811 Grand Consistory gave assurance that Masons would be made and advanced according to the style accustomed to the West Indies Masons from the degree of Entered Apprentice to Prince of the Royal Secret—and, even, Sovereign Grand Inspector General. There is nothing in their actions to suggest that the bodies being created were simply social clubs for the amusement of the members. It is clear that the rite was very much being propagated in New Orleans by the Kingston Masons. The action of having the Grand Consistory report to the Supreme Councils at Charleston and Kingston is also fully in keeping with a serious desire to create and preserve these bodies. While there is, also, very little information concerning the Supreme Council at Kingston, there are several facts that can be drawn out to help understand the situation a little better.

The Doszedardski and Bideaud Registers[26] indicate Comte Alexandre Francois Auguste de Grasse-Tilly founded the Kingston Supreme Council in 1804. Concerning this creation, Alain Bernheim writes:

> Grasse-Tilly had been made a prisoner in Saint-Domingue by the British toward the end of 1804[27] and taken to Kingston. The "letters of credence" which he had received from the Charleston Supreme Council, 21 February 1802, were "vised" in Kingston, 11 January 1804, by "Sol. Morales, P∴R∴S∴ Secretary" and by "J^{n} Morales, G∴I∴ Gal, 33^{d}." This was asserted by Baron de Marguerittes during the masonic trial of Grasse-Tilly before the "Prado" Supreme Council. It seems likely that "Jn" is a misprint (or a wrong reading) for "Ic". The mention of the 33d degree after the name of Morales seems to be the earliest mention of the degree in Jamaica where Grasse-Tilly founded a Supreme Council during the short time he was there. He returned then to Charleston (where he was present at a meeting of his former Lodge, La Candeur, 15 February 1804) and went to France where he arrived in July.[28]

26. In 1994 this writer discovered the Antoine Bideaud Register and ritual book in the archives of the New Orleans Scottish Rite Bodies. Bideaud was a S.G.I.G. from de Grasse-Tilly's 1802 West Indies Supreme Council who would, in 1804, travel to New York and establish there a Grand Consistory from which would give birth, in 1813, to De La Motta's Northern Supreme Council.

27. Misprint for 1803.

28. Alain Bernheim, "Further Light on the Masonic World of Joseph Glock," *Ars Quatuor Coronatorum*, vol. 100, (1987) 45.

It is not reasonable to think that Grasse-Tilly could have founded a Supreme Council in Kingston and not mention its existence to the members of the Charleston Council when he arrived there before leaving for France. It should also be noted that Grasse-Tilly was not the only one in a position to inform the Charleston Council of the creation of the Kingston Council. Solomon Morales of the Kingston Council and Emanuel De La Motta of the Charleston Council had been friends at least twenty years prior to the establishment of the Charleston Council.[29] In addition, Lusson was in Charleston when Jean Baptiste Aveilhé made him a Deputy Inspector General (25°) on December 12, 1797.[30] Lusson was not an unknown Mason in Charleston. The chances of there having been no communications between the two Councils are highly improbable to non-existent. The fact that the creation of the 1811 Grand Consistory in New Orleans included the instruction to make the creation known to the Councils of Charleston and Kingston makes the relationship evident.

Events of 1812 & 1813

The establishment of the 1811 Grand Consistory in New Orleans was a creation in an area that was but a territory of the United States; Louisiana was not granted statehood until April 30, 1812. Once statehood was achieved, the 1811 Grand Consistory was placed in a somewhat awkward position. Without question, the area was then under the jurisdiction of the Charleston Council. The area, in fact, was claimed by the Charleston Council as early as 1804 when Charleston issued a patent to Jean Baptiste Marie Delahogue (father-in-law of Grasse-Tilly and Lt. Grand Commander of the 1802 Supreme Council in the West Indies) to establish bodies in New Orleans.[31] While Delahogue is shown as the Master of Charity Lodge in New Orleans in 1804, there is no record, whatsoever, suggesting that he created any Masonic body in New Orleans during his stay there. Once Louisiana became a state, action obviously had to be taken in regard to the 1811 Grand Consistory. To allow it to remain under

29. Bernheim, Glock, 45.

30. McClenachan, 652.

31. Ray Baker Harris & James D. Carter, *History of the Supreme Council, 33° Southern Jurisdiction, USA 1801–1861* (Washington: The Supreme Council, 33°, S.J., 1964), 92.

the jurisdiction of the Kingston Council would mean to allow more than one Council to have bodies in an occupied area.

On May 17, 1830, Moses Holbrook, Grand Commander of the Charleston Council, sent a letter to John Holland, Grand Master of the Grand Lodge of Louisiana and Grand Commander in Chief of the Grand Council of Louisiana, which gave a report of a Consistory being formed in New Orleans on May 12, 1812, consisting of Louis Jean Lusson, Pierre Chameau, Sr., Jean Baptiste Pinta, Louis Casimir Moreau Lislet,[32] Jean Baptiste Casteret, Jean Baptiste Gillard "and some others" under the jurisdiction of the Charleston Council.[33] With no complete membership list for the Grand Consistory, we are left to assume, as should be expected, that the 1811 Grand Consistory was passing under the jurisdiction of the Charleston Council. Events then take an interesting turn.

From Charles Laffon de Ladébat's *Procés Verbal,* p. 72:

> On the 4th of December, 1812, Mr. Emanuel Gigaud, giving himself the title of Deputy Sov. Gr. Insp. Gen. 33d Degree, and Representative of the Grand Consistory established at New York by Joseph Cerneau, assembled certain persons possessing, regularly or irregularly, the high degrees of the A. and A. Rite, and raised them successively to the 32d Degree, and with them formed, provisionally, the so-called Grand Consistory of Louisiana.
>
> On the 8th of February, 1813, certain persons, whose names were Jean Pinard, Noel Fournier, Raymond Deveze, and Pierre Thomas Jarrié, asked from the Grand Consistory of J. Cerneau, at New York, a charter for a Grand Consistory of S.: PP.: R.: S.: 32d Degree, which they proposed to establish in Louisiana.
>
> On the 10th of April 1813, the petitioners received a letter from New York, which informed them that their request had been granted and that the charter would be sent them without delay. The charter is dated April 24, 1813, but it was not received until August of the same year. On the 19th of June, 1813, the said Grand Consistory was regularly installed....[34]

While the information that de Ladébat provides is quite significant, it should be pointed out that the organizational structure of the Cerneau Sovereign Grand Consistory provided for Grand *Councils* of Princes of the Royal

32. Lislet was the third Grand Master of the Grand Lodge of Louisiana serving in 1818 and serving as Deputy Grand Master from 1812–17. He was a most respected jurist whose decisions are discussed and remembered by the Louisiana Supreme Court to this day.

33. Alain Bernheim, Introduction, *Outline of the Rise and Progress of Freemasonry in Louisiana* (1873; reprint, with an introduction by Alain Bernheim, New Orleans, La.: Michael Poll Publishing, 1995) 13.

34. Charles Laffon de Ladébat, *Procés Verbal* (New Orleans: 1857) quoted by Scot, *Outline* 21

Secret and not Grand *Consistories* of Princes of the Royal Secret. De Ladébat's (and most future historians) use of the term "Grand *Consistory* of Louisiana" is incorrect for the body that was created in 1813 and existed under Cerneau. The first officers of the 1813 Grand Council of Princes of the Royal Secret in Louisiana were:[35]

Commander in Chief	Emanuel Gigaud
1st Lieutenant Commander	Jean Pinard
2. Lieutenant Commander	Noel Fournier
Grand Minister of State	Francis Martinez y Pizarro
Grand Treasurer	Raymond Deveze
Grand Secretary	Pierre Thomas Jarrié

With only scant secondary sources to piece together the creation and evolution of the Grand Consistory of Louisiana, we are left to draw assumptions as to the actual chain of events. The reports, in this case, lead one to believe that a consistory was created in New Orleans in 1811, passed under the jurisdiction of the Charleston Council in 1812 and then, again, switched jurisdictions to the Cerneau Bodies in 1813. This writer, however, is not wholly satisfied that this is the only possible and logical scenario. It is possible that divisions in the consistory began early on and that there were mixed opinions as to the direction the body should take. Moses Holbrook reported in 1830 that a consistory under the Charleston Council was "formed" and we, also, hear from Charles Laffon de Ladébat that a "Grand Consistory" [*sic*] was "formed" under Cerneau in 1813. We simply can not know if the 1811 body moved as a complete body to the Charleston Council or if the 1811 body fractured and the 1812 Charleston body was "formed" by only elements of the 1811 body (and, possibly, new members) as would be the 1813 body under Cerneau. Given the highly emotional and divided state of Louisiana Masonry in later years, it is not unreasonable to imagine that three separate "creations" took place in New Orleans in three years.

But Why Cerneau?

By 1813, there was significant activity in high grade Scottish Rite Masonry in New Orleans. But many pieces of a puzzle now exist. The 1811 Grand

35. Laffon de Ladébat, quoted by Scot, 21

Consistory was clearly the original body from which would spring (directly or indirectly) the 1812 Charleston Grand Consistory and the 1813 Cerneau Grand Council, but we must wonder what happened to cause the switch from Charleston to Cerneau. Since the 1811 Grand Consistory was instructed upon its creation to report not only to the Supreme Council at Kingston, but also to the one in Charleston (establishing Charleston as a "superior"), why did the New Orleans Scottish Rite Masons, even after a Charleston Consistory was established in New Orleans, move to or prefer the jurisdiction of Cerneau in 1813? Was there any reason that Cerneau Masonry should be considered "regular" by the New Orleans Masons in 1812?

To quote further from de Ladébat:

> It is worthy of remark that on the 3rd of May, 1814, the Grand Consistory of Louisiana received the denunciation of J. Cerneau by the Supreme Council of Charleston, and that on the 13th of November, 1814, Bro. Louis Jean Lusson, 33°, who on the 4th of December, 1812, had refused to subscribe to the conditions imposed by J. Cerneau, renewed his opposition to the said Grand Consistory. For this he was tried and condemned by that body, August 14, 1815. He was a member of the Supreme Council of Charleston, and, as such, had published in New Orleans the denunciation of Joseph Cerneau by Emanuel de la Motta.[36]

The first reported consideration given to passing under the Cerneau Jurisdiction came at a meeting on December 4, 1812, when a "provisional" Grand Council was formed. This was over six months after Lusson had created a Consistory in New Orleans under the Charleston jurisdiction. At this December 4 meeting, Gigaud was already a Cerneau "Representative" clearly establishing that "some" movement towards Cerneau had taken place prior to such a remarkable meeting. It would, also, seem predictable that Lusson (because of his role in the Charleston Consistory) would object to the Cerneau body being created in New Orleans, but his objection, itself, is a bit mystifying. There was no mention of irregularity concerning the Cerneau body, or with the area already being occupied by the Charleston Council. Lusson only seemed to object to some unspecified conditions imposed by Cerneau. Does this suggest that if the resulting obstacles from these conditions had been overcome, Lusson would have supported the Cerneau Grand Council of Louisiana?

36. Laffon de Ladébat, quoted by Scot, 21.

The fact is that the Charleston Council did not act against Cerneau (and might not have even known of his creation) until the spring or early summer of 1813 when Emanuel De La Motta traveled to New York and discovered the Cerneau and Bideaud Bodies.[37] The condemnation of the Cerneau Bodies did not officially come to New Orleans until over a year after the Grand Council of Louisiana was created. We must also recognize the fact that the *Grand Constitutions of 1786* did provide for two Supreme Councils in the United States (or North America, depending on which version you read) and from the information contained in those *Grand Constitutions*, and lack of published objections from Charleston, the Cerneau bodies could have been viewed, to many New Orleans Masons, as regular.[38]

That there was no apparent reason to view the Cerneau body as irregular at the time of the 1813 Grand Council creation does not, however, explain why the New Orleans Masons opted for Cerneau over Charleston. Even if the Cerneau Sovereign Grand Consistory had been welcomed with opened arms by the Charleston Council and declared perfectly regular, why would any reasonable New Orleans Scottish Rite Mason favor Cerneau over Charleston? New Orleans was clearly within the jurisdiction of the Charleston Council and a Consistory under Charleston was already established in New Orleans by Lusson. In order for the New Orleans Masons to embrace Cerneau it was necessary to make the considered decision to reject the Charleston Council. Logic dictates that there must have been a compelling reason for these Masons to take this seemingly extraordinary action.

The Situation in South Carolina

In December 1808 a union took place between two rival Grand Lodges in South Carolina. The Grand Lodge of Free and Accepted Masons and The Grand Lodge of the State of South Carolina, Ancient York Masons (AYM) merged to form The Grand Lodge of South Carolina. The battle between the two Grand Lodges had been long and hostile and the union lasted only a matter of weeks. The AYMs withdrew from the union and were, in turn,

37. La Motta would create the Supreme Council Northern Masonic Jurisdiction out of the "healed" Bideaud Bodies.

38. See: Michael R. Poll, "The Controversy of Joseph Cerneau: A Brief Examination," *Heredom* 4(1995): 47–61.

recognized as the regular Grand Lodge in South Carolina by most of the other US grand lodges. All of the members of the Charleston Supreme Council were members of the Grand Lodge of South Carolina which, at that time, was deemed irregular by most US grand lodges.[39] While this would have no effect on the regularity of the Charleston Supreme Council, it did, in fact, make all of the *members* of the Charleston Council "unrecognized" and unable to sit in a regular lodge of Master Masons in most US jurisdictions. This clearly presented the Charleston Council (and any Masonic body in relations with them) with a problem.

With all the members of the Charleston Council belonging to an unrecognized Grand Lodge, it is quite possible that the newly formed Grand Lodge of Louisiana did not desire to risk the possibility of being shut out of the regular Masonic community by a consistory in their jurisdiction, which was composed of many members of the grand lodge, entering into an association with a Supreme Council whose members were unrecognized and could be considered irregular. At that time, there was no mention of the Cerneau council, or any of its members, being irregular and Cerneau's deputy grand commander was the very influential Dewitt Clinton, long time grand master of the Grand Lodge of New York. Compounding the situation further was that Perfect Union Lodge (the senior Lodge in the formation of the Grand Lodge of Louisiana) obtained its charter in 1794 from the Grand Lodge of South Carolina, A.Y.M. The Worshipful Master of Perfect Union Lodge in 1812 was Pierre Francois Dubourg (a member of the 1811 Kingston Grand Consistory of Louisiana) who would become the first Grand Master of the Grand Lodge of Louisiana.

The fact, however, that York Rite grand lodges viewed the Charleston Council members and their grand lodge as "unrecognized" might not have been enough to influence a Grand Consistory of the *Scottish* Rite. Since the decision was made, however, to pass under the Cerneau Sovereign Grand Consistory, we must examine if there could have been any influence from other Scottish Rite Bodies to make this switch.

Remarkably, the grand commander of the Kingston Supreme Council, J. J. Itter, is listed as an honorary member of the Cerneau Sovereign Grand

39. Bernheim, Introduction to *Outline*, 7–8.

Consistory in its 1818 register of members.[40] The register is reprinted in Folger's 1862 *Ancient and Accepted Scottish Rite in Thirty-three Degrees* and carries the note: "This Pamphlet is annexed because it is a much more perfect one, than those published in 1813, 1814, 1815, and 1816. The others are not as full, and this is precisely like the preceding ones in every respect, the Author has preferred the one of this date."[41] While there is no known information establishing how long prior to 1818 Itter was an Honorary Member of Cerneau's body, Folger's report is supported by John James Joseph Gourgas (then Secretary General of the Supreme Council Northern Masonic Jurisdiction) who wrote to Emanuel de La Motta on July 3, 1815:

> ... we have one [communication] which says that I. I. [*sic,* read J. J.] Itter, the Sn. Gr. Cr. there, loves money much, is a second Joseph Cerneau there and entirely devoted to him, that it is needful to take precautions for the correspondence with the Supe. Gd. Council, and even that the said Itter is the grand director and manager of everything; it is recommended, however, as a precaution, to correspond and direct to Ill. Br. Morales, formerly the Sn. Gd. Comr., &c., &c., &c.[42]

Regardless of the austere comments made by Gourgas towards Itter, it is apparent that the Kingston Council (or, at least, its Grand Commander) had switched to the Cerneau camp. Given that the Kingston Council was the parent of the 1811 Grand Consistory of Louisiana, the action of the Kingston Council could reasonably be viewed as influential, if not, an expected "road map of action" for the New Orleans Masons to follow. The Kingston Council, however, was not the only Supreme Council to recognize Cerneau. In 1813 the Supreme Council of France entered into Communications with Cerneau as would the Grand Orient of France in 1816.[43]

Considering the Grand Lodge regularity dilemma of the Charleston Council Members and the position taken by the Supreme Councils of Kingston and France, it should be of little surprise that the many New Orleans Scottish Rite Masons abandoned the Charleston Council for Cerneau. Given the known

40. Robert B. Folger, *Ancient and Accepted Scottish Rite in Thirty-three Degrees* (New York: Robt. B. Folger, 1862), 186.

41. Folger, 181.

42. *Transactions of the Supreme Council of the 33d Degree for the Southern Jurisdiction U.S.A.* (reprint, Washington: Supreme Council, 33°, S.J., 1878), 46.

43. Folger, 109.

facts of that time, the New Orleans Masons could be viewed as irresponsible had they acted in any other manner.

THE ANALYSIS

De Ladébat stated in 1857 that Lusson was a "member of the Supreme Council of Charleston." It is possible that de Ladébat confused the fact that Lusson was appointed a "Representative" of the Charleston Council in order to deliver the Charleston denunciation of Cerneau with his being a "Member" of that Council. Because of Lusson's action, de Ladébat says that he was "tried and condemned by that body [the Grand Council of Louisiana], August 14, 1815." While the minutes of the Grand Council (and later Grand Consistory) of Louisiana from 1822 to 1846 have been recently re-discovered by this writer, there are no known minutes prior to 1822 for the Grand Council. This is, indeed, unfortunate as the record of the Lusson "trial" would prove most interesting. It is unknown how a body controlling degrees no higher than the thirty-second could hold a trial for a thirty-third, who would be under the jurisdiction of a Supreme Council.

Just as interesting as the "trial" of Lusson in 1815, is Lusson's own actions in 1813. Lusson was a party to the creation of the 1812 Consistory acting on behalf of the Charleston Council and would again act on behalf of the Charleston Council, as their Representative, in publishing the Cerneau denunciation in New Orleans in 1814. Despite this, the Doszedardski Register shows that Jean Doszedardski was made a thirty-third on 5 May 1813 in New Orleans by Lusson! The register is verified by Lusson's own signature. Lusson, while carrying the Charleston banner in one hand, created a thirty-third in the jurisdiction of the Charleston Council. On whose authority did Lusson act? Lusson's action of creating a thirty-third in the jurisdiction of the Charleston Council displays some defiance for the authority of the Charleston Council—or a bit of confusion.

To throw one more interesting tidbit into the "soup," Solomon Morales, long time friend of Emanuel De La Motta and Grand Secretary of the Kingston Supreme Council, wrote to La Motta on July 13, 1815, asking for various rituals and included a current list of Members of the Kingston Supreme Council. The names of Lusson, Lefebvre, Jastram, and Doszedardski are nowhere to be found on the list.[44] Were they suspended? Did they resign? Did they retire? Were they ever really Members? Did Morales "forget" them? What happened? It also must not be forgotten that by 1815 the Grand Commander of the Kingston Council had joined the Cerneau camp. Was the Kingston Council split? Was Morales acting on his own "behind the back" of Itter? Did Morales create a *second* Supreme Council in Kingston (explaining his need for rituals)? What is not known is equal to (or surpasses) what is known.

Regardless of the reasons behind the creation of the Grand Council under Cerneau in 1813 and any later questions regarding its regularity, this was the body that was to survive. While there are only fragmented records of the members composing the Grand Council of Louisiana from 1813 to 1822, the minutes from 1822 to 1846 show that members of both the 1811 and 1812 Grand Consistories became members of the 1813 Grand Council. Lefebvre (1811 Kingston Grand Consistory) and L. C. Moreau Lislet (1812 Charleston Grand Consistory) both became commanders in chief of the Cerneau Grand Council of Louisiana as well as grand masters of the Grand Lodge of Louisiana. The Grand Council of Louisiana was undoubtedly the body that was accepted by the majority of the New Orleans Scottish Rite Masons and the members of the Grand Lodge of Louisiana. Scot's statement (reprinted by *A Library of Freemasonry*[45]), "The regularity of the New Orleans Consistory [*sic*] was questioned from the first, and several members of the Grand Lodge and its constituents in possession of the high degrees of the A. and A. Rite, refused to have anything to do with it"[46] displays a serious lack of understanding of the New Orleans, Kingston, and Charleston situations during the time of the creation of the Grand Council or a failure to acknowledge the accurate state of affairs.

The next chapters of the Grand Council/Consistory of Louisiana become even more remarkable, involved, and far too voluminous for one paper. The "found" minutes book reveals that the grand council would again pass under the jurisdiction of the Charleston Council on February 21, 1831, due to the slumber of the Cerneau Council. The Grand *Council* of Louisiana again becomes the Grand *Consistory* of Louisiana. It was during this time that the

44. Bernheim, Glock, 46.
45. Gould, etc., *Library of Freemasonry*, 332.
46. Scot, 23.

Grand Consistory of Louisiana created two Scottish Rite craft lodges leading to the 1833 Concordat between the Grand Consistory and Grand Lodge of Louisiana. The stay under the jurisdiction of the Charleston Council is short and, due to Charleston entering into a slumber, the Grand Consistory of Louisiana passes under the jurisdiction of the United Supreme Council of the Western Hemisphere in New York on September 1, 1832. Upon this body also entering into a slumber, the Grand Consistory of Louisiana (after a time as a "Sovereign Grand Consistory") passes under the jurisdiction of the Supreme Council of the United States of America sitting in New Orleans (The Supreme Council of Louisiana) on October 9, 1846. On February 16, 1855, a concordat is entered into between the Charleston and New Orleans Supreme Councils and the Grand Consistory of Louisiana once again passes under the jurisdiction of the Charleston Council. Here the Grand Consistory of Louisiana remained until its conversion into a statutory consistory by Sovereign Grand Commander Henry Clausen in 1973.

The Early Years of the Grand Consistory of Louisiana (1811–1815)—A Rejoinder

Arturo de Hoyos, 33°, G.·.C.·.

"What is not known is equal to (or surpasses) what is known." With these words Brother Michael Poll summarizes his interesting article, "The Early Years of the Grand Consistory of Louisiana (1811–1815)," *Heredom*, vol. 8 (1999–2000). The early history of hauts grades Masonry in New Orleans is indeed fascinating, and Brother Poll is to be commended for approaching this difficult topic. Having said this, however, I believe some of the evidence supports interpretations differing from his. As I do not intend to rewrite Brother Poll's article, and because of the technical nature of this "rejoinder," the reader will be greatly benefited by reviewing his article. This will render the duplication of large parts of his text unnecessary.

Brother Poll attempts to account for the disappearance of the earliest Grand Consistory in New Orleans and for the emergence of subsequent bodies. Much of what we know about early Scottish Rite history is based on little-known documents in Masonic and private archives. My position as Grand Archivist and Grand Historian of the Supreme Council gives me liberal access to both types of collections, including primary sources that Brother Poll references only second-hand. Further, I have seen additional documents completely unknown to Brother Poll. These materials provide information to help us form a more accurate and complete picture of the early days of the Scottish Rite. This rejoinder seeks to explore several issues connected with the early history of the Scottish Rite and "Cerneauism," which may be defined as Masonic authority derived from a Frenchman named Joseph Cerneau (see frontispiece for a portrait). I suggest that the following points require reconsideration of some of Brother Poll's assumptions:

- The New Orleans Consistory that was granted a Charter on March 28, 1811, by the Supreme Council at Kingston, Jamaica, may not have been the same Consistory which submitted a return to the Supreme Council at Charleston on May 12, 1812.

- The above-mentioned "Jamaica Consistory" may have died out, rather than merged with the Cerneauists.

- Another Consistory may have been "established" in New Orleans on September 28, 1814, by the Supreme Council at Charleston.

- The Supreme Council at Charleston had both legitimate and practical reasons for not becoming involved in the Cerneau controversy before 1813.

- Joseph Cerneau's creation of a "Supreme Council" was in direct violation of the *Grand Constitutions of 1786.*

- The Supreme Council at Kingston, Jamaica, rejected Cerneauism.

A Consistory "Formed" on May 12, 1812?

As stated above, Brother Poll attempts to account for the disappearance of the earliest Grand Consistory in New Orleans, and for the emergence of subsequent Bodies. The earliest document I am aware of, relative to this first body, is in the Archives of the Supreme Council, Southern Jurisdiction (rather than in the "Doszedardski Collection" as Brother Poll conjectured). Addressed "To M[ost]∴ Ill[ustrious]∴ and M[ost]∴ P[uissan]t∴ P[rin]ce∴ J[ea]n∴ L[ouis]∴ Lusson, Sovern∴ Grd∴ Inspr∴ Gal∴ 33d D[egree]∴"[1] the document is a notice stating that the installation ceremonies were set for Sunday, April 7, 1811, at 5:00 pm.[2] Concerning this body, Brother Poll writes:

> The 1811 Grand Consistory was clearly the original Body from which would spring (directly or indirectly) the 1812 Charleston Grand Consistory and the 1813 Cerneau Grand Council....

Brother Poll's admittedly "scant secondary sources" led him to "draw assumptions" that the 1811 Consistory first passed under (whether complete, expanded or fractured) the authority of the Charleston Supreme Council in 1812, and then under authority of the Cerneau Grand Consistory. To support his thesis Brother Poll refers to a letter, written by Moses Holbrook, Grand Commander of the Supreme Council at Charleston, on May 17, 1830, to John H. Holland, Grand Commander in Chief of the Grand Council of Louisiana. Brother Poll writes:

> On May 17, 1830, Moses Holbrook, Grand Commander of the Charleston Council, sent a letter to John Holland, Grand Master of the Grand Lodge of Louisiana and Grand Commander in Chief of the Grand Council of Louisiana, which gave a report of a Consistory being formed in New Orleans on May 12, 1812, consisting of Jean Lusson, Pierre Chameau, Sr., Jean Baptiste Pinta, Louis Casimir Moreau Lislet, Jean Baptiste Casteret, Jean Baptiste Gillard "and some others."

Brother Poll uses the words "being formed" and "consisting of" to indicate two separate things: (1) the creation of a Consistory, and (2) the composition of that Consistory. Actually, Holbrook's letter does not use two separate and distinctive terms. Let us examine Holbrook's actual words to John Holland:

> Now I observe, dated at New Orleans, 12 May 1812 in a return on file that Louis Jean Lusson, Pierre Chameau aîné, Jean Baptiste Pinta, Louis Casimir Moreau

1. Au t∴ ill∴ et t∴ p^{t}∴ p^{ce}∴ Jn∴ L∴ Lusson, Souv∴ Grd∴ ins∴ g^{al}∴ 33e D∴, Archives, the Supreme Council, 33°, S.J., Washington, DC.

2. Pike reprinted the document, with minor transcription errors, in *Official Bulletin of the Supreme Council of The 33d Degree, for the Southern Jurisdiction of the United States,* vol v, no. 1 (Jul. 1882), 330.

> Lislet, Jean Baptiste Casteret, & Jean Baptiste Gillard are regularly recorded as constituting a Consistory of S.P.R.S. under this jurisdiction with some others.[3]

Notice that Holbrook merely referred to a "return on file," from "a Consistory" in New Orleans, which was "under this jurisdiction" (i.e., the Supreme Council at Charleston). I offer three points for consideration:

- The "return on file" was simply dated May 12, 1812, and listed the names of several members who were "recorded as constituting a Consistory."
- The "return on file" might have simply been a periodic return (perhaps annual or semi-annual?)
- The context of the word "constituting" is not completely clear. It may have simply meant comprising or composing, rather than creating.

Did Holbrook's letter refer to the New Orleans Consistory established by the Supreme Council at Kingston, Jamaica? If it was formed in April 1811, then it is plausible and understandable that an annual return might be dated May 1812. Or, is something else meant? The words "with some others" (not "and some others") could imply either "with some other members" or "with some other Consistories." There were other Consistories in New Orleans, including one reportedly "established" by Charleston in 1814, and another from Baracoa, Cuba.

A Consistory "Established" on September 28, 1814?

There is some evidence that a Consistory in New Orleans was "established" on September 28, 1814. On that date Emanuel De La Motta, as a Sovereign Grand Inspector General of the 33°, and third Grand Dignitary Officer (en ma qualité de Souverain Grand Inspecteur Général du 33e.·. dégré & de troisième Grand Offiçier Dignitaire) of the Supreme Council at Charleston, issued a document appointing Louis Jean Lusson a Representative of the Supreme Council at Charleston, for New Orleans.[4] The document also included a section addressed to all "regular sublime Masons in Upper or Lower Louisiana." The latter group was authorized and given full power to "... summon to order, duty

3. Moses Holbrook, Charleston, S.C., May 17, 1830, to J. H. Holland, Esq., New Orleans, La., copy in the Archives, the Supreme Council, 33°, S.J., Washington, DC.

4. *Universi Terrarum orbis Architectonis per Gloriam Ingentis—Ordo ab chao—Deus Meumque Jus—Au Nom et sous les auspices du Grand et Suprême Conceil ...*, untitled Ms., Sept. 28, 1814, Archives, the Supreme Council, 33°, S.J., Washington, DC.

and submission the adherents and pretended councils of S∴P∴ of the R∴S∴ established in New Orleans by the said Joseph Cerneau and his representative Emmanuel Gigaud...."

Ten months later Gourgas wrote to De La Motta mentioning "a communication from the Brethren in New Orleans." The document De La Motta issued to Lusson made him Charleston's Representative; it was not a patent for the New Orleans bodies. Thus, it apparently did not satisfy the "regular sublime Masons" in New Orleans, and they ceased their labors. According to Gourgas:

> ... on account of the situation of affairs there by the malignant and calumnious reports spread about by Joseph Cerneau and his adherents, they had deemed it prudent not to re-open their works until you send them from the Sup'e Gd. Council in Charleston a Constitutional Patent on parchment, in ample form, under the title of Grand Council of S∴P∴R∴S∴ for Upper and Lower Louisiana, to that effect you will also find herewith their petition and submission to your Sup'e Gd. Council.[5]

Whether the "Constitutional Patent" was ever issued I cannot say, since I have not seen such a document in the Archives of the Supreme Council, 33°, Southern Jurisdiction. However, if Emanuel De La Motta or other members of the Supreme Council at Charleston decided against sending a patent, we must wonder why they failed to do so. Fourteen years later, on October 11, 1828, Gourgas wrote to Moses Holbrook about this body:

> Are you in correspondence at New Orleans with the Subl∴ Cons^{y}∴ of S∴P∴R∴S∴ 32d established there in your name & under your authority 28 Sept 1814—by the late Ill^{s}∴ Brother Emanuel De La Motta? who are the present members? Did Ill^{s}∴ B^{r}∴J. B. M. De La Hogue in virtue of your Sup∴ Coun∴'s powers to him 29th July 1804—establish any Subl∴ Lod∴, Coun of P^{ces}∴ Jer^{m}∴ & Chap∴ R✠ at New Orleans—If so please furnish us with the names of the present members—[6]

Holbrook's response, written six days later, did not satisfy Gourgas's inquiry:

5. J. J. J. Gourgas, New York, NY, Jul. 3, 1815, to Emanuel De La Motta, Charleston, S.C., *Transactions of the Supreme Council of the 33d Degree, Ancient and Accepted Scottish Rite of Free-Masonry, for the Southern Jurisdiction of the United States of America. 1857 to 1866,* reprint, (Washington: Joseph L. Pearson, Printer, 1878), 14–16.

6. J. J. J. Gourgas, New York, NY, Oct. 11, 1828, to Moses Holbrook, Charleston, S.C., copy in the Archives, the Supreme Council, 33°, S.J., Washington, DC.

> At New Orleans—I have made several attempts to obtain information—and from Br Perez Snell R.✠. K–H. S.P.R.S. I lately received a letter dated 3d May 1828—It is not so definite as I could wish—he says "I have had some conversation with Mr Holland the Gr. Commander of the Consistory established in this City (New Orleans) by a body that was called the S. G. Council of the U.S. of A. under the direction of Mr Cerneau—Mr Holland intimated that the Sup. Council at Charleston was not acknowledged in Europe. I endeavored to convince him that it was, which I believe I did—as no longer than yesterday he wished to know if your S. Coun—would grant them a Charter if they should apply." (query—would it be best so to do?) "I informed him if they had the degrees correct & would swear allegiance to the S. C. of Charleston that there was no doubt of your willingness to receive them—Mr Holland replied that they would wait until he could hear from Mr Chapman in N York to whom he had written upon the subject. Mr H. also informed me that they hold a Charter from the Gr. O. of France to hold a Sov. Chapter of Princes of the Rose Cross granted 1798 and that they are in full correspondence with them an that they were directed by them (the G. O of France) to acknowledge Cerneaus authority as supreme in the U.S." This is all the information I can give you on the subject at New Orleans—There are no documents on file later than you are in possession of—No tableau—[7]

Because I have not thoroughly investigated the matter of this 1814 Consistory I am not prepared to offer a conclusion. However, as we shall soon see, Laffon de Ladébat implied that the Jamaica Consistory might have died out before 1814, while John H. Holland, writing in 1828, also suggested it had ceased to exist.

Holland corresponded with both Moses Holbrook, and J. J. J. Gourgas regarding New Orleans Masonry. Gourgas, interested to learn what happened to the Consistory formed in 1811 by the Supreme Council at Kingston, Jamaica, wrote to Holland. The latter responded on October 30, 1828, stating, "I believe that you will not be able to obtain here the information you desire Relative to the Composition of the Jamaica Consistory *if it still exists,* and that of Baracoa I believe has not existed for many years"[8] (emphasis added). If the "Jamaica Consistory" in New Orleans had "passed under" (to use Brother Poll's term) the authority of the Cerneau Grand Consistory, it is surprising that Holland would not have been aware of that. Indeed, the words "if it still exists" suggest

7. Moses Holbrook, Charleston, South Carolina, Oct. 17, 1828, to J. J. J. Gourgas, New York, NY, copy in the Archives, the Supreme Council, 33°, S.J., Washington, DC.

8. John Henry Holland, New Orleans, La., Oct. 30, 1828, to J. J. J. Gourgas, New York, NY, copy in the Archives, the Supreme Council, 33°, S.J., Washington, DC.

two things: (1) the Jamaica Consistory had a separate existence from the body with which Holland was affiliated, and (2) the Jamaica Consistory may have gone dark. Laffon de Ladébat suggested that it might have ceased to exist before 1814:

> If the Consistory of 1811 was in existence at this date [1814], the opposition to the New Consistory [i.e., the Cerneau Grand Council] could be easily accounted for. But as this is not probable, it more likely arose from the fact that the Cerneau Council at New York, and all bodies created by it, had been declared irregular.[9]

Thus, John H. Holland and Laffon de Ladébat, who had both been Cerneau Masons in New Orleans, give no indication that the 1811 Jamaica Consistory "passed" into the Cerneau Council. Rather, the Jamaica Consistory seems to have closed; however, it seems that some members of the 1811 Consistory joined the Cerneau Council.

LOUIS JEAN LUSSON: HIS "TRIAL" AND "DEFIANCE"

In questioning why some New Orleans Masons turned to Joseph Cerneau for a charter, Brother Poll brings to our attention the Masonic "trial" of Lusson, one of the founders of the 1811 Consistory, and the Representative of the Supreme Council at Charleston. He recites James B. Scot's translation of Laffon de Ladébat's account. Scot's translation, although fair, omitted italics that conveyed de Ladébat's intent:

DE LADÉBAT'S ACCOUNT	SCOT'S TRANSLATION OF DE LADÉBAT
Il est bon de remarquer que le 3 mai 1814 le Grand Consistoire de la Louisiana reçut la dénonciation de J. Cerneau par le Suprême Conseil de Charleston et que le 13 novembre 1814, le F∴ Ls. Jn. Lusson, 33e, qui, le 4 Décembre, 1812, n'avait point souscrit aux conditions imposées par J. Cerneau, renouvela son opposition au dit Grand Consistoire. Il fut jugé et condamné par ce corps le 14 août, 1815. Il était membre du *Suprême Conseil de Charleston,* et, comme tel, il avait publié, dans	It is worthy of remark that on the 3d of May, 1814, the Grand Consistory of Louisiana received the denunciation of J. Cerneau by the Supreme Council of Charleston, and that on the 13th of November, 1814, Bro. Louis Jean Lusson, 33°, who on the 4th of December, 1812, had refused to subscribe to the conditions imposed by J. Cerneau, renewed his opposition to the said Grand Consistory. For this he was tried and condemned by that body, August 14, 1815. He was a member of

9. Laffon de Ladébat, in James B. Scot, *Outline of the Rise and Progress of Freemasonry in Louisiana. From its Introduction to the Re-organization of the Grand Lodge in 1850* (1873; reprint, New Orleans: 1923), 23.

cet Orient, la dénonciation de J. Cerneau par Emanuel de la Motta.[10]

the Supreme Council of Charleston, and, as such, had published in New Orleans the denunciation of Joseph Cerneau by Emanuel de la Motta.[11]

This extract tells us that as early as December 4, 1812, (the day when Emanuel Gigaud, Representative of the Cerneau Grand Consistory in New York, formed his provisional Grand Council of P.R.S. in New Orleans), Louis Jean Lusson opposed Cerneauism. De Ladébat italicized his original text to emphasize that Lusson was a "member" (actually "Representative") of the Supreme Council of Charleston, not of the Cerneau bodies; therefore, his "trial" by the Cerneauists would have had no effect on his standing as a regular Scottish Rite Mason.

After discussing this "trial" Brother Poll states that Jean Doszedardski was made a Thirty-third Degree Mason by Lusson on May 5, 1813, in New Orleans. Questioning Lusson's authority to perform this act, Brother Poll suggests this either demonstrated "some defiance for the authority of the Charleston Council—or a bit of confusion." I am unaware of any record that suggests the Supreme Council at Charleston was displeased with Lusson's act. The lack of documents does not allow us to assume either ignorance or defiance; indeed, the Supreme Council at Charleston seems to have had much confidence in Lusson, going so far as to have appointed him their special Representative in New Orleans the following September.

Charleston's Intervention Against Cerneau

Why did the Supreme Council wait until 1813 to move against Cerneau? Brother Poll suggests that it may have been because Charleston was unaware of Cerneau's activities until that year:

> The fact is that the Charleston Council did not act against Cerneau (and might not have even known of his creation) until the spring or early summer

10. [Charles Laffon de Ladébat], *Procès-Verbal de la Session Annuelle du Supreme Conseil des Souv∴ Grands Inspecteurs Generaux, 33e et dernier Degré du Rit Ancien et Accepté, pour la Jurisdiction Meridionale des E.U.A. Tenue en la Vallee de la Nouvelle-Orleans* (Nouvelle-Orleans: Imprimerie de E. C. Wharton, 1857), 72.

11. James B. Scot, *Outline of the Rise and Progress of Freemasonry in Louisiana. From its Introduction to the Re-organization of the Grand Lodge in 1850* (1873; reprint, New Orleans: 1923), p. 22.

> of 1813 when Emanuel De La Motta traveled to New York and discovered the Cerneau and Bideaud Bodies.

To the contrary, the Supreme Council at Charleston was aware of Cerneau's activities as early as November 1808, but there were practical reasons why it could not act against him until 1813. A brief rehearsal of early events in New York helps us understand the circumstances.

Antoine Bideaud, a member of the Supreme Council of the French West India Islands, illegally created a "Sovereign Grand Council and Consistory of Sublime Princes of the Royal Secret" in New York on August 6, 1806. Members of this group later stated that because Bideaud was tempted by the prospect of making some quick money he exceeded his authority. Gourgas, who was one of the members of Bideaud's group, recalled:

> This act of Bideaud's was completely irregular, unconstitutional. He had no right or power within any part of the United States of America, but then he was tempted and did succumb at the rate of five times $46, or $230. As to us, we were then new and raw in these matters, believing all was right....[12]

Upon learning of their mistake, the members of the Consistory sought Masonic regularity and were subsequently "healed" by authority of the Supreme Council at Charleston in 1813, when De La Motta created the Supreme Council, Northern Masonic Jurisdiction.[13]

On the other hand, Cerneau's "Grand Consistory" was not created until October 1807, more than a year after the Bideaud Council and Consistory. Like Bideaud, Cerneau may also have been tempted by the lure of money. At the time of this creation, however, Cerneau did not pretend any Scottish Rite authority. Rather, his only powers derived from a patent (Appendix 1 of this book) he received in 1806 under authority of the Order of the Royal Secret[14] (improperly called the "Rite of Perfection"). The patent limited his authority to the northern part of Cuba and only authorized him to confer the "highest Degrees" on one person per year. In part it stated:

12. Robert Freke Gould, ed., *A Library of Freemasonry* (Philadelphia: John C. Yorston Pub. Co., 1911), vol. 5, 300–301. Samuel Harrison Baynard, *History of the Supreme Council, 33°,* 2 vols. (Boston: 1938), vol. 1, 153.

13. Arturo de Hoyos, "The Union of 1867," *Heredom,* vol. 4 (1995), 12.

14. The *Circular throughout two hemispheres,* also known as the 1802 Manifesto, uses the term "order of Prince of the Royal Secret."

> ... we create him our Deputy Inspector General, Deputy Grand Inspector, for the Northern part of the Island of Cuba ... we give him full and entire power to confer in the name of our aforesaid Grand Council , the highest Degrees of Masonry on a Kt: Prince Mason, one only each year....[15]

It is unlikely that Cerneau's members knew of, or understood, the limitations of his patent. And, unlike members of the Bideaud Consistory, the members of Cerneau's group never sought to be "healed" by legitimate authority.

Members of the Bideaud Consistory also joined a Council of Princes of Jerusalem (15°–16°) established by Abraham Jacobs in October 1808. As early as 1788 Jacobs knew John Mitchell, Grand Commander of the Supreme Council at Charleston, and, as early as 1801, he had worked with Emanuel De La Motta in Georgia.[16] On November 11, 1808, Jacob's Council was visited by Joseph Cerneau and John Mulligan, who announced themselves as an investigating committee from another Council of Princes of Jerusalem in the city. Jacobs balked at Cerneau's overtures and contacted the Supreme Council at Charleston.[17] Jacobs may have been aware that Cerneau's Council of Princes of Jerusalem had been organized prior to his own. Consequently, fearing they had infringed on another Council's rights, several members of Jacob's group abandoned him and joined the Cerneau Council. Jacobs waited in vain for relief from Charleston. A likely reason for its failure to become involved in this dispute was Article 6 of the *Constitutions, Statutes, Regulations* (Dalcho version), which stated,

> The power of the Supreme Council does not interfere with any degree below the 17th or Knight of the East and West. But every Council and Lodge of Perfection are hereby required and directed, to acknowledge them in quality of Inspectors General...."

However, even if the Supreme Council at Charleston desired to confront Cerneau, it would have been difficult. Charleston and New York City were

15. Gould, vol. 5, 302–3. Joseph Cerneau's original French patent is in the Archives, the Supreme Council, 33°, S.J., Washington, DC. See Appendix 1 of this book.

16. Baynard, vol. 1, 77–80. See extracts from Jacob's diary in Robert B. Folger, *The Ancient and Accepted Scottish Rite, in Thirty-three Degrees*, 2 vols. (New York: By the Author, 1862, 1881), vol. 2, 94.

17. The Supreme Council, Northern Masonic Jurisdiction complained to the Supreme Council at Charleston, "... the mischieves persisted in by that nefarious Joseph Cerneau never would have gone on to such a length, had you taken the business in hand, when we informed you of it in November 5808...." *Official Bulletin of the Supreme Council,* vol. 7 (1885), 311–13.

some 760 miles distant from each other. Because the Supreme Council at Charleston was still in an organizational stage, with few members and fewer resources, it would have been a burdensome, expensive, and time-consuming endeavor.

In 1813, however, an opportunity presented itself when Emanuel De La Motta traveled to New York City for cataract surgery. In a June 18, 1814, letter written by De La Motta to Auguste De Grasse-Tilly (reproduced in full in Appendix B of this article), he stated, "Shortly after arriving here, I received complaints from everywhere about the terribly anti-Masonic behavior of some obscure character called Joseph Cerneau. . . ." De La Motta soon received a copy of Cerneau's tableaux, which listed members of the Cerneau "Supreme Council." Examining Cerneau's tableaux, it became obvious to De La Motta that Cerneau's "Supreme Council" was a parody of the Supreme Council at Charleston. He enclosed one of Cerneau's tableaux, with his letter to De Grasse Tilly, and added:

> . . . please notice that neither the number of its officers, nor their true names, their positions nor functions are what they really should be, that the seal of the 33rd degree has the sword on the wrong side. . . .[18]

Although these irregularities were just the tip of the proverbial iceberg, this present article cannot explore all the problems of Cerneauism. However, in addition to the letter in Appendix B, a further account of De La Motta's contact with Cerneau may be found in my article, "The Union of 1867."

CERNEAU OPPOSES THE GRAND CONSTITUTIONS OF 1786

Brother Poll argues that because the *Grand Constitutions of 1786* provided for two Supreme Councils in the United States, Cerneau's body might have been viewed as regular. He writes:

> We must also recognize the fact that the Grand Constitutions of 1786 did provide for two Supreme Councils in the United States (or North America, depending on which version you read) and from the information contained in those Grand Constitutions, and lack of published objections from Charleston, the Cerneau Bodies could have been viewed, to many New Orleans Masons, as regular.

18. Emanuel De La Motta, Jun. 18, 1814, to De Grasse Tilly, copy in the Archives, the Supreme Council, 33°, S.J., Washington, DC.

The issue is much more complicated than Brother Poll suggests, because the above view ignores several fundamental problems, including the following:

- The *Grand Constitutions of 1786* did indeed call for two Supreme Councils in the United States.[19] However, Cerneau's Supreme Council did not claim itself to be a second Supreme Council in the United States, but rather Cerneau claimed his Supreme Council was the only Supreme Council for the United States. In an 1814 circular the Cerneau Council emphasized its uniqueness by denying the very existence of the Supreme Council at Charleston when it wrote, "no such Council in fact exists" and "if there ever was a Council at Charleston, it has long ceased to exist...."[20]
- Beginning in 1809 the Cerneau Council also claimed exclusive control over all the Scottish Rite Degrees throughout the United States, by stating "... the right of granting Constitutional patents for Masonic Institutions within the United States of America, their territories & dependencies, from the Secret Master, Fourth Degree, to that of Grand Inspector General, Thirty Third, both inclusive, exists only with the Sov. Gr. Consistory of Sup. Chiefs of Exalted Masonry."[21]

19. The oldest copy of the *Constitutions of 1786* is in the handwriting of Frederick Dalcho, Article 5 of which states, "There shall be but one Council of this Degree, in each nation or Kingdom in Europe—two in the United States of America, as remote from each other as possible...." See photo reproduction of Dalcho's copy in James D. Carter, ed. and Ray Baker Harris, *History of the Supreme Council, 33°—1801–1861* (Washington: Supreme Council, 33°, S.J., 1964) 337–46.

20. These statements appear in an untitled circular (To the Glory of the Grand Architect of the Universe.... Extract from the Minutes of the Grand Consistory, at Its Session the 28th Day of the 12th Month, Anno Lucis 5813 [New York(?): 1814]), reproduced in full in Charles S. Lobingier, *The Supreme Council, 33° Mother Council of the World Ancient and Accepted Scottish Rite of Freemasonry, Southern Jurisdiction, USA* (Louisville, Kentucky: The Standard Printing Co., 1931); see especially 94.

21. Extract from the Oct. 28, 1809, minutes of the "Most Potent Grand Consistory of the Sup. Chiefs of Exalted Masonry of the Ancient Constitutional Scottish Rite of Heredom for the United States of America, their Territories and Dependencies" as quoted in Robert B. Folger, *A History of the Ancient and Accepted Scottish Rite in the United States: More Especially as Connected with the Operations of the so-called Cerneau Supreme Council from its Organization in New York, in 1807 to its Final Absorption into the Supreme Council of the Northern Jurisdiction of the U.S. in 1867* (Unpublished Typescript prepared for E. T. Carson, Cincinnati, 1877), 74; emphasis added. Copy in the Archives of the Supreme Council, 33°, S.J., Washington, DC. According to Folger, the edict was published annually from 1809 to 1820. It also appears with minor spelling corrections in Cerneau's 1819 tableau.

- It is sometimes asserted that Cerneau's Supreme Council and/or Grand Consistory only claimed authority within the state of New York. In fact, the Cerneauists used a title which represented themselves as possessing exclusive control of the Scottish Rite within the United States: "The Most Potent Sovereign Grand Consistory of Princes of the Royal Secret & Grand∴ Inspectors∴ General∴ 33d∴ degree∴ Supreme Chiefs of the Exalted∴ Masonry, of the Ancient and Accepted Scottish Rite, for the United States of America and dependencies."[22] The fact that they sometimes added "held in the City of New York" did not detract from their claims to exclusive control over the Scottish Rite Degrees.

- There is no evidence or reason whatsoever to suggest that *non*-Thirty-third Degree Masons living in New Orleans would have been familiar with the *Grand Constitutions.* To the contrary, the *Grand Constitutions, Statutes and Regulations* of the Thirty-third Degree were deliberately withheld from Masons of lower degrees.

Archival manuscripts reveal that early Thirty-third Degree Masons were required to sign a promise not to share the *Grand Constitutions* without written permission. For example, on April 3, 1813, Jean Doszedardski, then residing in New Orleans, signed his letter of submission to the statutes, regulations and constitutions of the Thirty-third Degree. He promised never to give a copy to any person without written permission from the Sovereign Senate, 33°, at Kingston, Jamaica (figure 1).[23] A similar promise occurs in the Obligation

22. Le T∴P∴S∴Gr∴ Consistorie des Pces∴ du Rl∴ Sect∴ & GG∴ Insprs∴ Genl∴ 33e∴ deg∴, Chefs Supr∴ de la h∴ Mie∴, du Rite Ecoss∴ ancien et accepté, pour les Etats-unis Amérique et dépendces∴, Aux TT∴ Ill∴ & T∴P∴ Souv∴ Gr∴ Commandeur, GG∴ Offcrs∴ & Membres du Supr∴ Consl∴ pour la France, des P∴, & Souv GG∴ Insp∴ Gl∴ 33e∴ et dernier deg∴ du Rit Ecoss∴ ancien et accepté. Unpublished letter, signed by Joseph Cerneau, De Witt Clinton, John W. Mulligan, et al. dated "5th day of the 7th month Anno Lucis 5814" (le 5e∴ jr∴ du 7e∴ m∴ Anno Lucis 5814). Archives of the Supreme Council, 33°, S.J., Washington, DC. Cerneau's use of the words "Ancient and Accepted Scottish Rite, for the United States of America and dependencies" (Rite Ecoss∴ ancien et accepté, pour les Etats-Unis Amérique et dépendces∴) contradicts Robert B. Folger's statement that from the 1807 to 1827 the Cerneauists "without variation" called themselves "The Ancient Constitutional Scottish Rite of Heredom." See Folger's *The Ancient and Accepted Scottish Rite in Thirty-three Degrees* (New York: By the Author, 1862), 186.

23. Jean Doszedardski, "Petition ... Soumission," Apr. 3, 1813, Archives, the Supreme Council, 33°, S.J., Washington, reproduced in *Official Bulletin of the Supreme Council of The 33d Degree, for the Southern Jurisdiction of the United States,* vol. v, no. 1 (Jul. 1882), 331

D'A[n]toine Bideaud, Pour L'Execution des Statuts & reglements Des Gd∴I∴. generaux du 33me Degré in the *Antoine Bideaud Register* (1803), which Brother Poll rediscovered in New Orleans.[24] Because Thirty-third Degree members were obliged to withhold the *Constitutions* from non-Thirty-thirds, we cannot safely make any assumptions as to how they "could have been viewed ... [by] New Orleans Masons."

Indeed, any appeal to the *Grand Constitutions of 1786* is actually quite damaging to Cerneau. Soon after his encounter with Cerneau in 1813, Emanuel De La Motta published an account of their meeting, and explained why Cerneau's actions were contrary to the *Grand Constitutions of 1786*.

> It was not a contention between Mr. Cerneau and myself for the Grand Commandership; it was not a competition with Mr. Cerneau for his crown of straw, attempting, at the same time, to wrest it from his brows to deco-rate my own; but imperious duty as a lawful Sovereign Grand Inspector General of the 33d degree, necessitated me either to bring by friendly means Mr. Cerneau to a due sense of his antimasonic proceedings, so long persisted in, or to exhibit him to the public view of the fraternity. I beg leave to insert here the following articles from the Grand Constitutions of the 33d degree, as ratified at Berlin on the 1st of May, 5786.
>
> Article 9th. "No Deputy Inspector can use his patent in any country, where a Supreme Council of Inspectors General is established unless it is signed by said council!"
>
> Article 10th. "No deputy Inspector heretofore appointed, or who may hereafter be appointed, by virtue of this Constitution, shall have power to grant patents nor to give the degree of K+H; or the higher degrees."
>
> Article 11th. "The degree of K+H. and the degrees of prince of the Royal Secret, are never to be given but in the presence of three Sovereign Grand Inspectors General."
>
> Article 12th. "The Supreme Council shall exercise all the Sovereign Masonic power, of which his August Majesty, Frederick 2d. King of Prussia, is now possessed, in recalling the patents of Deputy Inspectors for improper unmasonic conduct," &c. &c. &.
>
> And the patents of every lawful Sovereign Grand Inspector General of the 33d degree contain the following paragraph: "And we hereby authorize our said

24. Ill∴ Joseph Marcel Montagnet, 33° (1886–1964), a member of Ionic Lodge No. 374, New Orleans, studied the untitled Bideaud Register in 1953, but the document seems to have languished from then until rediscovered by Bro. Poll in 1994. The Obligation appears on folio 68; copy in the Archives, the Supreme Council, 33°, S.J., Washington, DC.

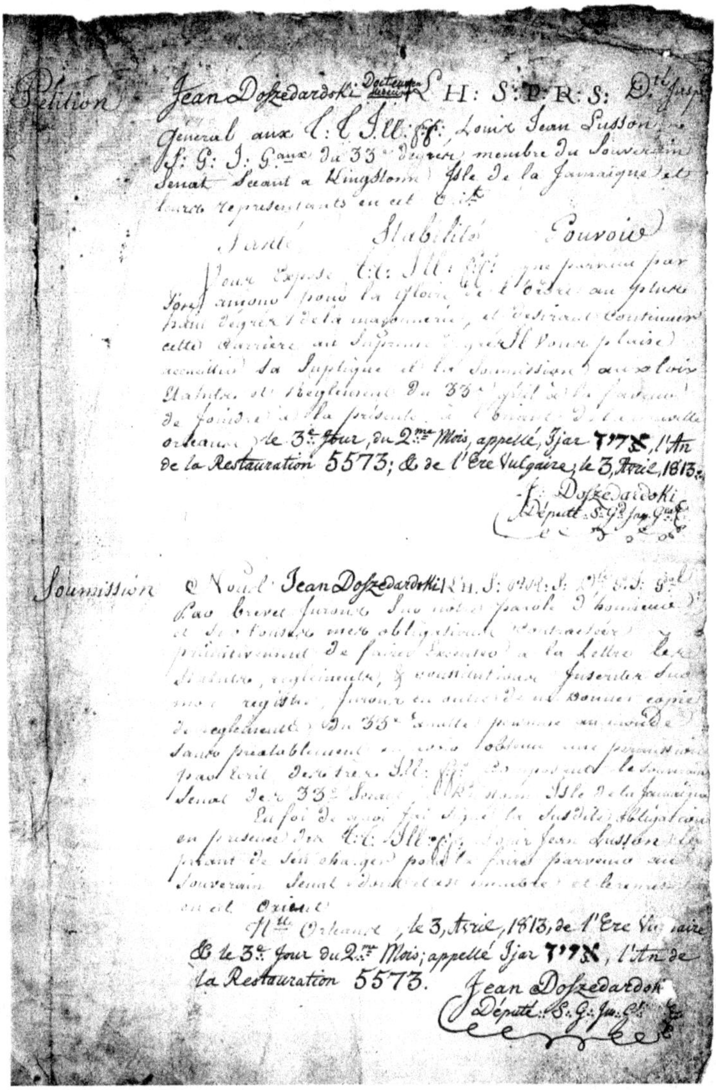

Petition — Jean Doszedardski Docteur en Medecine H: S: P: R: S: D.t Insp. General aux C: C: Ill: ff: Louis Jean Lusson S: G: I: G.aux du 33.e degré, membre du Souverain Senat Seant a Kingstown Isle de la Jamaique et leurs representants en cet O.t

Santé Stabilité Pouvoir

Vous expose C: C: Ill: ff: que parvenu par son amour pour la gloire de l'Ordre au plus haut degrés de la maçonnerie, et desirant continuer cette carriere au Suprême degré Il vous plaise accueillir sa Supplique et sa Soumission aux lois Statuts et Reglemens du 33.e [illegible] de joindre à la présente à l'Orient de la nouvelle orleans le 3.e Jour, du 2.me Mois, appellé, Ijar אייר, l'An de la Restauration 5573; & de l'Ere Vulgaire, le 3, Avril, 1813.

J. Doszedardski
Député S: G: Ins: G.al

Soumission — Nous Jean Doszedardski H: S: P: R: S: D.t I: G.al par brevet jurons sur notre parole d'honneur et sous toutes mes obligations contractées précédemment de faire executer à la lettre les Statuts, reglements, & constitutions inserées sur nos registres, jurons en outre de ne donner copie de reglements du 33.e [illegible] sans prealablement en avoir obtenu une permission par écrit des tres. Ill: ff: composant le Souverain Senat du 33.e Seant a Kingston Isle de la Jamaique
En foi de quoi j'ai signé la susdite obligation en presence des C: C: Ill: ff: Louis Jean Lusson [illegible] de s'en charger pour la faire parvenir au Souverain Senat dont il est membre et [illegible] en cet Orient
N.lle Orleans, le 3, Avril, 1813, de l'Ere Vulgaire & le 3.e Jour du 2.me Mois; appellé Ijar אייר, l'An de la Restauration 5573.

Jean Doszedardski
Député S: G: In: G.al

Figure 1. Jean Doszedardski's "Petition and Submission," executed April 3, 1813 in New Orleans. Like other early 33° Masons, Doszedardski promised both to abide by the statutes, regulations, and constitutions of the Order, and to never share these documents without written permission. From the Archives of the Supreme Council 33°, S.J., Washington, DC.

> Illustrious Brother to establish, congregate, superintend and inspect, all Lodges, Chapters, Councils, Colleges and Consistories of the Royal and Military Order of Ancient and Modern Free Masonry, over the surface of the two hemispheres, agreeably to the Grand Constitutions," &c. &c. &.
>
> From the latter clause in my patent, it became a bounden duty to interest myself in exposing Mr. Cerneau's impositions, for so many years practiced with impunity on the Masonic World.[25]

It is important to note that there are three early versions of the *Grand Constitutions.* In the above extract, De La Motta quotes from the Frederick Dalcho version (circa 1801), which is the oldest known.[26] The next oldest is the "French version" (circa 1802) which was J. B. M. Delahogue's translation of the Dalcho version;[27] and finally, there is the "Latin version" (first published in 1834). The wording of the French version is very similar to Dalcho's, and retains the same prohibitions. Although the language of the "Latin Constitutions" differs somewhat, they likewise contradicted Cerneau's actions.[28] There is ongoing debate regarding the authenticity of the *Grand Constitutions,* but there is no doubt that they are the law by which Supreme Councils were created.[29]

25. De La Motta's encounter with Cerneau was first publicly recounted in his untitled "manifesto" (Universi Terrarum orbis Architectonis per Gloriam Ingentis. Deus Meumque Jus. Ordo ab Chao. In the Name of the Grand and Supreme Council.... [New York: Sept. 5, 1814]). The was reprinted in Joseph M'Cosh, *Documents Upon Sublime Free-Masonry in the United States of America. Being a Collection of All the Official Documents Which Have Appeared on Both Sides of the Question. With Notes, and an Appendix* (Charleston: 1823), 52.

26. See photo reproduction of Dalcho's copy of the Grand Constitutions in James D. Carter, ed. and Ray Baker Harris, *History of the Supreme Council, 33°—1801–1861* (Washington: The Supreme Council, 1964), 342.

27. The original Delahogue manuscript is in the Georg Kloss Collection, Grand Lodge Library, The Netherlands. Copy in the Archives of the Supreme Council, 33°, S.J., Washington, DC. Delahogue's certified translation page is reproduced in Carter and Harris, *History of the Supreme Council,* 75–76. For a complete copy of the French version, see *Recueil des Actes du Suprême Conseil de France* (Paris: Sétier, 1832), reproduced by Alain Bernheim in *Renaissance Traditionnelle* no. 68 (1986), 301–3. Albert Pike, comp., *Ancient and Accepted Scottish Rite of Freemasonry. The Constitutions and Regulations of 1762. Statutes and Regulations of Perfection, and Other Degrees, Vera Instituta Secreta et Fundamenta Ordinis of 1786* [Grand Constitutions] (New York: Masonic Publishing Co., 1872), 279–96. There are several versions of the French version. see *Renaissance Traditionnelle,* no. 69 (1987), 74–84.

28. Pike, *Grand Constitutions,* 248–51.

29. Because the Dalcho version was lost until the 1930s, Albert Pike never had a chance to study it. His arguments against the imprecise language of the French version led him to believe that the Latin version was the oldest, and that the French version was an imperfect copy. Studying the Dalcho version, and the Thirty-third Degree ritual that accompanied it would have alleviated

De La Motta's extract above is important because it reveals how the first Supreme Council understood the *Grand Constitutions.* Their recital is not a convenient historical reinterpretation, but reveals the view held at the time the events occurred. In fact, De La Motta's recital is the first known application of Articles 9, 10, 11, and 12 and establishes precedent for their interpretation.

Created in 1801, the Supreme Council at Charleston was not only the first Supreme Council in the United States, but the first one in the world. Therefore, according to the *Grand Constitutions of 1786,* which form the fundamental law of the Rite, Emanuel De La Motta observed that:

1. If Cerneau claimed to be a lawful Deputy Inspector, he was prohibited from using his patent in the United States unless the officers of the Supreme Council at Charleston signed it.
2. If Cerneau claimed to be a lawful Deputy Inspector, or claimed authority under the *Grand Constitutions of 1786,* he was prohibited from granting patents and/or conferring the highest Degrees of the Rite; that is, from Knight Kadosh upward.
3. If Cerneau claimed authority under the *Grand Constitutions of 1786,* he was prohibited from conferring the Degree of Sublime Prince of the Royal Secret, unless three Sovereign Grand Inspectors General were present. The only other Sovereign Grand Inspectors General in the United States were made by the Supreme Council at Charleston.

Cerneau violated all three of these Articles. Thus, Cerneau's actions were in direct violation of the fundamental law that created and governed the Rite. The Cerneau "Supreme Council," having been organized contrary to the law that governed the Rite, was an unlawful body.

In his article "The Controversy of Joseph Cerneau" (*Heredom,* vol. 4), Brother Poll offered two options for viewing Cerneau:

> To date, there is no convincing evidence that Cerneau received the 33° initiation.... If Joseph Cerneau was not a 33° Mason then there seems to be only two reasonable explanations for the actions that he took: 1) He was a man of low moral character (or delusional) who sought to advance himself and capitalize

many of Pike's concerns.

> on a new masonic system; or 2) he believed that he was a 33° and believed that he was acting with proper authority.[30]

I do not know if Cerneau was "a man of low moral character," although this view was expressed by Emanuel De La Motta, "Joseph Cerneau [was] chased from Havana for embezzlement, [and is] a man of low class background, ignorant, a scoundrel..."(See Appendix B of this article.)

In light of his actions contrary to the *Grand Constitutions*, it is difficult to accept the position that Cerneau actually "believed that he was acting with proper authority." The only "proper authority" by which Supreme Councils could be created was the very *Grand Constitutions* which Cerneau contradicted.

Emanuel De La Motta also observed that his own personal patent, as a Sovereign Grand Inspector General, granted him the power to "... establish, congregate, superintend, and inspect all Lodges, Chapters, Councils, Colleges and Consistories of the Royal and Military Order of Ancient and Modern Free Masonry, over the surface of the two Hemispheres, agreeably to the Grand Constitutions...."[31] If Cerneau had truly been invested with the Thirty-third Degree, he would have been aware of this and, in conformity with the *Grand Constitutions of 1786,* he should have presented his documents to De La Motta for inspection. When asked to present them, however, Cerneau refused to comply. Additionally, because De La Motta was a lawful Sovereign Grand Inspector General, his powers went still further. According to Article 12 of the *Grand Constitutions of 1786,* De La Motta was empowered to revoke the patents of Deputy Inspectors guilty of un-Masonic conduct. Cerneau, whose highest patent was only that of a Deputy Inspector, was subject to De La Motta's authority. Cerneau abused his patent as a Deputy Inspector in at least two broad ways: (1) he acted outside of his limited jurisdiction in Cuba and (2) he erected a "Supreme Council" in opposition to the *Grand Constitutions of 1786,* as outlined above. Because of these abuses, the Supreme Council at Charleston was obliged to denounce Cerneau as an impostor, which it did on December 24, 1813.

Cerneau's so-called Supreme Council also had peculiarities which distinguished it from true Supreme Councils:

30. Michael R. Poll, "The Controversy of Joseph Cerneau," *Heredom,* vol. 4 (1995), 48.
31. M'Cosh, 52.

1) the Cerneau Supreme Council was subordinate to his Grand Consistory, rather than vice versa, and
2) its Thirty-third Degree was not conferred by a ritual, but was somehow bestowed—without ceremony—as an honor for merit and seniority.

Cerneau's disregard for the *Grand Constitutions of 1786,* his misunderstanding of the relationship between Supreme Councils and Grand Consistories, and his lack of the Thirty-third Degree ritual are all powerful evidence against his claims of legitimacy.

The Kingston, Jamaica, Supreme Council Rejects Cerneauism

Brother Poll refers to the 1818 register of members of Cerneau's Supreme Council,[32] to demonstrate that J. J. Itter, Grand Commander of the Supreme Council at Kingston, Jamaica (formed in 1804), was an Honorary Member of Cerneau's Supreme Council. Brother Poll writes, "there is no known information establishing how long prior to 1818 Itter was an Honorary Member of Cerneau's body...." Contrary to Brother Poll's statement, we discover that five years earlier, in 1813, the Cerneau Supreme Council's first tableau (figure 2) listed Itter among the "Honorary Members."[33] Brother Poll also mentions a letter written by J. J. J. Gourgas, on July 3, 1815, to Emanuel De La Motta, of the Supreme Council at Charleston.[34] In this letter Gourgas referred to a communication which stated that J. J. Itter was "a second Joseph Cerneau there [in Kingston] and entirely devoted to him...." On this basis, Brother Poll surmised that the Supreme Council at Kingston had "switched to the Cerneau camp":

32. According to Kent Walgren, the 1818 document is only known from Folger's reprint. See Walgren, "A Bibliography of Pre-1851 American Scottish Rite Imprints (non-Louisiana)," *Heredom,* vol. 3 (1994), 85; Folger, [Document No. 20], Appendix, 81–93. In his footnotes, Brother Poll omits reference to Folger's Appendices, which have their own pagination.

33. List of the Grand Officers, Members, Honorary Members &c.... 5813, 4.

34. Brother Poll's footnote 42 omits complete source citation and gives the wrong page number. See J. J. J. Gourgas, New York, NY, Jul. 3, 1815, to Emanuel De La Motta, Charleston, S.C., *Transactions of the Supreme Council of the 33d Degree, Ancient and Accepted Scottish Rite of Free-Masonry, for the Southern Jurisdiction of the United States of America. 1857 to 1866,* reprint (Washington: Joseph L. Pearson, Printer, 1878), 14–16.

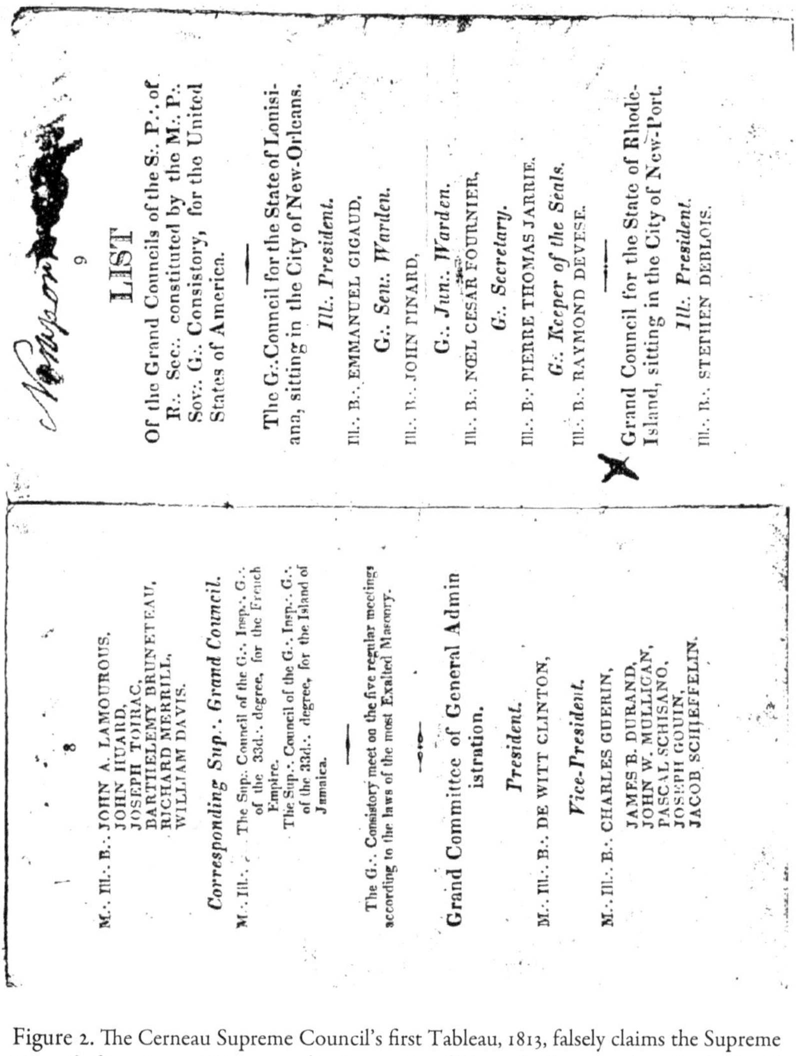

8

M.·. Ill.·. B.·. JOHN A. LAMOUROUS,
JOHN HUARD,
JOSEPH TOIRAC,
BARTHELEMY BRUNETEAU,
RICHARD MERRILL,
WILLIAM DAVIS.

Corresponding Sup.·. Grand Council.

M.·. Ill.·. The Sup.·. Council of the G.·. Insp.·. G.·. of the 33d.·. degree, for the French Empire.
The Sup.·. Council of the G.·. Insp.·. G.·. of the 33d.·. degree, for the Island of Jamaica.

The G.·. Consistory meet on the five regular meetings according to the laws of the most Exalted Masonry.

Grand Committee of General Administration.

President.

M.·. Ill.·. B.·. DE WITT CLINTON,

Vice-President.

M.·. Ill.·. B.·. CHARLES GUERIN,
JAMES B. DURAND,
JOHN W. MULLIGAN,
PASCAL SCHISANO,
JOSEPH GOUIN,
JACOB SCHIEFFELIN.

9

LIST

Of the Grand Councils of the S.·. P.·. of R.·. Sec.·. constituted by the M.·. P.·. Sov.·. G.·. Consistory, for the United States of America.

The G.·. Council for the State of Louisiana, sitting in the City of New-Orleans.

Ill.·. President.

Ill.·. B.·. EMMANUEL GIGAUD,

G.·. Sen.·. Warden.

Ill.·. B.·. JOHN PINARD,

G.·. Jun.·. Warden.

Ill.·. B.·. NŒL CESAR FOURNIER,

G.·. Secretary.

Ill.·. B.·. PIERRE THOMAS JARRIE.

G.·. Keeper of the Seals.

Ill.·. B.·. RAYMOND DEVESE.

Grand Council for the State of Rhode-Island, sitting in the City of New-Port.

Ill.·. President.

Ill.·. B.·. STEPHEN DEBLOIS.

Figure 2. The Cerneau Supreme Council's first Tableau, 1813, falsely claims the Supreme Council of Jamaica as a "Corresponding Sup.·. Grand Council." Contrast this with the denial by Solomon Morales in his letter to Emanual de la Motta (Appendix A).

> ... it is apparent that the Kingston Council (or, at least, its Grand Commander) had switched to the Cerneau camp. Given that the Kingston Council was the parent of the Grand Consistory of Louisiana, the action of the Kingston Council could reasonably be viewed as influential, if not, an expected "road map of action" for the New Orleans Masons to follow. The Kingston Council, however, was not the only Supreme Council to recognize Cerneau.

I do not know that we can safely accept Brother Poll's assumption. Cerneau's 1813 tableau also claimed that Supreme Council of Jamaica was a "Corresponding Sup∴ Grand Council" (figure 2).[35] After Emanuel De La Motta encountered the tableau, he wrote several letters to that Supreme Council at Kingston, Jamaica, to inform them of Cerneau's activities, and to inquire whether they were involved with him. These letters brought a definitive and speedy response from Solomon Morales, Secretary General of the Supreme Council at Kingston. Morales declared that the Supreme Council at Kingston had never corresponded with Cerneau, and would never recognize him or his adherents. Morales's letter is transcribed verbatim in Appendix A of this article.

Three days after writing this letter, Morales wrote another one to De La Motta. In this letter, Morales provided a list of members of the Supreme Council at Kingston and asked for copies of various rituals.[36] Brother Poll mentions this letter, and then speculates that Morales may have "create[d] a second Supreme Council in Kingston" acting "behind the back" of Grand Commander Itter. In and of itself Morales's request for copies of rituals was not unusual. The extensive correspondence in the archives of the Supreme Council, 33°, Southern Jurisdiction, includes many requests for rituals from other active Supreme Councils, including many requests from the Northern Masonic Jurisdiction. The correspondence of Gourgas and Holbrook includes many such requests. A random examination of just a few of their letters reveals

35. *List of the Grand Officers, Members, Honorary Members &c. of the Supreme Council Of Grand Inspectors General, of the 33d Degree, Regularly established according to the Ancient Constitutional Scottish Rite of Heredon, for the United States of America their Territories and dependencies, held in the City of New-York. Also of the Grand Consistory Of Supreme Chiefs of Exalted Masonry, and the Constituted bodies of its Jurisdiction. Anno Lucis, 5813.* (New-York: Printed by Hardcastle and Van Pelt, No. 86, Nassau-st., 1813)., 8.

36. Solomon Morales, Kingston, Jamaica, Jul. 13, 1815, to Emanuel De La Motta. Copy in the Archives, the Supreme Council, 33°, S.J., Washington, DC. Brother Poll's source for the letter was Alain Bernheim, "Further Light on the Masonic World of Joseph Glock," *Ars Quatuor Coronatorum,* vol. 100 (1987), 45–46; however, it was extracted from *Official Bulletin of the Supreme Council of The 33d Degree, for the Southern Jurisdiction of the United States,* vol iv, no. 1 (Jan. 1880), 331–33.

that requests for sharing rituals were made on the following dates: September 18, 1827, January 10, 1828, March 7, 1828, August 9, 1828, November 4, 1828, letters make it clear that the additional rituals were solely for comparison and study. Even today, many Supreme Councils desire large ritual collections in their Archives. In fact, in 1999 one of my first acts, as Grand Archivist, was to write to all Supreme Councils world-wide with whom we are in amity, requesting copies of their current rituals. In itself, Morales's request does not suggest that he was acting "behind the back" of his Grand Commander, any more than my own request did.

CONCLUSION

The problems in Brother Poll's article do not materially detract from the other pieces of interesting history he recites; and his statement remains true, "What is not known is equal to (or surpasses) what is known." I, for one, look forward to the next chapters of his writings, expecting even more surprises.

AUTHOR'S ACKNOWLEDGEMENT: *The author wishes to acknowledge Ill∴ Alain Bernheim, 33°, who proofread this paper.*

APPENDIX A

Letter of Solomon Morales to Emanuel De La Motta, July 10, 1815

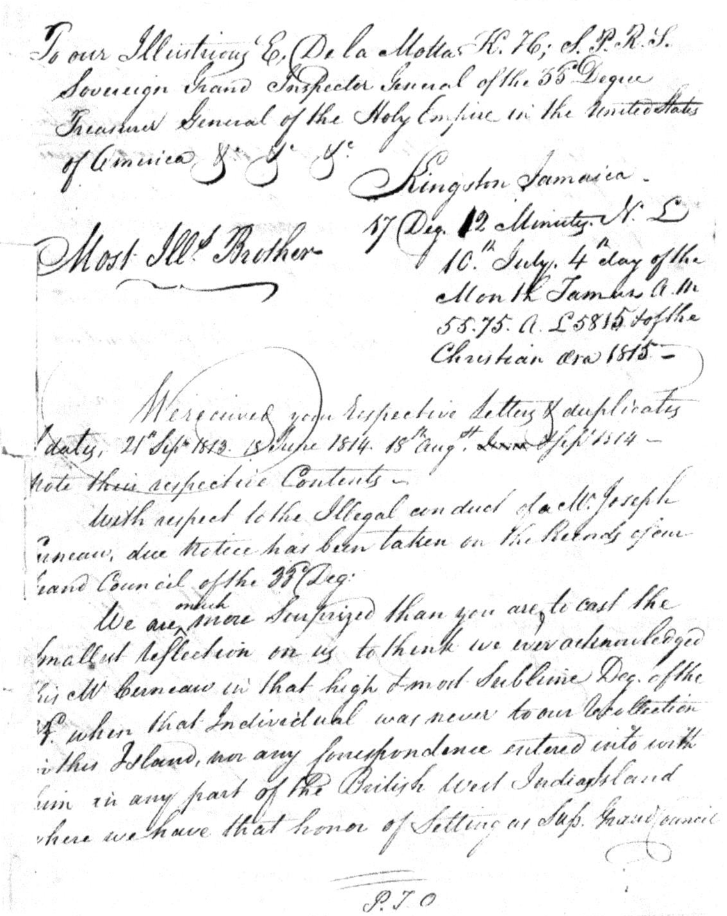

To our Illustrious E. De la Motta K.H.; S.P.R.S.
Sovereign Grand Inspector General of the 33d Degree
Treasurer General of the Holy Empire in the United States
of America &c &c &c
Kingston Jamaica.
Most Illt Brother— 17 Deg. 12 Minutes N. L.
10th July. 4th day of the
Month Tamus A.M.
5575. A. L 5815 & of the
Christian Aera 1815—

We received your respective letters & duplicates
dated, 21st Sept 1813. 18 June 1814. 18th Aug. & Sept 1814—
note their respective Contents—
With respect to the Illegal conduct of a Mr Joseph
Cerneau, due Notice has been taken on the Records of our
Grand Council of the 33d Deg.
We are much more surprized than you are, to cast the
smallest reflection on us to think we ever acknowledged
Mr Cerneau in that high & most Sublime Deg. of the
33 when that Individual was never to our Recollection
in this Island, nor any Correspondence entered into with
him in any part of the British West India Island
where we have that honor of Sitting as Sup. Grand Council

P.T.O

On July 10, 1815, Solomon Morales, Secretary General of the Supreme Council of Kingston, Jamaica, informed Emanuel De La Motta that the Jamaican body had never been in contact with Cerneau, and that this spurious New York body had never been recognized by their Supreme Council. The first page is shown here, and the transcription follows. From the Archives of the Supreme Council, 33°, S.J., Washington, DC.

To our Illustrious E. De la Motta, K.H; S.P.R.S.
Sovereign Grand Inspector General of the 33^d^ Degree
Treasurer General of the Holy Empire in the United States
of America &c &c &c.

Kingston Jamaica—
17 Deg. 12 Minutes N.L
10th July 4th day of the
Month Tamuz A.M
55.75. A.L 5815 & of the
Christian era 1815—

Most Ill^s^ Brother

We received your respective Letters & duplicates of dates, 21st Sep 1813, 18 June 1814, 18th Au^st^ ~~June~~ & Sep 1814—note their respective Contents—

With respect to the Illegal conduct of a Mr Joseph Cerneau, due notice has been taken on the Records of our Grand Council of the 33^d^ Deg.

We are ^much^ more surprized than you are, to cast the smallest reflection on us to think we ever acknowledged this Mr Cerneau in that high & most Sublime Deg. of the 33^d^ when that individual was never to our recollection in this Island, nor any Correspondence entered into with him in any part of the British West India Island where we have the honor of setting as Sup. Grand Council. —PTO— This we have to say for yours & the Satisfaction of the Sup. Grand Council, setting in the United States of America, that he nor any of his Adherants or supporters will ever be acknowledged by us, after having received such information from you—

Whatever may occur in our Grand Council, we shall give your Respectable Grand Council early information and be assured nothing will be more Gratifying to our Grand Concil than to keep up a strict Correspondence with you.

Receive the Assurance of our most fraternal sentiments by the sacred numbers & with all due Honor

Most Ill & Puiss^t^ Brother —

Your Affectionate Brothers

By Command *Sol Morales*—
K.H. S.P.R.S. Grand
Inspector ^Genl^ of the 33^d^ Deg &
Grand secretary of the Holy
Empire of the West India
British Islands

APPENDIX B

Letter of Emanuel De La Motta to
Alexandre Françoise Auguste De Grasse Tilly, June 18, 1814,
Regarding Joseph Cerneau's Masonic Imposture
Translated from a copy in the Archives of the Supreme Council, 33°, S.J.

Grand Orient of New York, under the C.·. C.·. at 40 degrees 41 minutes Northern Lat.·., the 18th day of the 4th month called Tamus A.·.M.·. 5574, of the Restoration 2344, A.·.L.·. 5814, & of the Christian Era on the 18th day of June 1814.—

To

The V.·. Ill.·., V.·.P.·. & V.·.D.·. Brother A^e.·.F^s.·.A^e.·. De Grasse Tilly—Sovereign Grand Commander of the 33° ad vitam for the French Winward Islands—&c. &c. &c.

V.·. D.·. and V.·. Ill.·. Brother—

Approximately one year ago I came to this place for a cataract operation, I am extremely unhappy because the operation was not successful and another cataract has developed on the other eye, which is very painful and I find myself almost blind. Due to these circumstances I will be forced to remain in this Orient for another year. Shortly after arriving here, I received complains from everywhere about the terribly anti-Masonic behavior of a certain obscure character by the name of Joseph Cerneau, who has been expulsed from Havana because of embezzlement of Masonic funds. Since his arrival here towards the end of 5805—he has constantly promoted schisms, disunion and confusion among the Sublime Masons of the United States of America. He started his speculative activities by covering himself with the heavy veil of darkness. He created at the beginning a Chap.·. of R.·.✠, which was composed mainly of the same caliber of characters as he is. In short time he dissolved it, *he* took its funds, while the Secretary took the accounting books, &c. After that, having become acquainted with some Frenchmen a little more respectable, he established another, and thanks to the patents he received from *Baracoa* on the island of Cuba, signed by *Germain Hacquet, Mathieu Dupotet* and others (the first had been received R∴✠ on the 13th day of the 4th month of 5798, and the second on the 1st day of the 7th month—5798—in the regular Chapter *La Triple Union* No. 5946—of that Orient) he founded here on the 28th of October—1807—a Sov^{n}∴ G^{d}∴ Coun^{l}∴ for *all* the U.S. of America and under its auspices a second Consistory in Newport, R.I., and a third one in New Orleans. Realizing the power he had, he has constantly *published* in the *Gazettes* and in the *public Directories* several of his acts, which prove their ignorance, presumption and impudence. I am enclosing the most striking of them all dated on the 25th day of the 5th month of 5812. He topped it all off a year ago last May by publishing and circulating his tableaux signed, sealed and stamped as Supreme Council of the S∴G∴I∴G∴ of the 33^{d}∴ Degree for *all* the United States of America, their Territories and Dependencies, *claiming for himself* the title of V∴P∴ Grand Commander—please notice that neither the *number* of officers, nor their *true names,* their positions nor functions are what they really should be, that the seal of the 33^{d}∴ has the sword on the wrong side, and the seal of S∴P∴R∴S∴ has a crown on both heads of the eagle & a collar uniting both heads, &c. that the seal for the Sublime has stars without numbers (not one of their numbers is perfect) in the place of 27—he engraved them himself, &c., &c., &c. that the jewels which he makes and sells for $40 are *one white eagle* with two heads of *polished silver,* a golden crown with a fleur de lys. — *Please also take notice that all of this started in 5807—and still is going on in 5814—and that it will not come to an end as long as this man feels backed by several Brothers of your Grand Orient, who may have had the shrewdness of letting him be recognized entirely or partially. It is a fact that his followers proclaim very loudly the fact that they are recognized by the Supreme Council, 33^{d}∴ for France.* We cannot respond on this point nor believe it, because they have not produced any evidence to prove this improbability. All of this has been done (as the expression goes) under the nose of the Supreme Council at Charleston, the *five* deputies Inspectors at *New York,* & *three* at *Philadelphia,* all *eight* well-known and *recognized*; several regular Chapters of R∴✠ having been established for *some years* in New York, Philadelphia, Baltimore, Portsmouth, Charleston & New Orleans; and of a Sovereign Grand Consistory of the 30°, 31° & 32° regularly established here since August 6—5806—by the most respectable BB∴ who are members of the Sov∴ Chap of R∴✠ *The*

Triple Union, which *paid* to *your* Ill∴ *Deputy,* Brother *Antoine Bideaud* $45 a piece for the 19th∴ to the 32^{d}∴. This Consistory had been recognized by us in Charleston. — What did *Joseph Cerneau* do to attain his goals? He started by declaring the Sov∴ Chap∴ The Triple Union, the Consistory and the Deputies as being irregular, & the S∴C∴ of the 33^{d}∴ in Charleston as *extinguished* & *null*—he did not visit me nor call for help and did not consult anybody with high degrees, experience, regular or instructed, although New York is full of such people. He took mainly *symbolic Masons* of which several had not belonged to Lodges for many years—*He,* by *himself* and *alone* gave by communication, and in just a *few* hours, *all the Sublime Masons, all the R∴✠, all the K–H∴, all the S∴P∴R∴S∴; He consecrated and installed them all by himself.* Concerning his Supreme Council of S∴G∴I∴G∴ 33^{d}∴ for *all* the United States of America, its Territories and Dependencies, *this is an enormous Masonic imposture, the most shameless and the most monstrous, which has ever been done.* It is true that right now he and his companions hope to get out of the difficulty by saying that they believed that the 33^{d}∴ was not *a Degree,* but only an honorary position won through merit and seniority, &c., &c., &c. — All these beautiful acts have taken place *thanks* to the patents of BB∴ *Hacquet* & *Dupotet* and *others*; please tell me, *how* and with *what rights* could those Brothers, relegated to the small Port of Baracoa, interfere and bestow such powers in a foreign jurisdiction, of which they could not know the localities? And moreover, how could (*if this is true*) *the Supreme Council, 33°* for the *Kingdom of France* recognize such a man and such behavior; wasn't the Supreme Council, 33^{d}∴ at Charleston well known by it? And didn't it deserve to be respected? And why by all means was it necessary to choose an adventurer of the caliber of Mr. Joseph Cerneau? Furthermore, isn't the Ill∴ Brother Fred: Dalcho since April 19, 5802, *your* patented Representative of the S∴C∴ of the 33^{d}∴ for the French Windward Islands in the United States of America?

Has Charleston ever declared that it would abandon its rights? And how can *foreign* BB∴ who do not know our localities, send with impunity a shameless emissary to sow trouble and discord among the BB∴? *No,* Charleston will never allow such a thing—It is Supreme in its territory as any other is elsewhere.

V∴ D∴ & V∴ Ill∴ Br∴ all I write about this man is based on well known facts, and among the local Masons here, all the most respectable know them in detail. Last year, when I arrived, although I was very sick, I immediately tried to put things back in order, and this if possible through fraternal love, which by the way had already been tried without any success. The BB∴ who had spoken with Cerneau had always been rejected from the start by his arrogance and insolence. — After having written to Charleston and having received *ad hoc* powers, I went on the 14th of September 5813 to see *Joseph Cerneau,* taking with me four of the most respectable BB∴ of the 33^{d}∴ as witnesses (*a very necessary precaution*); two were French and two American. He recognized without difficulty the S∴C∴of the 33^{d}∴ of Charleston, and myself as its Deputy. I thus told him that I came to see him as a good Brother, friend and gentleman. I asked him if *certain* tableaux had been published and distributed, and by pointing with the finger, I asked if he recognized having called himself *"Most Puissant Sovereign Grand Commander, 33^{d}∴ for all the United States of America, its Territories and Dependencies."*

He answered with an affirmation to all these questions. I then made some advances in the 33^{d}∴ for recognizing each other, having explained to him beforehand that all the Ill∴ BB∴ who accompanied me were also of the same Degree; I showed him, among other things, a certain ring, but he had never seen another like it before. He nevertheless examined it carefully and since then he has had some other similar rings made for all *his* Sov^{n}∴Gr∴ Inspr^{s}∴ G^{l}∴—I then asked him to show me his Patents and Powers by virtue of which he established *one* Chapter of R∴✠, *three* Consistories of which one is Sovereign, & his Supreme Council of the 33^{d}∴ for *all* the United States of America, its Territories and Dependencies, &c., &c., &c.

This he obstinately refused to do and replied that he had solemnly promised to his Consistory and Supreme Council of the 33^{d}∴ never to show them, but to refer to them for any kind of examination, information or other requests and that *he was recognized by the Grand Orient of France.* I answered him, that I, as a *regular* S∴G∴I∴G∴ of the 33^{d}∴, could not present myself until he had given me definite proofs of the regularity of all the different bodies created by him. Again he refused to give any explanation. I then asked him in the name of the Supreme Council, of the 33^{d}∴ of South Carolina to show me his Patents, Powers, &c., &c., &c. As he continued refusing, I gave him some time for reflection, to commune with himself, and to consult his people and left leaving my address; he refuses and will continue to refuse any cooperation. I have not seen him again.

On September 15, 5813—I went accompanied by an Ill∴ & R∴ Bro∴ of the 33[d]∴ to *his pretended* Deputy Grand Commander for *all* the U∴S∴ of Amer[ca]. Their Bro∴ and D∴ recognized me in the same way that he was recognized. By inquiring about the 33[d]∴ he told me that he received from *Cerneau all* of the high Degrees in one afternoon, that this happened about 4 to 5 years ago & that he did not remember anything and that his small son of 7 or 8 years of age who was present knew as much as he did.

Concerning the tableaux of the 33[d]∴ which were published & distributed by Cerneau, he considered this a *Collision* against the other Consistory, but that he would inquire about it, which he has not done, and that he would satisfy us, which he hasn't done either. — We waited until January 31, 5814, to end these shameful disorders by publishing and distributing on both hemispheres the enclosed circular. Please give this letter the widest circulation possible and ask the Grand Orient of France to distribute those which we enclose for them, as this is certainly the best method to make them reach their destination. Cerneau and his followers have persisted, and have circulated as late as last February a very insolent answer which is *full of falsehoods*; you will find that letter also enclosed herewith. Please note that it is just a pompous nonsense which does not comply with the forms of a Consistory, nor that of a Supreme Council of the 33[d]∴ Also notice that those people abjure the sacred principles of our Illustrious Order, and that it is the party spirit which dictated it, that of the infernal politics of Federalism, and their aim has also been to bluff the Symbolic Masons of this Orient to ward off the blow they received. Please think, Very D∴ and V∴ Ill∴ Bro∴ of the immeasurable damage, evil, disorder and trouble caused by some foreign characters who interfered and created new Bodies in a foreign jurisdiction, where they did not have any right. Was it, I ask you, up to a man like Joseph Cerneau, chased from Havana for embezzlement, a man of low class background, ignorant, a scoundrel and jeweler of trade, to be sent and conferred the power to establish High Masonry in this Country, when those who started it had the right to do it? The Grand Constitutions of the 33[d]∴ ordered *two* Supreme Councils of the 33[d]∴ to be established for the Jurisdiction of the United States of America—but it is only natural and correct that Charleston shall help establish the *second* one, and this is what they will do while I am here, and in very short time. I am also enclosing a little booklet which has been published and circulated here in English and French in 5810—by a Brother who was mistreated by Cerneau in his Chap∴ of R∴✠. This booklet is far from being correct, but it contains several interesting facts, among others that of a certain Mr. Toussaint Midi, a *profane* who was from the outset raised by Cerneau into the sublime degree of R∴✠—I am right now having other documents written about Joseph Cerneau and his gang; I shall have the pleasure to send it to you within a short time.

Please note and let the others know that another *pretended Supreme Council of the 33^{d}∴* was established last fall in Philadelphia under the auspices of Cerneau by *Blocquerst* and *Hurtel,* printers and refugees from St. Domingo. I would like to impress on you that the set-up of Mr. Cerneau is so active and we suppose so lucrative that if we cannot stop it in its monstrously anti-Masonic course, in a very few years even the remotest corners of the United States of America, its Territories and Dependencies will obtain from this noble Sov^{n}∴ G^{d}∴ Commander (who created himself) their Chap∴ of R∴✠, their Consistory and Supreme Council of the 33^{d}∴.

In order to give you an idea of the evil that this man spreads wherever he starts working, you should read the two ballustres enclosed herewith which were sent to me from New Orleans. The one comes from the Ill∴ Bro∴ Louis J^{n}. Lusson, Representative of Jamaica and the other from the Ill∴ Bro∴ Chamau, Sr. whom he defrauded.

We ask you V∴ D∴ and V∴ Ill∴ Bro∴ to send all of these documents and information to the Ill∴ Masonic Bodies of France, *and answer this letter as soon as possible here to New York.* We sincerely hope that you will not refuse this service to be a friend and Brother.

Could you also make me the favor by sending to me the book of *Vattel about the Crusades* and let me know all the news of your Orient since the reinstitution of the Rite of the 33^{d}∴ and of the different events which took place since then in that Illustrious Body, as well as all that is related to the *Reunion* of the different Rites and systems. This is a small collection of information which would be very useful to us and make us very happy. On the other hand if I can be of any help to you, I shall be glad to do anything to please you. I express to you my most affectionate feelings which should unite forever the true and good Brothers in the Grand Masonic Camp, with all the Honors due to you and by the sacred numbers.

T∴D∴ & T∴ Ill∴ Your affectionate Brother,
E. De La Motta
R∴✠ Eco; K–H∴; S∴P∴R∴S∴;
Sov^{n}∴ Grand Insp^{r}∴ G^{al}∴ of the 33^{d}∴
Ill∴ Treas^{r}∴ of the H^{y}∴ Empire
in the United States of Amer^{ca}∴ & its Deputy

By Command of the Sov^{n}∴ G^{d}∴ Insp^{r}∴ G^{al}∴ of the 33^{d}∴
& Deputy
Jacob De La Motta
R∴✠. K.H. S.P.R.S.

A Few "Rejoinder" Comments

Michael R. Poll, 32°

I was flattered when I received e-mails from Illustrious Brothers Arturo de Hoyos and S. Brent Morris inviting me to comment following Bro. de Hoyos' "rejoinder" to my last paper in *Heredom,* volume 8. Bro. de Hoyos wrote to me,

> Of course, there are still many unknown things, and naturally, places where you and I simply interpret things differently. In any case, with the resources we both provide, our readers should benefit by knowing more than they did before. I think that's a good thing.

I agree. In addition to providing as accurate a record as possible, a researcher should provide a reason for further inquiry and consideration. The fact is, we simply do not have the documentation to conclusively determine many events in Masonic history. Until the documentation can be found, researchers must apply their best interpretation of what they believe took place based on available information or records. Of course, one theory may invite differing views with which we will have a basis to weigh and examine more than one opinion.

Time does not now permit my writing a proper point-by-point response to Bro. de Hoyos's thought-provoking rejoinder. I must admit to disagreeing with some of Bro. de Hoyos's conclusions and will be happy to accept his invitation to write further "chapters" in this most fascinating aspect of Ancient and Accepted Scottish Rite history. For now, I would like to address several points raised by Bro. de Hoyos in connection with the early Grand Consistory of Louisiana aspect of the paper and several points concerning the Cerneau question.

Bro. de Hoyos writes that mine was an attempt to "account for the disappearance of the earliest Grand Consistory in New Orleans, and for the emergence of subsequent bodies." The goal was, actually, to lay a foundation from which we might explore the development and popularity of Cerneau Masonry in Louisiana during the 1800s. We have but speculation as to the actual chain of events that resulted in the Masons once on the rolls of the 1811 Grand Consistory of Louisiana arriving on the rolls of the Cerneau Grand Council of Louisiana. As we are able to uncover further documentation, we will have a clearer picture of the actual events. Until then, we will all have our opinions based on our readings and perceptions of the available documents.

Bro. de Hoyos also commented on my statement about Louis J. Lusson's elevation of Jean Doszedardski to the 33° in New Orleans. I wrote that Lusson displayed some "defiance" of the Charleston Council or "a bit of confusion." Bro. de Hoyos' response is interesting. He writes, "I am unaware of any record that suggests the Supreme Council at Charleston was displeased with Lusson's act."

I, likewise, admit to being unaware of any documentation suggesting the displeasure of this act by the Charleston Council. However, the lack of a report expressing displeasure should hardly condone such action. Article 17 of the *Grand Constitutions* limits the authority of a Sovereign Grand Inspector General in an area occupied by another Supreme Council.[1] At the time Lusson elevated Doszedardski to the 33°, Louisiana was a part of the United States, and New Orleans was clearly under the jurisdiction of the Charleston Council.[2] Lusson could have only legally elevated Doszedardski to this degree by acting under the jurisdiction of the Charleston Council (directly or as their

1. "No Inspector General possess any individual power in a Country where a Supreme Council is established...." Ray Baker Harris and James D. Carter, ed., *History of the Supreme Council, 33° (1801–1861)* (Washington, DC: The Supreme Council, 33°, S.J., 1964) 345.

2. New Orleans was claimed by the Charleston Council as early as 1804.

Deputy). Lusson, however, elevated Doszedardski by authority of the Kingston Council. I have, to date, found no suggestion that Lusson acted with the knowledge, permission or recognition of the Charleston Council.

The Lusson elevation of Doszedardski is noteworthy because Lusson, like many of the early Sovereign Grand Inspectors General, was a former Deputy Inspector of the older 25-degree system. The new 33-degree system, however, cannot be viewed as a duplication of the 25-degree system with a few degrees added on for good measure. There were significant differences built into the structure of the new system that made it different from the older one. Regardless of the distinctiveness of the new system, we find cases of former Deputy Inspectors acting under the authority of the new system in a manner suggestive of the older system. We do find examples (as Lusson) where there seems to be some uncertainty on the part of Sovereign Grand Inspectors General in regard to proper conduct as defined by the *Grand Constitutions of 1786.*

The Doszedardski Register is detailed and composed with obvious care. Had Lusson acted under the authority of the Charleston Council when he elevated Doszedardski, it would have been so recorded. This was not the case. The only possible explanations for Lusson's action were that he did not recognize the authority of the Charleston Council (highly unlikely due to his later actions) or that he had a degree of uncertainly of the actual meaning or laws as laid down in the *Grand Constitutions of 1786.* He would have simply misunderstood certain points and made a mistake with no ill intent. It was a brand new system with different rules. This writer believes that the later is the case.

Since my paper sought to explore, even on a limited, foundational basis, the popularity of Cerneau Masonry in Louisiana during the early to mid 1800s, it is logical that Bro. de Hoyos would wish to revisit the long-standing legitimacy questions of Cerneau in his rejoinder.

I will divide my comments concerning the Cerneau legitimacy into two sections. The first, to directly answer some of the questions and challenges poised by Bro. de Hoyos and the second part to further explore the circumstances.

Bro. de Hoyos offers three Articles from the French version of the *Grand Constitutions of 1786* in support of his position that Cerneau established his Supreme Council in violation of the *Grand Constitutions.*

Bro. de Hoyos quotes from Article IX:

> No Deputy Inspector can use his patent in any country where a Supreme Council of Inspectors General is established unless it is signed by said Council.

Since Article V of the *Grand Constitutions of 1786* provides for two Supreme Councils in the United States "as remote from each other as possible," it could only be a misreading or misunderstanding to suggest that Article IX would have, in some way, prevented Cerneau, or any S.G.I.G. (as well as any Deputy Inspector of the equal rank of Cerneau), from establishing a Council in the northern portion of the USA (just as De La Motta did). Article IX is clearly written to further clarify Article V. If it were desired to create a new Council in an occupied area, then permission from the senior Supreme Council in that jurisdiction would be necessary if the creation were to be considered legal according to the *Grand Constitutions.* Bro. de Hoyos associates "a country" with "a jurisdiction." In most areas of the world, this association is workable, but not in the United States. Article V provides for two councils (and two jurisdictions) in the USA. Permission to create another council in the USA would not be necessary unless a third council were created. Article IX does not in any way prevent a Sovereign Grand Inspector General (or a Deputy Inspector) from establishing a council in a manner agreeable to Article V (just as Cerneau did).

Bro. de Hoyos quotes from Article X:

> No Deputy Inspector heretofore appointed, or who may be hereafter appointed, by virtue of this Constitution, shall have power to grant patents, nor give the degree of K.H. or the higher degrees.

If this article is correctly written, then it is truly difficult to see how Joseph Cerneau, a Deputy Inspector General (not created as such until 1806), could have legally given any degree at or above the K.H. (Kadosh). Of course, since these Constitutions were reported to have been written and executed in 1786, then John Mitchell, also a Deputy Inspector General (and not created as such until 1795), would have been equally prevented from such action. But are we speaking of a Deputy Inspector (25-degree system) or a Sovereign Grand Inspector General (33-degree system)? Bro. de Hoyos makes the blanket statement, "If Cerneau claimed to be a lawful Deputy Inspector, or claimed authority under the *Grand Constitutions of 1786,* he was prohibited from granting patents and/or conferring the highest degrees of the rite; i.e, from Knight

Kadosh upward." I would be most interested to learn how Bro. de Hoyos would interpret Article II of the *Grand Constitutions.* The 33° is the highest degree in the A.&A.S.R. How could Mitchell have elevated Dalcho to the 33° if what Bro. de Hoyos writes is correct and complete? The *Grand Constitutions of 1786* actually do provide a means for a S.G.I.G. to elevate a qualified Mason up to the 33°.

Bro. de Hoyos quotes from Article XI:

> The Degree of K.H. and the Degree of Prince of the Royal Secret, are never to be given but in the presence of 3 Sovereign Grand Inspectors General.

If this Article is a correct transcription of the article that was written and approved on May 1, 1786, then we must ask who were the other two Sovereign Grand Inspectors General who were present on May 24, 1801, when John Mitchell gave the degree of Prince of the Royal Secret to Frederick Dalcho (one day before Mitchell elevated Dalcho to the 33°). If the *Grand Constitutions* were not the authority that was used to elevate Dalcho to this degree, then how can we be so certain that it was the authority used by Cerneau until the prescribed number of Sovereign Grand Inspectors General was achieved?

Regardless of Bro. de Hoyos' assertions, these articles, in themselves, do not automatically condemn Cerneau. In fact, we must ask if an appeal to these articles is even necessary to incriminate Cerneau.

Bro. de Hoyos was kind enough to provide us with the very useful appendix giving us the text of the 1814 letter from Emanuel De La Motta to Alexandre de Grasse-Tilly. In this letter, we can see the first reported exchange between De La Motta (or anyone from the Charleston Council) and Cerneau. De La Motta writes, "... I then asked him [Cerneau] to show me his Patents...." De La Motta goes on to write, "This he obstinately refused to do and replied that he had solemnly promised to his Consistory and Supreme Council of the 33d∴ never to show them...."

This writer can find nothing unreasonable in De La Motta's request to review Cerneau's patents. Cerneau publicly claimed to be a S.G.I.G. and the Grand Commander of a Supreme Council of the 33°. It is reasonable that another S.G.I.G. might wish to verify this claim of authority. Is it possible that Cerneau had questions regarding the legitimacy of De La Motta and, possibly, felt that either De La Motta was not a legal S.G.I.G. or that he might belong to an illegal Supreme Council? This is doubtful as De La Motta writes, "He recognized without difficulty the S∴C∴ of the 33d∴ of Charleston, and myself as its Deputy." And "I then made some advances in the 33d∴ for recognizing each other...."

If this is an accurate record, then how could Cerneau not accommodate such a justifiable request from one whom he "recognized" as a Deputy of the Charleston Council? It is simply not reasonable for Cerneau to have denied De La Motta's request if, that is, Cerneau was in possession of such a patent.

This first exchange with Cerneau might have been enough to give De La Motta cause to believe that Cerneau was not a legitimate S.G.I.G. If Cerneau were not a legitimate S.G.I.G. of the new 33-degree system, then he would not be qualified to establish a Supreme Council of the 33°. The story should end. Why is it necessary for Bro. de Hoyos (or anyone else) to examine the various Articles of the *Grand Constitutions* (or any of the many other charges levied against Cerneau) in order to support the charges of fraud? The argument should go no further than the fact that Cerneau did not produce a patent for the 33° and did not substantiate his claim that he was a legitimate S.G.I.G.

Cerneau's lack of a patent for the 33° is not sufficient to establish his irregularity because there is, likewise, no 33° patent for John Mitchell, the first Sovereign Grand Commander of the Charleston Council. In fact, this writer knows of no mention of his ever having possession of a 33° patent. The notion that a 25° Mason might have given the 33° to Mitchell is unacceptable. We do, however, have a mention of how Mitchell might have received the 33°. Moses Holbrook (Grand Commander of the Southern Jurisdiction from 1826–1844) wrote to J. J. J. Gourgas (of the Northern Jurisdiction) in 1829:

> I took the opportunity in mentioning it to Br. Dalcho, to ask how Mitchell got the 33rd. He replied that he could not ... recollect; but he [Mitchell] had signed some obligation in French for it. He thinks it came from some ~~German~~ Prussian [strikeout in original text] who was in Charleston, who was authorized to communicate it to him.[3]

3. Samuel Harrison Baynard, Jr., *History of the Supreme Council, 33° Ancient and Accepted Scottish Rite Northern Masonic Jurisdiction of the United States of America and its Antecedents*, 2 vols. (Boston: The Supreme Council, 33°, N.M.J., 1938) vol. 1, 89.

As I questioned in my 1995 *Heredom* paper,[4] why would a Prussian give an Irishman living in America an obligation for the 33° in French?[5] Albert Pike tells us that it is "probable" that Mitchell could not understand French. Dalcho's account of Mitchell's receiving the 33° simply makes little to no sense. We must wonder if Dalcho's recollection of this event is accurate.[6] Interestingly, we have cause to believe that Dalcho's memory of detail may not have been reliable. Thirteen days after Emanuel De La Motta established the Supreme Council for the Northern Jurisdiction, Dalcho wrote to De La Motta concerning the Cerneau Council, "It is well known to those who have lawfully received the 33d degree, that there can be but one Council in a nation or kingdom; & that the Council for the US was lawfully established in this City, May 31st 1801, consequently any other assuming its prerogatives must be surreptitious."[7]

This statement from Dalcho directly contradicts Article V of the *Grand Constitutions of 1786* in Dalcho's own hand.[8] Article V of the *Grand Constitutions* clearly provides for two Councils in the USA. How could Dalcho have made such a mistake? Given the lack of logic for his account of how Mitchell obtained the 33°, there seems to be little reason to doubt that his recollection of this matter was also a bit skewed.

John Mitchell's response to the news of Cerneau is, likewise, astonishing and makes it impossible to believe that Mitchell received the 33° from a Sovereign Grand Inspector General. Mitchell writes to De La Motta, "I am truly surprised and astonished at the conduct of the man you say is called Mr. Joseph Cerneau. No person ever had the degree but the Count de Grasse, & perhaps, but I am not sure, Mr. Delahogue. . . ."[9]

4. Michael R. Poll, "The Controversy of Joseph Cerneau: A Brief Examination," *Heredom,* vol. 4 (1995), 47–61

5. Albert Pike, *The Grand Constitutions of Freemasonry* (New York: The Supreme Council, 33°, S.J., 1872), 134.

6. Former Southern Jurisdiction Grand Historian Ray Baker Harris writes of Dalcho's apparent questionable memory, "Since the earliest known English copy of the document [the Grand Constitutions of 1786] is in the handwriting of Dr. Dalcho, it seems strange that its origin was not impressed upon his mind at the time he made the copy. It is the most intriguing of the unanswered questions relating to the beginnings of the Supreme Council." Harris and Carter, 95.

7. Harris and Carter, 118.

8. Harris and Carter, 340.

9. Harris and Carter, 117.

If no one else had the degree prior to Mitchell, then who gave the degree to Mitchell? Like Cerneau, there is simply no sound evidence that John Mitchell ever received the 33° from a S.G.I.G.

If, however, Mitchell, a Deputy Inspector General of the old 25-degree system, came into possession of a copy of the *Grand Constitutions of 1786* and accepted them as legitimate, he might have felt himself qualified to advance himself to the 33°. If this was the belief of Mitchell and his goal was to propagate a new system created by Frederick and with Frederick as the Sovereign Grand Commander of the "Supreme Council of the 33° in Berlin," (as stated in the opening of the French version of the *Grand Constitutions of 1786*),[10] then Mitchell would have had to believe that the degree existed prior to his obtaining it. But, clearly, Mitchell's statement concerning Cerneau makes such a conclusion impossible. How did John Mitchell then come into possession of the 33° and what was his understanding or beliefs of the *Grand Constitutions of 1786*?

If Cerneau Masonry was/is so very fraudulent, then how could both the Charleston and De La Motta Councils merge with Cerneau Councils in the mid-1800s? Did Cerneau bend or break any "rules"? It would be hard to imagine that he did not. Did Cerneau bend or break any more "rules" than Stephen Morin, John Mitchell, Frederick Dalcho, Louis Lusson, Alexandre de Grasse-Tilly, Albert Pike, or Albert Mackey? This writer finds no more or less evidence of guilt with Cerneau than with any of the above named Masons. So why has Masonic history so persecuted Joseph Cerneau? Maybe the next "chapters" in this history will tell us.

10. Harris and Carter, 337.

The Supreme Council of the 43rd Degree

Arturo de Hoyos, 33°, G.·.C.·.

The 33d degree is the *ne plus ultra* of Masonry.
—Frederick Dalcho

If historians have taught us anything, it's that complete histories are seldom written. This is more so true when a subject is prone to an emotional defense, when deliberate attempts are made to obscure facts, or when history and tradition are confused. Freemasonry is curiously able to combine all of these challenges simultaneously. Beginning with the Old Charges (Gothic Constitutions), Masonic "histories" are often an entertaining but unreliable combination of fact and fantasy, myth and mystery. Even today, our degrees continue to include a lecture—often called a "history"—which is allegorical, but accepted as literal by some members. To them, Solomon King of Israel, Hiram King of Tyre, and Hiram Abif, chief architect of the Temple, actually were the principal officers of an ancient grand lodge at Jerusalem, if not the founders of Freemasonry itself.

For the past 130 years readers of *Ars Quatuor Coronatorum* have enjoyed these transactions of Quatuor Coronati Lodge No. 2076 (London) as an archive of scientific research into the history of Freemasonry. As the first research lodge, it raised a new standard for integrity and rational thought in exploring our history, which has been happily emulated by dozens of other Masonic research groups although none, perhaps, as successfully as in our own Scottish Rite Research Society. Over the past quarter-century readers of *Heredom* have witnessed cherished notions of Masonic history dissected and put under the microscope, for the sake of truth. The goal and purpose of historical research is to arrive at the truth, and the truth alone, irrespective of the "traditional histories" of the Fraternity. And, however inspiring and noble the words "let there be light" might sound to a candidate kneeling at the altar, the reality is that the truth does not always arrive gently like warm sunlight on a Spring day—it may also burst forth with the uncomfortable and scorching heat of a full summer sun. The only question is: are we willing to receive it, or will we retreat to the shadows?

Although many examples of could be cited, I will point out one example of how good history can be both novel and challenging. Ill. Alain Bernheim recently argued that the Supreme Council, 33°, Northern Masonic Jurisdiction, was not founded in August 1813, as has been traditionally celebrated, but rather the evidence (the writings of the founders themselves) reveals it actually occurred in 1815.[1] Bernheim's thesis was challenged in a rejoinder by Mr. Jeffrey Croteau,[2] Manager of the Library and Archives at the Northern Masonic Jurisdiction's "Scottish Rite Masonic Museum & Library" in Lexington, Massachusetts. In turn, Bernheim and I coauthored a response, with additional evidence, which challenged and refuted Croteau's objections.[3] As enjoyable as they are, exchanges such as these are more than intellectual exercises. They are the whetstone which puts a razor's edge on the finer points of history. Accepting a preponderance of the evidence leads to writing "authentic history," which helps us understand how and why things are what they are, rather than writing a "faithful history," which is apologetic and/or serves idealistic or political purposes. Sometimes, it is even possible to establish facts from the absence of

1. Alain Bernheim, "Emanuel De La Motta in New York, 1813–1815: A Retrograde Chess Problem," *Heredom* (Washington, DC: Scottish Rite Research Society, 2013), vol. 21, 9–85.

2. Jeffrey Croteau, "'Emanuel De La Motta in New York, 1813–1815': A Rejoinder," *Heredom* (Washington, DC: Scottish Rite Research Society, 2014), vol. 22, 9–78.

3. Alain Bernheim and Arturo de Hoyos, "A Response to Jeffrey Croteau's Rejoinder," *Heredom* (Washington, DC: Scottish Rite Research Society, 2015), vol. 23, 79–94.

evidence—just as we can discern the precise shape of missing puzzle pieces, when the surrounding pieces are present.

The stability of today's Freemasonry is the product of yesterday's battles. Our Masonic forefathers were subject to the common passions and weaknesses which agitate humanity, and they responded to challenges precisely as we do today. Thus, it is only natural that our early history includes incidences of apathy, cover-ups, false-starts, frustrations, indecisiveness, misunderstandings, and everything else which attends the human condition. However one might be tempted to idealize our Masonic ancestors, authentic history asks us to see them as they were: as men who occasionally slipped, but recovered and persevered. Personally, I find the truth far more inspiring than any myth of perfection, and I believe it is healthier to embrace fact over fiction. In the present article I will briefly review examples of some challenges and frustrations experienced by the early Scottish Rite and show how, in response, the Supreme Council at Charleston attempted to alter the landscape of American Masonry. Had they succeeded, we'd be living in a much different Masonic world today. Not enough information survives to give us definitive account of this heretofore unrecorded incident, but enough of the surrounding puzzle pieces survive to assure us that it happened.

Nota bene: This article will be best understood when the reader is somewhat familiar with the early history of the Scottish Rite in the United States, i.e., from 1801–ca. 1830. Of necessity, I must abbreviate most of the early events, and focus primarily on incidents during this period which will punctuate this "new history."

The Royal Secret

On August 27, 1761, the French Grand Lodge at Paris (the Grand and Sovereign Lodge of St. John of Jerusalem), acting with a body of the superior degrees (the Council of the Emperors of the East and West, Sovereign Ecossais Mother Lodge), issued a patent to *Éstienne (Stephen) Morin*, a French merchant and enthusiastic Mason, as a Grand Inspector, "authorizing and empowering him to establish perfect and sublime Masonry in all parts of the world." Around 1763 Morin, then in Saint-Domingue (now Haiti), created and promulgated a Masonic rite of twenty-five degrees which he called the "Order of the Royal Secret" or "Order of Prince of the Royal Secret." This Order included many of the most popular degrees worked at the time. Although it was once commonly believed that the Council of the Emperors of the East and West created the Order of the Royal Secret, research by Alain Bernheim offered powerful evidence that Morin himself was more likely responsible for its organization.[4] There is also compelling evidence that, to bolster his authority, he created and backdated documents known as the *Constitutions and Regulations of 1762*[5]—an act that was not discovered for over 220 years.

In late 1762 Morin introduced the Order of the Royal Secret to Kingston, Jamaica, and by 1764 high degrees were brought to North American soil, when they were established in New Orleans, Louisiana.[6] About this time Morin empowered an enthusiastic Dutch Mason, Henry Andrew Francken, to establish Masonic Bodies throughout the New World, including the United States. Francken sailed to New York where he established the "Ineffable Lodge of Perfection" in Albany on December 20, 1767. As a Lodge of Perfection it was limited to conferring the Fourth to the Fourteenth Degree. The Ineffable was only active for seven years, and held its last meeting on December 5, 1774.[7] Fortunately, Francken also transcribed several manuscript copies of the rituals of the Order of the Royal Secret, some of which survive today. These copies are known as the *Francken Manuscripts*.[8]

4. For arguments favoring the view that Morin forged his authority, see Alain Bernheim, "Une decoverte etonnante concernant les Constitutions de 1762," *Renaissance Traditionnelle* No. 59 (July 1984), 161–97; A. C. F. Jackson, "The Authorship of the 1762 Constitutions of the Ancient and Accepted Rite," *Ars Quatuor Coronatorum* 79 (1984), 176–91. A. C. F. Jackson, *Rose Croix: A History of the Ancient and Accepted Rite for England and Wales* rev. & enl. (London: Lewis Masonic, 1980, 1987), 46–54. For the opposite view see Jean-Pierre Lassalle, "From the Constitutions and Regulations of 1762 to the Grand Constitutions of 1786," in *Heredom* 2 (1993), 57–88.

5. See Albert Pike, *Ancient and Accepted Scottish Rite of Freemasonry. The Constitutions and Regulations of 1762. Statutes and Regulations of Perfection, and Other Degrees. Vera Instituta Secreta et Fundamenta Ordinis of 1786. The Secret Constitutions of the 33d Degree* (New York: Masonic Publishing Co., A.M. 5632 [1872]; New Edition Printed by J. J. Little, &c., 5664 [1904]; reprint ed. Np., n.d.)

6. Gerry L. Prinsen, *The Story of the Ecossais Lodge of New Orleans* (New Orleans: Cornerstone Book Publishers, 2011)

7. "The Original Minutes of Ineffable and Sublime Grand Lodge of Perfection of Albany, NY, from 1767 to 1774," in *1906 Proceedings of the Thirty-seventh Council of Deliberation for the Bodies of the State of Ancient Accepted Scottish Rite Northern Masonic Jurisdiction, U.S.A., of the State of New York* (Printed by Order of the Council, 1906), supplement, 3–132.

8. For the complete rituals of a pre-1800 copy of an undiscovered Francken manuscript see Arturo de Hoyos and Alain Bernheim, *Freemasonry's Royal Secret: The Jamaican "Francken Manuscript" of the High Degrees* (Washington, DC: Scottish Rite Research Society, 2014). The most well-known copy, which is in the archives of the Northern Masonic Jurisdiction, was almost completely

On December 6, 1768, Francken appointed Moses Michael Hays, of Dutch parentage, a Deputy Inspector General of the Rite, for the West Indies and North America. The Hays patent granted authority to confer all the Degrees of Morin's Order of the Royal Secret. The following year Francken returned to Jamaica, and by 1780 Hays immigrated to Newport, Rhode Island. In 1781, Hays traveled to Philadelphia where he met with eight brethren whom he appointed Deputy Inspectors General over given American States, with the exception of Samuel Myers who presided over the Leeward Islands in the West Indies in the Caribbean. Barend Moses Spitzer, one of the Deputy Inspectors General, lived in Charleston from 1770 to 1781 and moved to Philadelphia where he was appointed Deputy for Georgia and, after traveling briefly abroad, returned to Charleston by 1788. On April 2, 1795, Spitzer appointed the Irish-born John Mitchell, then living in Charleston, a Deputy Inspector General of the Order of the Royal Secret. Colonel Mitchell had served as Deputy Quartermaster General of the Continental Army, and was an acquaintance of George Washington.

THE SUPREME COUNCIL AT CHARLESTON

On May 24, 1801, Colonel John Mitchell created the Reverend Frederick Dalcho a Deputy Inspector General of the Order of the Royal Secret, and one week later, on May 31, "the Supreme Council of the 33d Degree for the United States of America, was opened … agreeably to the Grand Constitutions" in Charleston, South Carolina, with Col. Mitchell and Rev. Dalcho presiding. The Supreme Council was a superior system to Morin's Order of the Royal Secret. The new Supreme Council would administer thirty-three degrees, including all twenty-five of Morin's rite.

The traditional authority of the Supreme Council stems from the "Grand Constitution of the 33d degree" (a.k.a. *Grand Constitutions of 1786*), ostensibly ratified by Frederick II ("the Great"), King of Prussia. The earliest known copy dates from about 1801–02, and is written in Rev. Dalcho's hand. Its eighteen articles are preceded by the title "Constitution, Statutes, Regulations &c. for the Government of the Supreme Council of Inspectors General of the 33rd

transcribed by Ill. Jerry A. Roach, Jr., 33°, and later published as *The 1783 Francken Manuscript. With Essays by Jeffrey Croteau, Alan E. Foulds, Aimee E. Newell* (Lexington, Mass.: The Supreme Council, 33°, NMJ, 2017).

and for the Government of all Councils under their Jurisdiction."[9] The *Circular throughout two Hemispheres*, or "1802 Manifesto" (the first printed document issued by the Supreme Council), also asserted that Frederick the Great instigated its creation:

> On the 1st of May, 5786 [1786], the Grand Constitution of the 33d degree, called the Supreme Council of Sovereign Grand Inspectors General, was finally ratified by his Majesty the King of Prussia, who as Grand Commander of the order of Prince of the Royal Secret, possessed the Sovereign Masonic power over all the Craft. In the new Constitution this high Power was conferred on a Supreme Council of nine Brethren in each Nation, who possess all the Masonic prerogatives in their own district, that this majesty individually possessed; *and are Sovereigns of Masonry.*

The involvement of Frederick II, King of Prussia, was repeated in the "History" which was delivered in the original Thirty-third Degree ritual:

> The Most Puissant Grand Sovereign—Grand Master Commander in Chief—Sovereign of Sovereigns of the degree of Prince of the Royal Secret, was our Illustrious brother, Frederick the 2:nd King of Prussia. He established this degree, in concert with our brother, his Serene Highness, Louis of Bourbon, Prince of the Blood Royal of France, and other Illustrious characters, who had received the degrees of K.H. and prince of the Royal Secret.... This new Degree he called "Sovereign Grand Inspectors General, or Supreme Council of the 33:rd"[10]

Like Morin's *Constitutions and Regulations of 1762*, many modern Masonic historians view the *Grand Constitutions of 1786* as "traditional" rather than historical documents. After a detailed investigation into its possible origins, however, Albert Pike accepted the tradition regarding the king's involvement, and his reputed role in the creation of the Supreme Council, even though there was no direct evidence that he did so. Pike did correctly argue, however, that whatever the origin, the formal adoption of any law forms a legal basis

9. A photographic facsimile of Dalcho's copy is in James D. Carter, ed., R. Baker Harris, *History of the Supreme Council, 33° (Mother Council of the World) Ancient and Accepted Scottish Rite of Freemasonry Southern Jurisdiction, U.S.A. 1801–1861* (Washington, DC: The Supreme Council, 33°, 1964), 337–46. For the "French" and "Latin" copies of the *Grand Constitutions of 1786*, as well as his defense, see Pike, *Ancient and Accepted Scottish Rite of Freemasonry. The Constitutions and Regulations of 1762 ...* (1872, 1904).

10. "33rd Degree Called, Sovereign Grand Inspectors General, or Supreme Council of the 33:rd" [folios 20r, 22r]. Unpublished manuscript in the handwriting of Frederick Dalcho, ca. 1801–02, with emendations made ca. 1804. Copy in the Archives of the Supreme Council, 33°, SJ, Washington, DC.

for government. Modern opinion agrees with the latter, and maintains that, at a minimum, the stories regarding the origins of the *Constitutions of 1762* and the *Grand Constitutions of 1786* are akin to the legends preserved in the Old Charges, providing a traditional environment for the degrees, just as the Biblical account of King Solomon's Temple forms the symbolic setting for Craft Freemasonry's origins.

Since its creation, the Supreme Council has embraced two mottos: *Deus Meumque Jus* (God and my right) and *Ordo ab Chao* (order from confusion). The latter has sometimes been mentioned by historians as referring to the order and structure which the first Supreme Council brought to its somewhat less-organized parent, the Order of the Royal Secret. Although appropriate to circumstance, the motto was likely inspired by the patents of La Candeur Lodge No. 12, a lodge that was chartered in Charleston, South Carolina, on May 24, 1796, with Alexandre François Auguste de Grasse-Tilly as the founding Master. In the upper part of its early patents appear two scenes. The first shows the earth as a globe in space; nearby is a crescent moon near seven

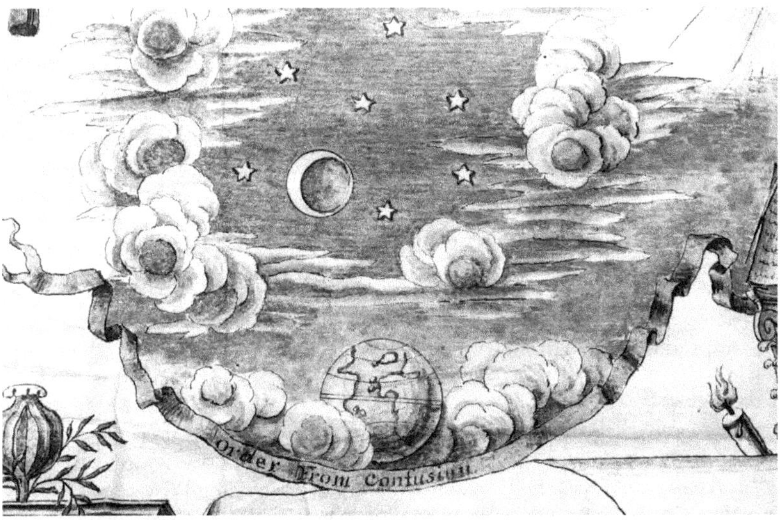

Figure 4. Detail from the patent of Lange Borman, issued in 1801 by La Candeur Lodge No. 12, Charleston, showing the motto "Order from Confusion." —*Archives of the Supreme Council, 33°, SJ.*

Figure 5. Detail from the patent of Claude Marin Girardin issued in 1800 by the "Grand Council and Sublime Orient," a body of the Order of the Royal Secret, at Charleston, showing the signature of Alexandre François Auguste de Grasse-Tilly as Sovereign Grand Commander. —*Archives of the Supreme Council, 33°, SJ.*

stars. Beneath this is a banner bearing the words "Order from Confusion." The second scene depicts the sun rising over the waters, beneath which is a banner with the motto "*La Lumière des Ténèbres*" (the light from the darkness). On November 12, 1796, de Grasse-Tilly was made a Deputy Inspector General of the Order of the Royal Secret and, in October 1799, he was Deputy Sovereign Grand Commander of the "Grand Council and Sublime Orient" at Charleston.[11] By 1800 his name appears as "Sovereign Grand Commander" on a patent issued by them in Charleston;[12] the following year this title would be adopted by Col. Mitchell as the head of the Supreme Council.

11. See Albert Pike, *Ancient and Accepted Scottish Rite of Freemasonry. The Constitutions and Regulations of 1762. Statutes and Regulations of Perfection, and Other Degrees. Vera Instituta Secreta et Fundamenta Ordinis of 1786. The Secret Constitutions of the 33d Degree* (New York: Masonic Publishing Co., A.M. 5632 [1872]; New Edition Printed by J. J. Little, &c., 5664 [1904]), 187–89.

12. Although the patent of Claude Marin Girardin is undated it is signed on the back, "Seen by us, Deputy Inspector General, Grand Commander at the Orient of Santo Domingo, the 27th of the 1st month 5800. [Dominique] Saint Paul" (vu à par nous Député insp^{r} G^{l} G^{d} Commd^{r} a L'O de St^{o} Domingo Le 27e Du 1e mois 5800 / Saint Paul).

When the Supreme Council was founded by Col. Mitchell and Rev. Dalcho, it did not, as Charles S. Lobingier reminds us, spring forth fully formed as Athena did from the head of Zeus.[13] Among other things, its officers bore different titles and were fewer in number, it presided over fewer degrees, and it was not known as the "Scottish Rite." At this early period the Supreme Council was what Alain Bernheim called "The Rite in 33 Degrees."[14] The name "Ancient and Accepted Scottish Rite" was not used until 1804, when the same de Grasse-Tilly, then a member of the Supreme Council at Charleston, organized a Supreme Council for France. In an agreement made that year between the newly-created Supreme Council and the Grand Orient of France (which operated as a Grand Lodge), the title "Ancient and Accepted Scottish Rite" (Rite Écossais Ancien et Accepté) was used for the first time.[15]

As the premiere Supreme Council in the world the Charleston body exercised authority over the entire country. For at least the first two years Col. Mitchell was called and identified as both the "Grand Commander in the U[nited]. States of America,"[16] as well as "President of the Supreme Council of Masons of the United States,"[17] while the nine members of the Supreme Council were denominated "Sovereigns of Masonry" who "possessed the Sovereign Masonic power over all the Craft." In its early days the Supreme Council did not directly preside over a system of thirty-three degrees or even thirty degrees (if we ignore the Blue Lodge). In fact, it did not yet possess all the degrees over which it would eventually preside. This is evident from early lists of the degrees, such as in the model "Letter of Credence" (patent) in Dalcho's Thirty-third Degree manuscript (ca. 1801–1802). The following extract from this document reveals that the only degrees known, at the creation of the Supreme Council, were the twenty-five degrees of the Order of the Royal Secret, with one new

13. [Charles S. Lobingier,] *The Supreme Council, 33°* (Louisville, Kentucky: The Standard Printing Co., 1931), 4.

14. Alain Bernheim, *Le rite en 33 grades De Frederick Dalcho à Charles Riandey* (Paris: Dervy, 2011)

15. *Acta Latomorum* (Paris: Grand Orient du France, 1805), vol. 1, 225.

16. *Circular throughout two Hemispheres* (Charleston, 1802)

17. Frederick Dalcho, *An Oration Delivered in the Sublime Grand Lodge, in Charleston, South-Carolina, on the 23d of September, 5801* (Charleston, S.C.: T. B. Bowen, [1801]), [ii]; reprinted in *Orations of the Illustrious Brother Frederick Dalcho Esqr. M.D.* (Dublin: John King Westmoreland, 1808)

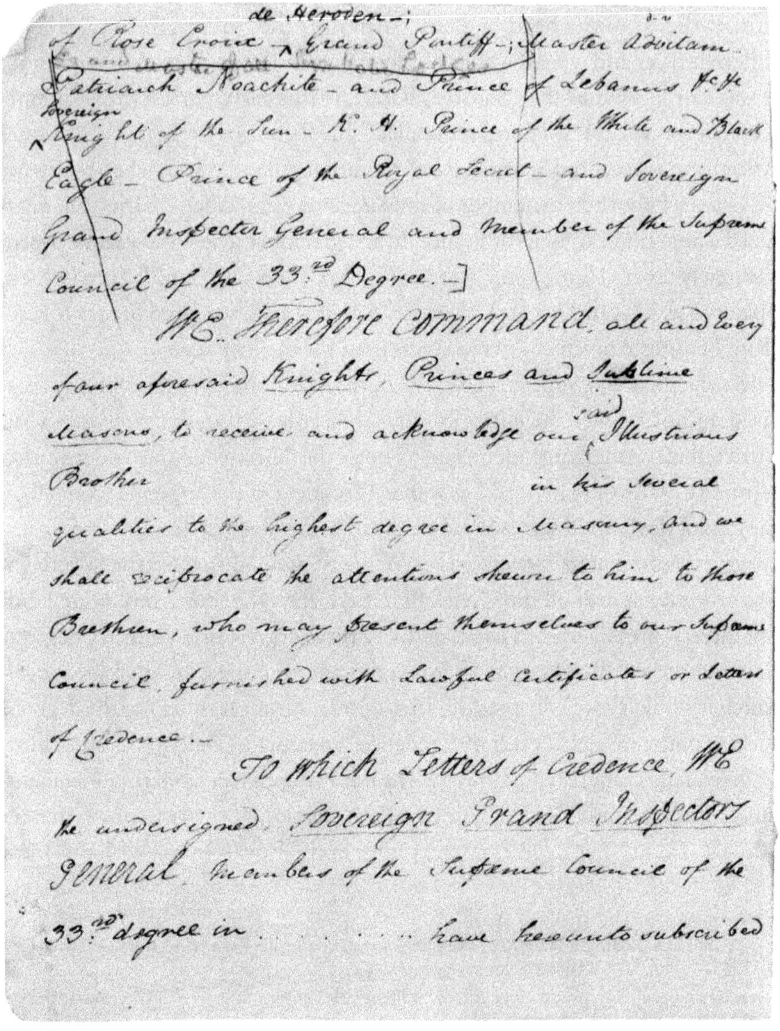
de Heroden—;
of Rose Croix—Grand Pontiff—; Master Ad Vitam
Patriarch Noachite—and Prince of Lebanus &c &c
Sovereign Knight of the Sun—K. H. Prince of the White and Black
Eagle—Prince of the Royal Secret—and Sovereign
Grand Inspector General and Member of the Supreme
Council of the 33.rd Degree.—]
We therefore command all and every
of our aforesaid Knights, Princes and Sublime
Masons, to receive and acknowledge our said Illustrious
Brother in his several
qualities to the highest degree in Masonry, and we
shall reciprocate the attentions shewn to him to those
Brethren, who may present themselves to our Supreme
Council, furnished with Lawful Certificates or Letters
of Credence.—
To which Letters of Credence, We
the undersigned Sovereign Grand Inspectors
General Members of the Supreme Council of the
33.rd degree in . . . . have hereunto subscribed

Figure 6. Page from the model "Letter of Credence" (patent) in Frederick Dalcho's Thirty-third Degree manuscript (ca. 1801–02), showing where the new degrees would be inserted. —*Archives of the Supreme Council, 33°, SJ.*

addition: "Sovereign Grand Inspector General and member of the Supreme Council of the 33rd Degree."

> *Know Ye* That we, the undersigned, *Sovereign Grand Inspectors General*, duly and lawfully established and Congregated, in *Supreme Council* of the 33rd <*degree*> have carefully and duly examined our Illustrious Brother _____ in the several degrees which he has lawfully received, and at his special request, *we do hereby* Certify, Acknowledge and Proclaim, our Illustrious Brother _____ (add civil <*or Military*> titles)— (Citizen or Subject of) residing in _____ to be an Expert Master and past Master of the Symbolic Lodge, And also a Secret Master – Perfect Master – Intimate Secretary – Provost and Judge, Intendant of the Building <*or Master in Israel*> – Master Elected of 9, Illustrious Elected of 15 – Sublime Knight Elected – Grand Master Architect – Royal Arch – and Grand Elect Perfect and Sublime Mason – *We do also certify* him to be a Knight of the East or Sword – Prince of Jerusalem – [Knight of the East and West – Knight of the Eagle and Prince of Rose Croix – <*de Heredon -;*> Grand Pontiff –; Master Ad<->vitam <*Grand Master of all Symbolic Lodges*> — Patriarch Noachite — and prince of Lebanus &c. &c. <*Sovereign*> Knight of the Sun – K.H. Prince of the White and Black Eagle – Prince of the Royal Secret – and Sovereign Grand Inspector General and Member of the Supreme Council of the 33:rd Degree. –]

THE SUPREME COUNCIL'S "NEW DEGREES"

Looking closely at this Letter of Credence we notice that the Prince of Lebanus Degree is twice followed by "&c."—an abbreviation for *et cetera*—precisely at the point where five of the Scottish Rite's new degrees would later be inserted. The names of these new degrees (23°–27°) would first appear in the *Circular throughout the two Hemispheres* (issued December 4, 1802), which included a calendar of the degrees conferred under its authority.

This means that between 1801 (when Dalcho received the Thirty-third Degree and transcribed the ritual) and December 1802 (when the *Circular* was written), the Supreme Council added the new degrees. Thus, the early Supreme Council effectively exercised control only over fifteen degrees, from the 17° Knight of the East and West, through the 33° Sovereign Grand Inspector General. The work, however, was not yet complete. Notice that the *Circular* still omitted some degrees and aggregated others. For example, the "Prince of the Royal Secret" constituted the three degrees 30°–32°. As any student of religion knows, describing the mystery of a three-in-one trinity is not an easy task, and Charleston avoided any explanation as to how this degree accomplished the task.

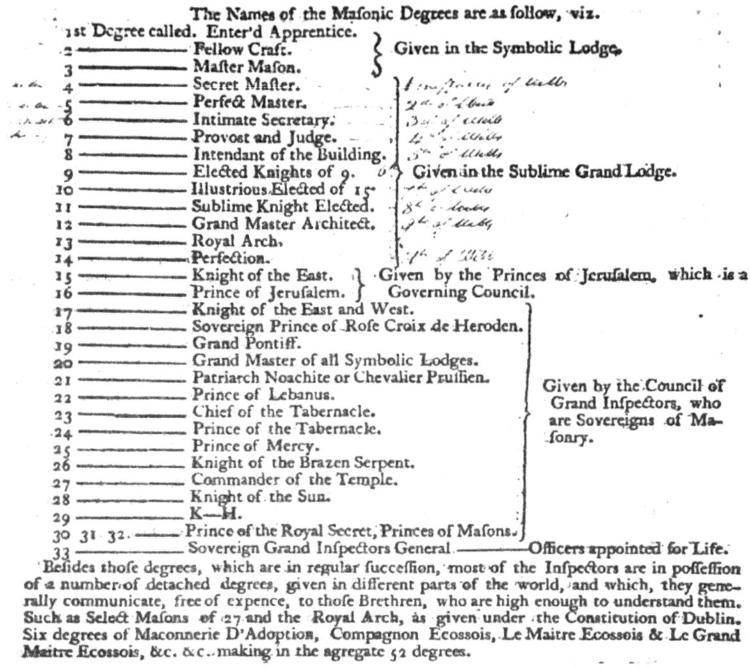

The Names of the Masonic Degrees are as follow, viz.

1st Degree called. Enter'd Apprentice.
2 ——— Fellow Craft.
3 ——— Master Mason. } Given in the Symbolic Lodge.
4 ——— Secret Master.
5 ——— Perfect Master.
6 ——— Intimate Secretary.
7 ——— Provost and Judge.
8 ——— Intendant of the Building.
9 ——— Elected Knights of 9. } Given in the Sublime Grand Lodge.
10 ——— Illustrious Elected of 15.
11 ——— Sublime Knight Elected.
12 ——— Grand Master Architect.
13 ——— Royal Arch.
14 ——— Perfection.
15 ——— Knight of the East.
16 ——— Prince of Jerusalem. } Given by the Princes of Jerusalem, which is a Governing Council.
17 ——— Knight of the East and West.
18 ——— Sovereign Prince of Rose Croix de Heroden.
19 ——— Grand Pontiff.
20 ——— Grand Master of all Symbolic Lodges.
21 ——— Patriarch Noachite or Chevalier Prussien.
22 ——— Prince of Lebanus.
23 ——— Chief of the Tabernacle.
24 ——— Prince of the Tabernacle.
25 ——— Prince of Mercy.
26 ——— Knight of the Brazen Serpent.
27 ——— Commander of the Temple.
28 ——— Knight of the Sun.
29 ——— K—H.
30 31 32. ——— Prince of the Royal Secret, Princes of Masons. } Given by the Council of Grand Inspectors, who are Sovereigns of Masonry.
33 ——— Sovereign Grand Inspectors General ——— Officers appointed for Life.

Besides those degrees, which are in regular succession, most of the Inspectors are in possession of a number of detached degrees, given in different parts of the world, and which, they generally communicate, free of expence, to those Brethren, who are high enough to understand them. Such as Select Masons of 27 and the Royal Arch, as given under the Constitution of Dublin. Six degrees of Maconnerie D'Adoption, Compagnon Ecossois, Le Maitre Ecossois & Le Grand Maitre Ecossois, &c. &c. making in the agregate 52 degrees.

Figure 7. Detail from the *Circular throughout two Hemispheres* (1802) listing the degrees over which the Supreme Council claimed authority. —*Archives of the Supreme Council, 33°, SJ.*

Interestingly, when we compare the *Circular* with Dalcho's personal patent (dated May 31, 1801), we find other differences. Dalcho's patent includes the "Grand Master Ecosé – Knight of St. Andrew" between the Prince of Libanus and Chief of the Tabernacle Degrees. Significantly, an unnumbered degree by this very name, Grand Master Ecosé, was included of Dalcho's collection of Supreme Council rituals, although it was mentioned in the *Circular* as one of the degrees communicated "free of expence, to those Brethren, who are high enough to understand them."[18] It's a matter of curiosity that the Grand Master Ecosé is the only degree named on his patent, and included in his collection,

18. For two versions of this degree see Arturo de Hoyos, *Freemasonry's Royal Secret* (Scottish Rite Research Society, 2014), 285–301; Arturo de Hoyos, *Reprints of old Rituals* (Scottish Rite Research Society, 2015), 167–95.

which is not currently a part of the Scottish Rite. This begs the question if it perhaps was once conferred as such, or if it was the inspiration for the title of the later 29°, Grand Ecossais of St. Andrew.[19]

The degree order would be further altered and expanded with additional degrees. Following these changes help to understand that although Frederick Dalcho's Thirty-third Degree patent is dated May 31, 1801, it must have been prepared between then and December 1802, since it includes an expansion and revision to the degrees found in *Circular*.

The Commander of the Temple Degree, which became the Twenty-seventh in the Scottish Rite, had been conferred as a detached (independent) degree by Louis Claude Henri de Montmain in Charleston, South Carolina, from 1798 to 1802. Brother de Montmain conferred it upon *Auguste* de Grasse-Tilly in 1801,[20] and he likely introduced it into the Supreme Council system. Other degrees came later, such as the 31° "Grand Inquiring Commander" (a.k.a. Grand Inspector Inquisitor Commander), which was not introduced until 1804. It is not known when Charleston's complete schedule of degrees was completed, but it was first printed in Joseph M'Cosh, *Documents upon Sublime Freemasonry* (1823).[21] The origin of the new degrees has been a bit of a mystery. However, on July 9, 1827, Grand Commander Moses Holbrook offered his opinion that "22–23–24–25–26–27 are very incorrect, [and] that they were modeled if not wholly manufactured in Charleston."[22]

19. For an early copy, see Arturo de Hoyos, *Masonic Formulas and Rituals Transcribed by Albert Pike in 1854 and 1855* (Washington, DC: Scottish Rite Research Society, 2010), 506–07.

20. [Albert Pike,] *The Inner Sanctuary. Part IV. The Book of the Holy House.* ([New York: Macoy,] 5644 [1884]), 272. A copy of de Montmain's "Grand, or Sovereign, Commander of the Temple" ritual, dated April 25, 1801, appears in Arturo de Hoyos, *Masonic Formulas and Rituals Transcribed by Albert Pike in 1854 and 1855* (Washington, DC: Scottish Rite Research Society, 2010), 477–84

21. Joseph M'Cosh, *Documents upon Sublime Freemasonry in the United States of America. Being a Collection of all the Official Documents Which Have Appeared on Both Sides of the Question. With Notes, and an Appendix.* (Charleston: [Sebring,] 1823). When M'Cosh reprinted the 1802 *Circular* he expanded the list to include all the degrees, but did not note this in his text. M'Cosh's list was later copied by and circulated by anti-Masons. See Arturo de Hoyos, *Light on Masonry. The History and Rituals of America's Most Important Masonic Exposé* (Washington, DC: Scottish Rite Research Society, 2008), 562–63.

22. Moses Holbrook, Charleston, South Carolina, July 9, 1827, to J. J. J. Gourgas, New York, New York. Copy in the Archives of the Supreme Council, 33°, SJ, Washington, DC.

COMPARISON OF THE NAMES OF THE DEGREES ON FREDERICK DALCHO'S PATENT WITH THE 1802 *CIRCULAR*

Dalcho's Patent (May 31, 1801)	Circular (December 4, 1802)
[18] Sovereign Prince of Rose Croix de Heroden	[18] Sovereign Prince of Rose Croix de Heroden
[19] Grand Pontif	[19] Grand Pontif
[20] Master ad Vitam – Grand Master of all Symbolic Lodges	[20] Grand Master of all Symbolic Lodges
[21] Patriarch Noachite Chevalier Prussian	[21] Patriarch Noachite or Chevalier Prussian
[22] Prince of Lebanus	[22] Prince of Lebanus
[23] Grand Master Ecosé – Knight of St. Andrew, &c &c &c	[23] Chief of the Tabernacle
[24] Chief of the Tabernacle	[24] Prince of the Tabernacle
[25] Prince of Mercy	[25] Prince of Mercy
[26] Knight of the Brazen Serpent	[26] Knight of the Brazen Serpent
[27] Commander of the Temple	[27] Commander of the Temple
[28] Sovereign Knight of the Sun, Prince Adept	[28] Knight of the Sun
[29] K.·.H.·. Knight of the White and Black Eagle	[29] K—H
[30] Prince of the Royal Secret	[30] Prince of the Royal Secret
[31] Prince of the Royal Secret	[31] Prince of the Royal Secret
[32] Prince of the Royal Secret	[32] Prince of the Royal Secret
[33] Sovereign Grand Inspector General	[33] Sovereign Grand Inspector General

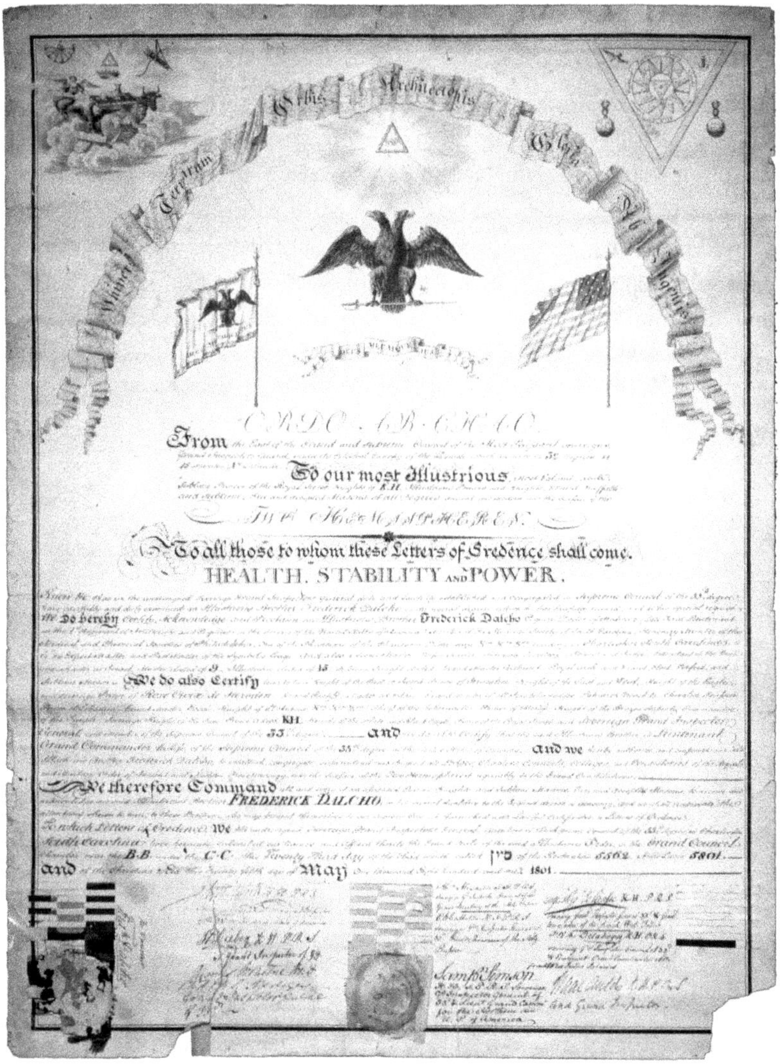

Figure 8. Frederick Dalcho's Thirty-third Degree patent (ca. 1801–02). Its inclusion of the "Grand Master Ecosé" and lack of "Prince of the Tabernacle" reveals it must have been written after the 33° manuscript, but before the *Circular*. —*Archives of the Supreme Council, 33°, SJ.*

Authority over the Degrees

The "Ineffable Lodge of Perfection," which Francken established in Albany, was active from December 20, 1767, until December 5, 1774.[23] From that time until 1801, the Sublime Grand Lodges of Perfection (which administered the 4°–14°), and Grand Councils of Princes of Jerusalem (administering the 15°–16°) operated under the Order of the Royal Secret. After its creation, the Supreme Council also issued "warrants of Constitution" to new Sublime Grand Lodges of Perfection and Grand Councils of Princes of Jerusalem, as well as to bring existing bodies under their protection. As intimated earlier, the Supreme Council did not involve itself directly in their government or administration. This was explained in the Article 6 of Frederick Dalcho's manuscript copy of the *Grand Constitutions of 1786*:

> [Article] 6th
>
> The power of the Supreme Council does not interfere with any degree below the 17th or Knights of the East and West. But every Council and Lodge of Perfect Masons are hereby required to acknowledge them in quality of inspectors General, and to receive them with the high honors ~~due them~~ <to which they are entitled>.

The limitation over the degrees was repeated in the original manuscript ritual of the Thirty-third Degree:

> The King on the first of May 5786, formed and established the 33:rd Degree to give some elucidations of the K.H.—
>
> The King was also conscious, that agreably [*sic*] to the common course of human events nature, he could not live many years; & he conceived and executed the glorious design of investing the Sovereign Masonic power which he held, as Sovereign Grand Commander of the order of Prince of the Royal Secret—in a Council of Grand Inspectors General—that they might, after his decease, regulate, agreably [*sic*] to the Constitution and Statutes which he then formed, the government of the Craft in every degree, from the 17:th or Knights of the East & West inclusive, leaving the control over the symbolic Lodge—the Grand, Ineffable and Sublime Lodge of Perfect Masons, and the Knights of the East or sword—to the Grand Council of Princes of Jerusalem, whom he conceived to be justly entitled to that Honor and power.[24]

23. "The Original Minutes of Ineffable and Sublime Grand Lodge of Perfection of Albany, NY, from 1767 to 1774," in *1906 Proceedings of the Thirty-seventh Council of Deliberation for the Bodies of the State of Ancient Accepted Scottish Rite Northern Masonic Jurisdiction, U.S.A., of the State of New York* (Printed by Order of the Council, 1906), supplement, 3–132.

24. "33rd Degree Called, Sovereign Grand Inspectors General, or Supreme Council of the 33rd,"

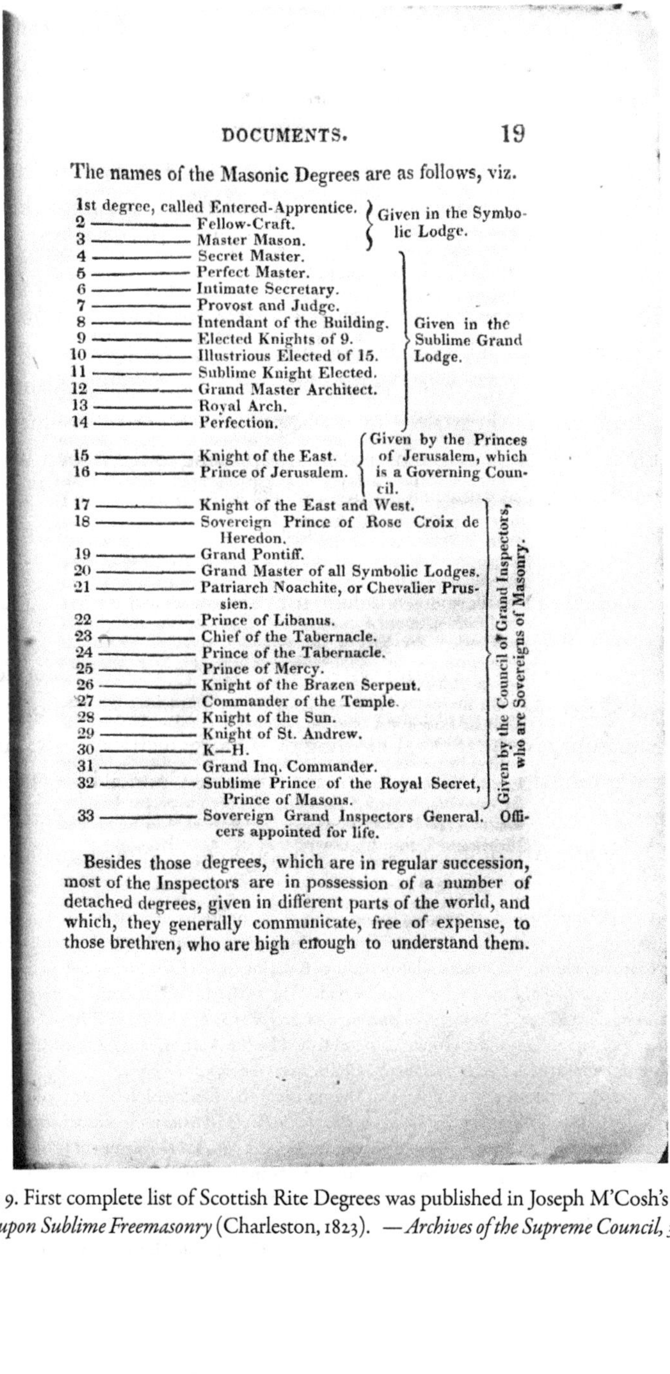

DOCUMENTS. 19

The names of the Masonic Degrees are as follows, viz.

1st degree, called	Entered-Apprentice.	Given in the Symbolic Lodge.
2 ——	Fellow-Craft.	
3 ——	Master Mason.	
4 ——	Secret Master.	Given in the Sublime Grand Lodge.
5 ——	Perfect Master.	
6 ——	Intimate Secretary.	
7 ——	Provost and Judge.	
8 ——	Intendant of the Building.	
9 ——	Elected Knights of 9.	
10 ——	Illustrious Elected of 15.	
11 ——	Sublime Knight Elected.	
12 ——	Grand Master Architect.	
13 ——	Royal Arch.	
14 ——	Perfection.	
15 ——	Knight of the East.	Given by the Princes of Jerusalem, which is a Governing Council.
16 ——	Prince of Jerusalem.	
17 ——	Knight of the East and West.	Given by the Council of Grand Inspectors, who are Sovereigns of Masonry.
18 ——	Sovereign Prince of Rose Croix de Heredon.	
19 ——	Grand Pontiff.	
20 ——	Grand Master of all Symbolic Lodges.	
21 ——	Patriarch Noachite, or Chevalier Prussien.	
22 ——	Prince of Libanus.	
23 ——	Chief of the Tabernacle.	
24 ——	Prince of the Tabernacle.	
25 ——	Prince of Mercy.	
26 ——	Knight of the Brazen Serpent.	
27 ——	Commander of the Temple.	
28 ——	Knight of the Sun.	
29 ——	Knight of St. Andrew.	
30 ——	K—H.	
31 ——	Grand Inq. Commander.	
32 ——	Sublime Prince of the Royal Secret, Prince of Masons.	
33 ——	Sovereign Grand Inspectors General. Officers appointed for life.	

Besides those degrees, which are in regular succession, most of the Inspectors are in possession of a number of detached degrees, given in different parts of the world, and which, they generally communicate, free of expense, to those brethren, who are high enough to understand them.

Figure 9. First complete list of Scottish Rite Degrees was published in Joseph M'Cosh's *Documents upon Sublime Freemasonry* (Charleston, 1823). —*Archives of the Supreme Council, 33°, SJ.*

Although the earliest history of the Supreme Council at Charleston is lost, one account is preserved which shows how its authority was recognized. In the earliest known reference to the Supreme Council (just five months and one day after its founding), we read that on November 1, 1801, Emanuel De La Motta, its Treasurer General, visited Savannah, Georgia. The Masonic record of Abraham Jacobs records that at a meeting of Sublime Masons held there on that date, two members informed the body that "Ill.∴ Bro.∴ Emanuel De La Motta, K.H. P. of the R.S., and member of the Supreme Council of the Thirty-third Degree in Charleston, had arrived in the city, and proposed that a Committee from this body should wait on him and tender an invitation to visit us...." At a meeting held on November 9 the Brethren entreated De La Motta to "put themselves under the protection of the Sublime Council of Princes of Jerusalem in Charleston, by applying to them for a Warrant and Constitutions, to establish a Lodge of Perfection in this city."[25] We are informed in the 1802 *Circular* that the petition was favorably received: "On the 4th of December, 5802, a warrant of Constitution passed the seal of the Grand Council of Princes of Jerusalem, for the establishment of a Sublime Grand Lodge in Savannah, Georgia."[26]

The government of the entire system, from the 4° Secret Master, to the 32° Royal Secret inclusive, was not assumed until after the revival of American Freemasonry in the 1840s, following the "Morgan affair."[27] The authority to govern the degrees was ceded to the Supreme Council by Article 8 of the *Grand Constitutions of 1786*, which denominated them "Sovereigns of Masonry," while Article 12 states that "The Supreme Council shall exercise

[folios 21v–22r]. Unpublished manuscript in the handwriting of Frederick Dalcho, ca. 1801–02, with emendations made ca. 1804. Copy in the Archives of the Supreme Council, 33°, SJ, Washington, DC.

25. [Abraham Jacobs,] "Minutes and Proceedings Relating to Applications Received from Brethren Initiated into the Sublime Degrees. Commended the 26th May, 1792, in the State of Georgia, North America," in Robert B. Folger, *The Ancient and Accepted Scottish Rite, in Thirty-three Degrees ... A Full and Complete Appendix* (New York: Published by the Author, 1862), Appendix, 94.

26. *Circular throughout two Hemispheres* (Charleston, 1802), 5.

27. For more on the Morgan Affair, and the political machine which benefitted from anti-Masonry, see Charles McCarthy, PhD, *The Antimasonic Party: A Study of Political anti-Masonry in the United States, 1827–1840* (American Historical Association: US Government Printing Office, 1903); William Preston Vaughn, The Anti-Masonic Party in the United States: 1826–1843 (University Press of Kentucky, 1983). To see how it impacted Freemasonry and led to an exposure of some of the Scottish Rite's early rituals, see Arturo de Hoyos, *Light on Masonry: The History and Rituals of America's Most Important Masonic Exposé* (Washington, DC: Scottish Rite Research Society, 2008)

all the Sovereign Masonic power ~~with~~ <of> which his August Majesty Frederick the 2nd king of Prussia ~~was~~ <is now> possessed...." This was reiterated in the 1802 *Circular* which noted that the Supreme Council "possessed the Sovereign Masonic power over all the Craft."

Trouble in the High Degrees

On February 21, 1802, the Supreme Council at Charleston issued a patent to de Grasse-Tilly making him Grand Commander for life of the Supreme Council in the French West India Islands.[28] In the early part of that year he established a Supreme Councils at Santo Domingo before leaving for France where he established another Supreme Council in 1804. In 1806, Antoine Bideaud, one of the members Supreme Council in the French West India Islands was traveling to Bordeaux, France, when he stopped in New York City. While there on August 6, he conferred the 4° through 32° of the Scottish Rite on John James Joseph Gourgas, and four others,[29] and created the "Sublime Grand Consistory of Princes of the Royal Secret of the 30th, 31st, & 32^{d} Degrees." Bideaud's authority was to be "conformable to the Grand Constitutions,"[30] which should have prevented him from establishing bodies in any country where a Supreme Council had been established.[31] This meant that the new Consistory was "irregular," and had no legitimacy within the Supreme Council system. Gourgas later stated

> The act of Bideaud's was completely irregular, unconstitutional. He had no rights or power within any part of these United States, but then he was tempted and did succumb at the rate of five times $46, or $230. As to us, we were then new and raw in these matters, believing all was right; however, it was afterwards

28. *Official Bulletin of the Supreme Council of the 33d Degree, for the Southern Jurisdiction of the United States,* vol. 2 (Charleston: August 1872), No. 1, 209–11.

29. *Proceedings of the Supreme Council of Sov. Gr Inspectors General 33° for the Northern Masonic Jurisdiction of the United States. Gourgas Body, 1813–1851. Raymond Body, 1851–1860. Van Rensselaer Body, 1860–1862.* (Portland [Maine:] Stephen Berry, Printer, 1876), 15–16.

30. See Bideaud's patent in *Proceedings of the Supreme Council ... Gourgas Body, 1813–1851. Raymond Body, 1851–1860. Van Rensselaer Body, 1860–1862.* (1876), 14.

31. The *Constitutions, Statutes, Regulations* of the Thirty-third degrees stated, "9th No Deputy Inspector can use his patent, in any Country, where a Supreme Council of Inspectors General is established, - unless it shall be signed by the said Council." See facsimile of Dalcho's copy in Carter and Harris, *History of the Supreme Council, 33° ... 1801–1861* (1964), 342.

> made all correct by the wiping off of our Illustrious Brothers at Charleston, S.C., and Philadelphia.[32]

When the members of this Sublime Grand Consistory learned that they were irregular, their President, John G. Tardy, travelled to Philadelphia to meet with Pierre le Barbier Duplessis, a Deputy Inspector General of the Order of the Royal Secret, who presumably "healed" them, and reappointed Tardy on October 4, 1807, to the same office. However, Duplessis's patent, which he received in 1790 from Augustin Prevost, was limited in authority to the twenty-five degrees of the Order of the Royal Secret,[33] and could not bestow legitimacy to a Sublime Grand Consistory of the 30°–32°.

The next event involved Abraham Jacobs, whom we recall helped secure a warrant for the Sublime Grand Lodge in Savannah, Georgia. In October 1808, Jacobs, now in New York, acted on his own authority and organized a Council of Princes of Jerusalem, and from then through November 3, 1808, he conferred the high degrees of the Order of the Royal Secret, up through the second to the last degree, the 23° Knight of the Sun. Two days later, however, when the new Council of Princes of Jerusalem was again opened, they were visited by John Tardy, who proceeded to investigate them under authority of the patent he had received from Duplessis in 1807. Jacobs related that on November 6, 1808, they opened a Council of Princes of Jerusalem, when "Brother Tardy having produced his Warrant and other credentials, investigated our proceedings, sanctioned and approved of the same, and promised his protection and every assistance in his power. . . ."[34] Tardy did not, however, reinstall the officers of three days earlier, but rather installed others of his own choice. On November 8, 1808, he issued a Warrant of Constitution or Charter for *Aurora Grata* Lodge of Perfection No. 1, and *Concordia Crecimus* Council of Princes of Jerusalem.

32. Enoch Terry Carson in Robert Freke Gould, *The History of Freemasonry its Antiquities, Symbols, Constitutions, Customs, etc. Derived from Official Sources throughout the* World 4 vols. (New York, Cincinnati, and Chicago: John C. Yorston & Co., 1889), vol. 4, 655.

33. See Duplessis's patent in *Proceedings of the Supreme Council . . . Gourgas Body, 1813–1851. Raymond Body, 1851–1860. Van Rensselaer Body, 1860–1862.* (1876), 17–18.

34. Diary of Abraham Jacobs, in Robert B. Folger, *The Ancient and Accepted Scottish Rite, in Thirty-three Degrees . . . A Full and Complete Appendix* (New York: Published by the Author, 1862), Appendix, 108.

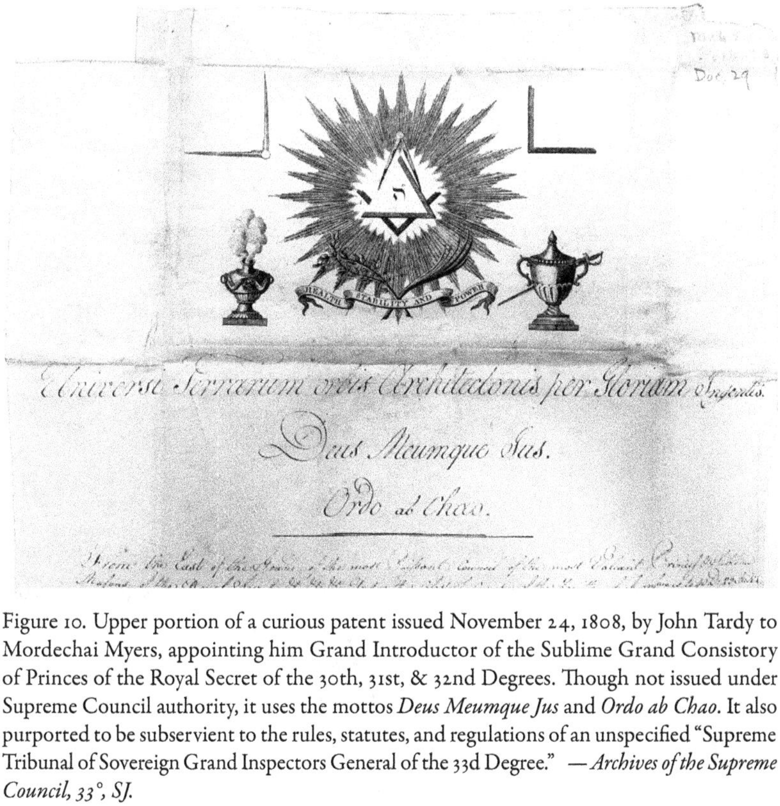

Figure 10. Upper portion of a curious patent issued November 24, 1808, by John Tardy to Mordechai Myers, appointing him Grand Introductor of the Sublime Grand Consistory of Princes of the Royal Secret of the 30th, 31st, & 32nd Degrees. Though not issued under Supreme Council authority, it uses the mottos *Deus Meumque Jus* and *Ordo ab Chao*. It also purported to be subservient to the rules, statutes, and regulations of an unspecified "Supreme Tribunal of Sovereign Grand Inspectors General of the 33d Degree." —*Archives of the Supreme Council, 33°, SJ.*

Although Tardy was not a member of the Supreme Council, the patents he issued imply that he somehow acted under their authority, or at least with their knowledge. Many of his patents[35] include the phrases *Deus Meumque Jus* and *Ordo ab Chao*, which mottos were unique to the Supreme Council. We can see this, for example, on the patent he issued on November 24, 1808, to Mordecai Myers, which appointed him Grand Introductor of the Sublime

35. Several examples appear in the back of Abraham Jacobs' *Register, Rules & Statu[te]s of the Sublime Degrees of Masonry.*

Grand Consistory of Princes of the Royal Secret of the 30th, 31st, & 32^{d} Degrees. This same patent also includes the following curious statement:

> ... We have installed him with all Honors and according to Our Ancient Usages; & Do hereby Approve, Ratify and Confirm, Whatever our Said Illustrious Brother may Do, which belong or in any Ways appertain to his above Special Eminent Situation, amongst Us, Conformable however to all the Rules, Statutes & Regulations of all the Different Degrees, which have or may be enacted hereafter, By the Supreme Tribunal of Sovereign Grand Inspectors General of the 33d Degree.[36]

In spite of this language there is no evidence that Tardy acted with either the authority or approbation of the Supreme Council at Charleston—or any other Supreme Council. If there are answers to these quandaries, they may have been in the lost minutes of these bodies.[37]

The Beginnings of Cerneauism

Antoine's Bideaud's act may have been the first in a long history of confusion regarding authority over the "Ineffable and Sublime Degrees" in the United States, but it would pale in comparison to the Masonic career of Joseph Cerneau. The latter's impact upon the Scottish Rite has long been a subject of argument, inquiry, and speculation. Because the matter has been the subject of several articles in *Heredom*,[38] I will recite only scant details. In brief, we know that Cerneau received a patent, while he lived in Cuba, from

36. Patent issued by John G. Tardy, New York, November 24, 1808, to Mordecai Myers. Archives of the Supreme Council, 33°, SJ, Washington, DC.

37. Robert Freke Gould, *The History of Freemasonry its Antiquities, Symbols, Constitutions, Customs, etc. Derived from Official Sources throughout the World* 4 vols. (New York, Cincinnati, and Chicago: John C. Yorston & Co., 1889), vol. 4, 655.

38. For articles on Cerneauism in *Heredom* see Arturo de Hoyos, "The Union of 1867," vol. 4 (1995), 7–45; Alain Bernheim, "An Introduction to Joseph Cerneau and His Biographers," vol. 6 (1997), 21–34; Michael R. Poll, "The Early Years of the Grand Consistory of Louisiana (1811–1815)," vol. 8 (1999–2000), 39–53; Arturo de Hoyos, "The Early Years of the Grand Consistory of Louisiana (1811–1815)—A Rejoinder," vol. 9 (2001), 69–99; Michael R. Poll, "A Few 'Rejoinder' Comments," Michael R. Poll vol. 9 (2001), 103–9; Alain Bernheim, "Joseph Cerneau, His Masonic Bodies, and His Grand Consistory's Minute Book – Part 1," 18:25–84; "Joseph Cerneau, Part 2—The Charleston Grand Council of P.R.S. & the Supreme Council of the U.S.A.," vol. 20:11–178; Alain Bernheim, "Emanuel De La Motta in New York, 1813–1815: A Retrograde Chess Problem," vol. 21 (2013), 9–85; Jeffrey Croteau, "'Emanuel De La Motta in New York, 1813–1815': A Rejoinder," vol. 22 (2014), 9–78. Alain Bernheim and Arturo de Hoyos, "A Response to Jeffrey Croteau's Rejoinder," vol. 23 (2015), 79–94.

Antoine-Mathieu Dupotet on July 15, 1806, creating him a "Deputy Inspector General, Deputy Grand Inspector, for the Northern part of the Island of Cuba," with authority to promote a Knight Prince Mason to the highest degrees of Masonry once a year. In November 1806 he traveled to New York and set up business as a jeweler, and organized a Grand Consistory on October 28, 1807. His body styled itself "The Grand Consistory for the United States of America, their Territories and Dependencies, of Supreme Chiefs of Exalted Masonry, according to the Ancient Constitutional Rite of Heredon." Like Bideaud before him, Cerneau's act exceeded his authority. He may not have known about Bideaud's (irregular) Consistory organized in 1806, but he soon learned about Tardy's reorganization of Abraham Jacobs's bodies, as the latter recorded in his diary:

> November 11th, 1808. This day Mr. Mulligan and a French gentleman (J. Cerneau) called on me at the school about 11 o'clock, informed me, that their visit was a Committee from a Council of Princes of Jerusalem, to desire my attendance on them as they were then sitting.
>
> I replied, "I know of no such body of men but the one I had established, and in order to prevent any other such body from infringing on the Constitution and Ancient Landmarks, we had made ourselves public by advertizing in the public prints of this city, and would say nothing further on the subject." They asked what reply they should return to their Council. I told them, "it was out of my power to wait on them."[39]

This encounter would be the first contact in what would become a war over the high degrees, which would last until 1867, although residual effects persist even today. Concerned about the encounter, Jacobs *et al.* wrote to the Supreme Council at Charleston, and warned them about Cerneau, but nothing was done because Charleston simply failed to act.[40] They would soon have cause to regret their lack of action.

39. Diary of Abraham Jacobs, in Robert B. Folger, *The Ancient and Accepted Scottish Rite, in Thirty-three Degrees . . . A Full and Complete Appendix* (New York: Published by the Author, 1862), Appendix, 107.

40. About 1815 the officers of the Supreme Council, 33° in New York complained to the Supreme Council 33° in Charleston, ". . . the mischieves persisted in by that nefarious Joseph Cerneau would never have gone on to such length, had you taken the business in hand, when we informed you of it in November, 5808, and as in duty we were bound to do it." [Albert Pike,] *Official Bulletin of the Supreme Council of The 33d Degree for the Southern Jurisdiction of the United States* (Gr.·. Or.·. of Charleston, 1885), vol. 7, 311–12. This fact was underscored in a letter written eighteen years by the Grand Commander Moses Holbrook of the Supreme Council at Charleston: "Of this S.C. you

At some point Cerneau became aware of the Supreme Council at Charleston, and in 1813 he also created his own version in New York, which he called "The Supreme Council of Grand Inspectors General, of the 33d Degree, Regularly established according to the Ancient Constitutional Scottish Rite of Heredon, for the United States of America their Territories and dependencies."[41] At present, we are not concerned with Cerneau's reasons or justifications for having created his groups, but are rather interested in the results of his actions.

It is notable that Cerneau's Supreme Council was the first to use the terms "Scottish Rite" and "Ancient and Accepted Scottish Rite"[42] in the United States. As previously noted these titles had been used by Alexandre-Auguste de Grasse-Tilly (a member of the Supreme Council at Charleston) in France in 1804, and I suspect that Cerneau learned about the Supreme Council from French sources. This could explain how he had "heard that a Council had existed at Charleston, South Carolina, which might yet be in activity."[43] Cerneau also stated he had attempted to contact Supreme Council by writing to Col. John Mitchell, but without success.

In the beginning Cerneau's Supreme Council was not a copy of the one in Charleston. Differences included their views on the Thirty-third Degree, the authority of the Supreme Council, the number and names of the principle officers, and other matters. To the average person on the outside, however, it would be difficult to appreciate any difference. Originally, the Supreme Council at Charleston used an *embossed seal* which included a double-headed eagle clutching a sword in its talons. On the upper part of the seal it read "• SUPREME • COUNCIL • 33 •" and on the lower part, "DEUS • MEUMQUE • JUS." When the Supreme Council for France was created

have a very correct view, and of the evils which have followed since 1801 and perhaps since 1808, when prudence and firmness might have remedied all the misfortunes under which we now labor∴ or it would have wholly prevented them." ∴*Moses Holbrook, Charleston, S.C., July 12, 1827, to J. J. J. Gourgas, New York, NY.* Copy in the Archives of the Supreme Council, 33°, SJ, Washington, DC.

41. See *Heredom* vol. 18 (2010), 71–77, for a facsimile of Cerneau's *List of the Grand Officers, Members, Honorary Members &c of the Supreme Council* (New York: Hardcastle and Van Pelt, 1813).

42. See transcript of the certificate issued to Cerneau by his successor Elias Hicks in 1827, in Alain Bernheim, "An Introduction to Joseph Cerneau and his Biographers," *Heredom* (Washington, DC: Scottish Rite Research Society, 1997), vol. 6, 33–34 (for a photograph of the original see 9–11).

43. Robert B. Folger, *The Ancient and Accepted Scottish Rite, in Thirty-three Degrees ... A Full and Complete Appendix* 2d ed. (New York: Published by the Author, 1862), 148.

Figure 12. *Left*: The embossed seal of the Supreme Council, 33°, of Masons of the United States of America, founded in Charleston in 1801. *Middle:* Printed seal of the Supreme Council, 33°, for France, founded in 1804. *Right*: The printed seal of Joseph Cerneau's Supreme Council, 33°, for the United States of America, founded in New York in 1813. —*Archives of the Supreme Council, 33°, SJ.*

in 1804, they created and used a *printed seal* for their documents which read "SUPREME COUNCIL OF THE 33d IN FRANCE" and on the lower part, "• DEUS MEUMQUE JUS •". The Cerneauists created a printed seal which was a close copy: it included a double-headed eagle, clutching a sword in its talons, surrounded by the words "SUP.·. COUN.·. OF THE 33.·. FOR THE U.·. S.·. OF AM.·. • DEUS MEUMQUE JUS •"

In an effort to regain control of the "Rite in 33 Degrees" the Supreme Council at Charleston created another Supreme Council in New York, in 1815 (documents were back-dated to make it appear that the act occurred in August 1813[44]), which presided over the "Northern District" of the United States, while the Charleston body would preside over the "Southern District." The members of the new Supreme Council for the Northern District, were largely the members of the Bideaud, Jacobs, and Tardy organizations.

For the purposes of this article it is not necessary to recite the years-long battle with Cerneau's Supreme Council. The subject has been discussed in many other publications, and need not detain us now.[45] It can be noted, however, that

44. Alain Bernheim, "Emanuel De La Motta in New York, 1813–1815: A Retrograde Chess Problem," vol. 21 (2013), 9–85; Jeffrey Croteau, "'Emanuel De La Motta in New York, 1813–1815': A Rejoinder," vol. 22 (2014), 9–78. Alain Bernheim and Arturo de Hoyos, "A Response to Jeffrey Croteau's Rejoinder," vol. 23 (2015), 79–94.

45. See for example, Arturo de Hoyos, "The Union of 1867," *Heredom* vol. 4 (1995), 7–45.

on December 24, 1813, the Supreme Council at Charleston, concluded that "Joseph Cerneau & his abettors & followers, are unworthy of Masonic communion with any regular Free Masons, whether of high or low degree, or wheresoever dispersed, & that each and every of them are hereby expelled from, even every or any lawful degree, or Masonic Society, in which they may have been received or admitted. . . ."[46] As "Sovereigns of Masonry," the Supreme Council at Charleston may have believed they possessed the power to expel Cerneau and his associates, but in reality they overreached their boundaries. At that time DeWitt Clinton, Mayor of New York City, was Grand Master of the Grand Lodge of New York, as well as Deputy Grand Commander of the Cerneau Supreme Council. However noble they were as individuals, and whatever rights they possessed over their own organization, the Supreme Council at Charleston had no power to expel the Grand Master of New York, or any other Masons.

Some Order, Some Chaos

Matters were further complicated on August 17, 1815, when Cerneau opened a Grand Council of Princes of the Royal Secret in Charleston itself. My discovery of their original minute book in 2010 (which was misfiled in the Archives of the Supreme Council, 33°, SJ) opened the door to understanding the fascinating and troubling interaction between these two groups. The story is told in Alain Bernheim's thorough article "Joseph Cerneau, Part 2—The Charleston Grand Council of P.R.S. & the Supreme Council of the U.S.A." (*Heredom* 20(2012): 11–178). The unfortunate loss of the original minutes of the Supreme Council at Charleston, however, prevents us from knowing their side of the story, the subjects of their deliberations, and what efforts were made to promote their rite. All that we know is gleaned from a few patents and warrants, and some surviving correspondence, but it's limited at best.

Cerneau not only established bodies of the Order of the Royal Secret, Grand Consistories, and created a Supreme Council, but he also conferred the degrees of Knighthood now connected with the York Rite. Robert B. Folger noted that "Cerneau also conferred the degrees of Knighthood on individuals by virtue of his Patent, and all the Knights Templar, Knights of the Red Cross,

46. See photographic facsimile of the original manuscript, signed by Mitchell and Dalcho, in Carter and Harris, *History of the Supreme Council, 33° . . . 1801–1861* (1964), 121.

and Knights of Malta, in New York at that time, of the present system practiced, were made so by Cerneau."[47] Folger continued:

> It must be borne in mind that there were Encampments of *Knights Templar* in existence many years before Mr. Cerneau arrived in this country from St. Domingo, as well as *Knights of St. John*, and of *Malta*. None of these, however, were esteemed as Masonic bodies, or in any way connected with Masonry. Many received these orders of Knighthood who were not Masons. Brother Elias Hicks was initiated a Knight of St. John of Jerusalem one year before he was initiated into Masonry, and all Master Masons were eligible to the Knight of Malta and Mediterranean Pass, as late as the year 1820. It was a very common thing at that period, to confer this Order in Lodges of Master Masons.[48]

The orders of knighthood held a peculiar position in their early history in the United States. When Thomas Smith Webb (himself a Knight Templar and Knight of Malta) published the first edition of *The Freemason's Monitor* (1797), he noted their unusual situation:

> OBSERVATIONS on the ORDERS of
> KNIGHTS TEMPLARS, and KNIGHTS of MALTA
>
> ALTHOUGH these degrees compose no part of the system of Masonry, yet, as they are not at present conferred on any but Masons, and as many encampments are established in different parts of the world, under sanction of Masons' Lodges, it may not be unuseful to give a sketch of their history.[49]

Five year later, when he published the second edition of the *Freemason's Monitor* (1802) Webb revised the statement: "As several orders of knighthood are conferred in Europe and America, reputedly under the sanction of masonic assemblies, it may be expected that some notice will be taken of them in this work."[50] It should be noted that Webb himself organized the Grand Encampment of Rhode Island in 1805 and served as Grand Master thereof until 1817. He was also instrumental in organizing the General Grand Encampment of

47. Robert B. Folger, *The Ancient and Accepted Scottish Rite, in Thirty-three Degrees ... A Full and Complete Appendix* (New York: Published by the Author, 1862), 122.

48. Robert B. Folger, *The Ancient and Accepted Scottish Rite, in Thirty-three Degrees ... A Full and Complete Appendix* (New York: Published by the Author, 1862), 123.

49. [Thomas Smith Webb,] *The Freemason's Monitor; or Illustrations of Masonry: In Two Parts. By a Royal Arch Mason, K.T.—K. of M.—&c. &c.* (Albany: Spencer & Webb, 1797), 181.

50. Thomas Smith Webb, *The Freemason's Monitor; or Illustrations of Masonry: In Two Parts.* (New York: Southwick and Crooker, 1802), 165.

the United States in 1816, when he was elected Deputy General Grand Master, which office he held until his death.

In June 1814 the Cerneau Grand Consistory further expanded its domain by creating the Grand Encampment of Knights Templar for the State of New York.

> The Grand Encampment of Sir Knights Templars and Appendant Orders, for the State of New York, regularly constituted by the Sovereign Grand Consistory of the Chiefs of Exalted Masonry for the United States of America, its Territories and Dependencies, sitting in New York.
>
> This day, the 18th of the 4th month, A. L., 5814, answering to June, A. D., 1814, &c., agreeably to notice assembled at the place assigned for their deliberations, this Grand Encampment was opened in due form and becoming solemnity. *Brother Jonathan Schieffelin* officiating as Thrice Illustrious Grand Master; *James B. Durand* as Senior "Warden, and *Toussaint Midy* as Junior Warden.
>
> The object of the meeting being announced, the Grand Orator took occasion to deliver a discourse, in which he stated the proceedings and ceremonial which took place at the formation of the Grand Encampment by the Sovereign Grand Consistory, in the city of New York, in January, 1814.
>
> That the numerous Encampments of Knights Templars, now existing within this State, *being self created bodies*, are consequently governed by their own private and individual laws, acknowledging no superior authority, because, in fact, none heretofore existed. A longer continuance of this state of things could be but productive of ill consequences, inasmuch as it was to be apprehended that these sorts of unconstituted Associations, so rapidly increasing in number, would sooner or later have lessened, if not entirely destroyed, that commanding respect due to so dignified a degree as that of Knight Templar, &c.
>
> Accordingly, the Sovereign Grand Consistory, fully impressed with the necessity and importance of this subject, has, at its session on the 22d of January, A. D., 1814, as aforesaid, decreed by a unanimous vote, the establishment of a "GRAND ENCAMPMENT OF KNIGHTS TEMPLAR AND APPENDANT ORDERS FOR THE STATE OF NEW YORK," and immediately proceeded to its formation by choosing the Grand Officers thereof, taken (for this time only) from among its own members, as follows:
>
> Dewitt Clinton, Thr.·. Illustrious Grand Master,
> Martin Hoffman, Grand Generalissimo,
> John W. Mulligan, Grand Captain General,
> James B. Durand, Senior Grand Warden,
> Jacob Schieffelin, Junior Grand Warden,
> Elias Hicks, Grand Orator,
> Anthony Rainetaux, Grand Recorder,
> Joseph Gouin, Grand Treasurer,
> Jonathan Schieffelin, Grand Marshal.

> They were accordingly installed into their respective offices, and the establishment of the Grand Encampment of Sir Knights Templars and Appendant Orders for the State of New York was next proclaimed in AMPLE FORM.[51]

The rapid progress and successes of Cerneau Masons must have troubled the Supreme Council at Charleston, more so because the Supreme Council for the Northern District in 1815 was ineffective and unwilling to work. J. J. J. Gourgas, its Grand Secretary and driving force, had personally borne the expenses and troubles associated with its organization, while the other officers displayed a casual disregard. Almost immediately after its organization Gourgas saw no option but to suspend the work of the Supreme Council for the Northern District, as he later confessed in a remarkably frank letter marked "confidential."

> In 1814–15, disgusted as I was with the total want of *true* masonic zeal & every thing else absolutely requisite so as to maintain it in prosperity according to the *right* principles of the masonic Order – I did let go and stopt entirely from troubling myself any more about it, from which time it remained in a profound sleep, until the receipt of your five circulars dated January 1826.[52]

It's important to note that a Supreme Council, unlike other bodies of Masonry, continues to exist as long a single member survives.[53] Thus, the Supreme Council for the Northern District continued, even in its "profound sleep" from 1815–26, when only the Cerneau and Charleston Supreme Councils were active. However, with a distance of 760 miles between Charleston and New York City, there was little that could be done to slow the growth of Cerneauism.

51. Samuel G. Risk, ed., *Proceedings of the General Grand Encampment of Knights Templar of the United States of America, from its formation, A.D. 1816, A.O. 698, to A.D. 1856, A.O. 738.* (New Orleans: Printed at the Bulletin Book and Job Office., 1860), as quoted in Robert B. Folger, *The Ancient and Accepted Scottish Rite, in Thirty-three Degrees . . . A Full and Complete Appendix* (New York: Published by the Author, 1862), 125–26.

52. *J. J. J. Gourgas, New York, June* [5], *1832, to Moses Holbrook, Charleston, South Carolina.* Archives of the Supreme Council, 33°, SJ, Washington, DC.

53. "[A] Supreme Council once lawfully, constitutionally established, represents a Sovereign, who never dies, or at least, never need to die, for the very youngest member who survives, has the right and power within himself to renovate the Council at pleasure." — *Proceedings of the Supreme Council of Sov.·. Gr.·. Inspectors General 33°, for the Northern Masonic Jurisdiction of the United States. Gourgas Body, 1813–1852. Raymond Body, 1851–1860. Van Rensselaer Body, 1860–1862* (Portland, [Maine]: Stephen Berry, Printer, 1876), 77.

On February 23, 1816, John Mitchell, the first Grand Commander of the Supreme Council at Charleston died. As we shall see, this would have unforeseen and dire consequences for the "Mother Supreme Council." His Lieutenant Grand Commander, Frederick Dalcho, advanced and assumed the vacated office. At this time the Supreme Council was still relatively new and unknown. With the exception of its recently published pronouncements against Joseph Cerneau, which had limited circulation, there is no reason why it would have come to the notice of the average American Mason. Coincidentally, however, soon after the death of John Mitchell, a well-known Masonic lecturer named David Vinton[54] published his book *The Masonic Minstrel*[55] which would offer the Scottish Rite some notoriety. Although it best known for introducing the dirge "Solemn Strikes the Funeral Chime," Vinton's book also included a list of forty-three "Masonick Degrees," which began with Entered Apprentice and ended with Sovereign Grand Inspector General.

Vinton's list is an enlarged version of that printed in the Supreme Council's 1802 *Circular throughout the two hemispheres*. Its heading, which mentions the Sublime Grand Lodges in Charleston, New York, and Newport, did not differentiate between bodies established by the Supreme Council at Charleston, with those of Joseph Cerneau, and Vinton did not appreciate the differences. His personal unfamiliarity with the degrees also caused him to ignore the divisions listed in the *Circular*, i.e., the Sublime Grand Lodge, the Princes of Jerusalem, and the Supreme Council of Grand Inspectors. Vinton also misunderstood the meaning of the abbreviation "K–H," which he thought meant "Knight of the Holy Ghost," although it actually means

54. In 1821 the Grand Lodge of North Carolina expelled Vinton for selling Masonic degrees, calling him "a base and unprincipled man, undeserving the continuance of the Masonic fraternity ... [a] wretch, who would build up his fortunes by the prostration of our sacred Order." See *Proceedings of the Grand Lodge of North-Carolina, at a Special Communication Held in the City of Raleigh on the 30th Day of April, 1821, A.L. 5821* (Raleigh: Thomas Henderson, Jr., 1821), 6–7. Among other things, he was accused of conferring the Mark and Past Master's degrees without authority, and of selling manuscripts of Masonic lectures. In fact, Vinton's actions were in common with other "itinerant degree lecturers"—a.k.a. "degree peddlers." It is likely that merely Vinton encroached on a local lecturer's territory.

55. [David Vinton,] *The Masonick Minstrel, a Selection of Masonic, Sentimental, and Humorous Songs, Duet, Glees, Canons, Rounds and Canzonettes Respectfully Dedicated to the Most Ancient and Honourable Fraternity of Free and Accepted Masons. With an Appendix, Containing a Short Historical Account of Masonry: And Likewise, A List of all the Lodges in the United States.* (Dedham, [Mass.]: Printed by H. Mann and Co. for the Author, 1816).

421

The names of the MASONICK DEGREES *are as follow, and such as are conferred in the Sublime Grand Lodges in Charleston, S. C. in the city of New-York, and in Newport, R. I.*

1. Entered Apprentice.
2. Fellow-Craft.
3. Master Mason.
4. Mark Master.
5. Past Master.
6. Most Excellent Master.
7. Royal Arch.
8. Royal Master.
9. Knight of the Red Cross.
10. Knight of Malta.
11. Knight of the Holy Sepulchre.
12. Knight of the Christian Mark.
13. Knight Templar.
14. Secret Master.
15. Perfect Master.
16. Intimate Secretary.
17. Provost and Judge.
18. Intendant of the Building.
19. Elected Knights of Nine.
20. Illustrious Elected of Fifteen.
21. Sublime Knight Elected.
22. Grand Master Architect.
23. Knight of the Ninth Arch.
24. Perfection.
25. Knight of the East.
26. Prince of Jerusalem.
27. Knight of the East and West.
28. Sovereign Prince of Rose Croix de Heroden.
29. Grand Pontiff.
30. Grand Master of all Symbolic Lodges.
31. Patriarch Noachite or Chevalier Prussien.
32. Prince of Libanus.
33. Chief of the Tabernacle.
34. Prince of the Tabernacle.
35. Prince of Mercy.
36. Knight of the Brazen Serpent.
37. Commander of the Temple.
38. Knight of the Sun.
39. Knight of the Holy Ghost.(*)
40. 41. 42. Prince of the Royal Secret, Prince of Masons.
43. Sovereign Grand Inspectors General.(†)

Besides those degrees, which are in regular succession, most of the Inspectors are in possession of a number of detached degrees, given in different parts of the world, and which they generally communicate, free of expense, to those brethren, who are high enough to understand them. Such as Select Masons of 27, and the Royal Arch, as given under the Constitution of Dublin. Six degrees of Maconnerie d'Adoption, Compagnon Ecossais; le Maître Ecossais, et le Grand Maître Ecossais, &c. &c. making, in the aggregate, 53 degrees.

(*) His Royal Highness Prince Edward, Duke of Kent, &c. is at present the presiding officer of the degree of K—H. in England.

(†) The 1st, 2d and 3d degrees are given in the Symbolic Lodge. From the 14th to the 24th inclusive, in the Sublime Grand Lodge, and the officers of both, are elected annually. The 25th and 26th are given by the Council of Princes of Jerusalem, the officers of which are also elected annually. From the 27th to the 43d inclusive, are given by the Inspectors, who are Sovereigns of Masonry. The Officers of the Supreme Council are appointed for life.

Figure 13. David Vinton's list of the Masonic degrees. —From *The Masonick Minstrel* (1816)

"Knights Kadosh." Vinton's list would be the first time that many Masons would encounter the Scottish Rite degrees, and his errors were perpetuated by the power of the printed word. The following year Samuel Cole reprinted Vinton's chart—including the "Knight of the Holy Ghost" blunder—in his own book, *The Freemasons' Library and General Ahiman Rezon* (1817), and the mistake would later be seized upon and exploited by anti-Masons.[56]

Revival in Albany

In the same year that John Mitchell died, Giles Fonda Yates, a gifted seventeen-year-old from Schenectady, New York, and member of Phi Beta Kappa, graduated from Union College with honors and the degree of Master of Arts.[57] He would become one of the most important Masons in the history of the Scottish Rite in the United States. Raised a Master Mason on October 27, 1820, he soon made an accidental discovery of the rituals and documents of Albany's Ineffable Lodge of Perfection. Yates reflected on these events in 1851:

> I turned my attention to the history of the Sublime degrees very soon after my initiation as a Mason. My intercourse, in 1822, with several old Masons in the city of Albany, led to the discovery that an Ineffable Lodge of Perfection had been established in that ancient city on the 20th December 1767. I also discovered, that not only the Ineffable, but the Superior degrees of our rite, had been conferred at the same time on a chosen few, by the founder of the Lodge, Henry A. Francken, one of the Deputies of Stephen Morin of illustrious memory. It was not long, moreover, before I found the original warrant of this Lodge, its book of Minutes, the Patents of Ill. Bros. Samuel Stringer, M.D., Jeremiah Van Rensselaer, and Peter W. Yates, Esquires, Deputy Inspectors General under the old system; also the Regulations and Constitutions of the nine Commissioners, &c., 1762—and other documents that had been left by Bro. Francken with the Albany brethren—when he founded their Lodge. With the concurrence of the surviving members of said Lodge in Albany, Dr. Jonathan Eights, and the Hon. and R. W. Stephen Van Rensselaer, P.G.M., of the Grand Lodge of New

56. Samuel Cole, P.M., *The Freemasons' Library and General Ahiman Rezon; Containing A Delineation of the True Principles of Freemasonry, Speculative and Operative, Religious and Moral. Compiled from the Writings of the Most Approved Authors, With notes and occasional remarks* (Baltimore: Printed and Published by Benjamin Edes, 1817), 316. See also *House No. 73 Report by a joint Committee of the Legislature of Massachusetts, on Freemasonry* (March 1834), 13, which stated that the letters "were supposed to stand for King of Heaven, or Knight of the Holy Ghost."

57. *The First Semi-centennial Anniversary of Union College. Celebrated July 22, 1845* (Albany: W. C. Little & Co.; Schenectady: I. Riggs, 1845), 78; *Centennial Catalog: New York Alpha of the Phi Beta Kappa, Union College* (Schenectady, 1922), 15.

> York, I aided in effecting its revival. The necessary proceedings were thereupon instituted to place the same under the superintendence of a Grand Council of Princes of Jerusalem, as required by the old Constitutions; and such Grand Council was subsequently opened in due form in said city.[58]

This reminiscence, made some thirty years after the event, is slightly off by a couple of years. Yates's discovery was actually made near the time of his raising in 1820. The twenty-one year old Yates displayed remarkable enthusiasm. Before the end of the year he had revived the Francken's "Ineffable" and moved it to Schenectady. He likely first called it "Tito Lodge of Perfection,"[59] which became "Delta Lodge of Perfection" after 1822; he also organized a Grand Council of Princes of Jerusalem. According to the records of the Supreme Council, 33°, Northern Masonic Jurisdiction:

> In the fall of 5820, with the concurrence of its surviving members, the forementioned [Ineffable] Lodge of Perfection was re-established under the appellation of a "Delta Lodge of Perfection," and placed under the jurisdiction of a Grand Council of Princes of Jerusalem, which had been opened previously in the City of Schenectady, by authority emanating from Ill.·. Bros.·. [SAMUEL] STRINGER and [PETER W.] YATES, above named.[60]

There are two gross errors in this statement. The first is that Dr. Samuel Stringer died in 1817,[61] three years before Yates discovered Francken's documents, which occasioned the revival. The second is that Giles F. Yates asserted that the Grand Council of Princes of Jerusalem was organized under the authority of Peter W. Yates, who "had authority from Br. Francken to establish

58. "Address of Ill. Br. Giles F. Yates, before the Sup. Council 33d, at Boston, Sept. 5, 1851," in Charles W. Moore, ed., *The Freemasons' Monthly Magazine* vol. 11 (Boston, January 1, 1852) No. 3, 83–84. See also *Proceedings of the Supreme Council of Sov.·. Gr.·. Inspectors General 33°, for the Northern Masonic Jurisdiction of the United States. Gourgas Body, 1813–1852. Raymond Body, 1851–1860. Van Rensselaer Body, 1860–1862* (Portland, [Maine]: Stephen Berry, Printer, 1876), 234–35.

59. In 1822 Yates wrote, "I am not certified that the ineffable degrees are conferred 'in forma' by any other masonic body in the United States, than by the sublime grand lodges in Charleston, South Carolina, in the city of New York, in Newport, Rhode-Island, and by 'Tito Lodge of Perfection,' in the city of Schenectady, New York." —Giles F. Yates, "Sublime Masonry," in Luther Pratt, ed., *The American Masonic Register, and Ladies' and Gentleman's Magazine* vol. 2 (New York: Benedict Bolmore, November, 1822) No. 3, 87.

60. *Proceedings of the Supreme Council of Sov.·. Gr.·. Inspectors General 33°, for the Northern Masonic Jurisdiction of the United States. Gourgas Body, 1813–1852. Raymond Body, 1851–1860. Van Rensselaer Body, 1860–1862* (Portland, [Maine]: Stephen Berry, Printer, 1876), 45.

61. Joel Munsell, *The Annals of Albany* (Albany: J. Munsell, 1855), vol. 6, 124.

Lodges, Councils, &c. of all Degrees." To the contrary, the minutes of Francken's Ineffable Lodge of Perfection reveal that Peter W. Yates did not possess that authority; he had only received the Thirteenth Degree at the time the Ineffable had ceased to function in 1774.[62] Even though Giles F. Yates was a practicing lawyer, and *Surrogate* of Schenectady County, his legal training yielded to Masonic zeal as he admitted to Gourgas, "When we established ourselves in 1820 prudence did suggest the idea we might not be acting right...."[63] At this early period, with the Ineffable and Sublime degrees little-known and its laws less understood, Giles F. Yates's irregular initiation into the higher degrees, and the unlawful creation of a Grand Council of Princes of Jerusalem would not be insurmountable issues. Ultimately, his enthusiasm and activity in the Scottish Rite would help save the Supreme Council, 33° for the Northern District of the United States.

The Charleston Association

Readers unfamiliar with the fascinating story of the Charleston Association are encouraged to review Ill. Alain Bernheim's article in *Heredom* 20 (2012), as I will only outline enough of the events to provide context to the ensuing history.[64] The Charleston Association was a group of enthusiastic Masons who, although not "Sublime Masons," acquired copies of the rituals for study. When they learned about the Cerneau Grand Consistory in Charleston, they petitioned for membership, but were denied. After this, they discovered the Supreme Council at Charleston, were initiated, and received a charter. The following abbreviated account demonstrates that their admission ultimately led to the success of the "Mother Supreme Council."

The birth of the Charleston Association began with the death of John Mitchell. The Grand Commander's passing resulted in hardships for Supreme

62. "The Original Minutes of Ineffable and Sublime Grand Lodge of Perfection of Albany, NY, from 1767 to 1774," in *1906 Proceedings of the Thirty-seventh Council of Deliberation for the Bodies of the State of Ancient Accepted Scottish Rite Northern Masonic Jurisdiction, U.S.A., of the State of New York* (Printed by Order of the Council, 1906), supplement, 130.

63. *Giles F. Yates, Schenectady, April 17, 1828, to J. J. J. Gourgas, New York.* Copy in the Archives of the Supreme Council, 33°, SJ., Washington, DC.

64. See also Joseph M'Cosh, *Documents upon Sublime Freemasonry in the United States of America. Being a Collection of all the Official Documents Which Have Appeared on Both Sides of the Question. With Notes, and an Appendix.* (Charleston: [Sebring,] 1823).

Council at Charleston. Not only had they lost their first leader but, as Albert G. Mackey informs us in his *History of Freemasonry in South Carolina*, Mitchell's death placed a financial burden on his widow, resulting in the sale of her late husband's Masonic papers.[65] Years later, on the twenty-fifth anniversary of the creation of the Supreme Council at Charleston, Moses Holbrook recounted this incident, and others, in a "Private & Confidential" letter. He noted that although he was able to secure Col. Mitchell's rituals, the Supreme Council at Charleston unfortunately lost correspondence, minute books, charters, seals, and other items, some of which were apparently acquired by the Cerneau Grand Consistory in Charleston:

> The day after Col Mitchell died—Mr J. W. Bacot sent a servant for all his Masonic papers—he being grand Mas<ter> at the time <of the Gr. Lodge of the state> she imprudently gave them, she says, two large trunks full <of papers>—Peter Javain says [...] it was only one big trunk full and a <big> basket full of papers—it was the vast correspondence formerly carried on by this Supreme Council—the minutes and the charters of different sublime bodies—hence came the bulk of the papers—with regard to the "*Auction*" the secretary of the 14th or 16th degree died, and his things were sold, for rent due—among them a few things were seen belonging to the Sublime Lodge—his wife's father Col. Rouse brought them in—Col. R. is not a Mason—but he kept them safely until the great fire 1818 when his house <being in imminent danger> was stripped of all moveables—but eventually saved—Col. R. has never seen any of these things since—<I believe> They however soon adorned P. Javains Sublime Lodge room—I have by accident seen some pieces of furniture that answers the description of some of the older members—I know of no other *auction* where any things were ever sold that belonged to the sublime body—Of the seals—a Merchant named Porter was the keeper—he died and his partner named Cassin administered upon his effects <& estate> and soon after died when Conly Cassin the other Cassins nephew administered upon his estate Conly Cassin to obtain some Cash immediately gave the set of silver seals which had come into his hands in the <manner> above mentioned, as a collateral pledge for the sixty or seventy Dollars which he borrowed of Thos. W. Bacot—who continues to keep them to this day—The Supreme Council was not incorporated at that day and could not at that time come in for them—the body had a much better set of seals—but stealing or detaining a set of seals from a body can certainly never destroy the body—Brs Col Mitchell <De La Motta> abd S. Harby died about this time—Doctr Dalcho was up the Cape of Good Hope—Doct Auld on Edisto's Island about 70 miles from the city where he resides—so that you see that a concurrence

65. Albert G. Mackey, *The History of Freemasonry in South Carolina from its Origin in the Year 1736 to the Present Time* (Columbia, S.C.: Steam Power Press, 1861), 175–76.

> of circumstances allowed Cerneau to make headway at the time he did—They were not able to obtain a set of manuscripts—Those belonging to Doctr Dalcho, Doct Auld an to the body were in the hand of late brother De La Motta—They have since been sold to a Brother by Jacob de La Motta for a considerable some of money—so the body lost these—Co Mitchells came into my hands & <then> to Doct Aulds possession, and are now used by us.[66]

Dr. Holbrook shared Col. Mitchell's rituals with the members of a small group of Masons, to which he belonged, known as the "Charleston Association." The purpose of the group was to "read over" Mitchell's rituals in order to learn more about the Ineffable and Sublime degrees. Since Mitchell death the hostilities between the Charleston Supreme Council and the Cerneauists in New York had come to a standstill. Rev. Dalcho, who had served as Grand Chaplain of the Grand Lodge of South Carolina, had several close friends who were members of Cerneau's Grand Consistory in Charleston, including Thomas W. Bacot, who was Grand Master of the Grand Lodge of South Carolina. Dalcho had wearied of the conflict, and refused to assemble his own Supreme Council. As we saw, the Supreme Council, 33° for Northern District, was also dormant, having been put into a "profound sleep" since its birth, by J. J. J. Gourgas, because its members lacked "true Masonic zeal."

In August 1821 the Cerneau Grand Consistory learned about the Charleston Association, and sent representatives, including Past Grand Master Bacot, to meet with Holbrook and his friends. They were informed that their actions were illegal and un-Masonic, and were told to deliver up the rituals or suffer the consequences. Holbrook sought the help of Rev. Dalcho, whom he informed of the details, but Dalcho offered no assistance. To the contrary, Dalcho actually aided Bacot in creating a list of all members of the Association.

Upon deliberation, and having received no help from Dalcho, Holbrook and other Association members resolved to submit, and in September they created, signed, and sent a petition to the Cerneau Grand Consistory, asking to be admitted into their Order. In a lengthy and condescending response, the Cerneauists questioned their worthiness, stated that their request was too casual, and summarily denied their petition. Unable to obtain relief from the

66. *Moses Holbrook, Charleston, S.C., May 31, 1826, to J. J. J. Gourgas, New York, NY.* Copy in the Archives of the Supreme Council, 33°, SJ, Washington, DC.

Cerneau Consistory or Rev. Dalcho, Holbrook and company investigated further. They learned that Cerneau's group had previously been denounced by Mitchell, Dalcho, and others of the Supreme Council at Charleston, and they hastened to make contact with and petition other members of Dalcho's Supreme Council for relief.

The two sides turned this private Masonic matter into a public one, publishing derogatory remarks about each other in the local newspapers. With additional information against Cerneau and his group, Association member Joseph M'Cosh published *Documents upon Sublime Freemasonry* in 1823, which did everything except foster the spirit of Masonic brotherhood. It is a fascinating document to read, but it is also strong proof that an angry man should not put a pen to paper.

On February 9, 1822, Dr. Isaac Auld, Lieutenant Grand Commander of the Supreme Council, with fellow Supreme Council member Dr. James Moultrie and others, called upon Rev. Dalcho and again asked him to assemble the Supreme Council. When he refused, the Supreme Council opened without him and transacted business. At that time Dr. Auld became "Acting Grand Commander in the United States of America." Assisted by James Moultrie, "Acting Lieut. Grand Commander in the United States of America," and Moses C. Levy, "Treasurer general of the Holy Empire in the United States of America," they created, congregated, and established a Chapter of Sovereign Princes of Rose Croix and a Grand Council of Princes of Jerusalem in the city, and granted a Charter to the Chapter and Council to make and perfect Masons in the Sublime Degrees, up to the 18th Degree agreeably to the Constitutions. Holbrook, and his associates received their degrees therein and became Scottish Rite Masons.

It is interesting that Dr. Auld called himself "Acting Grand Commander *in the United States of America*" (emphasis added), which jurisdictional claim was also reflected in the title held by Col. Mitchell. Could this imply that Dr. Auld and his Supreme Council were aware that the Gourgas had placed the Northern District into a "profound sleep" and that they then saw themselves as the only active legitimate body?

Although he was unwilling to help his own Supreme Council, Frederick Dalcho made an unusual offer to Peter Javain, who was representative of the Cerneau Grand Consistory for the State of South Carolina. Dalcho asked if a line of demarcation might be established, dividing the United States into two divisions: that south of Washington, DC, Dalcho asked to be placed under his own jurisdiction, while the north would be ceded to the Cerneauists. The latter, likely aware that they now had the only active high degrees in the northern part of the United States, ignored Dalcho's request. In spite of this, Dr. Dalcho continued to have friendly contacts within Cerneauism. In March 1822 Javain informed Dalcho that Dr. Auld had transacted business within the Supreme Council (issuing the aforementioned charter), and he asked Dalcho if had given him permission to do so. Dalcho's response, which is recorded in the minutes of the Cerneau Grand Consistory, reveals that he was unaware of this and that he still considered himself Grand Commander.

Charleston April 1st 1822

Most Ills Brother

In reply to your letter of the 29th ulto I have to observe that, until you informed me of the Circumstance, I was ignorant that any publication, with my name, have been made by any persons Connected with masonry, & it, unquestionably, does not meet with my approbation.

My answer to your other interrogatory will I trust be equally satisfactory. Dr Auld has no authority from me to perform any masonic acts, the power with which I am invested by the Constitution of the 33d Degree, I have not transferred to any person under the Canopy of Heaven.

I am my Dear & Ills Brother and friend
Fredk Dalcho
K.H. P.R.S. Sovn Gd Inspr Genl of the 33d and Gd∴ Commr
To the Ills Brother P. Javain Gd Inspr &c[67]

Contrary to the view expressed here by Rev. Dalcho, the *Constitutions of 1786* did not empower him to retain his office. Rather, Articles 12 and 17 bestowed the "sovereign Masonic power" to the Supreme Council which, with a "majority of their votes" granted "legality to their proceedings." No record exists to show when and how Dalcho learned of his removal from office, but he would have been aware by December 1823, when he was listed as "Past Grand Commander" at the legal incorporation of the Supreme Council at Charleston.[68] Whatever

67. Unpublished minutes of the *Most Potent Grand Consistory of the United States if America for the State of South Carolina*, April 26, 1822, folio 69 verso. Archives of the Supreme Council, 33°, SJ., Washington, DC.

68. *Acts and Joint Resolutions of the General Assembly of the State of South Carolina* (Columbia: J. M. Faust, 1824), 73–74.

Figure 15. Charter of the Charleston Council of Princes of Jerusalem, established February 9, 1822, by Isaac Auld, *Acting Grand Commander.* —*Archives of the Supreme Council, 33°, SJ.*

the case, Dalcho eventually accepted his position as Past Grand Commander and, from about this time forward, he signed charters and patents alongside Dr. Holbrook and the other members of the Supreme Council.

In the Spring of 1822 the eager new members of the high degrees at Charleston sent the following communication[69] to the Supreme Council for the Northern District, in an effort to establish contact. Among other things, it explained that during the War of 1812 the high degrees suffered, and although the Supreme Council survived it also recounted how Dr. Dalcho had been influenced by the Cerneauists.

> *To our thrice Illustrious Brother Daniel D Tompkins R. ✠ – K.H. – P.R.S. Sovereign Grand Inspector General of the 33^{d} Degree, and Grand Commander for the Northern District of the United States of America.*
>
> *Health Stability and Power*
>
> *Illustrious Brother*
>
> *Owing to the late war in which our Country was engaged, and the death of' a Great many of its members, the Grand Council of Princes of Jerusalem and the grand lodge of Perfection for this State ceased to exist. The Grand Council of the 33^{d} degree continued to flourish untill the Death of our late illustrious Brother Colonel Mitchell who was known to you as Grand Commander. At his death Doctor Frederick Dalcho became G^{d} Com^{r}, but he, being influenced by certain members of an illegal body established here by Joseph Cerneau, and De Witt Clinton refused to call his Council together, altho' there were never less than 3 Grand inspectors of said council in this city at any one time. On the 9th day of February last our illustrious Brethren Doctors Isaac Auld & Ja^{s} Moultrie R. ✠, K–H – P.R.S and Sovereign G^{d} Inspectors of the 33^{d} both officers in said Council called on the said Fred^{k} Dalcho and requested him to open the Grand Council of So. G^{d} In. Genl of the 33^{d} degree which he refused to do, on which the aforesaid Brothers congregated and established a Chapter of So. Princes of R: ✠ and a G^{d} Council of Princes of Jerusalem in this city, & gave a Charter to said chapter and council to Make and perfect masons in the Sublime Degrees to the 18th Degree agreeably to the Constitutions. The Grand consistory of So. Ps: Rl. S^{t} and Grand Council of So. G^{d} Ir of the 33^{d} Degree will be opened in this City in the month of May by our Illustrious Brother Isaac Auld acting G^{d} Commander, he at present being absent from the City.*
>
> *We are in a prosperous way, and no doubt, with your assistance and that of your grand council, we shall be able to destroy in this section of the country the influence of Mr Cerneau and his adherents, we have already put a stop to any more of the*

69. Moses Holbrook, et al. Charleston, South Carolina to "His Excellency Daniel D. Tompkins. Vice President of the United States, New York." Although undated, Gourgas wrote "Spring of 1822" on the letter. Copy in the Archives of the Supreme Council, 33°, SJ, Washington, DC.

fraternity being taken in and duped by these impostors, and have been very active in exposing their illegality and also published the documents issued in 1814 by our late illustrious Brother Dela Motta, one of which will be handed you by his son, who we understand is one of your Council. We solicit your fostering care, and trust you will ever be ready to Protect and encourage the honorable proceedings of those whose wish is to add dignity to our Sublime Institution. As we have been regularly established, and charter'd, we hope a communication will take place between the two councils, and your attention to this will be gratefully acknowledged, to which we look with patience.

Illustrious Brother, we salute you by the Sacred Numbers.

James W Rouse
Moses Holbrook
Committee of Correspondence

The following is a list of officers and members of the Grand Lodge of Perfection:

Sublime G^{d} Mr Moses Holbrook, M.D.
D^{y} S G^{d} M H. G. Street, Merchant.
SSGW James W. Rouse Dep^{y} Comp^{t} General State S. C^{a}
JGW Robert Carr MD
GC & K of the S. E. Gates Teacher of Classics
GM of C A McDonald Merchant
G Sy Jas M'Cosh Merchant
G Tr N Bachelder D^{o}
C.G. James Little Millwright
G Tyler Wm Dyer Late of the Army

Members

M. McKenzie — Fr^{s} Rolando — Wm Wright — John La Roach — E^{d} Sebring — Jno C. Duke — Ja^{s} May — Jno Dawson — S M Hart — Jno Roche — Henry Cohun — Jas Moon —

There is no evidence that the Supreme Council for the Northern District responded to this letter. A couple of months later Dr. Holbrook made another attempt to contact them. In a letter written in July 1822 he explained to Gourgas that his letters to the Northern District "have received no answer yet."[70] This letter was also ignored.

THE SUPREME COUNCIL, 43°

When we consider the confrontations, interruptions, and sundry tribulations of the Supreme Council at Charleston we may understand a bold endeavor

70. Moses Holbrook, Charleston, South Carolina, July 15, 1822, to J. J. J. Gourgas, New York, *New York.* Copy in the Archives of the Supreme Council, 33°, SJ, Washington DC.

they made to expand their grasp over American Freemasonry. Unfortunately, without surviving records, we only have circumstantial evidence to suggest why and when these things occurred. And, although no minute books are known to survive which explain how this happened, we have other witnesses. The surviving records of the Cerneau bodies reveal that the Supreme Council at Charleston had reasons to be concerned. The Cerneauists were not only active in the Scottish Rite, but they were also aggressively claiming other Masonic authority and territory. With the Supreme Council for the Northern District in a "profound sleep," there was nothing to stop the Cerneau Masons from expanding, and they quickly helped organize the grand bodies of what would become the York Rite.

The Supreme Council at Charleston would not sit idly by and watch more of American Masonry slide away into Cerneauism. Aware that Cerneau Masons conferred the degrees of knighthood, the Charleston "Sovereigns in Masonry" also decided to confer other degrees. Perhaps inspired by David Vinton's list of forty-three Masonic degrees they too would seek to expand their domain over American Freemasonry. No records survive to give us details, but Moses Holbrook's attitude and opinions to the notion survive in correspondence written soon thereafter. The idea to expand the domain of the Supreme Council likely occurred around 1822. Perhaps the first hint appears in a manuscript book of sundry rituals transcribed by Moses Holbrook, intermittently from 1817–29. The collection includes a copy of the ritual of Order of the High Priesthood, an honor conferred upon the presiding officer of Royal Arch Chapters. The ritual, which is dated 1822, includes an interlineation which obligated the recipient to observe the bylaws of the Royal Arch Chapter and those of the Supreme Council, 33°:

> ... I will stand to and abide by all the laws, rules & Regulations and Decrees of the <Sup Coun of SGIG of 33d degree> Presiding body under which, this chapter is holden. – And that I will faithfully endeavor to observe all the Bye Laws of this Chapter <and of the Sup Council of 33 or Grand Chapter under it> and to see them carefully enforced.[71]

71. "Order of the High Priesthood. (As contained in the Archives of the Supreme Council of Sov. Gr. Insp. General of the 33d Degree in Charleston – S. Ca. 1822 – M. Holbrook – Copyist – Partly received from Dr. J. M. Wilson – 1818," in untitled manuscript ritual book of Moses Holbrook, 76. Archives of the Supreme Council, 33°, SJ, Washington, DC.

Logically, the Supreme Council would have no cause to confer the Order of the High Priesthood unless they were also conferring the Royal Arch Degree. Although this suggested to me that something was happening, all doubt was removed by my discovery of a ritual of the "43^d Degree called Sovereign Grand Inspectors General, or Supreme Council of the Forty Third Degree." This seventy-five page ritual, which is entirely in the handwriting of Moses Holbrook, is a revision of the Dalcho manuscript of the Thirty-third Degree. In every instance where Dalcho's ritual reads "33" and "thirty-three" Holbrook has replaced it with "43" and "forty-three."

Although this ritual was known to Albert Pike, he incorrectly attributed it to Horatio G. Street, a member of the "Charleston Association," who joined the Supreme Council with Holbrook on November 15, 1822. Not only did Pike fail to recognize Holbrook's handwriting, but he also avoided any reference to the Forty-third Degree and described it as "... a manuscript book remaining in the Archives of the Supreme Council at Charleston, made in 1822, in the handwriting of Horatio G. Street, containing the ritual and Ordinances of the 33d Degree, the French *Grand Constitutions of 1786,* and the Constitutions or Regulations of 1762."[72] In truth, Pike knew it was a ritual of the Forty-third Degree, and he considered it important enough to transcribe a copy of it for himself.

In addition to the ritual, Holbrook's manuscript includes the following list of the living members of the Supreme Council.

List of Supreme Council

Gr. Comm Fr. Dalcho	*initiated*	*25*	*May*	*1801*
Lt. Gr. Comm Is. Auld, M.D.		*10th*	*Jan*	*1802*
Secy G. H.E. Jas. Moultrie, M.D.		*Aug*	*3*	*1802*
Treas. G. H.E Moses C. Levy		*May*	*9*	*"*
Moses Holbrook MD		*Nov*	*15*	*1822*
Hor. Gates Street		*"*	*"*	*"*
Alex. McDonald		*Nov*	*"*	*"*
Jos M'Cosh		*"*	*"*	*"*

72. [Albert Pike,] *Official Bulletin of the Supreme Council of The 33d Degree for the Southern Jurisdiction of the United States* (Gr.·. Or.·. of Charleston, 1885), vol. 7, 313.

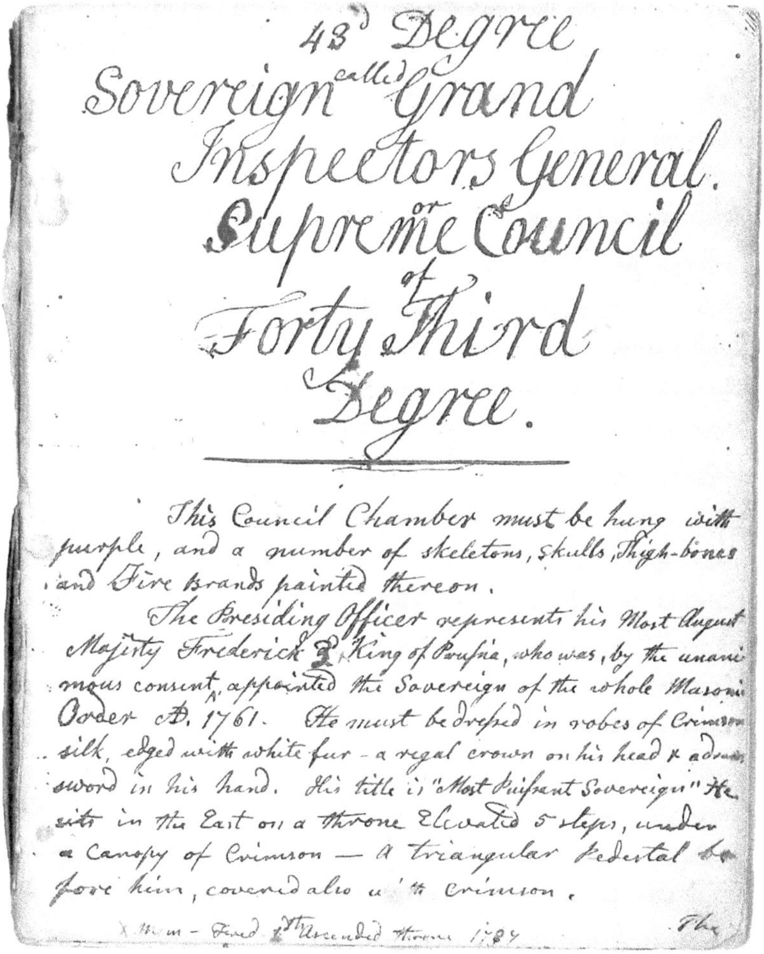
43d Degree
Sovereign called Grand
Inspectors General.
or Supreme Council
of
Forty Third
Degree.

This Council Chamber must be hung with purple, and a number of skeletons, skulls, Thigh-bones and Fire Brands painted thereon.

The Presiding Officer represents his Most August Majesty Frederick 2d King of Prussia, who was, by the unanimous consent, appointed the Sovereign of the whole Masonic Order AD. 1761. He must be dressed in robes of Crimson silk, edged with white fur - a regal crown on his head & a drawn sword in his hand. His title is "Most Puissant Sovereign" He sits in the East on a throne Elevated 5 steps, under a Canopy of Crimson — A triangular Pedestal before him, covered also with crimson.

The

Figure 16. First page of Moses Holbrook's ritual of the "43d Degree" (ca. 1822–25). —*Archives of the Supreme Council, 33°, SJ.*

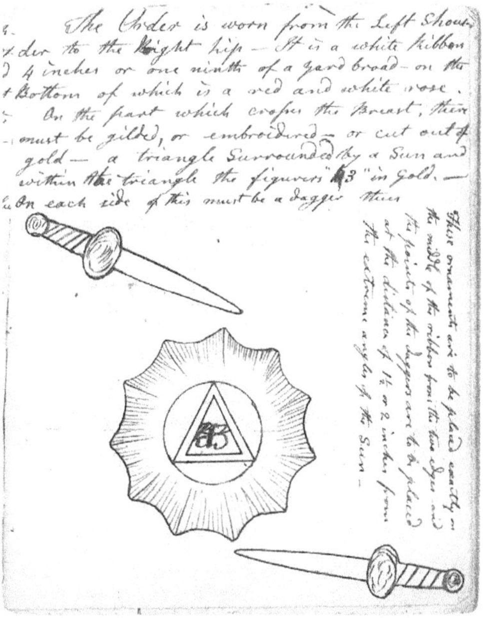

Figure 17. *Left:* A page from Moses Holbrook's "43ᵈ Degree" manuscript which describes and depicts the "order" (sash) of the degree. Copying the text directly from Dalcho's 33d ritual, Holbrook occasionally wrote "33," which he corrected to "43."

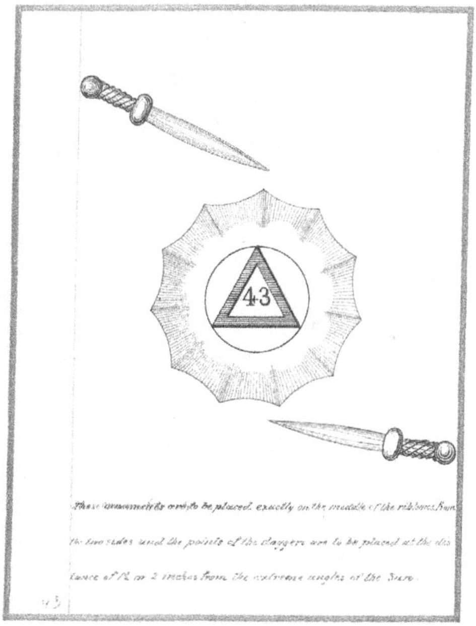

Figure 18. *Right:* The complimentary page in Albert Pike's copy of Holbrook's manuscript. —*Archives of the Supreme Council, 33°, SJ.*

John Barker – agent for Cou.	*May*	*13*	*1823*
~~*Jacob De L. Motta from N.Y. S. Council*~~	~~"~~	~~"~~	~~"~~
Joseph Eveleth	*March*	*30*	*1825*
John Roche	"	"	"
Giles F. Yates	*Oct*	—	*1825*
C. C. Sebring	*Oct*	*28*	*1826*

Also of interest is a list (dated November 16, 1822) at the back of the manuscript, which shows the costs of the regalia for the degree. It included a jewel, saber, rings for the 24° and 43°, and other items. If that is the date on which the Supreme Council, 33° was reorganized into the Supreme Council, 43°, it means that this occurred the day after Moses Holbrook, Horatio G. Street, Alexander McDonald, and Joseph M'Cosh were admitted members of the Supreme Council at Charleston, and exactly one week after Frederick Dalcho was removed from office. It also means that the innovation was approved or conceived by Isaac Auld, who was Grand Commander from 1822–26, although I suspect that he was influenced by Moses Holbrook, and possibly his fellow former members of the Charleston Association.

Even if Holbrook's ritual of the Supreme Council, 43°, was written in 1822, they likely had not yet begun to function as such. This would explain why, at their lawful incorporation in 1823, the Supreme Council at Charleston registered under their traditional title and only claimed thirty-three degrees:

> Dec. 1823.} Inspectors General of the thirty-third Degree incorporated.
>
> Sec. 33. *And be it further enacted by the authority aforementioned,* That Isaac Auld, M.D. as Grand Commander; the Reverend Frederick Dalcho, M.D., as Past Grand Commander; James Moultrie, M. D. as Secretary General, and Acting Lieutenant Commander; Moses C. Levy, Esquire, as Treasurer General; Moses Holbrook, M.D. Horatio Street, Alexander McDonald and Joseph M'Cosh, Esquires, with their associates and successors, be, and they are hereby incorporated, and declared a body politic and corporate, in deed and in law, by the name and style of Inspectors General of the thirty-third Degree: And the said Inspectors General of the thirty-third Degree, shall have power to regulate all orders and degrees of Masonry, from the sixteenth to the said thirty-third degree, according to the constitutions of said several degrees; and the said corporation, by its name and style as or said, shall have a common seal, with power to

> alter the same, and to make all necessary by-laws for their better government; and the said corporation shall have power to purchase lands or personal estate, and to accept any devise, bequest or donation: *Provided* the same shall not exceed the sum of ten thousand dollars: *And provided also,* that nothing herein contained shall be construed to interfere with any powers, rights or privileges heretofore granted to the "Most Worshipful Grand Lodge in this State," or any other Grand Lodge of Masons heretofore incorporated.[73]

Further evidence shows that throughout the following year they still functioned as before. The patents of Jeremy Cross (June 24, 1824), and Lucius Levy Solomon (November 16, 1824), were issued under the authority of the "Supreme Council of the Thirty-third Degree."[74] Thus, other than having the date 1822 written in Holbrook's ritual, we have no other evidence that the Supreme Council, 43°, was active as such as late as November 1824.

The first piece of evidence which suggests a date for its activity appears in a manuscript book of ten of the degrees, transcribed by John Roche,[75] who was admitted to the Supreme Council at Charleston on March 30, 1825. Roche's manuscript rituals reveal that the degrees were renumbered by adding a value of ten to their common positions, just as they were in David Vinton's list.

The rituals in Roche's collection include material translated and extracted from the *Manual de la Mazoneria* (1822).[76] Interestingly, just the month before Roche was admitted to the Supreme Council, Holbrook alluded to this when he wrote to Giles F. Yates on February 7, 1825,[77] that he was "translating from

73. *Acts and Joint Resolutions of the General Assembly of the State of South Carolina* (Columbia: J. M. Faust, 1824), 73–74.

74. Copies in the Archives of the Supreme Council, 33°, SJ, Washington, DC.

75. In 1817 John Roche served as Master of Washington Lodge No. 7, in Charleston. *Proceedings of the Two Grand Lodges in South-Carolina, called the Grand Lodge of South-Carolina Ancient York Masons, and the Grand Lodge of South Carolina, and of the Masonic Bodies under their Respective Jurisdictions: for the Purpose of Uniting the Mystic Order into One Harmonious Body, under the Jurisdiction of the Grand Lodge of Ancient Free Masons of South Carolina, Completed in Charleston on the 26th December, A.L. 5817. Together with The Address of the M.W. Grand Master, and a Sermon, Preached in St. Michael's Church by the M.R. The Grand Chaplain* (Charleston: Printed by A. E. Miller, [1818]), 18.

76. *Manual de la Mazoneria o sea Retejador de los Ritos Escoses, Frances y de Adoption* (Cadiz, [Spain]: En la imprenta de Roquero, 1822). In Holbrook's January 8, 1827, to Gourgas he mentions the book by name, noting that it was "sent me from Cadiz in 1822."

77. Moses Holbrook, Charleston, South Carolina, February 7, 1825, to Giles F. Yates, Schenectady, New York. Copy in the Archives of the Supreme Council, 33°, SJ, Washington DC. The letter was also printed in the *Official Bulletin of the Supreme Council of the 33d Degree for the Southern Jurisdiction of the United States of America* vol. 9 (March, 1889), No. 1, 251–53.

DEGREES IN THE MANUSCRIPT RITUAL BOOK OF JOHN ROCHE

"Eighteenth Degree (or 28th) Knights of the Eagle or Sovereign Prince of Rose Croix de Heroden"

"Nineteenth Degree (or 29th) or Grand Pontiff Sublime Scot[c]h Masonry"

"Thirtieth Degree <or 20th> Venerable Grand Master of all Symbolic Lodges. Sovereign Princes of Freemasonry or Master 'Ad Vitam.' (for Life)"

"Thirty first Degree (or 21st) called Noachite or Prussian Knight or Patriarch Noachite. Seventh Grand of Freemasonry"

"Thirty second Degree (or 22nd) Knight of the Royal Axe or Prince of Libanus (Lebanon)"

"Thirty third Degree or 23rd or Chief of the Tabernacle"

"Thirty fourth Degree or 24th or Prince of the Tabernacle"

"Twenty fifth or Thirty fifth Degree or Knights of the Brazen Serpent"

"Twenty sixth or 36th Degree Called Prince of Mercy or Scotch Trinitarian"

"Twenty seventh or 37th Degree Called Grand Commander of the Temple at Jerusalem" the Spanish." Thus, the Supreme Council, 43°, may have been conceived in 1822, but came into being between November 1824 and March 1825.

In addition to renumbering the degrees and revising the titles, the contents of the rituals were also modified. For example, looking at the obligation of the Sovereign Prince of Rose Croix Degree, we find that the candidate pledged "And I do furthermore swear, promise & engage, on my sacred word of Honor, to observe & obey all decrees which may be transmitted to me by the Grand Inspectors General in Supreme Council of the 43rd Degree."

Holbrook's drastic revision of the Dalcho's Thirty-third Degree ritual also tells something about the Supreme Council's opinion of the *Grand Constitutions of 1786*. Holbrook's manuscript ritual of the Forty-third Degree also includes a copy of the *Grand Constitutions of 1786* or "Constitutions, Statutes, & Regulations," as they were then called. These were similarly amended to refer to the Forty-third Degree, which was said to have been created by Frederick II, King of Prussia. In other words, Holbrook viewed the "Frederick tradition" as Masonic mythology, rather than historical fact, which made it something that could be amended and revised as needed.

If the Supreme Council, 43°, met with any success as such it did not leave any evidence thereof. With the unfortunate loss of the records of the early Supreme Council at Charleston, I know of no correspondence or records which mention it by name. Although we have evidence in the rituals, I have not discovered any patents which refer to the Supreme Council, 43°, during this period. To the contrary, a patent issued on May 30, 1825, to Isaac T. Cushing, admitting him to the 32° Sublime Prince of the Royal Secret, was issued under authority of the Supreme Council, 33°, at Charleston.[78] It's possible, of course, that they simply did not update the patents. Although absence of evidence is not evidence of absence, I find it very peculiar that, apart from the rituals, there are no surviving documents.

A second set of rituals, also in the handwriting of John Roche, shows that the idea of a Supreme Council, 43°, was also abandoned in 1825. The Charleston rituals sent to Giles F. Yates later in that year referred simply to the Supreme Council, 33°. One degree, however, retained an unintentional artifact

78. Patent of Isaac T. Cushing, May 30, 1825. Archives of the Supreme Council, 33°, SJ, Washington, DC.

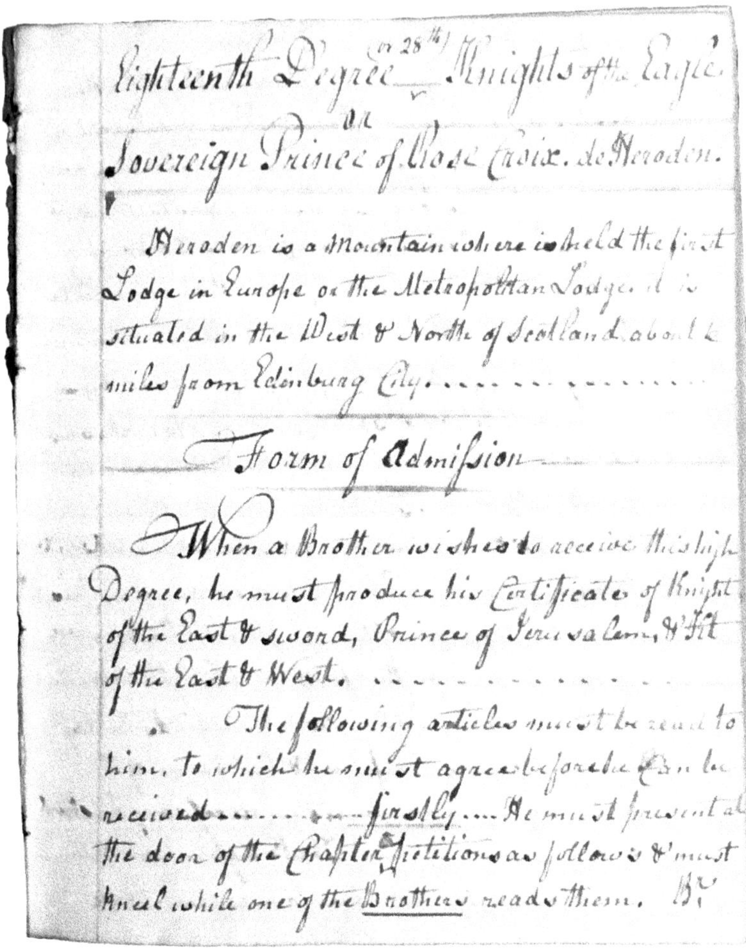
Eighteenth Degree (or 28th) Knights of the Eagle or
Sovereign Prince of Rose Croix de Heroden.

Heroden is a Mountain where is held the first Lodge in Europe or the Metropolitan Lodge. it is situated in the West & North of Scotland about [illegible] miles from Edinburg City. ....

Form of Admission

When a Brother wishes to receive this high Degree, he must produce his Certificate of Knight of the East & sword, Prince of Jerusalem, & Kt of the East & West. ....

The following articles must be read to him, to which he must agree before he can be received........ firstly.... He must present at the door of the Chapter Petitions as follows & must kneel while one of the Brothers reads them. Br.

Figure 19. Title page of the "Eighteenth Degree (or 28th) Knights of the Eagle or Sovereign Prince of Rose Croix de Heroden." From the manuscript ritual of John Roche (early 1825). —*Private collection.*

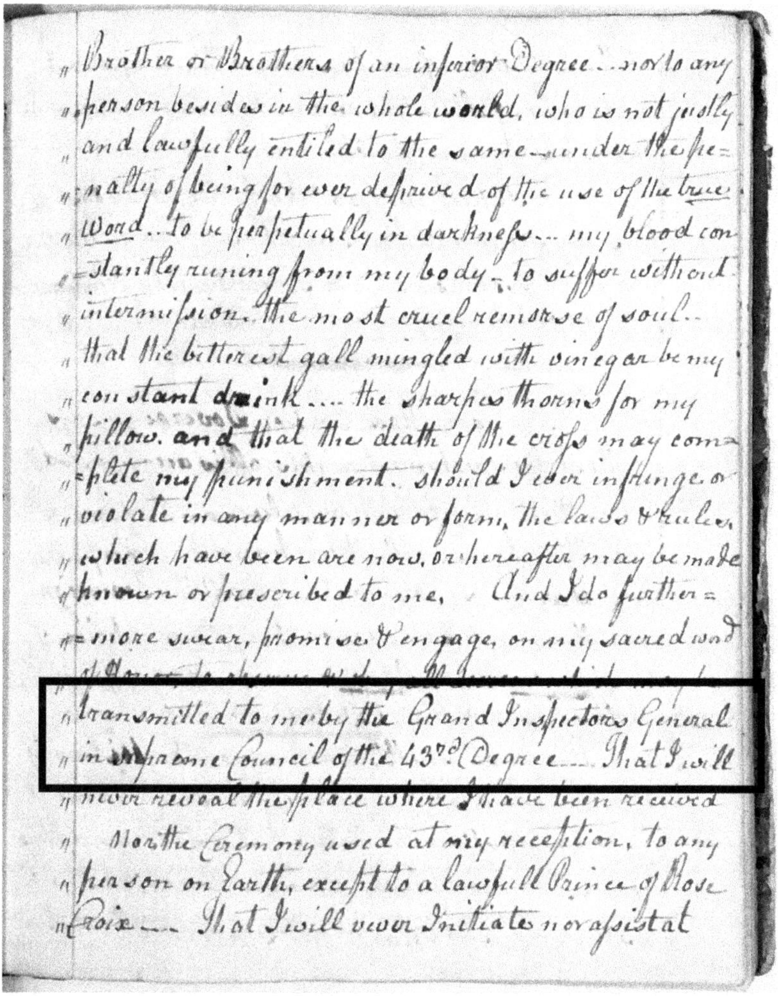

Figure 20. Excerpt from the obligation of the "Eighteenth Degree (or 28th) Knights of the Eagle or Sovereign Prince of Rose Croix de Heroden" which later refers to the Supreme Council of the 43rd Degree. From the manuscript ritual of John Roche (early 1825). —*Private collection.*

of this novel system, which escaped Charleston's notice. In the ritual of the 27°, Grand Commander of the Temple at Jerusalem (or "Sovereign Commander of the Temple at Jerusalem"[79]), appears a remark calling it the "37th Degree of Sublime Freemasonry." The note was so incidental that it escaped notice when the ritual was redacted to the earlier form. These latter rituals, which were loaned to Giles F. Yates in 1825, were later taken and copied without his authority by a former officer, and used in creating David Bernard's exposure *Light on Masonry* (1829), where the anomalous remark was reprinted.[80]

There were several reasons why the idea of the Supreme Council, 43°, could have proved impractical. Perhaps the greatest hurdle was the fact that by the 1820s there were several Supreme Councils in the world, all of which (excepting Cerneau's) traced their authority to Charleston, and with whom they were in fraternal recognition. How would this change affect their relationships? Would other Supreme Councils have also been obliged to add the additional degrees? Whatever the opinion of the Supreme Council at Charleston, it couldn't be denied that great strides were made by Cerneau Masons in organizing the Grand Chapters and Grand Encampments, which helped stabilize Masonic government.

THE SCOTTISH RITE IN NEW YORK

While the Supreme Council for the Northern District slept, Charleston found an ally in Giles F. Yates of Schenectady. As early as 1823, just three years after reviving Francken's Lodge of Perfection, he made substantial improvements

79. The aforementioned *Manual de la Mazoneria* (1822), which was used by Holbrook in his ritual revisions, calls it "Gran Comendador del templo, ó Soberano Comendador del templo de Jerusalem," 95.

80. David Bernard's *Light on Masonry* (Utica: William Williams, 1829) ran through five enlarged and improved editions in a single year. The complete fifth (largest) edition of Bernard's book is reprinted in facsimile, with much additional material, in Arturo de Hoyos, *Light on Masonry: The History and Rituals of America's Most Important Masonic Exposé* (Washington, DC: Scottish Rite Research Society, 2008). For the statement on the "thirty-seventh degree" see 258 [478].

Henry Dana Ward, "a renouncing and seceding Mason" also noted in his *Free Masonry: Its Pretensions Exposed in Faithful Extracts of Its Standard Authors ...* (New York, 1828), 393, "In 1801, the sovereign grand inspectors announced *thirty-three in direct ascent and twenty collateral degrees.* (See *Dalcho's Orations.*) In 1816, the number in direct ascent was increased to *forty-three.* (See *F.M.L.*)." Ward's remark did not actually refer to any Supreme Council, but to his misunderstanding of the chart reproduced in Cole's aforementioned *The Freemasons' Library and General Ahiman Rezon* (1817).

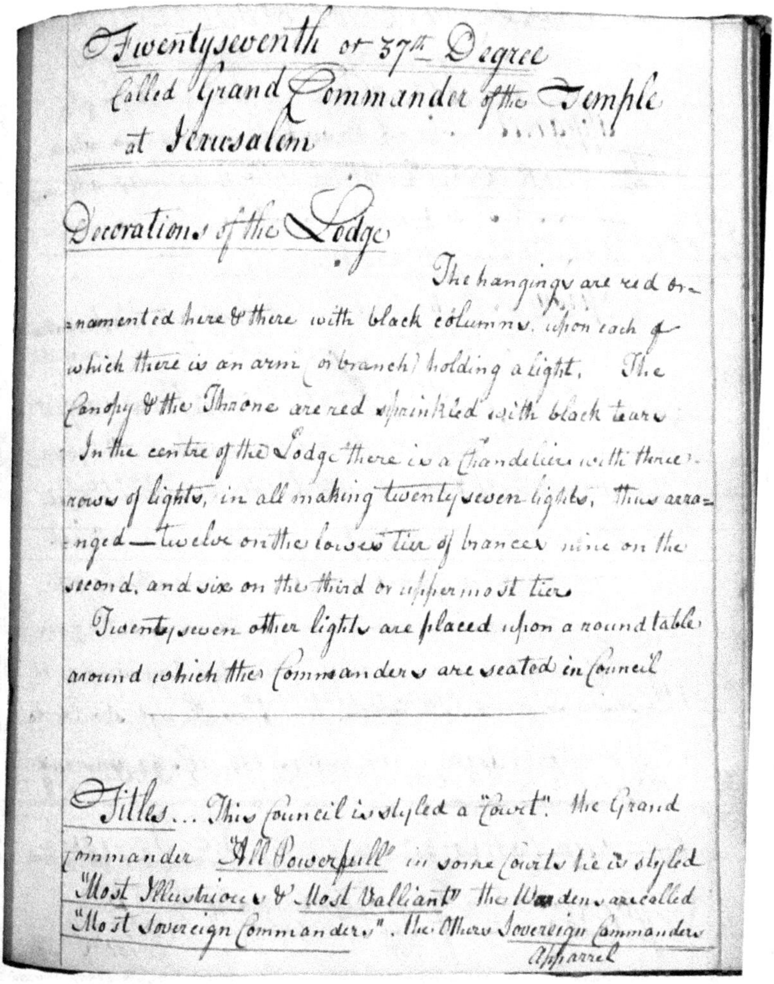

Twentyseventh or 37th Degree
Called Grand Commander of the Temple
at Jerusalem

Decorations of the Lodge

The hangings are red ornamented here & there with black columns, upon each of which there is an arm (or branch) holding a light. The Canopy & the Throne are red sprinkled with black tears

In the centre of the Lodge there is a Chandelier with three rows of lights, in all making twentyseven lights, thus arranged—twelve on the lower tier of branches nine on the second, and six on the third or uppermost tier

Twentyseven other lights are placed upon a round table around which the Commanders are seated in Council

Titles... This Council is styled a "Court". the Grand Commander "All Powerfull" in some Courts he is styled "Most Illustrious & Most Valliant" the Wardens are called "Most Sovereign Commanders". The Others Sovereign Commanders

Apparrel

Figure 22. Title page of the "Twenty seventh or 37th Degree Called Grand Commander of the Temple at Jerusalem" in this early 1825 manuscript ritual of John Roche. —*Private collection.*

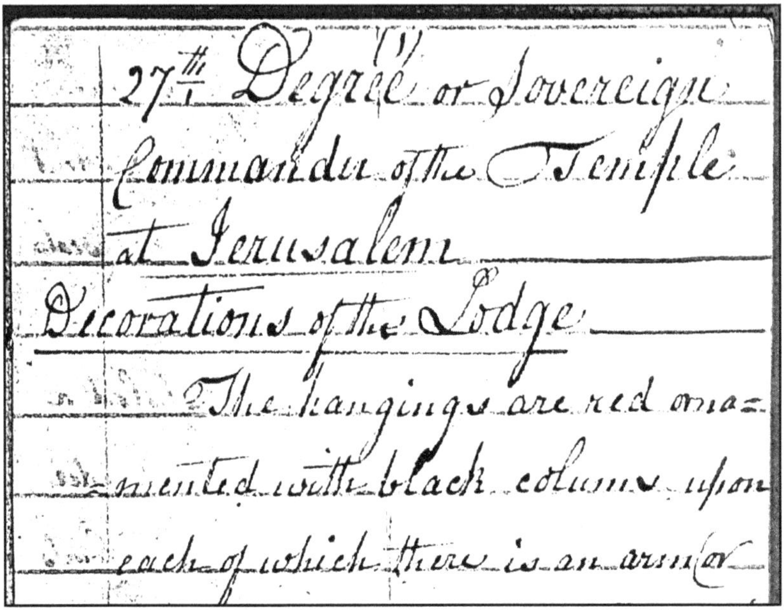

27th Degree (1) or Sovereign
Commander of the Temple
at Jerusalem

Decorations of the Lodge

The hangings are red orna=
mented with black columns upon
each of which there is an arm (or

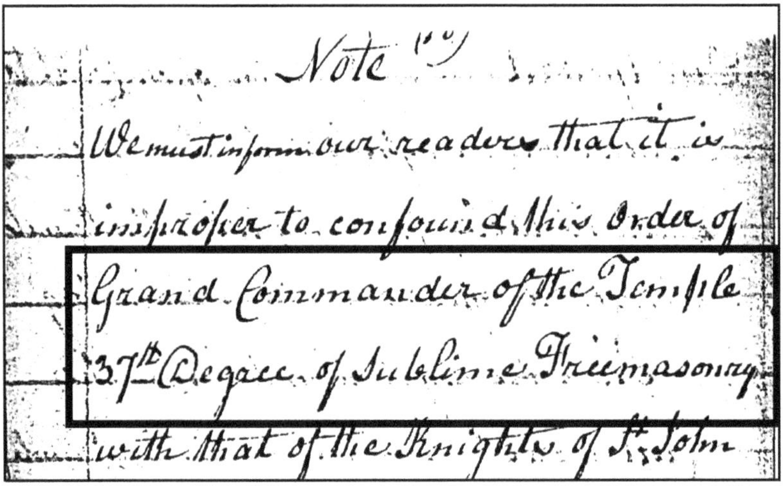

Note (10)

We must inform our readers that it is
improper to confound this Order of
Grand Commander of the Temple
37th Degree of Sublime Freemasonry
with that of the Knights of St. John

Figure 23. The title page of John Roche's 1825 manuscript shows the traditional title & number of this degree restored. However, near the end of the ritual remains an artifact calling it the "37th Degree of sublime Freemasonry." —Copy in the *Archives of the Supreme Council, 33°, SJ.*

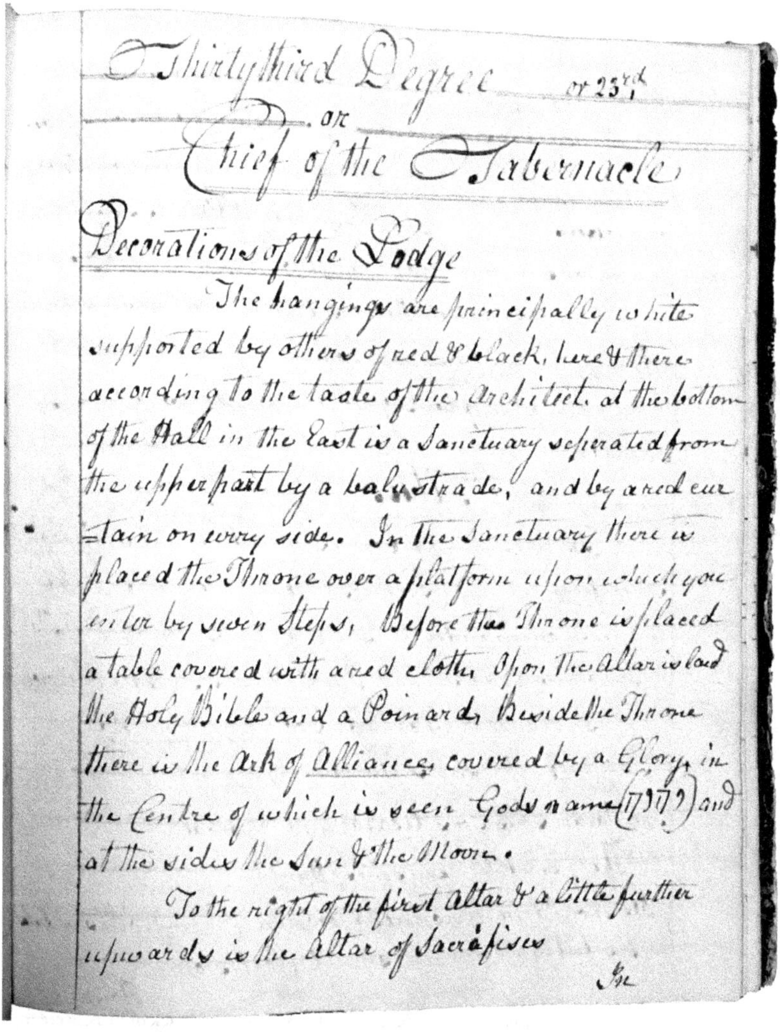

Thirtythird Degree or 23rd
or
Chief of the Tabernacle

Decorations of the Lodge

The hangings are principally white supported by others of red & black, here & there according to the taste of the Architect. at the bottom of the Hall in the East is a Sanctuary seperated from the upperpart by a balustrade, and by a red cur=tain on every side. In the Sanctuary there is placed the Throne over a platform upon which you enter by seven Steps, Before the Throne is placed a table covered with a red cloth, Upon the Altar is laid the Holy Bible and a Poinard, Beside the Throne there is the Ark of Alliance, covered by a Glory, in the Centre of which is seen Gods name (יהוה) and at the sides the Sun & the Moon.

To the right of the first Altar & a little further upwards is the Altar of Sacrafices

The

Figure 24 Title page of the "Thirtythird Degree, or 23rd, or Chief of the Tabernacle" in this early 1825 manuscript ritual of John Roche. —*Private collection.*

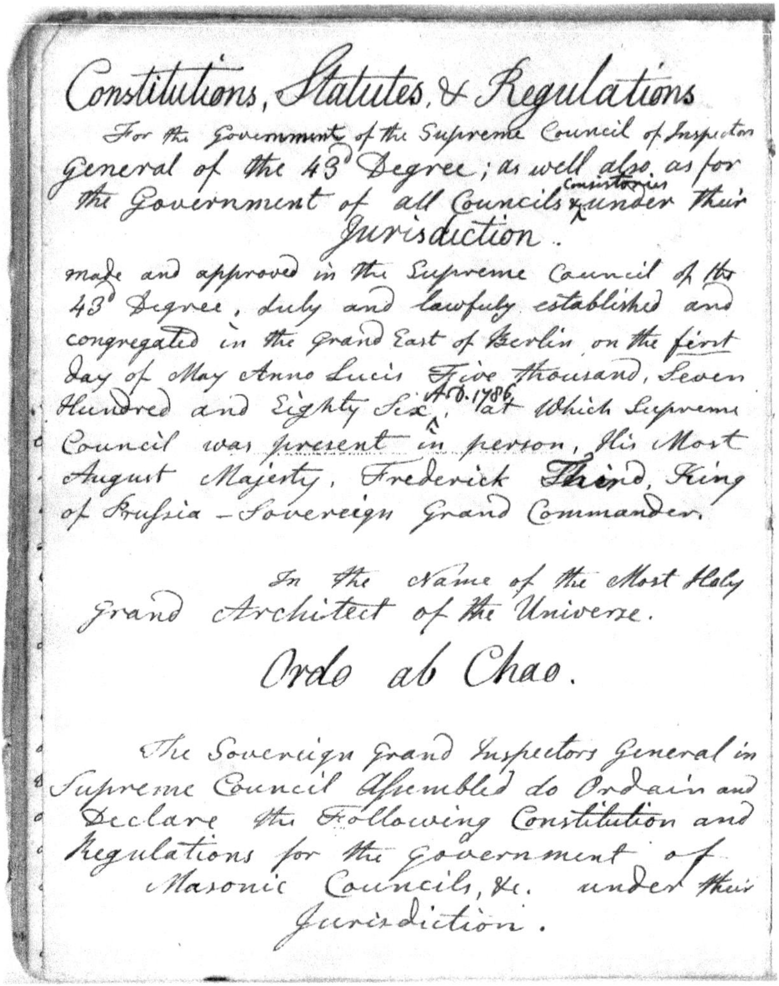

Constitutions, Statutes, & Regulations
For the Government of the Supreme Council of Inspectors
General of the 43^{d} Degree; as well also as for
the Government of all Councils & Consistories under their
Jurisdiction.
made and approved in the Supreme Council of the
43^{d} Degree, duly and lawfuly established and
congregated in the Grand East of Berlin on the first
day of May Anno Lucis Five thousand, Seven
Hundred and Eighty Six, A.D. 1786, at Which Supreme
Council was present in person, His Most
August Majesty, Frederick Third, King
of Prussia – Sovereign Grand Commander.

In the Name of the Most Holy
Grand Architect of the Universe.

Ordo ab Chao.

The Sovereign Grand Inspectors General in
Supreme Council Assembled do Ordain and
Declare the Following Constitution and
Regulations for the Government of
Masonic Councils, &c. under their
Jurisdiction.

Figure 25. The *Grand Constitutions of 1786* were modified to say that Frederick of Prussia created the "Supreme Council of Inspectors General of the 43^{d} Degree" and was present on the occasion. —*Archives of the Supreme Council, 33°, SJ.*

and revisions to the rituals of the Lodge of Perfection.[81] The following year he learned about the Supreme Council at Charleston, and contacted them. Moses Holbrook sent their agent John Barker to Yates to "heal" or "regularize" him, as he recalled a quarter of a century later:

> [O]n the twenty-fourth day of October, 5829 (Anno Domini, 1825), I received from Ill. Bro. JOHN BARKER (who received a special authority for that purpose from the Grand and Supreme Council of the 33d degree, sitting in the Grand East in the city of Charleston, in the State of South Carolina), the several degrees of the Rite, to Sovereign Grand Inspector General of the 33d degree, inclusive.[82]

Yates enthusiastically worked to spread the Ineffable and Sublime degrees, and soon joined the Supreme Council at Charleston, as this brief summary demonstrates:

> [O]n November 16, 1824, he was appointed Sovereign of Sovereigns of the Consistory he established at Albany.
>
> On September 13, 1825, in his capacity of Most Equitable Grand Sovereign of the Grand Council of Princes of Jerusalem, he issued a Dispensation empowering some of the Albany members of Delta Lodge of Perfection at Schenectady to confer the Ineffable degrees to and including perfection in Albany. This eventually terminated in the removal of the Lodge of Perfection back to Albany, late that year.
>
> On October 24, 1825, he was crowned a Sovereign Grand Inspector General of the 33° and admitted an Active member of the Southern Supreme Council....[83]

It is important to bear in mind that Yates's authority over these bodies came from the Supreme Council at Charleston and, on February 7, 1825, Holbrook informed Yates that he had forwarded a Charter for their Consistory.[84] In

81. See Arturo de Hoyos, *Light on Masonry: The History and Rituals of America's Most Important Masonic Exposé* (Washington, DC: Scottish Rite Research Society, 2008), 86, 727–52.

82. *Proceedings of the Supreme Council of Sov.:.Gr.:. Inspectors General, for the Northern Masonic Jurisdiction of the United States. Gourgas Body, 1813–1851. Raymond Body, 1851–1860. Van Rensselaer Body, 1860–1862* (Portland, [Maine]: Stephen Berry, Printer, 1876), 36. However, in a talk on Aug. 25, 1852, Yates confused names, and credited Joseph M'Cosh with the act, stating, "In 1825 I took my vows as a 'Sovereign Grand Inspector General' 'between the hands' of our Brother Joseph M'Cosh, he having been specially deputized for that purpose." Ibid., 233–50.

83. Baynard, *History of the Supreme Council, 33°* (1938), 1:231–32.

84. Moses Holbrook, Charleston, South Carolina, February 7, 1825, to Giles F. Yates, Schenectady, New York. Archives of the Supreme Council, 33°, SJ, Washington, DC. Also reprinted in [Albert Pike, ed.,] *Official Bulletin of the Supreme Council* ... vol. 9 (March 1889), No. 1, 251–53.

the public Masonic newspapers Yates proudly noted that his Grand Council had been "recognized by the Supreme Council of the 33d, &c. for the United States of America" (i.e., at Charleston).[85]

In order to assist Yates with his work, in July 1825 Holbrook promised to send "the rough translations of the remaining from 17th to 22d Degrees."[86] Although all their correspondence is not extant, we know that in early September Holbrook also sent the rituals from the 18°–21°, and "some observations upon 33d." In 1825 Barker also supplied Yates with copies of the Supreme Council's rituals (17°–32°). Holbrook expressed to Yates his concern about the slumbering Supreme Council in New York and the Cerneau problem stating that the Northern District could reassemble, or possibly come under Yates's management:

> The remaining members of the 33^{d} in New York have a right to organize themselves at pleasure and a storm might be brewed by neglecting them[.] I wish some way you could get the management of their concerns into your own – or your friend power (S. Van *Rensselaer*) – it would put all things right and you would silence Cerneau and his interlopers.[87]

Four months later, on January 28, 1826, Holbrook contemplated the need to reinstitute another Supreme Council in the Northern District, and again hinted that "someone" could take control:

> I sometime since wrote to S. Simpkins, R. Riker, J. J. J. Gourgas & MLM Peixotto – I have received no answer – I forwarded a resolution of this Supreme Council – As they have never written a line to this S.C. for thirteen years – we have kindly reminded them of their neglect – it will be followed by further resolutions upon the subject – founded upon their reply, if they should deign to make one – If they will not act by a friendly request – someone else can surely be appointed.[88]

85. *American Masonic Record, and Albany Saturday Magazine*, Vol. 1 (Albany, Saturday, February 10, 1827), No. 2, 14.

86. Moses Holbrook, Charleston, South Carolina, July 14, 1825, to Giles F. Yates, Schenectady, New York. Copy in the Archives of the Supreme Council, 33°, SJ, Washington, DC.

87. Moses Holbrook, Charleston, South Carolina, September 7, 1825, to Giles F. Yates, Schenectady, New York. Copy in the Archives of the Supreme Council, 33°, SJ, Washington, DC.

88. Moses Holbrook, Charleston, South Carolina, January 28, 1826, to Giles F. Yates, Schenectady, New York. Copy in the Archives of the Supreme Council, 33°, SJ, Washington, DC.

Two days later Holbrook wrote to Gourgas, "Several notices have at different times been communicated to the members of the N.Y. Supreme Council, but there is nothing in the Archives of this S. Council from yours or from any of its members for the last thirteen years."[89] Holbrook's frustration continued to find its way into his letters to Yates, as he again lamented in March and July concerning the inactivity of the Supreme Council for the Northern District:

> With regard to the silence of the New York Supreme Council, I am half inclined to believe that there is some agreement that they shall not work in the business. I have, some months since, written a polite letter to each of them and have never received any answer whatever – they have been written to as a body and have never answered – and we do no hear of their having met for these twelve or more years past.[90]
>
> I would hope that you will go on as a body as of no body existed in N.Y. leaving us to regularly turn you over you over to them. – perhaps they may take another 14 years nap of undisturbed *tranquility*.[91]

These facts differ from a narrative printed by the Supreme Council, 33°, NMJ, almost two centuries later. The history of Francken's Ineffable Lodge of Perfection, and Yates's association with the Supreme Council at Charleston was apparently forgotten when the Northern Masonic Jurisdiction published the following curious remarks:

> This year, 2001, marks a special occasion for Scottish Rite Freemasonry. You may recall that Scottish Rite Freemasonry first came to be practiced in what was to become the United States in 1767 at Albany New York, where a Lodge of Perfection was formed and still is in operation under the auspices of the Northern Masonic Jurisdiction.
>
> Some 34 years later, in 1801, the first Supreme Council was formed in Charleston, South Carolina. Our Northern Masonic Jurisdiction was subsequently chartered in 1813.[92]

As has been demonstrated, "Scottish Rite Freemasonry" was not practiced in Albany, New York, in 1767. Francken's Ineffable Lodge of Perfection

89. Moses Holbrook, Charleston, South Carolina, January 30, 1826, to J. J. J. Gourgas, New York, New York. Copy in the Archives of the Supreme Council, 33°, SJ, Washington, DC.

90. Moses Holbrook, Charleston, South Carolina, March 20, 1826, to Giles F. Yates, Schenectady, New York. Copy in the Archives of the Supreme Council, 33°, SJ, Washington, DC.

91. Moses Holbrook, Charleston, South Carolina, July 10, 1826, to Giles F. Yates, Schenectady, New York. Copy in the Archives of the Supreme Council, 33°, SJ, Washington, DC.

92. *Abstract of Proceedings of the Supreme Council, 33° A.A.S.R., N.M.J., U.S.A. . . . Annual Meeting Held in Indianapolis, Indiana September 23–25, 2001* ([Lexington, Mass.], 2001), 127.

(4°–14°) in Albany was never a part of the Scottish Rite, but rather belonged to the Order of the Royal Secret, the 25-degree system created by Stephen Morin. The Albany body was only active for seven years, and ceased to function completely in 1774. It was revived, *forty-six years later*, without authority, in 1820 by Giles F. Yates, which was nineteen years *after* the creation of the Supreme Council at Charleston. When Yates was finally "healed" and received authentic Scottish Rite authority, it came from the Supreme Council at Charleston, because the Supreme Council for the Northern District, was in "a profound sleep."

"Sovereigns of Masonry" and the York Rite, 1826–32

Within weeks of Holbrook writing the abovementioned letters, and after more than a decade of slumber, Gourgas was ready to awaken the Supreme Council for the Northern District. Unfortunately, however, the year 1826 would not be kind to American Freemasonry. Almost immediately after the reawakening of the Supreme Council for the Northern District, William Morgan, of Batavia, New York, disappeared following his unwise boast that he would expose and publish the rituals of the Fraternity. His disappearance, and presumed murder, would ignite the infamous "anti-Masonic episode" which lasted until 1842. During that period most Masonic activity throughout the United States ceased.

For the first five years of the anti-Masonic period, from 1826–32, Gourgas and Holbrook carried on an extensive correspondence which benefitted both Supreme Councils. Their correspondence evinced a warm affection for each other and a genuine concern over the welfare of each other's Supreme Councils. Each was willing to share documents, books, manuscripts, rituals, and opinions. During this same period Gourgas corresponded with Giles F. Yates, on matters of mutual concern.

With several Grand Lodges inactive, it is no surprise that the members of the Supreme Councils retained their notion of superiority. The attitude was also fueled by a dislike of anything connected with Cerneau's name. In December 1826, Gourgas wrote to Holbrook, expressing a dislike of the York

Rite's Red Cross, Malta, Templar, and other degrees, suggesting that they were "Priest Craft Masonry."

> The modern degrees of R: ✠ — Knight Malta — Templars, Holy Sepulchre, Mediterean Pass &c. &c. &c. is Priest Craft Masonry, they have nothing to do with otherwise *true* ancient Sublime Free and accepted Masonry they had better be left alone to their own fate, along with their mammoth Septennial Grand Chapters & Encampments.[93]

Holbrook was more open-minded than Gourgas, and in 1823 he served as the first Grand Commander of South Carolina Encampment No. 1, Knights Templar, under authority of the General Grand Encampment of the United States.[94] As noted, the General Grand Encampment was largely formed by and included many Cerneau Masons. Although he appreciated some of the York Rite's degrees, Holbrook did not generally hold the grand bodies in high esteem. His disdain was increased when, on September 16, 1826, the General Grand Royal Arch Chapter passed the following resolution: "That no Royal Arch Mason, within the jurisdiction of this General Grand Chapter, shall be permitted to confer any degree in Masonry, not recognized as a Constitutional degree, nor to establish any Society of Masons, not recognized as a Constitutional body." Holbrook interpreted this as a direct attack on the Scottish Rite and, on July 12, 1827, he informed Gourgas that the General Grand Royal Arch Chapter "intended to put a stop to the Sublime Degrees" adding "Do tell me what right has this Gen[eral]. Gr[and]. Body to interfere with us? Since 1783 we have had our rights in full operation and do not mean to have them abridged by these modern upstarts."[95] In actuality Holbrook misunderstood the resolution which had nothing to do with the Scottish Rite. It was simply intended to limit the degrees conferred *within* the York Rite, not those of other Orders,[96] and to stop "new degrees in what they *miscall* Masonry . . . [by conferring] them upon persons *as inducements* to them to enter the Masonic

93. J. J. Gourgas, New York, NY, December 5, 1826, to Moses Holbrook, Charleston, S.C. Copy in the Archives of the Supreme Council, 33°, SJ, Washington, DC.

94. *Proceedings of the Grand Encampment of Knights Templar Triennial Session*, vol. 22 (1884), "Appendix F. Copies of papers relating to South Carolina Commandery No. 1," 170–76.

95. Moses Holbrook, Charleston, S.C., July 12, 1827, to J. J. Gourgas, New York, NY. Copy in the Archives of the Supreme Council, 33°, SJ, Washington, DC.

96. Benjamin B. French, ed., *A Compendium of the Proceedings of the General Grand Chapter of Royal Arch Masons of the United States: From the 24th Day of October, 1797, to the 2nd Tuesday of September 1856* (Baltimore: Joseph Robinson, 1859), 162.

fraternity—to confer them, and others, which they call honorary degrees, on women, and to induce them to walk in Masonic processions, clothed in the insignia of the fraternity!"[97]

Holbrook's harangue continued, and the following month he called the York Rite "... the new fangled Freemasonry of the present day—It is a complete farce."[98] Three months later he suggested that Gourgas confer the York Rite degrees under authority of the Supreme Council:

> ... the State of South Carolina has no authority to issue charters for Royal Arch or K[nigh]t. Templars <out of state>—the General Grand Chapter and the General Grand Encampment of the United States agreeably to "*ancient custom*" (say eleven years last June) have the sole authority to issue charters out of the different states [...] I will loan you from our archives the Orders of K[nigh]t T[emplar] an Red + [Cross]—With the Maltese Order as conferred by the Ge[neral]. Gr[and]. Enc[ampmen]t—and by the time you will have copied these I will endeavor to find the Mark Master, M[ost]. Ex[cellent]. Master, Royal Arch and Royal Master to loan you [...] I think they had better receive their authority from your Supreme Council of the 33^{d} to give the degrees and Orders, it is much *more ancient* in real truth[.] They will be enabled to do so from the manuscripts and it will really be better for them—In June (about the 6th) 1816 at New York Cerneau & Co. made up the degrees and Orders as we now have them.[99]

On December 13, 1827, Gourgas expressed similar views, telling Holbrook that he thought it was proper to communicate the Knight Templar Degree, and other orders of knighthood, as well as the "Rose Croix Ecossais – d'Hérédom de Killwinning" (Royal Order of Scotland) on Scottish Rite Masons holding the Thirty-second and Thirty-third Degrees. He added, "Further, it is very desirable for the general good & prosperity of the Masonic Order in this Country — that the 'U.S. Genl G^{d} Encamp^{t} should be very soon entirely dispensed with — and that *every* 'State G^{d} Encamp^{t}' be transformed into *a State* Grand Coun^{l} & Consistory of 30—31—32—*Submitted* to the Sup. Coun. of 33^{d} of their own Jurisdiction."[100] He justified this with the statement that the Supreme Council

97. French, ed., *A Compendium of the Proceedings of the General Grand Chapter of Royal Arch Masons ...* (1859), 142.

98. Moses Holbrook, Charleston, S.C., August 22, 1827, to J. J. J. Gourgas, New York, NY. Copy in the Archives of the Supreme Council, 33°, SJ, Washington, DC.

99. Moses Holbrook, Charleston, S.C., November 4, 1827, to J. J. J. Gourgas, New York, NY. Copy in the Archives of the Supreme Council, 33°, SJ, Washington, DC.

100. *J. J. J. Gourgas, New York, NY, December 13, 1827, to Moses Holbrook, Charleston, S.C.* Copy

acted as the "Guardians & Supreme Chiefs of the whole of Free Masonry ancient and modern, over the surface of the two Hemispheres." The words echoed the 1802 *Manifesto*, and were in spirit with the idea of Holbrook's Supreme Council of the 43°.

On January 10, 1828, Gourgas thanked Holbrook for sending the lectures Mark Master, Most Excellent Master, and Royal Arch Mason Degrees and, at the same time, he requested complete copies of the rituals of Past High Priest, Mediterranean Pass, Christian Mark, Holy Sepulchre, "and any other orders of knighthood." Two months later, Holbrook sent an old copy of the Mediterranean Pass ritual. In August Gourgas wrote again, reminding Holbrook to send him the "detached degrees of Knighthood—particularly the Holy Cross—Holy Sepulchre conclave & others."[101]

The requests for rituals soon came to a halt as the work of anti-Masonry progressed. A "Convention of Seceding Free Masons," held in the village of Le Roy, Genesee County, New York, on February 19–20, 1828, appointed a committee of fifteen seceding Masons to prepare the several Degrees, above that of Master Mason, for publication. The Le Roy Convention's work, which included most of the rituals Gourgas sought, was approved and published under the title *A Revelation of Free Masonry, as Published to the World by a Convention of Seceding Masons* (1828).[102] This work would later be corrected and superseded in David Bernard's *Light on Masonry* (1829), while additional degrees appeared in Avery Allyn's *A Ritual of Freemasonry* (1831).[103]

Gourgas's opinion was that since 1806, when the Sovereign Grand Consistory 30°, 31°, 32° was founded, and since 1813, the traditional founding date

in the Archives of the Supreme Council, 33°, SJ, Washington, DC.

101. *J. J. J. Gourgas, New York, NY, August 9, 1828, to Moses Holbrook, Charleston, S.C.* Copy in the Archives of the Supreme Council, 33°, SJ, Washington, DC.

102. *A Revelation of Free Masonry, as Published to the World by a Convention of Seceding Masons, held at Le Roy, Genesee County, N.Y. on the 4th and 5th of July 1828: Containing a True and Genuine Development of The Mode of Initiation, and also of the Several Degrees: To Wit: in the Chapter, Mark Master, Past Master, Most Excellent Master, and Royal Arch. In the Encampment, Knight of the Red Cross, Knight Templar, Knight of the Christian Mark, and Guards of the Conclave, and Knights of the Holy Sepulcher. In the Ancient Council of the Trinity, Denominated the Holy and Thrice Illustrious Order of the Cross, The Illustrious, Most Illustrious, and Thrice Illustrious Degrees. Published by the Lewiston Committee* (Rochester, NY: Printed by Weed & Heron, 1828).

103. *A Ritual of Freemasonry, Illustrated by Numerous Engravings. To Which is Added a Key to the Phi Beta Kappa, the Orange, and Odd Fellows Societies. With Notes and Remarks.* (Philadelphia: John Clarke, 1831).

of the Supreme Council for the Northern District, that "all and every power and authority *whatsoever* they might be *ceased* to have any force within this Jurisdiction, *even* those of the Th.·. Ills.·. Br Stephen Morin himself & all his Deputies been alive & here present—his and their power & authority would have become null and void within this Jurisdiction—unless endorsed and confirmed by it."[104]

In October 1827 a territorial division was made between the two Supreme Councils and on July 5, 1828, Yates transferred his membership to the Northern District. The opinions of these Sovereigns of Masonry were simply theoretical, not practical. Hampered by anti-Masonry, they were unable to effect any changes, and the final correspondence we have from them is dated June 1832, followed by a silence of twelve years. Following this there are only hints of Scottish Rite activity in the Northern District, while in the Southern District occasional certificates and patent survive to show that the work continued quietly, and infrequently. To the certain chagrin of these two Supreme Councils, during the anti-Masonic period, most of the high degrees were conferred by Cerneau Masons.

Later Opinions and Limitations of Authority

Following the general revival of American Freemasonry in 1842, there would be many changes in the Scottish Rite. Over the next couple of years Giles F. Yates successfully urged Gourgas to reawaken the Northern District and Jurisdiction, when on

> June 15, 1844. Gourgas and *Yates* met, consulted, examined "*a mass of foreign communications*" and resolved to "resume the activity of all our former private as well as official, home and foreign correspondence." Of their former associates, three were dead, and one removed probably in diplomatic service. Five months later three Brethren from Boston were admitted to the Council. In a year the membership had grown to eight, and the brethren with great regularity attended to the duties of supervision and regulation. . . .[105]

104. J. J. J. Gourgas, New York, NY, March 29, 1829, to Giles F. Yates, Schenectady, NY. Copy in the Archives of the Supreme Council, 33°, SJ, Washington, DC.

105. *Proceedings of the Supreme Council of Sovereign Grand Inspectors-General of the Thirty-third and Last Degree of the Ancient Accepted Scottish Rite of Freemasonry for the Northern Masonic Jurisdiction of the United States of America. In Annual Meeting held in the City of Philadelphia Commencing on the Thirteenth Day of the Month Ellul, A.M. Fifty-six Hundred and Seventy-four, September Sixteenth A.D. Nineteen Hundred and Thirteen* (Boston: 1913), 20.

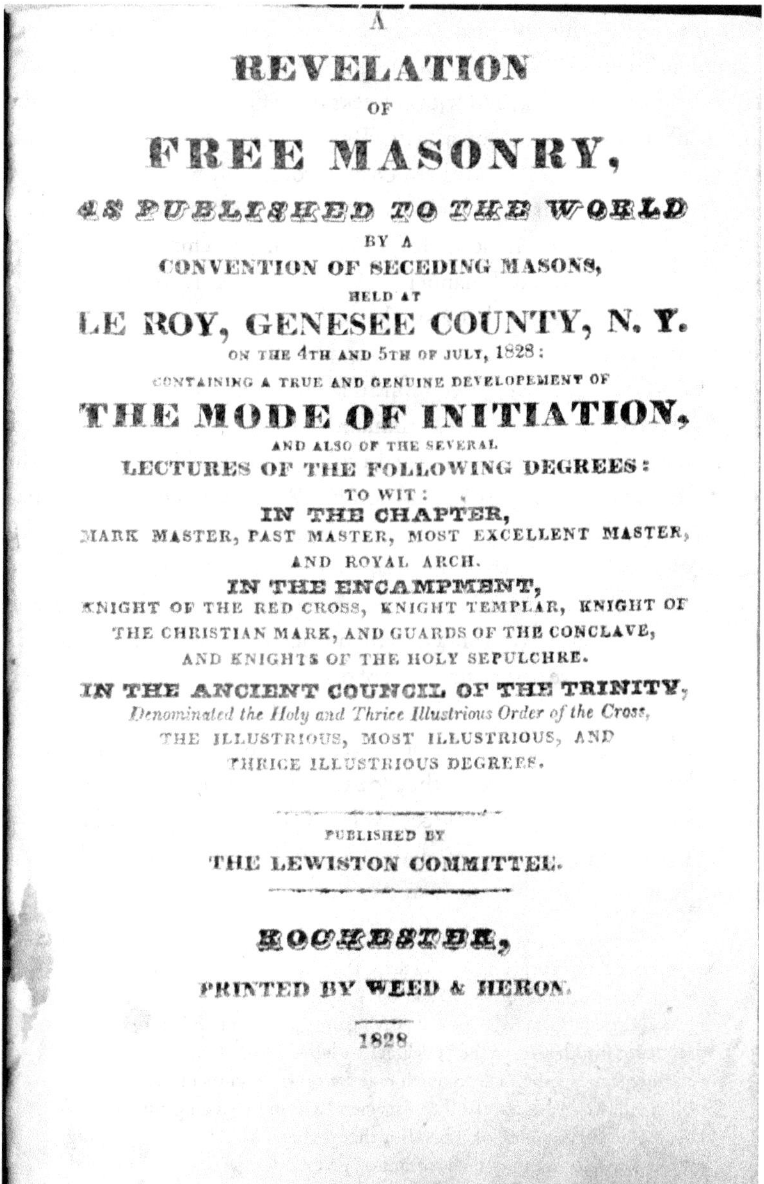

A

REVELATION

OF

FREE MASONRY,

AS PUBLISHED TO THE WORLD

BY A

CONVENTION OF SECEDING MASONS,

HELD AT

LE ROY, GENESEE COUNTY, N. Y.

ON THE 4TH AND 5TH OF JULY, 1828:

CONTAINING A TRUE AND GENUINE DEVELOPEMENT OF

THE MODE OF INITIATION,

AND ALSO OF THE SEVERAL

LECTURES OF THE FOLLOWING DEGREES:

TO WIT:

IN THE CHAPTER,

MARK MASTER, PAST MASTER, MOST EXCELLENT MASTER, AND ROYAL ARCH.

IN THE ENCAMPMENT,

KNIGHT OF THE RED CROSS, KNIGHT TEMPLAR, KNIGHT OF THE CHRISTIAN MARK, AND GUARDS OF THE CONCLAVE, AND KNIGHTS OF THE HOLY SEPULCHRE.

IN THE ANCIENT COUNCIL OF THE TRINITY,

Denominated the Holy and Thrice Illustrious Order of the Cross,

THE ILLUSTRIOUS, MOST ILLUSTRIOUS, AND THRICE ILLUSTRIOUS DEGREES.

PUBLISHED BY

THE LEWISTON COMMITTEE.

ROCHESTER,

PRINTED BY WEED & HERON.

1828

Figure 2.6. The publication of ritual exposés such as *A Revelation of Free Masonry* proved useful to J. J. J. Gourgas, and other officers of Masonic bodies, who sought to collect copies of as many degrees as possible.

In practicality, this commenced the first stable activity of the Northern Masonic Jurisdiction. It had been put into a "profound sleep" almost immediately following its creation, and within weeks of its first awakening in 1826 the Morgan affair caused it to slumber again. Thus, from its creation in 1815 to 1844, the Supreme Council in the Northern District could only been active for a few weeks to a few months. In 1844 however, it awoke in earnest and with great success.

In the Southern Jurisdiction, Holbrook died in December 1844, and Dr. Jacob De La Motta (son of Emanuel De La Motta, founder of the Northern Supreme Council) presided at a single session of the Supreme Council at Charleston, when Albert G. Mackey was appointed Grand Secretary General. Dr. De La Motta passed away two months later, in February 1845, when Alexander McDonald became Grand Commander. On May 1, 1845, the Supreme Council for the Northern District issued a circular notice which reaffirmed the lawful authority of both jurisdictions, adding, "At no time since the organization of our said Supreme Councils have we been without our constitutional number of members."[106] What this meant was unclear. Two months later, on August 2, the Southern Jurisdiction also announced that it was working, and issued its own "Manifesto of 1845," which traced its lineage, but curiously reprinted the primitive degree structure of original 1802 *Circular*, which listed the "Prince of the Royal Secret" as 30°–32°.

From this time forward Charleston made no claims to the degrees outside of those mentioned, or alluded to, in the 1802 *Circular* which, it should be remembered, amounted to fifty-two degrees. As late as 1845, however, the Northern District still briefly mused with the idea of wider control. In September 1845 Yates (who was now Lieutenant Grand Commander) wrote to Gourgas:

> We *claim* as a Sup[reme]. Council jurisdiction of every detached degree *subsidiary* to our principal degrees. Some of them are straying away under other jurisdictions & we have but as you say, to take our property wherever we find it.
>
> As a Supreme G[rand]. Council, leaving out "of the 33d degree" *co nomine* LIMITS our jurisdiction to the 33 degrees ~~we have~~, we can I think accomplish what then appears so much so much rage for on the continent of Europe & in England, Ireland & Scotland & elsewhere, without changing out name ~~of~~ to Supreme Gr^{d} Council of Rites. But that perhaps would only be keeping our old *name* & assuming the jurisdiction properly belonging to S[upreme].

106. Charles W. Moore, ed., *The Freemasons' Monthly Magazine,* Vol. IV (Boston: [Tuttle & Dennet], October 1, 1845), No. 12, 356–59.

(2)

Since that period the Supreme Council has continued to hold its sessions in this City, and to exercise the powers and prerogatives delegated to it by the Secret Constitutions of the 33d degree. An interruption to its active operations occurred during the disastrous period when the dark spirit of anti-masonry was moving like an incubus over our unhappy land. But its constitutional powers were never surrendered, and its authority has been always acknowledged by the possessors of the sublime and ineffable degrees. Vacancies having occurred by the deaths of members, these vacancies were duly and constitutionally supplied, by the appointment of competent brethren as S. G. I. G. and the Council, now completed, consists of the following members:—

ALEXANDER McDONALD, Most Puissant Sovereign Grand Commander.
JOHN H. HONOUR, Most Illustrious Lieutenant Grand Commander.
JAMES C. NORRIS, Illustrious Treasurer General of the Holy Empire.
ALBERT G. MACKEY, M. D., Illustrious Secretary General of the Holy Empire.
CHARLES M. FURMAN, Illustrious Master of Ceremonies.
JAMES S. BURGES, Illustrious Captain of the Life Guards.
C. C. SEBRING, Sovereign Grand Inspector General, 33d.
JOSEPH McCOSH, Sovereign Grand Inspector General, 33d.
ALBERT CASE, Sovereign Grand Inspector General, 33d.

The Supreme Council thus organized claims Masonic jurisdiction over all the southern and south-western district of the United States, as the Supreme tribunal for the sublime and ineffable degrees of the Scotch rite. In deference to the Constitutions of the York rite, practised in this country, it waives its rights and privileges, so far as they relate to the degrees of Ancient Craft Masonry, which, long before the establishment of a Supreme Council in this hemisphere, were under the control of a Symbolic Grand Lodge. But this Council does claim the exclusive right to confer the following degrees, which now are, and always have been communicated by Grand Inspectors, or by bodies deriving their authority from a Supreme Council of the 33rd degree.

4. Secret Master. 5. Perfect Master. 6. Intimate Secretary. 7. Provost and Judge. 8. Intendant of the Building. 9. Elected Knights of 9. 10. Illustrious Elected of 15. 11. Sublime Knight Elected. 12. Grand Master Architect. 13. Royal Arch of Solomon. 14. Sublime and Perfect Mason. 15. Knight of the East. 16. Prince of Jerusalem. 17. Knight of the East and West. 18. Sovereign Prince of Rose Croix de Heroden. 19. Grand Pontiff. 20. Grand Master of all Symbolic Lodges. 21. Patriarch Noachite. 22. Prince of Libanus. 23. Chief of the Tabernacle. 24. Prince of the Tabernacle. 25. Prince of Mercy. 26. Knight of the Brazen Serpent. 27. Commander of the Temple. 28. Knight of the Sun. 29. Grand Elect Knight K—— H——. 30. 31. 32. Sublime Prince of the Royal Secret, Prince of Masons. 33. Sovereign Grand Inspectors General.

On the 5th day of August, 1813, as appears from authenticated documents in the possession of this Council, a similar Supreme Council was, in accordance with the Secret Constitutions, duly and lawfully established and constituted at the city of New-York, by Emanuel De La Motta, as the Representative and under the sanction and authority of the Council at Charleston. The Masonic jurisdiction of the New-York Council is distributed over the northern, north-western and north-eastern parts of the United States. And this, with the Council at Charleston, are the *only* recognized Councils which exist or *can exist*, according to the Secret Constitutions, in the U. States. Both bodies are now in active operation. Their labors have never been suspended, though withdrawn for a time from the public eye—their authority has never been, and cannot be, abrogated. They hold in their archives certified copies of the Secret Constitutions, derived from the Grand Consistory held at Paris, in 1761. Their succession of officers and members has been regularly and duly continued, and the Great Light of Sublime Masonry, which has been confided to their keeping, like the sacred fire of the Vestals has been preserved unextinguished on their altars.

The object of these Supreme Councils is not to interfere with the rights of any other Masonic bodies, but simply to preserve from decay or innovation, those sublime truths and ineffable mysteries, which, while they throw a brighter light upon the pure system of Ancient Craft Masonry, can be attained only by those who, with constancy unwavering, with fidelity unshaken, with courage unflinching, and perseverance unabated, have travelled rough and rugged roads, and sought for light in the deepest recesses of the Masonic temple. They ask, therefore, as the legal guardians of these invaluable treasures, the sympathy and fraternal kindness of their brethren, to whom they take this occasion of offering the right hand of brotherly love and affection.

Lastly, this Supreme Council, in common with its thrice illustrious sister of New-York, does most emphatically protest against the false and scandalous statements made by J. F. B. Clavel in his "Histoire Pittoresque de la Franc Maçonnerie"—statements which exhibit, on the part of their author, either a deplorable ignorance of the

Figure 27. The Southern Jurisdiction's *Manifesto of 1845* reasserted its authority over the Scottish Rite Degrees, but omitted several, by reprinting the outdated list from the 1802 *Circular*.

> G[rand]. Council of rites. ~~A new~~ To accomplish the purpose hinted at, we will doubtless have to remodify & rearrange & extend & amplify our powers & increase the *number* of our superintending body. [...] Let this Sov[ereign]. Gr[and]. Council be called if you please "Sovereign Grand Council of Rites for the N[orthern]. D[istrict]. & J[urisdiction]. of the U.S.A. In this way we can get over the difficulty.[107]

Gourgas, however, realized that to build the Supreme Council for the Northern District, it was impractical to overextend their reach. Two and half months later, he implored Yates to abandon his ideas and focus on the Scottish Rite.

> I only have to beg of you let the Red [Cross] and the Encampments to themselves — let us attend to none but the *blues* — ineff[able] — & our own degrees — *solely* — beware to create any kind of jealousy — it will all come on gradually right of its own self — when once we are what we ought to have been and be.[108]

Yates heeded the advice and the Northern District focused on making progress, both ritualistically and organizationally. In Charleston, there was only one last effort to work additional degrees, which brief attempt occurred in 1866, under the administration of Albert Pike. Aware that the "Maçonnerie d'Adoption" was included in the 1802 *Circular*, Pike rewrote the rituals, and printed the first three as *The Masonry of Adoption* (1866).[109] In his introduction he noted, "The Masonry of Adoption is regularly attached to the Ancient and Accepted Scottish Rite, and under the protection of the Mother Supreme Council of the 33d degree, at Charleston, South Carolina." Although he hoped it would become a viable alternative to Eastern Star, it garnered little interest and the rituals of the four higher degrees were never printed. Finally, in 1868 the Supreme Council at Charleston "relinquish[ed] all control over the degrees of Royal and Select Master."[110] This final act ended any attempts at control over degrees not unique to the Scottish Rite.

107. Giles Fonda Yates, Albany, New York, September 23, 1845, to J. J. J. Gourgas, New York, NY. Copy in the Archives of the Supreme Council, 33°, SJ, Washington, DC.

108. J. J. J. Gourgas, New York, NY, December 17, 1845, to Giles F. Yates, Schenectady, NY. Copy in the Archives of the Supreme Council, 33°, SJ, Washington, DC.

109. [Albert Pike,] *The Masonry of Adoption* (N.p., 1866).

110. Albert Pike, *Ancient and Accepted Scottish Rite of Freemasonry. The Constitutions and Regulations of 1762. Statutes and Regulations of Perfection, and Other Degrees* ... (New York: Masonic Publishing Co., A.M. 5632 [1872]; New Edition Printed by J. J. Little, &c., 5664 [1904]; reprint ed. Np., n.d.), 389.

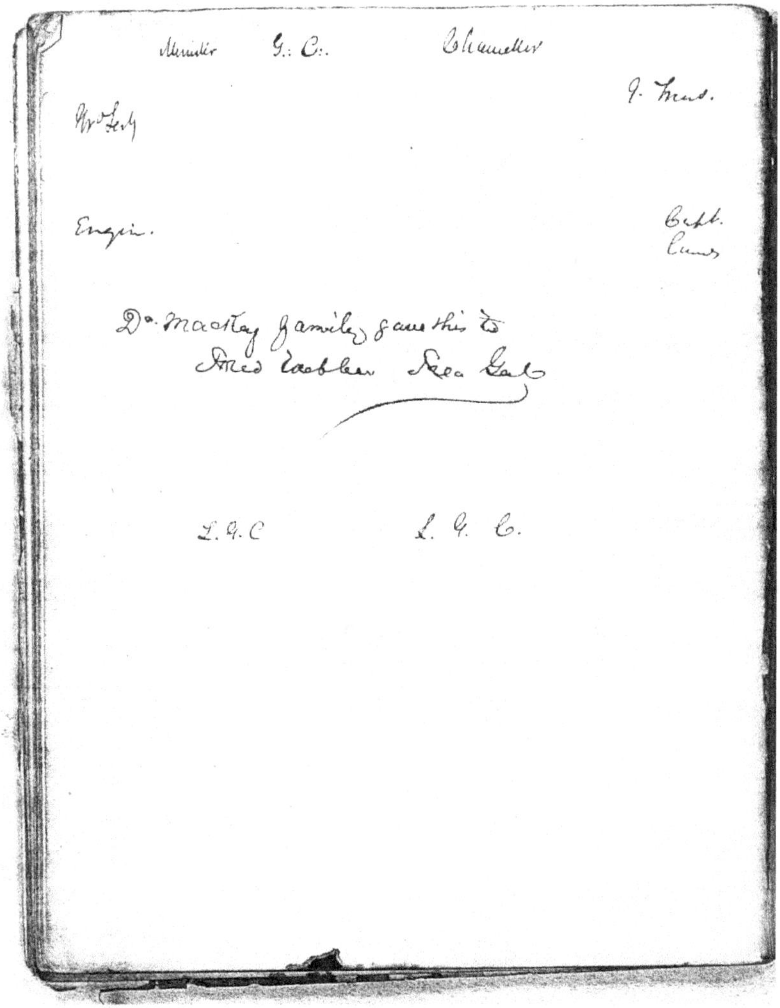

Figure 28. The penultimate page from Moses Holbrook's "43[d] Degree" manuscript shows the Supreme Council's layout (seating arrangement), with a line added after 1881: "Dr Mackey['s] family gave this to Fred Webber[,] Trea[surer] G[ener]al." —*Archives of the Supreme Council, 33°, SJ.*

MAGNA EST VERITAS

The story of the Supreme Council of the Forty-third Degree would not be complete without the oblique mention found in Albert G. Mackey's *History of Freemasonry*.

> In David Vinton's *Short Historical Account of Masonry* appended to his *Masonic Minstrel,* which was published at Dedham, in Massachusetts, in the year 1816, will be found a list of the degrees said to be conferred in Charleston, New York, and Newport. The number is 43, and the last, or 43d, is Sovereign Grand Inspector-General. The number is made up by adding to the thirty-three degrees of the Scottish Rite ten others, embracing the degrees of the American Rite and several Orders of Knighthood. In this enumeration the Knight of the Sun is made the 38th, and therefore I suppose that the number "28" prefixed to that degree in the extract above quoted is also an error. This enumeration of 43 degrees was never accepted nor used by the legitimate bodies of the Scottish Rite, but only by some spurious associations which then existed.[111]

Mackey's comment was not caused by ignorance or misunderstanding. It was simply untrue, and he knew better. In fact, Moses Holbrook's 43d Degree manuscript was actually kept by Albert G. Mackey until his death, when his family gave it to Frederick Webber, who was Treasurer General of the Supreme Council, 33°, SJ.

Why did Mackey omit the truth about the Supreme Council of the Forty-third Degree from his seven-volume Masonic history? Knowing that Mackey was a wide reader, the only charitable response I can offer is that he may have had in mind a line from James Anderson's *The New Book of Constitutions of the Ancient and Honorable Fraternity of Free and Accepted Masons* (1738):

"It is good to know WHAT NOT TO SAY!"[112]

111. Albert Gallatin Mackey, *The History of Freemasonry: Its Legends and Traditions, Its Chronological History,* William James Hughan, William Reynolds Singleton eds. (New York and London: Masonic History Company, 1898, 1906), vol. 5, 1277.

112. James Anderson, *The New Book of Constitutions of the Ancient and Honorable Fraternity of Free and Accepted Masons* (London: Caesar Ward and Richard Chandler, 1738), x.

James Foulhouze: S.G.C. of the Supreme Council of Louisiana

Michael R. Poll, 32°

> Mr. Pike is altogether unknown to me, and I have never seen him, which is perhaps to be regretted, because in the event he spoke to me pursuant to the information which he has received from ill-disposed individuals, I suppose that he will be sorry for having allowed his pen to write what is neither correct nor rational.
>
> —James Foulhouze, 1858.[1]

James Foulhouze was, unquestionably, the arch-nemesis of Albert Pike in the latter's early days as Grand Commander of the Southern Jurisdiction. Judge James Foulhouze, former Roman Catholic priest, Sovereign Grand Inspector General of the Grand Orient of– France and Sovereign Grand Commander of the New Orleans Supreme Council in the pre-Concordat of 1855 period along with some of the leading New Orleans Masons,

1. *The Masonic Delta,* Mar. 1858.

including the very respected Judge T. Wharton Collens and the powerful United States Senator Pierre Soulé, nearly destroyed the concordat between the New Orleans and Charleston Supreme Councils—an official agreement which was the breath of life to the newly reorganized Charleston Supreme Council. Who was this man who could have caused such a disturbance? Did he cause the disturbance or was he, himself, swept along in a tidal wave of events?

The following is a glimpse into the life and tumultuous Masonic times of a most significant, but highly controversial, figure in the history of the US Scottish Rite. It is to be regretted that no photograph or likeness of Foulhouze is known to exist. It is also unfortunate that some areas of his life are simply lost in the midst of time.

On October 1, 1800,[2] Jacques Foulhouze was born to Michel and Jeanne Cronier Foulhouze in Riom, France. The young man received a Catholic education at the Seminary of St. Sulpice in Paris culminating in his ordination as a Roman Catholic priest. The Reverend James Foulhouze then traveled to the United States and labored in the Diocese of Philadelphia in 1834 and 1835.[3] The next record concerning Foulhouze in the US comes in 1835 when his name appears in a Philadelphia court records book of aliens declaring their intention to take the oath of allegiance to the United States.[4] Foulhouze would not long remain a priest nor keep his domicile in Philadelphia. An 1858 New Orleans publication contains interesting comments about Foulhouze and his possible reasons for leaving the priesthood. The comments were written by Charles Laffon de Ladébat, a leading figure in mid-19th century New Orleans Scottish Rite Masonry, who will be discussed later in this paper. De Ladébat says that Foulhouze might have remained a priest had not, "Mr. (now bishop) Hughes been appointed, in his stead, to the important rectorship of a northern parish, to which Mr. Foulhouze was, for his long service, justly entitled."[5]

2. This date was obtained from the tombstone of James Foulhouze located in St. Thomas the Apostle Church Cemetery, Pointe a la Hache, Louisiana.

3. Personal letter: Christine McCullough, Assistant Archivist, Archdiocese of Philadelphia to Michael R. Poll, Apr. 23, 1993.

4. *Passenger and Immigration List Index Vol. I,* P. William Filby, Mary K. Meyer eds. (Detroit, Michigan: Gale Research Co., 1981), 314.

5. Charles Laffon de Ladébat, translator, notes, *A Masonic Trial in New Orleans* (New Orleans, La.: J. Lamarre, 1858), 62.

John Hughes (1797–1864) served with Foulhouze in the Diocese of Philadelphia and founded there the *Catholic Herald* newspaper. Hughes was consecrated coadjutor to Bishop John Dubois of New York in 1838. He succeeded Dubois in 1842 and became archbishop of New York in 1850.[6] Foulhouze, regardless of de Ladébat's comments, could not have been affected by the 1838 Hughes appointment as the *Journal Notes* of Philadelphia Bishop Francis Kenrick record Foulhouze's faculties being suspended on February 5, 1836.[7] As with many areas of Foulhouze's life, it is unclear what could have taken place to cause his separation from the priesthood. Foulhouze was a graduate of the highly respected Seminary of St. Sulpice. Most Catholic dioceses consider such graduates to be a highly desirable prize. The accounts of Foulhouze for that time, however, tell a different story. The records of the Archdiocese of Philadelphia,[8] while confirming that Foulhouze was, indeed, a priest assigned to them, show had he had "no specific assignment."[9] This is a remarkable situation. Why would the Diocese of Philadelphia not take advantage of the quality education that Foulhouze received by putting his abilities and education to use? Foulhouze, himself, may provide this answer. In 1843 he was asked if he had taken the vows of the priesthood, he replied, "No, but it is true that they were given to me, against my will."[10] Regardless of what philosophical point Foulhouze was making, his statement reflects that he may have never wholly embraced the priesthood. If his work reflected the same lack of interest, then it is very likely that, regardless of what seminary he attended, he would not have been given assignments nor appointments to higher positions. All conjecture aside, Foulhouze did leave the priesthood, pursued a career in law, and moved to New Orleans.

6. *Encyclopedia Britannica,* vol. xi (Chicago: William Benton, Publisher, 1965), p. 814.

7. McCullough to Poll, Apr. 23, 1993. It should be noted that a priest having his faculties suspended is akin to a physician having his medical license suspended. The affected priest would no longer be able to carry out the duties of a priest such as hearing confessions, preforming wedding, baptisims, Mass, etc. While a priest who has had his faculties suspended is, in fact, prevented from doing all that makes one a priest, it is only the Vatican who can separate a priest from his vows as a priest. This would mean that Foulhouze might have, technically, remained a priest, without powers, until his death.

8. At the time that Foulhouze was a priest, Philadelphia was a "Diocese" and not yet an "Archdiocese."

9. McCullough to Poll, Apr. 23, 1993.

10. De Ladébat, notes, *A Masonic Trial in New Orleans,* 62.

Foulhouze began his law career in Philadelphia after leaving the priesthood. In 1842, he published a book in Philadelphia that reflected the same interest in philosophy that was maintained throughout his life. The 200-page work was titled, *A Philosophical Inquiry Respecting the Abolition of Capital Punishment.*[11] It is possible that Foulhouze was in New Orleans when this book was released, but it is clear that he was in that city the following year. Philadelphia Bishop Francis Kenrick (Foulhouze's former superior) wrote in a 1843 letter:

> Here affairs go on smoothly but at New Orleans an infidel faction are struggling to destroy or subjugate the Episcopal authority. A fallen French priest, Foulhouze, is the editor of an impious paper,[12] the organ of the Marguillers.... The leaders in disorder are Freemasons, and they contrived to set apart a lot in the Cemetery for their Masonic brethren, and had it dedicated by a speech from their Grand Master who is a Marguiller.[13]

The Marguillers were the wardens of the St. Louis Cathedral in New Orleans. The Grand Master that Kenrick spoke of was E. A. Canon, who was not only a Marguiller, but the President of the Marguillers. The Marguillers (many of whom were Freemasons) controlled the appointments of the priests for the St. Louis Cathedral during the early to mid-1800s. There was, of course, a great division within the congregation over Freemasons having a say in the appointment of their parish priests (regardless of the fact that these Freemasons were, themselves, Roman Catholic and members of the parish). The matter becomes more convoluted when we consider that the first Bishop of the St. Louis Cathedral was the brother of the first Grand Master of the Grand Lodge of Louisiana. In New Orleans, Masonry and the Roman Catholic faith were tightly intertwined for a number of years in a love/hate relationship. It was a situation not without some hostile conflicts. An event that took place in 1842 is worth mentioning.

> On the feast of All Saints, an incident took place in the Cathedral which was in itself trivial, but which shows to what lengths the two factions[14] would go. While Father Jamey was preaching, E. A. Canon, the president of the Marguillers, entered the sanctuary by way of the choir entrance, and made a tour of the

11. Philadelphia: U. Hunt, 1842.

12. The paper which Bishop Kenrick mentions was *Le Penseur* (The Thinker).

13. *Records of the American Catholic Historical Society,* vol. viii, 1896, Bishop Kenrick to Dr. Cullen, Nov. 23, 1843, 311–12.

14. Masonic and anti-Masonic.

> altar towards that place assigned to the president of the wardens (side opposite the door of the sacristy by which he entered). He remained there for a few minutes, but not being able to hear very well, he advanced to the balustrade of a neighboring chapel, in order to hear better. He had only heard a few words, and then decided to retire by the way he had come in, that is, behind the altar. As he was going out he was greeted by Octave de Armas, a parishioner loyal to [Bishop] Blanc, (who was also seated in the sanctuary) with the words, "Get out; you are not in your place...." Canon answered this with apparent sharp disdain and was preparing to leave when he was pushed. He was near the door of the sacristy and fell on the steps. On getting up he heard Armas distinctly cry, "I, I alone will get rid of the wardens." The services were interrupted for about five minutes, but the Mass was soon continued and all ended calmly.[15]

The event may have ended "calmly" at that time, but the incident was far from over. As a result of his being pushed in the St. Louis Cathedral, Canon, following typical Creole custom, sought satisfaction from Armas by means of challenging him to a duel. Armas, however, refused the challenge on the grounds that he was a Roman Catholic.[16] Friends of Canon would not let the matter drop and charges were filed against Armas with the City Recorder. Armas was found guilty of assault. The incident is reflective of the growing tensions between the factions within the New Orleans Catholic community. It was in this atmosphere and, likely, through the contacts with the Marguillers that Foulhouze was introduced to Louisiana Masonry. It obviously attracted him, and he sought to be a member.

From Priest to Freemason

The Marguillers might have introduced James Foulhouze to Louisiana Masonry, but it was not his first exposure to Freemasonry itself. Foulhouze stated in 1857, "Being a Grandson of Free-masons, I, in my early years, conceived and entertained a desire to enter the fraternity...."[17] Foulhouze fulfilled that early desire by becoming a member of *Los Amigos del Orden,* a Spanish speaking,

15. *The Louisiana Historical Quarterly,* vol. 31, no. 4, Oct. 1948. New Orleans, LA, 918.

16. Roman Catholic law forbid duels regardless of the fact that, for many years, the traditional site for duels was in the gardens directly behind, and on the grounds of, the St. Louis Cathedral.

17. *The Masonic Delta,* Nov. 1857.

New Orleans Scottish Rite lodge.[18] Foulhouze also stated, "Within a year from my initiation I was made a Master Mason in the same Lodge."[19]

There are, unfortunately, no known records of the initiation of Foulhouze nor can an exact date be placed on his initiating, passing or raising. Foulhouze did state in his *Historical Inquiry* that he was initiated by Antonio Costa.[20] Costa was Worshipful Master of *Los Amigos del Orden* in 1843. An 1843 initiation followed by an 1844 raising meant rapid advancement for Foulhouze. Foulhouze was, apparently, viewed as a Mason of promise. On February 14, 1845, he was appointed Grand Translator by the Grand Lodge. The office of Grand Translator did not exist prior to Foulhouze receiving the appointment. The office was created due to the growing need for English to French and French to English translation in Grand Lodge records and documents.

In the summer of 1845 (about a year after Foulhouze became a Master Mason) Foulhouze traveled to France carrying a letter of introduction from Robert Preaux, Grand Master of the Grand Lodge of Louisiana and Active Member of the New Orleans Supreme Council. During his stay in Paris, Foulhouze received all of the degrees of the A.&A.S.R. culminating in the 33rd degree on September 27 from the Grand College of Rites of the Grand Orient of France. There has never been an explanation as to why such an honor was given to such a young Master Mason nor has the contents of the letter from Preaux ever been revealed. Regardless of what activities Foulhouze later engaged in, he was, in the eyes of the US Masonic community, a legitimate Sovereign Grand Inspector General. Of this event, Foulhouze comments:

> The Scotch Rite ... pleased me on account of its truly philosophical principles, and the more I studied it, the more I felt anxious to take its superior degrees, when a fair opportunity so to do offered itself to me in 1845.
>
> I was in France, and on the recommendations and letters of my Scotch brothers here, the worshipful Lodge "Clémente Amitié" opened its door to me, and after a short stay among them I was made a Knight R.∴ + and a Knight Kadosh, which I am bound to say, rendered still clearer to my eyes and intellect the views which I had long entertained on the merits of the Scotch Rite, and for ever attached me to its admirable and useful tenets.

18. *The Masonic Delta,* Nov. 1857.
19. *The Masonic Delta,* Nov. 1857.
20. James Foulhouze, *Historical Inquiry into the Origin of the Ancient and Accepted Scottish Rite* (New Orleans: True Delta Job Office, 1859.), 17.

116 GG.∴ INSP.∴ GÉN.∴.

7 février 1842.

EMM. DE LAS-CASES (Comte), 1er *G.∴ M.∴ Adj.∴ de l'Ordre.*

12 août 1843.

MADAULE, capitaine du génie.

28 juin 1845.

DUPONT, Négociant à la Pointe à Pitre (Guadeloupe).

FURNELL, Député Lieutenant du comté de Limerick (Irlande).

JONES (J.), Haut Sheriff et Magistrat de Dublin (Irlande).

KENNY, ancien Officier au service britannique, à Dublin.

27 septembre 1845.

FOULHOUSE, Avocat à la Louisiane.

MEYERBEER, Membre de l'Institut, etc. à Paris.

KASTNER, Membre de l'Académie royale des Beaux-Arts de Berlin, à Paris.

BUGNOT, *Off.∴ du G.∴ O.∴.*

FUZIER, Docteur-médecin à Lyon.

In the 1846 *Calendrier Maçonique du G.∴ O.∴ de France* listing of Grand Inspectors General (GG.∴ INSP.∴ GÉN.∴), James Foulhouze is shown as receiving his degree on September 27, 1845. Courtesy Pierre Mollier, Bibliothècaire, Grand Orient de France.

> The favors thus bestowed on me, were unexpected, and I certainly desired no others, when on a special and unasked resolution of the Supreme Council in the Grand Orient, I was called and raised in that body to the thirty third degree.[21]

Following the death of Sovereign Grand Commander Jean-Jacques Conte, New Orleans Judge Jean-François Canonge, a powerful Past Grand Master of the Grand Lodge of Louisiana, became the Grand Commander of the New Orleans Supreme Council on September 20, 1845.[22] Foulhouze said of Canonge, "As long as he lived, I had but little to do, and contented myself with studying the rite...."[23]

Foulhouze, who had affiliated with the New Orleans Council in 1846, was, regardless of his comments, not idle during this period. Foulhouze was appointed grand secretary of the New Orleans Council in 1847.[24] He also advanced through the chairs of *Los Amigos del Orden* serving as its worshipful master in 1847. Once serving his term as worshipful master, he was elected a life member of the grand lodge. It must also be pointed out that the invasion of the jurisdiction of the Grand Lodge of Louisiana by the Grand Lodge of Mississippi and the creation of the Louisiana Grand Lodge in 1848 would, surely, have occupied a considerable amount of time with all the worshipful masters of New Orleans Lodges.

The Grand Lodge of Mississippi and the Union of 1850

A faction within the New Orleans English-speaking York Rite Masons felt that the 1844 Constitution of the Grand Lodge of Louisiana sanctioning the cumulation of the three rites worked by lodges in Louisiana (French, Scottish,

21. *The Masonic Delta,* Nov. 1857.

22. Canonge served the Grand Lodge of Louisiana as Grand Master in 1822–24 & 1829 and, also, served as Commander in Chief of the Grand Consistory of Louisiana from 1843–46. Canonge had served as the Grand Senior Warden of the Cerneau Grand Council of Princes of the Royal Secret, 32° in Philadelphia in 1818 and was an early member of the New Orleans Supreme Council, being appointed Grand Expert on Nov. 7, 1839. It was during Canonge's administration as Commander in Chief of the Grand Consistory that this body passed under the jurisdiction of the New Orleans Supreme Council. Prior to his election to the office of Sovereign Grand Commander, Canonge served as the Lt. Grand Commander of the Council. Canonge had the reputation of being a "no nonsense" and "ready to act" individual with an amazing memory. As a criminal court judge he once ordered the arrest of the entire state Supreme Court for interfering in one of his capital trials. *New Orleans Times Democrat,* Jan. 8, 1893, "Louisiana Families."

23. *The Masonic Delta,* Nov. 1857.

24. Foulhouze, *Historical Inquiry* 62.

& York) altered the grand lodge into a body that was no longer a true York Rite Grand Lodge.[25] The decision was made by these Masons to sever their association with the grand lodge and organize themselves into what they felt was proper York Rite Masonry. A committee was formed and a letter of grievance was brought before the Grand Lodge of Mississippi on January 23, 1845.[26] The Grand Master of the Grand Lodge of Mississippi was Mexican War hero and former governor of Mississippi, John Anthony Quitman. The Grand Lodge of Mississippi appointed a committee to go to New Orleans in order to examine the situation. On January 21, 1846, the committee from the Grand Lodge of Mississippi appointed to examine the charges presented by the York Masons from New Orleans presented three reports concerning the events. The first report was presented on behalf of the majority of the committee and concluded that there was "no Grand Lodge of Ancient York Masons within the limits of the State of Louisiana" and that the Grand Lodge of Mississippi had "the power, and it is its duty on proper application, to issue Dispensations and Charters to bodies of Ancient York Masons within the limits of the State of Louisiana, until the constitution of a Grand Lodge within that State."[27] Two "counter" reports were then presented which advised against the Grand Lodge of Mississippi issuing charters within the jurisdiction of the Grand Lodge of Louisiana. The outcome of the events of January 21 (despite the efforts of the two "counter" reports) was the chartering of George Washington Lodge in New Orleans and Lafayette Lodge in Lafayette[28] by the Grand Lodge of Mississippi on February 22. Relations were severed between the Grand Lodges of Louisiana and Mississippi. The Louisiana lodges chartered by the Grand Lodge of Mississippi were declared irregular by the Grand Lodge of Louisiana. In total, the Grand Lodge of Mississippi charterd seven lodges in the New Orleans area by 1848.[29] These seven lodges united to form the "Louisiana Grand Lodge of Ancient York Masons" on March 8, 1848. The

25. See: *The Elimination of the French Influence in Louisiana Masonry* (Charlottesville, Va.: Michael Poll Publishing, 1996).

26. *Report of the Committee on Foreign Correspondence of the Louisiana Grand Lodge of Ancient York Masons* (New Orleans: Cook, Young & Co., 1849.), 5.

27. *Report of the Committee on Foreign Correspondence,* 5.

28. The town of Lafayette was a suburb of New Orleans in the 1800s located in what is now considered the "uptown" area of New Orleans.

29. George Washington, Lafayette, Warren, Marion, Crescent City, Hiram & Eureka.

Grand Lodge of Mississippi received admonishment from most US Grand Lodges and the majority openly condemned its action.[30] While the future for this splinter group of the Grand Lodge of Louisiana may have looked bleak, several events took place to not only strengthen the position of the English-speaking New Orleans Masons, but to assure them of total victory by the loss of French control over all forms of Louisiana Masonry.

One of the last official acts of Grand Commander Jean-François Canonge was a speech made on November 3, 1847, in Baton Rouge in which he is reported as stating that a circular issued by the Mississippi lodges in New Orleans was "unworthy of notice."[31] Canonge died on January 19, 1848. On January 31, 1848, James Foulhouze was elected Grand Commander of the New Orleans Supreme Council. The Foulhouze election bypassed a number of senior members of the council and, clearly, established the popularity of Foulhouze with the council. Foulhouze had brought with him various rituals from France[32] which he edited for the New Orleans Council.[33] During the same month as the death of Canonge and the election of Foulhouze, the Charleston Council was talking an action that greatly strengthened its own position and further weakened the hold of the French-speaking New Orleans Masons. Albert Mackey (the Grand Secretary of the Charleston Council) sent a notice to the *Freemason's Monthly Magazine*[34] (Boston) which read:

> At a special session of the Supreme Council ... for the Southern Jurisdiction of the United States of America, our Illustrious Brother, John A. Quitman ... Major General in the Army of the United States, was elected to fill a vacancy in this Supreme Council, and was duly and formally inaugurated a Sovereign Grand

30. *Grand Lodge of the State of Louisiana Report and Exposition* (New Orleans: J.L Sollée, 1849), 5–34.

31. James B. Scot, *Outline of the Rise and Progress of Freemasonry in Louisiana* (1873; reprint, Charlottesville, Va.: Michael Poll Publishing, 1995), 76.

32. Charles Laffon de Ladébat, *Ancient and Accepted Rite. Thirtieth Degree* (New Orleans: 1857), xxvii.

33. De Ladébat states in a footnote of his published 18° ritual, "The philosophical explanation of this and of all the other Degrees from the First up to the Thirtieth inclusive, is taken from the work of Ill.·. Bro.·. J. Foulhouze, 33d, with some slight alterations, of which, the author willingly assumes the responsibility." De Ladébat, *Ancient and Accepted Scotch Rite. Eighteenth Degree* (New Orleans: 1856), 123. Foulhouze had, also, rewritten the 33° for the New Orleans Council. See James D. Carter *History of the Supreme Council, 33° S.J., U.S.A. (1861–1891)* (Washington, DC: The Supreme Council 33°, 1967), 37.

34. The title of this magazine is sometimes given as *Freemasons' Magazine*. Many thanks to Alain Bernheim for this discovery.

SUPREME COUNCIL

OF THE

SOVEREIGN GRAND INSPECTORS GENERAL

33d and Last Degree of the Scotch Rite,

In the United States of America, sitting in the City of New Orleans.

JAMES FOULHOUZE, Sovereign Grand Commander.
FRANCOIS VERRIER, Lieut.·. S.·. Gr.·. Comm.·. Founder.
JEAN LAMOTHE, Gr.·. Chanc.·. Sec.·. of the H.·. Empire.
J. B. FAGET, Gr.·. Treas.·. of the H.·. Empire.
J. H. HOLLAND, Gr.·. Master of Cerem.·.
ROB. J. L. de PREAUX, Gr.·. Capt.·. of the Guards.
RAMON VIONNET, Gr.·. Almoner or Chaplain.
FRANCOIS MEILLEUR, Standard Bearer.
FELIX GARCIA, S.·. G.·. T.·. G.·.
PIERRE SOULE, S.·. G.·. T.·. G.·.
G. A. MONTMAIN, S.·. G.·. T.·. G.·.

REPRESENTATIVE AND WARRANTER OF FRIENDSHIP

Of the Grand Orient of France near the Sup.·. Council.

N——————.

N. B.—The Supreme Council, regularly constituted according to the Scotch Rite, is in friendly and fraternal correspondence with the Grand Lodge of the State of Louisiana, and the foreign Grand Orients; and the members of the Sup.·. Council are all officers and members in activity of the Grand Lodge.

Officers of the Supreme Council in the United States of America, sitting in New Orleans, showing James Foulhouze as Sovereign Grand Commander. From the 1848 *Proceedings of the Grand Lodge of Louisiana.*

> Inspector General of the 33d. All Consistories, Councils, Chapters and Lodges under this jurisdiction are hereby ordered to obey and respect him accordingly.[35]

On January 29, 1849, the Grand Lodge of Louisiana published a report that Foulhouze wrote for them concerning the cumulation of the rites practiced by the grand lodge and on February 26 the grand lodge published Foulhouze's report on the 1833 concordat. Both reports upheld the positions of the Grand Lodge of Louisiana and encouraged the continued practice of the cumulation of the rites in Louisiana.

On September 14, 1849, Foulhouze, along with a several other New Orleans Masons, were honored by Friends of Harmony Lodge (whose Worshipful Master was elder Past Grand Master and New Orleans Supreme Council Member John Henry Holland) by being made honorary members of the lodge. An excerpt from the minutes of the Lodge reads:

> WHEREAS by their great ability and impartiality our well beloved Brethren JOSEPH WALKER, JAS. FOULHOUZE, P. WILLMAN, JOHN D. KEMPER & R. PREAUX have earned the destination of Honorary Membership, their services in the Masonic vineyard entitling them to some suitable token or tribute of appreciation of their worth, and of the high respect entertained for their estimable personal and Masonic character—they being Brethren to whom a burdened may pour out his sorrows, to whom distress may prefer its suit; Brethren whose hands are guided by justice and whose hearts are expanded by benevolence.
>
> Therefore be it now decreed, that the aforesaid distinguished Brethren be and they are hereby created Honorary Members of the Friends of Harmony Lodge of F & A Masons, this as a testimony of regard for the inestimable services as Masons, and their courtesy, affability and kindness as men—well worthy of imitation and the foregoing preamble and resolution being seconded and put is carried unanimously.[36]

THE UNION OF 1850

The 1848 Louisiana Grand Lodge obtained recognition from only one other Grand Lodge—the Grand Lodge of Mississippi. In 1849 John Gedge, a New Orleans attorney, was elected Grand Master of the Louisiana Grand Lodge. Despite the irregularity of the Louisiana Grand Lodge and the lack of support

35. Charles S. Lobingier, *The Supreme Council, 33°* (Louisville, Ky.: The Standard Printing Co., Inc., 1931), 172; Ray Baker Harris, James D. Carter, *History of the Supreme Council, 33° S.J., U.S.A. (1801–1861)* (Washington, DC: The Supreme Council 33°, 1964), 236.

36. Minutes Book, Friends of Harmony Lodge No. 58,. Sep. 14, 1849.

for this new grand lodge within the Masonic community, the Grand Lodge of Louisiana entered into negotiations and finally merged with this body in 1850. The Grand Lodge of Louisiana was left with little choice in this matter. The fact that the Grand Lodge of Louisiana was overwhelmingly considered the "regular" Grand Lodge was not sufficient to overcome the internal problems stemming from the cultural divisions in New Orleans. By mid-1849, it was likely realized that the English-speaking lodges that had remained loyal to the grand lodge were showing signs that continued loyalty would, most likely, not happen. Obviously realizing that the total collapse of the Grand Lodge of Louisiana was a very real possibility, the Grand Lodge of Louisiana and the Louisiana Grand Lodge entered into talks designed to merge the two bodies.[37] That merger took place in June of 1850 with the approval of a new constitution of the Grand Lodge of Louisiana of Free and Accepted Masons. Under the terms of the agreement of the merger, the Louisiana Grand Lodge members became recognized as "regular" by the Grand Lodge of Louisiana. All lodges chartered by the Louisiana Grand Lodge (or by the Grand Lodge of Mississippi in Louisiana) passed under the jurisdiction of the new Grand Lodge of Louisiana. While the new constitution appeared to merge the two grand lodges, the Grand Lodge of Louisiana was, in effect, taken over by the Louisiana Grand Lodge. All non-York Rite lodges were instructed to turn in their charters to receive new York Rite charters from the new grand lodge. Three Scottish Rite lodges, *Étoile Polaire, Los Amigos del Orden,* and Disciples of the Masonic Senate, sought relief from the New Orleans Supreme Council. Of these events Foulhouze wrote:

> It was agreed that the Grand Lodge should no more *cumulate* the rites, that it would have and keep its own forms, but that each Lodge in the East might freely work according to its particular and more favorite rite and tenets.
>
> Had that agreement been faithfully observed, another series of quiet days might have ensued in Louisiana: but the newcomers in the Grand Lodge soon showed that far from being sincere, they had crept into our bosom with the only view to tear it to pieces and to build their powers on the ruins of ours....
>
> They made as I had foreseen and foretold, a Constitution by which the Scotch lodges of the East were reduced to nought and the life members of the

37. James Scot, *Outline of the Rise and Progress of Freemasonry in Louisiana* (Charlottesville, Va.: Michael Poll Publishing, 1995), 78–80.

> Grand Lodge expelled from it[38] the better to secure the triumph and power of those invaders.
>
> But from the moment that the constitution began to work, the Scotch lodges understood their mistake; and not withstanding the blame thrown upon them by the new Grand Lodge which was as it was expected, did not fail to say that they were bound by the vote of the majority at Baton Rouge, they all parted from it, averting and showing that they had been deceived, and could not thus be fetted and annihilated by a paltry trick.
>
> That event occasioned a good deal of rumor. The Mississippians who had snatched the power began promulgating their bulls of excommunication. John Gedge, like his imitators of this present Consistory, wrote his reports, made his speeches, sent his circulars, but it was to no purpose.
>
> The Supreme Council of Louisiana resumed its authority on the blue lodges of the Scotch rite, and the separation was consummated.[39]

If the goal of the new 1850 grand lodge constitution and the merger with the Louisiana Grand Lodge was to bring peace to all the Louisiana Masons, it was a total failure. If the goal was to remove the power base in the grand lodge from the French-speaking New Orleans Masons, it was, indeed, a success. The French-speaking New Orleans Masons became split after 1850. One faction, outraged at the turn of events, wished nothing more to do with the grand lodge and saw the supreme council as the only hope of maintaining the French interests. The other French faction, most likely very tired of the squabbles, remained with the grand lodge in the hopes of possibly still bringing unity to the troubled grand lodge.

The 1850 Union of the Grand Lodge resulted in a perceived need for action in the New Orleans Council. Foulhouze believed that he could strengthen the New Orleans Scottish Rite by expanding the number of 33rds in the Council. Foulhouze says of this:

> Brother Canonge died and I was elected commander in his place. My first move was to promote to the 33d degree one or two members of each of the lodges then established and of some importance in the city of New Orleans,

38. Prior to the Grand Lodge Constitution of 1850 Past Masters of the constituted lodges were made Life Members of the Grand Lodge with voting rights in the Grand Lodge. Following the Constitution of 1850, voting rights were only given to Grand Lodges Officers, the three principal members of each lodge, Past Grand Masters and Grand Lodge Committee members.

39. *The Masonic Delta,* Nov. 1857.

hoping that their initiation would be the best means to secure the masonic peace in our East, as it would contribute to carry light where it was most needed."[40]

During Foulhouze's administration of the New Orleans Supreme Council prior to the concordat, he elevated approximately thirty Masons to the 33rd Degree in the New Orleans Council.[41] Those elevated to the 33rd degree by Foulhouze included Charles Claiborne, Thomas Wharton Collens (June 22, 1849), Claude Pierre Samory, and Charles Laffon de Ladébat (February 11, 1852). The wisdom of expanding the membership of the Supreme Council was recognized by Albert Pike on March 25, 1859, (Pike's first Supreme Council Session as Grand Commander) when he expanded the membership in the Charleston Council from nine members to thirty-three members.

Charles Claiborne assumed the post of Secretary General for the New Orleans Council and T. Wharton Collens, that of Lt. Grand Commander. The Foulhouze/Collens relationship was a very close one which continued until Foulhouze's death in 1875—years after both had resigned from Masonry. Foulhouze and Collens would, in the early 1850s, even share a law office.

THE LOPEZ EXPEDITION AND JAMES FOULHOUZE

If the Union of 1850 between the Grand Lodge of Louisiana and the Louisiana Grand Lodge, along with the many bomb shells from that event, were not enough to occupy the minds of the Louisiana Masons, an event took place simultaneously that over-shadowed the Masonic events in Louisiana and thrust into the forefront of the minds and thoughts of all Americans. This international event directly played a part in future New Orleans Masonic "battles."

In 1849 Narciso Lopez, an adventurous Venezuelan, began a campaign to take control of Cuba and replace the Spanish government on the island with his own government. Lopez received limited support from various US politicians, but was unable to raise a suitable sized army for his mission. Lopez found better luck in New Orleans were he was able to raise an army of approximately 750 men, mainly veterans of the Mexican War, and to sail out of New Orleans in April of 1850 with the goal of capturing the island. The mission was

40. *The Masonic Delta,* Nov. 1857.

41. The numbers vary according to the source. *The Annual Grand Communication of the Supreme Council,* 1859, viii, lists 26 new 33rds. Albert Pike, *Official Bulletin VIII*, 1886, 571–72 lists 31 new 33rds.

a complete failure. The US troops were slaughtered and Lopez was eventually captured and executed. Reports quickly came to the US and the newspapers of the day reported the "murder" of the US troops along with the capture and execution of not only troops, but vacationing US tourists who happened to be on the island. New Orleans was an obvious "hot spot" for the Lopez Expedition as, not only did the expedition leave from New Orleans, but the city contained many Spanish-speaking citizens from Cuba. During its early years the Grand Lodge of Louisiana had also chartered two Lodges in Cuba.[42] The tie between New Orleans and Cuba was close for both the general and Masonic population.

James Foulhouze became entwined in the Lopez Expedition when he traveled to Cuba at the height of the crisis. A New Orleans newspaper, the *Daily Delta,* ran a story on Foulhouze vehemently criticizing his trip, and suggesting that he was, possibly, a spy for the Spanish government.[43] The very evening following the publication of the article concerning Foulhouze, T. Wharton Collens and Robert Preaux published an article in the *Daily Picayune* explaining that Foulhouze's trip to Cuba was with the goal of, hopefully, securing the release of vacationing US citizens who were caught in the conflict.[44] Foulhouze, being made a Mason in a Spanish-speaking Lodge, had numerous interactions with New Orleans Masons from Cuba. In addition, Foulhouze had gained the confidence of various Spanish officials on the island of Cuba through acting as legal council for them several years earlier. Along with the article published by Collens and Preaux, the *Delta* article on Foulhouze received censure by a number of competing New Orleans newspapers. The *Delta* article was exposed to be a newspaper "thriller" story with little basis in fact. One newspaper entitling an article critical of the *Delta's* lack of support for its charges "Newspaper Intolerance"[45] and another paper calling a report on Foulhouze's trip "A Mission of Humanity."[46] The *Delta* ran one more article in defense of its position claiming that the matter would be settled when Foulhouze returned to

42. *Reunion Fraternal de Caridad* in Havana, Jul. 12, 1815, and *El Templo de la Devina Pastora* in Matanzaz, Jul. 12, 1818, *Proceedings of the Grand Lodge of Louisiana,* 1995 (A–2 & 3).

43. *New Orleans Daily Delta,* May 31, 1850.

44. *The Daily Picayune,* New Orleans, Louisiana, May 31, 1850.

45. *The Daily Crescent New Orleans,* Louisiana, Jun. 1, 1850.

46. *Daily Orleanian, New Orleans,* Louisiana, Jun. 2, 1850.

New Orleans and the entire event would be brought to the attention of the public.[47] Nothing more, however, was published on the matter by the *Delta*. The event passed from the public's attention and was attributed to one newspaper's attempt to sensationalize anything concerning a recent event with the possible goal of increasing its sale of newspapers.

ENTER THE CHARLESTON SUPREME COUNCIL

John Gedge, who in 1849 was the grand master of the irregular Louisiana Grand Lodge, was elected grand master of the Grand Lodge of Louisiana for the year 1851. On March 27, 1858, the New Orleans Council issued a manifesto in its own defense. This manifesto examined the New Orleans situation and was an appeal for the establishment of fraternal relations between the New Orleans Council and other Masonic Bodies world-wide. With Louisiana Masonry in a state of turmoil and the once powerful New Orleans Supreme Council fighting for order and stability, the time for the Charleston Council to act was at hand.

At the invitation of John Gedge, Albert Mackey came to New Orleans in February of 1852 and established, for the Charleston Council, a Consistory of the Thirty-second Degree. Gedge served as Commander in Chief. The establishment of this Charleston Consistory in New Orleans resulted in a new wave of turmoil and paved the way for the Concordat of 1855 merging the Charleston and New Orleans Councils.

The New Orleans Supreme Council responded to the Charleston Consistory in New Orleans by taking several measures. A notice critical of the new consistory was place in the *New Orleans Bee* by the New Orleans Supreme Council on February 27, 1852.[48] The notice carried the names of the then twenty-nine Active Members[49] of the New Orleans Council. The New Orleans Council, also, incorporated itself under the official name of "Supreme Council of the Thirty-three [*sic*] and last degree of the Ancient and Accepted Scotch

47. *New Orleans Daily Delta*. Jun. 1, 1850.

48. *New Orleans Bee,* Feb. 27, 1852.

49. James Foulhouze, T. W. Collens, Charles Claiborne, J. B. Faget, Felix Garcia, F. A. Lumsden, Joseph Walker, John L. Lewis, Robert Preaux, Charles Murian, S. Heriman, Jean Lamothe, Antonio Costa, A. P. Lanaux, G. A. Montmain, F. Correjolles, J. H. Holland, R. D. Fanis, J. E. Jolly, J. Bachino, Aug. Broué, M. Prados, F. Ricau, J. J. E. Massicott, François Meilleur, C. M. Emerson, H. G. Duvivier, C. Samory & Charles Laffon.

Rite for the United States of America, sitting at New Orleans, State of Louisiana." The act of incorporation was signed on June 7, 1852, and approved by the secretary of state, the noted Charles Gayarre, on January 13, 1853.[50]

In July of 1852 Foulhouze traveled to New York to install Henry C. Atwood as grand commander of the "Supreme Council of the Thirty-third Degree of and for the Free, Sovereign and Independent State of New York" and then journeyed on to France in an attempt to enlist French support for his cause. It is noteworthy that Foulhouze embraced the concept that supreme councils should be limited to state jurisdictions just as grand lodges.[51]

THE CONCORDAT OF 1855

The speed in which the total loss of the Grand Lodge of Louisiana by the French-speaking Masons occured caused obvious confusion and uncertainty as to the future. James Foulhouze, as Grand Commander of the New Orleans Supreme Council, sought to unite all of the French-speaking Masons under his banner. Whether it was because of the rapid advancement of Foulhouze (resulting in uncertainty in his ability) or simply personality conflicts, Foulhouze was unable to unite all of the French Masons. The conflict of opinions within the New Orleans Supreme Council as to the direction in which to proceed can reasonably be seen as a contributing factor to the resignation of Foulhouze on July 30, 1853, and nearly all of the officers of the New Orleans Council by December of 1853. The final break for Foulhouze appears to have occurred at the June 22 meeting of the New Orleans Council. At that meeting,

50. *The Masonic Delta,* Aug. 1857.

51. An interesting document resides in the New Orleans Scottish Rite Library and Museum. It is a handwritten copy of the 1846 General Regulations of the New Orleans Supreme Council. This document is of special interest as it was used as a "working copy" for the 1848 General Regulations which were approved on Jul. 20, 1848. The document contains the notes and changes throughout made by James Foulhouze with his signature. Clearly the various changes were presented to the Council for approval. The official name "The Supreme Council for the United States of America Sitting in New Orleans" at the head of the Regulations has portions scratched out leaving the only "The Supreme Council sitting in New Orleans." In addition, the side margins contain the proposed changes. In addition to the official name being altered to remove "for the United States of America," the proposed change to "for the State of Louisiana" written in the margin was also scratched out. Presumably the new title did not pass the vote of the Council or Foulhouze decided not to propose this name change—at that time. It is significant, however, to realize that Foulhouze, from the early days of his administration, considered the Supreme Council structure as possibly being limited to state boundaries just as Grand Lodges.

T. Wharton Collens had prepared a series of resolutions to present to the council. After a reading of the resolutions, the floor was opened for comment, but instead of addressing the points of the various resolutions, Charles Claiborne apparently began a series of attacks on Foulhouze's clothing. The meeting fell into shouting matches and the deep-rooted feelings of frustration from the events of the past years seemingly boiled up. Foulhouze, realizing that control of the meeting was lost, closed the council and departed.[52]

In the absence of the minutes of the New Orleans Council during the Foulhouze years[53] it can only be presumed that T. Wharton Collens assumed the post of acting grand commander for the remainder of 1853 until his own resignation on December 19 of that year. The day following the resignation of Collens, the grand treasurer, Jean Baptiste Faget, turned in his letter of resignation, and an undated letter of resignation from the grand secretary, J. J. E. Massicott, was also accepted by the Council.

On January 7, 1854, Charles Claiborne was elected grand commander of the New Orleans Council. Claude Pierre Samory was elected lt. grand Commander and Charles Laffon de Ladébat was appointed grand secretary. Samory and de Ladébat were part of the French-speaking faction that split from Foulhouze during the 1850–53 turmoil. The year 1854 was devoted to negotiations with the Charleston Supreme Council. February 6 & 17, 1855, the concordat merging the New Orleans and Charleston Supreme Councils was signed. Present in New Orleans for the signing of the concordat, and representing the Charleston Council, were Albert Mackey and John Quitman. John Gedge, who had spearheaded the movement of the Louisiana Grand Lodge and the 1852 consistory, did not live to see the concordat between the New

52. This account can not be confirmed in totality by any existing official record, but is recounted in an old unsigned handwritten paper located in the New Orleans Scottish Rite Library and Museum. In the notes of the 1859 A Masonic Trial in New Orleans, Charles Laffon de Laébat writes of the event: "... An opportunity offered and that was ther address of Ill.·. Bro. Chas. Claiborne who, instead of arguing the point at issue, that is, the merits and demerits of the 20 articles, amused himself by ridiculing the masonic costumes of Mr. Foulhouze. Mr. Foulhouze was stung to the quick and swore, in leaving the hall, that he had done with Masonry! He sent in his letter of resigination on the 30th of July 1853." 43.

53. Alain Bernheim located the minutes of the New Orleans Council from its creation to Feb. 15, 1847, in the Bibliothèque Nationale in Paris in 1987. This writer located the minutes of the New Orleans Council from the election of Charles Claiborne to the Concordat of 1855 in the Library of the New Orleans Scottish Rite Bodies in 1994.

Orleans and Charleston Councils—he died on April 13, 1854, during a yellow fever epidemic in New Orleans.

The death of Gedge must have created some concern for the future of the newly reorganized Scottish Rite Masonry in New Orleans. Gedge had led a complete and total coup of the grand lodge, dramatically altering its nature. It was, also, Gedge who had written to Mackey to bring a Charleston consistory to New Orleans and took control of this consistory as he did the grand lodge. The introduction of the Charleston consistory paved the way for the Concordat of 1855. His influence on the events of the times is unquestionable. It is reasonable to assume that Gedge might have taken some position of leadership in the post-concordat days—had he lived. It is logical that Gedge would have become an active member of the Charleston Supreme Council and led the reorganized Grand Consistory of Louisiana. The death of Gedge made this impossible, yet the basic problem remained. A powerful figure was needed to lead and unite the very fragmented New Orleans Scottish Rite. Regardless of the fact that the concordat had taken place, there were still quite a number of former New Orleans Council 33rds unaffiliated with the Charleston Council—or any council. The potential for uprising was undeniable. In a letter to Claude Samory, Albert Mackey suggested that the man to lead and unite the New Orleans Scottish Rite Masons had been found and it was believed that only the formalities remained. Mackey wrote:

> I hope to be present at the installation of that Bro∴ as S∴G∴I∴G∴ whose adhesion to us will heal all difficulties.... The moment we receive your nomination, the nominated Bro∴ will be elected.[54]

The man Mackey wrote of was James Foulhouze. The choosing of Foulhouze to join the Charleston Council and lead the New Orleans Scottish Rite *for* the Charleston Council is very reasonable and, given the situation, the only logical choice that could be made. Foulhouze was viewed as a regular 33rd from the Grand Orient of France. As Foulhouze was also a former grand commander of the New Orleans Supreme Council who had resigned prior to the concordat, he might have been viewed as something of a prominent "free agent." The fact that Foulhouze was a member (and even grand commander) of the New Orleans Council was irrelevant from a regularity stand point. If

54. *Official Bulletin viii,* 1886, p 536.

he agreed to join with the Charleston Council then this matter could be easily settled. Samory and de Ladébat were also members of the New Orleans Council (and both given the 33rd degree *by* Foulhouze), yet both became active members and officers of the Charleston Council. If James Foulhouze agreed to lead the New Orleans Scottish Rite, under the Charleston Council banner, the Charleston Council would have a much easier road to travel in bringing the remainder of the New Orleans Scottish Rite Masons under their control. Foulhouze was approached by Albert Mackey and Claude Samory in the summer of 1856 and offered the position of commander-in-chief of the Grand Consistory and active membership in the Southern Jurisdiction providing that he joined the Charleston camp.[55] Of this event Foulhouze wrote:

> About a year or fifteen months ago, M. Antonio Costa asked me whether I had any objection to converse with M. Claude Samory about the then state of affairs with regard to the Scottish Rite in Louisiana. I answered that I had none. On the following day M. Samory together with M. Costa called on me, and in his presence, told me that he had long been anxious to see me, that he was always my friend, that the course which he and other members of the Supreme Council of Louisiana had followed since I left it was with the only view of putting an end to any further contest and quarrel both with the Grand Lodge of our state and the Supreme Council of Charleston, that many a York mason of this east was now initiated to the high degrees of the Scottish Rite, that they all had heard of me as being well versed in its tenets and ceremonies, and were anxious to see me join the Consistory thereto assume the command of the Rite in Louisiana, that indeed I had just cause to complain of the conduct of some BB.·. towards me both in the Supreme Council and in the Polar Star Lodge, but that they all acknowledged it, and were ready on my joining the Grand Consistory, to offer me any apology I might wish, that there was a vacancy in the Supreme Council of Charleston which he had been offered to fill, and which he was ready to give up in my behalf if I would unite with them, that my presence in that Council would do immense good both here and at Charleston, and that the best I could do was to accept, if I desired to carry out my opinion and views with regard to the right which Louisiana has to its Supreme Council.
>
> My answer to M. Samory was as follows:

55. Foulhouze, *Historical Inquiry*, 78. *The Masonic Delta*, Aug. 1857 & March 1858. Charles Laffon de Ladébat, trans., *A Masonic Trial in New Orleans* (Lamarre's Defense) (New Orleans: J. Lamarre, 1858), 43–44. Note: *A Masonic Trial in New Orleans* was written by Joseph Lamarre and originally published in French. The work was translated into English and republished that same year. The name of the translator is not given in this work. Charles Laffon de Ladébat states on 83 of *Dissection of the Manifesto of Mr. Charles Bienienu* (New Orleans: privately published, 1858) that he was the translastor for Lamarre's work and author of the notes in that book.

I need no apology, for any thing which may have been done or said in any masonic body to hurt my feelings. Masonry, thank God, has taught me better desires, and it is enough for me to hear from you that all those who may have had an intention to offend me, do now regret it. As to your proposal, I can in no way or manner accept it. My position is clear and well defined. The Supreme Council of Louisiana was not founded by me. It existed before I was a mason. In 1845 I received, not in the Supreme Council of France founded by M. Grasse de Tilly, but in the Supreme Council of the Grand Orient, the 33d degree. That most Illustrious body treated me as a future member of the Supreme Council of Louisiana with which it corresponded, and I was commissioned by its Grand Commander and other members to be the interpreter of their good feelings near our Supreme Council. A short time after my return here, our Grand Commander Jean François Canonge died, and I was elected to replace him. On doing so, I bound myself to obey it and protect its rights: and I must say that after a most serious inquiry into its origin and the sources from which it emanates, I am more than ever convinced that my opinion with regard to the fundamental authority of the Scottish Rite is correct, and that the views of Charleston thereon are altogether erroneous. From the moment you and other 33rds of this East judged fit to recognize the Council of Charleston as your superior, I and two other members of our Supreme Council, did immediately exercise what, in such case we considered to be our right, and continued the work of our Supreme Council. It is true that on account of the momentary excitement which has prevailed, we have chosen to be silent, but we exist nevertheless and have resolved to safeguard our power and authority for any case of emergency. I certainly feel much honored with the proposition which you make me to accept an appointment as an active member of the Supreme Council of Charleston and as such to preside your Consistory here, but neither such a flattering offer, nor any other consideration can make me deviate from what I consider to be my duty towards a body which I have sworn to protect. I have personally no pretension whatsoever to power. I know that I am good only to make an initiation, and I acknowledge that the privilege of commanding should be better placed in other hands than mine. Many a person, no doubt, will attribute my determination to a spirit of opposition, but as I feel good will towards all and even those who condemn me both in York and Scottish [*sic*] ranks of Masonry, I will, happen what it may, persevere following the line which I believe to be the only correct one.

Thereupon, M. Samory expressed his hope that I would change my mind, and asked me whether I would like to converse with M. Albert G. Mackey on that subject. I answered affirmatively and two or three days afterward, he called at my house with that Gentleman.

M. Mackey began by expressing a desire that his visit to me should not be considered as official. I replied that being both knights templars, we were authorized to meet as such and talk of the questions relative to the Scottish Rite, as if we were perfect strangers to it; and it being so agreed, he repeated to me all that

> M. Samory had said before with regard to the desire expressed by a large number of masons that I should join the consistory, and with regard to my being made an active member of the Council of Charleston and taking as such command of the Scotish rite in Louisiana. I answered him what I had already answered M. Samory. A few words where then exchanged between him and me, with regard to the origin of the council of Charleston, the constitutions [*sic*] of 1786, the authority which the Supreme Council of the Grand Orient of France claims on the Scotish degrees and the differences which exists between the York and Scotish rites. He admitted that difference and that the reasons which I gave upon all the other points presented a strong matter of consideration, but that he could not accept them as conclusive, which I immediately understood and acknowledged to be with him a matter of course.
>
> He then insisted that I should again consider the proposition made by Mr. C. Samory, and confirmed by himself; and in conclusion he wished me to let him know what my determination would be after more mature reflection.
>
> I promised to do so through Mr. Samory: and this Gentleman having called on me some weeks afterwards, and repeated all that he had been kind enough to say at his first interview with me, I again answered that I could not accept: and I remember having thus addressed him in the end:
>
> "My dear Sir, in the same manner as the masons whom you now represent, express a desire to have me in your Consistory for their best interest, so a time may come when Scotish masons of this East, tired of a foreign dominion, shall be glad to know that there is in New Orleans a 33d of some value who has never varied, and can at any time be the strong hold around which they may gather as Louisianians."
>
> Thereon we parted good friends as I parted with Mr. Mackey, after due interchange of kindness and politeness.[56]

In 1858, Charles Laffon de Ladébat, while clearly bitter towards Foulhouze, commented on this meeting between Foulhouze, Samory, and Mackey:

> Ill Bros. Mackey and Samory knew very well that with a few persons, amoung the weak minded and the ignorant, Mr. Foulhouze was "somebody," and that if they could prevail on him to join the Grand Consistory of Louisiana, peace would be finally restored, and it was solely for the purpose of securing that peace, that they paid him a visit, against the advise of many who knew Mr. Foulhouze better than they.[57]

With John Gedge dead and Foulhouze no longer in consideration, Claude Samory became the first New Orleans Mason to be elected an active member of the Charleston Council. His election was on November 20, 1856. On

56. *The Masonic Delta,* Aug. 1857.

57. De Ladébat, *A Masonic Trial in New Orleans,* 43.

December 17, 1856, the grand consistory filled the vacancy offered to James Foulhouze. The choice was a Mason of promise but of little training in the Scottish Rite. The attorney from Arkansas, Albert Pike, was unanimously (and in his absence[58]) elected Commander in Chief of the Grand Consistory of Louisiana.

Prior to the election of Samory and Pike, Foulhouze took part in an activity which sealed his fate with the Charleston Council. James Foulhouze, along with T. W. Collens, J. J. E. Massicott, J. B. Faget and other former members of the New Orleans Supreme Council declared, in effect, the Concordat of 1855 invalid and publicly resumed the activities of the New Orleans Council. The date that the New Orleans Council was re-opened is sometimes disputed. Foulhouze stated in November of 1857:

> From the moment I had noticed of that nameless act [the Concordat of 1855], I called upon some 33ds, whom I knew to be true to their obligations, and with them I immediately opened the Supreme Council and continued its work, in order that it might not even be said that it had slept a single instant....[59]

If such a meeting of 33rds did take place, it was still not until October 9, 1856, that J. J. E. Massicott would be elected Grand Commander of the reorganized New Orleans Supreme Council and their activities become public. That action was the "shot" which started a new round of Masonic turbulence which dramatically altered the nature of the US Scottish Rite.

THE RE-ORIGINATION OF THE SUPREME COUNCIL OF LOUISIANA

The days/months/years following the concordat were a time of great uncertainty with many New Orleans Masons. The arguments made by all sides sounded somewhat reasonable. An examination of who chose to associate with the Charleston Council after the concordat, who choose to associate with the revived New Orleans Council, and who chose to associate with neither body provides an interesting look into the divided, confused, and emotional state of affairs. Of the Grand Lodge of Louisiana officers who were active members of the New Orleans Council in the pre-concordat days, two of the five past

58. *Albert Pike, His Address before the Grand Consistory of Louisiana, April 29, 1857* (Charlottesville, Va.: Michael Poll Publishing, 1997), 1.

59. *The Masonic Delta,* Nov. 1857.

grand masters[60] chose to affiliate with neither body. One affiliated with the Charleston Council[61] and two with the revived New Orleans Council.[62] Of the eight senior grand lodge officers, two chose to affiliate with neither body,[63] two with the Charleston Council[64] and four with the revived New Orleans Council.[65] Of the non-grand lodge New Orleans 33rds in the pre-concordat days, eight chose to associate with neither body, fifteen with the Charleston Council and four with the revived New Orleans Council. The totals then would be: twelve choosing to affiliate with neither body, nineteen with the Charleston Council and ten with the revived New Orleans Council. These figures should not, however, be viewed as the final tally as they were, over the following years, modified as members moved from one body to the other in a most disconcerting manner. L. E. Deluzain, who was a participant in the 1855 concordat affiliating with the Charleston Council, reaffiliated with the revived New Orleans Council upon its revival. Joseph Lamarre, who was created a 33rd in the revived New Orleans Council on February 25, 1858, was tried and expelled by that Council on May 22, 1858. He then affiliated with the Grand Consistory of Louisiana becoming an honorary 33rd. Neither side could truly claim clear victory as the severely bitter strife left both sides with ragged edges. Many of those who chose one side or the other eventually retired from any Masonic affiliation.

Possibly concerned over the reorganization of the New Orleans Council, the Grand Consistory of Louisiana sought to organize itself into a state corporation in early 1857. On March 19, 1857, the General Assembly of the Louisiana State Senate and House of Representatives approved the incorporation of the Grand Consistory of Louisiana. Listed as members were two future Sovereign Grand Commanders of the Charleston Council—Albert Pike and James C. Batchelor. On April 22, 1857, Foulhouze was elected Grand Commander of the revived New Orleans Council; T. Wharton Collens resumed his former position as Lt. Grand Commander. With Foulhouze back in command, the New Orleans Council began to grow in strength and size. The year 1858 was

60. Felix Garcia, Lucien Hermann.
61. John Henry Holland.
62. Jean Lamothe and Robert Preaux.
63. Ramon Vionnet and Stephen Herriman.
64. François Meilleur and Charles Murian.
65. Jean B. Faget, Jean J. E. Massicott, Romain Brugier and Joseph Lisbony.

pivotal for Foulhouze, and for the reorganized New Orleans Supreme Council. In February, Albert Pike delivered a lecture before the Grand Lodge of Louisiana. His lecture was a sharp assault on Foulhouze and the New Orleans Council. The lecture by Pike, and arguments against it, occupied most of the March 1858 issue of the *Masonic Delta.*[66] Clearly the Charleston camp had found a Mason as capable of the "stinging pen" as Foulhouze. February 1858 also brought a commanding new (returning) member to the New Orleans Council. The announcement in the *Masonic Delta* was sure to cause great concern in the Charleston/New Orleans camp:

> We are happy to say that our most Ill∴ and worthy Bro∴ Pierre Soulé has joined the Supreme Council of the 33d, in and for the Sovereign and Independent State of Louisiana. This eminent citizen and learned Free-mason admits thus the State Rights masonically as well as politically.[67]

The return of this fiery and powerful former United States Senator and US Minister to Spain to the rolls of the New Orleans Supreme Council was the equivalent of a shot of adrenaline for the New Orleans Council. Soulé was created a 33rd on March 8, 1838, by Jean Jacques Conte and was, actually, a member of the New Orleans Supreme Council prior to the election of Foulhouze as Grand Commander. Soulé resigned from the Council at some point following Foulhouze's election as his name is no where to be found in any of the records concerning the Concordat of 1855. There are no known records giving the reasons for the resignation of Soulé from the Council nor his Masonic activities during, or thoughts of, the concordat. Soulé was elected a US Senator in 1847 and served in that office until 1853 followed by his appointment as Minister to Spain from 1853–55. Soulé was a vocal, resourceful and respected addition to the New Orleans Council.

The addition of Pierre Soulé as an active member of the New Orleans Council was answered by the addition of Albert Pike as an active member of the Charleston Council on March 20, 1858.[68] At the very session which elected

66. The revived New Orleans Council's monthly publication.

67. *The Masonic Delta,* Feb. 1858.

68. Although Pike was elected an Active Member in March, it was not until Jul. 7 that Mackey would send the official general notification of his election. Harris, Carter, *History,* 260. Mackey would, however, inform Claude Samory of Pike's election on May 8, 1859. *Official Bulletin,* vol. VIII, 544.

Pike as an Active Member, Foulhouze was formally "expelled" from the Scottish Rite by the Charleston Council. Since Foulhouze was never a member of any body controlled by the Charleston Council, this action was more of a public statement of disapproval than an actual expulsion. What followed next was a series of "sledge hammer" verbal and written attacks from and upon both the New Orleans and Charleston Councils. The extremely bitter attacks surpassed even the Cerneau "war" (ca. 1813–1830s) which resulted in the death of all "High-Grade" Scottish Rite Masonry in the US with the exception of in New Orleans. Foulhouze released his *Mémoire à Consulter* in French in 1858 and, then in 1859, issue his *Historical Inquiry into the Origin of the Ancient and Accepted Scottish Rite* in English.[69] The book served as the platform from which Foulhouze stated his case, defined his actions and views on regularity, as well as his concepts of the history of the Scottish Rite. Foulhouze also used the *Masonic Delta* as a platform. This monthly publication was the official organ of the revived New Orleans Supreme Council. Joseph Lamarre released his *A Masonic Trial in New Orleans* in French in 1858 and Charles Laffon de translated and added notes to the work for an English edition. The next major New Orleans Masonic publication was a work designed to answer Foulhouze's *Mémoire à Consulter* and further state the position of the Charleston Council. *A Dissection of the Manifesto of Mr. Charles Bienvenu* was released 1858 and opened a very regrettable door for the Charleston Council. The work, while originally issued as an anonymous publication, was later learned to be the work of Albert Pike and Charles Laffon de Ladébat. While the *Dissection* was as harsh in tone as Foulhouze's *Mémoire à Consulter*, it went back to the Lopez Expedition period and reprinted in the end of the booklet the article published on Foulhouze by the *Daily Delta* and the retort by T. Wharton Collens and Robert Preaux. What was not published, nor mentioned, was the response of nearly all of the competing New Orleans newspapers condemning the yellow journalistic style of the article. The illusion created in the *Dissection* was that the *Delta's* article on Foulhouze was factual and Collens and Preaux were only attempting to deny the obvious. In 1873, James Scot published his

69. Foulhouze's *Historical Inquiry* can not be viewed as an English translation of his *Mémoire à Consulter.* Upon examination by Alain Bernheim, it has been determined that the *Historical Inquiry,* while closely following *Mémoire à Consulter,* has enough significant changes to consider it a rewrite rather than a translation.

Outline of the Rise and Progress of Freemasonry in Louisiana and revealed that the *Dissection* influenced his thinking and beliefs (and assuredly that of many others) of Foulhouze. Scot says of Foulhouze:

> At this time [1850] he [Foulhouze] was charged with being a spy of the Spanish Government, and was afterwards denounced as such in the newspapers of the day when the news of the fate of the Lopez expedition reached New Orleans. During the excitement he was concealed by some friends to prevent his falling into the hands of the mob, until he was able to effect his escape to Havana. He afterward returned, and resigned his membership in the Supreme Council, July 30, 1853.[70]

James Foulhouze was not viewed as one who simply held a very strong opposing Masonic opinion and followed a course of action that he felt was correct, he was now portrayed as a charlatan of low moral character. This was quite a different picture than the Mason who was approached by Albert Mackey to become an Active Member of the Charleston Council. The statement by Scot is erroneous. The only newspaper which published such a opinion of Foulhouze was denounced by the balance of the newspapers in New Orleans. Foulhouze went to Havana in an attempt to secure the release of American citizens *prior* to the article by the *Delta*. He did not "escape" to Havana. The Scot quotation is an example of the emotional and confused state of affairs in Louisiana Masonry and the fact that inaccuracies were, sadly, sometimes accept as fact.

On October 3, 1858, Foulhouze informed the New Orleans Council, in Session, of a communication he received from the Grand Orient of France. Foulhouze, as a Grand Orient 33rd, was officially instructed to disassociate himself from the revived New Orleans Council. Foulhouze refused this mandate. On February 4, 1859, the Grand Orient of France struck Foulhouze's name from its list of 33rds.

Despite the actions taken and the decrees and publications written against Foulhouze and the New Orleans Council, there was no sign that the Council was weakening. In fact, the New Orleans Council showed every indication of strengthening. By 1859 the New Orleans Council was at its peak of power in the post concordat days. Twenty-five active lodges were under its

70. Scot, *Outline*, 4.

jurisdiction[71] and the Council was composed of thirty-four active members.[72] Of the lodges under the jurisdiction of the New Orleans Council, seven were located outside of New Orleans in various regions of Louisiana. The make-up of the lodges reveal that the popularity of the New Orleans Council was not solely with the French speaking New Orleans Masons. Twelve lodges worked in the French language, seven in the English language, two in German, one in Italian, and one in Spanish. Remembering the fact that the Louisiana Grand Lodge (with its "irregular" stamp) grew in power and took over the Grand Lodge of Louisiana in 1850 with no outside support, save the Grand Lodge of Mississippi, the matter of the New Orleans Council had to be addressed. It was not simply a growing threat to the Charleston Council, but, also, to the Grand Lodge of Louisiana.

With no real structure, rituals or organization, the Charleston Council began to realize that it was, indeed, in trouble. Of this time Charles S. Lobingier, 33°, G.C. writes in his 1931 *The Supreme Council, 33°:*

> Both Pike and Mackey had by this time decided that the Supreme Council needed reform. On January 20, 1858, the former had written the latter urging an increase in the membership and the introduction of the elective system.[73]

For reasons that are, at best, ambiguous, Grand Commander John Honour resigned his office in the Charleston Council on August 13, 1858. It was not until January 2, 1859, that Albert Pike was proclaimed, by Albert Mackey, *elected* to the office of grand commander of the Charleston Council. It is logical that the actions of Foulhouze and the New Orleans Council influenced the change of command in the Charleston Council. Pike immediately began to reform the Charleston Council and make the changes necessary for its survival.

In 1860 Foulhouze was elected to the judgeship of the Second District Court in Plaquemines Parish. While the election of Foulhouze as a district court judge advanced his profession, the twenty-mile Mississippi River boat ride from his home in New Orleans to his new court office in Plaquemines must have grown wearisome. In 1861 Foulhouze moved his domicile from New Orleans to Plaquemines Parish. That same year former judge and Lt. Grand

71. *The Masonic Delta,* Sep. 1859.
72. *The Masonic Delta,* Apr. 1860.
73. Lobingier, *Supreme Council,* 249.

Commander T. Wharton Collens was elected Judge of the Seventh District Court in New Orleans. On January 2, 1861, the New Orleans Council re-incorporated itself taking, for the first time, the name "The Supreme Council of Louisiana." Due to the pressures of his new position, T. W. Collens resigned in 1861 as Lt. Grand Commander of the New Orleans Council. He was replaced by Sam Brown, who was created a 33rd by Foulhouze March 5, 1860.

THE CIVIL WAR

Arguably there has been no lower point in the history of the United States then the Civil War years of 1861–65. The divided country nearly destroyed itself in four years of devastating war, the effects of which plagued the county for a century to follow. While there have been numerous accounts of Masonic acts of charity during the war years, the war weakened Masonry in the US due to the loss of life, property, and the economic hardship that followed the war years. There is no sign or record that any of the Supreme Councils in the US were active during the Civil Wars years. Pierre Soulé was imprisoned for a time upon the capture of New Orleans in 1862. Upon his release from prison, he lived out the remaining war years in Cuba. Albert Pike was charged with war crimes stemming from the Battle at Pea Ridge (his only war command) and was left out of the general amnesty afforded at the close of the war. Pike fled to Canada awaiting a Presidential pardon allowing him to return to the US

There is no known records of the New Orleans Supreme Council during the war years and it is unknown what events, if any, took place in the council during this time. James Foulhouze, who prior to the war was a district court judge is shown to be a Parish Attorney for Plaquemines Parish following the war. There are no records of the exact date that he left office as a judge, nor giving the reasons. It is possible that the then 65 year old Foulhouze simply retired from his judgeship or his leaving office might have been required by the Union in the post war years. A series of events that can best be described as "amazing" then takes place concerning Foulhouze and the New Orleans Council.

On May 3, 1866, T. Wharton Collens, Pierre Soulé, and eight other 33rds of the New Orleans Council signed an "oath of allegiance" to the New Orleans Council.[74] Foulhouze's name is not included in this apparent reorganization.

74. Original document in the George Longe Collection in the Amistad Research Center at

On May 10, 1866, the New Orleans Council obtained the oath of allegiance of Robert Preaux and created two 33rds. One of the 33rds created was a New Orleans music teacher, music shop owner, and composer of moderate note who corresponded with many of the artistic and literary figures in Europe including Victor Hugo. His name was Eugene Chassaignac. On January 7, 1867, Chassaignac was elected Grand Commander of the New Orleans Council. It is unknown who was Grand Commander or "acting" Grand Commander at the time that Chassaignac was elevated to the 33d degree or why Chassaignac was selected to lead the New Orleans Council. There is a total veil of mystery over the election of Chassaignac and the departure of Foulhouze.

The May 1, 1867, minutes of Liberty Lodge No. 19 (under the New Orleans Council's jurisdiction)[75] show that O. J Dunn, Grand Master of the Eureka Grand Lodge of Louisiana (Prince Hall) and five other Prince Hall Lodges in various locations in the US had officially accepted the invitation to attend Liberty Lodge and noted that this Lodge admitted visitors with no regard to race. The worshipful master of Liberty Lodge was Eugene Chassaignac. The New Orleans Council, likewise and that same year, officially announced that membership to its lodges were not be based on race. That announcement, in itself, seems a curious restatement of the obvious, as the New Orleans Council (and the whole of New Orleans Masonry) had a long history, prior to the Civil War, of having little concern over race and Masonic membership.

In an amazing and dramatic move, the Grand Orient of France, ignoring its past action against James Foulhouze, re-recognized the New Orleans Council on November 5, 1868. Eugene Chassaignac commented on James Foulhouze and the relations with the Grand Orient of France in the April-May 1869 issue of the *Bulletin:*[76]

> It is true that in 1858, following the writings of Mr. J. Foulhouze, (writings that were not at all the acts of the Supreme Council) our relations with the Grand Orient were interrupted; but since I have had the honor of being the Grand Commander and Grand Master of the Scotch Rite, in Louisiana, I had the pamphlets disavowed by a solemn resolution; on the other hand, Mr.

Tulane University, New Orleans, La.

75. Photocopy reproduction of the minutes in *The Perfect Ashlar* (current publication of the Supreme Council of Louisiana), Oct. 1969.

76. *The Bulletin* replaced *The Masonic Delta* in 1869 as the official publication of the Supreme Council of Louisiana.

> Foulhouze not being any longer a member of our order, there no longer exists a reason for the relations between the Grand Orient of France and the Supreme Council of Louisiana to be interrupted.[77]

What happened? Without James Foulhouze, the reorganization of the New Orleans Council would have failed before it started. The Chassaignac statement can only be viewed as incredible and shows an almost contempt for Foulhouze. Why? There is no clue as to what could have taken place during the Civil War years. Prior to the war the New Orleans Council was at its height of power and could have in a matter of a few years, realistically, overpowered the Charleston Council and seriously threatened the Grand Lodge of Louisiana had the war not interrupted its growth. James Foulhouze was the power and the driving force of this movement. It simply could not have happened without him. There is not a hint as to why Foulhouze left office, why Chassaignac was made a 33rd, why Chassaignac was elected Grand Commander, or why Chassaignac seemingly turned on Foulhouze. Just as perplexing as the Chassaignac statement on Foulhouze is the re-recognition of the New Orleans Council by the Grand Orient. The Grand Orient had stripped Foulhouze of his 33rd Degree for his participation in the reorganization of the New Orleans Council. Why would they now recognize that very same body? The re-recognition of the New Orleans Council by the Grand Orient of France unquestionably caused great concern in the Supreme Councils S.J. and N.M.J. In a bold move, relations between the Grand Orient and the S.J. and N.M.J. were suspended by a join resolution of the S.J. and N.M.J. dated May 2 and June 15, 1870. The resolution made the following points (presumably written by Pike).

> The Grand Orient of France well knew, for it had so decided in a sane interval, in 1858, that an Inspector-General created by itself could exercise no powers within the jurisdiction of another Supreme Council. It knew that the Chassaignac body was created by the sole authority of M. Jacques Foulhouze, whom it had denuded of his privileges as an Inspector-General, for "*forfaiture d'honneur*," in establishing it. And yet, without any new light upon the subject, without any reconsideration or reexamination, without restoring M. Foulhouze, and while in alliance with us, it recognized this spurious organization as a lawful Supreme Council."[78]

77. Eugene Chassaignac, *Bulletin* (New Orleans, A. Simon, 1869), 28.
78. Carter, *History*, 431.

THE DEATH OF JAMES FOULHOUZE

There is no suggestion that Foulhouze had any connection with Masonry following the Civil War years. In 1869 Foulhouze co-authored a book with William M. Prescott titled *The Ordinances of the Police Jury of the Parish of Plaquemines.* Foulhouze is listed as "Parish Attorney" and Prescott as "Parish Judge." Foulhouze apparently busied himself with legal matters and spent the remainder of his life in the Mississippi River town of Pointe-a-la-Hache, Louisiana.

On December 21, 1875, the following article appeared in the *New Orleans Bee*: "Deceased the 18th of December 1875 at Pointe-a-la Hache, parish of Plaquemines, the Hon. James Foulhouze at the age of seventy-five. A native of Riom, Auvergue, France."

Foulhouze was buried at St. Thomas the Apostle Church Cemetery in Pointe-a-la-Hache. T. Wharton Collens, who had by then also resigned from all Masonic activities, handled the legal matters concerning Foulhouze's succession. Collens wrote of Foulhouze:

> I was very intimately acquainted with the late James Foulhouze during the thirty years that preceded his death. He was a native of Riom in France, and during the thirty years that I knew him he frequently spoke to me of his relatives in that country, and showed me his correspondences with them. His father died previous to 1830, his mother a few years before he "J. Foulhouze" did. He had a brother who died before he did—that brother left one heir a daughter. Foulhouze himself was never married.[79]

While Foulhouze was not, by any means, a man of great wealth, he did own a home in Pointe-a-la-Hache and some property. Foulhouze's entire estate was willed to Odéalie Collens McCaleb, the married daughter of his long time friend T. Wharton Collens and Odéalie's son, James Foulhouze McCaleb.

The many unanswered questions concerning Foulhouze, and the events surrounding him may never be fully answered or understood. It is clear, however, that Foulhouze followed a path which he honestly felt to be correct. Regardless of which side of the issue one takes, it must be objectively recognized that the impact that Foulhouze had on the whole of US Scottish Rite Masonry is undeniable. It must, also, be pointed out that those who supported and held the same opinion as Foulhouze were neither "weak minded" nor "ignorant" as sometimes charged. Differing opinions are frequently held by

79. Foulhouze Secession Papers, 1875, Court House Pointe-a-la Hashe, Louisiana.

intelligent people. It is unfortunate when judgment is colored by emotion and it is tragic when erroneous conclusions born of skewed judgment makes its way into accepted history.

Joseph Cerneau, Part 1—His Grand Consistory's Minute Book

Alain Bernheim, 33°

I wrote once that "little is known about Joseph Cerneau's life and nothing definite about his death."[1] In October 2009 in Washington, I regretted publicly that we know next to nothing about the Minute Book of Cerneau's Grand Consistory. I now have new information about both topics.

1. Cerneau's Biographical Dates

In 1800, Joseph Cerneau was a member of *La Réunion Désirée*, warranted in 1784 by the Grand Orient of France in Port-au-Prince. He appears in the

1. Alain Bernheim, "An Introduction to Joseph Cerneau and His Biographers," *Heredom*, vol. 6 (1997), 21–34.

same town as a goldsmith merchant (*marchand orfèvre*), Royal Arch and Rose Croix, on the printed Tableau (June 1801) of *La Réunion des Cœurs* No. 47 (of which Germain Hacquet was then Wor. Master), warranted in 1789 by the Grand Lodge of Pennsylvania. He was chosen Jr. Gr. Warden of the Prov. Gr. Lodge of St. Domingo, founded at Port-Républicain (the new name of Port-au-Prince) in January 1802 by the Grand Lodge of Pennsylvania, with Antoine Mathieu-Dupotet, Prov. Gr. Master. In December 1804, he petitioned Pennsylvania to warrant Lodge *Le Temple des Vertus Théologales* in Havana and was its Wor. Master. When in New York, he was naturalized an American citizen on 15 April 1809 and affiliated in 1810 with Washington Lodge No. 21 (Grand Lodge of New York) of which he remained a member until his return to France in 1827.

For the past twenty-five years Mr. Gilles Lorillon researched the history of his village, Villeblevin. In August 2010, he wrote to me that he discovered in the local archives, among many remarkable figures, "that of Joseph Cerneau, born there 14 November 1765" and added: "I have a copy of his birth certificate. He was first a goldsmith in Sens, as many youngsters of his generation." Mr. Lorillon realized that Cerneau was a prominent Mason and asked me for further information. I did my best to help him and he was kind enough to send me three remarkable documents: Cerneau's birth certificate, his death certificate, and that of his wife, all of which are reproduced in the Appendix to this paper. They confirm Cerneau's birth day[2] and show that his wife, Marie Roch, died in Villeblevin on 14 March 1837 and Joseph Cerneau died in Melun, 3 February 1848.[3]

2. THE MINUTE BOOK

Former Mentions and Recent Reappearance

In 1891, Josiah H. Drummond mentioned, presumably for the first time, a Minute Book of Cerneau's Grand Consistory:

2. Bernheim, "An Introduction," 22 and note 10.

3. In the most useful "'Bento' Enhanced Computer Correlated AQC-Index: Vol. 1–109" Cerneau's biographical dates are given as 1763–1828.

> Returning now to the Cerneau bodies in New York; the Grand Consistory was exceedingly active and kept itself before the public by numerous publications; for some years it published a Tableau annually; its early records are lost, but a volume covering the years from 1816 to 1826 is in the archives of the Northern Supreme Council.... In this book is pasted a leaf containing the record of a meeting of the Grand Council of Princes of the Royal Secret, held October 12, 1827.[4]

In 1938, Samuel H. Baynard Jr. devoted a few pages to that Minute Book in his *History of the Supreme Council, 33°*.[5] In 1950, the Northern Masonic Jurisdiction created a History Committee which met until 1955. Its mentions of the Cerneau Minute Book in 1951 are commented below.

George Adelbert Newbury and Louis Lenway Williams, co-authors of *A History of the Supreme Council, 33°, of the Ancient and Accepted Scottish Rite of Freemasonry for the NMJ of the USA* (1987), were familiar with the minutes of the History Committee.[6] However the five pages of chapter 15 "Cerneau and Cerneauism," authored by Williams,[7] did not mention the Minute Book once.

In 2010, Aimee E. Newell[8] described it this way:

> The Scottish Rite Masonic Museum and Library is fortunate to have a minute book kept by Cerneau's group covering the years from 1816 to 1825 [*sic*]. The records in the book resemble those of countless lodges, The entries track the group's business – they document meetings, note charters granted and members nominated, review reports by subcommittees, and discuss correspondence and accounts. In short, these pages present a group that had a common aim and went about its business with its members thinking they were doing nothing wrong.

Lastly, Mr. Jeffrey Croteau[9] sent a Letter to the Editor of *The Plumbline,* ("Restless Sleepers"), illustrated with the first folio of the Minute Book. His Letter was published in the Summer 2010 issue and began with:

4. Stillson & Hughan, eds., 1891, 814–15 (see Bibliographical Notes).

5. Baynard 1938, vol. 1, 203–13. See also vol. 1, 186.

6. The Minutes of the History Committee are quoted or discussed 44, 49, 50, 54, 57–59 (indexed), as well as xix, xxi, 230–32, 269, 274 (not indexed).

7. The respective authors of the 46 chapters of the book, Past Sovereign Grand Commander George Adelbert Newbury and Active Emeritus Member Louis Lenway Williams, are listed xix.

8. Aimee E. Newell, "Joseph Cerneau's Supreme Council – Misunderstanding or Malice?" *The Northern Light*, May 2010, 4–7. The author is Director of Collections at the Scottish Rite Masonic Museum and Library. His paper quotes books by Newbury & Williams, Peter Ross, Mackey, Folger and Baynard, as well as two articles issued in *Heredom* by Michael Poll and myself.

9. Jeffrey Croteau is the Manager of the Van Gorden-Williams Library & Archives, Scottish Rite Masonic Museum & Library, Lexington, Massachusetts.

> I very much enjoyed reading Alain Bernheim's "My Approach to Masonic History,"[10] although I'd like to clear up some misimpressions that Mr. Bernheim has relayed both to his original audience and now to the greater membership of the Scottish Rite Research Society.
>
> Despite Mr. Bernheim's view that the minutes of Joseph Cerneau's Grand Consistory "sleep in the archives of the Northern Masonic Jurisdiction," I can assure him that they sleep restlessly, waiting for historians like himself and others to avail themselves of this important material and, as Mr. Bernheim has begun to do, re-examine previous assumptions about men like Joseph Cerneau. The minute book of Cerneau's Grand Consistory, which covers the years 1816–1825 [*sic*], is cataloged and has been available to researchers here at the Scottish Rite Masonic Museum & Library for many years.

And ended thus:

> With the upcoming 2013 bicentennial celebrating the founding of the Northern Masonic Jurisdiction in 1813, I hope that Mr. Bernheim and others will, indeed, be ready, willing, and anxious to provide new perspectives on the Scottish Rite by re-examining primary sources, especially those here at the Scottish Rite Masonic Museum & Library.

Whereupon I asked Mr. Croteau per email if a copy of that Minute Book was available. He answered on August 17:

> As for the Cerneau minutes, we do not currently have an access/preservation copy of the Cerneau minutes and the minutes themselves are in a bound volume that would not withstand photocopying.

A few days later, I had the pleasant surprise to find in my (snail-) mail – without the shadow of an accompanying note – a full photocopy of the Cerneau Minute Book. I wish to express my thanks to the anonymous contributor who allows me to describe that most interesting document, to try and elucidate obscure parts of Masonic history and, incidently, to correct some remarks of my predecessors.

10. As guest speaker to the Scottish Rite Research Society meeting in Washington in October 2009, I said: "We know next to nothing about the Minutes of Cerneau's Grand Consistory. They sleep in the archives of the Northern Masonic Jurisdiction and have never been published... yet. It would be very interesting to read them and see what they have to say. It would be a great sign of generosity if their lawful owners would make this possible." My speech was printed in the Spring 2010 issue of *The Plumbline*.

Quick Survey

Part of the Minute Book was (re)copied in June 1823 as showed by the Minutes of 16 January 1823, 110th Sitting (extraordinary meeting) and of 8 September 1823 (117th Sitting):

> [f° 68] The Minutes of the Proceedings of the Gd Consistory and the Gd Council of PRS for the State of New York (which have remained unengrossed since the year 1815) to be written up and also to cause the archives and papers relating or belonging to either of the two bodies, which now are in a very disarranged state, to be placed in due and proper order. The necessity and importance of causing the above to be effected with as little delay as possible, and the expediency of appointing some proper person (a member of this Sov. Gr. Consistory) to execute the same, as well as the propriety of allocating the person so appointed a suitable compensation [f° 69] for the time and trouble attendant thereon, having been duly considered, on motion from Bro. Dubuar duly seconded it was
>
> Resolved that the Bro. Tobias W. Bedell be and he hereby is duly appointed to carry the above into effect. And also resolved that the Bros. Francis Dubuar, Jonathan Schieffelin, and Alexander Glass be a Committee to superintend the execution of the above Resolution....
>
> [f° 98] The Committee appointed on the 16th day of Jany. 1823, to Superintend the copying, arranging, filing &c. of the minutes, proceedings, Documents, Archives &c. of the Sov∴ Grand Consistory, which by a resolution of said date the Ill∴ Br∴ J. W. Bedell was appointed to execute.
>
> Respectfully report that the minutes of the Grand Consistory from 18th Feby. 1815. to the 9th of June 1823 containing 34 pages and Index to Ditto from the 8th June 1811 to 9th June 1823 containing 34 pages,[11] as also the minutes of the Grand Council from 12th October 1817 to 24th November 1822 containing 22 pages & Index 4 pages; likewise a General Index to books & papers containing 7 pages: in all amounting to 190 folios pages have been copied, & carefully compared with the originals, and found to be correctly transcribed and entered in their proper books & files. Your committee further report that the rough minutes, having [f° 99] been taken down by various brethren & being in possession of different individuals, Br∴ Bedell has been at much pains & trouble to collect the same. The voluminous documents comprising the Archives of the Grand Consistory have been judiciously and correctly filed from its commencement to the present date; and that your Committee have drawn on the Gr∴d Treaurer for One hundred & thirty dollars, which Br∴ Bedell has received in part payment for his services.
>
> All of which is respectfully submitted.
>
> New York 8th day of September 1823.

11. The mention of "containing 34 pages" repeated twice is presumably the result of a mistake.

= Signed = *Francis Dubuar.*
Jonathan Schieffelin.

Mistakes did happen by copying. A note at the end of folio 19 says: "NB The minute of the above sitting was by accident copied before the following which is of an earlier date."

Number and Numbering of Meetings[12]

When the Minute Book was recopied in 1823, the sittings of the Grand Consistory were numbered consistently from 78 to 143 (Table 1).

Sitting	Folio	President	Coded Date	Date	Year
78	1	Cerneau	8/9/5816[13]	8 November	1816
79	3	Cerneau	30/9/5816	30 November	1816
80	5	Cerneau	18/10/5816	18 December	1816
81	11	Cerneau	12/5/5817	12 July	1817
82	11	Cerneau	30/9/5817	30 November	1817
83	14	Cerneau	12/10/5817	12 December	1817
84	15	Cerneau	30/9/5818	30 November	1818
85	17	Cerneau	20/12/5818	20 February	1819
86	18	Cerneau	25/3/5819	25 May	1819
87	19	Cerneau	21/4/5819	21 June	1819
88	20	Cerneau	19/4/5819	19 June	1819
89	22	Cerneau	15/3/5820	15 May	1820
90	24	Cerneau	15/4/5820	15 June	1820
91	26	Cerneau	10/9/5820	10 November	1820
92	29	Cerneau	6/2/5821	6 April	1821
93	31	Cerneau	17/3/5821	17 May	1821
94	34	Cerneau	13/5/5821	13 July	1821
95	36	Cerneau	15/10/5821	15 December	1821
96	39	Mulligan	19/10/5821	19 December	1821
97	42	Mulligan	24/10/5821	24 December	1821
98	44	Mulligan	28/12/5821	28 February	1822
99	46	Mulligan	26/1/5822	26 March	1822
100	48	Mulligan	8/3/5822	8 May	1822
101	49	Mulligan	9/3/5822	9 May	1822
102	50	Cerneau	14/4/5822	14 June	1822
103	52	Mulligan	21/4/5822	21 June	1822

Sitting Folio President Coded Date Date Year

12. All the meetings were entitled "Sittings" except the first, "78th Session," and the second, "79. Séance," part of which is in French.

13. This column shows the coded dates in an abbreviated form. Sitting 78 is dated "8th day of the 9th month, Year of T∴ L∴ [True Light] 5816. and of the Christian Era 1816," showed here as 8/9/5816.

104	54	Cerneau	10/6/5822	10 August	1822
105	56	Cerneau	29/8/5822	29 October	1822
106	57	Cerneau	16/9/5822	16 November	1822
107	61	Mulligan	23/9/5822	23 November	1822
108	64	Mulligan	26/9/5822	26 November	1822
109	65	Cerneau	2/11/5822	2 January	1823
110	68	Cerneau	16/11/5822	16 January	1823
111	71	Schieffelin	4/12/5822	4 February	1823
112	73	Cerneau	5/2/5823	5 April	1823
113	76	Cerneau	17/3/5823	17 May	1823
114	80	Cerneau	9/4/5823	9 June	1823
115	85	Cerneau	14/5/5823	14 July	1823
116	87	Cerneau	18/6/5823	18 August	1823
117	88	Cerneau	8/7/1823	8 September	1823
118	90	Cerneau	17/7/1823	17 September	1823
119	91	Cerneau	22/7/1823	22 September	1823
120	92	Cerneau	24/8/1823	24 October	1823
121	93	Cerneau	28/8/1823	28 October	1823
122	95	Cerneau	14/9/5823	14 November	1823
123	97	Cerneau	8/7/5823	8 September	1823
124	100	Hicks	28/8/5823	28 October	1823
125	103	Cerneau	14/9/5823	14 November	1823
126	107	Cerneau	24/9/5823	24 November	1823
127	108	Cerneau	6/10/5823	6 December	1823
128	110	Hicks	15/10/5823	15 December	1823
129	113	Hicks	12/12/5824 [*sic*]	12 February	1824
130	116	Hicks	23/12/5824 [*sic*]	23 February	1824
131	118	Hicks	10/2/5823 [*sic*]	10 April	1824
132	121		22/7/5823 [sic]	22 September	1824
133	123	Hicks	25/8/5824	25 October	1824
134	127	Hicks	25/8/5824	25 October	1824
135	130	Hicks	9/9/5824	9 November	1824
136	139	Hicks	22/9/5824	22 November	1824
137	142	Hicks		Tuesday 25 January	5825
138	145	Hicks		17th day of June	1825
139	147	Cerneau		26th day of August	5825
140	150	Hicks		Friday evening October the 14th	5825
141	151	Schieffelin		Monday the 14th day of November	5825
142	154	Hicks		Thursday the 30th day of March	1826
	166		BLANK FOLIO		
143	167	Hicks		Monday the 24th day of April	1826
	178		LAST FOLIO		

Table 1. Sittings of the Grand Consistory as recorded in the Minute Book

However Minutes of three sittings were completed at a later date and numbered as if they were new sittings (TABLE 2).

SITTING	FOLIOS	DATE	YEAR
117	88–89	8 September	1823
121	93–94	28 October	1823
122	95–96[14]	14 November	1823
123*	97–98	8 September	1823
124*	100–102	28 October	1823
125*	103–106	14 November	1823

TABLE 2. Three sittings minuted twice

Accordingly sixty-three meetings were recorded in the Minute Book between 1816 and 1826 (TABLE 3).

YEAR	NUMBER OF MEETINGS
1816	3
1817	3
1818	1
1819	4
1820	3
1821	6
1822	11
1823	17
1824	8
1825	5
1826	2
Total	63

TABLE 3. Number of meetings of the Grand Consistory from 1816 to 1826

DATING OF MINUTES

The Minute Book describes meetings of the "M∴ P∴ Sov∴ Grd∴ Consistory for the U∴S∴ of America." The first one ("78th Session") is dated "8th day of the 9th Month, Year of T∴ L∴[15] 5816 and of the Christian Era 1816" after the classical French Masonic dating code in which the first month is March,

14. Marginal note on folio 95, Sitting 122, 14 November 1823: "This sitting is copied over again complete on page 103."

15. Year of T∴ L∴ (True Light), translation of the Masonic expression: *An de la Vraie Lumière.*

the twelfth one February,[16] and 4000 is added to the year. The date is equal to 8 November 1816 of the Gregorian Calendar. The date of the 98th Sitting, 28th day of the 12th month 5821, corresponds to 28 February 1822.[17]

The Grand Consistory made use of that dating code until its 137th Sitting, dated Tuesday 25 January 5825, and remained by it until its 141st Sitting, dated Monday the 14th day of November 5825. The last two sittings (142nd and 143rd) are dated Thursday the 30th day of March 1826 and Monday the 24th day of April 1826.[18]

3. CERNEAU'S GRAND CONSISTORY

3.1 The Consitory (1807)

Creation and earliest list of members

The *Statutes and Regulations* (1862) describes in two different places the creation by Joseph Cerneau in 1807 of a Grand Consistory in New York:

In August, 1806, Ill.·. Bro.·. Joseph Cerneau arrived at New York from Cuba, and by virtue of his patent as Grand Inspector General, and in accordance with the Secret Articles, hitherto alluded to, established on the 28th day of the 8th month of True Light, in the year 1807, a Most Puissant Sovereign Grand Consistory of Supreme Chiefs of Exalted Masonry, its officers being:—[19]

On the 28th day of the 8th month of True Light 1807, the Most Puissant Sovereign Grand Consistory of Sublime Princes of the Royal Secret; Supreme Chiefs of Exalted Masonry, according to the Ancient Constitutional Scottish Rite of Heredom, for the United States of America, their territories and dependencies, was opened in the City of New York, with all the high honours of Masonry, by Most Puissant Joseph Cerneau, Sovereign

16. See The Coding of the Month in Alain Bernheim, "The Dating of Masonic Records" (Norman B. Spencer Prize Essay 1986, Quatuor Coronati Lodge No. 2076, London). *AQC* 99, 1987, 18.

17. Four successive entries of the Minute Book (Sittings 129 to 132) show that the then Secretary was at a loss with the French dating code. The first two bear the dates 12 and 23 February 1824 of the Christian Era, coded 12th and 23rd day of the 12th month 5824 (instead of 5823). The next two, 10 April and 22 September 1824 of the Christian Era, coded 10th day of the 2nd month and 22nd day of the 7th month 5823 (instead of 5824).

18. Aimee Newell and Jeffrey Croteau, quoted above, stated that the Minute Book covers the years "from 1816 to 1825."

19. *The Statutes and Regulations* (New York 1862), "Introduction," 19 (see Bibliographical Notes).

Grand Inspector General, 33d. and constituted in due form, with its organization complete. The following illustrious brethren composed the list of officers, as appears by the records:[20]

T∴P∴S∴G∴C∴[21]	Joseph Cerneau, Past Master
D∴G∴C∴[22]	John W. Mulligan, Past Master
G∴P∴A∴[23]	De Witt Clinton, Grand Master of the Grand Lodge, and Mayor of the City of New York
1st Lieut∴ G∴C∴	Dr. Charles Guerin, Past Master
2d Lieut∴ G∴C∴	Jacob Schieffelin
G∴C∴ and G∴O∴[24]	Cadwallader D. Colden, Past Senior Grand Warden of the Grand Lodge of New York
G∴S∴G∴[25]	J. P. Berard
G∴T∴ and G∴K∴ of S∴[26]	Martin Hoffmann, Deputy Grand Master of the Grand Lodge of New York
G∴A∴I∴[27]	J. B. Subrau
G∴I∴G∴[28]	Jonathan Schieffelin
G∴C∴ of C∴[29]	John Bleecker
A∴G∴S∴G∴[30]	John B. Ponzolz
A∴G∴I∴G∴	John C. Ludlow[31]

A Committee of General Administration was also formed....[32]

During the year 1808, the officers of the Sovereign Grand Consistory remained the same, with the exception of Ill∴ Brother Charles Clinton, who was of the 28th day of the 8th month, appointed Grand Keeper of the Seals....

20. *Statutes and Regularions*, "History of the Supreme Council 33d, Ancient and Accepted Scottish Rite, for the United States of America, its Territories and Dependencies," 179.

21. From the abbreviation, T∴ P∴ S∴ G∴ C∴, which I understand as meaning *Très Puissant Souverain Grand Commandeur*, I presume that the original list was written in French. An identical list, 19 of the same book, has: "M∴ P∴ Sov∴ Gr∴ Com."

22. Dep∴ Gr∴ Com∴, 19.

23. D∴ G∴ I∴ and G∴ P∴ A∴, 19.

24. G∴ Ch∴ and G∴ Or∴, 20. Likely Grand Chancellor and Grand Orator.

25. Grand Secretary General.

26. G∴ K∴ of S∴, 20.

27. Grand Assistant Introductor?

28. Grand Introductor General?

29. Misprint for G∴ C∴ of G∴ [Guards]?

30. Likely Assistant Grand Secretary General.

31. An identical list stays on pages 19–20 of *The Statutes and Regulations* (New York 1862) with a few differences for the abbreviations of offices, mentioned above in foot-notes.

32. See § 3.2 below.

> In the early part of the year 1809, a petition was presented for the reorganization and affiliation of the "Sovereign Chapter of Rose Croix," under the definitive title of "Triple Alliance"....[33]
>
> During this year, a Grand Council of Sublime Princes of the Royal Secret, for the State of New York, was also constituted, its officers being: ...[34]
>
> In the year 1810, there was a change in the officers of the Sovereign Grand Consistory, Ill.·. Brother Elias Hicks was elected G.·.A.·.I.·. in the place of Ill.·. Brother J. B. Subrau, and Ill.·. Brother Joseph Gouin was elected Grand Hospitaler....
>
> In the year 1811, the Ill.·. Brother De Witt Clinton became Deputy Grand Commander of the Sovereign Grand Consistory, and John W. Mulligan, Minister of State. There were also other changes, which made the officers rank as follows:[35]

The list of sixteen officers which follows is identical with that of the printed list for 1813 except that it does not mention the offices of Gd Secretary and Assist. Gd Secretary and that both Charles Clinton and J. P. Berard are listed as G.·. Orator.

The existence of a Grand Council of Sublime Princes of the Royal Secret in 1809 was mentioned by La Motta:[36]

> That this Mr. Cerneau had first made his appearance in Longworth's Directory for the year 1809, as "G. I. G. P. S. G. C." (meaning I suppose) "Grand Inspector General, Potent Sovereign Grand Commander, (of his) Most Potent Sovereign Grand Council of Sublime Princes of the Royal Secret, Supreme Chiefs of High Masonry," &c.

It was confirmed by the American historian Edward Cusick:[37]

> In a letter to Voorhis, Cusick has this to say: "In 1809 he (Cerneau) is listed as a member of the Most Potent Sovereign Grand Council of Sublime Princes of the Royal Secret, Supreme Chiefs of High Masonry – Regularly Constituted by Constitutional Patent the 28th day of the 8th month, 5808. Grand Officers – Joseph Cerneau, G. I. G., P. S. G. C. I believe it has been overlooked that in 1809 Brother Cerneau is reported as a Grand Inspector General and Puissant Grand Commander, which is four years before Emanuel de la Motta appeared on the scene in New York City. Baynard (Vol. 1, page 155) says that in the New York City Directory of 1809–10 that it is reported as the 'Sovereign Grand

33. See § 3.3 below.

34. The words "for the State of New York" are likely the result of a mistake. See § 3.5. below.

35. *The Statutes and Regulations* (New York 1862), 179–82. See Table 5.1.

36. La Motta's *Rejoinder* (1814), 4.

37. Minutes of the History Committee of the Northern Masonic Jurisdiction, 3 August 1953, 2.

Consistory.' For once Brother Baynard is mistaken. It is as above quoted – 'Most Potent Sovereign Grand Council (underscoring mine) of Sublime Princes.'"

Le Souverain Grand Consistoire de la Sainte Trinité

The Grand Consistory is mentioned several times in the documents of the Supreme Council of France 1804–1815. On 5 August 1811, the French Supreme Council mentioned it had received a copy of the Grand Consistory's deliberation from 8 February 1810, together with its Tableau under the distinctive title of "Sov∴ Gr. Consist∴ de la Ste Trinité à New York."[38] The minute of the deliberation and an accompanying letter from 15 February 1810 are extant,[39] the Tableau, unfortunately, is not.

Le Grand Consistoire des Etats-Unis d'Amérique & dépendances

In the French Supreme Council's documents is also the copy of an extract of the sitting of the "*Grand Consistoire des chefs supr∴ de la h∴ Maç∴ pour les Etats-Unis d'Amér∴ et dépendances, régt∴ constitué au rit ancien écossais d'Heredom, séant à New York,*" dated "30e∴ jr∴ du 9e∴ m∴ A∴ L∴ 5811.," signed by its Grand Chancellor, John Pascal Schisano, "R∴C∴ K∴H∴ S∴P∴ du Rl∴ St∴ G∴Insp∴ Gal∴ 33e degr∴":[40]

> à ces causes et pour d'autres bonnes raisons déduites dans le cours de la délibération a arrêté et arrête que le Gr∴ Consistoire constitué sous le titre de la Ste. Trinité ne sera plus à l'avenir reconnu que sous celui de Grand Consistoire des Etats-Unis d'Amérique & dépendances, et se proclame dès à présent et pour toujours comme tel; que les actes et pièces émanés de ce Gr∴ Consistre∴ ne porteront d'autre titre que celui sous lequel il est proclamé ce jour, le titre de la Ste Trinité, par lequel il était désigné jusqu'à cette époque, ne devant plus exister, comme de fait il n'existe plus par l'effet de la présente délibération.

The above means that on 30 November 1811, the Grand Consistory of the Holy Trinity decided that, henceforward and forever, its title shall be Grand Consistory of the United States of America & Dependencies.

38. SCDF tome I, folio 611 (see Bibliographical Notes).

39. SCDF tome III, folios 518–21. I have transcribed both documents in my book, *Le Rite en Trente-Trois Grades*, Paris: Dervy, which will be issued in March 2011.

40. SCDF tome II, folios 429–31.

The Most Puissant Sovereign Grand Consistory of Supreme Chiefs of Exalted Masonry – Elections mentioned in the Minute Book

This title is found page 5 of the printed list of 1813 and page 8 of the printed one for 1818. "Grand Consistory of Supreme Chiefs of Exalted Masonry" is the translation of "*Grand Consistoire des chefs supr*[*êmes*]∴ *de la h*[*aute*]∴ *Maç*∴," which stayed at the head of the French Minute of 30 November 1811.

Several mentions of elections are recorded in the Minute Book beginning with 30 November 1817 (82nd Sitting):

> [f° 11] The Sov∴ Grd∴ Commander [Joseph Cerneau] stated that according to a long established rule of this Grand Consistory, the nomination of new officers is to take place on the 28th∴ day of October in every third year and their installation on the 30th∴ day of November following being St∴ Andrews day;[41] but that owing to some unavoidable cause the Grd∴ Consistory did not meet on the 28th∴ of October last, the day on which the choice of new officers should have been made: he therefore had called this meeting for the purpose both of Electing and Installing the New Officers who are to govern the labours of the Sov∴ Grand Consistory for the three years succeeding the said 28th∴ day of October last past.

15 December 1821 (95th Sitting):

> [f° 36] The Sov∴ Prest∴ [Joseph Cerneau] opened the Sitting of the Grand Consistory … stated that this meeting was called for the purpose of Electing Officers for the three years succeeding the 28th of October 1820, circumstances having prevented the Election from taking place on that day, the Sov∴ Grd∴ Com∴ stated that as he was about to leave this country for France, he should decline a reelection to that office … the following Pces∴ were unanimously elected.… [f° 37] When on motion of the Sov∴ Grd∴ Commander Elect seconded by the Ill∴ Bro∴ 2d∴ Minister of State Resolved unanimously that the thanks of this Sov∴ Grd∴ Consistory be presented to the Most Ill∴ Bro∴ Joseph Cerneau Past Grd∴ Commander of this Grd∴ Consistory for the zeal and ability with which he has presided over this Body since its Establishment, and that a Patent be granted him, constituting him an Honorary Grd∴ Commander of this Sov∴ Grd∴ Consistory Ad Vitam. On like Motion & duly seconded Resolved that the Ill∴ Bro∴ Dewitt Clinton be appointed an Honorary Grand Commander of this Sov∴ Grd∴ Consistory, and he is hereby and from this time forward declared to be such.

28 October 1823 (121st Sitting):

41. This mention of St. Andrews day in the Minute Book is so remarkable that it would deserve comments outside the scope of this paper.

> [fº 93] An election was held and the following Ill. Brethren chosen for the ensuing three years.

6 December 1823 (127th Sitting):

> [fº 109] After the ceremony of installation the following Resolution was submitted by Br.·. J. Cerneau seconded by Br J. Schieffelin Viz. That the M. P. S. G^{d}. Commander, Ill D^{y}. Gd. C., 1. & 2nd Lieut. G^{d}. C. be chosen triennially and that annual elections take place in future for the remaining Gd. Officers of this M. P. Sov. G^{d}. Consistory.

9 November 1824 (135th Sitting, fº 137) when "the remaining Gd. Officers" were elected viva voce, and 14 November 1825 (141st Sitting) when they were balloted:

> [fº 151] It being the night of election of officers from the first Minister of State down to the Assistant Capt.·. of the Guard, (the first four G.·. Officers being elected for three years)....

The Grand Officers of the Sovereign Grand Consistory between 1813 and 1826 are listed in Table 5.1., its other members in Table 5.2.

3.2 THE COMMITTEE OF GENERAL ADMINISTRATION (1807)

A Committee of General Administration was formed by the Grand Consistory in 1807[42] and was still in existence in 1823.

1807	1811[43]	1816[44]	1823[45]
De Witt Clinton, *President*	De Witt Clinton, *President*	De Witt Clinton, *President*	Elias Hicks, *Dep^y G^d∴ Com∴*
Dr. Charles Guerin	Dr. Charles Guerin	Dr. Charles Guerin, *Vice-President*	Jonathan Schieffelin *1st Lieut. G^d Com.*
John W. Mulligan	James B. Durand	James B. Durand	Francis Dubuar *2nd d^o*
Jacob Schieffelin	John W. Mulligan	John W. Mulligan	A. H. Palmer *1st M of State*
J. P. Berard	John P. Schisano	Pascal Schisano	John Telfair *G^d Chancellor*
Martin Hoffman	Joseph Gouin	Joseph Gouin	A. S. Glass *G^d Treasurer*
J. B. Subrau	Jacob Schieffelin	Anthony Rainetaux	Thomas Lownds *G^d Keeper of the Seals*
		Jacob Schieffelin	

TABLE 4. Members of the Committee of General Administration

42. "A Committee of General Administration was also formed, consisting of the following Illustrious Brethren: ...." *The Statutes and Regulations* (New York 1862), 180.

43. "The Grand Committee of General Administration, charged with the supervision of the affairs of the Order, and through whose hands all applications for Warrants, Patents, &c., &c., must pass, consisted of...," *The Statutes and Regulations* (New York 1862), 183.

44. Grand Committee of General Administration, *The Statutes and Regulations* (New York 1862), 205.

45. Committee of General administration. Minute Book, 128 Sitting, 15 December 1823, f° 111.

OFFICE	1813[46]	1817 (1818)[47]	1821[48]	28.10.1823[49]
M∴ P∴ Sov. Gd Commander	Joseph Cerneau	Joseph Cerneau	John W. Mulligan	De Witt Clinton
Honorary Gd Commander			Jos. Cerneau De Witt Clinton	[J. Cerneau]
Dy Gd Commander	De Witt Clinton	De Witt Clinton		James B. Durand [*declined*]
1st Lieut Gd Commandern	Charles Guerin	Charles Guerin	Joseph Bouchaud	Jonathan Schieffeli
2d Lieut Gd Commander	James B. Durand	James B. Durand	Jonathan Schieffelin	Francis Dubuar
1st Minister of State	John W. Mulligan	John W. Mulliganr Past Master Ex∴ D∴ G∴ Commander	Aaron H. Palmer Past Maste	Aaron H. Palmer
2d Minister of State	Cadwallader D. Colden	Cadwallader D. Colden	Harman Westerwelt	Martin Hoffmann
Gd Chancellor	I. Pascal Schisano	Anthony Rainetaux	Elias Hicks	John Telfair
Gd Secretary	Anthony Rainetaux	Aaron H. Palmer	John Telfair	
Assistant Gd Secretary	Joseph Bouchaud	Joseph Bouchaud		Mariano Velasquez
2d Assistant Gd Secrety		Francis Dubuar		

TABLE 5.1. Grand Officers of the Most P∴ Sov∴ G∴ Consistory of Sup∴ Chiefs of Exalted Masonry

46. Printed List for 1813. *The Statutes and Regulations* (New York 1862) mentions 190 that "John Bleeker [was elected] G∴ O∴, in place of J. P. Berard." The printed list shows Bleeker among the "Present Members" and does not mention the office of Grand Orator.

47. Minute Book, 82. Sitting, 30 November 1817, folio 12. This list of Officers is identical with the printed list for 1818. However it does not mention 1st and 2d before Minister of State, Grand Master of Ceremonies, and Grand Expert Introductor but only the title of office instead of 1st and "Assistant to" instead of 2d. The four Assistants are listed last in the Minute Book

48. Minute Book, 95. Sitting, 15 December 1821, folios 36–37.

49. Minute Book, 121. Sitting, 28 October 1823, folios 93–94.

OFFICE	6.12.1823[50]	9.11.1824[51]	14.11.1825[52]	30.3.18[53]
M.·. P.·. Sov. Gd Commander				De Witt Clinton
Honorary Gd Commander				Joseph Cerneau
Dy Gd Commander	Elias Hicks			Elias Hicks
1st Lieut Gd Commandern				Jonathan Schieffelin
2d Lieut Gd Commander				Francis Dubuar
1st Minister of State		Aaron H. Palmer	Martin Hoffmann	Martin Hoffmann
2d Minister of State		Martin Hoffmann	George Scriba	George Scriba
Gd Chancellor		John Telfair	Velasquez de la Caetña	Mariano Velasquez de la Cateña
Gd Secretary		Oliver M. Lownds	Hampton Dunham M.D.	Hampton Dunham
Assistant Gd Secretary	Mariano Velasquez			
2d Assistant Gd Secrety				

Table 5.1. Grand Officers of the Most P.·. Sov.·. G.·. Consistory of Sup.·. Chiefs of Exalted Masonry

50. 50. Minute Book, 127. Sitting, 6 December 1823, folios 108–9.
51. 51. Minute Book, 135. Sitting, 9 November 1824, folios 137–38.
52. 52. Minute Book, 141. Sitting, 14 November 1825, folio 152.
53. 53. Minute Book, 142. Sitting, 30 March 1826, folios 160–61.

OFFICE	1813	1817 (1818)	1821	28.10.1823
Gd Treasurer	Joseph Gouin	James Gelston	Alex[r] S. Glass	Alexander Glass
Gd Keeper of the Seals	Jacob Schieffelin	Joseph Gouin	Francis Dubuar	Jacob Schieffelin [*declined*]
Gd Chaplain				
1st Gd Master of Ceremonies	Jonathan Schieffelin	Jonathan Schieffelin	Tobias W. Bedell	Tobias W. Bedell
2d Gd Master of Ceremonies	Thomas Lownds	Thomas Lownds	Gerret Morgan	Gerret Morgan
1st Gd Expert Introductor	Toussaint Midy	Toussaint Midy	Thomas Lownds	Thomas Lownds
2d Gd Expert Introductor	Elias Hicks	John Telfair		William J. Hunter
Gd Capt of the Guards	Martin Hoffmann	Martin Hoffmann	Martin Hoffmann	Oliver M. Lownds
Asst. Gd Capt of the Guards				
Gd Hospitaler	John C. Ludlow	Gasper Gr. Eddy	Gasper Gr. Eddy	
Gd Standard Bearer				Abraham Lott
Past Sov. Gd Commander				

Table 5.1. Grand Officers of the Most P∴ Sov∴ G∴ Consistory of Sup∴ Chiefs of Exalted Masonry

OFFICE	6.12.1823	9.11.1824	14.11.1825	30.3.18
Gd Treasurer		Alexander Glass	Alexander Glass	Alexander Glass
Gd Keeper of the Seals	Thom. Lownds	Thom. Lownds	Thom. Lownds	Oliver M. Lownds
Gd Chaplain			Revd F. C. Schaeffer	Revd F. C. Schaeffer
1st Gd Master of Ceremonies		Gerret Morgan	Gerret Morgan	Gerret Morgan
2d Gd Master of Ceremonies		Joseph Bouchaud	August T. Cerneau	August T. Cerneau
1st Gd Expert Introductor	William J. Hunter	William J. Hunter	Oliver M. Lownds	Elisha King
2d Gd Expert Introductor	George Scriba		Louis Timolat	Louis Timolat
Gd Capt of the Guards		James Gelston	Henry March	Henry March
Asst. Gd Capt of the Guards	Henry March			
Gd Hospitaler	H. Dunham	Hampton Dunham	Hypolite Barerre	George Smith
Gd Standard Bearer				
Past Sov. Gd Commander				John W. Mulligan

Table 5.1. Grand Officers of the Most P∴ Sov∴ G∴ Consistory of Sup∴ Chiefs of Exalted Masonry

MOST P∴ SOV∴ G∴ CONSISTORY OF SUP∴ CHIEFS OF EXALTED MASONRY

Members Present

1813 • Charles Clinton, • John Bleecker, • Louis Labourdette, • Francis Dubuar.[54]

1817[55] (1818) • Jacob Sheiffelin [*sic*], Past Master, • John P. Schisano, • Elias Hicks, Gd Sec. of the GL, • Abraham Lott, Past Master, • Alexander Glass, Past Master, • William T. Hunter, Past Master.

1826 • Cadwallader D. Colden, • Jacob Schieffelin, • James B. Durand, • Joseph Bouchaud, • Toussaint Midy, • William J. Hunter, • G. W. Eddy, • James Gelston, • Aaron H. Palmer, • John Telfair, • Harman Westerwelt, • Peter Lammay, • Wm H. Wetmore, • Hugh J. Roberts, • Joseph N. Widmer, • C. B. Wessels.

Members Absent

1813 • J. P. Berard, Ex Grand Chancellor, G∴ Honorary Off∴, P∴M∴, • J. B. Subran, Ex G∴ Exp∴ Introd∴, • J. P. Pouzols [*sic*], Ex 2d∴ M∴ of Cer∴, • Moreau Lillet, • Stephen Deblois.

1817 (1818) • J. P. Berard, Ex Grand Chancellor, G∴ Honorary Off∴, P∴M∴ • Charles Clinton, • J. B. Subran, • Louis Labourdette, • Lalung Montrop, • Emmanuel Gigaud, • J. B. M. Lefebvre, • W. Davis, • D. D. Dessesarts, • Stephen Deblois, • R. Merrill, • J. F. Hurtel, • P. Duler, • T. W. Bacot, • P. Desportes, • J. Dumaine, • J. Asemonti.

1826 • Charles Guerin, • John P. Schisano, • J. Gouin, • Charles Clinton, • J. B. Subran, • Louis Labourdette, • Lalung Montrop, • Emmanuel Gigaud, • J. B. M. Lefebvre, • W. Davis, • D. D. Dessesard, • Stephen Deblois, • J. F. Hurtel, • Peter Duler, • Peter Javain, • Thomas W. Bacot, • J. Dumaine, • J. Azemonti[56]

Deputies in the Provinces

1813 • Emmanuel Gigaud, for the State of Louisiana, • John A. Shaw, for the State of Rhode-Island.

1817 (1818) • J. Pinard, for the State of Louisiana. • John A. Shaw, for the State of Rhode-Island. • A. J. Blocquerst, for the State of Pennsylvania. • Peter Javain, for the State of South-Carolina. • Louis Le Loup for the State of Maryland.

54. Present, Absent, and Honorary Members, Deputies in the Provinces, and Corresponding Grand Councils are only in the printed list for 1818. They are not mentioned in the Minute Book.

55. All "Past Master" except Labourdette.

56. And twenty-five more Absent Members listed 162 of the Minute Book.

1826	[same as 1818, except no name for Louisiana, and:] Benj. C. Howard (Maryland), J. M. Canalejo (Cuba), F. Terreforte (Puerto Rico), Seth Driggs (Trinidad), Doc^r Spofford (Mass.), Doc^r Dazet Senac (Virginia).

HONORARY MEMBERS

1813	• Germain Hacquet,[57] • J. J. Itter,[58] • A. M. Dupotet,[59] • John A. Lamourous, • John Huard, • Joseph Toirac, • Barthelemy Bruneteau, • Richard Merrill, • William Davies.
1817 (1818)	• Germain Hacquet,[57] • J. J. Itter,[58] • A. M. Dupotet,[59] • John A. Lamourous, • John Huard, • Joseph Toirac, • Barthelemy Bruneteau.
1826	• Germain Hacquet, • Lefevre d'Aumale, • Barthélémy Bruneteau, • Joseph Toirac, • Simon Bolivar, • Francisco de Paula Santander, • José Francisco Bermundez, • Carlos Soublette, [*and sixteen more*]

CORRESPONDING SUP.·. GRAND COUNCIL

1813	• The Sup.·. Council of the G.·. Insp G.·. of the 33d.·. degree, for the French Empire. • The Sup.·. Council of the G.·. Insp G.·. of the 33d.·. degree, for the Island of Jamaica.

REPRESENTATIVES OF THE CORRESPONDING BODIES NEAR THE M.·. P.·. SOV.·. GRAND CONSISTORY

1817 (1818)	• Joseph Cerneau, for the G.·. O.·. of France, Supreme Council of Rites, and Sovereign Grand Consistory. • James B. Durand, for the Sov.·. G.·. Council of the Sub.·. P.·. of R.·. Sec.·. for the State of Louisiana. • Thomas Lownds for the Sovereign Grand Council of the Sub.·. P.·. of R.·. Sec.·. for the State of Rhode-Island. • John W. Mulligan, for the Sovereign Grand Council of the Sub.·. P.·. of R.·. Sec.·. for the State of Pennsylvania. • Jacob Schieffelin, for the Sovereign Grand Council of the Sub.·. P.·. of R.·. Sec.·. for the State of South-Carolina. for the Sov.·. Grand Lodge, Astrée, of Russia.

Table 5.2. Most P.·. Sov.·. G.·. Consistory of Sup.·. Chiefs of Exalted Masonry

57. G.·. Honorary Commander, Representative near the Sup.·. Council of G.·. Inspectors General of the 33d.·. degree for the French Empire.

58. Representative near the Sup.·. Council of G.·. Inspectors G.·. of the 33d.·. degree, for the Island of Jamaica.

59. G.·. Honorary Commander.

3.3 The "Triple Alliance" Rose Croix Chapter (1809)

According to *The Statutes and Regulations*,

> In the early part of the year 1809, a petition was presented for the reorganization and affiliation of the "Sovereign Chapter of Rose Croix," under the definitive title of "Triple Alliance," sitting in the Valley of New York. It was the oldest Chapter of that grade in the United States, and its application being favorably entertained, it was resuscitated with the following officers:

John W. Mulligan	M∴ R∴ and P∴ President
Jonathan Schieffelin	Senior Warden
Francis Dubuar	Junior Warden
Thomas Lowndes	Orator
Martin Hoffman	Secretary
Harman Westervelt	Treasurer
James B. Durand	Grand Keeper of the Seals
John P. Schisano	Expert
Garrett Morgan	M∴ of Ceremonies
Tobias W. Bedell	Hospitaller
Caspar W. Eddy	Guard of the Temple
Elias Hicks	Assistant Orator
Aaron H. Palmer	Assistant Grand Secretary
Josh Telfair	G∴ M∴ of Ceremonies
Joseph Colbert	Assistant Guard of the Temple

> There was also constituted at the same time with the above Chapter, a Lodge of Perfection, and a Sublime Council of Princes of Jerusalem, under the same title. In succeeding years these three bodies – Lodge, Council and Chapter,– composed as they were of the most respectable and influential citizens, and Masons became the most numerous in membership of any in the United States.[60]

60. *The Statutes and Regulations* (1862), 180–81. The abbreviation M∴ R∴ and P∴ (Most Respectable and Perfect) is as remarkable as that of St. Andrews mentioned before (note 41). It is characteristical of the ritual of the R∴ C∴, 4th Order of the *Grand Chapitre Général* [*du Grand Orient*] *de France* (1784). Eleven years later, it appears ("a Petition ... signed by the most Resp∴ and Perfect Brethren") in the charter delivered to the Sovereign Chapter of P^{ces}∴ R∴✠∴ under the title of *La Triple Unité* in Baltimore on 15 May 1820 by the Grand Consistory. The charter is transcribed in Edward T. Schulz, 32°, *History of Freemasonry in Maryland*, vol. 4 (1888), 684–86. The petition was read in New York on that day (Minute Book, f° 23).

3.4 THE SUPREME COUNCIL OF GRAND INSPECTORS GENERAL OF THE 33D DEGREE

The original members of the Supreme Council were listed in *The Statutes and Regulations* (New York 1862):

> On the 15th day of the month *Sivan*, 5572–25th of May, 1812,[61] the Supreme Council of Sovereign Grand Inspectors General of the 33d Degree, for the United States of America, its territories and dependencies, was opened with the high honours of Masonry in the City of New York, with its number of officers complete, viz: ...[62]

Its members are enumerated in the printed lists for 1813 and 1818. A detailed list of its Officers, Honorary, Present and Absent Members, stays at the end of the 142nd Sitting, 30 March 1826, of the Minute Book. It was printed the same year.[63] Table 6 shows the members of the Supreme Council and their respective offices since 1812.

3.5 THE GRAND COUNCIL OF PRINCES OF THE ROYAL SECRET FOR THE STATE OF NEW YORK (1816)

On 18 December 1816 (80th Sitting), the Grand Consistory created a Grand Council of Princes of the Royal Secret for the State of New York, similar to those in Louisiana, Rhode-Island, Pennsylvania, and South Carolina, mentioned in the 1816 printed list:

> [f° 5] Resolved that there shall be formed in the body of the Sov∴ Grd∴ Consistory, a Grd∴ Council of Pces∴ of the Royal Secret for the State of New York, to be held in the City of New York in the Chamber of the Sov∴ Grd∴ Consistory and vested with all the rights, Priveleges [*sic*] and Prerogatives appertaining to a Council of the Ral∴ Sect∴ ...
>
> [f° 6] Resolved also that from and after the installation of the Grand Council of Pces∴ of the Royal Secret for the State of New York, the Sov∴ Grd∴

61. *The Statutes and Regulations* (1862), 180–81. The abbreviation M∴ R∴ and P∴ (Most Respectable and Perfect) is as remarkable as that of St. Andrews mentioned before (note 41). It is characteristical of the ritual of the R∴ C∴, 4th Order of the *Grand Chapitre Général* [*du Grand Orient*] *de France* (1784). Eleven years later, it appears ("a Petition ... signed by the most Resp∴ and Perfect Brethren") in the charter delivered to the Sovereign Chapter of Pces∴ R∴X∴ under the title of *La Triple Unité* in Baltimore on 15 May 1820 by the Grand Consistory. The charter is transcribed in Edward T. Schulz, 32°, *History of Freemasonry in Maryland*, vol. 4 (1888), 684–86. The petition was read in New York on that day (Minute Book, f° 23).

62. Equivalent dates according to the Jewish and the Gregorian Calendars.

63. Page 183. Same list ibid. 21.

Consistory will cease to confer the Degrees within the competence of the Gr^{d}∴ Council and subordinate bodies and will confine itself to the exercise of its powers as supreme supervisor, Legislator and administrator of Exalted Masonry in the United States of America, their Territories and Dependancies [*sic*].

Whereupon the Sov∴ Gr^{d}∴ Consistory proceeded to choose the officers of the Grand Council of P^{ces} of the Royal Secret....

OFFICE	25 May 1812[64]	1813[65]	1818[66]	30 March 1826[67]
M∴ P∴ Sov∴ G∴ Commander	Joseph Cerneau	T∴ M∴ Ill∴ B∴ Joseph Cerneau, Past Master	T∴ M∴ Ill∴ B∴ Joseph Cerneau, Past Master	T∴ M∴ Ill∴ B∴ Joseph Cerneau, P. M.
M∴ Ill∴ Dep∴ G∴ Commander	De Witt Clinton	T∴ M∴ Ill∴ B∴ Dewitt Clinton, Grand Master of the Grand Lodge of the State of New York	T∴ M∴ Ill∴ B∴ Dewitt Clinton, Grand Master of the Grand Lodge, and Governor of the State of New York	T∴ M∴ Ill∴ B∴ Dewitt Clinton, Past G∴ Master of the G∴ Lodge, and Governor of the State of N. York
M∴ Ill∴ Lieut∴ G∴ Commander	John W. Mulligan	T∴ M∴ Ill∴ B∴ John W., Mulligan Past Master	T∴ M∴ Ill∴ B∴ John W., Mulligan Past Master	T∴ M∴ Ill∴ B∴ John W., Mulligan Past Deputy G∴ Master of the G∴ Lodge of the State of N. York
Ill∴ Minister of State	Dr. Charles Guerin	T∴ M∴ Ill∴ B∴ Cadwallader D. Colden Senior Warden of the Grand Lodge	T∴ M∴ Ill∴ B∴ Cadwallader D. Colden, Senior Warden of the Grand Lodge, and Mayor of the City of New York	T∴ M∴ Ill∴ B∴ Cadwallader D. Colden, Past Senior G∴ Warden of the G∴ Lodge of the State of New York, Senator.

TABLE 6. Supreme Council of Grand Inspectors General of the 33d Degree

64. KW 61 (see Bibliographical Notes).
65. Printed List.
66. Printed List.
67. Minute Book, folios 158–60. This list was printed in 1826 (KW 61).

OFFICE	25 May 1812	1813	1818	30 March 1826
Ill∴ G∴ Treasurer of the H∴ E∴	Cadwallader D. Colden	T∴ M∴ Ill∴ B∴ Charles Guerin, Past Master	T∴ M∴ Ill∴ B∴ Charles Guerin, Past Master	T∴ M∴ Ill∴ B∴ Elias Hicks, G∴ Secretary of the G∴ L∴ of the State of New York.
Ill∴ G∴ Secretary of the H∴ E∴	John P. Schisano	T∴ M∴ Ill∴ B∴ Jacob Schieffelin, P∴ M∴	T∴ M∴ Ill∴ B∴ John P. Schisano	T∴ M∴ Ill∴ B∴ Francis Dubuar, P∴ M∴
Ill∴ assist∴ G∴ Secretary				T∴ M∴ Ill∴ B∴ M°. Velasquez de la Cateña.
Ill∴ G∴ K∴ of the Seals	Jonathan Schieffelin	T∴ M∴ Ill∴ B∴ Jonathan Schieffelin, P∴ M∴	T∴ M∴ Ill∴ B∴ Jonathan Schieffelin, P∴ M∴	T∴ M∴ Ill∴ B∴ Jonathan Schieffelin P∴ M∴
Ill∴ G∴ Expert				T∴ M∴ Ill∴ B∴ Martin Hoffman, G∴ Master of the G∴ Lodge of the State of N. York
Ill∴ G∴ M∴ of Cer. James B. Durand, P∴ M∴	J. P. Berard			T∴ M∴ Ill∴ B∴
Ill∴ C∴ of G.	Martin Hoffman			T∴ M∴ Ill∴ B∴ Joseph Bouchaud, P∴ M∴
Ill∴ Gr∴ Hospitalier				T∴ M∴ Ill∴ B∴ Alexander S. Glass, P∴ M∴
G∴ Insp∴ General		M∴ Ill∴ B∴ J. Pascal Schisano, James B. Durand, Joseph Gouin.		

Table 6. Supreme Council of Grand Inspectors General of the 33d Degree

OFFICE	25 May 1812	1813	1818	30 March 1826
Honorary Members		M∴ Ill∴ B∴ A. M. Dupotet, G∴ Honorary Com∴, • G. Hacquet, G∴ Honorary Com∴, • J. J. Itter, Emmanuel Gigaud, • J. P. Berard, • John Huard, • J. B. Modest Lefebvre,[68] • Peter Chamau Sr		T∴ M∴ Ill∴ B∴ Simon Bolivar, Most Serene G. Master of the Grand Orient and President of the Republic of, Columbia • Francisco de Paula Santander, Vice Presidente [*sic*] of the Republic of Columbia, • Genl∴ José Francisco Bermundes, • Carlos Soublette Secretary of War of the Republic of Columbia[69]
Present Members			T∴ M∴ Ill∴ B∴ • Jacob Schieffelin, • James B. Durand, • Joseph Gouin, • Elias Hicks, • Toussaint Midy, • Anthony Rainetaux, • Thomas Lownds, • Francis Dubuar, • Joseph Bouchaud, • Martin Hoffman.	T∴ M∴ Ill∴ B∴ • Jacob Schieffelin, • Toussaint Midy, • Gerrit Morgan • John Telfair, • William J. Hunter.

TABLE 6. Supreme Council of Grand Inspectors General of the 33d Degree

68. The last two names were added in handwriting on the printed list.
69. And 18 more names from Central and South America.

OFFICE	25 May 1812	1813	1818	30 March 1826
Absent Members			T∴ M∴ Ill∴ B∴ • A. M. Dupotet,[70] • G∴ Honorary Com∴, • G. Hacquet, G∴ Honorary Com∴,• J. J. Itter, Gigaud, • J. P. Berard• John Huard, • John P. Le Febvre, • A. J. Blocquerst, • J. F. Hurtel, • P. Duler,• Louis Le Loup, • J. Pinard, • P. Javain, • P. Desportes, • J. Dumaine	T∴ M∴ Ill∴ B∴ • Germain Hacquet, Honorary G. Commander, • Lefevre d'Aumale, Representative of the G∴ Orient of France in his Supr∴ Council of G∴ Insp∴ G∴ of the 33 Degree, • Charles Guerin, • John P. Schisano, • Joseph Gouin, • Emmanuel Gigaud,• J. J. Itter, • A. J. Blocquerst, • J. F. Hurtel, • Peter Duler, • Peter Javain, • Peter Desportes, • J. Dumaine, • P. A. Garcia, • B. S. • Damajo de la Luz, • José Maria Casalejo, • Francis Terreforte, • Seth Driggs, • John S. Cogdell, • Thomas W. Bacot, • P. Laurens, • Genl∴ Lafayette, • George W. Lafayette, • Charles S. Tucker

Table 6. Supreme Council of Grand Inspectors General of the 33d Degree

70. Note printed in the list: *Dead.

The list of offices and names of the Grand Officers of the Grand Council follows on folios 6–7 of the Minute Book. It is identical with pages 13–14 of the printed list for 1818.[71]

OFFICE	18 DECEMBER 1816	30 MARCH 1826[72]
Ill.·. President	John W. Mulligan	John Telfair
Grd Senr Warden	Jacob Schieffelin	Hampton Dunham
Grd Junr Warden	Jn. P. Schisano	Jonathan Schieffelin
Grd Orator	Gasper W. Eddy	Rev. F. C. Schaeffer
Grd Secretary	Aaron H. Palmer	M. Velasquez de la Cadena
Gen.·. Grd Treasurer	Joseph Gouin	Alexander S. Glass
Assistant Grd Treasurer	James Gelston	
Grd Keeper of the Seals	Jn. Schieffelin	———
Grd Master of Ceremonies	Francis Dubuar	Augustus S. Cerneau
Grd.·. Expert	Thomas Lownds	Lewis Timolat
Grd.·. Standard Bearer	John Telfair	
Grd Capn.·. of the Guards	Abraham Lott	Henry Marsh
Grd Hospitaler	Alexr S. Glass	J. Widmer

TABLE 7. Grand Officers of the Grand Council for the State of New York

CHARLESTON, THE HISTORY COMMITTEE OF THE NMJ, AND THE MINUTE BOOK

THE HISTORY COMMITTEE OF THE NORTHERN MASONIC JURISDICTION

In 2009, I said in my Washington address to the Scottish Rite Research Society:

> You know of course that along the 19th Century up to the present day, Cerneau is described with rather unflattering words such as impostor of the first magnitude, irregular, spurious.... However, what you may not know is something you will not find in Masonic books. Namely that Grand Commander Dalcho, in December 1821, suggested to the Cerneau representative in

71. Same list with the date 1809 in *The Statutes and Regulations* (1862), 181 (see note 34).
72. Minute Book, f° 164–65

> Charleston that Cerneau's Grand Consistory in New York and Dalcho's Supreme Council in Charleston should divide the whole territory of the United States between them. This Dalcho's offer stays in the Minutes of Cerneau's Grand Consistory....
>
> Now let me explain why I am familiar with Dalcho's offer. In 1950, the Northern Jurisdiction created a History Committee. It met eleven times until 1955 and kept Minutes which were written down with a typewriter for private circulation only. At one of these meetings, on 21 September 1951, Harold Voorhis made a report. He had gone through Cerneau's Consistory's Minutes and found what I just told you about Dalcho's offer to Cerneau.[73]

One year later, I am now able to compare the manuscript of the Minute Book with the quotes made in the Minutes of the History Committee of the Northern Masonic Jurisdiction in 1951. This is what stays in their Minutes:

> Harold V. B. Voorhis who had been given the task of delving into the Masonic Libraries of Boston, New York and Baltimore reported upon a rather startling minute from the records of the Sovereign Grand Consistory (Cerneau) New York, which are now in the archives of the Supreme Council at Boston.
>
> The minute dated December 28, 1821, states that Peter Javain, who was the Grand Consistory's representative to Charleston, South Carolina wrote New York as follows:
>
> "Another Communication from the Ill. Bro. Javain covering a communication from Frederick Dalcho, who pretends to the possession of the degrees of Exalted Masonry and to the dignity of Grd. Inspector Gen'l, or 33°, and in consequence of such pretended quality, asks this Sov. Gd. Consistory to divide the jurisdiction with him by a line of demarkation, dividing the United States of America into two distinct Masonic divisions; that South of the City of Washington he modestly asks to be placed under his jurisdiction and to allow the Gd. Consistory the command of all that [*sic*] north of the said City of Washington.[74]

The words quoted by Voorhis stay on folio 45 of the Minutes of the 98th Sitting, however the date of that sitting is "the 28th day of the 12th∴ Month, Year of T∴ L∴ 5821, Christian Era 1822," which corresponds to 28th February 1822, not to "December 28, 1821." He reported further:

> Another interesting item in the Grand Consistory Minute Book dated May 12, 1817, states: "The Ill∴ Bro. Jean Batiste Aveihe, formerly a member of the Sov. Gd. Cons. of St. Domingo was announced." He was then made a member.

73. *The Plumbline*, Spring 2010 (see note 10).

74. Minutes from 21 September 1951, 18. The discovery of the offer made by Frederick Dalcho startled the NMJ History Committee who appears to have doubted its genuineness. The exact text of Cerneau's Minute Book is quoted below.

The date of the Minute relating the reception of Bro.·. Aveilhé is not 12 May 1817, but "the 12th day of the 5th Month Year of True Light 5817 Christian Era 1817," that is, 12 July 1817. The full passage is worth quoting:

> The Ill.·. Br.·. Jean Batiste [*sic* for Baptiste] Aveihé, formerly Member of the Sov.·. Grd.·. Cons.·. of St.·. Domingo was announced at the exterior of the hall, when he was admitted with the usual acclamations which were returned by him, with his expressions of gratitude for the favorable reception and marks of attention evinced by this Grand Consistory towards him. – After which the Grd.·. Com.·. proposed his admission as a member of this Grd.·. Consistory, he having retired, it was unanimously Resolved that he be admitted as such, whereupon he was again introduced and subscribed to the requirements of this Grd.·. Consist.·. and was proclaimed with all due ceremonies a member of the same, when it was
>
> Resolved that the Grd Chancellor furnish to the Ill.·. Br.·. Aveilhé a copy of this Evenings proceedings signed by at least five Grd.·. Officers.

Voorhis said lastly:

> A third item appearing in the (Cerneau) Grand Consistory, minute book also bears repeating. August 10, 1824–131st sitting – Page 119 of Minute Book. "Notice of Charleston advertisement showing incorporation of the body from 16 to 33 degrees signed by Auld, Holbrook, Dalcho, Moultrie, Levy, Street, McDonald, and McCash [*sic*]. A Committee was appointed to look into the matter."

This item belongs to folios 118 & 119 and the date reads: "the 10.th day of the 2.nd mo. Year of T.·. L.·. 5823 & of the Christian Era April 10th 1824."[75] I wonder how Voorhis came to "August 10, 1824"? Although the words set between quotations marks suggest an actual entry from the Minute Book, such is not the case (see below).

CHARLESTON ENTRIES IN THE MINUTE BOOK[76]

12 July 1817 (81st Sitting, f° 10):

75. See note 17.

76. The coded dates of the sittings are converted into those of the Gregorian Calendar (see Table 1).

A Tableau of the Members composing the Grd∴ Council of Subl∴ Pces∴ of the Royal Secret for the State of South Carolina sitting in Charleston was next presented when it was ordered that the same together with the above communications be deposited in the archives.

30 November 1817 (82nd Sitting, fo 12–13):

Resolved that the Ill∴ Br∴ Grd∴ Secretary be requested to write to the Grd∴ Councils of Philadelphia, Charleston, and Rhode Island separately to remind them of their solemn obligations to forward to the Grand Consistory a detailed and faithful account of their respective operations and labours which have for a long time been anxiously expected by this Sov∴ Grand Consistory (The Sov∴ Grd∴ Commander will furnish the Grd∴ Secretary with proper instructions & material to enable him to frame his correspondence to each of the above Councils to meet the sense of the present decree).

30 November 1818 (84th Sitting, fo 16):

A communication was next received from the Grand Council for the State of South Carolina at Charleston, announcing that the Brother John S. Cogdell[77] has been elected President thereof, accompanying which was a Tableau of the Grd Council and Chapter R∴ +∴ at that place, which were read and Deposited in the Archives.

6 April 1821 (92nd Sitting, fo 29–30)

Several communications received by the Grd∴ Commander were next laid before the Grd∴ Consistory respecting Joseph de Glock D'Obernay,[78] alias D'Obernay de Glock, one of which was from the Grd∴ Council of Pces∴ of the Ral∴ Sect∴ for the State of Maryland dated the 17th∴ day of the 10th Month ad 1820, and the other from the Ill∴ Br∴ P. Javain, our Representative for the State of South Carolina, dated Charleston, the 14th day of the 1st∴ Month ad 1821.

15 December 1821 (95th Sitting, fo 37–38):

A communication was next presented & read from the Grd∴ Council of Pces∴ of the Ral∴ Sect∴ for the State of South Carolina containing a list of members &c. with other documents relating to irregular proceedings of sundry persons at Charleston, who pretend to the possession of the Degrees of Exalted

77. John S. Cogdell (1778–1847), lawyer, was Grand Secretary (1815) then Junior Grand Warden (1817) of the Grand Lodge of South Carolina before succeeding T. W. Bacot as Grand Master of the Grand Lodge of Ancient Free-Masons of South-Carolina on 15 December 1820.

78. See Alain Bernheim, "Further Light on the Masonic World of Joseph Glock," *AQC* 100 (1987), 33–60.

Masonry which Documents were referred to a Special Committee consisting of the Ill.·. Brethren Joseph Cerneau, J. W. Bedell, J. W. Mulligan, Jno Scheiffelin [*sic*] and Harman Westerwelt with directions to report thereon with all convenient speed.

19 December 1821 (96th Sitting, f° 39–41):

Report

The com.·. to whom was referred the communications received at the last sitting of this Gr^{d}.·. Consistory respectfully report.

That many of them being the usual communications from our correspondents only require to have the usual notice of them entered in the minutes and the order for acknowledging the receipt of them entered,

That those from the Gr^{d}.·. Council of P^{ces}.·. of the R^{al}.·. Sec^{t}.·. of South Carolina, contain important information of the irregular proceedings on the part of some persons who profess to have acquired possession of some papers relative to the higher degrees of Masonry under the [40] Jurisdiction of this body; and of the course the same Gr^{d}.·. Council has taken in relation to the same.[79]

The proceedings of the Gr^{d}.·. Council of Charleston S. C.·. have been in the opinion of your Committee marked with a prudence, discretion and firmness and a regard to the principles of Masonry, and the just rights, as well of themselves as of this body which entitle them to its warm approbation and acknowledgment and the confirmation of their proceedings in that behalf, as communicated.

The committee therefore recommend, that this body pass a resolution to that effect, and at the same time declaring its condemnation of the proceedings of the persons by name who have been complained of and that this body doth not acknowledge them; and pronounce their proceedings to be irregular and void and that notice thereof be given to all Masonic bodies under the jurisdiction of, and in correspondence with it, and to all others,

Signed with the following initials Viz.—

J. W. M. — J^{h} C — J. S. — J. W. B.

On motion the above report was accepted and in conformity with its recommendation the following resolution was unanimously adopted Viz.

Resolved that the proceedings of the Gr^{d}.·. Council of Subl.·. P^{ces}. of the R^{al}.·. Sec^{t}.·. for the State of South Carolina so far as relate to the irregular proceedings of certain persons named in their communications above alluded to, be, and the same hereby are approved and confirmed, And that this Sov.·. Gr^{d}.·. Consistory condemns the proceedings of these persons.

Viz. H. G. Street, Moses Holbrook, Elijah Gates, Robert Carr, Alexander Mc.·. Donald, John G. La Roche, N. Bacheldor, Henry Cross, William M

79. See the Appendix of Joseph M'Cosh's *Documents upon Sublime Free=Masonry in the United States of America . . .*, Charleston, 1823.

Dyre, Michael Mc Kenzie, James Little, Joseph Mc Cosh, James W Rouse[80] & Isaac Auld, as unmasonic and irregular, and [41] declare that that [*sic*] it does not recognize the said persons as possessed of any Masonic quality, and directs that all masonic bodies and persons under this jurisdiction govern themselves accordingly and that the preceding recital and resolutions be communicated to all regular masonic bodies in the usual manner,

Whereupon it was resolved unanimously that the Ill∴ Brothers, the Two Ministers of State together with the Grand Secretary, be a committee to make known the meaning of the above report and resolution to the Gr^{d}∴ Council of Subl∴ P^{ces}∴ of the R^{al}∴ Sec^{t}∴ for the State of South Carolina sitting at Charleston, and to carry the same in all its parts into full effect.

24 December 1821 (97th Sitting, f° 43):

On motion, Resolved that the Ill∴ Bro^{s}∴ the Two Ministers of State and the Gr^{d}∴ Secretary be a committee to answer such communications from Charleston, South Carolina, as now remain unanswered.

28 February 1822 (98th Sitting, f° 44–45):

4th∴ a letter from the Ill∴ Bro∴ P. Javain representative of this Gr^{d}. Consistory for the State of South Carolina dated Charleston 28th∴ Dec^{r}∴ 1821, recommending the Ill∴ Bro∴ John Z. Wright as his assistant at Charleston to this Gr^{d} Consist∴ and also Bro. T. W. Bacot,[81] and John S. Cogdell to be Gr^{d}∴ Inspect^{rs}∴ Genl∴ whereupon Resolved that the Bro∴ John Z. Wright, T. W. Bacot, and John S. Cogdell be clothed with that Dignity.

5th∴ Another letter from Bro∴ Javain requesting his Certificate or Diploma as Dep∴ Gr^{d}∴ Inspector Genl∴ and Representative of this Sov∴ Gr^{d}. Consistory for the State of South Carolina; whereupon Resolved that the same be granted & forwarded to him without delay free of expense.

6th∴ Another communication from the Ill∴ Bro∴ Javain covering a communication from Frederick Dalcho, who pretends to the possession of the Degrees of Exalted Masonry and to the dignity of Gr^{d}∴ Inspector Genl∴. or 33^{d}∴ Degree, and in consequence of such pretended quality, asks this Sov∴

80. All these Brethren, except Henry Cross, will belong to the Grand Lodge of Perfection founded in Charleston together or immediately after the creation of a Grand Council of Princes of Jerusalem on 9 February 1822 by Isaac Auld (facsimile Harris-Carter 1964, 140). Their names are listed in the letter Moses Holbrook and James W. Rouse sent to His Excellency Daniel D. Tompkins, Vice-President of the United States, New York, in the Spring of 1822 (*Proceedings* NMJ 1866, 79).

81. "Thomas Wright Bacot … was appointed Postmaster at Charleston by President George Washington in 1794. He retained the position with increasing honor for more than forty years" (Arthur Henry Hirsch, Ph. D., *The Huguenots of Colonial South Carolina* [Duke University Press, 1928; reprinted 1962 by Archon Books; http://listsearches.rootsweb.com/th/read/DuBose/1998-09/0905909567]). Grand Master of the Grand Lodge of South Carolina 1814–17 and of the Grand Lodge of Ancient Free-Masons of South-Carolina 1817–20.

Gr^{d}∴ Consistory to divide the jurisdiction with him by a line of demarkation, dividing the United States of America into two distinct Masonic divisions; that South of the City of Washington he modestly asks to be placed under his jurisdiction and to allow (underlined) the Gr^{d}∴ Consistory the command of all that part North of the said City of Washington.

The subject was referred to the committee on papers from Charleston respecting irregular Proceedings of sundry persons.

26 March 1822 (99th Sitting, f° 46–47):

The Sov∴ Pres^{t}∴ then presented a communication from the Grand Council of Subl∴ P^{ces} of the Ry^{al}∴ Sec^{t}∴ for the State of South Carolina, sitting at Charleston dated the 11th∴ of the present month related to the pretentions to Masonic authority of Doct^{r}∴ Isaac Auld of that city, which he has evinced by the formation and Organization of a Sublime Lodge of Perfection at Charleston, thereby interfering with the Jurisdiction of this Sov∴ Gr^{d}∴ Consistory together with a report of their proceedings on that subject.

Whereupon On Motion of the Ill∴ Bro∴ Cerneau, seconded by the Ill∴ Bro∴ Bedell,

Resolved that a committee of three be appointed to consider, answer, and in all respects to attend to this communication, and all others on the same subject from Charleston, and that said committee be directed to forward the result of their deliberations to our representative for the State of South Carolina, at Charleston in order that it be laid before the said Grand Council, with the least possible delay.

The Ill∴ Bro^{s}∴ Westervelt, Eddy, and Dubuar, were named the above committee.

16 January 1823 (110th Sitting, f° 70):

The Ill∴ Gr^{d}∴ Commander then presented a communication addressed to him by the Ill∴ Bro∴ P. Javain, Depy Gr^{d}∴ Inspect^{r}∴ Genl∴ and Representative of this Sov∴ Gr^{d}∴ Consistory for the State of S∴ Carolina Sitting at Charleston, and hinting at the neglect of this Gr^{d}∴ Consistory, in not answering the communications formerly received from that body after reading which it was mentioned that a committee appointed by this Grand Consistory on the 26th 1st∴ Month 5822 to consider answer and attend to such communications from Charleston of which Bro∴ Westervelt is Chairman had not performed the duty assigned them. Therefore

Resolved that the said committee be discharged from the further consideration of the subject.

Also Resolved that the Bro^{s}∴ Francis Dubuar, Jno∴ Schieffelin and Tobias W Bedell be a committee to consider, answer, and in every respect attend to all communications that have been recd∴ from said Gr^{d}∴ Council, or our

Representative at Charleston which now remain unanswered and report the result of their deliberations without delay.

4 February 1823 (111th Sitting, f° 71):

The committee to whom were referred the communications from Charleston at the last sitting of this Grd∴ Consistory reported that they had compleated [*sic*] the duty assigned them and submitted the Paper by them drawn up with intent to forward to the Grd∴ Council at that place through the Ill∴ Bro∴ Javain our Representative for South Carolina, for the sanction of this Grd∴ Consistory, and in order that it may receive the proper Seals that it was not in the power of a Committee to attach, the said paper having been read and considered, it was on motion Unanimously

Resolved that the document drafted by the Committee consisting of Bros∴ Dubuar, Scheiffelin [*sic*] & Bedell to be forwarded to the Grd∴ Council Sitting at Charleston S∴ C∴ is expressive of the views of this Grd∴ Consistory, and that the same is hereby approved and sanctioned, and that the proper seals, and a certificate from this Grd∴ Consistory be attached thereto agreable [*sic*] to the request of the Committee, and in order that it may bear the fullest marks of authenticity; The proper officer is therefore directed to perform that duty, and cause a copy of the same together with the report of the Committee to be deposited in the Archives of this Grd∴ Consistory.

14 July 1823 (115th Sitting, f° 85):

A Letter was received and read from the Ill∴ Brother P. Javain dated Charleston May 17, 1823, tendering his Resignation as our Representative for S°∴ Ca∴ On motion Resolved that the Grand Chancellor be directed to write to the Ill∴ Br. Javain convening a Com∴ to the Grd Council at Charleston requesting said Council to name an Ill. Bro. of their Body who would be agreeable to its Members, to act as our Representative at that place.

17 September 1823 (118th Sitting, f° 90):

A Communication was received from the Ill∴ Brother John W. Mulligan Grand Commander tendering his Resignation of that dignity and Retiring as a member. Ordered to remain for consideration until the 28. day of the 8. month.

With the above was also Received two Communications from the Ill. Brr P. Javain under dates of 24. & 28. of August accompanying a Pamphlet[82] Published and circulated by a Spurious Assembly at Charleston Sh Ca and a Statement of their Iniquiteous [*sic*] proceedings.

On motion of Brother Bedell seconded by Brr Dubuar Resolved unanimously that the following Brethren Viz. Brr Wm J Hunter, Alexander S. Glass, Elias Hicks, John Telfair & J W Bedell be a committee to consider the Said

82. The M'Cosh book mentioned note 79.

Communications & Report what measures are necessary to Suppress the further proceedings of sais Spurious assembly and insure the future Order and Harmony of the Institution.

14 November 1823 (122d Sitting, f° 95):

The Committee appointed at the meeting of the 17th of the 7th Month 118th Sitting on the subject of a Pamphlet published and circulated by a spurious Assembly at Charleston S. C. made their report & presented the following circular, which was discussed and with sundry amendments unanimously adopted – See page 103.

14 November 1823 (125th Sitting, f° 104):

The committee appointed at the meeting of 17th of 7 m.·. 1823 on the subject of a Pamphlet published & circulated by a spurious Assembly at Charleston S. C. made their report & presented the following circular, which being discussed was adopted.

Ordo ab Chao.

To the Glory of the Grand Architect of the Universe

Most Potent Sov.·. Grand Consistory of the Supreme Chiefs of Exalted Masonry of the ancient Scottish rite of Heredom, for the United States of America, their Territories and Dependencies.

Extract from the Minutes of its Session of the 14th day of the ninth month Anno Lucis 5823 – christian era 14 November 1823.

Under the cel.·. canopy of the zenith, at the central point answering to the 40th degree, 41 min.·. N.·. L.·.

The Sovereign Grand Consistory regularly convoked, met in general assembly on the day above mentioned, at the usual place for holding its sittings, and its labours opened by the Sovereign Grand Commander in the accustomed form and manner.

The subject of the following Resolution being under consideration and the motives that led to this measure being maturely weighed and appreciated, several members having evinced their opinion upon it and the Illustrious Bro.·. Minister of State being heard, it was unanimously adopted in these words.

The Sov.·. Gr[d].·. Consistory having heard read a communication from our representative for the State of South [105] Carolina, respecting the Gr[d].·. Council in the said State, and having seriously deliberated on the same, has felt it a duty thus promptly and expressly to conntain [*sic*] all Councils and Chapters deriving their authority from under this Sov.·. Gr[d].·. Consistory, against having connection or holding correspondence with any Councils or Chapters or with any person or persons, professing to be member or members of any Council or Chapter located in the United States of America, particularly with certain societies under the assumed title of K.·. H.·. whose members are unworthy of professing the Sub.·. Deg.·. of Philosophic Masonry, which is founded on the christian religion, to which they are enemies in principles, and not recognized by this Sov∴ Gr^{d}∴ Consistory; All and every such Chapters being Spurious and Irregular, and their members Impostors. And in order that it may be fully understood who are and who are not regular, it has been deemed expedient to promulgate, that Patents have been granted by this Sov∴ Gr^{d}∴ Consistory for the formation and establishment of Gr^{d}∴ Councils of P^{ces} of the Ryal∴ Sec^{t}∴ and capitulary charters for Sov∴ Chap∴ of R∴ +∴ in the following places, vis.

New York,	State of New York	New Orleans	State of Louisiana
Charleston	d° South Carolina	Baltimore	d° Maryland
Philadelphia	d° Pennsylvania	Newport	d° Rhode Island
Havana	Island of Cuba	Mayaguez	Island of Puerto Rico

Cumana
Barcelona and — Republic of Columbia, South America
Laguayra,

all which are now in the active operation of their powers and functions. And further, that this Sov∴ Gd∴ Consistory has at this moment Dep∴ Gr∴ Insp∴ Gls∴ and Repres∴ residing in all the above mentioned States, Provinces and Departments, to either or all of which Gd∴ Councils, Sov∴ Chap∴ of R∴ +∴ or representatives, application may be made by any brother regularly possessing the degrees of Exalted Masonry, as also by all other Masonic bodies connected with this Sovereign Grand∴ Consistory, either by affiliation or correspondence for information on any and on all subjects relating to the order and without whose recognition, no person claiming the privileges of the same should or ought to be received and admitted into said Councils and Chapters, and acknowledged by the respective members of the same.

This Sov∴ Gr∴ Consistory cannot avoid considering the present a very apt and proper occasion for enjoining upon all the Gd∴ councils and Sov∴ Chap∴ of R +∴ subordinate to its authority, and upon all its Dep∴ Gd∴ Insp∴ Genl∴ and representatives wherever located, strictly to abstain from entering into any public controversy on the subject of its regularity or constitutional organization; its recognition by the Gr^{d}∴ Orient, Gd∴ Consistory, and sup∴ council of Gd∴ Insp∴ Genl∴ of the 33d∴ Deg∴ of France and by all other regularly constituted Sov∴ Gd∴ Consistory in Europe, bearing ample testimony to the order and solidity of its foundation.

On motion ordered 300 copies of the foregoin [*sic*] report be printed and five copies to be sent to each Gd∴ Council & Chap∴ R∴ +∴ under the jurisdiction of the balance [*sic*] deposited in archives for future occasions. The Grand Chancellor is charged with the execution of the same with the least possible delay.

10 April 1824. (131st Sitting, folio 118–19):

A communication was also received from Br.·. P. Javain inclosing an advertisement of an act of incorporation to certain persons as Inspectors Gen.l of 33rd degree with certain powers &c. Resolved that this communication be referred to B^r^.·. Colden with a request for this legal advice with regard to this advertisement for the govt. of our Gr^d^. Council at Charleston.

The tenor of the said advertisement is as follows :

Extract from An Act to incorporate certain Societies.

"Section 33. And be it further enacted, &c. That Isaac Auld, M.D. as Grand Commander; Moses Holbrook, M.D. as Lieutenant Grand Commander; Rev. Frederick Dalcho, M.D. as Past Grand Commander; James Moultrie, M.D. as Secretary General; Moses C. Levi, Esquire, as Treasurer General; Horatio Gates Street, Alexander M'Donald, and Joseph M'Cosh Esqrs., with their associates and successors, be, and they are hereby incorporated and declared a body politic and corporate, in deed and in law, by the name and style of Inspectors General of the Thirty-Third Degree; [And the said Inspectors General of the Thirty-Third Degree] shall have power to regulate all Orders and Degrees of Masonry, from the Sixteenth to the Thirty-Third, (inclusive,) according to the Constitutions of the said several degrees; and the said Corporation, by its name and style aforesaid, shall have a common seal, with power to alter the same, and to make all necessary bye-laws for their better government; and the said Corporation shall have power to purchase lands or personal estate, and to accept any devise, bequest, or donation : Provided, the same shall not exceed the sum of Ten Thousand Dollars : And provided also, that nothing herein contained shall be construed to interfere with any powers, rights, or privileges heretofore granted to the "Most Worshipful Grand Lodge in this State," or any other Grand Lodge of Masons heretofore incorporated.

In the Senate, the twentieth day of December, in the year of our Lord one thousand eight hundred and twenty-three, and in the forty-eighth year of the Independence of the United States of America.

Jacob Bond I'on, President of the Senate.

Patrick Noble, Speaker of the House of Representatives."[83]

26 August 1825 (139th Sitting, f° 148):

A report was then read from the Sub.·. P^ces^.·. Roy.·. Secret in South Carolina, and of the Chapt.·. of Knights R.·. X. sitting in the valley thereof acquainting the Sov.·. G.·. Consistory with the respective elections of the Supreme Council & of the Chapt of R.·. X.

83. See *Official Bulletin ... for the Southern Jurisdiction*, vol. VII (1885), 314–15; Lobingier 1931, 132, with a reference to *Masonic Mirror and Mechanics' Intellgencer* dated 27 June 1825; Harris-Carter 1964, 141 and 147.°

FOREIGN MEMBERS OF THE GRAND CONSISTORY

Some members of the Grand Consistory were foreigners. The Iznaga family is mentioned in the English Peerage. The mention of Jose Macedonio de Chavez in the Minute Book is quoted extensively because it shows the detailed administrative measures taken when daughter bodies were founded by the Grand Consistory outside the United States. The Marquis of Sant'Angelo's name is intimately tied with the first mention of the *Grand Constitutions*' Latin version.

Joseph Azimonti

12 December 1817

> It was proposed that the Ill.·. Brother Joseph Azimonti, a member of Gr^d.·. Council of Princes of the Royal Secret, be admitted a member of this Gr^d.·. Consistory. Thereupon on motion Resolved unanimously that he be admitted....

Joseph Azimonti was "a Milanese gentleman", described p. 255 of *A Narrative of Excursions, Voyages, and Travels*... by George Rapelje, Esq. New York. 1834, available from Google Books.

The Iznaga Family

14 June 1822

> Resolved that the Ill.·. Bro.·. Felix Iznaga, P^ce.·. of the Royal Sec^t.·., recently received a member of the Gr^d.·. Council of Subl.·. P^ces.·. of the R^al.·. Sec^t.·. for the State of New York be admitted to the right of membership to this Sov.·. Gr^d.·. Consistory.

Felix Maria Iznaga y Borrell, christened 11 Apr 1802 in Trinidad, Cuba, died 1876. He married Francisca Rendon y Mesa. http://iznaga.webs.com/gen11.htm (114 xiii).

21 June 1822

> Resolved that the Ill.·. Bro.·. Felix Iznaga be clothed with power and authority to confer the several Degrees to that of P^ce.·. of the R^al.·. Sec^t.·. inclusive, on the Bro.·. Jose Carel at present a resident of the Island of Trinidad and that he be exempted of the payment of further fees therefor, ... translating the manuscripts

> and Documents relating to the several Degrees inferior to and including the last named Degree of Sub.·. P^{ce}.·. of the R^{al}.·. Sec^{t}.·. 32^{d}.·. Degree.
>
> A motion was made and duly seconded that the Bro.·. Joseph Anisetto Iznaga, P^{ce}.·. of the R^{al}.·. Sec^{t}.·., and member of the Gr^{d}.·. Council of Subl.·. P^{ces}.·. for the State of New York be received a member of this Sov.·. Gr^{d}.·. Consistory.

Jose Aniceto Iznaga y Borrell, born 21 Apr 1791 in Trinidad, Cuba; christened 8 Jan 1792 in Trinidad, Cuba; died 3 Dec 1860 in Sancti Spiritus, Cuba. He married (1) Luisa Mariana del Camino y Pablo Velez; (2) Maria Dolores Castillo y Lopez. http://iznaga.webs.com/gen11.htm (105 iv).

29 October 1822

> A Petition was then presented from the Ill.·. Bro. José Antonio Iznaga, praying to be admitted a member of this Gr^{d}.·. Consistory. Whereupon the Prayer of the Petitioner was granted. . . ."

Jose Antonio Iznaga y Borrell, born 8 Jan 1790 in Trinidad, Cuba; christened 8 Jan 1793 in Trinidad, Cuba; died 12 Jan 1827 in Kingston, Jamaica. He married Maria Francisca Del Valle y Castillo. http://www.thepeerage.com/p41281.htm#i412806 & http://iznaga.webs.com/gen11.htm (104 iii).

> The Yznaga's did live in Cuba for many years between 1860–85 or so. The Yznaga's are a Basque family from North-Eastern Spain. They left Spain after being asked to leave by the King as they were wealthy members of the Basque resistance. Moving to Cuba for less then a generation, they had to leave Cuba (for supporting the rebels against the Spanish Crown) and ended up in a few places. Jose Antonio Yznaga was the patriarch and his children settled in Texas, Louisiana and New York.

This is one of several messages concerning the Yznaga family in: http://boards.ancestry.co.uk/thread.aspx?mv=flat&m=357&p=surnames.snead).

JOSE MACEDONIO DE CHAVEZ

2 January 1823

> The petition of Ill.·. Bro.·. Jose Macedonio de Chavez, a member of this Sov.·. Gr^{d}.·. Consistory was received praying that he may be appointed Representative of this Sov.·. Gr^{d}.·. Consistory for the South of the Island of Cuba and be clothed with power and authority to take the preparatory steps towards forming a Sov.·. Chap.·. R.·. +.·. and Gr^{d}.·. Council of Subl.·. P^{ces}.·. of the R^{al}.·. Sec^{t}.·. for the South of the Island of Cuba, his present residence, which having

been read, and the importance of Establishing in a legal & regular manner an assemblage of Masons of the higher degrees at that place having been considered, a number of Brethren and the Ill∴ Minister of State having been heard thereon

Resolved unanimously that the Ill∴ Bro∴ Jose Macedonio de Chavez be and he hereby is appointed our Dep^{y}∴ Gr^{d}∴ Insp^{r}∴ Genl∴, and Representative for the South of the Island of Cuba, and in consequence of his Dignity as such, is empowered, and authorised to advance seven persons already possessing the three Degrees of Symbolic Masonry to the Subl∴ Degree of Sov∴ P^{ce}∴ of the R^{al}∴ Sec^{t}∴ 32 deg∴ for each and every of which seven persons so advanced by & under the authority hereby delegated, he shall pay, or cause to be paid to this Gr^{d}∴ Consistory the sum of Twenty five Dollars; and so soon as the same shall have been effected shall proceed to form a Chap∴ R∴ +∴ and a Provisional Provincial Grand Committee of P^{ces}∴ of the R^{al}∴ Sec^{t}∴ for the South of the said Island of Cuba and cause report of his proceedings in the premises and a list of Officers elected for said Chap∴ R∴ +∴ and Provincial Gr^{d} Committee to be forwarded together with applications for a Capitulary Charter for the Establishment of a Chap∴ R∴ +∴ and a Gr^{d}∴ Council of P^{ces}∴ of the R^{al}∴ Sec^{t}∴, to this Sov∴ Gr^{d}∴ Consistory without delay, and after the number of seven shall have been so advanced, it shall not be lawful for our said representative, or the said Chap∴ R∴ +∴, or Gr^{d}∴ Provisional Provincial Committee to confer the degrees, or any of them on any person or persons until such Capitulary Charter and Warrant shall have been obtained from this Gr^{d}∴ Consistory and the fees therefor fully paid."

> Dimanche 19 janvier 1817. Port de La Havane. A midi, j'ai pris une volante (voiture du pays, attelée d'une mule), et je me suis rendu chez dom Macedonio de Chavez, riche propriétaire de l'île. (Anon. [Baron de Montlèzon]. *Voyage fait dans les années 1816 et 1817, de New-Yorck a la Nouvells-Orléans et de l'Orénoque au Mississippi*, Paris, Librairie de Gide Fils. 1818. Tome Second, pp. 25–26, available from Google Books).

Orazio de Attelis, Marquis of Sant'Angelo

25 October 1824

Ill∴ Br∴ Jonathan Schieffelin put a sealed package into the hands of the Sov∴ G∴ Commander, stating, that he had received it from the Marquis Sant Angelo, who being a member of the G∴ Consistory at Naples, solicited to be acknowledged and received as such by the Sov∴ G∴ Consistory of the U∴S∴A∴ On opening said package it was found to contain several diplomas written in the Italian language, setting forth, that Orazio de Attelis, Marquis Sant Angelo had been initiated in the several degrees of Masonry up to the [*blank*] On motion of said Ill∴ Br∴ Schieffelin the diplomas were considered issued in due & regular form, and the Ill∴ Br∴ Orazio de Attelis, Marquis

Sant Angelo, was admitted member of this Sov∴ G∴ Consistory : the M∴ P∴ Dep∴ Sov∴ G∴ Commander being requested to inform him thereof."

25 January 1825

The Il∴ Br∴ Orazio de Attelis Sant Angelo, being introduced by the G∴ M∴ of Ceremonies, took the oath of allegiance & affiliation & was duly proclaimed a member of this G∴ Consistory."

The Register (Golden Book) of Saint Laurent includes the earliest-known Latin version of the Constitutions dated from 1 May 1786 (folios 22–37).[84]

At the bottom of folio 37 Saint Laurent wrote the following note : "Nta. J'avais confié ce manuscrit (rare et précieux par lui-même autant que par les signatures qui s'y trouvent) au marquis de St Angelo, qui l'a égaré pendant plusieurs mois. Comme je voulais avoir sur mon registre les copies de toutes mes pièces je continuai à y écrire laissant la place présumée suffisante pour copier les lois de l'ordre. Mais les copistes ayant mal pris leurs dimensions, le certificat de ces pièces se trouve compris dans celui qui est porté à la page 49 de ce registre." (signé) Cte de St Laurent.[85]

At the bottom of folio 49 is the following :

The foregoing writings are the true copies by abstract of the respective originals thereof, from page 22 vo to this present

Witness my hand and the seals and stamps of the United Sup. Council & sections

The Grand Secretary and Chancel∴ of the H∴ E∴

Geo Smith 33°

84. The (second) Register of Saint Laurent belongs to the archives of the Grand Lodge of Pennsylvania whose Associate Librarian and Curator, Bro. John H. Platt, sent me a photocopy some twenty-five years ago (Alain Bernheim, "Le 'Bicentenaire' des Grandes Constitutions de 1786: Essai sur les cinq textes de référence historique du Rite Écossais Ancien et Accepté" (3rd part), *Renaissance Traditionnelle* Nr. 70, 1987, 99–115). The Latin version of the Constitutions of 1786 belongs to the Register's first part which was certified on 15 August 1832. It first appeared in print in 1836 as an annex to the Treaty signed in Paris on 23 February 1834 between the Supreme Councils of France, Brazil, and the United Supreme Council of the Western Hemisphere. The latter Council was the result of a Treaty signed in New York in February 1832 between Saint Laurent's Council and that founded by Joseph Cerneau, then headed by Elias Hicks. In the United States, the Latin version was first "Published by Authority of the Supreme Council for the Southern Jurisdiction of the United States of America" in 1859 in New Orleans and in New York by Albert Pike.

85. "I entrusted this manuscript (rare and valuable because of the signatures it includes) with the Marquis of St Angelo who mislaid it several months long. Since I wanted to have the copies of all my documents in my register, I kept on writing in it leaving what I thought to be room enough to copy the laws of the order. But the copists having miscalculated the necessary space, the authentification of these documents is included in the one which stays page 49 of this register."

QUESTIONS . . . AND A LAST DOCUMENT

> I shall tell *only* what I believe to be true, which is easy. I shall tell *everything* I believe to be true, which is more difficult....
> — Léon Blum

Mr. Jeffrey Croteau ended his Letter to the Editor with words I quoted at the beginning of this paper:

> With the upcoming 2013 bicentennial celebrating the founding of the Northern Masonic Jurisdiction in 1813, I hope that Mr. Bernheim and others will, indeed, be ready, willing, and anxious to provide new perspectives on the Scottish Rite by re-examining primary sources....

I modestly tried to fulfill Mr. Croteau's hopes with the present paper's first part. That is, I brought part of the evidence which was known to all the historians who were lucky enough to read the Cerneau's 1816–26 Minute Book. The second part of this paper will presumably appear next year in *Heredom*. It will attempt to elucidate a question which I purposely refrained from approaching here, namely the legality, the legitimacy, of Cerneau's doings in New York, which is related to a further question: Which were the laws followed by Cerneau? A question which can hardly be approached without taking a good look at the legality of the creation of both contemporary American Supreme Councils. Let us give it a glance.

Mr. Croteau mentions as an established fact the founding of the Northern Masonic Jurisdiction in 1813. How can he explain then that the founder of that Supreme Council, Emanuel De La Motta, wrote on 18 June 1814:

> The Grand Constitutions of the 33d∴ ordered *two* Supreme Councils of the 33d∴ to be established for the Jurisdiction of the United States of America – but it is only natural and correct that Charleston shall help establish the *second* one, and this is what they will do while I am here, and in a very short time.[86]

"Shall help ... will do ... in a very short time...." In the middle of June 1814, La Motta mentioned *in the future* something which supposedly had happened several months earlier. Isn't that odd?

86. Letter of Emanuel De La Motta to Alexandre François de Grasse-Tilly, original French in the Archives of the Supreme Council, 33°, S.J., published by Arturo de Hoyos in *Heredom*, vol. 9 (2001), 90–95.

Let us take a close look at the official documents issued in Charleston between February 1822 and May 1825.[87] All of them show that the Officers of Charleston Supreme Council added "U.S. America" after their names and office titles. Such was the name of the Mother Supreme Council since its celebrated *Circular throughout the two Hemispheres*, approved on 4 December 1802:

> On the 31st of May, 5801, the Supreme Council of the 33d degree for the United States of America, was opened....

In the documents issued in Charleston during the 1820s, the mention of "Southern Jurisdiction" happens *for the first time* in the Balustre sent to New York on 22 January 1827![88] Even then, a document drawn up four months later has – again! – "in the U.S.A." added after the names of the Officers of the Charleston Supreme Council.[89] And the last document signed by Frederick Dalcho, 14 March 1830, shows he added "Past Grand Commander *in the U.S.A.*" (my emphasis) after his signature although Holbrook on the same document signed as "Sov. Gr. Commander of the S.D. & J. of the U.S.A."[90]

Was the Northern Masonic Jurisdiction legitimately created in 1813 – or slightly later – by a member of the Charleston Supreme Council and with its approval? Whoever thinks it was, should find a good answer to the above questions.

However Mr. Croteau should not think that my inquisitive critical mind is turned exclusively against, or toward, the Northern Masonic Jurisdiction.

I also find very strange La Motta's words from 18 June 1814 ("The Grand Constitutions of the 33d∴ ordered *two* Supreme Councils of the 33d∴ to be established for the Jurisdiction of the United States of America.") when compared with what Frederick Dalcho had written to La Motta a few months earlier:

> It is well known to those who have received the 33d degree, that there can be but one Council in a nation or kingdom; & that the Council for the U. S.

87. Facsimiles in Harris-Carter (1964), 140, 142, 150, 160.
88. Harris-Carter (1964), 172–75.
89. Harris-Carter (1964), 178.
90. Southern District and Jurisdiction, Harris-Carter (1964), 202.

> was lawfully established in this City, May 31st 1801, consequently any other assuming its prerogatives must be surreptitious.[91]

"*The* Council for the U.S." ... And no mention of "*two* Supreme Councils for the Jurisdiction of the United States of America" ... How strange again!

And these are the two Supreme Councils who judged that Joseph Cerneau's Supreme Council was illegal ... spurious ... irregular ... !?

Masonic history should maybe experience an "agonizing reappraisal" ... which is what the second part of this paper will attempt to do.

A Last Document

Almost all historians – except of course those who belonged to the Cerneau system – laid stress on the fact that not one single extant document shows that meetings of the Supreme Council founded by Cerneau were held before November 1827. And, consequently, such an absence implies that it never met. For instance, William Sewall Gardner:

> It is well known that Joseph Cerneau had not for some years any Supreme Council. He had what he called a Sovereign Grand Consistory in and for the State of New York.... Previous to his sailing, – to wit, Nov. 28, 1827, – a Supreme Council (so called) was opened in the city of New York, by Joseph Cerneau, and, as I believe, for the first time. I can find no allusion to it before this time among the papers and records of the Cerneau body in my possession.[92]

Albert Pike:

> and no Body claiming to be a Supreme Council of the 33d Degree, with any powers, was established by him until November 28, 1827.[93]

Samuel Baynard:

> Of the meetings and transactions of this "Supreme" Council there are no known minutes. As a matter of fact, it is the consensus of opinion of all authorities whom it has been our privilege to consult, that there were no meetings or transactions to record. The body existed in name only, was subject and

91. Letter from 23 August 1813, Harris-Carter (1964), 118.

92. "The Spurious Supreme Councils in the Northern Jurisdiction," *Proceedings* NMJ 1864, 109–73 (here 110, 114, & 115) where a footnote, 109, shows that Gardner's article originally appeared in the *Freemason's Monthly Magazine*, vol. 23.

93. *The Sup∴ Council for France and its Dependencies in re Joseph Cerneau* (1886), quoted in Baynard 1938, Vol. I, 211.

> appendant to the Sovereign Grand Consistory for the United States of America, Their Territories and Dependencies.[94]

Of course, the absence of documents does not, by itself, prove that a Masonic body did not exist or hold meetings. Do we have the Minute of a single meeting of the Charleston Supreme Council after 4 December 1802 and before … the 1820s ? Pike himself admitted in rather strong words that

> written record-books are by no means necessary to prove the continued existence of Masonic Bodies.… All the babble about the want of records has been addressed by knavery to ignorance.… A Masonic Power that performs its functions publicly for three quarters of a century and more, and an officer known to have acted as such for a quarter of a century, need no other proof of title.[95]

Faced with such contradictory points of view, I happened to notice the importance of a hand-written sheet headed:

> The Supreme Council of Grand Inspectors General of the 33d Degree for the United States of America their Territories & Dependencies … Extract from the minutes of the Sitting of the 11th day of the 5th M∴M∴ A∴L∴ 5823.

It is signed by nine members of Cerneau's Supreme Council.[96] Its date, 11 July 1823, stays between two sittings of the Grand Consistory, 9 June and 14 July. Which, at least for me, is the palpable evidence that Cerneau's Supreme Council *did* hold (at least) one sitting of its own.

The evidence should be brought before the eyes of a jury, that is, the readers of this paper. Which is why it is reproduced in facsimile in the Appendix.

BIBLIOGRAPHICAL NOTES

Primary Sources

Except one,[97] the Grand Consistory founded several bodies in New York before the beginning (8 November 1816) of the Minute Book analyzed in

94. Baynard 1938, Vol. I, 203.
95. Albert Pike, *Of Cernauism* (New: York 1884), 77–78.
96. Bibliothèque Nationale, FM1307.
97. "The Grand Encampment of Sir Knight Templars and Appendant Orders for the State of New York" is not mentioned in this paper. According to *The Statutes and Regulations* (1862), it was established "on the 22d day of January, 1814" (190) and "opened" (191) or "regularly constituted

this paper. The following sources suggest dates for their creations and show the names of their officers and members.

Documents of the Supreme Council of France 1804–1815, three volumes of manuscript and printed items,[98] rediscovered in the archives of Washington by Ill.·. Arturo de Hoyos who copied and put them at my disposal.

Two lists printed in New York, copies of which were also put at my disposal by Ill.·. de Hoyos. One for 1813[99] is reproduced in the Appendix. It was entitled:

> *List of the Grand Officers, Members, Honorary Members &c. of the Supreme Council of Grand Inspectors General, of the 33d Degree, Regularly established according to the Ancient Constitutional Scottish Rite of Heredom, for the United States of America their Territories and dependencies held in the City of New York, also of the Grand Consistory of Supreme Chiefs of Exalted Masonry, and the Constituted bodies of its Jurisdiction.* Anno Lucis, 5813. – New-York: Printed by Hardcastle and Van Pelt, No. 86, Nassau-st. – 1813.[100]

The other list, for the year 1818, brings information not included in the Minute Book. It is entitled:

> *List of the Grand Officers, Members, Honorary Members &c. of the Supreme Council of Grand Inspectors General of the 33D Degree, and of the Sovereign Grand Consistory of Supreme Chiefs of Exalted Masonry, of the Ancient Constitutional Scottish Rite of Heredom, for the United States of America, their Territories and Dependencies, held in the City of New York. Also, of the Constituted Bodies of its Jurisdiction, and of the Grand Bodies Correspondent.* Anno Lucis 5818. New York: Printed by Br. J. Seymour, 49 John-St. 1819.[101]

by the Sovereign Grand Consistory" on "the 18th day of the 4th month, A.·. L.·. 5814, answering to June, A.·. D.·., 1814" (21).

98. In French: *Décisions du Suprême Conseil des Inspecteurs généraux du 33e et dernier degré du Rite ancien et accepté, pour la france, depuis L'année 1804. Jusques et Compris l'année 1815.* The existence of these three volumes was (first?) mentioned in *Dissection of a Manifesto* (1858), 63, and by Pike in *Official Bulletin*, vol. VIII (September 1887), 274.

99. KW 32.

100. This title was quoted verbatim twice by Emanuel De La Motta in his *Rejoinder*: "In the early part of May, 5813, I arrived here, not on any *speculative*, *office hunting*, or *masonic* errand, but in quest of health. Some time in July a certain pamphlet or tableau, signed, sealed and stamped, was placed in my hands, entitled...." (3) and 60, where La Motta mentions "their *alias cidevant* [*sic*] Supreme Council."

101. KW 43. Walgren wrote that this list was printed in 1818 (which is wrong) and notes that not having found an original copy, he copied Folger's Document No. 20. That list was also transcribed in William H. Peckham, *The Ancient and Accepted Scottish Rite in the United States of America from 1801 to 1883 inclusive*, 158–66 (New York 1884).

Original in the collection of the San Antonio (Texas) Scottish Rite Library. It was formerly the property of Nathan Hammett Gould, 33°, who moved to San Antonio in 1876 (Baynard 1938, Vol. I, pp. 426–28). N. H. Gould's copy belonged to William Douglas (Member of the Consistory in Rhode Island). It was given to him by John A. Shaw, Deputy "for the State of Rhode-Island" on the 1818 list (see Table 5.2.).

The Cerneau file FM1307 from the Bibliothèque Nationale de France, which was sent to me by Ill.∴ S. Brent Morris, 33°. It includes 23 manuscript documents issued between 1802 and 1842 in Port-Républicain, Havana, Baracoa, New York, and Villeblevin.

De La Motta, Emanuel. 1814. [Rejoinder]. 61 pp. + 1 p. Errata. Dated 5 September 1814, p. 51. KW 35. Original in the Archives of the Supreme Council, 33°, S.J., Washington, DC. A photocopy was put at my disposal by Ill.∴ Br.∴ Arturo de Hoyos, 33°. It is transcribed in Lobingier 1931, pp. 99–122, except for the page of Errata.

Secondary Sources

The Statutes and Regulations, Institutes, Laws and Grand Constitutions of the Ancient and Accepted Scottish Rite with Notes, from Authentic Documents, Prepared by the Supreme Council 33° of the United States of America. New York, 1862.

A book of 278 pages, printed in 1862 by Macoy & Sickels, 430 Broome Street, New York. It is mentioned and its contents summarily described in Baynard 1938, Vol. II, pp. 112–13. It was reprinted by Kessinger Publishing, 2003, and a limited preview is available from Google Books.

Although the book was published anonymously, its authors can be ascertained.[102] They mention "the records" several times and relied likely on original documents.[103] Its Appendix, entitled "The History of the Supreme Council 33d, Ancient and Accepted Scottish Rite for the United States

102. The *Supplement* inserted in Folgers's 2nd edition (1881) shows under 8 October 1860 (27): "Resolved, That a Committee of Three be appointed to prepare and publish a correct history of this Supreme Grand Council. Thrice Ill.∴ Bros.∴ Edmund B. Hayes, Hopkins Thompson and George L. Osborne were appointed such committee."

103. The list of Officers for 1816 which it reproduces, 203–5, is strictly identical with that of the Minute Book (18 December 1816, 80th Sitting, f° 6–7).

of America, its Territories and Dependencies" (pp. 179–257), appears as a reasonably reliable source for the period 1807–15 because the lists of officers, the Minutes and documents for the years 1816–26 it includes are almost identical with those of the Minute Book.

In my copy stays a letter written on 27th August 1862 in Paris by Harry Seymour "Sov.·. S.·. Mas.·. of Ceremonies.·.," showing that he brought it "To his Excellency Maréchal Magnan 33rd, Grand Master of Masons composing the Grand Orient of France" (About Seymour's visit to Europe, see Peckham 1884, pp. 206 sq.). Folger likely used some indications from that book (see Chapter Tenth, Statistic Account, pp. 287 sq. of the 1862 first edition) though with some inaccuracies and without mentioning his source. Folger also mentions "the records of the Sovereign Grand Consistory."[104]

History of the Ancient and Honorable Fraternity of Free and Accepted Masons and Concordant Orders. Illustrated. Written by a Board of Editors: Henry Leonard Stillson, Editor-in-Chief. William James Hughan, European Editor. Boston and New York, U.S.A.: The Fraternity Publishing Company. London, England: George Kenning, 16 Great Queen Street, European Publisher. 1891.

A collective work of 904 pages. Josiah H. Drummond, Past Sovereign Grand Commander for the Northern Masonic Jurisdiction of the United States of America and Past Grand Master of Maine, was the author of the chapter devoted to the Ancient and Accepted Scottish Rite. Pages 652, 714, 814–15, & 854 concern Cerneau. The book is available from Google Books.

CLASSICAL WORKS

Baynard, Samuel Harrison, Jr. 1938. *History of the Supreme Council, 33°, Ancient and Accepted Rite of Freemasonry, Northern Masonic Jurisdiction of the United States of America and its Antecedents.* 2 vol. Boston, Massachusetts: Privately printed. Press of Grit Publishing Company, Williamsport, Pa.

Folger, Robert. 1862. *The Ancient and Accepted Scottish Rite in thirty-three Degrees … With an Appendix containing numerous documents….* 2nd edition, 1881. New York: Published by the author.

104. Folger 1862, 111. Also Peckham 1884, vi.

Harris-Carter. 1964 [Harris, Ray Baker. Prepared for Publication by James D. Carter, 33°]. *History of The Supreme Council, 33° (Mother Council of the World) Ancient and Accepted Scottish Rite of Freemasonry Southern Jurisdiction, U.S.A. – 1801–1861.* The Supreme Council, 33°: Washington, DC.

[Lobingier, Charles S.] 1931. *The Supreme Council, 33°, Mother Council of the World. Ancient and Aceepted Scottish Rite of Freemasonry, Southern Jurisdiction, U.S.A.* Louisville, Kentucky: The Standard Printing Co. Incorporated.

Walgren, Kent. 1994. "A Bibliography of Pre-1851 American Scottish Rite Imprints (non-Louisiana)." *Heredom*, Volume 3 (1994), pp. 55–119.

Abbreviations

KW Refers to one of the 105 numbered documents listed in Walgren 1994.
SCDF Refers to Documents of the Supreme Council of France 1804–1815.

APPENDIX

The transcriptions of the first three documents were made by Mr. Gilles Lorillon who put them at my disposal.

1. Birth Certificate of Joseph Cerneau[105]

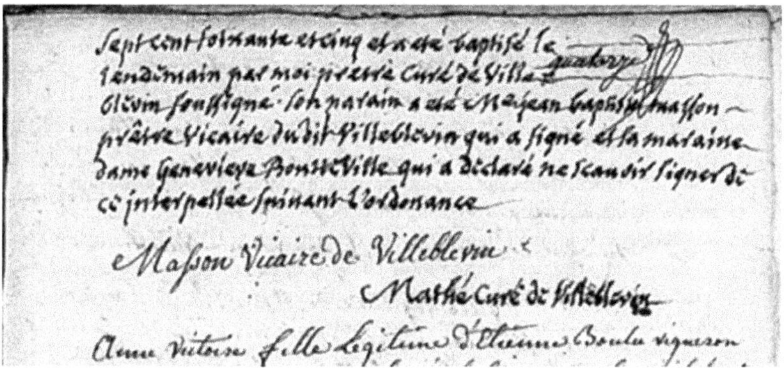

Joseph fils légitime du sieur Edme Etiene Cerneau recteur des petites ecoles de Vileblevin et de félicité perpetue gateau est né le quatorze novembre mil sept cent soixante et cinq et a eté baptisé le lendemain par moi prêtre curé de Villeblevin soussigné. Son parrain a eté Mr jean baptiste masson prêtre vicaire du dit villeblevin qui a signé et la maraine dame Genevieve Boutteville qui a déclaré ne scavoir signer de ce interpellée suivant l'ordonnance
Masson Vicaire de Villeblevin
Mathé curé de Villeblevin

105. ADY (Archives Départementales de l'Yonne) – 4E450 / 10 - 5 Mi 1024/3.

2. Death Certificate of Joseph Cerneau's Wife[106]

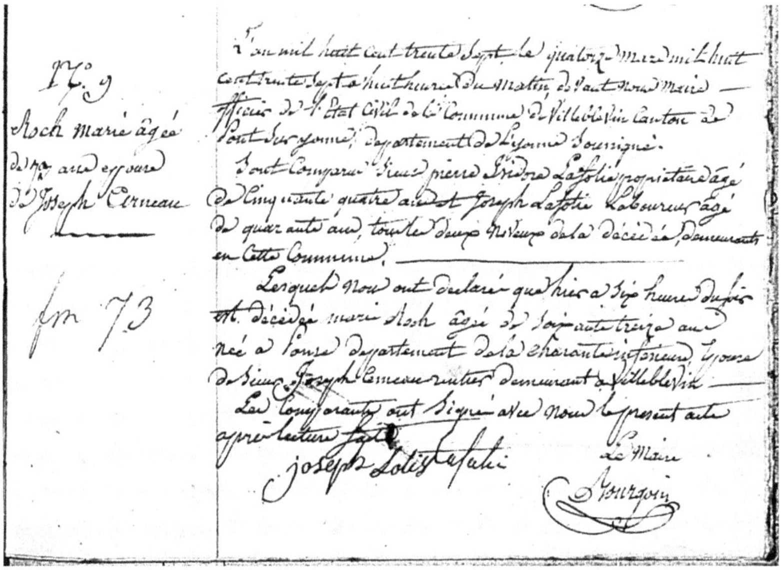

L'an mil huit cent trente sept, le quatorze mars mil huit cent trente sept a huit heures du matin, devant nous maire officier de l'Etat Civil de la Commune de Villeblevin Canton de Pont sur Yonne, departement de L'Yonne soussigné.

Sont comparus Sieur pierre Isidore Lafolie propriétaire âgé de cinquante quatre ans et Joseph Lafolie Laboureur âgé de quarante ans, tous les deux neveux de la décédée, demeurant en Cette Commune

Lesquels nous ont declaré que hier a six heures du soir est décédée Marie Roch âgée de soixante treize ans née a Pouze departement de la Charente inférieure, Epouse de Sieur Joseph Cerneau rentier demeurant a Villeblevin

Les comparants ont signé avec nous le present acte après lecture faite

joseph Louis Lafolie Le Maire

Bourgoin

106. ADY – 2E450 / 15 – 5 Mi 1025/5.

3. Death Certificate of Joseph Cerneau[107]

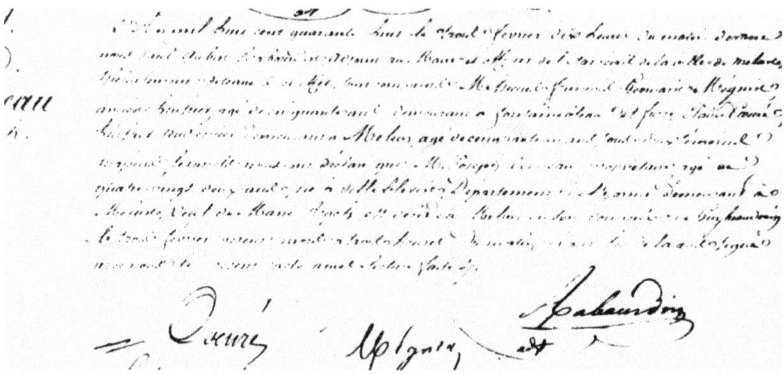

L'an mil hui cent quarante huit le Trois février dix heures du matin devant nous Paul Aubin Rabourdin, 2ième adjoint au Maire et officier de l'état civil de la ville de Melun, spécialement dévolu à cet effet, ont comparus Messieurs françois Germain Mégnien ancien bijoutier agé de cinquante ans demeurant a fontainebleau et Eloi Coeuré huissier ordinaire demeurant à Melun âgé de cinquante un ans tous deux témoins majeurs, lesquels nous ont déclaré que M. Joseph Cerneau propriétaire, agé de quatre vingt deux ans, né à Villeblevin Département de l'Yonne demeurant à Melun, veuf de Marie Roch, est décédé à Melun en son domicile rue Guy baudouin le trois février présent mois à trois heures du matin ... ont signé avec nous le présent acte apres lecture faite.

107. ADSM (Archives Départementales de Seine-et-Marne) 6E306/58 – 5 MI6039 (1848–49), vue 18.

Joseph Cerneau, Part 2— The Charleston Gr. Council P.R.S. & the Supreme Council of the U.S.A.

Alain Bernheim, 33°

Because a story has been related, in one way, for an hundred years past, is not, alone, sufficient to stamp it with truth.

— Frederick Dalcho
An Oration, 1803

Shortly after the reappearance in November 2010 of the second Minute Book of Cerneau's Grand Consistory in New York, an unknown manuscript of an even greater significance comprising some 170 folios foolscap came to light: the Register (Minute Book) of the Cerneau's Grand Council of Princes of the Royal Secret at Charleston discovered by Ill. Arturo de Hoyos, 33°, in the archives of the Supreme Council in Washington.[1] The Minutes begin on 17 August 1815 (first meeting), they end with the 74th meeting held on 21 May 1825.

Before getting acquainted with the new information provided by the *Register*, readers who wish to refresh their knowledge of the Masonic situation in South Carolina – the successive state Grand Lodges and the Supreme Council of the United States of America – will take a look at Appendix 1 which also includes information about some of the protagonists mentioned in this paper (Who's who in Charleston, Appendix 1.4).

THE *REGISTER*

The *Register* opens with two unnumbered folios bearing the titles of the officers, a few notes about its organization and the Hebrew names of the months, followed with a certification signed by Peter Javain showing that he delivered the *Register* in Charleston, 'the 17th Day [of] the Sixth Month 5815', that is on 17 August 1815 (transcribed in Appendix 2.1).

Next come the Minutes of the first meeting of the Grand Council on the same day and the text of the Warrant from 10 April 1815 (transcribed in Appendix 2.2 and 2.3).

Then comes a series of laws written in French followed with fifteen 'Articles of Regulations and General Police, decreed by the Gd Consistory of the United States ... to be observed by the Grand Councils of its Jurisdiction' dated 26 September 1812, and an 'Abstract of the Sitting [of the Grand Consistory in New York] of the 19th day of the 7th month A.L. 5812,' that is, 19 September 1812 (see Appendix 2.4).

The rest of the *Register* is devoted to the Minutes of the meetings of the Charleston Grand Council from 16 September 1815 to 21st May 1825.

1. In 'Joseph Cerneau, His Masonic Bodies, and His Grand Consistory's Minute Book – Part I.' (*Heredom* 18, 2010, 25–84), I enumerated biographical dates concerning Joseph Cerneau and thanks to the rediscovery of the second Minute Book of the Grand Consistory founded in New York in 1807, I was able to describe the various bodies under his authority. Since that Minute Book began with the 78th sitting of this Grand Body on 8 November 1816, the preceding period remained somewhat obscure.

NEW INFORMATION PROVIDED BY THE REGISTER

1. A Grand Council of Princes of the Royal Secret was opened in Charleston on 17 August 1815 under a Warrant from the Cerneau Grand Consistory in New York.[2] Thomas Wright Bacot, its first President, was chosen for a period of three years. He was then Grand Master of the Grand Lodge of South Carolina and became the first Grand Master of the Grand Lodge of Ancient Free-Masons of South Carolina founded in December 1817.

2. Together with the Warrant, the New York Grand Consistory communicated to Charleston its laws in French. A copy is included in the *Register* under the general title *Extraits des Lois Generales et des Instructions sur les principes G.ˣ de la h∴ mie – Instituts, Statuts et reglements Generaux de la Haute Maconnerie.* The *Register* includes no *Reglements Generaux. Instituts* and *Statuts* are followed with an *Extrait des Instructions sur les Principes Generaux de la Haute Maconnerie.*

3. Specific minutes of the *Register* describe the origin of a controversy which began in Charleston on 21 August 1821, five weeks after the death of Emanuel De La Motta. By that time John Cogdell had succeeded T. W. Bacot as President of the Cerneau Grand Council as well as Grand Master of the Grand Lodge. Frederick Dalcho had become Grand Commander in 1816 after the death of John Mitchell and as Most Rev. Grand Chaplain was the fifth-ranking Grand Officer of the Grand Lodge.

On that day Cogdell informed the Grand Council that '*Books and other documents which it is understood belonged to Grand Commander John Mitchell*' had come into the hands of a group of Charleston Blue Masons called 'the Association' which met at the New England Coffee House held by Horatio Gates Street. Cogdell named Bacot president of a committee to investigate the situation. The committee entered in contact with members of the Association. Bacot alone had several conversations on the matter with Frederick Dalcho. Members of the Association had talks with Dalcho. The committee's report delivered on 21 September showed who were the members of the Association whose names were never listed before in a Masonic book. Four

2. The exact date of the creation of the Charleston Grand Council was uncertain until the discovery of the *Register.* Mackey showed the correct year date, 1815, but termed the body 'a Grand Consistory' (Mackey 1861, 526); Folger set the date after 1816 (Folger 1862, 170); according to Carlson it was instituted in 1814 (Carlson 1889, 697).

of them were Moses Holbrook, Horatio Gates Street, Joseph M'Cosh, and Alexander McDonald.

4. Documents which do not belong to the *Register* show that on 9 February 1822 Grand Commander Dalcho refused to open the Supreme Council – which apparently had not met since John Mitchell's death – and that Isaac Auld signing as *Acting Grand Commander*, together with James Moultrie, *Acting Lieutenant Gr. Commander*, and Moses Levy delivered a Charter to six members of the Association appointing them 'a regular Council of Princes of Jerusalem'.

On 15 November 1822, signing as *Grand Commander of the United States of N.A.*, Isaac Auld delivered a patent of 'Sovereign Grand Inspector General, and Member of the Supreme Council of the Thirty-third Degree' to Horatio Gates Street.[3] According to a memorandum drawn up by Street, Moses Holbrook on the same day, Alexander McDonald and Joseph M'Cosh two days later, also became members of the Supreme Council.[4]

5. In a rare book printed in Charleston by Cornelius C. Sebring in the Summer of 1823, *Documents upon Sublime Freemasonry*,[5] Joseph M'Cosh gave his version of how the controversy originated. It differed from the information provided by the *Register*. Moses Holbrook added further details in letters written in 1822 and some more in 1826 after he became Grand Commander of the Charleston Supreme Council. Their writings are transcribed in APPENDIX 3 together with other relevant contemporary documents.

6. The publication of M'Cosh's book brought the controversy to a climax. Through the intercession of Frederick Dalcho, it ended on 28 October 1823 with an agreement termed 'amicable arrangement', between M'Cosh, Sebring, and Holbrook on one part, Grand Master John Cogdell and Past Grand Master T. W. Bacot on the other. It is reproduced further down. The agreement was considered 'highly satisfactory' by the Grand Lodge which adopted the stipulation that reciprocal complaints would be expunged from its *Proceedings*.

7. The *Register* includes copies of letters dated 14 and 18 October 1823 from T. W. Bacot and from John Cogdell resigning from the Grand Council and

3. Appendix 3.3. Facsimile Harris-Carter 1964, 142.

4. *OB* VII, 313.

5. KW 55. Walgren noticed that 'All copies examined have had the imprint on the title page cut out'.

from Freemasonry. Grand Lodge *Proceedings* show that Frederick Dalcho resigned as Grand Officer of the Grand Lodge on 31 October. All three became honorary members of Grand Lodge on 19 December.

Did Frederick Dalcho 'withdraw' from the Supreme Council? Did he ever resign as Grand Commander?[6] A copy of a letter he wrote on 1 April 1822 also belongs to the *Register*. It includes the following words:

> Dr Auld has no authority from me to perform any Masonic acts. The power with which I am invested by the Constitution of the 33^d Degree, I have not transferred to any person under the Canopy of Heaven.

A Major Discovery

It was a major discovery to ascertain that the *Instituts* and *Statuts* of the *Register* are nearly identical with the *Instituts* and *Statuts* included in the *Recueil des Actes du Suprême Conseil de France*, a book printed in 1832 in Paris; and that the *Extrait des Instructions* of the *Register* is identical with article 12 of the *Instructions sur les Principes Généraux de la Haute Maçonnerie* of the *Recueil* (see Appendix 2.4). The constitutional laws of the high degree bodies founded by Joseph Cerneau in the United States have always been ignored and no historian ever realized that they were printed in the *Recueil des Actes*.

Progressive Discovery of the Laws Governing the Ancient & Accepted Scottish Rite

The first Supreme Council in the world was opened in 1801 in Charleston. The existence of its laws was mentioned for the first time in the *Circular throughout the two Hemispheres*:[7]

> On the 1st of May, 5786, the , called the Supreme Council of Sovereign Grand Inspectors General, was finally ratified by his Majesty the King of Prussia....

The Grand Constitution of the 33d degree was printed for the first time in its entirety thirty years later, namely on pages 36 to 41 of a book issued in 1832 in Paris: *Recueil des Actes du Suprême Conseil de France*. Its first article included the following stipulation:

6. Harris 1959, 27. Harris-Carter 1964, 43, 137, 141, 167, 208, 209.
7. Approved by the Supreme Council on 4 December 1802 and dispatched on 1 January 1803.

> The Constitution and Regulations made by the Nine Commissaries, nominated by the Grand Council of Princes of the Royal Secret in the year 5762 shall be strictly adhered to in all its parts, except in those which militate against the articles of the present Constitution – And which are hereby repealed.[8]

The 'Constitution and Regulations' said to have been made in 1762, also appeared for the first time in print pages 1 to 19 of the *Recueil.* They comprised 35 articles preceded with a lengthy introduction of some 400 words and were entitled:

> Règlemens et Constitutions faits par les neuf commissaires nommés par le Souverain Grand Consistoire des Sublimes Chevaliers de Royal Secret et Princes de la Maçonnerie, le 20 septembre 1762, au Grand Orient de Bordeaux.

Another set of rules, entitled *Instituts, Statuts, Règlemens Généraux* and *Extrait des Balustres Constitutionnels*, appeared between the other two on pages 19 to 36 of the *Recueil.* They were not mentioned separately in the Table of Contents and printed as if they belonged to the Constitutions of 1762.

Grand Commander Pike's Succesive Comments

Shortly after he became Grand Commander, Albert Pike published in 1859 *The Statutes and Regulations, Institutes, Laws and Grand Constitutions of the Ancient and Accepted Scottish Rite* which opened with the facsimile of a two pages hand-written note signed by him and Mackey in which he wrote:

> I Albert Pike . . ., do hereby certify that the foregoing Constitutions and Regulations in French, of the year 1762, with the Statutes, Regulations, Institutes and Balustres that follow have been accurately copied by me from the ancient manuscripts in the Archives of the Supreme Council at Charleston. . . .[9]

Pike recopied and translated the 1762 Constitutions as printed in the *Recueil* and added before the set of rules that followed:

> The following Institutes, Statutes and Regulations are translated from the *Recueil des Actes du Suprême Conseil de France*; where they are given as a part or sequence of the Constitution of 1762, without any indication of date or parentage. I have not succeeded in learning any thing in regard to 'Adington,

8. Art. 1 of *Constitutions, Statutes Regulations for the Government of the Supreme Council of Inspectors General of the 33*rd (facsimile in the handwriting of Frederick Dalcho (Harris-Carter 1964, 337–46). Same wording in the French version included in the *Recueil* (Pike 1874, 285).

9. Pike 1859, a book of 168 pp.

TABLE

PAR ORDRE NUMÉRIQUE,

DES DÉCRETS, ARRÊTÉS ET DÉCISIONS,

CONTENUS DANS CE VOLUME.

Top of page vii of the *Recueil* (1832)

> Chancellor;' but as they seem to have emanated from the Orient of 17° 58' North Lat., I presume they came from Gaudaloupe [*sic*].[10]

One year later, before his Supreme Council, he underlined the importance of his book:

> No *complete* collection of our Constitutions, Regulations, Institutes, Laws and Statutes has ever been made, in French or English. The "*Recueil des Actes du Supreme Conseil pour* [*sic*] *la France*," published in 1832, in French, contained a part, very inaccurately and imperfectly; and a copy of the Grand Constitutions of 1786, in Latin, was annexed to the Treaty of Alliance of 1834, between the Supreme Councils of France, Belgium and Brazil, and the pretended Supreme Council for the Western Hemisphere, of Elias Hicks of New York.
>
> ... I have transcribed from the manuscripts in your archives, and translated, the Regulations and Constitutions of 1762, and the Statutes and Institutes subordinate to them; and have induced our Ill.·. Bro.·. Robert Macoy, of New York, to publish these, ... this is the only complete collection, the only collection

10. Pike 1859, 82.

> *approaching* completeness, of the Law of the Ancient and Accepted Rite ever published....[11]

In 1872 Pike published *Ancient and Accepted Scottish Rite of Freemasonry*[12] in which he did not include the Constitutions and Regulations of 1762 as they appeared in the *Recueil* but instead reproduced and translated the version included in the Register of Delahogue[13] made in Charleston between 20 June 1798 and 12 October 1799.[14] Pike explained in the *Prefatory*:

> Copies of these Constitutions and Regulations of 1762 and of the subsequent Statutes, Institutes and Regulations, of unknown date and uncertain authenticity, which follow the Constitutions in this volume, were published in French, at Paris, in the "*Recueil des Actes du Supreme Conseil de France*," in 1832, by authority of that body.[15]

Nevertheless he kept from his earlier book the translation of the set of laws which followed them in the *Recueil* but set them apart from the Delahogue version.[16] He also kept the beginning of his earlier comments concerning them but changed his conclusion as to their origin:

> I have not succeeded in learning anything in regard to "ADINGTON, CHANCELLOR;" but as they seem to have emanated from the Orient of 17° 58' North Lat., they were, no doubt, enacted by the Sov∴ Gr∴ Council of Sub∴ Princes, of the Royal Secret (25th degree) at Kingston, Jamaica, which, in 1797 and 1798, claimed, and was admitted to have power of discipline and control over that at Charleston, according to authentic documents in the Archives of the Sup∴ Council at Charleston.[17]

Such was the state of knowledge of the early Masonic laws of what was to become the A&ASR. Nothing new appeared on the subject during the next hundred years.

11. Grand Commander's allocution, *Transactions 1860*, 18–19, quoted in Lobingier 1931, 416.
12. A book of 467 pages which includes many texts which were not reproduced in 1859 such as the French version of the Grand Constitutions and the 'Secret Constitutions'.
13. Pike 1872, 10–55.
14. Pike letter to Daruty, 20 September 1877 (Daruty 1879, 196).
15. Pike 1872, 5–6.
16. Pike 1872, 110–22.
17. Pike 1872, 110. Bernheim 1986–1987 .

Discoveries Made During the Past Thirty-five Years

In 1977 a manuscript certified by Francken on 30 August 1771 was re-discovered by Arthur Reginald Hewitt in the Library of the Supreme Council for England and Wales.[18] It included

> The great Statutes & Regulations, Made in Prussia and France Sepbr 7th 7762. Resolved by the Nine Commissioners named by the grand council of the sublime Princes of the Royal Secret at the grand East of France, Consequently by the Deliberation dated as above, to be Ratified and observed by the aforesaid grand Council of the Sublime Princes of France and Prussia, and by all the Particular & regular Councils spread over the two Hemispheres.

Brigadier Jackson published these great Statutes & Regulations in 1980 and wrote:

> These Constitutions ... are an English translation of the 1762 document and, as such, are the earliest known version of a document whose original has never been found.[19]

In 1984 I demonstrated first the identity between the text of the Francken manuscript and the *Statuts* voted by the Grand Lodge of France on 21 February 1763[20] which were sent to Estienne Morin who had left France for the West Indies one year before. I suggested that he had adapted them as rules for The Order of the Royal Secret he was creating.[21] I also explained why nobody had noticed before the near identity of both texts:

> The main difference between the Francken version and all the others consists in the fact that neither the long introduction nor articles 1, 2 and 35 belong to the Francken manuscript. Accordingly all mentions of the title Sovereign Grand Commander ... as well as the enumeration of 25 degrees – which is indeed included in the Francken manuscript but not as a part of the Constitutions – must be considered as late additions.

But once the version of the Statutes & Regulations, said in the Francken manuscript to have been made in Prussia and France on 7 September 1762, was set side by side with the French *Statuts* of 1763, their identity was obvious. This

18. Hewitt 1977, 208–10.
19. Jackson 1980, 256.
20. The Statuts of 1763 were published for the first time by Arthur Groussier in *Compte Rendu des Travaux du Grand Orient de France*, July 1929. Also see Sitwell in *St. Claudius*, 1929–1930, 7–35.
21. Bernheim 1984.

was readily acknowledged by Brigadier Jackson in the paper he published in volume 97 of *Ars Quatuor Coronatorum*.

The Major Discovery

Recently, Ill∴ Arturo de Hoyos, 33°, re-discovered in the Archives of the Supreme Council in Washington a set of three volumes containing about 500 documents, mostly manuscript, covering the first years (1804–1815) of the activity of the Supreme Council of France.

The third volume included eight folios entitled *Statuts généraux de la h^te^ maçon∴*, certified by [Louis Charles] Bailhache[22] on 27 August 1805.[23] They comprised three parts: *Instituts*, *Statuts* and *Reglemens generaux*. The first two were identical with the laws copied at the beginning of the Charleston *Register*.

Copied in the Register of Saint-Laurent,[24] made in 1832, they received the following heading:

> Lux ex tenebris, Instituts, Statuts et Reglements Généraux de la haute Maçonnerie révisés d'après les observations de nos très illustres et très puissants frères des SS∴ EE∴ D'Ec∴ de Su∴ de Fr∴ d'Al∴ et les notres, par notre tres illustre royal et très puissant grand président et frère S∴ M∴ le roi Frédéric second de Prusse, et sanctionnés par lui le 25e jour du 2e mois Yiar 5763.

With the same heading, they were also included in the Golden Book, made in 1835, of Dr Charles Morison of Greenfield and, as such, were transcribed in the *Report* presented on 5 August 1948 to the Supreme Council for Scotland by its Grand Secretary General, R. S. Lindsay.[25]

Conclusion

No historian could ever explain why these laws were printed in the *Recueil* or suggested which were the Masonic bodies regulated by them. It was never realized that they were the constitutional laws used by the high degree bodies founded by Cerneau. The *Register* is the first piece of evidence which ties them

22. Bailhache received the 33rd Degree from Grasse-Tilly in Paris on 8 October 1804 (Bernheim 1987, 137. Grasse-Tilly 2003, 260).

23. *SCDF* III, folios 898–905. Kloss was familiar with this Bailhache manuscript (Kloss 1853, II, 389).

24. Bernheim 1987, 99–115.

25. Lindsay 1948, 40–52. Bernheim 1986, 264–66.

to the Masonic bodies he created in the United States. It is obvious that the laws inserted in the *Recueil* were never part of the 1762 Constitutions.

The letter of these laws explains comments made by Emanuel De La Motta in the *Rejoinder* he issued in New York in 1814, such as:

> the gentlemen composing the committee of Mr. Cerneau's Society have made a jumble of different points under different heads.[26]

I approached the truth in a paper twenty-five years ago which devoted several pages to the various sets of regulations included in the *Recueil* when I wrote:

> It appears to me that this polemic can only be explained if one admits that La Motta as well as Cerneau owned different sets of regulations and that each of them ignored the existence of the set owned by the other.[27]

CHARLESTON 1815–1823

MARCH 1815–MAY 1821

Emanuel De La Motta left New York on 8 March 1815 and returned to Charleston with Sampson Simson. His activity in New York[28] could well be the reason why the (Cerneau) Grand Consistory issued a Warrant for the creation in Charleston of a Grand Council of Princes of the Royal Secret on 10 April.

According to a letter written by Lieutenant Grand Commander Dalcho on 2 May 1815,[29] the Supreme Council intended to meet and hear La Motta, likely about his creation of a Supreme Council in New York. On 3 July Gourgas wrote to La Motta and sent him the draft of a Circular Letter antedated 7 January 1815 which he wished to have signed by Dalcho and other members of the Charleston Council. The following words, also in the handwriting of Gourgas, 'We think the ratification ought to be dated 21st of May, 1815', were apparently sometimes later pasted upon it'.[30] It was not returned to New York and La

26. La Motta's 'Rejoinder', 40 (KW 36). Lobingier 1931, 114.

27. Bernheim 1986–1987, 51.

28. In my last book, *Le rite en 33 grades – De Frederick Dalcho à Charles Riandey* (Dervy, 2011), I devoted some fifty pages to the activity of Emanuel De La Motta in New York between 1813 and 1815. It includes copies of the original English documents issued there under his signature during that period.

29. Harris-Carter 1964, 127.

30. *TSJ* 1878, 49–51. *OB* VII, 306–8. De Hoyos 2010, 33. Bernheim 2011, 259, note 210.

Motta never replied. Mitchell died a few months later.[31] Nothing shows that the Supreme Council had any activity afterwards. La Motta died 17 May 1821.

The first meeting of the Grand Council of Princes of the Royal Secret for the State of South Carolina was held in Charleston on 17 August 1815. The meeting was convened by Ill.·. Peter Javain, 'Deputy Grand Inspector General.·. 33°, Representative of the Most Puissant Grand Consistory of the U.·. S.·. & its Dependencies'. Present were P. Desportes and J. Dumaine, both G.·. I.·. G.·. 33°, Thomas W. Bacot, John S. Cogdell, Anthony E. Ulmo, Charles S. Tucker, and Isaac M. Wilson, all P.R.S.

The Warrant received from New York was read and the Brethren took an oath of fidelity which included their submission to the Institutes & Regulations. After being installed by Javain, Thomas W. Bacot as President of the Gd.·. Council delivered a short address in which he said:

> Our noble Institution is now in its infancy, in this State; and we are (at least most of us) I may say, novices in the art we are about to establish. We have not only to Create a character for our Sublime Council, that will make us honored and respected abroad, *but we shall have perhaps to Combat with the prejudices, if not the hostility, of a few members of the former Grand Council in this place which it appears, had become extinct from ceasing to perform their necessary functions.*[32]

John Dumaine and John S. Cogdell were installed as Senior and Junior Wardens, Anthony E. Ulmo as Grand Orator, Peter Desportes Grand Treasurer, Isaac M. Wilson Grand Secretary, and Chs. S Tucker Grand Master of Ceremonies. The Names of the Officers of the Grand Council were ordered to be published in one or more of the Gazette of the City.

During the first six years of its existence, the Grand Council enjoyed a quiet life. Pierre Fayolle was its first new member. The Minutes of 16 September 1815 mention his 'kindness in offering to this Council the use of his Room Gratis'. He received the degrees from Past Master to the 13th Degree between 16 September and 5 October 1815, the 14° to the 18° in the Rose Croix Chapter founded in Charleston on 16 October 1815, and from 19° to 32° in the Grand Council between 24 November 1815 and 25 June 1816. He was the only member who received the degrees in so many separate meetings. The Minutes list the

31. See John Mitchell in APPENDIX 1.4.

32. My emphasis. The words '*former Grand Council in this place which it appears, had become extinct*' allude likely to the *Supreme Council for the United States.*

names of the degrees he received, but no particulars of the rituals (APPENDIX 2.6, Table 5). Their succession is different from other lists of degrees mentioned in various documents drawn up or printed in the United States between 1802 and 1823 (APPENDIX 2.6, Table 6).

In 1816 Grand Commander John Mitchell died. Lieutenant Commander Dalcho became his successor but we do not know if he ever appointed a Lieutenant.

In January 1817, committees agreed upon Articles of Union between the two rival Grand Lodges of South-Carolina which existed side by side since 1809 and after several meetings the Grand Lodge of Ancient Free-Masons of South-Carolina was opened and its Grand Officers installed.

On 21 September 1818, T. W. Bacot declined being re-elected as President of the Grand Council and John Cogdell became his successor. The Minutes add:

> The Ill^s President presented sundry Papers which he had received from the widow of the Ill^s Brother J. W [*sic*] Mitchell late Gd Comander [*sic*]. also a register from Brother E. Elizer of the names of the members of the late Grand Consistory to this Council.

There was indeed a John Wroughton Mitchell born in 1796 in Charleston, S.C., who was elected Charleston city attorney in October 1817[33] and died in New York in 1878. He was the son of John Hinckley Mitchell[34] who lived next door to Colonel Mitchell's house in 1813.[35] They do not appear to have been related to each other.[36]

MAY 1821–JANUARY 1822

Emanuel De La Motta's death on 17 May 1821[37] left the Charleston Supreme Council with four active members only: Grand Commander Dalcho, Isaac Auld, Moses Clava Levy and James Moultrie.[38]

33. http://www.lib.unc.edu/mss/inv/m/Mitchell,John_Wroughton.html.
34. http://wc.rootsweb.ancestry.com/cgi-bin/igm.cgi?op=GET&db=syf&id=I18583.
35. Harris 1959, 19.
36. Colonel John Mitchell's father was Irish, John Hinckley Mitchell's father was English.
37. http://wc.rootsweb.ancestry.com/cgi-bin/igm.cgi?op=GET&db=steinmann&id=I228.
38. Thomas Bowen, Israel de Lieben and Joseph Dickinson died in 1807, Abraham Alexander on 21 February 1816.

June 1821

In the Appendix of *Documents upon Sublime Free-Masonry* issued in Summer 1823, Joseph M'Cosh wrote:

> Early in the summer of the year 1821, several Blue Masons discovered, that many valuable Masonic papers were scattered abroad in the hands of different persons. On reflection, they concluded that it would be an object of some importance to the cause of Freemasonry, which they had much at heart, to gather and unite them in one common collection. The attempt was made, and attended with almost complete success. Every Brother Master Mason, (none of lower degree being admitted) signed a solemn written agreement, "never to communicate to any person whatever, any information he might obtain from the manuscripts." (The original is before me, dated June 22, 1821.) To this instrument they invariably adhered—and so far was their number from increasing, though repeated intercessions were made for admission, that it actually decreased from, *twenty-eight* to ELEVEN, agreeably to a certain rule, which was adopted for their government.[39]

M'Cosh did not specify who were these 'several Blue Masons', the nature of the 'many valuable Masonic papers', nor how they had come into their hands.

August 1821

John Cogdell, then President of the Grand Council, learned about it. On Friday 17 August 1821, at the 46th meeting of the Grand Council, he said:

> Certain number of Bro[r] Masons ... had illegally associated them selves, to work and given the Sublime Degrees of free Masonry which right alone exists in this Sov[n] G[d] Council....

The Minutes of the *Register* reproduce Codgell's list of the members of the Association. It included 13 names – among which Joseph M'Cosh, James W. Rouse, Alexander McDonald and Moses Holbrook (TABLE 1) – qualified 'clandestines', said to 'have signed the bye Laws' and 'meeting at H. G. Street's East Bay'. Their names was followed with those of eight 'Applicants'.

A committee of three, Thomas W. Bacot, John Izard Wright[40] and Peter Laurans, was formed

39. M'Cosh 1823, 91. The whole Appendix of this book is transcribed in APPENDIX 3.4.

40. At the 44th meeting of the Council, on 22 June 1821, a letter was received from John Izard Wright, "a Knight of R.·.✠ praying to Receive the Degrees up to 32 inclusive, ... he was unanimously Elected to received [*sic*] all the degrees Which was done in due form."

> to wait on such persons, as have been reported to have had meetings.... That they be requested to discontinue their further meetings or proceedings and that they be also requested to deposit in the Grand Council all the Books and other documents which are now in their possession and which it is understood belonged to the late Sovn Gd Inspr General Brother John Mitchell.

On 21 September, at the next meeting of the Grand Council, it delivered their report accompanied with documents marked A to F (APPENDIX 2.5).

∴

On Monday 20 August,[41] the committee went to the New England Coffee House which was kept by Horatio Gates Street.[42] The committee spoke with him and with Nathaniel Batchelder who resided there. The committee told both of them what had been reported to the Council three days before and asked if its information was correct. Street admitted 'without hesitation' that they had associated

> for the purpose of reading over the Degrees in Sublime Masonry, of which they had obtained manuscript Copies, being the same which belonged to the late Brother Collenel [*sic*] Mitchell.

The committee warned them that if they kept on, 'they would insure the risk of expulsion from the symbolic Degrees'. The committee was told that their Association had a meeting that very evening at the New England Coffee House and was invited to meet them, which the committee declined to do, as their instructions 'were not, in any manner, to recognize them as a body of Masons'.

M'Cosh's version of this first encounter:

> About the 20th of August, (for these usurpers did not affix any date,) a long string of "Resolutions" from some persons pretending to be S. P. R. S. evidently originating in false information of the meetings at the New-England Coffee House, was communicated to "the eleven;"[43]

On Thursday 23 August, Bacot had 'a pretty long conversation' with Frederick Dalcho.[44] Dalcho informed Bacot that two days before, he had the visit of three members of the Association, James W. Rouse, Alexander McDonald, & John Laroche, who were in 'possession of the Manuscript copies of the

41. APPENDIX 2.5, Document A.
42. 'New England Coffee House, 175 E Bay St.' (City directory Charleston 1822, 100).
43. M'Cosh 1823, 92.
44. APPENDIX 2.5, Document B.

several degrees ... asking his advice'. He told them that before he could advise them, they must give him 'from under their hands a promise not to divulge or to disclose except to those who should be lawfully entitled to the same any thing relating to those degrees which had thus come to their knowledge. They promised him to do so.' Bacot informed Dalcho of the resolution of the Grand Council and of his interview with Street and Batchelder.

An hour later Dalcho 'called again at the Bank' and informed Bacot that after their conversation, he had met with Dr. Holbrook going down Broad Street, 'who pressed him to go into his house, where several of the associators were, as they wished much to see him ... they then tendered him a paper signed by thirteen persons, being the written promise that they had said they would give him. Bacot and Dalcho had a further conversation together. Back home, Bacot made a note from memory of the paper which Dalcho had showed him:

> We do hereby now solemnly promisse and swear (or declare) that we will always hail, keep, & conceil, and never will reveal, any of the part or parts, the point or points of the mysteries of Sublime Masonry, which we have obtained, (or are in possession of) (or are to come to our knowledge) or which we may hereafter obtain (or be intrusted in) to any persons in the world. except it be to a Brother who shall be lawfully intitled to receive the same. To this we swear (or declare) without any hesitation, mental reservation, or self evasion of mind whatsoever, under the penalty of having all our former obligations on force, (or put in force) against us. So help us God keep us in our senses to enable us to perform the same. Signed as follows H. G. Street, Moses Holbrook, Elyzah Gates, Robert Carr, Alexr Mc Donald, John P. Laroche, N. Batchelder, Henry Cross, W. M. Dyer, Ml Mc Kenzie, James Little, and James W. Rouse. 13 Persons.[45]

Before or after the conversations Bacot had with Dalcho, a long letter of some 1,900 words[46] was sent by the committee to Horatio Gates Street accompanied with a note[47] begging him to 'communicate its contents to such brethren as are associated with you for the purposes connected with the Sublime Degrees of masonry and we request your answer on Monday morning'.

M'Cosh version:

> this was followed August 23d, 1821, by a huge folio letter of *seven pages*, large paper, and closely written, very officially communicated, and like the former,

45. Bacot lists only twelve names and appears to have forgotten M'Cosh (see TABLE 1).
46. APPENDIX 2.5, Document D.
47. APPENDIX 2.5, Document F.

evidently founded in mistaken information, which to this day, they have obstinately refused to correct. This frightful communication accused "the eleven" of violating TRUTH, VIRTUE and JUSTICE. In a spirit of bitterness and domineering vengeance, they ungraciously assert that "the eleven" "*have violated every thing held dear and sacred* among Masons;" that their conduct "was *contrary to the principles of Justice and Morality, and calculated to destroy* ail the *social* and *moral virtues*." They are several times, in this terrible letter, accused of "violating *truth*"—of "having forgotten the first principles of virtue, as well as their solemn obligations," and of "robbing "—aye, of "robbing!"—of "*striving to force from them by violence* (as was attempted with our D.G.M. of old) and by unmasonic means, what their sacred obligations bound them to preserve." They add: that "the eleven" "stand upon the brink of a precipice—another step and their fall is certain;" that if they do not give up every thing to these usurpers and acknowledge their fault "to save themselves from *certain destruction*," "they will find (when perhaps *too late*) that there is a *strength* and *power to punish* every offender." To avoid these empty threats, these *robbers*, these *liars*, these *assassins*, these *ruffians* (for these are the charming epithets which are implied in the above extracts from this uncharitable letter, "written," as they say, "in the spirit of" *their* "candour and" of *their* "brotherly love,") "these eleven" are finally informed "that they must unequivocally see their *error*, and abandon in the most *solemn manner* their unmasonic conduct, and thus prevent the steps which *must be pursued* against them, and the *consequences* which *must inevitably follow*."

By this violent proceeding "the eleven" were deprived of using their own judgment, nor were they allowed to have any opinion of their own, or to reflect upon the best course to be pursued; but were at once held up as a "mark for the finger of scorn to point at;" and, as it were, already turned without the pale of the Masonic Family. The accusations it contained, were so *indefinitely* made that they could not be replied to, and the bitter threats which were strewed throughout the virulent mass of cowardly wrath and incivility, so overbearingly directed against eleven peaceful and quiet brothers of correct morals and domestic habits, aroused them to a consideration of the subject and taught them to examine for the cause of such uneasiness in these persons who pretended to such deference and demanded such respect.[48]

Horatio Gates Street answered on 27 August:[49]

Dear Brother

Your Packet has been duly received, which my respect for you, Would lead me to notice had not the persons to whom you allude communicated their intentions to the rev^{d} Dr Dalcho by whose advice they purpose to be regulated,

48. M'Cosh 1823, 92–93.
49. APPENDIX 2.5, Document E.

> it is my earnest hope that every thing will be amicably setled in Brotherly love and friendship—
>
> I remain dear sir yours fraternaly
>
> Signed H. G. Street

On that evening, at the request of Dalcho 'whom they had just left, [... and who] declined to do any thing', Holbrook, McDonald & Rouse visited Bacot.[50] They said their number was thirteen and that they did not wish to obtain more than the Degree of Perfection. Bacot advised them in the first place to deliver all the manuscripts in their possession to the Grand Council.

On Thursday 30 August, the committee sent another note[51] to H. G. Street:

> The committee of the G. C. of the P. R. S. Who addressed you a few days since, being desirous of make their report to that body on Monday next, request that if you have any further written communication to make to them, than that received from you under the date of 27th inst, you will favour them with the same on or before tomorrow evening, addressed to Bro Bacot as their chairman.

M'Cosh version:

> Aug. 30th, 1821—they received another Communication from the Committee of the spurious—and as honest, upright Brothers, having no reasons for concealment, they openly informed the committee of impostors of their purpose. But as the vengeance of the intruders was about to fall heavily on one, whom the usurpers could seriously injure, and deprive of his living,[52] "the eleven" withdrew their application and patiently waited the event of the storm that was gathering.[53]

September 1821

M'Cosh added the following information which does not appear in the committee's report:

> Sept. 10th, 1821, a chief of the spurious and illegal sent for one of "the eleven" and entreated him to use his best endeavours to heal the wounds which would be likely to ensue in the Masonic family, and begged him to use his influence with the Brothers at the New-England Coffee House to sign an application to his body, and they should be received. The Brother stating some objections to

50. APPENDIX 2.5, Document C.

51. APPENDIX 2.5, Document F.

52. In his letter from 18 August 1826 to Gourgas, Moses Holbrook will explain that this remark alluded to Dalcho (APPENDIX 3.6).

53. M'Cosh 1823, 95.

> this plan, the Spurious Chief concluded his intercession with the following pathetic appeal to his feelings: "Will you not do it," (that is, exert his influence to have "the eleven" apply to him;) "will you not do it for my sake—for the sake of Masonry will you not do it?" The Brother informed "the eleven" of the proposition which had been made to him, and the promise annexed to it.[54]

On Friday, 21 September, Bacot presented the report of the committee to the Grand Council, with the recommendation that it be sent to the Grand Consistory in New York.

After which a letter sent on Friday 14 September by Alexander McDonald 'To the Grand Council of Princes of the Royal Secret &c &c—Charleston S. C.' was read:

> Brethren
>
> We the undersigned Brothers of the Masonic Fraternity, having in our possession the manuscript degrees of sublime masonry—feeling an anxious desire to retain those degrees among us, and prevent their circulating, beg leave, with all fraternal love and duty as Brothers to offer ourselves as candidates for initiation into your Grand Council of Princes of the Royal Secrets, and to solicit your suffrages in our behalf.—As some false and malicious reports have been promulgated respecting our having formed an association for the purpose of receiving candidates and conferring on them said degrees; we think it necessary here to state, that such reports are unfounded and without the least shadow of Truth, in as much as our number has not increased from the period of our first meeting which was to take into Consideration, the manner of addressing you as regarded becoming members of your Council, but, which desirable object has been unhappily prevented by Circumstances, which we do not think proper or necessary, to advert to at present, as our sole motive is Harmony, Peace and Goodwill to all the Fraternity; and an anxious desire to become one and the same Body.
>
> If therefore, the Grand Council, which we now have the honor to address, as Brother Masons, deem us worthy of a participation of the Rites and Mysteries of sublime Masonry, (being already acquainted with the Degrees) we shall acknowledge their concurrence with all due consideration, and hail, them with unity, strength & Harmony. We have the honor to be Brethren
>
> Respectfully your Obt servant
>
> Signed H. G. Street, James W. Rouse, James Little, Robt Carr, Alexander Mc Donald, Joseph McCosh, Moses Holbrook, Wm M. Dyer, Nathl Batchelder, Henry Cross, M. Mc Kinsie.

54. M'Cosh 1823, 96.

The Grand Council resolved

> That as the said letter applies for initiation direct into the G[d]. Council, of the several brethren whose names are thereunto subscribed, the same is informal, and the usual ceremony of reference to a Committee cannot be complied with, in as much as that neither of the applicants for initiation has obtained the indispensable, previous degrees of Rose ✠ and until such step shall have been taken by them respectively, no application from either of the said brethren to this Body can be acted upon.
>
> Resolved that the Secretary do inform them of the same....

Which was done on 25 September:

> Secretary's letter
> to B[rs] Street & al.
>
> To Brothers A. B. C. & al. Your letter to G[d] Council of Sov. P. of Royl Secrets praying for initiation therein was presented to that Body on Saturday evening, and I now enclose you copy of a resolution adopted by the Gd Council on reading the same and remain fraternally
>
> Ch. S. Tucker Sec[y]

M'Cosh explained in his own way why the letter from 14 September was sent to the Grand Council:

> Upon mature deliberation "the eleven" concluded, that after being received, it would be lawful for them to retire again, should the documents of the spurious, upon a careful inspection, be found illegal; and as it was then, and is still believed, that in ail disagreements *gentlemen can make propositions which gentlemen can receive without any derogation from principles of honour or urbanity,* "the eleven," on the 14th of September, 1821, consented, (to use the words of the application,) "for the sake of HARMONY, PEACE and GOOD-WILL, and an anxious desire of healing ail difficulties in the craft."
>
> Further, in their letter of application, these individuals, in reply to the repeated assertions in writing and in common conversation of the illegal pretenders, use these words: "as some false and malicious reports have been promulgated respecting our having formed an 'Association' for the purpose of receiving candidates and conferring on them said" [Sublime] " Degrees, we think it necessary here to state, that such reports are unfounded and without the least *shadow* of TRUTH, inasmuch as our number has *not increased* from the period of our first meeting."
>
> This letter was signed by "eleven" individuals—and they were all, who, *at that date*, had any right, title or claim to Masonic papers of any kind, or who in any way belonged to the meetings at the New-England Coffee House. This application was handed "*unsealed*" [*M'Cosh footnote*: We challenge an investigation

> upon this point. They officially say it was "*sealed*"—which is positively denied.] to the Chief, as they call him, at whose earnest solicitation it had been made; nor did "the eleven" ask this as a gratuity; they proffered a handsome remuneration or fee at their reception.[55]

Then M'Cosh mentions facts which again are not confirmed by the *Register*. He writes "the eleven" signed another letter of application on 25 September and

> while this letter was in their hands unacted upon, an earnest attempt was made by them to have a petition signed for the Grand Lodge of this State to expel these eleven Blue Masons from the Masonic Family.[56] … But many whose signatures were applied for to this petition, had too much honour and nobleness of soul to lend their aid in support of these overbearing usurpers; hence the sorrowful paper with some signatures, was never presented to the Grand Lodge—and some of its signers have confessed that they were imposed upon, and asked pardon for ever having listened to the deceivers on a subject that would so deeply affect any Brother's welfare.[57]

November 1821 – January 1822

For this crucial period, M'Cosh brings much information which is not otherwise confirmed. The *Register* records no meetings between 21 September and 5 November.

On 5 November, Cogdell

> informed the Grand Council that he had convened them for the purpose of aiding the Chapr of R.·. ✠.·. with regard to the application of Sundry persons who had illegally assembled on Sublime Masonry[.] in consequence of a resolution adopted at the last meeting that the Documents &c. relating those persons was order to be sent to the Sovn. Grand Consistory of the United States of America, whereupon it was Resolved that the operation of the resolution be suspended until the 20th Inst^{t}.

55. M'Cosh 1823, 96–97.

56. M'Cosh renews here an accusation he had made in a foot-note added by him (M'Cosh 1823, 31) to the Grand Consistory's reply of 28 February 1814 (KW 34. Lobingier 1931, 93–99): 'Remember how J. C.'s body of usurpers proceeded in Charleston S. C., in the summer of 1821; they strained every nerve to have certain brothers who had never been initiated into the sublime degrees, expelled by the Grand Lodge of South-Carolina.'

57. M'Cosh 1823, 97–98.

On 28 November, he

> informed the Grand Council that he had convened this Body for the purpose of deliberating on the Documents respecting the unmasonic proceedings of Certain persons interfering with the rights, and promulgating the Degrees soly belonging to this Gd. Council, which was ordered to be sent on to the Sov^{n}. Grand Consistory of the United States, but which was suspended until the 20th Instant.
>
> Whereupon it was Resolved, that the Ill^{s}. President be requested forthwith to send on the report & documents accompanying it, to the Sov^{n}. Grand Consistory of the U^{d}∴ States of America to gether with the Proceedings relative to them in the Chap^{r} of R∴ ✠∴
>
> The Council was informed by one of its Members, that Mr. Laroche of whom the Committee had reported favorably, had again joined the unmasonic association. Information was likewise given to the G^{d}. Council, that a Day or Two after the meeting of the Chapr of R∴ ✠∴ those associates had again assembled, and increased their numbers to Twenty seven. They also received Information from one of its Members, that Mr. Dyer had declared that the Members of that Association had entered into a Compact that should a single Applicant be refused admission, none of them would go in our Sublime order; a similar information was received from an other Member, that another of the associates had declared the same thing to him; in confirmation of their unmasonic proceedings a printed blank Summons was procured from one of the Associates and handed in to this Council.
>
> Whereupon Resolved that copy of these Minutes be forwarded to the G^{d} Consistory of the U. States.

On 27 December Cogdell announced that he had forwarded the documents to New York.[58]

M'Cosh mentions 'four or five' and 'seven or more meetings' of the Grand Council, which does not fit with the *Register* but may cover meetings of the R∴ ✠ Chapter:

> After the usurpers had held four or five meetings and admitted such as members of their "Friends of Peace," as would vote to reject the application, Nov. 9th 1821, this spurious body, (to use their own words,) "resolved to notify"

58. During the meeting of 27 December, Cogdell said that 'the R^{ble} Brother J. Jones a Sublime Mason quite infirm and old had plassed [*sic*] into his hands sundry m^{que} Manuscripts and Seals.' John Jones was an English inn-keeper in Curaçao and a forceful personality who was later appointed Provincial Grand Master of the Dutch Province of Curaçao (Seal-Coon 1976, 73–74; also Valette, *AQC* 44, 65 & Seal-Coon in *AQC* 104, 168). Jones affixed his signature on a copy of Grasse-Tilly's patent certified by Gourgas (*NMJ* 1876, 13).

> ["the eleven"][59] "that their application was informal," "and to inform them" how they might again apply.[60]

And after a few digressions,

> Nov. 11th 1821—"The eleven" met at the New-England Coffee House, and after reading the communications of the spurious which have been alluded to, and these being under consideration, but more particularly the resolves in reply to the solicited applications and promised admission which had been made in the utmost good faith and in a respectful manner by "the eleven," it was "*Resolved*, That after waiting with much patience and anxiety from Sept. 14th 1821, to Nov. 10th 1821, during which time the illegal body had had seven or more meetings—during which time others had applied and been admitted by them,[61] that the conduct of the pretenders must inevitably be considered as an equivocation, not compatible with their solicitations, nor consonant with the deportment of one Freemason to another; more particularly, 'the eleven' protest against their low artifice to obtain the names of the persons who had met at the New-England Coffee House, with a view to their expulsion,—therefore, unanimously resolved, never to have any thing further to do with these ungenerous usurpers."[62]

He states that contacts were taken between some of 'the eleven' and members of the Supreme Council:

> A part of "the eleven" once more applied to the regular Supreme Council, which had been founded in 1783,[63] (the Grand Commander having withdrawn from the Council during the present disturbance, from the nature of his vocation, and having desired to have no voice either directly or indirectly in the transactions which might ensue, desired not to be consulted in any respect about the business;) the Supreme Council correctly organized under the next officer,[64] was in possession of all the requisite documents—and happily for the cause of Freemasonry, he, and the remaining members of the Council were not within the reach of the "tender mercies" of their revengeful charity.[65]

One piece of circumstancial evidence supports M'Cosh's assertion: on 19 December 1821, when the New York Consistory commented on the report received four days earlier from Charleston, it 'condemned the proceedings' of

59. Two words in square brackets in M'Cosh.
60. M'Cosh 1823, 98.
61. The *Register* shows no admissions in November.
62. M'Cosh 1823, 99–100.
63. *Sic*!
64. An assertion which a letter quoted below from Grand Commander Dalcho will disprove.
65. M'Cosh 1823, 100. An allusion also explained in Holbrook's letter from 18 August 1826 (APPENDIX 3.6).

fourteen persons and listed their names. These were the thirteen signatories of the promise from 23 August (see Table 1) to which was added last that of Isaac Auld (*Heredom* 18, 51–52).

And that contacts were also taken between the Supreme Council and the Grand Council:

> The legal Council proceeded to a consideration of the subject which by this time had obtained some adventitious importance: scarcely had they engaged in the discussion, when, like Virgil's harpies, the illegal body attempted to stop their progress by professing a great desire for harmony, and for healing all difficulties and removing every obstacle to a complete union of all parties, and about the last of Nov. 1821, begging the Council to defer all further consideration of the subject for a few days, and naming the coming Christmas (1821) as ample time to accomplish this project. This proposition was readily acceded to. But on the 9th January 1822, a further time of ten days or a fortnight was interceded for to complete their arrangements. As the object was important, this further delay was also granted.[66]

The Minutes of the New York Consistory show that Javain sent several letters to New York where they were read on 28 February 1822.[67] The last one included an essential piece of information which could be interpreted as a confirmation of one of M'Cosh's statements:

> Another communication from the Ill.·. Bro.·. Javain covering a communication from Frederick Dalcho, who pretends to the possession of the Degrees of Exalted Masonry and to the dignity of Gr^{d}.·. Inspector Genl.·.. or 33^{d}.·. Degree, and in consequence of such pretended quality, asks this Sov.·. Gr^{d}.·. Consistory to divide the jurisdiction with him by a line of demarkation, dividing the United States of America into two distinct Masonic divisions; that South of the City of Washington he modestly asks to be placed under his jurisdiction and to allow (underlined) the Gr^{d}.·. Consistory the command of all that part North of the said City of Washington.

The above shows the friendly relation entertained by Dalcho and Javain with each other and could be seen as their private diplomatic attempt to save a situation dangerous for all concerned. The *Register* does not mention it at all.

66. M'Cosh 1823, 101.

67. The New York Minutes were transcribed in my previous paper (*Heredom* 18, 2010, 52–53). Javain recommended that 'his assistant', John Z. Wright, as well as T. W. Bacot and John S. Cogdell be Grand Inspectors General, and the Consistory resolved that 'they be clothed with that dignity'. He requested a Certificate or Diploma showing him as Deputy Grand Inspector General and Representative of the Grand Consistory for the State of South Carolina.

FEBRUARY–NOVEMBER 1822

The Grand Council of Princes of Jerusalem

A completely new situation happened on 9 February 1822 when three members of the Supreme Council delivered a Charter for a Grand Council of Princes of Jerusalem to six members of the Association (Table 1). It was signed by Isaac Auld 'Acting Grand Commander in the United States of America', James Moultrie 'Acting Lieut Gr: Commander in the United States of America' and Moses Clava Levy 'Treasurer General of the Holy Empire in the United States of America' (APPENDIX 3.1).[68]

M'Cosh described it thus:

> Saturday 9th Feb. 1822, all postponements agreed on having completely expired, the Supreme Council determined to be trifled with no longer, and proceeded to commence the initiation of six of "the eleven," and at different meetings from that date until Christmas 1822 these six received S. P. R. S. with all the lower degrees.[69]

The last words show that he is far from being a reliable witness. Then he and three other members of the Association – Horatio Gates Street, Moses Holbrook, and Alexander McDonald – became members of the Supreme Council in November 1822, that is, more than half a year before he issued his book.

They beg further the question: What happened on 9 February 1822? Unfortunately, there are no testimonies from the members of the Supreme Council who signed the Charter. But one is included in a letter written within a matter of weeks after the delivery of the Charter.

The Letter to Daniel D. Tompkins

A letter signed jointly by 'Moses Holbrook, James W. Rouse, Committee of Correspondence', was received in New York in the Spring of 1822.[70] The envelope was addressed to 'His Excellency Daniel D Tompkins, Vice Presi-

68. The Charter was transcribed more than a century ago by Grand Commander Pike (*OB* VIII, 747 & *OB* IX, 115). Its facsimile is reproduced in Harris-Carter 1964, 140.

69. M'Cosh 1823, 101.

70. Appendix 3.2. According to the Balustre sent from New York to Charleston on 1 March 1827 (*OB* VII, 340), this letter was brought by Dr Jacob De La Motta. It was wholly reproduced in *NMJ* 1866, 79, and in *NMJ* 1876, 26; partly in Lobingier 1931, 124; it is not mentioned at all in Harris-Carter 1964. See my notes in Appendix 3.2.

dent of the United States, New York', and the letter was headed 'To our thrice Illustrious Brother Daniel D Tompkins, R+ – K.H. P.R.S. Sovereign Grand Inspector General of the 33^{d} Degree and Grand Commander of the Northern District of the United States of America'.[71] The beginning of the letter stated:

> Owing to the late war in which our Country was engaged, and the death of a Great many of its members, the Grand Council of Princes of Jerusalem and the grand lodge of Perfection for this State, ceased to exist. The Grand Council of the 33^{d} degree continued to flourish until the Death of our late illustrious Brother Colonel Mitchell who was known to you as Grand Commander. At his death Doctor Frederick Dalcho became G^{d}. Com^{r}; but he being influenced by certain members of an illegal body established here, by Joseph Cerneau, and Dewit Clinton refused to call his council together, altho' they were never less than 3 Grand inspectors of said council in this city at any one time.

If we believe the above, it means that during the six years which followed John Mitchell's death, Grand Commander Dalcho had not once called the Supreme Council together because he was 'influenced' by members of the Cerneau Council.

The letter described what happened on 9 February 1822:

> On the 9th day of February last, our illustrious Brethren Doctors Isaac Auld & Ja^{s} Moultrie, R:+. K–H – P:R:S and Sovereign G^{d} Inspectors of the 33^{d} both officers in said Council, called on the said $Fred^{k}$ Dalcho and requested him to open the Grand Council of So. G^{d}. In. Genl. of the 33^{d} degree which he refused to do, on which the aforesaid Brothers congregated and established a chapter of So. Princes of R: +, and a G^{d} Council of Princes of Jerusalem in this City, & gave a Charter to said Chapter and Council to Make and perfect Masons in the Sublime Degrees to the 18th Degree agreeably to the Constitutions.

The word *Acting* used by both Isaac Auld and James Moultrie under the signatures they affixed on the Charter supports Holbrook's statement that Dalcho refused to open the Supreme Council on 9 February 1822.

The letter added a list of Officers & Members of a Grand Lodge of Perfection of which Moses Holbrook was Sublime Grand Master and Rouse Senior Grand Warden. The six Masons named in the Charter delivered on 9 February were members of the Association and of the Grand Lodge of Perfection listed in Holbrook's letter (TABLE 1).

71. See the facsimile of the patent he received from Emanuel De La Motta in New York on 5 August 1813 in Baynard 1938, I, 171. Transcribed in Bernheim 2011, 248.

Mackey's Narration (1861)

Forty years later, Mackey will write the following imaginative lines:

> The fact that Dr. Dalcho had, when the question was proposed to him, candidly acknowledged the illegality of the Consistory,[72] although he at the same time declared that he intended to take no part in the pending difficulty, caused him, involuntarily, to become mixed up with these troubles, for it was supposed by the Consistory that the influence and advice of Dr. Dalcho alone, kept the associators from surrendering the manuscripts and applying for admission into their body.
>
> In consequence of this a long, and in many respects an unpleasant correspondence, took place between Messrs T. W. Bacot and Jno. S. Cogdell on the one part, and Dr. Dalcho on the other.[73] Mortified at the estrangement of feeling which seemed on the point of being engendered by this Masonic dispute, between himself and two old friends, who were bound to him also by the close tie of membership in the Church of which he was the assistant Minister, Dr. Dalcho withdrew from the Supreme Council, having peremptorily refused to heal the associators. As soon as he had retired, Dr. Isaac Auld, the next officer of the Supreme Council, and who then constitutionally succeeded to the prerogatives of the Grand Commander [*an extremely questionable statement*], having no such delicate relations with Bros. Bacot and Cogdell, proceeded to legalize the associators, and, on the 9th of February, 1822, conferred on six of them the degree of Sublime Prince of the Royal Secret [*another statement not supported either by facts or documents*].[74]

February–April 1822 – Essential New Information from the Register

The Grand Council met two weeks later on February 26. A communication of the New York Grand Consistory was read[75] which was referred to a Committee consisting of T. W. Bacot, P. Laurens and P. Javain. Being approved by New York for their 'prudence, discretion and firmness' applied to a situation which was a thing of the past; Charleston was now confronted with an entirely new situation since a meeting of the Grand Lodge of Perfection mentioned in Holbrook's letter had been advertised in a local newspaper. Accordingly a

72. Mackey means the Charleston Grand Council, not the New York Grand Consistory.

73. That 'unpleasant correspondence' is not supported otherwise.

74. Mackey 1861, 175–76. APPENDIX 3.7. I suspect that Mackey's statement, 'Dr. Dalcho withdrew from the Supreme Council', was nothing but an echo of M'Cosh's words, 'the Grand Commander having withdrawn from the Council during the present disturbance'. The word *withdrew* is set twice between commas in Harris-Carter 1964, 137 and 139.

75. It is not transcribed in the *Register* but we know its substance from the New York Register under 19 December 1821 (*Heredom* 18, 2010, 51–52).

	17 Aug. & 21 Sept. 1815	**21 Sept. 1816**	**21 Sept. 1817**	**21 Sept. 1818**
President	T. W. Bacot	T. W. Bacot	T. W. Bacot	J. Cogdell
Dty President		J. Cogdell	J. Cogdell	Anthony Ulmo
Gd Sr Warden	J. Dumaine (21 Sept.)	Peter Desportes	Peter Desportes	Isaac M Wilson
Gd Jr Warden	J. Cogdell (21 Sept.)	Anthony Ulmo	Anthony Ulmo	Peter Fayolle
Gd Orator	Anthony Ulmo	L'Herminier	L'Herminier	L'Herminier
Gd Treasurer	Peter Desportes	Simon Jude Chancognie		Desportes
Gd Secretary	Isaac M Wilson	C. S. Tucker	C. S. Tucker	C. S. Tucker
Gd Master of C.	C. S Tucker	Peter Fayolle	Peter Fayolle	Achille Le Prince
Gd Keep. of the S		Alex Carivene	Alex Carivene	Alex Carivene
Gd Expert [Introductor 1823]		J. F. Prentice		
Gd Capt. of the G		August Follin	August Follin	Samuel Richards
Gd Hospitaler		Magnan	Magnan	Magnan
Tyler				

TABLE 3. Grand Officers of the Grand Council of Princes of the Royal Secret in Charleston (1815–1824)

	21 Sept. 1819	21 Sept. 1821 & 22 Sept. 1822	18 Oct. 1823	22 Sept. 1824
President	J. Cogdell	J. Cogdell	Joel Poinsett	Joel Poinsett
Dty President	Ulmo	Ulmo		Tucker
Gd Sr Warden	Joel Poinsett	Joel Poinsett	Tucker	Peter Laurens
Gd Jr Warden	Peter Fayolle	Isaac M Wilson	Peter Laurens	C. C. Chitty
Gd Orator	T. W. Bacot	J. I. Wright		
Gd Treasurer	Desportes	Desportes	Desportes	Desportes
Gd Secretary	C. S. Tucker	C. S. Tucker	Norris	Norris
Gd Master of C.	Achille Le Prince	Achille Le Prince	Achille Le Prince	John Philip
Gd Keep. of the S	Alex Carivene	Alex Carivene	Alex Carivene	Alex Carivene
Gd Expert [Introductor 1823]			C. C. Chitty	Vincent Barré
Gd Capt. of the G	Samuel Richards	C. C. Chitty	Samuel Richards	Samuel Richards
Gd Hospitaler	Magnan	Peter Laurens	John Inness	John Inness
Tyler	E. Elizer	Richards	Samuel Seyles	Samuel Seyles

Table 3. Grand Officers of the Grand Council of Princes of the Royal Secret in Charleston (1815–1824)

second Committee consisting of Dr I. M. Wilson, Richard Pearce and C. C. Chitty was appointed

> to take into consideration the advertisement which took place in the Southern Patriot of this City on the 21st instant respecting a meeting of a Sublime G^{d}. Lodge under such a Title, and that they should also make inquiry to know from whom these persons may have obtained a Charter if they have any.

On 11 March, the Charleston Council sent a letter to the Consistory in New York[76]

> related to the pretentions to Masonic authority of Doct^{r}.·. Isaac Auld of that city, which he has evinced by the formation and Organization of a Sublime Lodge of Perfection at Charleston, thereby interfering with the Jurisdiction of this Sov.·. Gr^{d}.·. Consistory together with a report of their proceedings on that subject.

The report of the second Committee was not ready at the stated meeting of 22 March and reported only on 26 April:

> That they have been informed that those persons who have been advertising in the newspapers are the same that have found the manuscripts of old Col^{l} Mitchell. that they had solicited from Two or Three persons who stiles themselves as G.^{d} Inspectors General 33° to obtain warrants signed by them in order to appear to work with some sort of regularity, and they [*sic*] Committee was further informed that these persons were M. C. Levy the old Doc^{r} Moultrie & a Doctor Auld. not being that they were told that Doc^{r} Dalcho was one also, but for reasons they could not pay no Credit to. the Committee further report that they have Heard that those spurious Masons have been applying to Brother Josep [*sic*] Jahan and to Doctor Fronty to sanction their acts that this Two last Brothers have formally reffused them after much importunity[.]

Although the 'advertising in the newspapers' (plural) is not otherwise described, the Manifesto calling Cerneau '*an Impostor of the first magnitude … whom we have expelled from every Masonic Asylum within our Jurisdiction*' signed by Dalcho and Mitchell which Emanuel De La Motta had issued in New York at the end of January 1814, was reprinted by the Association and circulated in Charleston in the mean time.

The question was now to find out whether Grand Commander Dalcho had played a part in this reprint. During the 26 April meeting, Javain was

76. It was read there on 26 March (*Heredom* 18, 2010, 53).

able to bring an information which illustrates the relationship which existed between him and Dalcho, both calling each other 'Illustrious Brother', Dalcho adding 'and friend'.

> The Ill.^{s} Grand Insp^{r} Genl rep^{tive} of the Sov^{n} G^{d} Consistory Communicated to this Council a Copy of his letter to Doc^{r} f. Dalcho dated the 29th ultimo and the answer from the Doc^{r} Dalcho thereof Dated the 1st Instant. Which Letters on Motion the Ill.^{s} Grand Insp^{r} General have agreed to have them copied on the minutes
>
> Copy
>
> Charleston the 29. March 1822.
>
> To the Mt Ill^{s} & Revd Doctor Dalcho
>
> M. Ill^{s} Br^{r}
>
> I have to inform you that the publication Formerly issued out against our Ex G^{d} Comm^{r} Joseph Cerneau (which publication was signed by E Delamotta and Countersigned by Col^{l} Mitchell & your self) has been recently sent from the press by a body of men terming themselves a regular Body of Sublime Masons, I thought proper to apprise you of it, as it will appear, that it might be done by your Sanction, as your name appears in the said publication. I am satisfyed that you must be highly displeased with their Conduct & from late Communication with the Sov^{n} Grand Consistory for the United States respecting your sentiments on the subjects, I am warranted in my opinion.
>
> I would thank you me dear Brother to favour me, by stating whether that publication was printed without your sanction or not.
>
> I would further request of you to inform me whether Doc^{r} Auld has any regular documents to authorise him to proceed (as I have heard) he has done.
>
> These Communications my most Ill^{s} Brother I hope you will receive in the same spirits of Charity in which they are written—
>
> Yours with sentiments of Respect
>
> Signed P. Javain G^{d} Ins^{r} Genl 33 –
> Rep^{tive} of the G^{d} Consistory of the U. States
> Of America sitting in New York –
>
> *An early answer is requested*[77]
>
> Copy – of the answer
>
> Charleston April 1st 1822
>
> Most Ill^{s} Brother

77. Five words underlined.

> In reply to your letter of the 29th ult^{o} I have to observe that, until you informed me of the Circumstance, I was ignorant that any publication, with my name, have been made by any persons Connected with Masonry, & it, unquestionably, does not meet with my approbation.
>
> My answer to your other interrogatory will I trust be equally satisfactory. Dr Auld has no authority from me to perform any Masonic acts. the power with which I am invested by the Constitution of the 33^{d} Degree, I have not transferred to any person under the Canopy of Heaven
>
> I am my Dear & Ill^{s} Brother and friend
>
> Fred^{k} Dalcho
>
> K.H. P.R.S. Sov^{n} G^{d} Insp^{r} Genl of the 33^{d} and G^{d}.·. Comm^{r}
>
> To the Ill^{s} Brother P. Javain G^{d} Insp^{r} &c

Dalcho's letter brings new essential elements to the information sent by Holbrook and Rouse to Tompkins. If Auld had no authority from Dalcho to perform any Masonic acts, and if Dalcho had not transferred to any person the power he was invested with, then the affirmation that Dalcho had, at any time, named a Lieutenant appears more than doubtful.[78]

Had he named as such one from the three members of the Supreme Council who signed the Charter on 9 February, that member would have mentioned his quality under his signature instead of 'Acting Grand Commander' or 'Acting Lieutenant Grand Commander'. In other words, Dalcho's words question the legality of the issue of the Charter.

Furthermore, the fact that the signatories of the Charter accompanied their unusual titles with the words 'in the United States of America' strongly suggests that as late as 1822 the three of them deliberately ignored the creation of a 'Northern District' or of a 'Northern Jurisdiction' in New York between 1813 and 1815 by Emanuel De La Motta.

M'Cosh thought fit to write 'the Supreme Council correctly organized under the next officer', which is not surprising because as a party, his aim was to support the legality of the Charter and he may not have been familiar with the wording of Art. 3 of the Grand Constitution of 1786. But it is surprising

78. 'it was Dr. Dalcho who had appointed him [Dr. Auld] Lieutenant Grand Commander' (Harris-Carter 1964, 166)! 'On February 9, 1822, with the other members of the Council, Dr. Auld called upon Dr. Dalcho, requesting him to assemble the Council to take needed action. While he was unwilling to do so, *he also displayed no disposition to prevent the Lieutenant Grand Commander from acting on his own authority.*' (Harris-Carter 1964, 167. My emphasis).

to see the author(s) of a book printed two centuries later make M'Cosh's argument their own and write without blushing: 'With Dr. Dalcho taking no part in the controversy, Auld Moultrie and Levy constituted the minimum three members required to conduct business'.[79]

May–November 1822

During the following May, Javain as the representative of the New York Consistory and M'Cosh, then Secretary of the Grand Lodge of Perfection and member of the Grand Council of Princes of Jerusalem, expanded the controversy further in the Charleston press. Their exchange of letters was partly reproduced by M'Cosh.[80] Nothing relevant appears in the Minutes of the next meetings of the Grand Council on 24 June and 22 September.

On 15 November 1822 Horatio Gates Street received a patent which certified that he was a 'Sovereign Grand Inspector General, and Member of the Supreme Council of the Thirty-third Degree.'[81] It was signed by Isaac Auld 'Grand Commander of the United States of N. A.', Moses Holbrook 'Lieut. Grand Commander in the U. S. A.', James Moultrie Secretary General, and M. C. Levy Treasurer General; and further by Alexander McDonald, Joseph M'Cosh SGIG of the 33rd Degree, and John Barker SGIG.

A hand-written Memorandum by Horatio Gates Street 'made in 1822'[82] lists Holbrook and Street as members of the Supreme Council since 15 November, McDonald and M'Cosh since 17 November. A manuscript list of the members of the Supreme Council certified on 29 April 1830 by Moses Holbrook[83] shows he became the 33° on 13 November, Street on 15 November, McDonald and M'Cosh on 17 November. The *Register*'s Minutes say nothing about these four promotions which the Cerneau Council may have ignored.

79. Harris-Carter 1964, 139. One of them, James D. Carter, was the author of 'A Research Report on Fundamental Masonic Law Relating to Symbolic Masonry, the Scottish Rite and Fraternal Relations', a pamphlet of 18 pages published by the Supreme Council in Washington, DC, in 1966.

80. Appendix 3.4. The first Javain's letter, in the *Southern Patriot* of 3 May 1822, alludes to two M'Cosh letters issued on the previous Thursday and Friday, which M'Cosh did not reproduce.

81. Appendix 3.3. The patent was twice copied by Grand Commander Pike (*OB* VIII, 745 and *OB* IX, 116), a facsimile was included in Harris-Carter 1964, 142.

82. *OB* VII, 313.

83. Harris-Carter 1964, 208.

AUGUST–SEPTEMBER 1823

> We now arrive at an eventful period in the history of Masonry in this State, which nothing but the fidelity of an historian induces me to record.
>
> —ALBERT G. MACKEY[84]

The story could have ended here. But during the Summer 1823, Joseph M'Cosh issued *Documents upon Sublime Free-Masonry in the United States of America being a collection of all the official documents which have appeared on both sides of the question. With Notes and an Appendix.* From what had been until then a controversy, these 104 pages gave way to a tragedy.

On Friday 22 August, Past President T. W. Bacot who was a honorary member of the Council since 21 June 1821 requested to be re-activated as a member and was duly elected. Then

> The Ill[s] President [Cogdell] presented a Pamphlet signed M[c] Cosh containing lybellous Insults against the members of this Council which was reffered to a Committee with all power to act on the same. To Draft a Petition to the Gd Lodge on Fryday Evening next charging the said M[c] Cosh and his adderent with gross unmasonnick Conduct && the Committee appointed to that effect Isaac M. Wilson, Benj[n] Mathews, John Inness, J. C. Norris & Ch[s] Tucker.[85]

The 'lybellous insults' probably referred to the foot-note added by M'Cosh to the article from the Charleston Mercury from 7 May: 'two large trunks of papers were obtained from a widow lady, in rather a clandestine manner'.[86]

Javain informed the Consistory in two letters (24 and 28 August) read in New York on 17 September, accompanying

> a Pamphlet Published and circulated by a Spurious Assembly at Charleston S[h] C[a] and a Statement of their Iniquiteous Proceedings.... Resolved [that five Brethren] be a committee to consider the Said Communications & Report what measures are necessary....[87]

On 27 August a Knights Templar Encampment was opened in Charleston. This opening may or may not have had an influence upon the next two months and was not related to the Grand Council or the Supreme Council,

84. Mackey 1861, 174.

85. Wilson was Deputy Grand Master. Matthews, PM of Union Kilwinning, received the 32° on 21 September 1818. Inness and Norris were Junior Grand Deacons, Tucker Grand Treasurer.

86. APPENDIX 3.4. M'Cosh 1823, 86. Harris-Carter 1964, 146.

87. *Heredom* 18 (2010), 55.

but some of the members of the Association, notably Moses Holbrook and Joseph M'Cosh, were directly involved. Details are given below in "Moses Holbrook and the Knights Templar."

The next stated meeting of the Grand Council, 22 September, was adjourned to 18 October 'in consequence of the Inclemency of the weather this being our night of Election of officers – and so few present'. The adjournment had probably other reasons.

The *Abstract of the Proceedings of the Grand Lodge of Ancient Free-Masons of South-Carolina from St. John the Evangelist's Day, 5822, until St. John the Evangelist's Day, 5823,* printed in 1824, records a Grand Lodge meetings on Friday 26 September 1823 which includes nothing relevant to the petition mentioned in the Council's Minutes of 22 August.

OCTOBER–NOVEMBER 1823

> If you have one source only, no problem. They begin when you have several ones.
> — ÉTIENNE GOUT

The Grand Council Minutes

Under the presidency of Javain, the Grand Council met on 18 October and

> Two letters were received and read. the first being from Brother Th. W. Bacot our beloved Past President Sending his resignation to this body as a member.

Both letters are fully transcribed in the Minutes. The most salient parts of Bacot's letter, dated 18 October said:

> Circumstances of so painful a nature have since occurred that I have upon the most mature deliberation, made up my mind to withdraw my self altogether from the active Concerns of free masonry, and more especially from that called Sublime.... I feel it my duty to declare that I am not impelled to it by any doubts on my mind of the Legitimacy of the Supreme Grand Consistory in New York, from which the Council in Charleston derives its authority, but solely from an anxious desire to retire from most of the Societies of what I have been a member....

The other letter, dated 14 October, was from John Cogdell. He also retired from the Council as its President and as a member as well. He ended his letter with these words.

> Here then terminates my masonic career and has been as painful and as unhappy as the beginning was pleasing and interesting.

Grand Lodge Proceedings will indirectly explain the reasons for both resignations.

The Grand Lodge Proceedings Printed in 1824

The *Abstract of the Proceedings* printed in 1824 includes the Minutes of a Special Communication held on 31 October 1823, which are worded thus:

> The Grand Lodge was opened in ample form.
>
> A letter from the Most Reverend Brother F. Dalcho, M. D. Grand Chaplain, was read, and, on motion,
>
> *Resolved, unanimously*, That the same be accepted, and that the Resolution recommended therein be adopted.
>
> [Which letter and proceedings consequent thereon, have already been published and communicated to the fraternity in a pamphlet form, entitled "*Proceedings of the Grand Lodge of Ancient Free-Masons of South-Carolina, held in Charleston, on Friday Evening, the 31st of October*," as stated by the Most Worshipful Grand Master in the records of the 19th December, 5823. It is, therefore, considered unnecessary here to republish the same.]
>
> His Excellency Brother John L. Wilson, Worshipful Master of Lodge No. 40, and Brother David Ross, Worshipful Past Master of Lodge No. 7, gave in their names to be recorded Members of the Grand Lodge.
>
> A letter was read from Brother Rev. F. Dalcho, stating that it would be inconvenient for him to perform the service on the celebration of St. John's Day next, as he should not then be a Member of the Grand Lodge, and requesting the Grand Secretary to record his resignation at the end of the Masonic Year, and, as a matter of course, of the proxy held by him for Lodge No. 17.
>
> On motion, *Resolved*, That a Committee be appointed to wait upon and engage some Clergyman of the fraternity to officiate in the duties of the day, in the place of our Reverend Brother Dalcho, who has declined his services.
>
> The following Brethren were appointed a Committee, viz. Brothers William Waller, Richard Maynard, and Eliab Kingman.
>
> The Grand Lodge was then closed in ample form and harmony.[88]

I found an original copy of the Proceedings of 31 October 'in a pamphlet form' at the Bibliothèque Nationale in Paris.[89] It included a hand-written

88. *PRO* 1824, 16–17.

89. Reference in the *Fonds Maçonnique*: FM² 560. 14 pages. The cover-page shows it was 'Printed by Bro. C. C. Sebring, No. 44 Queen-street. 1823'.

letter dated 21 November 1823 from Past Grand Master Cogdell to 'the Grand Lodge of France' quoted below.

The Grand Lodge Proceedings of 31 October 1823 Printed in November 1823

These Proceedings opened with the following words set in square brackets:

> [The following Proceedings of the Most Worshipful Grand Lodge of Ancient Free-Masons of South-Carolina, are deemed, by the Grand Master, of sufficient importance, to communicate to the Fraternity, without waiting for the usual period of publication.]

All Grand Officers, with the exception of H. H. Bacot, were present, as well as

> Thomas W. Bacot, Past Grand Master; Brother Jervis H. Stevens, Past Deputy Grand Master;[90] and the Representatives, Past-Masters and Proxies, of twenty-eight Lodges. Brother Joseph M'Cosh, a member of Solomon's Lodge No. 1, was present by special invitation.
>
> The Grand Lodge was opened in ample form.
>
> A letter was received from the Most Rev. Dr. Dalcho, Grand Chaplain, which was read, and is as follows.

I do not deem it necessary to reproduce the whole of Dalcho's letter since it is correctly copied in Mackey's *History of Freemasonry in South Carolina*, 1861, which can be read on the Web.[91] At the end of it, Dalcho wrote:

> Intrusted with the "ministry of reconciliation," by divine authority, I interposed between our Brethren, who, unhappily, were at variance, and, as a mutual friend, endeavoured to heal the wounds which misrepresentation and misunderstanding had made. And it gives me real pleasure to state to the Grand Lodge, that from the candid and very honourable and brotherly manner in which my mediation was received and accepted by both parties, I felt the delightful assurance that the genuine principles of our ancient and honourable Order had neither lost their influence over the human heart, nor fled to other climes. I found in all with whom I had occasion to converse on the subject, a sincere disposition to restore harmony to the Grand Lodge, and to pour the balm of masonic affection into the troubled bosom. I cannot express to you, my dear Brethren, the delight it afforded me to be, under God, the happy instrument of producing this reconciliation. I know, however, that you will see, with me, the important effects it must necessarily produce on the respectability of our Order, and, with me, will rejoice in the success of my mediation.

90. An office he occupied last in 1817 in the former Grand Lodge of South Carolina.
91. http://www.archive.org/details/historyoffreemasoomack, 177–79.

I now, my Brethren, submit to you the evidence of this happy reconciliation, and respectfully suggest, that, after it shall have been read, the following resolution may be proposed for the unanimous consent of the Grand Lodge:

Resolved, that the agreement entered into between the M. W. Grand Master and Past Grand Master on one part, and Brothers McCosh, Sebring and Holbrook on the other part, be considered as highly satisfactory to this Grand Lodge; and that the "declarations and recommendations" of the said Grand Officers, as set forth in the 2d article, be now adopted in conformity with their wishes.

The evidence of 'this happy reconciliation' consisted in the following document which Mackey did not fully recopy:

UNION —— WISDOM —— STRENGTH.

Charleston, October 28th, 5823.

Whereas it is an object of primary importance among Free-Masons, to act upon the Square with all mankind, and to live in harmony and brotherly-love with each other, and to cherish those amiable feelings which should always distinguish the members of the mystic family: but from causes not necessary to mention, and more particularly from misinformation and misunderstanding, the harmony of the Grand Lodge has, in some degree, been interrupted: Therefore, with the sole and sincere desire, to restore peace and good-will to the Grand Lodge, and to promote the prosperity and unanimity of the Fraternity, as well as to show the triumph of masonic principles over personal considerations, they, who may on either side, have been considered as more immediately concerned, have, on a mutual explanation, cheerfully consented to make the following declarations; viz.

1st. Each of the Brothers named in the Appeal of the M. W. Grand Master, and Past Grand Master, to the Grand Lodge, doth, for himself, hereby positively declare, that nothing contained in any writing, pamphlet, or other publications, supposed to have been made by him or them, or with their knowledge, was, as they firmly believe, intended to injure the personal feelings, the honour, or private character, of the M. W. Grand Master, or the M. W. Past Grand Master, of the Grand Lodge of Ancient Free-Masons of South-Carolina; and the said publications are hereby considered as suppressed. And in consideration of the amicable arrangement agreed upon, Brothers Holbrook and Sebring will return the copy of the said Appeal, with which they were furnished by the Grand Secretary.

(Signed) JOSEPH M'COSH.
C. C. SEBRING.
MOSES HOLBROOK.

2d. The Grand Master, and Past Grand Master, declare, that as they are, and ever have been, sincerely desirous of promoting the harmony, happiness, and prosperity of the Craft; so they likewise declare, that if any thing like personal feeling has appeared on their parts, towards any Brother, or any reflection thought to have been cast on his honour, or character, it was never so intended by them: and in consideration of the amicable arrangement agreed upon, the Grand Master, and Past Grand Master, will respectfully recommend to the Grand Lodge, to permit every thing which has been laid before them, of every kind and nature whatsoever, connected with this subject, to be withdrawn; and every record of the same on the Grand Secretary's books, to be expunged; the Committee appointed upon this subject to be discharged, and these declarations, and recommendations, to be placed on the Journals of the Grand Lodge in their stead.

(Signed) JOHN S. COGDELL,
Grand Master of the Grand Lodge of A. F. M. of S. C.
THO. W. BACOT,
Past Grand Master of the Grand Lodge of A. F. M. of S. C.[92]

Grand Lodge followed Dalcho's respectful suggestion and adopted unanimously the resolution set forth in the last paragraph of his letter. The core of the resolution was

> to permit every thing which has been laid before [Grand Lodge], of every kind and nature whatsoever, connected with this subject, to be withdrawn; and every record of the same on the Grand Secretary's books, to be expunged;

Grand Master Cogdell addressed Grand Lodge – his address is fully transcribed in Mackey's *History*.[93] The Proceedings printed in 1823 end with a Cogdell letter not transcribed in Mackey:

> The following letter from the Grand Master was then read, and the several papers and documents laid before the Grand Lodge, were ordered to be inserted in the Journals.

The main part of which was:

> I now beg the liberty of announcing to you, that I am no longer a candidate for those honours and those distinctions, which are attendant upon the Chair of the Grand Lodge.

92. *Proceedings of a Special Communication of the Grand Lodge of Ancient Free-Masons of South-Carolina held in Charleston on Friday Evening, the 31st of October, 5823, 8–9.*
93. Mackey 1861, 179–81.

Grand Master Cogdell's Letter to the 'Grand Lodge of France'

On 21 November 1823, Grand Master Cogdell sent a copy of his Grand Lodge Proceedings to 'The Grand Lodge of France'[94] and a letter in which he wrote:

> In the Course of the last Summer, a Pamphlet over the signature of Bro: Joseph M^c^Cosh and printed by Bro: C. C. Sebring at Charleston was circulated – and subsequently two letters, one purporting to have been printed in Charleston, the other at New York and circulated thro the Post Office.
>
> The Pamphlet had induced an appeal on the Part of the Past Grand Master Bro. Thomas Wright Bacot and myself to the Grand Lodge against the conduct of the Brethren whose names you will find in the Printed Extracts from the Minutes of the Grand Lodge.
>
> _______But it is with pleasure I inform you, all the difficulties and all the differences have been masonically healed; superseding the necessity of further pursuing the appeal before the Grand Lodge, the same with all matters connected with it & the Pamphlet have been expunged from the Minutes, as you will perceive by the printed document which I have the honor now to transmit to your Most Worshipful Grand Lodge....

Holbrook's Version in Two Letters He Sent to J. J. J. Gourgas in 1826

In two letters,[95] Holbrook gave more details:

> I was arraigned before the Grand Lodge of the State, and after five meetings Mr. Cogdell and Mr. Bacot, my accusers, at the fifth meeting obtained a majority to try me and to punish me....
>
> To give you a better idea of the proceedings of the Grand Lodge, which were very voluminous: J. T. [*sic*] Cogdell was Grand Master of the Grand Lodge of the State and the presiding officer of the spurious 32d of Cerneau in this City; T. W. Bacot was a Past Gr. Master of the Gr. L. and a past presiding officer of Cerneau's Body. These two ordered an extra call of the G. L. of the State, and read a long memorial about the pamphlet called "Documents upon Sublime Free-Masonry," of which I had the honor to forward a copy to yourself in 1823. It accused Joseph McCosh of editing, C. C. Sebring of printing, and Br. Moses Holbrook "of offering it to be openly sold to the community at a public book-store, (perhaps from which pamphlet were read by him, (M. H.,) with the view deeply to injure them, the Gr. Master and Past Gr. Master, as *Masons* as well as citizens in a community among whom they were *born* and *reared* and have been thus far *respected*." There was the head and front of our offending.

Then Holbrook gives his version of how things were brought to an end:

94. APPENDIX 3.5. Obviously Grand Master Cogdell ignored that no Grand Lodge existed in France at that time, but a Grand Orient.

95. Both transcribed in APPENDIX 3.6.

> and we were put upon trial for expulsion under this sweeping charge, no point of which was true. Five meetings of the Grand Lodge were held, and the result was that Bacot and Cogdell were left out of office in the Grand Lodge with their adherents.

Holbrook mentions neither the document he signed together with M'Cosh and Sebring on 28 October nor the part played by Dalcho. In short, his narrative does not agree with the Grand Lodge Proceedings.

Mackey's Version Written in 1861

Mackey's version brings no new element but should be read out of curiosity.[96] He must have had a copy of the Minutes of 31 October 1823 parts of which he recopied accurately. His well-meant intentions resulted in a picture somewhat far from the facts:

> Irritated at the language used in this pamphlet [*the M'Cosh book*], and the accusations of perfidy and error with which they were charged, Brothers Bacot and Cogdell appealed to the Grand Lodge for protection. Here, however, the fraternal services of Dr. Dalcho were again called into requisition, and at a special Communication of the Grand Lodge, which was holden on the 31st of October, 1823, a solemn declaration was read, which had been obtained by the Grand Chaplain, and which was signed by Joseph McCosh, C. C. Sebring, and Moses Holbrook, the persons particularly named in the appeal of Brothers Cogdell and Bacot.[97]

Bacot and Cogdell were not 'charged with accusations of perfidy and error', neither did they appeal to the Grand Lodge 'for protection'. The Minutes of the Grand Council from 22 August show that Cogdell said the Mc Cosh pamphlet contained libelous Insults and that it was referred to a Committee to draft a petition to the Grand Lodge charging M'Cosh and his adherent with gross unmasonic Conduct.

Mackey added further:

> Immediately after these transactions, both Brothers Cogdell and Dalcho gave notice that they were no longer candidates for reelection to their respective offices, and at the expiration of the year they withdrew from membership in

96. Appendix 3.7.
97. Mackey 1861, 176.

> the Grand Lodge. Neither of them again took any interest in the proceedings of the Order.[98]

As far as Frederick Dalcho is concerned, Mackey is again inaccurate. The Grand Lodge Proceedings of 31 October mention that

> A letter was read from Brother Rev. F. Dalcho, stating that it would be inconvenient for him to perform the service on the celebration of St. John's Day next, as he should not then be a Member of the Grand Lodge, and requesting the Grand Secretary to record his resignation at the end of the Masonic Year....

Grand Lodge likely hoped that Dalcho would remain a Grand Officer. But of course, once he had achieved his '"ministry of reconciliation" by divine authority', he could hardly go further. He never expressed his feelings toward Holbrook but they appear in a letter written some seven years later by Moses Holbrook:

> With my present feelings, I think you will never see Dalcho's name on the same paper with mine. After reputedly calling to see him for 4 days – and he lives one mile from me nearly – he almost rudely shut the door in my face. He was shorter than pie crust.[99]

DECEMBER 1823

After its Special Communication on 31 October, Grand Lodge met in Columbia on 5 and 9 December. The letter from Grand Master Cogdell was read and Grand Lodge resolved unanimously That the thanks of this Grand Annual Communication be tendered to him 'for the faithful manner in which he has discharged the duties of his station, whilst in the office of Most Worshipful Grand Master'.

At the Quarterly Communication of Grand Lodge in Charleston on 19 December, a Preamble and Resolution 'presented by Brother C. C. Sebring' were read and adopted: The Grand Lodge

> having received with regret the resignation of their Chaplain, feel themselves called to express their sentiments on this occasion. Resolved, That the Grand

98. Mackey 1861, 181.

99. Holbrook to Gourgas, 6 March 1830 (Harris-Carter 1964, 205). The last document which bears both signatures is the Warrant for Natchez Consistory dated 14 March 1830 (facsimile Harris-Carter 1964, 202).

> Lodge deeply regret the late resignation of the Most Reverend Grand Brother Dalcho....

As a testimonial, Grand Lodge voted a sum not exceeding one hundred dollars for defraying the expense for

> an engraved likeness of him to be made, of such size, as that it may conveniently be placed in the second edition of the Ahiman Rezon; and that every Lodge, and every Brother having a copy of that work, be entitled to a copy of the engraving to place therein.

Grand Master Cogdell read his report in which he said:

> In obedience to the dictates of the most conciliatory and Masonic feelings, I have caused to be printed, a part of the Minutes of the late Special Meeting of the Grand Lodge, which eventuated in so much harmony and union of sentiments; and these extracts I have distributed to the Lodges subordinate through the Mail, and otherwise, and to our Brethren in neighbouring States, where it was known these extracts were necessary to justice, truth, and good feeling, to sustain the character of this Grand Lodge.

Brother Henry H. Bacot presented a Resolution expressing Grand Lodge's regrets that Brother Cogdell declined a re-election to the Chair. A Committee was appointed to cause the Resolution 'to be written on vellum and presented' to the Grand Master. John Cogdell gave notice that he should withdraw from being a Member of the Grand Lodge after St. John's Day next. Grand Lodge resolved that our venerable Past Grand Master Thomas W. Bacot and the Most Reverend Grand Chaplain F. Dalcho be admitted as honorary Members of the Grand Lodge. The election of Grand Officers followed. Moses Holbrook was elected 'Worshipful Corresponding Gd. Secretary'.

At the Adjourned Communication of Grand Lodge on 26 December,

> A letter from Brother Frederick Dalcho was read, acknowledging the receipt of the Resolutions passed at the last Communication , and tendering his sincere thanks for the many acts of kindness received by him from the Grand Lodge.
>
> Letters were read from Brothers Thomas W. Bacot, Most Worshipful Past Grand Master, and Peter Javain, Worshipful Senior Grand Deacon, giving notice that they should withdraw from being members of the Grand Lodge after St. John's Day next, and accepted.

At the General Grand Communication on 27 December, Moses Holbrook was installed as Corresponding Gd. Secretary, Alexander McDonald and

Horatio Gates Street as Senior Grand Deacons. In his address, the new Grand Master, His Excellency John L. Wilson, said:

> If there should be any differences existing amongst the Brethren, this Hall contains the sacred Altar upon which the asperities and irregularities of the passions should all be sacrificed.... When feelings of enmity produce acts of revenge—when the hands of some are uplifted against the hands of others, the order and beauty of this Institution are lost in chaos.
>
> If there be any of those feelings which I have described, now within these walls, let them be made a sacrifice this day on the Altar of Universal Love.

One week before, on 20 December, an *Extract from an Act of the Legislature of the State of South-Carolina* showed the incorporation of 'a body politic and corporate, in deed and in law, by the name and style of "*Inspectors General of the Thirty-third Degree*"' with the following members: Isaac Auld M.D. Grand Commander, Moses Holbrook M.D. Lieutenant Grand Commander, Rev. Frederick Dalcho M.D. Past Grand Commander, James Moultrie M.D. Secretary General, Moses C. Levy, Esquire, Treasurer General, Horatio Gates Street, Alexander McDonald and Joseph M'Cosh, Esquires.[100]

MOSES HOLBROOK AND THE KNIGHTS TEMPLAR

THE ROXBURY STORY

Moses Holbrook was born in Sherborn, Co. Middlesex, Mass., 1783. He was entered in Middlesex Lodge in 1804, two months after his 21st birthday, and raised February 12, 1805.[101] Sometimes afterwards he must have made friends with members of Washington Lodge in Roxbury, County of Norfolk, Mass., warranted in March 1796. The history of the Lodge recites:

> In August 1808, there appears to have been some irregularity in the proceedings of the Lodge. New officers were chosen; but why, the records do not state, although it was voted that the proceedings should be recorded. About this

100. *OB* VII, 314–15. Lobingier 1931, 132, with the reference: *Masonic Mirror and Mechanics' Intelligencer*, I, No. 27 (June 25, 1825). Harris-Carter 1964, 141 & 147.

101. http://www.middlesexlodge.org/About1.htm. The Lodge was warranted in June 1795, its seat was at Framingham, Co. Middlesex.

> time the powers and priviledges of the Lodge were suspended, and the Charter withdrawn by the Grand Lodge....
>
> At a meeting of the Grand Lodger, held June 13, A.L. 5808, "a letter from the ... Junior Grand Warden was read ... detailing certain recent transactions of the officers of Washington Lodge, in Roxbury, viz. their clandestinely using the Charter of the Lodge for purposes and designs never contemplated by this Grand Lodge; ... the following vote passed unanimously:" "It appears to this Grand Lodge that the Charter ... has been appropriated by the officers of the Lodge to the purpose of conferring and receiving other degrees that those known to this Grand Lodge: it is, therefore, voted that the same be returned." ...
>
> At the next quarterly communication of the Grand Lodge, Sept. 12, A.L. 5808, "a petition was presented from a number on members of Washington Lodge, praying for the restoration of their Charter....
>
> At a meeting of the Grand Lodge held Dec. 27, A.L. 5808, [a report] on the conduct of a number of the officers and members of Washington Lodge, *and other Lodges* [was adopted. It listed] the names of those Brethren at Roxbury, *and elsewhere*, who have signed their recantation ...: 'The subscribers, being associated as members of the Washington Encampment at Roxbury for the purpose of conferring various degrees in Masonry, in a way and manner which we are conscious is contrary to the principles of Masonry and ancient usages, and totally subversive of the harmony and prosperity of the Craft, do most heartily renounce and abandon said Association forever, and freely acknowledge our error, solemnly engaging to conform to all the Edicts and Regulations of the Grand Lodge'.

This 'recantation' was signed at Boston on 13 December 1808 by nineteen Brethren, Moses Holbrook's name was listed first.[102] Lobingier was aware of the above and wrote:

> Holbrook took the trouble three years later to become "formally healed" in Mt. Vernon Chapter, Portland, District of Maine, shortly after he had delivered the St. John's Day address before that body and Ancient Landmark Lodge of the same place.[103] Holbrook was then preceptor of Portland Academy; but that was evidently an avocation during his preparation for the medical profession.[104]

THE BATH STORY

We find new elements of Holbrook's career in a *History of Bath*:[105]

102. Dadmon & Newton 1866, 13–19.

103. http://catalogue.nla.gov.au/Record/3751662. 'An oration pronounced on the festival of St. John the Baptist, 24th June, A.L. 5811.: Before Ancient Land Mark Lodge, and Mount Vernon Chapter. By Br. Moses Holbrook, K.T. preceptor of Portland Academy.'

104. Lobingier 1931, 128.

105. Reed 1894, 384.

> Dr. Moses Holbrook was, for some years, in practice in Bath, and had the reputation of skill in his profession, as he was also in the art of Masonry, and was Master of Solar Lodge in the years of 1813, 1814, and 1815. Subsequently he became a resident of Charleston, S. C.

As in Roxbury, problems seem to have happened in 1813 in the Bath Lodge:[106]

> This feeling came to a head in 1813 when Solar Lodge of Bath, through a committee, addressed a circular letter to the twenty-three Lodges in the District of Maine, criticising the action of certain Grand Officers and airing the grievances of the Lodge against the Grand Lodge. The Bath circular complained that Solar Lodge had not, for three years past, received any copy of the annual communications of the Grand Lodge; that they had never received any Past Masters' diplomas, to which, by the Constitution, they were entitled; that their complaints to the Grand Lodge remained unanswered; and that they had only been furnished with diplomas printed on paper while entitled to have them engrossed on parchment. They also complained of the new constitutional provision requiring the payment of three dollars for each initiate, instead of two dollars as heretofore.
>
> There is no doubt that some of the Maine Lodges fully sympathized with Solar Lodge in her complaints. Others, however, felt that the Bath brethren were going at the matter in the wrong way. Copies of the Bath circular were transmitted to the Grand Lodge and were referred to a committee of distinguished brethren. This committee refused to consider the justice or injustice of the Bath charges, holding that these were not properly before them. They did, however, hold the proceedings of Solar Lodge to have been insubordinate and undutiful and recommended that the Master and Wardens of Solar Lodge be summoned to appear before the Grand Lodge and show cause, if any, why the charter of said Lodge should not be revoked.
>
> Realizing that they had made a tactical error, the brethren of Solar Lodge voted an apology declaring themselves to be faithful and liege subjects of the Grand Lodge and praying pardon and forgiveness for their mistake. The apology was accepted and further proceedings against the Lodge were quashed.

Holbrook's name appears in 1819 in the Charleston Directories. He is first listed in the Grand Lodge Proceedings in the *Report of Lodges* from 1823 as a Past Master, member of Washington Lodge No. 7[107] and in the same year in connection with a Charleston Encampment.

106. Pollard 1945, Chapter III online.

107. *PRO* 1824, 35. Horatio Gates Street was then WM and Cornelius Sebring Senior Warden of No. 7.

Gourdin's Version (1855)[108]

The South-Carolina Encampment, No. 1, of Knights Templars and the Appendant Orders was established in 1780, as is evident from the old seal in our archives. But, it does not appear from what source our ancestors derived their first charter, all of our records previous to Nov. 7th, 1823, having been lost or consumed by fire. It is clear, however, that this Encampment was in active operation in 1803, and continued so until long after the date of our oldest record, for, on December 29th, 1824, it was "Resolved that, in consideration of the long and faithful services of our Most Eminent Past Grand Commander, Francis Sylvester Curtis, *who regularly paid his arrears to this Encampment for more than twenty years,* he is considered a life-member of this Encampment, and that his life-membership take date from November, 1823."[109, A] In a "list of various Masonic degrees," in Cole's Ahiman Rezon, extracted from a publication in 1816, the *Knight of the Red Cross* is termed the 9th degree, the *Knight of Malta* the 10th, and the *Knight Templar* the 13th; and they are said to be conferred in the Sublime Grand Lodges in Charleston, S. C., in the city of New-York, and in Newport, R.I.[110, B]

On November 7th, 1823, our Encampment, which was then regularly working at Sir Knight Roche's Asylum,[111, C] under the Command of the M. E. Sir Moses Holbrook, M. D., Grand Commander, received *"the authority from the G. G. E."* to work. At the following meeting, (Nov. 15,) Moses Holbrook was re-elected to the office which he then held. John Barker was elected an honorary member, January 16th, 1824. It was, at this time, the practice to introduce the *candidates separately in both degrees.* On January 18th, 1824, James Eyland was created a Templar. The Encampment met, January 30th, 1824, at Sir Knights H. G. Street's Asylum,[112, D] and the meetings, which had hitherto taken place on *every* Friday evening, were changed, February 15, 1824, to the last Wednesday in each month; and the last Wednesday in November was fixed for the annual election. March 31st, 1824, our Encampment "voted to recommend our Ill. Sir John Barker to be Grand Visitor for the Southern States."[113, E]

Mackey's Version (1861)[114]

I have been unable to find any reference, in the contemporary journals of the day, to the existence of "South Carolina Encampment No. 1," at that early period.

108. Gourdin 1855, 29–31. The footnotes A to E are Gourdin's original ones.

109. Footnote A in original: MS. Records of S.C. Enct. No. 1.

110. Foot note B in original: The Freemasons' Library, 317.

111. Footnote C in original: At the S.E. corner of Church and Chalmers sts. Charleston, S. C., John May.

112. Footnote D in original: On East Bay street, in the rear of the establishment known as the "French Coffee House," Charleston, S.C., John May.

113. Footnote E in original: MS. Records of S.C. Encampment No. 1.

114. Mackey 1861, 487, 489, 491, 492.

I have, however, been more successful in obtaining indisputable evidence that the degrees of Knight of the Red Cross and Knight Templar were conferred in Charleston, in a regularly organized body, as far back as the year 1783, and I have no doubt that the seal, with the date "1780," to which Gourdin refers, belonged to that body and afterwards came into the possession of South Carolina Encampment....

I have no doubt that the degree of Knight Templar was conferred in Charleston by the members of the Supreme Council, which had been formed there in 1801. As strongly corroborative of this fact, it may be stated that, for a long time, in the early period of the history of Templarism in this State, the most prominent men in the Encampment were members of the Supreme Council....

But it is very probable, and indeed scarcely to be doubted, that there was an Encampment in Charleston in 1803. This is deduced from the fact that in 1823 a resolution was adopted by South Carolina Encampment No. 1 in these words: "Resolved, that in consideration of the long and faithful services of our Most Eminent Past Grand Commander, Francis Silvester Curtis, who regularly paid his arrears to this Encampment for more than twenty years, he be considered a life member of this Encampment, and that his life membership take date from November, 1823."

Now F. S. Curtis was a leading member of the Ancient and Accepted Rite in this State,[115] and as it is likely from his Masonic character that he would have been one of the founders of the Encampment, it is probable that the Encampment was formed in 1803, to which period the twenty years mentioned in the resolution of 1823 would carry us back.

One thing more is evident. If South Carolina Encampment No. 1 was in existence from the year 1803, of which I have already said there is scarcely a doubt, and derived its original authority from the Supreme Council, it continued its existence from that time until 1823, either under the same authority or acted as an independent body....

Such, I presume, was the case in South Carolina, and the true history of the Encampment in Charleston probably is, that, having been originally constituted as an honorary Order by the Supreme Council in or about 1803, it subsequently prolonged its existence by its own independent act.

But the General Grand Encampment was established in 1816, and the Templar Order from that time began to be organized on a more stable, and, I may add, more respectable footing. Accordingly on the 7th of November, 1823, South Carolina Encampment No. 1 received its warrant from the General Grand Encampment of the United States. Templarism was at that time in a very prosperous condition in the State.

115. An extraordinary statement unsupported by a single known document related to the A&ASR!

Parvin's Version (1889)[116]

Under the provisions of the Constitution the General Grand Encampment did not assemble again [after 16 September 1819] until the 18th of September, 1826, at which time Sir John Snow, G.G.G., presided over the Body.

The Grand Encampments of Massachusetts and Rhode Island, and of New York, were again represented. We find South Carolina Encampment No. 1 of Charleston, S. C., duly represented by Sir John Barker, prox. for Sir Moses Holbrook, Grand Master, the same whose name appears on the famous circular of 1823, announcing that a Charter of Recognition had been received from the General Grand Encampment. The records, however, of the Grand Body fail to show the fact.

And immediately afterwards:

[On 18 September 1826] The record contains no report from the General Grand Officers, who undoubtedly made such report as the committee to whom they referred the proceedings of the General Grand Officers since the last meeting submitted a report from which we learn that Encampments had been established in ... South Carolina and Georgia as follows:

"... That the General Grand Generalissimo had granted the following Charters, to wit: ... a Charter of Recognition to South Carolina Encampment, at Charleston, South Carolina, September 23, 1823."

Speed's Version (1890)[117]

Speed quoted a note signed by Joseph M'Cosh which he found in the Grand Encampment Proceedings from 1883:

"That on diligent search being made in the archives, it clearly appears that this encampment was in full operation under the sanction of the warrant of 'Blue' Lodge No. 40,[118] upwards of thirty years ago, and continued in operation many years subsequent; and has, time out of mind, caused to be made and used a common seal. It also further appears that the said encampment has been dormant for several years past....

"*Resolved*, That the M∴ E∴ Sir James C. Winter, together with the Recorder, be authorized to forward the necessary documents to prove the existence of this encampment prior to the year 1816, and obtain the desired recognition.

Extract from the minutes,

"[Signed] Joseph McCosh,
"Recorder *pro tem.*"

116. Parvin 1889, 592–93. But also see Parvin 566–69 with the facsimile of a patent and seal of St. Andrews Lodge No. 1, Charleston, from August 1783.

117. Speed 1890, 706.

118. In order to understand the various references to Lodge No. 40 at Charleston, formerly St. Andrews No. 1, see Sachse 1913, 184–96; Sachse 1815, 42–43; Bernheim 2007, 142–45.

SCHULTZ'S VERSION (1891)[119]

A short time prior to the holding of the Centennial referred to, the fraters of South Carolina Commandery came into possession of certain papers through Sir Knight S. Stacker Williams, of Ohio, which had been in the possession of the widow of a son of Sir John Snow, Grand Generalissimo of the General Grand Encampment from 1819 to 1826. These papers are published in a pamphlet containing an account of the so-called centennial celebration, and consist of extracts from the minutes of a meeting of nine Knights Templar held at Charleston, August 27th, 1823, for the purpose of reorganizing South Carolina Encampment No. I, in conformity with the Constitution, of the General Grand Encampment of the United States.

The minutes show that on the day named, the nine Sir Knights present authorized the reopening of the Encampment No. I. That it was thereupon duly convened, and the members severally signed the oath of fealty to the General Grand Encampment, and passed upon the form of a petition to that body for a Charter of Recognition, three additional names being attached to the petition, making it twelve. The preamble and first resolution read as follows (Italics mine):

At a meeting of South Carolina Encampment No. I, at their Asylum, in Charleston, South Carolina, a constitutional number of Knights Templar, members of said Encampment, present, among other things it was

Resolved, That on diligent search being made in the archives, it clearly appears that *this Encampment was in full operation, under the sanction of the Warrant of Blue Lodge No. 40, upwards of thirty years ago*, and continued in operation many years subsequent, and has, time out of mind, *caused to be made and used a common seal.* It also further appears that said Encampment has lain dormant for several years past.

The second resolution recognized the General Grand Encampment of the United States, and requested that a Charter of Recognition be forthwith issued by that body, and that it confirm the election held that day.

The third resolution authorized "Sir Knight James C. Winter and the Recorder to forward the necessary documents *to prove the existence of the Encampment prior to the year 1816, and to obtain the recognition.*"

Opposite the signatures of the Sir Knights present at the meeting, and also opposite the signatures of the twelve Knights signing the oath of fealty to the General Grand Encampment, is a seal (a fac-simile of which is here given).

In compliance with the request of these Sir Knights, a dispensation was issued by Sir John Snow, General Grand Generalissimo, dated at Providence, Rhode Island, September 23rd, 1823; in the preamble to which the facts are set

119. Schultz 1891, 202–4.

forth as in the petition, that said Encampment was in full operation upwards of thirty years ago, and that it was in existence prior to the year 1816, the date of organization of the General Grand Encampment.

The next paper exhibited in the pamphlet is a copy of a circular letter, now in the archives of the Grand Commandery of Massachusetts and Rhode Island, and which reads as follows (Italics also mine):

South Carolina Encampment No. I, Charleston, September 3rd, 1823.

I. N. P. E. F. E. S. S. I. *Pax Oblectatio et Unitas.*

Most Eminent Sir and Illustrious Companions—I have the honor to inform you that the Encampment of Knights Templar and the appendant Order, *established in this city in 1780*, has this day regularly acknowledged and come under the jurisdiction of the General Grand Encampment of the United States, and in behalf of our Encampment we crave from you that interchange of friendship and social intercourse between our respective members individually, and between our Encampment by correspondence, which characterizes our illustrious and magnanimous Order.

You have herewith *an impression from our old seal,* and the signatures of our officers, and I beg that you may reciprocate with us.

I salute you fraternally.

Joseph McCosh, *Recorder.*
M. Holbrook, M. D., *G. C.*
Th. W. Curtis, *Gen.*
David Ross, *Capt. Gen.*

To the M. E. Grand Commander, Sir Henry Fowle, Esq., G.M. and Illustrious Knights, Companions of the Grand Encampment of Massachusetts and Rhode Island.

P. S.— *We will give timely notice of the change which will take place in our seal.*

The impression of the seal (a fac-simile of which we also produce) attached to this letter, it will be seen, is precisely the same as those on the two papers referred to, *except* that in lieu of the words and figures, "Lodge No. 40," are the characters and figures. "S. Ca. No. 1, 1780," (meaning, of course, South-Carolina Encampment No. 1, 1780) which characters and figures are for the *first and only time* referred to, or are upon any paper or document exhibited in the pamphlet.

To my mind it is vey clear that after this paper was written, and before being sent to its destination, the contemplated "change" in the seal "took place," and therefore it was not an impression of the *old* seal that was sent to the Grand Encampment of Massachusetts and Rhode Island, but an impression, either of the *old* seal *altered*, or, what is more probable, an impression of a *new* seal. The old seal, as we have seen, used twice, *only seven days* previous to the date of this letter, bore the words and figures, "*Lodge No. 40.*"

SINGLETON'S VERSION (1898)[120]

On November 7, 1823, that encampment, which was then regularly working at Sir Knight Roche's Asylum, under the command of the M.E. Sir Moses Holbrook, M.D., Grand Commander, received "*the authority from the G. G. E.*" to work. At the following meeting (November 15th) Moses Holbrook was re-elected to the office which he then held.

MELCHER'S VERSION (1900)[121]

The first seal of the Commandery with Lodge No. 40 at the bottom was of the same description as the fourth design at the head of the diploma. The seal with South Carolina Encampment No. 1, 1780 at the bottom, with same design as formerly, was probably adopted after the Lodge became connected with the ancient York Grand Lodge of South Carolina, instead of Pennsylvania, or more likely when they severed their connection with Lodge 40, and acknowledged and came under the jurisdiction of the *General Grand Encampment of the United States*, as the following copies of documents preserved in the Archives of the Commandery, would indicate, viz:

Present:

Sir J. C. Winter, G. C. Pt., Sir F. S. Curtis, Gen'l, Sir Richard Maynard, C. G., Sir David Ross, Sir Caleb Duhadway, [*read*: Dunaway] Sir Joseph Cole, Sir John McAnally, Sir Jacob Mann, Sir Moses Holbrook, Sir Joseph Mc Cosh.

An Encampment was opened in short form; the members of said Encampment did severally sign a paper, purporting to be a desire and authority to reopen said Encampment, in conformity with the Constitution of said General Grand Encampment. The oath of allegiance was then duly administered to all Sir Knights present, Extract from the minutes of the said meeting on the 27th August, 1823.

Witness our hand and seal of the Encampment.

Signed:

J. C. Winter	Joseph McCosh
G.C. Pt.	Recorder Pt.

We the subscribers, Knights of the Red Cross, Knights Templar and of Malta, having taken the necessary obligation, do severally promise to conform to and abide by the Constitution, Laws and Edicts of the General Grand Encampment of the United States.

Charleston, S.C., 27th August, 1823.

120. Singleton 1898 & 1906, 1373, quoting *Gourdin MS. Records of South Carolina Encampment, No. 1*, 29, 30.

121. http://www.clansinclairsc.org/SouthCarolinaCommanderyNo1Hist.htm. The author wrote: 'The position taken by Brother Schultz is, therefore, too preposterous to be entertained'.

Signed
F. S. Curtis. Edwd. Hughes. David Ross. Richard Maynard. C. B. Duhadway. [*read*: Dunaway] M. Holbrook. Joseph McCosh. Joseph Cole. Jacob Mann. Jno. McAnally. Patrick McGann. John R. Rogers.
Sworn to and signed in open Encampment
Witness our hands and seal of said Encampment.

J. C. Winter — Joseph Mc Cosh
G.C. Pt. — Recorder Pt.

Both of these documents bear the seal of the Encampment, with Lodge No. 40 at the bottom, which shows that this seal was in use as the seal of the Encampment from the first day of August, 1783, where it appears on the diploma heretofore mentioned, until the twenty-seventh of August, 1823, where it appears for the last time....

The Commandery is also in possession of a copy of the original circular issued by them, September 3rd, 1823, to the several Grand Encampments of the United States;[122] it informs them that the Encampment of Knights Templar and the appendant Orders, *established in this City in 1780*, had been this day regularly acknowledged, and come under the jurisdiction of the General Grand Encampment of the United States, and in behalf of the Encampment craves an interchange of fraternal and social intercourse between the respective members, and with this circular is given an impression of the old seal; being signed by Joseph McCosh, Recorder; M. Holbrook, M.D., G. Comd.; Th. W. Curtis, Gen'l; David Ross, Capt. Gen. This seal is the same as that which we find on the diploma issued by the "Most Holy and Invincible Order of Knights of St. Andrew's Lodge No. 1, to Brother Sir Henry Beaumont, on the 1st day of August, 1783, with the exception Lodge No. 40 being replaced by *So. Ca. Enc. No. 1, 1780.*
(WEBMASTER'S NOTE: Image not available. KT est 1780)[123]

...

It appears that a *Grand* Encampment was established in South Carolina as early as 1826, for the records of the General Grand Encampment of the United States, held in 1826, the committee reported, with approval, that since the preceding conclave, the General Grand Officers had established a Grand Encampment in South Carolina....

The record book of South Carolina Encampment shows the following entry:

Sir J. W. Rouse (Recorder) handed me over the books and papers, all for me to deliver up to this Encampment, some time in 1832, with a letter of resignation, and at the same time the books and papers of Grand Encampment of South Carolina. All were flooded when Sir John May's workshop was burned. I received the remains in January, 1840.

(Signed) Moses Holbrook,
Past Grand Commander and Past G. M. of Grand Encampment of S. C.

122. See Parvin 1889, 569.
123. The seal attached to the Circular was reproduced by Schultz (see above).

Summary

An Encampment was opened or re-opened in Charleston on 27 August 1823. On 3 September, that Encampment sent a Circular Letter

> to the several Grand Encampments of the United States; it informs them that the Encampment of Knights Templar and the appendant Orders, *established in this City in 1780*, had been this day *regularly* acknowledged, and come under the jurisdiction of the General Grand Encampment of the United States....

The seal affixed to the Minutes showed *Lodge No. 40.* It appears to have been tampered with on the Circular sent one week later – as noticed by Schultz – and replaced with *So. Ca. Enc. No. 1, 1780.* Both documents – the Minutes of 27 August and the Circular Letter from 3 September – show the names of Moses Holbrook and Joseph M'Cosh.

Mackey writes: 'Accordingly on the 7th of November, 1823, South Carolina Encampment No. 1 received its warrant from the General Grand Encampment of the United States.'[124] Singleton gives the same date and adds 'At the following meeting (November 15th) Moses Holbrook was re-elected to the office which he then held.... Jos. M'Cosh, who was afterwards [*sic*!]' an Ins. Genl. of the thirty-third degree, resigned November 28, 1827.[125]

I wrote at the beginning of this paper: Did Frederick Dalcho 'withdraw' from the Supreme Council? Did he ever resign as Grand Commander? There could be more than a coincidence to see that the date at which the Charleston Encampment received a Charter is identical with the date when, according to Moses Holbrook writing on 29 April 1830, Frederick Dalcho 'Resigned the G^{d}. Commandership'.[126]

124. Mackey 1861, 492.

125. Singleton 1898, 1373 & 1375.

126. Facsimile in Harris-Carter 1964, 208. The author(s) thought fit to add the following italicized comment: 'This date appears to be incorrect, and may have been meant for 1822. Dr. Auld had already assumed the office of Grand Commander before Novermber 7, 1823.' (Harris-Carter 1964, 209).

APPENDIX

1. SOUTH CAROLINA

1.1 GRAND LODGES 1736–1817

The Provincial Grand Lodge of South Carolina was founded in 1736 and remained active at least until 1788. Within the next three years it took the name of *The Grand Lodge of the State of South Carolina, Free and Accepted Masons.*[127]

In 1787 a second Grand Lodge was founded in Charleston, *The Grand Lodge of the State of South Carolina, Ancient York Masons (AYM)*. In 1808 Frederick Dalcho was its Corresponding Grand Secretary.[128] Together with Colonel John Mitchell – both were Past Masters of No. 8, Union Blue Lodge – he was very active in promoting a union between both Grand Lodges which materialized with seven Articles of Union ratified on 24 and 27 September 1808. The new Grand Lodge, *The Grand Lodge of South-Carolina*, was opened in due form and its Grand Officers elect installed on 31 December 1808. Dalcho held the same office as in the AYM Grand Lodge.[129]

The union lasted but for a few months. Members of the AYM Grand Lodge re-constituted their body in 1809 and on 15 May expelled the ten Charleston Lodges 'with all the Officers and Members belonging thereto' which had ratified the union.[130]

On 18 June 1810, the Grand Lodge of South Carolina delivered a Bill of Complaint against the Grand Lodge of the State of South Carolina, Ancient York Masons. The trial took place in March 1813 before Judge Henry W. Desaussure, Chancellor in Equity, South Carolina District. Frederick Dalcho and Emanuel De La Motta were two of the witnesses for the complainants whose bill was dismissed without costs of suit by the Judgement rendered on 13 November 1813.[131]

127. In 'Little-Known Documents about the Early Masonic Life of South-Carolina', *Heredom* 15, 2007, 129–66, I explained the origin and particulars of South Carolina Grand Lodges.

128. An office distinct from Grand Secretary.

129. *An Abstract*, 1814, 17.

130. *An Answer*, 1809, *Appendix*, 35–36.

131. Desaussure 1815, a very rare pamphlet of 95 pages which was printed by Barnard Levy for the Grand Lodge of the State of South Carolina, Ancient York Masons.

Four years later, on 26 December 1817, both Grand Lodges reunited as *The Grand Lodge of Ancient Free-Masons of South Carolina* and heard 'an excellent and appropriate Sermon delivered by Brother Dalcho'[132] who had been elected one day before its Most Rev. Grand Chaplain.

In the mean time, Cerneau's Grand Consistory in New York had warranted a Grand Council of Princes of the Royal Secret[133] in Charleston which held its first meeting on 17 August 1815.

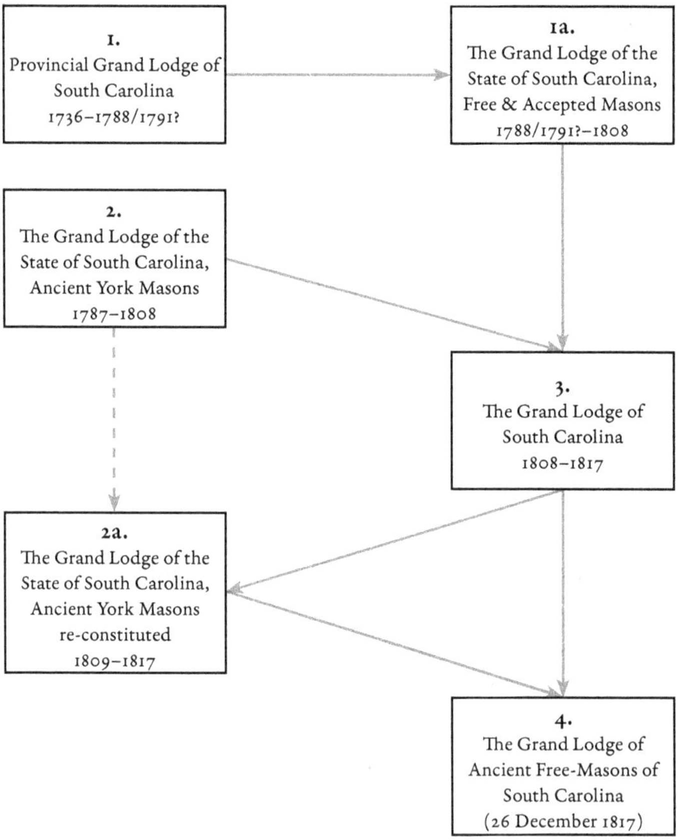

TABLE 2. Successive Grand Lodges in South Carolina 1738–1817

132. *The Masonic Family Re-united* [1818], 29. Dalcho's Sermon is printed on thirteen pages at the end of this pamphlet.

133. Not 'a Grand Consistory' as Mackey wrote (Mackey 1861, 174).

1.2 THE SUPREME COUNCIL FOR THE UNITED STATES OF AMERICA *10 October 1802–1 January 1803*

> At a meeting of Sovereign Grand Inspectors General in Supreme Council, of the 33d. degree, held ... on ... the 10th of October, 1802. The Grand Commander informed the Inspectors that they were convened for the purpose of taking into consideration, the propriety of addressing circular Letters to the different Symbolic Grand Lodges, and Sublime Grand Lodges and Councils throughout the two Hemispheres, explanatory of the origin and nature of the Sublime Degrees of Masonry, and their establishment in South-Carolina.... a committee, consisting of the Illustrious Brethren Doct. Frederick Dalcho, Doctor Isaac Auld and E. De La Motta, Esq., Grand Inspectors General, was appointed to draft and submit such letter to the Council at their next meeting.

The committee submitted its *Report* on 4 December 1802 'and the Council was pleased to express the highest approbation of the same.' Dispatched on 1st January 1803 under the title *Circular throughout the Two Hemispheres,*[134] it included famous words which have never been corroborated by another reliable contemporary document:

> On the 31st of May, 5801, the Supreme Council of the 33d degree for the United States of America, was opened with the high honors of Masonry, by Brothers John Mitchell and Frederick Dalcho, Sovereign Grand Inspectors General....[135]

Who were these two Brothers?

Colonel John Mitchell

In January 1788, John Mitchell was Worshipful Master of Union Blue Lodge No. 8 of the Grand Lodge of the State of South Carolina, AYM.[136] He became Junior Grand Warden in 1789 and 1790, then Deputy Grand Master in 1799 and 1800, in which capacity he signed Circular Letters promoting a union of

134. Facsimile in Harris-Carter 1964, 319–25. The first line of the *Circular* reads: 'From the East of the Grand and Supreme Council of the most Puissant Sovereigns, Grand Inspectors General, ...'. The possible importance of the comma set between the words Sovereign and Grand, here as in Grasse-Tilly's patent (*OB* VIII, 726), does not seem to have been noticed elsewhere.

135. Mackey used slightly different words: 'The Supreme Council of Sovereign Grand Inspectors General of the Ancient and Accepted Rite had been legally established in Charleston on the 1st of May 1801, and John Mitchell had been appointed the presiding officer, with the title of Sovereign Grand Commander' (Mackey 1861, 174).

136. Certificate of Stephen Girard, 28 January 1788 (facsimile in Harris-Carter 1964, 30). About this brother and how he got this certificate, see Dorian 1977, 58–60.

the United States Grand Lodges.[137] In May 1788, he was also Sublime Senior Grand Warden[138] of the Lodge of Perfection established in Charleston by Isaac Da Costa in 1783[139] and on 2 April 1795, he was appointed a Deputy Inspector General by patent of Brother Barend Moses Spitzer.[140]

Further, according to the *Circular throughout the two Hemispheres,*

> On the 2d of August 1795, Brother Colonel John Mitchell ... was made a Deputy General Inspector for this State, by Brother Spitzer, who acted in consequence of Brother Myers's removal out of the country. Brother Mitchell was restricted from acting until after Brother Spitzers death, which took place in the succeeding year.

Spitzer died on or about 1st January 1796, not in 1797 as asserted by Mackey.[141]

Dr. Frederic Dalcho, His Register, and Other Documents

In 1888, Albert Pike transcribed documents from what he described as

> The Register of Bro∴ Moses Holbrook, 33°, Grand Commander of the Supreme Council for the Southern Jurisdiction of the United States.[142]

137. The Circular from 24 June 1799 is transcribed in Schultz 1884, I: 287–90, that from 31 December 1799 in [Proceedings of the] *Grand Lodge of Pennsylvania, Free and Accepted Masons. 1730 to 1809*. Vol. I., 244–45. Excerpts in Lobingier 1931, 8–9.

138. Abraham Jacobs. Document No. 15, 75 (Folger 1862–1881).

139. The year-date 5783 stays page 2 of the *Annual Register for the year 5802* (Harris-Carter 1964, 306) and page 5 of the *Circular throughout the two Hemispheres*. The reproduction of what is described as 'the seal of this Lodge ... found among the Franklin papers at the American Philosophical Society' stays in Sachse 1915, 32–33. That seal bears the words 'Sublime Scotch Lodge Charleston S°. Carolina WILMANS ZUM TEMPEL – ARCANUM SCRUTATUS CUNCTA ADEPTUS'. However both seals affixed on the facsimile reproduction of the document drawn up in December 1788 appointing John Marshall as Captain of the Guards of the Lodge of Perfection (Fox 1997, first facsimile after 87) appear different

140. Document 3 of Frederick Dalcho's Register, *OB* VIII, 715–16. The patent reads: 'WE Barend M. Spitzer, ... Deputy Grand Inspector General by authority of a Convention of Inspectors convened at Philadelphia on the 25th day of June 1781, ... have thought proper to confer on him [John Mitchell] the degree of K. H. and further to the highest degrees in Masonry, and ... have consented to ... appoint [him] by these presents Deputy Inspector General ... this second day of April 1795'. About Spitzer's authority, see Bernheim 1996, 177, note 80.

141. Mackey 1861, 497.See SPITZER under APPENDIX 1.4.

142. *OB* VIII (October 1888), 711–39. This Register was described by Mackey as 'Book H' (Mackey 1861, 496–97). The mistake goes back to 1858 (Dissection of the *Manifesto* of Mr. James Foulhouze ..., 23).

That Register did bear the signature of Moses Holbrook on its flyleaf but was all in the handwriting of Frederick Dalcho and included fourteen copies of various patents and other documents.[143]

In the same volume, Pike transcribed six 'Copies of original parchments in the Archives of the Supreme Council for the Southern Jurisdiction of the United States'.[144] Four of them were delivered to Frederick Dalcho, they bear his signature 'ne varietur' but did not appear in his Register. The first two are certificates issued in Charleston by the Officers of the Grand Council of Princes of Jerusalem and by the Officers of the Sublime Grand Lodge for the other. The third one states that Dalcho is a Knight of the East and West and has been received and constituted a 'Knight of the Eagle, Sovereign Prince of Rose Croix de Heredon'. These three documents bear the equivalent years 5801 or 7801 and 1801 without a specific date. The fourth one was discovered in 1874.[145] Termed 'Letters of Credence', it is described and discussed below.

The last two bear the year dates 9 February and 15 November 1822.[146] They do not apply to Dalcho but are taken under consideration in this paper.

Frederick Dalcho's name appears for the first time in a Masonic context on 16 February 1801 on his own signed and dated copy of the 4th Degree, Secret Master.[147]

It appears next on two patents he received from John Mitchell on 24 May 1801 in Charleston (documents 4 and 5 of his Register). In the first one, Mitchell describes himself as 'Deputy Grand Inspector General' and signed it as 'K.H. P.R.S. Deputy Inspector General' whereas Dalcho added under his signature 'Secretary to the Inspector'. The patent reads: 'We have thought proper to confer on him the degree of K.H. and the degree of Prince of the Royal Secret, and ... have consented to ... appoint [him] by these presents Deputy Inspector General....'[148] In the second patent, worded in French and

143. Harris 1959, 67; Harris-Carter 1964, 15 note 22 & 91.

144. *OB* VIII, September 1887, 740–48.

145. It was found in the papers of the late husband of Mrs. Robert S. Breens [*sic* for Breen] by Bro.·. Wilmot G. de Saussure who announced his discovery in a letter to Commander Albert Pike from 14 November 1874 (*OB* III, July 1876, 349–50).

146. Facsimiles in Harris-Carter 1964, 140 and 142.

147. Arturo de Hoyos 2007, 911. Also see facsimiles of four Dalcho's Diplomas (Harris-Carter 1964, 331–34).

148. *OB* VIII, 717–18. Facsimile of the original Harris-Carter 1964, 329. See the remark of Lobingier who may have made it with his tongue in his cheek (Lobingier 1931, 9–10).

in English on two parallel columns,[149] Mitchell described himself as 'Deputy Inspector General ... by patent from Barend Moses Spitzer Deputy Grand Inspector[150] and Prince of Masons in South Carolina' and signed it as on the first patent. The patent reads: 'We have initiated him K.H. and Prince of the Royal Secret, Deputy Grand Inspector General &c. &c. &c....'[151]

A third document delivered to Dalcho, which is *not* included in his Register and was discovered in 1874,[152] termed 'Letters of Credence', is extremely suspect for several reasons. It is dated:

> this Twenty Third day of the Third month, called סיון [Sivan] of the Restoration 5562. Anno Lucis 5801.— **and** of the Christian Æra this twenty fifth day of **May** One thousand Eight hundred and one. 1801. —

Both dates are not equivalent. 25 May 1801 is equal to thirteenth Sivan 5561 in the Jewish Calendar; the twenty-third day of the third month, called Sivan [,] of the Restoration 5562 corresponds to 23 June 1802 in the Gregorian Calendar.[153] It describes Dalcho as a 'Member of the Medical Society of South Carolina' – to which he was elected on 1 July 1801[154] – and as 'one of the Physicians of the Charleston Dispensary'[155] which was first opened on 1st May 1802.[156] It bears ten signatures among which that of 'Sampson Simson Lieut. Grand Comm^{r} for the Northern dis^{t} U. S. of America' – a title he became many years later – which can have been affixed only about April 1815 when Simson came to Charleston.[157] This last element is immaterial and irrelevant

149. *OB* VIII, 719–20. Facsimile of the original Harris-Carter 1964, 334.

150. But in the French column, the text reads: 'Spitzer Député Grand Inspecteur Général'.

151. Notice the wrong statement: 'Two patents were issued by John Mitchell. The first, in his capacity as a Deputy Inspector General, designating Frederick Dalcho to the same [*sic*] rank, dated May 24, 1801' (Harris-Carter, 93).

152. Certificate of Stephen Girard, 28 January 1788 (facsimile in Harris-Carter 1964, 30). About this brother and how he got this certificate, see Dorian 1977, 58–60.

153. A discrepancy I mentioned twenty-five years ago (Bernheim 1986, 31).

154. http://collections.nlm.nih.gov/muradora/objectView!getDataStreamContent.action?pid=nlm:nlmuid-2563019R-bk&dsid=OCR&mimeType=text/plain. Harris 1959, 25.

155. In which he volunteered to serve on 5 April 1802 (Harris 1959, 56).

156. 'In 1802 ... an act was passed for the establishment of the Charleston Dispensary.... On the first of May, 1802, the institution was opened.' (*The Medical Repository*, Volume 3, New York 1806, 434–34). http://books.google.ch/books?id=dT9JAAAAYAAJ&pg=PA444&lpg=PA444&dq=%22the+medical+repository%22+Dalcho&source=bl&ots=10CbT_y5iC&sig=h_LzDy1-j67k7Y18hKlGyHiGZfQ&hl=fr&sa=x&ei=xFVfT7OYJ9SL4gSZ5uzzBw&ved=0CDcQ6AEwAg#v=onepage&q&f=false.

157. Letter from Dalcho to Moret, 2 May 1815 (Harris-Carter 1964, 127).

since it was not unusual, then as now,[158] to see signatures added to a Masonic document after its date of issue.

However the fact that these Letters of Credence begins with the words 'Know Ye, that we the undersigned Sovereign Grand Inspectors General', a plural repeated *twice* at the end of the document, 'To which Letters of Credence, We the undersigned Sovereign Grand Inspectors General, Members of the Supreme Council of the 33[d] degree, in Charleston, South Carolina, have hereunto subscribed our Names',[159] shows the impossibility that it could have been issued and drawn up on 25 May 1801, since the Supreme Council is said to have been opened by Mitchell and Dalcho alone six days later.[160]

As far as the date of the opening of the Supreme Council is concerned, one of the best and most accurate historians of the Supreme Council made the following strange remark:

> In the midst of his activity for the Scottish Rite, we find him [Frederick Dalcho] on February 1, 1802, a few weeks before the opening of the Supreme Council, listed as a visitor with De Grasse and others at the well-known Lodge *La Candeur*.[161]

From 1803 to the Death of the First Grand Commander in 1816

Along the next thirteen years, few documents attest to the activity of the Supreme Council.[162] Dalcho wrote to John Fowler, Grand Commander of

158. 'Members of our Supreme Council today are frequently invited to sign their names and titles to patents which were issued prior to the time they were Active Members' (Harris 1959, 9).

159. Same wording in Grasse-Tilly's Letters of Credence from 21 February 1802 (*OB* VIII, 726–27) as if the wording of Dalcho's Letters of Credence had been copied from it.

160. 'Other signatures than that of Mitchell's appear on these patents [24 and 25 May 1801], but the content of each clearly indicates they were issued by Mitchell alone in the capacities cited' (Harris-Carter 1964, 93). 'Dalcho's patent of May 25, 1801, in addition to citing his rank as a Sovereign Grand Inspector General, also designated him as being the Lieutenant Grand Commander' (Harris-Carter 1964, 96).

161. Lobingier 1931, 11. About Lobingier's first book, see my remarks in the Bibliography. Dalcho's visit to *La Candeur* on 1st February 1802 was recorded by Wilmot G. de Saussure in 1874 (*OB* III, 346).

162. The reason may have been that the members of the Supreme Council belonged to the Grand Lodge of South Carolina created in 1808, a body which had difficulties with many American Grand Lodges such as New Hampshire, Maryland, Georgia (see their letters in *An Answer*, Appendix, 24–26 & 33–34), Kentucky, Pennsylvania and Virginia (Mackey 1861, 110–11) who recognized the reconstituted the AYM Grand Lodge and not the Grand Lodge of South Carolina. A communication of the reconstituted AYM South Carolina Grand Lodge to the Grand Lodge of New York 'enjoyed a diplomatic sleep' (McClenachan, vol. II., 1892, 250).

the Illustrious College of Heredon, Knights of K.H. of Ireland, on 25 February 1807[163] and allowed him to reprint his Charleston Orations – they were reprinted with some emendations in Dublin in 1808 – and wrote to him again on 21 December 1809.[164] Then there is almost nothing[165] until an exchange of letters, August–December 1813, between Mitchell and Dalcho in Charleston and Emanuel De La Motta in New York, and La Motta's return to Charleston in May 1815.[166]

Colonel John Mitchell's death in 1816 does not seem to have been the object of any Masonic commemoration. It is mentioned twice in the Minutes of the Cerneau *Register.*[167] First on 21 September 1818 in this way:

> The Ill[s] President presented sundry Papers which he had received from the widow of the Ill[s] Brother J. W [*sic*] Mitchell late G[d] Comander [*sic*].

There was indeed a John Wroughton Mitchell born in 1796 in Charleston, S.C., who was elected Charleston city attorney in October 1817[168] and died in New York in 1878. He was the son of John Hinckley Mitchell[169] who lived next door to Colonel Mitchell's house in 1813[170] although they do not appear to have been related to each other.[171]

When John Mitchell died in 1816, Lieutenant Grand Commander Dalcho became automatically his successor according to article 3 of the Constitution of 1786.[172] Whatever the precise date of his death, it occurred after La Motta's return to Charleston from New York. Which brings the following question:

163. Dalcho was answering a letter from John Fowler from 17 October 1806 (Dalcho 1808, iii-iv). Wrong dates '17 October 1807' and '25 February 1808' in Harris-Carter 1964, 114.

164. Harris Carter 1964, 114.

165. On 27 January 1808, at a General Assembly of the Grand Lodge of the State of New-Hampshire: 'Letters and communications were read from various Grand Lodges and particularly one from the Sublime Council of the Ineffable Degrees, in South-Carolina, whereupon, *Voted*, To return a simple answer.' (*Proceedings of the Grand Lodge of New-Hampshire*, Concord 1860, 135). See the comments of MW Thomas Thompson, PGM, on the following 27 April (*ibid.*, 140–42).

166. Emanuel De La Motta left New York on 8 March 1815 (according to the letter Gourgas wrote to Holbrook on 5 December 1826, *OB* VII, 336) and was back in Charleston at the beginning of May (letter from Dalcho to Moret, 2 May 1815 , Harris-Carter 1964, 127).

167. The second time on 17 August 1821 (it is quoted below).

168. http://www.lib.unc.edu/mss/inv/m/Mitchell,John_Wroughton.html.

169. http://wc.rootsweb.ancestry.com/cgi-bin/igm.cgi?op=GET&db=syf&id=I18583.

170. Harris 1959, 19.

171. Colonel John Mitchell's father was Irish, John Hinckley Mitchell's father was English.

172. Dalcho's manuscript version (Harris-Carter 1964, 339).

when Dalcho was elected Most Rev. Grand Chaplain of the Grand Lodge of Ancient Free-Masons of South Carolina on 26 December 1817, was he, like Mitchell, Grand Commander of the Supreme Council of the United States of America or – since La Motta is reported as having founded a second Supreme Council during his stay in New York – was he Grand Commander of the Southern Jurisdiction?

Then on all the documents signed by Dalcho between 24 June 1824 and 14 March 1830, he always added under his signature "Past Grand Commander" adding on eight of them "Past Grand Commander in the U.S.A." Dalcho never used the words Southern Jurisdiction.[173]

1.3 GRAND OFFICERS

TABLE 3 lists the Grand Officers of the Grand Council of Princes of the Royal Secret in Charleston, 1815–1824, and TABLE 4 lists the Grand Officers of the Grand Lodges of South-Carolina, 1817–1823.

1.4 WHO'S WHO IN CHARLESTON[174]

Isaac AULD (25 February 1770–17 October 1826). See his biography in Harris 1959, 55–58. His father, Dr. Jacob Auld (http://boards.ancestry.com/thread.aspx?mv=flat&m=18&p=surnames.auld), was a member of Lodge No. 2, Grand Lodge of Pennsylvania (Sachse 1909, 236) and a visitor of Lodge No. 8 (same Grand Lodge) to which his son belonged (Sachse 1912, 245). No. 8 'virtually disbanded in the year 1789' (Sachse 1913, 293). Auld's name does not appear in the Proceedings of the Grand Lodge of South Carolina where he arrived a few years afterwards. As showed before, he had been in contact with the *Association* before December 1821, which explains why he 'regularized' six of their members – something Grand Commander Dalcho declined to do – and, together with James Moultrie and Moses Clava Levy, delivered them a Charter for a Grand Council of Princes of Jerusalem on 9 February 1822. On the following 1st of April, Dalcho wrote : 'Dr Auld has no authority from me to perform any Masonic acts. the power with which I am invested

173. See the foot-note under Javain's letter issued in the *Charleston Mercury* of 7 May 1822, printed in M'Cosh *Documents*, 86 (APPENDIX 3.4).

174. I found the following file useful and informative: http://ccplarchive.files.wordpress.com/2008/11/historicproperty_research.pdf

by the Constitution of the 33d Degree, I have not transferred to any person under the Canopy of Heaven'.

Thomas Wright Bacot. (1765–1834) 'The emigrant, Pierre Bacot, of the vicinity of Tours in France, and his wife, Jacquine Menesier, together with their two sons, Daniel and Pierre, went to Charles Town, South Carolina, late in the seventeenth century. In 1696 and in 1700 grants of land were made to Pierre Bacot, the elder, in St. Andrew's Parish, lands that are now a part of the well-known Middleton Place, near Charleston. He died in 1702. His wife, it seems, died in 1709. The two sons who survived moved over into the Goose Creek section, about twenty miles from Charles Town, not far from what is now Ladson's Station. In 1769, Samuel Bacot, grandson of the emigrant and the eldest son of Peter Bacot by his second wife, moved into the Darlington District, far into the back-country. In 1741 he had married Rebecca Foissin. The family was one of the highly respected and efficient planter and merchant class, several of whom entered public life. Thomas Wright Bacot of the Charles Town branch of the family, was appointed Postmaster at Charleston by President George Washington in 1794. He retained the position with increasing honor for more than forty years'.[175]

On 6 March 1788[176] he married Jane McPherson DeSaussure (1768–1801) (http://www.findagrave.com/cgi-bin/fg.cgi?page=gr&GRid=35107112), a daughter of Henry Desaussure. Grand Master of the Grand Lodge of South Carolina from 1814 to 1817 and from the Grand Lodge of Ancient Free-Masons of South-Carolina from 1817 to 1820, he remained President of the Grand Council of Princes of the Royal Secret until 21 September 1818.

Henry H. Bacot, his blood-brother and a lawyer, Senior Warden of Lodge No. 4 in 1817, was Grand Lodge's Corresponding Secretary (1819), Junior Grand Warden (1821), Senior Grand Warden (1822–1823) and Deputy Grand Master (1824).

Andrew Carivene. A bill of sale for four slaves, Charleston, 17 April 1817.[177]

175. Arthur Henry Hirsch 1928. *The Huguenots of Colonial South Carolina.* http://listsearches.rootsweb.com/th/read/DuBose/1998-09/0905909567

176. http://huguenots-france.org/france/loire/tours/genealogie/pago.htm#12

177. http://www.archivesindex.sc.gov/onlinearchives/RecordDetail.aspx?RecordId=46387.

Simon Jude CHANCOGNIE. In 1803 'Agent of the Commissary General's department of commercial relations on the part of the French Republic'.[178] *'Chargé de la gestion du Commissariat de Charleston; de la L. la Vérité O. du Cap Français, chev. d'Orient'.*[179] Photo of his house built on 5 Alexander Street in 1813.[180]

John Stephano COGDELL (19 September 1778–25 February 1847).[181] Lawyer. Member of the House of Representatives of South Carolina from 1810 to 1818, then Officer of the Admiralty from 1821 to 1832. President of the Bank of South Carolina from 1832 until his death. Past Master of Union Kilwinning No. 4. Grand Secretary (1815) and Junior Grand Warden (1817) of the Grand Lodge of South Carolina. Senior Grand Warden when the Grand Lodge of Ancient Free-Masons of South Carolina was founded on 24 December 1817. Succeeded Bacot as Grand Master, 15 December 1820. Grand Junior Warden of the Grand Council of Princes of the Royal Secret, then Deputy President in 1816–1817, succeeded Bacot as President from 21 September 1818 to 18 October 1823. His gravestone is in St. Michel's church.[182] Richard Walpole Cogdell, Grand Officer of the Grand Lodge since 1822 and its Grand Master in 1830 was his younger blood brother (http://files.usgwarchives.net/nc/wayne/collections/cogdell01.txt).

Frederick DALCHO. Elements about the early life of Frederick Dalcho in Harris 1959, 23–28. An earlier document from 6 July 1796 'Notifies [Capt. Michael] Kalteisen that surgeon's mate Frederick Dalcho will be under his command [at Fort Johnson] in Charleston'.[183] A *Resolution* presented before The Grand Lodge of Ancient Free-Masons of South Carolina on 19 December 1823 by Brother C. C. Sebring mentioned that 'Dr. Dalcho has been a distinguished Member of this body for upwards of four and twenty years.' (*Abstract*

178. Jefferson/calendar V2, 159. 'The papers of Thomas Jefferson: 1 July to 12 November 1802, 385–86.

179. Honorary member of the *'T∴ R∴ Loge de St. Jean de Jerusalem, sous le titre distinctif de la loge française La Candeur, No. 12, Etablie à Charleston (Caroline du Sud), le 24eme jour du 5eme mois, 5796 … Charleston 1803'* (*OB* VIII, 646).

180. http://www.ccpl.org/content.asp?id=15686&action=detail&catID=6029&parentID=5747.

181. Author of a bust of General Moultrie of which a reproduction is in the Library of Congress (http://freepages.genealogy.rootsweb.ancestry.com/~paday/dobbers/cogdell.htm).

182. Jervey 1906, 66.

183. http://wardepartmentpapers.org/searchresults.php?searchClass=fulltextSearch&fulltextQuery=Frederick+Dalcho.

of the Proceedings of the Grand Lodge of Ancient Free-Masons of South-Carolina, 1824, 21), which wasn't quite to the point: in 1801 Dalcho belonged to the Grand Lodge of the State of South-Carolina AYM, and from 1807 to 1817 to the Grand Lodge of South Carolina. His gravestone in St. Michael's church.[184]

Emanuel De La Motta (2 November 1760, St. Croix–17 May 1821, Charleston). His father Isaac was born in Copenhagen in 1726. He married Judith Canter (*1771) in Charleston on 26 December 1787. They had eight children, the first six were born in Savannah.[185] See below his eldest son Jacob.

Jacob Canter De La Motta (24 February 1789, Savannah–13 February 1845, Charleston). He married Charlotte Lazarus (*1804) 29 April 1835 in Charleston.[186]

Henry William Desaussure[187] (16 August 1763–26 March 1839). An American lawyer, state legislator and jurist from South Carolina who became a political leader as a member of the Federalist Party following the Revolutionary War. He was appointed by President George Washington as the 2nd Director of the United States Mint, was a co-sponsor of the legislation that established the South Carolina College which was to become the University of South Carolina and was given the title of Chancellor as a justice of the SC Equity Court, also known as chancery court. In this capacity he wrote and codified much of the state's equity law still in use today. He served as Intendant (Mayor) of both Charleston and Columbia, SC.[188] Father of Henry A. de Saussure (initiated in Union Kilwinning No. 4 in 1825 and its WM in 1827). Grand-father of Wilmot Gibbes de Saussure (1822–1886) Grand Master 1875–1877 and active member of the Supreme Council, 30 May 1876.

184. http://archive.org/stream/inscriptionsontaoojerv#page/14/mode/2up.

185. http://americanjewisharchives.org/pdfs/stern_po54.pdf.

186. http://americanjewisharchives.org/pdfs/stern_po54.pdf.

187. http://en.wikipedia.org/wiki/Henry_William_de_Saussure. http://ctwsearch.wesleyan.edu/vufind/Author/Home?author=De%20Saussure%2C%20Henry%20William%2C%201763–1839. http://www.greatercharleston.com/henry-william-de-saussure/. http://genealogytrails.com/vir/henrico/bios_pg2.html. Also the Guide to the Cataloged Collections in the Manuscript Department of the William R. Perkins Library, Duke University, 1980 (Item 1468): http://library.duke.edu/digitalcollections/rbmscl/guide/inv/pdf/ .

188. http://en.wikipedia.org/wiki/Henry_William_de_Saussure .

"This venerable man and useful citizen departed this life on Friday last, in this city, having passed the boundary of three score and ten, and reached the advanced age of seventy-five years. In the dawn of manhood he participated in our revolutionary struggle, having gallantly borne arms in defence of Charleston against the invading foe. After the achievement of our independence, and the organization of our present system of government, he received from the father of our country the appointment of director of the mint at Philadelphia, having been the second to fill that office, (the venerable and celebrated Rittenhouse having preceded him), and we learn that he retained, and took pleasure to the last in exhibiting to his friends and acquaintances, a piece of his own coinage, (one of the first gold coins ever struck at the mint, the very first one having been presented by him to Washington), in evidence of this incident in his life. This office he did not retain long, but returning to Charleston and resuming the practice of the law, he rose to eminence in his profession. In 1797–8, he filled the municipal office of intendant (or mayor) of Charleston, and for a number of years acted as chairman of the board of commissioners of that noble institution of benevolence, the Orphan House of Charleston. He bore a part in the convention of this state which adopted the constitution of the United States, and also in that which framed the present constitution of this state; was a member of the state legislature, and was one of the founders of the South Carolina college, an institution which he cherished with parental care. In December, 1808, he was elected one of the chancellors of the state, and continued to fill that high office for a period of twenty-nine years, until December, 1837, when increasing physical infirmity compelled him to tender his resignation to the legislature."[189]

Pierre Desportes. In 1803 '*habitant de St. Domingue, natif de Vitry le Français* [*sic*], *Maître de Cérémonies de la L∴ la Candeur No. 12, M∴*.'[190] In 1817, he belonged to La Candeur No. 36 and was listed as one of its PM in *Proceedings* 1825.

189. The *Charleston Courier*, 1 April 1839, q. in *The American jurist and law magazine*, Volume 21, Boston 1839, 486.

190. 'Tableau de la T∴ R∴ Loge de St. Jean de Jerusalem, sous le titre distinctif de la loge française La Candeur, No. 12, Etablie à Charleston (Caroline du Sud), le 24ème jour du 5ème mois, 5796 ... Charleston 1803 (*OB* VIII, 645).

	GL of SC, AYM	**GL of SC**	**GL Lof AFM of South Carolina**	
	26 Dec. 1817		26 Dec. 1817	18 Dec. 1818
Grand Master	John Geddes	T. W. Bacot	T. W. Bacot	T. W. Bacot
Deputy GM		J. H. Stevens	David Johnson	J. S. Cogdell
Sr Gd Warden	Eliab Kingman	Charles Kershaw	J. S. Cogdell	Charles Kershaw
Jr Gd Warden	Jacob Lankester	J. S. Cogdell	Eliab Kingman	I. M. Wilson
Gd Chaplain	Urban Cooper		F. Dalcho	F. Dalcho
Gd Lect & Insp				
Gd Treasurer	Charles Holmes	Langton	[Langton]	Tucker
Gd Secretary	Joseph Galluchat	J. H. Mitchell	J. H. Mitchell	J. H. Mitchell
Corr. Gd Secr.		I. M. Wilson	I. M. Wilson	H. H. Bacot
Gd Marshall		JamesSweeney	James Sweeney	James Sweeney
G Pursuivant			William Waller	William Waller
Sr Gd Deacon(s)	Moses Tennant	Charles Cleapor, C. S. Tucker	C. S. Tucker, Pearce	P. Javain, Pearce
Jr Gd Deacon(s)	C. C. Chitty	Pearce, Baxter O. Mynott	Baster O. Mynott	Benjamin Philipps, Baxter O. Mynott
Gd Stewards				
Gd Tyler	David Rechon	Robert Shand	Shand	Shand

TABLE 4. Grand Officers of the Grand Lodges of South Carolina (1817–1823) According to Contemporary Proceedings

Grand Lodge of Ancient Free Masons of South Cc\arolina				
27 Dec. 1819	27 Dec. 1820	Dec. 1821	13–23 Dec. 1822	19 Dec. 1823
T. W. Bacot	J. S. Cogdell	J. S. Cogdell	J. S. Cogdell	John L. Wilson
J. S. Cogdell	J. R. Poinsett	I. M. Wilson	I. M. Wilson	H. H. Bacot
Charles Kershaw	I. M. Wilson	H. H. Bacot	H. H. Bacot	William Waller
Maynard	H. H. Bacot	William Waller	William Waller	Norris
F. Dalcho	[Dalcho]	[Dalcho]	Dalcho	Robert S. Symes
				J. Barker
Tucker	Tucker	Tucker	Tucker	Tucker
Hughes	Hughes	Hughes	Hughes	Hughes
Galluchat	R.W. Cogdell	R. W. Cogdell	I. A. Johnson	Holbrook
Charles Cleapor	Charles Cleapor	Pearce (p.t.)	Pearce [?]	Cole
William Waller		Benjamin Philipps	Benjamin Philipps	Ross
P. Javain, Seyle	P. Javain, Seyle	P. Javain, Seyle	P. Javain, Seyle	Mc Donald, H. G. Street
Benjamin Philipps, C. C. Chitty	C. C. Chitty, R. W. Cogdell	Norris	Norris, Innes	Edw Sebring, George B. Eckhard
Pearce, Innes, Rechon, Benjamin Bailey	Innes, Rechon, Benjamin Bailey, Fraser			
Shand	Shand	Shand	Shand	Shand

Table 4. Grand Officers of the Grand Lodges of South Carolina (1817–1823) According to Contemporary Proceedings

Joseph DICKINSON. Native of South Carolina, Inspector of Exports, late a Captain of Infantry, aged 33 years, 'Appointed Captain of the Fourth Regiment of Infantry, from South Carolina, on the 20th of February, 1793' ("A Register of the Army of the United States, November 1, 1796" q. by Robert H. Hall, *OB* VIII, p. 548). Intimate Secretary (*Annual Register* 1802). Capt. of the Guards of the Supreme Council, 'Major Jos. Dickinson, Capt. of Guard (police) and Custom House Officer' (*Negrin's Directory*, 1806, q. in *OB* III, p.348). Grand Marshall of the Grand Lodge of South Carolina AYM (1802–1806), Orator and Past Master of Lodge No. 9 when Emanuel De La Motta was WM; Capt. of the Guards of the Supreme Council. *The Free-Mason's Vocal Assistant and Register of the Lodges of Masons in South-Carolina and Georgia*. Charleston. Printed by Brother J. J. Negrin 1807 (quoted. in *TSJ* 1787, pp. 52B, 52E and 52G; and in *OB* VII, p. 302). 'Joseph Dickinson was listed as a new member at the beginning of 1807, but he died on March 10 of that year' (Barnett A. Elzas 1907, *Leaves from my historical Scrap-Book* & Harris-Carter 1964, p. 128).

Jean DUMAINE. Listed as one of the three Honorary members of Lodge *les Sept Frères Réunis,* Or∴ of Cap-Français, on its Tableau dated 24 June 5802 (*OB* VIII, 684), where he is described as born in Blaye, aged 49, '*ex-ordonnateur en chef de la Marine et des Guerres de la colonie de St.-Domingue, … ex-président et fondateur du S∴ Ch∴ de la Vérité, à l'Or∴ du Cap, île Saint-Domingue*.' As 'Johann' Dumaine on the Tableau of the same Lodge one year later (Kloss 1852, I, 410). However the same Brother has Jean-Baptiste as first name in Le Bihan 1967, 394); Escalle & Gouyon 1993, 115 & 434 (born in Blaye ca. 1752); also in Jacques de Cauna. 2009. *Haïti, l'éternelle révolution: histoire de sa décolonisation (1789–1804)*, 266.

Eleazer ELIZER (1763–September 1821).[191] Notary public in 1803 and Justice of the Peace in 1813 (Elzas 1907, 141); office at 92 E. Bay St. (Charleston Directory 1819). Author of *A Directory for 1803: containing the names of all the house-keepers and traders in the city of Charleston, alphabetically arranged, their particular professions, and their residence. Collected with great care and attention by Eleazer Elizer* (Shaw & Shoemaker 4146). Joined St. John's Lodge at

191. Or 'Born about 7 October 1761 Newport, R.I.' (www. familysearch.org).

Newport in 1790.[192] As K.H. – P.R.S. signed the Warrant for the Sublime Grand Lodge of Perfection in Charleston and became its first Sublime Junior Grand Warden, 6 July 1801 (*OB* VIII, 721–22). Member of No. 17, Cheraw Hill, in 1808. PM of No. 12 in 1817.

Pierre FAYOLLE. 48 years old in 1816. 'During the quasi war with France and disturbance of commerce on the high seas by both England and France Charlestonians began to prepare for War. Following the 1807 episode of the HMS *Leopard* attack of the US Ship *Chesapeake* and continued impressments of American seamen, several Militia companies were organized in Charleston. Between 1792 and 1813, 23 such companied had been organized. One Company of particular interest was The Union Alarm Company, a company of French exempt men who raised a company and elected officers on 16 July, 1812. Six of the Officers were to become founders of La Société Française. Their Captain was Pierre Fayolle, who served with Lafayette during the American Revolution.' ('The Napoleonic and Celtic Influence in France and Charleston', Julian V. Brandt III).[193] 'Dancing Master' in 1815[194] also in the Charleston Directory for 1816 and 1822, 359 King Street.

Auguste FOLLIN.[195] Likely Augustin Follin aîné, Négociant, Member of *Les Amis Réunis* at Mole St. Nicolas (St. Domingo) in 1799.[196] The will of his father Michel Follin was drawn up in Charleston on 27 June 1812.

Michel FRONTY. Described as 'Doctor of Medicine, 50 years old', member of the Sublime Grand Lodge of Perfection of South Carolina and Grand Chancellor of the Grand Consistory of Princes of the Royal Secret, in the *Annual Register* 1802.

192. *Publications of the American Jewish Historical Society*, Number 19 (1910), 19.

193. http://www.frenchsociety.net/pb/wp_0976a6f2/wp_0976a6f2.html.

194. 'Rules or By–laws of the Union Kilwinning Lodge No. 4, Charleston under the jurisdiction of the Grand Lodge of Ancient Free-Masons of South-Carolina' (1822).

195. http://colemanyoung.familytreeguide.com/getperson.php?personID=I1561&tree=colemanyoung.

196. Escalle & Gouyon 1993, 473. The authors state, 153, the Lodge received a provisional Warrant from the 'Provincial Mother-Lodge at Kingston' (Jamaica) and was warranted in 1799 by the Grand Orient of France.

Étienne (Stephen) GIRARD. (20 May 1750, Bordeaux–25 December 1831, Philadelphia). According to Max Dorian, William Adcock, Grand Master of Pennsylvania, objected to Girard being made a Mason because he was one-eyed. Having arrived at Charleston on 2 January 1788, Girard sent a letter 'To the Worshipful Master, Wardens and Brethren of the Blue Lodge No. 8 of Free and Accepted Masons' showing that he was 'desirous of being admitted a member ... if found worthy.' He was made on January 28 and left Charleston on 2 February.[197] Girard and John Jacob Astor belonged to the first American millionaires.

Paul HAMILTON (1762–1816). South Carolina Governor, elected 7 December 1804. Born in St. Paul's Parish, South Carolina. Had to leave school at a relatively young age for financial reasons. He fought in the South Carolina Militia during the Revolutionary War. In addition to being an indigo and rice planter, he served as tax collector of St. Paul's Parish from 1785 to 1786 and as Justice of the Peace in 1786. He went on to serve in the South Carolina House of Representatives from 1787 to 1789 and was a member of the South Carolina Convention that ratified the US Constitution in 1789. He was a member of the South Carolina Senate for several non-consecutive terms and served as the state's Comptroller of Finance for five years before being elected governor by the South Carolina legislature. During Hamilton's single term as governor, the US Congress proposed to place a tax on imported slaves but withdrew its proposal after the South Carolina legislature threatened to repeal its own law (enacted during the administration of Hamilton's gubernatorial predecessor-James B. Richardson) restricting the importation of male slaves over the age of fifteen. After leaving office, Hamilton served as Secretary of the Navy under President James Madison from 1809 until 1812.[198]

Moses HOLBROOK (1783–1844). 'The preeminent Middlesex Mason, Moses Holbrook, gained most of his fame elsewhere. He was born in Sherborn, Middlesex, Mass., in 1783, probably descendent from the original settlers.

197. Max Dorian 1977, 58–60. Also see 'Stephen Girard and his Legacy', Chapter XXVII of Barratt & Sachse 1919, *Freemasonry in Pennsylvania 1727–1907*, Volume III, where the origin of the certificate reproduced in Harris-Carter 1964, stays 246.

198. http://www.nga.org/cms/home/governors/past-governors-bios/page_south_carolina/col2-content/main-content-list/title_hamilton_paul.html.

He was entered in Middlesex Lodge in 1804, two months after his 21st birthday, and raised February 12, 1805. He graduated with the class of 1808 from Harvard University. He became a physician and received a Doctor of Medicine degree (honoris causis) from the Medical College of South Carolina.[199] Sometime between 1811 and 1819, he moved to Charleston, South Carolina, where he raised a large family.... In 1843, after some 25 to 30 years in South Carolina, he became a homesteader in Florida near what is now Ft. Pierce. He died there 1 December 1844.'[200] 'Dr. Moses Holbrook was, for some years, in practice in Bath, Maine and had the reputation of skill in his profession, as he was also in the art of Masonry, and was Master of Solar Lodge in the years of 1813, 1814, and 1815. Subsequently he became a resident of Charleston, S. C. Dr. Holbrook was present at Fort Pierce on the night that it burned (December 11, 1843). His homestead was next to Captain Burnham on the south. He had come to the area from Charleston, South Carolina. Considered a talented physician he served the community for a time as a circuit riding doctor. Described as a man of powerful build, elderly, bald and usually hatless. He played flute and brought a valuable library with him to the settlement. He died after two years and was buried in an unmarked grave on the bluff.'[201] Not in the Charleston Directory for 1816. In 1819 as M.D., 18 Elliottt St.; in 1823 as Physician, 7 Broad St.; in 1825 at 123 Church St. and in 1829 at 64 Queen St.

Joseph JAHAN. 43 years old, WM of *La Candeur* No. 12, Deputy Grand Master of the Sublime Grand Lodge of Perfection of South Carolina and Lieutenant Grand Commander of the Grand Consistory of Princes of the Royal Secret.[202] In a letter written on 22 August 1811 from Paris by Delahogue to an unnamed Very Illustrious Brother, Jahan is said to be 'a member of the Supreme Council of the 33d Degree in Charleston'.[203] Listed in the Charleston Directory for 1819 as a carpenter, in the Directory for 1822 and 1825 as an architect, always in Meeting St.

199. I appreciate Arturo de Hoyos for bringing this to my attention.
200. http://wc.rootsweb.ancestry.com/cgi-bin/igm.cgi?op=GET&db=syf&id=I12661
201. http://wc.rootsweb.ancestry.com/cgi-bin/igm.cgi?op=GET&db=syf&id=I12661.
202. 1802 *Annual Register.*
203. *SCDF* 1, 633.

Pierre (Peter) JAVAIN. 'Mr Javain and sister, two orphans, one 20 and the other 14 years of Age. They have one thousand dollars at interest in this town, but the interest not sufficient to maintain them. Miss Javain wishes to go to France. The above is a list of the French Emigrants from St. Domingo, in and near this place, & as I am informed, I believe to be a Just statement. Given under my hand at Alexandria, the first day of February 1794. Dennis Ramsay, Mayor.' (*Calendar of Virginia State Papers and other Manuscripts* . . ., Vol. VII, Richmond 1888, page 24).[204] From 1816 to 1825, grocer in King St. In 1829, Farmer at W. corner St. Philip's St. and Lines, Neck.[205] His estate inventory[206] (next page) shows he was deceased in April 1843 in Chester.

Joseph M'COSH (*1782). [In the list written by Moses Holbrook on 29 April 1830[207] which includes several mistakes his birth year is given as 1786]. 'Married. At Chester Court House, South Carolina, on the 27th December last, by the Rev. John B. Davies, Mr. Joseph M'Cosh, formerly of Charleston, S.C., to Miss Mary Holden, of the former place.'[208] Became a member of the Charleston Supreme Council on 17 November 1822. Published *Documents upon Sublime Free-Masonry* in Charleston during the Summer of 1823.[209] Recorder of the South Carolina Encampment on 27 August 1823 from which he resigned on 28 November 1827 (Gourdin 1855, 27). He is first mentioned in the *Proceedings of the Grand Lodge of Ancient Free-Masons of South-Carolina* on 31 October 1823: 'Brother Joseph M'Cosh, a member of Solomon's Lodge No. 1, was present by special invitation' (*PRO* 1824, 4). He signed the *Revised Statutes . . . for the Southern Jurisdiction* from 20 March 1855 and lived then at York (S.C.).[210] Joseph McCosh, aged 78, born in Ireland, is mentioned as farmer in Boydton, York, SC, in the 1860 Census together with his wife, Mary, aged 61.[211]

204. http://archive.org/details/calendarvirginio8palmgoog.
205. *Charleston Directories.*
206. http://www.fold3.com/spotlight/20616/slave_etrenne_quotmulatto_woman_out/.
207. Facsimile in Harris-Carter 1964, 208.
208. *American Masonic Record, and Albany Saturday Magazine*, 19 January 1828, 40.
209. Mackey wrote it was published in 1825 (Mackey 1861, 501).
210. Facsimile in Harris Carter 1964, 246.
211. http://us-census.org/pub/usgenweb/census/sc/york/1860/pg0485a.txt.

Alexander M'DONALD. Not in Charleston Directories for 1816, 1819, 1822, 1825. In Directory 1829: 'SE. cr. King & George Sts'. Elected Grand Captain General of the Grand Encampment of Knights Templars, and the Appendant Orders, for the State of South Carolina, on 27 February 1827.[212] From the *Charleston Mercury*, Dec. 21, 1833: 'Cash will be paid for any number of single negroes, from the age of 10 to 35 years old, of either sex. Also, wanted, carpenters, blacksmiths, coopers, and bricklayers. Persons wishing to sell such property, will do well by calling at the City Hotel, East Bay, or at Alexander M'Donald's store, corner of King and George Streets, as the subscriber will continue to purchase during the season, and will give the highest prices for such property. {Signed) Hugh M'Donald.'[213]

Jacques Nicolas MAGNAN. '*Réfugié de St. Domingue*' according to his passport delivered on 21 February 1805.[214]

MITCHELL. The Mitchell family were merchants in Glenarm (Ireland) from the 17th century. John and James Mitchell were involved in the purchase of a trading vessel *The Rose* in 1698. Alexander Mitchell was a merchant in Dublin and died in 1712. His brother Hugh was a merchant in Cork. Of this Glenarm family came William Mitchell of Dickeystown (died before 1755) whose sons were Hugh (died before 1757) merchant in Philadelphia USA and then in Dublin; Alexander, merchant in Philadelphia and later in Dublin; Randle, merchant in Philadelphia from 1749 to retirement in 1774; and John, merchant in Dominica West Indies, then Philadelphia through 1784, then Alexandria Virginia.[215]

John MITCHELL. 'native of Ireland, Justice of the Quorum and Notary Public, late a Lieutenant-Colonel in the American Army. Member of the Cincinnati ... aged 60 years.'[216] 'In 1813 he is living at 60 East Bay, with John Hinckley

212. *American Masonic Record, and Albany Saturday Magazine*, vol. 1, 50.
213. Edwin Pitt Atlee, *An Address to the citizens of Philadelphia, on the subject of slavery.*
214. http://gael.gironde.fr/img-viewer/FRAD033/M/4M/4M681/viewer.html?name=FRAD033_4M681_0411_P.jpg.
215. http://www.antrimhistory.net/forum/view.php?topic_id=187.
216. 1802 *Annual Register.*

Mitchell residing in the adjoining house at 58 East Bay'.[217] Elements about the early life of John Mitchell in a letter of Robert H. Hall to Albert Pike (*OB* VIII, 550) and Harris 1959, 13–20. Harris writes that Mitchell had been in Charleston 'as early as 1784'. Colonel John Mitchell is reported as having died in January 1816 according to the *Charleston Courier* from 27 January 1816 in which an 'obituary notice gives age as 85' (Harris 1959, 13 & Harris-Carter 1964, 21; also Harris 1959, 20 & Harris-Carter 1964, 34). This does not fit with 'John Mitchell ... aged sixty years', page 6 of the *Annual Register* of 1802, a reliable document reproduced in facsimile in Harris-Carter 1964, 306–16. Another document states that Mitchell was re-elected at the *Standing Committee* of the *Society of Cincinnati*, on the 4th of July 1816 (letter from Robert H. Hall to Albert Pike, 9 June 1888, *OB* VIII, 550–52). However a Balustre sent on 21 June 1828 by the Charleston Supreme Council to the New York one includes the following: 'Br. Mitchell died 23d February, 1816, aged 74 years—while he presided over this Supreme Council' (*OB* X, 214). This is likely the origin of a Minute of the Supreme Council of the Northern Jurisdiction, dated 27 December 1844, which states that 'Our M∴ Ill∴ Bro∴ Colonel John Mitchell, First Grand Commander at Charleston, S.C., died as far back as the twenty-third February, 1816, aged 74 ...' (*NMJ* 1876, 65). Mackey wrote twice that Mitchell died in 1820 (Mackey 1861, 174 & 175).

John Hinckley **Mitchell** (January 1767–5 July 1832). Justice of the Peace & Notary public. Moses Mitchell, born in London ca. 1698, arrived in Charleston in 1730; his second wife was Sarah Hinckley, whom he married at St. Philipp's Parish in Charleston, 25 November 1760. John Hinckley Mitchell was the fourth of their five children.[218] A Notary Public, he is listed as a Secret Master in the 1802 *Annual Register*. He was Grand Secretary of the Grand Lodge of the State of South Carolina AYM since 1801 and kept the same office in the Grand Lodge of South Carolina (17 December 1808) and in the Grand Lodge of Ancient Freemasons of South Carolina (24 December 1817) until 17 December 1819. He 'was constitutionally read off for non payment of arrears'

217. Harris 1959, 19.

218. http://williamson.co.za/family/tree/GMitchell.htm, http://wc.rootsweb.ancestry.com/cgi-bin/igm.cgi?op=GET&db=syf&id=I18583

according to a letter from the Secretary of Lodge No. 8, read at the Quarterly Communication of Grand Lodge on 26 September 1823.

Antoine Louis MORET. Very likely merchant in St. Domingo and elder son of Antoine Michel Moret and Claude Marie Paillieux.[219] In 1802 a member of *L'Union Française* No. 14 in New York, then founding member and Senior Warden of *La Sincérité* installed on 10 April 1805 in New York.[220] Gourgas wrote to him on 26 November 1807.[221] Manly Palmer Hall [P.R.S.] MS. 209[222] belonged to *'la collection maçonnique du F: illustre F: Antoine Louis Moret fondateur, et Véné honoraire de la R.L. La Sincerite No. 122. Ex president du Souv: Chap: la Triple union Or: maitre, Elu, chevalier commandeur, patriarch, Prince & Govr: Prince des tous les ordres macon: et des tous les Rites: Francais, Ecossais, Anglais, irelandais, Prussiens, &c. &c. &c. Govr: G: insp: Gene: du 33e degre S: P: D: E: Or: de: New York Etats unis L'am: du Nord 5810'.*[223]

NEW ENGLAND COFFEE HOUSE. *See* Horatio Gates STREET

Seth PAINE. In December 1795 Clement [Paine] went to Charleston, S.C. where his brother Seth, in connection with Peter Freneau, Secretary of the State, and brother of Philip Freneau (well known as a poet and political editor of that period) was engaged in the publication of the *City Gazette* (from 1st January 1795) – the first daily paper ever printed in South Carolina. It had at the time reached a circulation of 1500 copies daily. Some friendly correspondence between Seth Paine and Philip Freneau is still preserved. Clement took charge of his brother's business during the absence of the latter Eastward, and returned to Athens in the following June, with pleasant impressions of Charleston and its society.... Seth Paine to Clement Paine: 'At the last election here I had the honor of being elected Jun. Grand Warden of the Grand Lodge of S.C.; a body so respectable as to have at present forty five lodges under its control.' The Eulogy, written and delivered by Seth Paine before the Grand Lodge of

219. http://doc.geneanet.org/registres/zoom.php?idcollection=121&page=385&r=1&Larg=1680&Haut=1050 & http://www.famillesparisiennes.org/patro/pa.html.

220. *L'Union Française* 1915, 48 & 111.

221. Also on 18 December 1822 and 10 April 1823 (private communication, Arturo De Hoyos).

222. http://www.revistaazogue.com/biblio.htm – Click on 'Box 34' to see the MS.

223. http://www.levity.com/alchemy/t_stgermain.html.

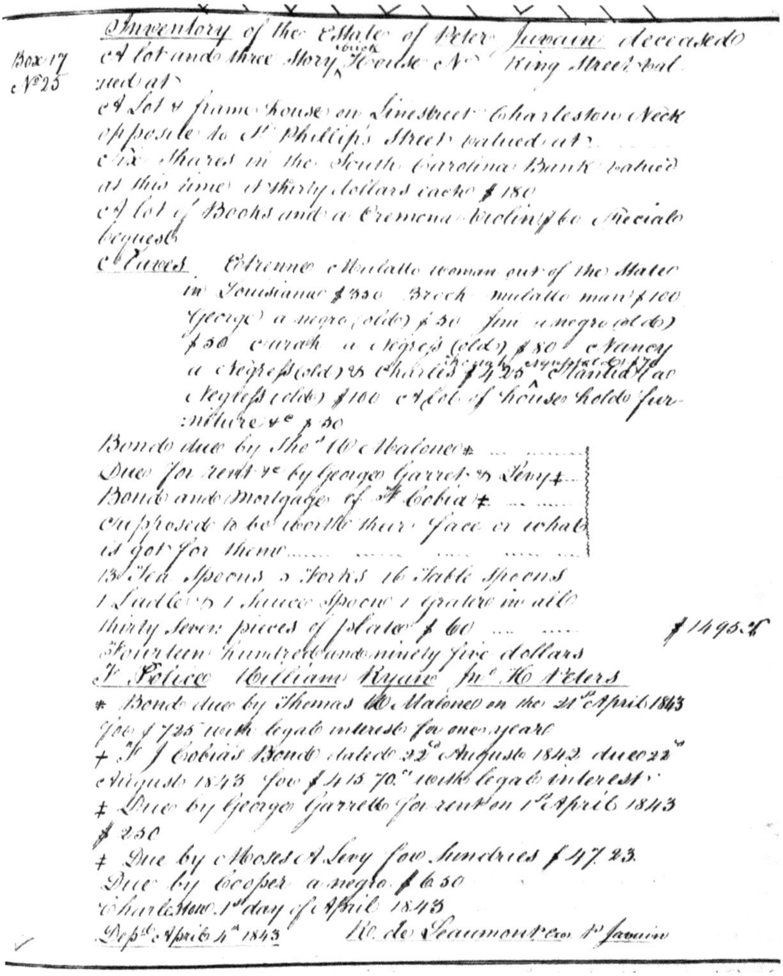

Box 17
No 25

Inventory of the Estate of Peter Javain deceased
A lot and three Story brick House No King Street valued at
A Lot & frame house on Line street Charleston Neck opposite to St Phillip's Street valued at
Six Shares in the South Carolina Bank valued at this time at thirty dollars each $ 180
A lot of Books and a Cremona Violin $ 60 Special bequest
Slaves Estienne Mulatto woman out of the State in Louisiana $ 350 Brock mulatto man $ 100 George a negro (old) $ 30 Jim a negro (old) $ 50 Sarah a Negress (old) $ 80 Nancy a Negress (old) & Charles $ 425 [illegible] Harriet a Negress (old) $ 100 A lot of house hold furniture &c $ 50
Bond due by Thos W Malone * ...
Due for rent &c by George Garret & Levy ‡ ...
Bond and Mortgage of J Cobia + ...
supposed to be worth their face or what is got for them ...
13 Tea Spoons 5 Forks 16 Table Spoons 1 Ladle & 1 Sauce Spoon 1 grater in all thirty seven pieces of plate $ 60 ... $ 1495.
Fourteen hundred and ninety five dollars
J. Police William Ryan Jno H Peters
* Bond due by Thomas W Malone on the 21st April 1843 for $ 725 with legal interest for one year
\+ J J Cobia's Bond dated 22d August 1842 due 22d August 1843 for $ 415 70/100 with legal interest
‡ Due by George Garrett for rent on 1st April 1843 $ 250
‡ Due by Moses A Levy for sundries $ 47 23.
Due by Cooper a negro $ 6 50
Charleston 1st day of April 1843
Dep'd April 4th 1843 R. de Beaumont Exor P Javain

Estate inventory of Peter Javain

the State, on the occasion of the first anniversary of the death of Washington, was a production of merit of which some copies are still in existence.[224] About

224. An eulogy, on General George Washington. Pronounced in the Friendship Lodge, no. 9, Antient York Masons, in presence of the Grand Lodge of South-Carolina, and a numerous assemblage of brethren, on the 22d of February, 1800—being the day recommended by

the same time Clement Paine was chosen to prepare and deliver an Oration on Masonry before St. John's Lodge of rural Amity at Athens of which he acted for many years as Secretary. This was also published. Seth Paine died at Charleston of yellow fever in October 1801.[225]

Joel R. POINSETT (1779–1851). Member of the House of Representatives of South Carolina from 1816 to 1819. Member of Congress (1821–1826). First representative of the United States in Mexico (1826–1830) and War Secretary (1837–1841).

Jacques Philippe (James Philip) PUGLIA. (~1760 Genoa–1831 Charleston). Interpreter for foreign languages in Philadelphia in 1794. He committed suicide in Charleston in August 1831.[226] Jacques Philippe Puglia was *Adjoint au Maître des Cérémonies* of Lodge N° 47, *La Réunion des Coeurs franco-américains, Négociant*, R.·.†.·., C.·.K.·.S.·. & C.·. de l'En.·. (Tableau from 27 December 1800, Bibliothèque de France, FM² 545). Louis Jean Lusson delivered a patent of Inspector on 24 May 1800 at Port-au-Prince to 'Jacques Ph. Puglia' (*OB* IX, 172), to 'Philipp Puglia' (Minutes of the *History Committee* Northern Masonic Jurisdiction, May 1955, 37). At the end of a letter signed by Simson, Gourgas and Tardy, which was sent on 7 February 1814 to Charleston, stays the following question: 'Is Br.·. James [*sic*] Joseph Puglia, Dy. Ir. Gl., at Philadelphia, acknowledged by you?' (*TSJ* 1878, 13).

Samuel RICHARDS. 'A very practical typographer... conducted the *Gazette and Daily Advertiser* in Charleston from 1812 to 1814' together with Samuel J. Elliott.[227] Proxy of seven Lodges in September and December 1808. PM of Solomon's No. 1. Received the 18° to 32° in Charleston on 30 May 1818.

Congress, to the people, to assemble and testify their grief, by "suitable eulogies, orations, and discourses."—Published by desire of the Grand Lodge. By Seth Paine, junior grand warden. Also Dalcho 1801, 28 and Mackey 1861, 84. http://openlibrary.org/works/OL11116039W/An_eulogy_on_General_George_Washington.

225. Paine Family History in handwritten notes by Charles Clement Paine (1818–1886) of Troy, Pa. (http://www.joycetice.com/families/painefreem.htm).

226. Richard N. Juliani, *Building Little Italy, Philadelphia's Italians Before Mass Migration* (Penn State Press, 1998) 21, 27 & 327.

227. William L. King, *The Newspaper Press of Charleston, S.C.* (1872), 57.

James W. Rouse (+ 23 April 1834). Three volumes of Mitchell's rituals were autographed by him, the second one dated August 18, 1821 (De Hoyos 2010, 35). Past Master of St. John No. 13 in 1825. Junior Grand Deacon in 1827.

William Rouse, Colonel (30 January 1756–Died 15 June 1829 in Charleston). Married to Mary Stuart.[228] Lived at 37 Market St. in Charleston in 1819. Lived together with James W. Rouse at 83 (in 1825) or 81 (in 1829) Market St.

Cornelius C. Sebring.[229] (20 August 1796, New York – 18 February 1863, New York). Elected a member of the New-England Society of Charleston, 22 December 1828. Cornelius C. Sebring was a printer in Charleston, S.C. In 1826, he lived 44, Queen Street. 'removed and vacated 1826' (Pike 1859, 151). Elder brother of Edward Sebring.[230] In 1824 Senior Warden of Washington Lodge No. 7[231] of which Horatio Gates Street was Master and Moses Holbrook Past Master. About 1831–1835 he was printing books in Mexico and in 1846 he was selling a restorative 'never-failing remedy for dyspepsia and nervous affections.'[232]

William Loughton Smith. (1758 – 19 December 1812) Representative from South Carolina; born in Charleston, S.C.; attended preparatory schools in England 1770–1774; studied law in the Middle Temple at London, England, in 1774; pursued higher studies in Geneva 1774–1778; returned to Charleston, S.C., in 1783; was admitted to the bar in 1784 and commenced practice in Charleston; engaged in agricultural pursuits on his estate near Charleston; member of the privy council in 1784; member of the state house of representatives 1787–1788; warden of the city of Charleston in 1786; elected as a Pro-Administration candidate to the First, Second and Third Congresses and reelected as a Federalist to the Fourth and Fifth Congresses; served from March 4, 1789, until July 10, 1797, when he resigned; chairman, Committee

228. http://genforum.genealogy.com/rouse/messages/753.html.

229. Also see Lobingier 1931, 152.

230. http://familytreemaker.genealogy.com/users/s/e/b/Richard-A-Sebring/GENE2-0005.html, 189.

231. Warranted 26 December 1818 (http://personal.bellsouth.net/t/r/trublu3/wash5.htm).

232. http://fultonhistory.com/Newspapers%206/New%20York%20NY%20Tribune/New%20York%20NY%20Tribune%201846%20June%20-%20Dec%20Grayscale/New%20York%20NY%20Tribune%201846%20June%20-%20Dec%20Grayscale%20-%200158.pdf.

on Elections (Third Congress), Committee on Ways and Means (Fourth and Fifth Congresses); appointed United States Minister to Portugal and Spain on July 10, 1797, and served until September 9, 1801, when he took leave of absence; commissioned Minister to the Ottoman Porte on February 11, 1799, but did not reach that court; returned to Charleston; unsuccessful Federalist candidate for election in 1804, 1806, and 1808 to the Ninth, Tenth, and Eleventh Congresses; lieutenant in the state militia in 1808; again a member of the state house of representatives in 1808; president of the Santee Canal Co.; vice president of the Charleston Library Society and of the St. Cecilia Society; died in Charleston, S.C.; interment in St. Philip's Churchyard.[233] Elected GM of the GL of South Carolina AYM in the month of June 1808, successor of Paul Hamilton.[234]

Barend Moses Spitzer. 'On Sunday last the body of Mr. Barend Moses Spitzer was found on Sullivan's Island; he had been missing for upwards of ten days past.' (*City Gazette* from [Tuesday] 12 January 1796. *The South Carolina historical and genealogical magazine*, vol. 23, 152, p. 152).[235]

Jervis Henry Stevens (1750–22 July 1828). His sister Mary Ann Elizabeth (+1827) married George Cogdell, one of their three sons was John Stephano Cogdell.[236] Grand Juror for the parish of St. George Dorchester in 1778. Church organist of St. Philip's 1784–1814. In 1820 coroner for Charleston. Many biographical details in *Votaries of Apollo – The St. Cecilia Society and the Patronage of Concert Music in Charleston, South Carolina 1766–1820* by Nicholas Michael Butler, University of South Carolina Press. Columbia, South Carolina. 2007 (pp. 70–74,. 167, 205).[237]

233. http://bioguide.congress.gov/scripts/biodisplay.pl?index=S000633.

234. Desaussure 1815, 19.

235. http://books.google.ch/books?id=gkMTAAAAYAAJ&q=barend+spitzer&dq=barend+spitzer&hl=fr&sa=x&ei=_CJST4_LFM744QTk8qTNDQ&redir_esc=y.

236. Jervey 1906, 65. http://www.findagrave.com/cgi-bin/fg.cgi?page=gr&GRid=36805832.

237. http://books.google.ch/books?id=GIizNkE7zzkC&pg=PA74&lpg=PA74&dq=jervis+henry+stevens&source=bl&ots=GRLTZBb2us&sig=m8yjBLm1LOt1OucqzC8j84RQft4&hl=fr&sa=x&ei=m6CWT6m2I8yfOuOYgeYN&ved=0CEgQ6AEwBA#v=onepage&q=jervis%20henry%20stevens&f=false.

Horatio Gates STREET (18 Nov. 1777–30 Oct. 1849). '[He] was born at Northford, Connecticut and made a Mason in Hiram Lodge (1) at New Haven. After engaging in coast-wide trade for a few voyages, he located at Charleston as a merchant and inn-keeper, and later became a plantation owner on Edisto Island. His record in South Carolina Masonry is long and honorable.' (James R. Case, F.P.S., Grand Historian of the Grand Bodies of Connecticut, 'Yankees In the Mother Supreme Council', *The Philalethes,* February 1973). Married 21 June 1801 Lois Holt.[238] 'A sea captain, store and hotel keeper. He was six feet four inches tall with a kind face, friendly eyes and manners. His wife was a commanding presence. They lived in Charleston, SC, and spent ther last years of his [*sic*] life on Edisto Island, where they are both buried'.[239] The New England Coffee House was held by Horatio Gates Street (Charleston 1822 Directory, 68); 'the Commercial Coffee House, on East Bay, kept [in 1826] by Bro. H. G. Street' (Mackey 1861, 208).

Daniel Decius TOMPKINS (21 June 1774–11 June 1825). Governor of the Sate of New York (1807–1817), Vice-president of the United States (1817–1825). Grand Secretary (1801–1805) and Grand Master (1820 & 1821) of the Grand Lodge of New York. On 5 August 1813 elevated to the 33° and 'proclaimed … Grand Commander of the Supreme Council … for the Northern District of the United States of America' by Patent of Emanuel De La Motta in New York (facsimile in Baynard 1938, I, 171). Remained Grand Commander until his death. See his biography in McClenachan's *History*, vol. II (1892), 324 and Baynard 1938 I, 195.

Charles S. TUCKER. PM, Senior Grand Deacon 1814–26.12.1817 and Member of the ritual committee of the GL of South Carolina (May 1817). Senior Grand Deacon 26.12.1817 and Gd Treasurer 1819–1824 of the GL AFM. In 1823 a PM of Prudence No. 35.

Anthony Entrope ULMO. In 1816 and 1819 M.D. & Druggist, 20 Queen St.; Physician, 45 Queen St. in 1822, 157 King St. in 1825; M.D., Druggist,

238. http://wc.rootsweb.ancestry.com/cgi-bin/igm.cgi?op=DESC&db=mscheffler&id=I80502

239. http://familytreemaker.genealogy.com/users/s/t/r/Thomas-B-Street/WEBSITE-0001/UHP-0259.html

92 Meeting St. in 1829.[240] 'M.D., late of St. Domingo' married in 1800 Mary Louisa Aimee Champy.[241] Elected a Vestryman of the Roman Catholic Congregation together with Conly Cassin and Joseph Jahan.[242]

Isaac Mazyck WILSON, Dr. WM and Corresponding Secretary of the Grand Lodge of South Carolina in 1817, then Corresponding Secretary 1818, Junior Grand Warden 1819, Senior Grand Warden 1821, Deputy Grand Master of the Grand Lodge of Ancient Free-Masons of South Carolina 1822–1823.

John Izard WRIGHT (11 April 1792–18 April 1822). 'With this object in view a site on the north side of Broad Street just east of the Catholic Cathedral, known then as St. John and St. Finbar, was purchased by Mr. John Izard Wright at a cost of $10,700. There was a house on the lot, and pending the completion of their arrangements the canny Scots rented it at $180 per annum.'[243] 23 Jan 1797. John Izard WRIGHT, Esq., youngest son of Alexander WRIGHT, Esq., [married] to Miss Rebecca IZARD, eldest daughter of Ralph IZARD, jun., Esq. by the Rev. Mr. MILLS. (SC Weekly Museum Newspaper, Issue_04 Feb 1797).[244]

Websites I visited[245] show 18 April 1822 as date of his death. There is likely a confusion of names since he is recorded as Senior Warden of *L'Étoile Renaissante* No. 3 in 1827 (*American Masonic Record, and Albany Saturday Magazine*, Saturday 8 March 1827, p. 34).[246]

240. *Charleston City Directories.*

241. *Charleston City Gazette* copied by Jeanne Hayward Register. http://www.jstor.org/discover/10.2307/27569666?uid=3737760&uid=2129&uid=2&uid=70&uid=4&sid=47698851878497

242. *Charleston Courier*, 18 January 1820. http://www.genealogbank.com/gbnk/newspapers/?p_field_base-0=gblname&action=search&p_text_base-0=Ulmo&kbid=5747&s_referrer=daddezioo2&p_multi=GBNEWS%7CGBOBIT%7CGBSSDI%7CGBBOOK%7CGBDOC

243. http://standrewssocietyofcharlestonsc.org/chapter-5-historic-hall/. http://wc.rootsweb.ancestry.com/cgi-bin/igm.cgi?op=DESC&db=michelotti&id=I002928. http://familytreemaker.genealogy.com/users/s/t/r/Thomas-B-Street/WEBSITE-0001/UHP-0263.html.

244. http://www.reocities.com/Heartland/Lake/3577/charlestonmarriages.html.

245. http://wc.rootsweb.ancestry.com/cgi-bin/igm.cgi?op=GET&db=syf&id=I7152 & http://www.chestnut-blue.com/Chestnut-0/p1041.htm.

246. http://books.google.ch/books?id=wENJAAAAYAAJ&pg=PA34&lpg=PA34&dq=%22John+Izard+Wright%22&source=bl&ots=CB41_fv28v&sig=gGoKO2y2q1uwlzR7zWtuhQRxE40&hl=fr&sa=x&ei=L5RHT6TaBsToOYu-oPEN&ved=0CGkQ6AEwCA#v=onepage&q=%22John%20Izard%20Wright%22&f=false

2. THE *REGISTER*

2.1 The First Two Unnumbered Folios

[*Unnumbered first folio*]

Titles of the officers

An Ill^{s} President or G.^{d} Master
a Deputy G.^{d} Master
a Senior G.^{d} Warden
a Junr G.^{d} Warden
a G.^{d} Secretary Keeper of the Archives
a G.^{d} Treasurer
a G.^{d} Keeper of the Seals
a G.^{d} Master of Ceremonies
a G.^{d} Expert Introductor – or Tyler
a G.^{d} Cap^{n} of the Guards
a G.^{d} Hospitaler

& Dep^{t} G.^{d} Inspr G.^{l} 33.° representing the Sov^{n} G.^{d} Consistory

---

Members
Not to Exceed – 27 – Viz
15 active members – and 12 supernumerary

Obligatory Meetings
21th March – 25 June, 21st September, and 27 December

Day of Election
21st of ~~December~~ September

President for 3 years
officers every year – and are reelegible

[*Unnumbered second folio*]

<u>Months</u>

1st Month Called	Nissan	ניסן	March
2d Month ″	Year		April
3d Month ″	Sivan		May
4th Month ″	Tamus		June
5th Month ″	ab		July
6th Month ″	Elul		August
7th Month ″	Tizry		September
8th Month ″	Hivan		October
9th Month ″	Kisleu		November
10th Month ″	Thebet		December
11th Month ″	Sebat		January
12th Month ″	Adar		february

[*folio 1 r°*]

We the Subscriber Peter Javain G^{d}∴ Insp^{r}∴ Gen.l 33.^{d} Degree representatif of the Most Pot.^{t} Grand Consistory of the united States of America for the State of South Carolina – do – declare that on the 17th Day of the אב Month called Elul . in the M^{que} year 5815 – We have delivred [*sic*] this present Register to the Sov^{g} Grand Council of P∴^{ces} of Royal Secret for the Said State a their Seatting of Installation to serve to record the Minuttes of all their proceedings Which Book Countains one hundred Seventy Seven Leaves – Including this one and which we have numbered – In Testimony there of we have Set to this the Grand Seals of our arms and the Seal of P^{ces} Masons

G.^{d} East of Charleston the 17th Day the Sixth Month 5815-

P. Javain
G. I G.l 33.d Deg, & Deputed

2.2 The First Meeting

To the Glory of the G∴ A∴ of the Un^{e}∴

Lux ex Tenebris

From the East of the Sov. G^{d}. Council of Princes of the R∴ S∴ for the State of South Carolina, under the Celestial Canopy of the zenith, answering to 32° 42^{m} N. Lat^{de}.

<u>Health</u>, <u>Stability</u> & <u>Powers</u>

At a Meeting of the Ill^{s}∴ Princes Ma^{ns}∴ held at their Council Chamber in Charleston in consequence of a Summons from the Mst∴ Ill∴ Bro^{r}. Peter Javain Dep^{ty}. G^{d}∴ Insp^{r}∴ Genl∴ 33° Degrees [*sic*], Representative of the Most Puiss^{t}∴ G^{d}∴ Consistory of the U∴ S∴ & its Dependencies, on the 17th day of the Month called אב[247] Elul of the Hebraic Year 7815. of M^{ry}∴ 5815 & of the Chris^{n}∴ era 1815 —

Presents

P. Javain D∴G∴I∴G^{l} 33°	J. S. Cogdell P.R.S∴
P. Desportes G∴ I∴ G∴ 33	A. E. Ulmo P.R.S.
J. Dumaine G∴ I∴ G∴ 33	C. S. Tucker P.R.S.
Th.^{s} W. Bacot P∴R∴S∴	I. M. Wilson P.R.S.

The Ill^{s}. Bro^{r}∴ P. Javain informed the Council that he had received from the Most Puiss^{t}. G^{d}∴ Consist^{y} of the United States sitting at New york the Constitutional warrant for the Establishing of a G^{d}∴ Council of P^{ces}∴ of Roy$^{l.}$ Sec^{t}. for the State of S^{o}. Carolina and that he had convened the Ill Brethren for the purpose of Inaugurating the Temple & Installing the officers Elect according to a Resolve of the Provisional Provincial Committee of the 12 Instant which was read.

New Light being obtained, The <u>Temple</u> was consecrated in a very solemn Manner according to the usual form.

The Council was afterwards open'd in due form.

247. Hebrew month אב! Elul would have been אלול.

The Constitutional warrant was then read and the Ill∴ Brethren took the following oath of fidelity.

Viz

We the undersigned Thomas Wright Bacot, John Dumaine, John S. Cogdell, Anthony E Ulmo, Peter Desportes, Charles S. Tucker, & Isaac M Wilson, do promise & swear in Presence of the G^{d}∴ Arch^{t}∴ of the Universe to support to the utmost of our power the Constitutional warrant & the Constitution of the Most Sov^{n}. Grand Consistory of the U∴ S∴ of America & to submit ourselves to all its Institutes & regulations, agreably to the Tenor of our former obligations.

		Tho. W. Bacot
A. Ulmo	Isaac M Wilson	Chs S Tucker
P.R.S	P.R.S	K–H & P.R.S

The Constitutional Warrant was ordered to be recorded in the Minute Book of the G^{d}∴ Council.

The Deputy Grand Insp^{r}. Genl. the proceeded to the Installation of the Ill^{s}. Brother Thomas W. Bacot as President of the G^{d}∴ Council of Princes of Roy^{l}∴ Sec^{t}∴ for the State of S^{o}. Carolina with the usual honors, after being Installed the Ill President delivered to the Brethren the following short but appropriate & affectionate address.

"Most Ill^{s}∴ Dep∴ G^{d}∴ Insp^{r}∴ Genl∴ and M∴ Ill^{s}∴ P^{ces}∴ of this M∴ Pot^{t}∴ and Subl∴ G^{d}∴ Council.

My dear and Respected Brothers

I feel sensibly affected by the high honor you have conferred upon me, in placing me at the *head* of this subl∴ Body, and am persuaded that I owe my elevation more to your kindness than to any great share of merit in my self. The duty which I shall be called upon to perform, will, I am aware, be somewhat arduous, with the slender abilities I possess, and from the numerous vocations which occupy my mind, and engage my services. It is alone upon your friendly cooperation with my humble endeavours (on which I confidently rely) that I shall under Divine Providence, presume to flatter my self with the expectation of a performance of these precious duties, or hope to be any way useful. I am not vain enough to anticipate an increase of the *splendor* of our Subl∴

order by any exertions of my own, but I flatter my self I may venture to assure you, that in my intercourse with my Brethren, I shall hold the scales of *Justice* in proper equilibrium – that I shall ever be mindfull to cultivate that *equality* which ought always to exist among Masons (and to which I have ever bowed with reverence) and that my never ceasing aim will be to promote, among our Illustrious household, *Peace, Union* & *Harmony*. So that our Sublime Lodge may be the abode of tranquility and Brotherly Love, and be humbly, typical of that Celestial Lodge above, where reigns, alone, true happiness.

Our noble Institution is now in its infancy, in this State; and we are (at least most of us) I may say, novices in the art we are about to establish. We have not only to Create a character for our Sublime Council, that will make us honored and respected abroad, but we shall have perhaps to Combat with the prejudices, if not the hostility, of a few members of the former Grand Council in this place Which it appears, had become extinct from ceasing to perform their necessary functions.

It is only, therefore, by Zeal and diligence in studying and comprehending our respective duties in the Lodge, and performing them with fidelity and firmness, that we can hope to obtain a reputation abroad and more specially with the most Potent & Sublime Grand Consistory of the United States, so as to merit the Confidence they have placed in us, and the Great Kindness they have shewn us, as well as to ward off the attacks of calumny or Jealousy, should they unfortunately assail us.

Deign to accept, then, my respected & Ill^{s}. Brethren! my unfeigned thanks for your partiality and kindness towards me, in *this* as well as *other* occasions. and I entreat you kindly to throw a veil over the many errors which it is too probable I shall commit in the performance of my duties, as President of this Subl^{me}∴ Council and to grant me your brotherly Indulgence and Support. And may the Great Jehovah who ruleth over all prosper each Individual of you in this life, and bless you in eternity."

The Ill∴ Dep∴ G^{d}∴ Insp∴ Genl∴ then Proclaimed our Ill∴ Bro^{r}∴ T. W. Bacot President of the Grand Council, afterwards Ill^{s}. Bro^{r}. John Dumaine was duly installed as Senr Warden & Ill. John S. Cogdell as Junr. Warden with the usual honors & were proclaimed as such.

The Constitutional Warrant, Seals, Register, & the Regalia of office were delivered to the President on his being Conducted to the Throne, an appropriate Charge was delivered to each of the above named officers by our worthy & Ill^{s}. Bro^{r}∴ Javain.

The Ills President proceeded to Instal the following Ills. Brethren in the offices to which they had been elected viz

Anthony E Ulmo	G^{d}∴ Orator
Peter Desportes	G^{d}∴ Treasurer
Isaac M. Wilson	G^{d}∴ Secretary
Chs, S Tucker	G^{d}∴ Master of Ceremonies

& they, after having each received an appropriate Charge were proclaimed as such.

The Names of the officers of the Gr^{d}∴ Council were ordered to be published in one or more of the Gazette of the City.

Ordered that extracts from the Minutes of this night be forwarded to the Sov∴ Gd∴ Consistory at New york & to the Grand Councils at Newport, New Orleans, Baltimore & Philadelphia, with an address to each.

The Committee appointed to frame the Bye Laws, will report to the President when they are ready, who will assemble the Council to hear them read & to discuss them.

Nothing having been offered for the Benefit of the Royal Art neither for this Grand Council the first reading of the Minutes being done and approved We proceeded to Close the Council in due form and made oath of Secrecy.

[*signed*] Tho. W. Bacot Presid^{t}
Chas S Tucker K–H, P.R.S

2.3 The Constitutional Warrant of the Grand Council

Constitutional Warrant

To the Glory of the G^{d}. Arch^{t}∴ of the Universe

Ordo ab Chao

from the O∴ of the M∴ high and M∴ Powerful Sov^{n}. G^{d}. Consistory of the Sup^{me}∴ Chiefs of exalted Masonry for the United States of America its Territories & dependencies, regularly Constituted according to the ancient

Scottish rite of Heredon Sitting at the Central point answering to the 40 Deg. 41 m.∴ N.∴ L.∴

Let the rebuilding of the Holy Edifice, began under the protection of the G^{d}. Arch.∴ of the U.∴ be Conducted to its End by his blessing our undertaking

Health

Stability & Power

We Most Ill.∴ P^{ces}.∴ Most powerful Sov.∴ G^{d}.∴ Commander, G^{d}.∴ Insp^{r}.∴ Genl.∴ of the 33^{d}.∴ Deg.∴ and G^{d}.∴ Dignitaries of the Most Powerful Sov^{g}.∴ G^{d}.∴ Consistory of the United States of America regularly constituted by Constitutional Patents bearing date the 28th. Day of the 8th. Month of the T.∴ L.∴ 5807. Do Declare and attest that all Breth^{n}. Knights and Princes Mas.∴ Spread throughout both Hemispheres, that having upon a "Convocation" extraordinary Met in General assembly of the G^{d}.∴ Consis^{ry}.∴ the Most Powerf.∴ Sov.∴ G^{d}.∴ Commander communicated to us a Petition, accompanied by an oath of Submission, to our G^{d}.∴ Consistory, by our beloved & Ill Breth^{n}.∴ Peter Desportes, John Dumaine, Thomas Wright Bacot, John S. Cogdell, Anthony Entrope Ulmo, Charles S. Tucker, and Isaac Mazyck Wilson, recommended by our Most Ill.∴ Brother P. Javain our Deputy G^{d}. Inspector for the State of South Carolina, all of whom being recognised in their Dignity and Subl.∴ Degree.∴ of P^{ces}.∴ of the Roy^{l}. Sec^{t}.∴ and residents of Charleston, State of South Carolina, zealously desirous of working for the advantage and improvement of the Roy^{l}. Art in its Greatest perfection, Sollicit from our G^{d}. Consistory that it may be please to authorise them by Constitutional Patents to Establish a Grand Council of the Sublime Princes of the Royal Secret in the said City of Charleston, under the distinctive title of Gd. Council of Subl.∴ Princes of the Royal Secret for the Sate of South Carolina, To this effect and for other Good reasons, considering that there exist no G^{d}.∴ Council of P^{ces}.∴ of the Royal Secret in the State of South Carolina, that a similar Establishment cannot but be conductive to the propagation of true Masonic principles; and that it is necessary the Mas^{ik}.∴ authority Should be confined to one single spot within the said State, reposing moreover the greatest Confidence in the zeal, and Mask. knowledge of the M.∴ Ill.∴ Bro.∴ Th.∴ W.∴ Bacot,[248] designated

248. Like Mitchell and Dalcho, Bacot belonged to Lodge No. 8.

by our M∴ Ill∴ Brethren to preside in the G^{d}∴ Council, and the M∴ Ill∴ Broth^{n} John Dumaine[249] and John S. Cogdell as Senr∴ and Junior Wardens, We have by an unanimous vote, Constituted and Invested them, as by these presents We do Constitute, Institute and Give full and intire powers to the M∴ Ill∴ Broth^{r}. Thomas W. Bacot, John Dumaine and John S. Cogdell to Establish a G^{d}∴ Council of the P^{ces}∴ of the Roy^{l}∴ Sec^{t}∴ in the City of Charleston, to take care that the Statuts and general regulations of exalted Masonnery, and those particular to the G^{d}∴ Consist^{ry}. of the United States of America be strictly observed, and never to admit none but true and legitimate Breth^{n}∴ of Subl∴ Mas.^{y} to regulate and govern the members composing the said Grand Council, under the distinctive Title of G^{d}∴ Council of Subl∴ P^{ces}∴ of the Roy^{l}∴ Sec^{t}∴ for the State of South Carolina. We empower the said Grand Council to appoint and Install its G^{d}∴ Officers, the said appointments and Installations to take place on the 21st Day of September in every year. And we enjoin the said Grand Council to Cause the List of the G^{d}. Officers and Members to be forwarded to us in the intermediate time between the 21st of September and the 30th of November under the penalty of being Deprived of the priviledge of having their names Inserted in the Genl∴ List of the G^{d}, Consistory, which closes every year at that period.

We Grant to and confer in the ^{above} Said Grand Council, thus established, the power of initiation (even to its compliment which shall not exceed the numbers of twenty seven present members) Masons already admitted to the Degree of P^{ce}. R∴ ✠∴ to the Sublime Philosophical Mas^{ry}∴ as far as and including the Subl∴ degrees of P^{ce}∴ of R^{l}∴ Sec^{t}. 32 Degrees, provided they discover in them the requisite virtues and qualities; to receive supplication in request of Capitulary and constitutional Charters for the establishment of Councils, Colleges, &∴ within the State of South Carolina; to authorize them to work the degrees appertaining to them by conforming strictly to all ^{the} laws, Institutes, Statutes, and general regulations of exalted Masonry; and to those peculiar to our Gr^{d}. Consistory, under the obligations of solliciting within the Term of six months our approbation and ratification; to form Demands in its own name to the G^{d}∴ Consistory of the United States of America, within six months from the Time of application made by the petitioners to the said

249. Possibly Jean Dumaine.

G^{d}. Council; To inspect and Survey the said establishment of Perfection and Philosophical Mas^{ry}∴ in their proceedings.

As it is of the essence of the Sacred principles, upon which the base of our Subl∴ Institution rests, not to tolerate the Correspondence of Instituted bodies, with isolated bodies, and Masons who should not exibit Diploms of perfect regularity; the Gr^{d}∴ Consistory accordingly invites every Mas∴ belonging to its Grand Jurisdictions whether united in bodies or separately, carefully to avoid Correspondence, and to conform themselves allways to the articles of the Genl. regulations upon that Subject.

We entreat all our R∴ & M∴ Ill^{s}∴ Broth∴ of every Degrees, to acknowledge the said Grand Council of P^{ces}∴ of the Roy^{l} Sec^{t}∴ for the State of South Carolina, and to welcome its members, whether in Lodge, Chap∴, College, or Subl∴ Council, promising to manifest the same kind attention towards those who in our s^{d} O∴ shall present themselves at the gates of our Sacred Sanctories furnished with Similar Titles and recommendations.

Given under our hands, the seal of our arms, the Gr^{t}∴ Seal of P^{ce} Masons and the Privy Seal of the Sov^{g} Grand Commander, in a place wherein are deposited the greatst∴ treasures the beholding of which creates in us infinite Consolation joy and gratitude for all that is Great and Good, under the C∴ C∴ the 10th Day of the 2^{d} Month Called , of the Heb∴ Year 7815; A∴ L∴ 5815, of the Restoration 5575, and of the Chris^{n} aera 1815. Signed

Joseph Cerneau Sov^{n}. G^{d} Commander

Dewitt Clinton G^{d}. I^{r}. G^{l}. 33° Dep∴ G^{d}∴ Comm^{r}

Ch^{s} Guerin G∴ I∴ G^{l}. 33° 1st Lieu^{t} G^{d} Comm^{r}

James B Durand G∴ I∴ G^{l}. 33° 2^{d} Lieut G^{d} Comm^{r}

John W. Mulligan G. I. G^{l}. 33° ex Dep^{t} G^{d} Comm^{r} & Minister of State

Cadwallader D. Colden G∴ I∴ G∴ 33° 2^{d} Minister of State

Rainetaux D. G∴ I∴ G^{l}∴ 33° Grand Chancelier

P. Schisano G∴ I∴ G∴ 33° G^{d} Secretary

J^{h}∴ Gouin G∴ I∴ G∴ 33° G^{d} Treasurer

Jo^{n} Schieffelin G∴ I∴ G∴ 33° G^{d} M^{r} of Ceremonies

Thos Lownds G∴ I∴ G∴ 33° 2^{d} G^{d} M^{r} of Ceremonies

Thos Midy G∴ I∴ G∴ 33° G^{d} Expert Introductor

F^{cis} Dubuar G∴ I∴ G∴ 33° ass^{t} G^{d} Secretary

Jacob Schieffelin G∴ I∴ G∴ 33° G^{d}∴ K∴ of the Seals

E. Hicks G∴ I∴ G∴ 33° 2^{d} G^{d} Exp^{t} Int∴ & S∴ B∴

Martin Hoffmann G∴ I∴ G∴ 33° G^{d} Cap^{n} of the Guards

Jos Bouchaud G∴ I∴ G∴ 33°

W. J. Hunter Prince of Roy^{l} Sec^{t}

We Pr. Javain Dep.^{ty} G^{d}. Inspector Genl 33° Representative of the most Puiss^{t} Sov^{g} Grand Consistory of the united States of america, for the State of South Carolina. do Certiffy that on the 17th Day of the 6th month called Elul of the Heb. year 7815 of mas^{ry} 5815 and of the Christ^{n} Era 1815, by virtue of Powers that we are vested of, we have Regullarly Called together on a General Assemble or meeting all the P^{ces}∴ of Roy^{l} Sec^{t} mentionned on the other part in the Constitutional Warrant and that we have in the name of the Sov^{g} G^{d} Consistory of the Sup^{me} Chiefs of Exalted Masonry for the united States of america proclaimed & Installed in the Sacred Azylum the Sov^{g} G^{d} Council of P^{ces} of Royal Secret for the State of South Carolina Sign P. Javain Dep^{y} G^{d} Insp^{r} G^{l} 33° Rep^{tive} of the G^{d} Consistory

2.4 The Constitutional Laws of the Cerneau Bodies

Folio 7 v° of the *Register* is blank except for the word "English" underlined on top of the folio. Folio 8 recto has the following:

French

A.·. L.·. G.·. D. G.·. A.·. of L'U

Ordo ab Chao

S.·. G^{d}. Consis^{re} des G^{ds}. Inspecteurs G^{x} 33e Deg.·. et P.^{ce} du Roy.^{l} Sec^{t} Chef Sup.·. de la h.·. M.·., du Rit Ec.·. ancien et accepté, pour les Etats Unis d'amerique et dependances, Seant Sous le C.·. C.·. au p^{r} Cent.·. rept.·. au 40° 41 m. La^{de} Nord.

Extraits des Lois Generales et des Instructions sur les principes G^{x}. de la h.·. M^{ie}.

Instituts*, *Statuts, Et reglements

Generaux de la haute Maconnerie.

This is followed with the French text of *Instituts* in 10 articles (f° 8 and 9), of *Statuts* in 18 articles (f° 9 to 14) and of '*Extraits des Instructions sur le* [*sic*] *Principes Generaux de la Haute Maconnerie*' (six lines only) underneath which stays:

> Signé et Timbré pour Extrait Conforme par mandement du G^{d}. Consistoire des Etats unis et Depend^{ces} P. Schisano. Gd. Chance^{r}.·. D.·. G.·. I.·. G.·. 33°.

These 'laws, Institutes, Statutes, and general regulations of exalted Masonry' are written in French on the recto of seven folios, the respective blank versos were likely intended for an English translation which was never made. They bear at the end:

> Signé et Timbré pour Extrait Conforme par Mandement du G^{d} Consistoire des Etats Unis et Depen^{ces} P. Schisano. Gd Chance.·. D.·. G.·. G.·. Gl. 33°—
>
> Pour Copie Conforme a L'original resté entre mes mains dans nos archives.
>
> P. Javain Dep^{t}.·. G.·. I.·. G.·. 33°
>
> Representant Le Sov^{n} G^{d}.·. Consist^{r}. des Etats unis pour L'état de la Caroline du Sud.

Then, on three folios (16 v° to 17 v°) come fifteen articles preceded by the following:

To the Glory∴ of the Gd∴ Arch∴ of the U.

Ordo ab Chao

The G^{d}∴ Consist∴ of the Sup∴ Chiefs of h∴ exalted Mas^{ry}∴, for the United States of America and dependencies regularly Constituted according to the ancient Scottish rite of Heredom Sitting in New york

---

Articles of Regulation and General Police, decreed by the G^{d}∴ Consistory of the United States &c. in its Sitting of the 26. Day of the 7th Month A∴ L∴ 5812 to be observed by the Grand Councils of its Jurisdiction.

[folio 18 r°]

Abstract of the Sitting of the 19th day of the 7th month A. L. 5812

The Grand Consistory Deems that Conformably to the 3rd & 4 ~~of the~~ articles of the Institutes, the President of G^{d}∴ Councils of P^{ces}∴ of the Roy^{l} Secret Constituted by that Sov^{g}. Body shall by natural right be members of the G^{d}∴ Consistory; and that they shall moreover be decorated with the Subl∴ Dignity of honor^{y} Lieu^{t}. G^{d}. Commandeur.

Sealed. & Certyfied Conform by P. Schisano. G^{d} Chan^{r}. G∴ I∴ G∴ 33°.

Delivered by us Deputy Grand Insp^{r} G^{l}. 33° representing the G^{d} Consistory of the United State of America near the Sov^{g} Council of P^{ces} of the Ro^{l}∴ Sec^{t}∴ for the State of South Carolina

P. Javain
D^{t} Gd Insp Gl 33°

2.5 The Committee's Report & Members of the 'Association' *17 August 1821*[250]

Lux ex Ténébris

At an Extra Meeting of the Sov^{n} Grand Council of P^{ces} of Royal Secret for the State of South Carolina held at B^{r} Pearce's Lodge Room on Friday Evening the 17th Day of the 6th month Called Elul of the H∴ Y∴ 7821 A∴ L∴ 5821 of the Ch^{n} Era the 17th August 1821—

Present

Illu^{s} Br John S. Cogdell--------President

" " Th^{s} W. Bacot -----------Ex president

" " Richard Pearce---------S.W. Prot–

" " A A A Carivene -------J^{r} W Prot

" " P. Javain -----------------D^{ty} G^{d} I. Genl

" " P. Desportes ------------Treasurer

" " Ch^{s} S. Tucker ----------Secretary

" " Saml Richards ----------Cap^{n} of the Guard.

" " Peter Laurans ----------

" " John Izard Wright-----

" " Ch^{s} C. Chitty----------

" " E. Elizer -----------------Tyler

The Council of P^{ce} of Roy^{l} Sec^{t} was opened in Due form the Ill^{s} President informed the Council that he had Convened them in consequence of information he had received that a Certain numbers of Bro^{r} Masons (as p^{r} List N° 1) had illegally associated them selves, to work and given the Sublime Degrees of free Masonry which right alone exists in this Sov^{n} G^{d} Council, when the following Resolutions where unanimously agreed to—"The Sov^{n} Grand Council for the state of South Carolina, P^{ces} of Roy^{l} Secret, have heard with deep regret, that *Certain Persons* who have claimed to themselves the distinction of membership in the great and honored family of the Craft, and who

250. Folio 52 recto.

are held and taken as such, have been induced to assemble for the purpose of working in the degrees which are only Constitutionally granted to this Sov^{n} G^{d} Council of P^{ce} of Roy^{l} Sec^{t}, that they have obtained the Books and documents, and Jewels, of a Brother of this degree, now deceased, and by and thro' means so obtained they are Giving, what they call degrees Corresponding with those embraced only in this G^{d} Council—the Sov^{n} Grand Council as Master Masons, but more particularly as Past Master, forbear here to express their opinion & their secret sorrow, at the impression such a step is calculated to make not only on their minds—but on the heart of every member of the Craft who has not enlisted this new association—

"The council feel it their duty to approach the personnes [*sic*] above mentioned with all that mild and Brotherly admonition and Counsel, which the obligations, and the morales lectures of the orders of Masonry in general, unceasingly inculcate. – With this view, and in the spirit of harmony and Love, The Sov^{n} grand Council have adopted the following Resolutions, doubting little, that its effect must be to restore to order the Brethren who have thus trespassed on the Sanctity and priviledge of our Council."

Resolved· that our Ill^{s} Brothers Thos W. Bacot, John Izard Wright, and Peter Laurans be a Committee to wait on such persons, as have been reported to have had meetings for, or have otherwise agreed upon, the establishment of a Society to be Governed upon the establishment of a society to be governed by Such Rules and Regulations as appertaining exclusively to this Grand Council. Which is alone regularly and Constitutionally established in this State. that they do represent, in the true spirit now moving this Body, that the Course taken by them us not in harmony with the duty they owe to Masonry in General, that as it would be their bounden duty to check every encroachment upon the *rights, Powers, harmony,* and *advancement* of their mother, the G^{d} Lodge, so should they be *prompt, Magnanimous, Brotherly* & *Zealous* to preserve to every order of Masonry established among us—Pure and undefiled all its Sacred Rights and Priviledges – That they be requested to discontinue their further meetings or proceedings and that they be also requested to deposit in the Grand Council all the Books and other documents which are now in their possession and which it is understood belonged to the late Sov^{n} G^{d} Insp^{r} General Brother John Mitchell—

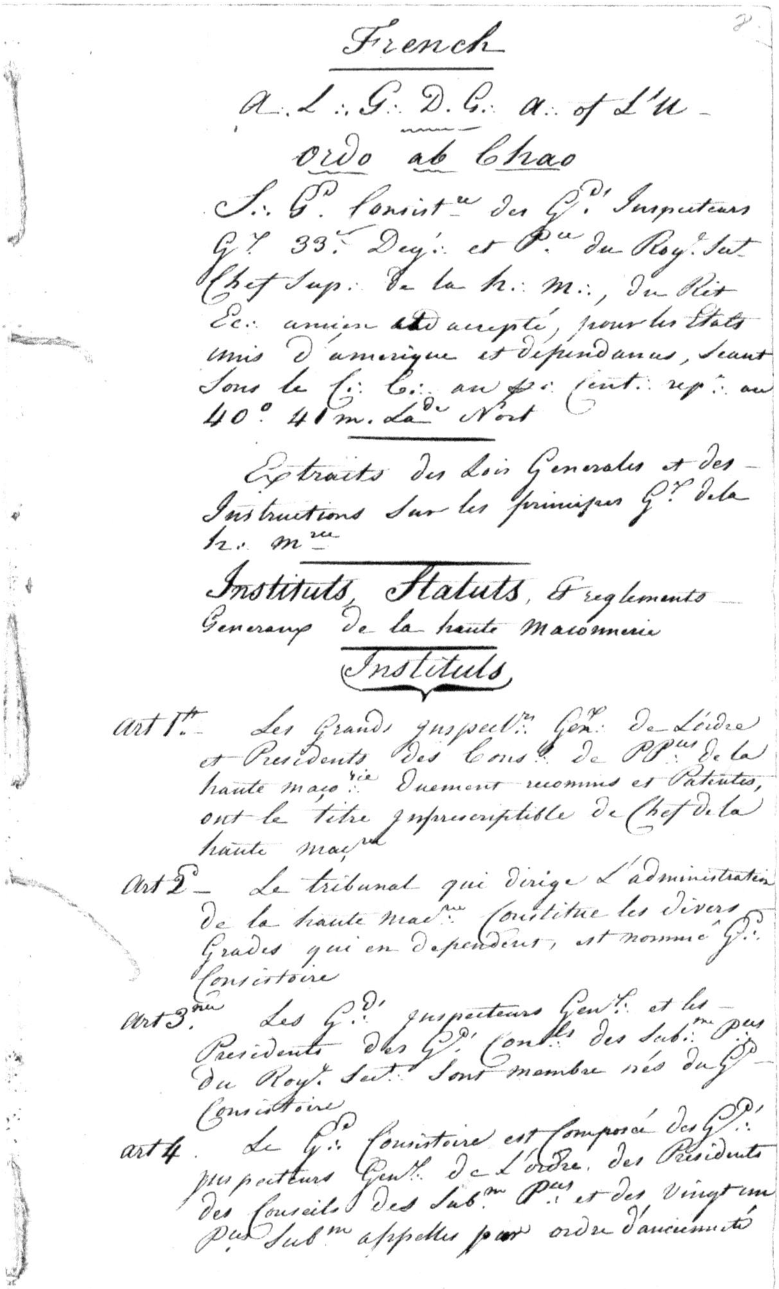

French

A∴ L∴ G∴ D∴ G∴ A∴ of L'U-

Ordo ab Chao

S∴ G.d Consist.re des G.ds Inspecteurs G.x 33.e Deg∴ et P.ce du Roy.l Sct Chef Sup∴ de la h∴ m∴, du Rit Ec∴ ancien ~~etc~~ accepté, pour les Etats unis d'amerique et dependances, Seant Sous le C∴ C∴ au p∴ Cent∴ rep∴ au 40° 41 m. La.de Nord

Extraits des Lois Generales et des Instructions sur les principes G.x de la h∴ m.rie

Instituts, Statuts, & reglements Generaux de la haute Maconnerie

Instituts

art 1.er – Les Grands Inspect.rs Gen.x de Lordre et Presidents des Cons.ls de PP.ces de la haute maço.rie Duement reconnus et Patentés, ont le titre Inprescriptible de Chef de la haute maç.rie

art 2 – Le tribunal qui dirige L'administration de la haute mac.rie Constitue les divers Grades qui en dependent, et nommé G∴ Consistoire

art 3.me Les G.ds Inspecteurs Gen.x et les Presidents des G.ds Cons.ls des Sub.mes P.ces du Roy.l Sct. Sont membre nés du G.d Consistoire

art 4. Le G∴ Consistoire est Composé des G.ds Inspecteurs Gen.x de L'ordre, des Presidents des Conseils des Sub.mes P.ces et des vingt un P.ces Sub.mes appelles par ordre d'ancienneté

Folio 8 recto of the *Register*

Resolved, that the Committee be at Liberty to read these Resolutions to as many persons as may be so, as aforesaid, associated for the purposes herein before complained of—

Resolved that the committee make a report as early as possible—

No other Business before this Council it was Closed in due form.

Charles S Tucker

No. 1 Copy of the list of the person Composing the association—

Clandestines (meeting at H. G. Street's East Bay)

✓ H. G. Street W. Master of the Mark Lodge ---------President ---------- 1st
✓ Moses Holbrook a Past Master ----------------------Vice Pres^{t} ---------- 2^{d}
✓ Elyah Gates --Sec^{ry} & Treasurer 3^{d}
✓ × Robt Carr W. Master of Solomons Lodge --------N° 1 ---------------- 4th
✓ × Alexander Mc Donald ---------------------- N° 13 ---------------------- 5
✓ John Laroche -------------------------------- N° 8 ---------------------- 6
✓ N. Bachelder W. Master of Lodge-------- N° 6---------------------- 7
✓ Henry Cross S.W. ----------------------- N°5 ---------------------- 8
✓ × W. M. Dyer -------------------------------- N° 5 ---------------------- 9
✓ M Mc Kinzie--------------------------------- N° 1 ---------------------- 10
✓ James Little -------------------------------- N° 5 ---------------------- 11
✓ Joseph Mc Cosh---------------------------- N° 1 ---------------------- 12
✓ James W. Rouse --- 13

the above have signed the bye Laws 13 in number

[Wm Proctor was not of the number among the signers. T W. B]

Applicants

Howland S.W. N° 8—
Dr Green – Lodg N° 1
Bell—Gofferey—Getsinger of Lodg. N° 5—
Rollando of Lodge N° 5—Wright & Sadler

21 September 1821[251]

At a Stated Meeting of the Sov^{g}. G^{d} Council of P. of Roy^{l} Secrets for the State of South Carolina held ... le [*sic*] 21 September 1821– ... The Committee appointed to wait on those Brother Masons who had illegally assembled – respecting Sublime Masonry made the following report —

Your Committee call'd upon Mr H. G. Street on Monday evening 20th August 1821, & had an interview with him & Mr Batchelder, who resides in the same house. Mr Street acknowledged himself to be President of that association, holding its meetings in his House, and informed the committee that the association were then in session, & proposed that (they Committee) should go into the room where they were assembled, & communicate with them; which was declined, your committee assigning as a reason that they could not know or acknowledge such illegal and unmasonic association as a regular Masonic body, for the same reason they refused to receive any part of such assembly into the room where they were for the more particular account of this interview you committee refer you to the paper mark'd (**A**)

Copy of DOCUMENT A

Monday 20th August 1821

The Committee appointed by the G^{d} Council of P^{es} of Roy^{l} Sec^{t} waited upon Brother Street, whom they understood to be at the head of the association of persons who had got possession of manuscripts of the Degrees of Sublime Masonry, and there meeting Brother N^{l} Batchelder the following is what passed between the Committee and those Brethren—

The Committee communicated to them the information which had been given to the G^{d} Council on friday evening 17th instant, as stated in their minutes, and requested to know if they had been correctly informed, and, if they had been, to know what were the objects proposed by this association.

Brother Street, without hesitation, acknowledged that there was an association of persons of which he was the head, (or President) that they were then in his house assembled; that they were thus associated for the purpose of reading over the Degrees in Sublime Masonry. of which they had obtained manuscript Copies, being the same which belonged to the late Brother Collonel [*sic*] Mitchell; that they had established regulations and formed bye Laws; that they had not worked, but had only read over, those degrees, and that they did not suppose,

251. Folio 53 verso. The following is a verbatim transcript of the committee's Report, folios 54 r° to 56 v°, which is followed in the *Register* with the Documents marked A to F (folios 57 r° to 63 v°). For the sake of clarity these six documents are inserted where the report mentions them first.

or believe, that in so doing they were Conducting them selves in a manner unmasonic. the Instructions from the G^d^ Council and their resolutions were then read to those Two Brothers, and they were affectionately exorted by the Committee to desist from any further proceedings, and were most solemnly warned of all the consequences which would inevitably insue, if they continue them, they were also assured they would insure the risk of expulsion from the Symbolic Degrees.

Brother Street seemed to be disposed to view the Business rather seriously; Brother Bachelder said "there is only one way to get over the Business". the question was immediatly asked, which is that? the answer was, "why admit the whole Body as Members of the G^d^ Council," it was then replyed by one of the Committee, "this ended, to use an old adage, in letting the cat from the Bag" these Brothers at same time acknowledged they Could do nothing in their Present state, but intend to apply for authority not saying whose.

One of the Committee asked, "why make regulations if they did not intend to proceed and do something? the answer was by (Brother Bachelder) to keep the secrets to our selves, and not to let others know it."!

they informed us that their association was then assembled, and wished the Committee to meet them, in an adjoining Room, and make any Communication to them. this the Committee declined to do. they then proposed that those persons should Come into the Room, where the Committee was, this was also declined, they then proposed that a few at a time should come in to meet the Committee, this was also objected to, as the Instructions to the Committee were not, in any manner, to recognise them as a body of Masons.

the committee, then requested and entreated the brothers, Street & Batchelder to pause & to reflect before they suffered themselves further to proceed in this injustiable business again warning them of the serious consequences, the Committee also begged Br^r^ Street to Communicate to those brethren who had been engaged in this business with him, what had passed between the Committee & himself and Br^r^ Batchelder. Bro^r^ Street very Earnestly replied he would do so, and said that Bro^r^ Bacot should hear from him, very shortly

The Committee and those / two / Brethren separated. Signed Th^s^ W. Bacot, John Izard Wright & Peter Laurens.

Your Committee beg leave to draw your attention to the paper marked (**B**) Which is a statement of part of a conversation between B^r^ Bacot (one of the committee appointed by this grand council) & Br^o^ fred^k^ Dalcho, containing a copy of the signatures of the individuals composing that association, to their written obligation, which he (Br^o^ Dalcho) consider'd as completely binding them. To Each name has been added the Lodge & R.A. Chapter of which each is a member excepting Dr Moses Holbrook's, Elizar Gate's & James Rouse's, who your members understand are not members of any Lodge or Chapter.

DOCUMENT B

In a conversation with the Rev[d] bro[r] Dalcho on the 23[d] August 1821, he informed me that three of the persons who had associated for purposes connected with Sublime Masonry, having possession of the Manuscript Copies of the several degrees, to Wit Brothers Rouse, M[c] Donald, & Laroche, had called upon him on 21st asking his advice; He said that previous to his giving it, they must give him from under their hands a promise not to divulge or to disclose except to those who should be lawfully entitled to the same any thing relating to those degrees which had thus come to their knowledge. they promised him to do so.

I informed him what the Grand Council had done relating to this association, showed him their resolves, and stated what had passed between the Committee at the G.·. Council, and brothers Street & Batchelder. We held a pretty long conversation upon the subject, the particulars of which were noted in writing, by me, in the afternoon of the same Day.

An hour (or more) afterwards Brother Dalcho Called again at the Bank, and informed me that after he had left me, in going down Broad street, he had met with D[r] Holbrook, who pressed him to go into his house, where several of the associators were, as the wished much to see him, he went in under an express declaration, & understanding that he did not, nor would recognise them as a Body. they then tendered him a paper signed by thirteen persons, being the written promise that they had said they would Give him—This paper he showed to me. I read it over three times to impress on my memory a full recollection of it, so as to Commit the same to writing as soon as might be practicable. It was after Two o clock when Brother Dalcho left me, we having had a further and free conversation together upon the subject, also particularly noted by me. The moment I had dined, I committed to writing all that had passed between Brother D. and myself, as before stated, and the following is a near as possible an exact copy of the Paper he exhibited to me. It was writing, I think, upon a large sheet of vellum paper, at the top of which was painted the Eye of omnipotent's, the whole in a large hand writing, and the name of that sacred being to whom the appeal was made in still large letters. – I called the attention of our Brother, in the most imphatic manner, to that holy name and to the Eye above, the words were these. "We do hereby now solemnly promisse and swear (or declare) that we will always hail, keep, & conceil, and never will reveal, any of the part or parts, the point or points of the Mysteries of Sublime Masonry, which we have obtained, (or are in possession of) (or are come to our Knowledge) or which we may hereafter obtain (or be Intrusted in) to any person in the world. except it be to a Brother who shall be lawfully intitled to receive the same. – To this we swear (or declare) without any hesitation, mental reservation, or self evasion of mind whatsoever, under the penalty of having all our former obligations in force, (or put in force) against us. – So help us God keep us in our senses & enable us to perform the same. Signed as follows H. G. Street, Moses Holbrook,

> Elyzah Gates, Robert Carr, Alex^{r} Mc Donald, John G. Laroche, N. Batchelder, Henry Cross, W. M. Dyer, M^{l} Mc Kenzie, James Little, and James W. Rouse."
>
> 13 Persons
>
> the names were compared by Brother Dalcho and my self, with those in a paper handed to the Committee in the hand writing of Saml Richards, and were adantically the same, and marked thus ✓ by me in ^{his} Bro^{r} D.s presence;__Brother Dalcho said the reason if his receiving the above written obligation from them was, that, he conceived it bound every individual among them, not to make use of the manuscripts in their possession, in an unlawful manner.
> Thom^{s} W. Bacot signed.

they beg leave to draw your attention likewise to the paper marked (**C**) being a statement of an interview between Br^{o} Bacot and Dr Holbrook, Alex^{d} M^{c}donald & J. W. Rouse

DOCUMENT C

> On Monday Evening the 27 august 1821, Bro Bacot one of the Committee of the Sov^{n} G^{d} Council of P^{ces} of Roy^{l} Secrets was waited upon by Bro^{s} Holbrook, Mc Donald & Rouse, (three of the associates; who stated that they had Called at the request of B^{r} Dalcho, whom they had just left, that he declined doing any thing. and had advised them to call on Brother Bacot. – they expressed a desire to have every things reconciled; they were told it depended upon them selves, they denyed any Intention to work untill authorised, said their number was thirteen they did not wish to obtain more than the Degree of Perfection. they wished advise, after being warned of the consequence of atempting to work or even to associate as Masons, they were advised in the first place to deliver up to the Grand Council all the Manuscripts in their possession; and if they wished to receive $^{the\ Degrees}$ as far as they mentioned, to make application in writing and to state what were their views and motives for having assembled, in the most candid manner, that no doubt every degree of Liberality would be extended to them, but they must have confidence in the Grand Council.—— a conversation of quite a desultory nature was carried on for some time; in substance as above, they then Departed.

Your committee judged it better under all circumstances, to represent in writing, & in the strongest manner possible, but in a brotherly & friendly spirit the Highly unmasonic conduct of that association. the paper marked (**D**) is a copy of what was Drawn up for that purpose; pointing out the Masonic tenets inculcated in the symbolic or blue degrees which had in the opinion of your committee been violated. this was addressed to Mr H. G. Street and left with him by one of the committee, with a request that he would communicate its contents to such persons as he knew to be members thereof.

DOCUMENT D

Masonry is universal, and consists of different Degrees and orders, previous to gaining admission into the Higher or Sublime Degrees, it is necessary that the candidate should have passed through the three first or Symbolic degrees; so Called, because operative tools, implements, and emblems, are used as Symbols to inculcate Brotherly Love, truth, virtue, and Justice.

By the rules of the Higher orders, the door is always open, (subject however to balot) for admission into the sublime degrees of all such Brethren as prove them selves worthy and well qualifyed; or in other words, who have faithfully fulfilled for a length of time the solemn obligations by which, they had bound themselves in the Symboliques Degrees; (which serve as probationnary Degrees to test their moral character) and who have faithfully and conscienciously Conformed to, and practised in every respect the moral precepts and sacred principes of the Institution. all of which are increasingly inculcated in the various charges, lectures, and explanations, of the several operative implements and emblems, symbolicaly used in those degrees, to illustrate the moral and masonic obligations; among which are to be found particularly those of Brotherly *Love, truth, virtue* & *Justice.*

Brotherly Love is forcibly brought to our view in the entred apprintice's degree, the charge read in opening the Lodge, has these words, "behold! how sweet and pleasant it is for *Brethren* to dwell in *Unity!*" the Prayer in closing the degree, means this "May the Blessing of Heaven rest *upon us* and *all regular Masons!* May Brotherly Love prevail, and may every *Social* and *Moral Virtue cement* us!" We would ask with *brotherly affection*, and in the *spirit* of *candor* whether your conduct at this moment Towards the Brethren of the sublime Degrees be *calculated* to *continue* that "*unity*", which we all as Brethren so frequently and devoutly pray for? Whether the steps you are now pursuing be not in *violation* of *every* thing held *Dear* and *sacred* among Masons; contrary to the principles of *Morality* and *Justice*, and Calculated, if persisted in, to *destroy* that *Brotherly Love*, and all those *Moral* and *Social virtues*, which should *Cement* us?

It can not be said that Sublime Masons, working under a *regular Charter* (all of whom have received in a Legally constituted Lodge, the Degrees of Masters and Past Masters) are other than *regular* Masons; nor can it be contended that such brethren as have associated without *Warrant, Charter,* or any *acknowledged Masonic authority;* who have framed *bye Laws* and signed them, *Elected officers,* by *whatever* names called; holding *association* or *meeting* for the avowed purpose of *communicating* the Sublime Degrees to others either by *reading them* or by *any other* mode, whether *under* the *solemn obligation* of a *Masonic oath*, or *without such obligation*, act in *conformity* to the *established principles* of the *Masonic Institution*. their conduct is Certainly highly *unmasonic, irregular* and in *violation* of the *long established principles* of *Masonry*.

the Sublime Degrees in this State belong solely to the Grand Council of Sov^{n} P^{ces} of Roy^{l} Sec^{ts} legally Established in Charleston for the State of South Carolina, by the Grand Consistory of the united States of america. Such Brethren therefore as have associated for the purpose of *communicating*, or *conferring*, (or by whatever names they chuse to call it) the Sublime degrees, belonging to the Grand Council at Charleston or even to read them in their illegal and unmasonic association, must surely have forgotten, not only the principles of *virtue* and *Justice*, inculcated in the lectures, but also the *solemn obligation* by which they bound them selves, "not to *wrong* a *Master Mason* to *the value of any thing*"! every Member of the Grand Council is a *Master Mason*, the Brethren therefore composing that *unmasonic* and *illegal*, association, as often as the *assemble* unquestionably *rob* the members of the G^{d} Council of Sov^{n} P^{ces} of Roy^{l} *Secrets* (*who are all Master Masons*) to the value of their Degrees.

"Truth" (we are informed in the lecture) "is a divine attribute, and the fondation of every virtue. To be good and true is the *first lesson* we are taught in Masonry, on this theme we contemplate & by its *dictates* endeavor to *regulate* our conduct; hence, while *influenced* by this principle, hypocricy & deceit are unknown among us, sincerity & plain dealing distinguish us, & the *heart* and *tongue join* in *promoting* each others *welfare* & rejoicing in each other *Prosperity*" we would ask in the same spirit of *Brotherly Love* & *Candor*, whether holding that illegal & *unmasonic association* for the purpose of *Conferring* the Sublime Degrees *or reading them* or for any other purpose *relating* to those Degrees, or to any others (which that unmasonic association have not obtained in a *just* and *legal* manner agreably to the *long Established Principles of Masonry*) or Communicating a Knowledge of them in any mode whatever to others, be not in *violation* of this *Principle* of truth, in as much as "the *heart* and *tongue*" do *not join* in *promoting* each others welfare & rejoicing in each *other's prosperity*." It cannot be denied that it tends to *injure* their "*welfare*" and to *destroy* their "Prosperity."

"*Justice* is that *standard* or *boundary* of *right* which enables us to render to EVERY *man* his *just due* without distinction. this virtue is not only *Consistent* with *divine* and *human laws*, but it is the very Cement and support of Civil *Society* and as *Justice* in a great measure Constitutes the real good man, so should it be the *Invariable practice* of *every Masons* never to *deviate* from the *minuttes* principles thereof"—Can any Brother of that *unmasonic association* hear this, & not be sensible that he has *violated* THIS *principle*, which "is the *standard* and *boundary* of *right*, & which enables us to *render* to *every man* his *Just* due? have not the members of that association (as Brother Masons we have the charity to hope unconsciously) *violated* this *sacred Tie*? Instead if the Brethren of that *illegal association* "rendering to us of the Sublime Degrees" our *just* due as men." (but more *particularly* as MASONS) they are endeavouring to *rob* is of our degrees, which is *contrary* to the *Principles* of Justice; when "it should be the *invariable practice* of EVERY *Mason never* to *deviate* from the *minutes* Principles thereof." You cannot have forgotten, My Brothers, that when you received your first degree, in Masonry & was invested of what you had been divested, that you was placed in the N. E. at the right hand of the Worshipful Master "where (you was pleased to say)" you stood as a *just* and *upright man*" & it was given to you in charge in the *strongest manner* possible "ever to act & walk as such."

With the *feeling* of *Brethren* whose *duty* it is to "*admonish* a brother of his faults," & to *point* them out to him, we would ask you whether your conduct towards the members of the Grand Council be "that of a *just* and *upright man?* You must recollect that "there is represented in every regular & well governed Lodge a *point within* a *Circle* , the point representing an individual Brother, the *Circle* representing the boundary line of his duty to God & man, beyond which he is never to suffer his passions, prejudices, or interests to betray him on any occasion. the Circle is emberdered by Two perpendicular parallel Lines representing St. John the Baptist & St. John the Evangelist, who were perfect parallels in Christianity as well as Masonry, & upon the vertex rests the Book of Holy=Scripture, which points out the *whole duty* of man, & while a Mason keeps himself *thus* circumscribed it is impossible he can materially err"

"The Book of *Holy Scripture* which points out the *whole duty* of man" teaches or rather *Commands* us "to render unto *Cesar* the things which are Cesar's"; which the principles of Justice, inculcated in the lecture of the 1st Degree teach us also, tho' in different Words, viz *Justice* is that *stendard* of *right* which enables us to *render* to *every* man his *just due* without distinction" how can you therefore retain the books of the sublime degrees, Which you have *not* obtained *lawfully* & *masonically*, without acting *contrary* to the command contained in the *Holy Scriptures,* and violating the *principles* of *Justice* as above stated, which is invariably impress'd upon the mind of every *candidate* in the first degree of Masonry. it is a *Masonic* Virtue as well as a cardinal one.

"The *Plumb* admonishes us to walk *uprightly* in our *several stations* before God and *Man*, square in our actions by the square of Virtue.," acting contrary to the *principles of Justice* as already incontrovertably pointed out *particularly* towards *brethren*, cannot *possibly* be said "to *square* own *actions* by the *square* of *Virtue*."

The *trowel* We are taught to make use of for the more noble & glorious purpose of *spreading* the *cement* of *Brotherly love* & *affection* that *cement* which *unites* us into one *sacred band* or society of *friends* & *brothers* among whom no *contention* should *ever exist*, but that *noble contention* or rather *emulation* of *who best can Work* or *best* agree" in the same *brotherly spirit* we would ask Whether the members of that association act in *conformity* to the *principles inculcated* in the *explanation* of the *trowel?* is that *unmasonic* meeting calculated "to *spread* the *cement* of *brotherly love* & *affection*, that *cement* which *unites* us into *one sacred band* or *society* of *friends* & *brothers*, among whom no *contention* should *ever exist*, but that *noble contention* or rather emulation of who *best can work* or *best agree*"? is it not rather calculated to *destroy* that *cement* which *unites* us into *one sacred band* or *society* of *friend* & *brothers*."?

We have been told by one of the members of that association, that he knows "but *one way* to put an end to that *unmasonic* association, which is, by *admitting* their *whole body* as *members* into our Gr^d Council." it is with sentiment of deep sorrow & regret, *easier conceived* by a true & zealous mason than Words can *possibly express*, that we are compel'd to state, *that such* a *sentiment* was utter'd by the *Master* of a *Lodge*. is this "that *noble contention* or rather *emulation* of who *best can work* or *best agree*"? this had more the *appearance* of a *contention* to *force* from the Grand Council (as was attempted with our deputy Grand Master of old) by *violence* & *unmasonic* means what our *sacred oaths* have bound us to *preserve*. let us remind you, my brother, that "*fortitude* is that noble & steady purpose of the mind, whereby we are enabled to undergo any pain, peril, or danger when prudentially deem'd expedient. this virtue is equally distant from rashness & cowardice, and like the former, (temperance) should be deeply impressed upon the mind of a *every Mason* as a *savegard* or *security* against ANY *illegal attack* that may be made by *force* or *otherwise* to *extort* from him *any* of those *secrets* with *which* he has been *entrusted*, and which was emblematically represented upon his first admission into the Lodge."

If such grounds be taken to extort from the G^d Council admission into their body, or any of those secrets with which they have ^been so solemnly entrusted; we must declare, using the sentiment so beautifully express'd in the charge to the candidate in the 3^d Degree that "no motive shall ever make us swerve from our duty, violate our vows, or betray our trusts; but be true and faithfull, and imitate the example of that famous artist whom we represented on the evening we were raised to that degree. as masons we feel mortified that any brother should have forgotten & acted contrary to that part of the same charge wherein you was emphatically told "you are now bound by *duty, honor*, & *gratitude*, to be faithful to your trust, to support the *dignity* of your character on *every* occasion, & to *enforce* by *precepts* & *example obedience* to the TENETS of our order". can the steps pursued by the members of that *unmasonic* association be consider'd as "*supporting* the *dignity* of their character as *Masons* or enforcing by *precepts* & *example, obedience* to the *tenets* of our order? are they not in open violation of them? in the character of a Master Mason you are authorised to correct the *errors* and *irregularities* of your uninform'd Brethren, and *guard* them against a breach of fidelity "can you, who are *committing errors* and *irregularities* be said to correct the *errors* and *irregularities* of others? "to *preserve* the *reputation* of the *fraternity unsullied* must be your *constant* care" By *violating* (as has been pointed out to you) all the *principles* nearly of the institution, have you not in a great measure *sullied* the *reputation* of the *fraternity*" When it was your bounded duty "to *preserve* it *unsullied?* We speak to you my brother as brethren & friends desirous of pointing out to you your errors in the clearest manner, which is our duty as Master Masons. What excuse however can be made for Masters of Lodges & past Masters, whose duty it is to *know all* these things &

to *inculcate* them in others? Who have been reminded when they inter'd office of "their *responsibility* for the *faithful* Discharge of the *duties annexed* to their appointment"? that the *honor reputation* & *usefulness* of their Lodge *materially* depend on the skill and assiduity with which they menage their concerns; whilst the *hapiness* of its members will be *generally promoted* in proportion to the zeal & abilities with which they *propagate* the genuine PRINCIPLES of the institution"? that it is their duty "*forcibly* to *impress* upon the members the *dignity* and *high importance* of *Masonry*, & *seriously* to *admonish* them *never* to *disgrace* it"? that their *hands* should be *guided* by *Justice* and their *Hearts expanded* by *benevolence*"? What *can* be said of those who have acted *contrary* to the principles they are *bound* to instil into others? as brethren We have to lament it, but sincerely hope, they will see their error and reform before it be too late. as Masons however it is our duty to warn you as our brother, of approaching danger and to solicit you to avoid it; to point out to you, that you stand upon the brink of a precipice—an other step and your fall is certain. the masonic edifice is supported by three pillars, viz, *wisdom, strength,* & *Beauty;* the Masonic *principles* and regulations are *framed* with such *Wisdom* that it is *impossible* for *any brother* to act *unmasonically* and *assail* the *beauty* & *harmony* of any part of the *masonic family* Without finding, when perhaps it is too late, that there is *strength* & *power* to *punish every brother* so offending, *more particularly after* a *friendly brotherly warning*—let us therefore *entreat* you to relinquish your *unmasonic* pursuits & to *save* yourself by authorising us to report to the G^{d} Council of S. P. of R. S. that you have *unequivocally* seen your *error* and have abandonned in the most solemn manner your *unmasonic* conduct; and thus *prevent* the *steps* which *must* be *pursued* against you; and the *consequences* which Must *inevitably* follow.

DOCUMENT F[252]

Thursday 23^{d} Augt 1821

Dear Brother

After reading attentively the inclosed paper we beg you will communicate its contents to such brethren as are associated with you for purpose connected with the Sublime degrees of masonry and we request your answer on Monday morning

We respectfully and fraternally—

signed TW B... JIW... P L...

to Br^{o} H. G. Street

252. Marked as Document F, an obvious mistake in copying. It was the letter accompanying Document D.

in reply to which the paper mark'd (**E**) was received whereby it appears that the members of that association had applied to Bro Dalcho for his advice.

DOCUMENT E

Charleston 27th August 1821

Dear Brother

Your Packet has been duly received, which my respect for you, Would lead me to notice had not the persons to whom you allude communicated their intentions to the revd Dr Dalcho by whose advice they purpose to be regulated, it is my earnest hope that every thing will be amicably setled in Brotherly love and friendship—

I remain dear sir yours fraternaly

Signed H. G. Street

Various reports having been communicated to your committee from different quarters stating at one time that the members of that unmasonic association were about to send an address to the Sov∴ Gd Council of P of R S. assuring them of their submission; giving up the manuscripts in their possession, which they had obtain'd in a manner far from legal & Masonic; & applying for admission agreably to the established rules of the order; at another that they were resolved to persevere; your committee thought it advisable to address a second letter to Mr H G Street (of which the paper is mark'd (**F**) is a copy) requesting of he had any further communication to make, he Would do it, on or before Friday (31st August) since, which time your committee have not heard from him

[DOCUMENT F][253]

Thursday 30 August 1821

Dear Brother

The committee of the G. C. of P. R. S. Who addressed you a few days since, being desirous of makeg their report to that body on Monday next, request that if you have any further written communication to make to them, than that received from you under the date of 27th inst, you will favour them with the same on or before tomorrow evening, addressed to Bro Bacot as their chairman

fraternally yours

Signed T. W B... J I W... P L... Commries

To Bro H G Street

Charles Tucker

253. This follows the document marked F.

It is proper to state that a paper corresponding precisely with that which was shown by Br° Dalcho to Br° Bacot, containing the oath and signatures of the 13 associates was torn up in the presence of a member of the G^d^ Council, by Mr Alex^d^ M^c^Donald on the evening of the interview with Br° Bacot, as stated in the paper marked (C)

> In an interview which Br° Wright had With Mr Laroach the letter authorized him (as one of the committee) to declare to the grand Council that he Would Withdraw his name from the association Which he intended to have done even if Br° Wright had not convinced him that the G^d^ council of Charleston Was a legal body, and that at their next meeting the associat. Would proceed to admit more members; Which he consider'd Would be a Violation of his obligation; which obligation altho' torn up, (as above stated) he still consider'd as Equally binding upon him.

Your committee begs leave to recommend that copies of this report & the document accompanying it be forwarded to the G^d^ Consistory of G^d^ Inspectors Generals of the 33^d^ Degree & Princes of the Royal Secrets, Supreme Chefs of exalted Masonry of the ancient Scotish Rite of Heredon for the United States of America sitting at New–york under the C∴C∴ at the central point answering to 40 Degrees 41 minutes North Latitude. That such steps may pursued as related to the persons implicated as the nature of the case may require

All of Which is respectfully submitted Charleston 21st September A L 5821 Signed Th. W. Bacot J I Wright P Laurens

On motion resolved that the thanks of the meeting be tendered to the committee for their able and indefatigable exertions and that he committee be discharged ***Resolved*** that the report of the committee be accepted

The President presented a letter which had been handed to him, sealed by Br. Alex^d^ Mc Donald and which being read is as follows

> To the Grand Council of Princes of the Royal Secret &^c^ &^c^—Charleston S. C. September 14, 1821—
>
> Brethren
>
> We the undersigned Brothers of the Masonic Fraternity, having in our possession the manuscript degrees of sublime masonry—feeling an anxious desire to retain those degrees among us, and prevent their circulating, beg leave, with all fraternal love and duty as Brothers to offer ourselves as candidates for initiation into your Grand Council of Princes of the Royal Secrets, and

to solicit your suffrages in our behalf.—As some false and malicious reports have been promulgated respecting our having formed an association for the purpose of receiving candidates and conferring on them said degrees; we think it necessary here to state, that such reports are unfounded and without the least shadow of TRUTH, in as much as our number has not increased from the period of our first meeting which was to take into Consideration, the manner of addressing you as regarded becoming members of your Council, but, which desirable object has been unhappily prevented by Circumstances, which we do not think proper or necessary, to advert to at present, as our sole motive is *Harmony, Peace* and *Goodwill* to all the Fraternity; and an anxious desire to become one and the same *Body*.

If therefore, the Grand Council, which we now have the honor to address, as Brother Masons, deem us worthy of a participation of the Rites and Mysteries of sublime Masonry, (being already acquainted with the Degrees) we shall acknowledge their concurrence with all due consideration, and hail, them with unity, strength & Harmony. We have the honor to be Brethren

Respectfully your Ob[t] servant

Signed H. G. Street, James W. Rouse, James Little, Rob[t] Carr, Alexander M[c] Donald, Joseph M[c]Cosh, Moses Holbrook, W[m] M. Dyer, Nath[l] Batchelder, Henry Cross, M. M[c] Kinsie.

Whereupon it was resolved That as the said letter applies for initiation direct into the G[d]. Council, of the several brethren whose names are thereunto subscribed, the same is informal, and the usual ceremony of reference to a Committee cannot be complied with, in as much as that neither of the applicants for initiation has obtained the indispensable, previous degrees of Rose X and until such step shall have been taken by them respectively, no application from either of the said brethren to this Body can be acted upon.

Resolved that the Secretary do inform them of the same....

Secretary's letter
to B[rs] Street & al.

25 September 1821

To Brothers A. B. C. & al. Your letter to G[d] Council of Sov. P. of Roy[l] Secrets praying for initiation therein was presented to that Body on Saturday evening, and I now enclose you copy of a resolution adopted by the Gd Council on reading the same and remain fraternally

Ch. S. Tucker Sec[y]

2.6 DEGREES 1802–1823

1815			
16 September		Past Master	Lodge
	4°	Secret Master	Lodge
	5°	Perfect Master	——
21 September	6°	Intimate Secretary	Lodge
	7°	Prevost & Judges	Lodge
28 September	8°	Super Intendant of the Building	Lodge
	9°	Knight of the nine Elect	Chapter
	10°	Elected Knight of 15	Chapter
	11°	12 Elected or Knight Elect	Chapter
5 October	12°	Gd∴ Master Architect	Lodge
	13°	Royal Arch	Colledge
12 October		"On Motion Resolved that the Sov^{g} Chapter of R∴ ✠∴ under the Title of Friends of Peace be Consecrated and Inaugurated on Monday next the 16th Instant."	
16 October		"this day being appointed to Inaugurate Consecrate and Installe the Sov^{g} Chapter of R∴ ✠ ..."	
23 November		"a Ballustre from Brother Fayolle a P^{ce} of R∴ ✠ having been read ... he was balloted for and unanimously Elected to be advance in all and every Degrees as far as this"	
24 November	19°	Gd Pontif	Lodge
	20°	Master ad vitam	Lodge
	21°	Patriarch Noachite Prussian Knight	Chapter
	22°	Prince of Libanus	Colledge
27 December	23°	Chief of the Tabernacle	Degree
	24°	Prince of the Tabernacle	Chapter
	25°	Knights of the Brazen Serpent	Chapter
	26°	Prince of Mercy	Chapter
	27°	Knight of the Sun	Council
1816			
27 March	28°	Knight of St Andrew	Chapter
	29°	Gd Commander of the Temple	Court
25 June	30°	Gd Knight Elect K∴H	Chapter
	31°	Gd Inquisitor	Tribunal
	32°	Prince of the Royal Secret	Sov Gd Council

TABLE 5. Degrees received by Pierre Fayolle in the Grand Council of Princes of the Royal Secret in Charleston

	4 Dec. 1802 CHARLESTON*	24 Nov. 1808 NEW YORK Gourgas†	1815–1816 CHARLESTON Pierre Fayolle	15 Nov. 1822 CHARLESTON H. G. Street‡	Summer 1823 CHARLESTON Joseph M'Cosh§
23°	Chief of the Tabernacle	Chief of the Tabernacle	Chief of the Tabernacle	Chief of the Tabernacle	Chief of the Tabernacle
24″	Prince of the Tabernacle	Prince of the Tabernacle	Prince of the Tabernacle	Prince of the Tabernacle	Prince of the Tabernacle
25°	Prince of Mercy	Knight of the Brazen Serpent	Knight of the Brazen Serpent	Prince of Mercy	Prince of Mercy
26°	Knight of the Brazen Serpent	Prince of Mercy	Prince of Mercy	Knight of the Brazen Serpent	Knight of the Brazen Serpent
27°	Commander of the Temple	Commander of the Temple	Knight of the Sun	Commander of the Temple	Commander of the Temple
28°	Knight of the Sun	Knight of the Sun††	Knight of St. Andrew	Knight of the Sun	Knight of the Sun
29°	K–H	K–H, or Knight of the White and Black Eagle†††	Grand Commander of the Temple	K–H	Knight of St. Andrew
30°	Prince of the Royal Secret, Princes of Masons**	Prince of the Royal Secret††††	Gd Knight Elect K∴H	Knight of St. Andrew	K–H
31°	Prince of the Royal Secret, Princes of Masons	Grand Inquisitor	Grand Inquisitor	Grand Inq. Commander	Grand Inq. Commander
32°	Prince of the Royal Secret, Princes of Masons**	Deputy Inspector General†††††	Prince of the Royal Secret	Sublime Prince of the Royal Secret,	Sublime Prince of the Royal Secret, Prince of Masons
33°	Sovereign Grand Inspectors General	Sovereign Grand Inspector General		Sovereign Grand Inspectors General	Sovereign Grand Inspectors General

TABLE 6. Names of the degrees from 23° to 33° – Charleston and New York 1802–1823[254]

* *Circular throughout the Two Hemispheres 1802* (facsimile Harris-Carter 1964, 319–25). **In the Appendix of Dalcho's *Oration* 1803, 79: 'Prince of the Royal Secret, Prince of Masons'.

† *NMJ* 1876, 20, 'Originally so written, afterwards amended in margin as follows: ††28.–Knight of St. Andrew; †††29.–Knight of the Sun; ††††30.–K–H, or Knight of the White and Black Eagle; †††††32.–Sublime Prince of the Royal Secret (*NMJ* 1876, 20).'

‡ APPENDIX 3.3. Facsimile Harris-Carter 1964, 142.

§ Reprint of the *Circular throughout the Two Hemispheres* in M'Cosh 1823, 19.

254. This TABLE should be compared with 'Early Scottish Rite Ritual Collection' (Arturo de Hoyos 2010, 34–39).

3. DOCUMENTS

3.1. Charter of the Council of Princes of Jerusalem. 9 February 1822

UNIVERSI TERRARUM ORBIS ARCHITECTONIS

PER DEUS	DEUS
GLORIAM	MEUMQUE
INGENTIS	JUS

ORDO AB CHAO

From the East of the Grand and Supreme Council of the Most Puissant Sovereigns, Grand Inspectors-General, under the Celestial Canopy of the Zenith which answers to the 32^{d} Degree 45 Min: North Latitude.
To all those whom these Letters shall come,

HEALTH, STABILITY & POWER

From the Chamber of the Supreme Grand Council of the 33^{d} Degree, duly established and congregated on the 17th day of the 11th Month called Shebat 5582, Anno Lucis 5826, and of the Christian Era the 9th day of February 1822.

— UNION, CONTENMENT & WISDOM —.

We, the Subscribers, having witnessed the ardour of our Valiant and Illustrious Brothers, Moses Holbrook, Horatio Gates Street, Alexander McDonald, Nathaniel Bachelder, Robert Carr, and Joseph McCosh, Knights of the East and Princes of Jerusalem, having scrupulously examined their lives, conduct and manners, and judged of their skill, capacity and zeal for the Most Excellent Order of Free Masonry – Reposing Special Trust and Confidence in their prudence and fidelity, have administered to them their Obligations, and do by these Presents, Constitute and Appoint them and their Successors, now and forever, a regular Council of Princes of Jerusalem, to be holden in the City of Charleston, State of South Carolina, investing Them with all the Titles,

Prerogatives, Powers, Privileges and immunities, which any where throughout the inhabited Globe, belong to such Council, of said Degree, hereby granting them full authority to assemble in the said City and legally initiate, make and perfect Free Masons in this and in all the previous degrees of the Order, and to do all other things which such Councils have a right to do, in any part of the World, according to the Laws and Constitutions of Free Masonry – and by this Instrument, we authorise and empower them to grant Charters or Warrants to any applicants legally qualified to hold Sublime Grand Lodges of Perfection in this or in any other State of this Union where there may not be one already established under this Jurisdiction of our Sovereign Grand Council agreeably to the Rules of the Order.

In testimony whereof, We have furnished them with this CHARTER, and signed the same with our own Hands, and affixed our Seals on the above named date and year, that full faith and credit may be given to all their Acts and Deeds, by all regularly constituted bodies throughout both Hemispheres.

James Moultrie
R.✕. K–H: P.·. R.·. S.
Sover:^{n} Gr: Inspec: Genl: of the 33^{d} Degree, and Acting Lieut Gr: Commander in the United States of America.

M. C. Levy
R.✕. K–H: P.·. R.·. S.
Sover:^{n} Gr:^{d} Inspec^{r} Genl of the 33^{d} Degree, and Treasurer Genl: of the Holy Empire in the United States of America

Isaac Auld
R.✕. K–H: P.·. R.·. S.
Sovereign Grand Inspector General of the 33^{d} Degree, and Acting Grand Commander In the United States of America

3.2 TWO LETTERS FROM MOSES HOLBROOK IN 1822[255]

His Excellency Daniel D Tompkins
Vice President of the United States
New York

255. My transcription from Xerox copies of both letters which Ms Gloria Jackson, *Assistant Librarian* of the *Museum of Our National Heritage* (Lexington), was kind enough to send me in September 1989. The first letter is not dated. Its transcription in *NMJ* 1866, 79, is preceded with: 'In March, 1822, the letter of which the following is a copy was addressed to ...' and at the end: 'Endorsed in the handwriting of J. J. J. Gourgas: "Spring of 1822"'. In *NMJ* 1876, 26, it is preceded with: 'The following letter was received in the Spring of 1822'.

To our thrice Illustrious Brother Daniel D Tompkins, R+ – K.H. P.R.S. Sovereign Grand Inspector General of the 33^{d} Degree and Grand Commander of the Northern District of the United States of America

Health Stability and Power

Illustrious Brother

Owing to the late war in which our Country was engaged, and the death of a Great many of its members, the Grand Council of Princes of Jerusalem and the grand lodge of Perfection for this State, ceased to exist. The Grand Council of the 33^{d} degree continued to flourish until the Death of our late illustrious Brother Colonel Mitchell who was known to you as Grand Commander. At his death Doctor Frederick Dalcho became G^{d}. Com^{r}; but he being influenced by certain members of an illegal body established here, by Joseph Cerneau, and Dewit Clinton refused to call his Council together, altho' they were never less than 3 Grand inspectors of said Council in this city at any one time. On the 9th day of February last, our illustrious Brethren Doctors Isaac Auld & Ja^{s} Moultrie, R:✕. K–H – P:R:S and Sovereign G^{d} Inspectors of the 33^{d} both officers in said Council, called on the said Fred^{k} Dalcho and requested him to open the Grand Council of So. G^{d}. In. Genl. of the 33^{d} degree which he refused to do, on which the aforesaid Brothers congregated and established a chapter of So. Princes of R: ✕, and a G^{d} Council of Princes of Jerusalem in this City, & gave a Charter to said Chapter and Council to Make and perfect Masons in the Sublime Degrees to the 18th Degree agreeably to the Constitutions.[256] The Grand consistory of of [*sic*] So. Ps: Rl: S^{t}: and Grand Council. of So. G^{d}. In. of the 33^{d} Degree will be opened in this City in the month of May by our illustrious Brother Isaac Auld acting Gr^{d} Commander, he at present being absent from the City.

We are in a prosperous way, and no doubt with your assistance and that of your grand Council, we shall be able to destroy in this section of the country, the influence of Mr Cerneau and his adherents, we have already put a stop to

256. The quote made by Lobingier began with 'The Grand Council of the 33^{d} degree' and ended here (Lobingier 1931, 124).

any more of the fraternity being taken in and duped by these impostors, and have been very active in exposing their illegality and also published the documents issued in 1814 by our late illustrious Brother De la Motta, one of which will be handed you by his son, who we understand is one of your Council. We solicit your fostering care, and trust you will ever be ready to Protect, and encourage the honorable proceedings of those whose wish is to add dignity to our Sublime Institution. As we have been regularly established, and chartered, we hope a communication will take place between the two Councils, and your attention to this will be gratefully acknowledged, to which we look with patience.

Illustrious Brother, we salute you by the sacred numbers.

James W. Rouse,
Moses Holbrook,
Committee of Correspondence.

The following is a list of Officers & Members of the G^{d} Lodge of Perfection:

Sublime G^{d} M^{r}	Moses Holbrook	MD
D^{y} S. G^{d} M.	H. G. Street	Merchant
S S G W	James W Rouse	Dep^{y} Comp^{t} General State S.C^{a}
J G^{d} W	Robert Carr	MD
G O & K of the S.	E. Gates	Teacher of Classics
G M of C	A Mc Donald	Merchant
G Sy	Jos McCosh	Merchant
G Tr	N Bachelder	D^{o}
C. G.	James Litle	Millwright
G Tyler	Wm Dyer	Late of the Army

Members

M. McKensie – Fr^{s} Rolando – Wm Wright – Jn La Roach – [Ed. Sebr]ing – Jno C Duke – Ja^{s} May – Jn Dawson – S M Hart – [Jno Ro]che – Henry Cohun – Jas Moon –

Direct to Doct. M. Holbrook
Broad Street
Charleston
S.C.

P.S. Our Illustrious Br Dr. De La Motta will be kind enough to make any explanations which may be required.

Charleston, S.C., 15th July 1822
To J. J. J. Gourgas Esqr

Respected Brother,

Doct. De La Motta desired me to write you individually upon the subject of the Higher Degrees of Freemasonry. In compliance with his desire, I forward you this by the hands of Mr Coleman who has this Spring been initiated to 18th or Rose Croix Degree in our Body. As he is a late made Brother, he is not probably so fully acquainted with all the items of the dispute which we have, for the present, silenced in this quarter. J. Cerneau's friend in this city – P. Javain – has been so in the contest and deserted by his party – as to quit his business (a grocery) and has gone on to N. York for some assistance in supporting his wanton attack upon us. All will remain at peace untill his return.[257]

We, under our Charter of 16th or P. of J. wrote your council to be acknowledged as such by you, as such acknowledgment would prove useful to us in maintaining the legal cause which we are engaged in. Doct. De La Motta promised to deliver the letter and make any explanations which might be acquired – we have received no answer yet – I should be happy to answer any inquiries, or give any information upon the subject – And I shall feel pleased if, Sir, you will individually (or if your Council have met, Officially) answer me upon the receipt of this by Mail – and give your opinion freely upon the subject – adding any observations and giving any hints which can be of any use to us, in this cause – we shall most cheerfully listen to any communications which you may be incli[ined] to make – a cooperation in this cause w[ould] be of very essential service to it.

I am requested to present Doct. De [La Motta our] best respects – he has departed for Savannah in good health.

I am with respect sincerely

257. From 'Cerneau's friend' to 'his return' quoted in Harris-Carter 1964, 139, without indication of a source and the last two words transcribed as 'he returns'.

Yours
M Holbrook
PS I have mislaid your address

Doct. M. Holbrook
Broad St.
Charleston

3.3. Horatio Gates Street's Patent, 15 November 1822

UNIVERSI TERRARUM ORBIS ARCHITECTONIS PER INGENTIS.

DEUS MEUMQUE JUS.

ORDO AB CHAO.

From the Grand East of the Supreme Council of the Most Puissant Sovereigns Grand Inspectors General of the thirty-third Degree, under the Celestial Canopy of the Zenith, which answers to the *thirty-second degree* and *forty-five minutes* North latitude.

To our Illustrious, Most Valiant, and Sublime Princes of the Royal Secret, Knights of K–H, Illustrious Princes and Knights, Grand, Ineffable, and Sublime Freemasons of all Degrees, ancient and modern, over the surface of the two hemispheres.

To all those to whom these Letters of Credence shall come,

HEALTH, STABILITY, AND POWER.

Know Ye, That we, the undersigned, Sovereign Grand Inspectors General, duly and lawfully established and congregated in Supreme Council of the Thirty-third Degree, have duly and carefully examined our Illustrious Brother Horatio Gates Street, in the several degrees which he has lawfully received; and at his especial request we do hereby certify, acknowledge, and proclaim our Illustrious Brother Horatio Gates Street, Merchant; citizen of the United States of America, residing in Charleston, South Carolina; to be an expert Master Mason and Past Master of a Symbolic Lodge; and also a Secret Master, Perfect Master, intimate Secretary, Provost and Judge,

Intendant of the Building, Elected of Nine, Illustrious Elected of Fifteen, Sublime Knight Elected, Grand Master Architect, Knight of the Royal Arch, and Grand Elect Perfect and Sublime Master.

We also certify him to be a Knight of the East or Sword, and Prince of Jerusalem; Knight of the East and West, Sovereign Prince of the Rose Croix de Heredon, Grand Pontiff, Master "*ad vitam*," Prussian Knight, Prince of Lebanon, Chief of the Tabernacle, Prince of the Tabernacle, Prince of Mercy, Knight of the Brazen Serpent, Commander of the Temple, Knight of the Sun, K—H, Knight of St. Andrew, Grand Inquiring Commander, Sublime Prince of the Royal Secret, **Sovereign Grand Inspector General, and Member of the Supreme Council of the Thirty-third Degree.** And we hereby authorize and empower FOR LIFE our said Illustrious Brother, Horatio Gates Street, to *Establish*, *Congregate*, *Superintend*, and *Inspect* all Lodges, Chapters, Councils, Colleges, and Consistories of the Royal and Military Order of Ancient Freemasonry over the surface of the two hemispheres, *agreeably to the Grand Constitutions.*

We therefore recommend all and every of our aforesaid Knights, Princes and Sublime Freemasons, to receive and acknowledge our said Illustrious Brother, Horatio Gates Street, to the highest degree in Freemasonry: and we will reciprocate the attentions shown him to those Brothers who may present themselves to our Supreme Council furnished with like lawful Letters of Credence.

To all which we the aforesaid Sovereign Grand Inspectors General and Members of the Supreme Council of the Thirty-third Degree for the United States of America, sitting in the City of Charleston, State of South-Carolina, and duly established the 31st of May, A.D. 1801, have hereunto subscribed our names and affixed upon the same the Grand Seals of the said Illustrious Order, in the Grand Council Chamber, near the B.B. under the C.C. this *Second* day of the *Ninth* month, called KISLIEU, and of the Restoration two thousand three hundred and fifty-*two*: in the year of the world five thousand eight hundred and twenty-*six*, answering to the Fifteenth day of *November*, in the year of our Lord one thousand eight hundred and twenty-*two*.

John Barker Grand
[*one and a half line illegible*]
K–H: S.P.R.S.
Sov: Gr: Inspector Genl

Joseph McCosh
K.-H S.P.R. S. [Sov.]
Grand Insp[ector] General of the
33d Deg[ree]

DEUS MEUMQUE JUS.

Isaac Auld M. D.
K–H: S.P.R.S.
Sov: Gr: Inspector Genl
of the 33d Degree, and Grand
Commander of the United States of
of N.A.

Moses Holbrook M. D.
K.H. S.P.R.S. Sov. G. Insp.
General of the 33d Degree and
Lieut: Grand Commander in the
U.S.A.

M. C. Levy K. H. S.P.R. S.
Sov Grand Inspec^r General of the
33^d Degree, and Treasurer
General of the Holy Empire

James Moultrie M: D:
K.H. S.P.R.S. and Sov^n G^d: Insp:
General of the 33^d Degree, and
[Secretary General of the Holy
Empire]

Alex^r Mc Donald K.H. S.P.R.S.
Sov. G. Insp. General of the 33^d
Degree

NOTE: *On the original, the signatures of John Barker and Joseph M'Cosh are set left and right of the last paragraph of the patent. I used the transcriptions made by Grand Commander Albert Pike in OB VIII, 745 and OB IX, 116 to fill the gaps of the facsimile, parts of which were cut off by the printers in 1964.*[258] *However in OB VIII, Pike set the name of John Barker without the text under his signature, and in OB IX he left his name out.*

3.4 *DOCUMENTS UPON SUBLIME FREE-MASONRY*, JOSEPH M'COSH (1823)
This small book has 104 pages. It opens with a five-pages introduction entitled 'To the Reader', dated at the end 'Charleston, June, 1823'.

[Pages iii–vii]

TO THE READER.

DEAR BROTHER,

HEARING much conversation upon the Sublime Degrees of Free-Masonry, and finding two parties in existence, one of which must be totally wrong, I have made it an object to embrace every opportunity of conversing with the well informed in these degrees, to obtain that information of which I was in pursuit. During the search, I have accumulated a vast bulk of letters, pamphlets, &c. upon the subject; and believing that a selection of them laid before the

258. Facsimile Harris-Carter 1964, 142.

public might be of essential service to the craft, in their search after the truth, I wrote a note to a friend more than a year since, for his opinion upon the subject. His advice was, "to defer it for the present, as there was a hope that matters would be all made up." I complied; but as the parties are now to appearance no nearer being reconciled, I have again written him, and I copy a portion of his answer below:

> "DEAR SIR AND BROTHER,
>
> "Your proposal to publish the papers you mention, containing a complete view of the subject in dispute, by inserting all the documents which have been published by both parties, partially meets my approbation. I beg you would not publish them all; better save such as I have marked for some future occasion; for they will be too voluminous.
>
> "The scarcity of the documents not marked, their want of durability in their present form, and the difficulty for any person to obtain them all at one time, and having a full view of the subject at once before him, will, in my opinion, authorize you to unite them in one volume; thus arranged, their usefulness must be apparent to every rational brother. But you must not calculate to please all; you cannot convince those of their error, who blindly follow names in opposition to truth; who endeavour to subvert the [iv] real principles of our most ancient institution; who, destitute of all nobleness of soul, will circulate falsehoods and substitute obstinacy in the place of benevolence; who show a disposition to overturn all the foundations of Free-Masonry, and, in their stead, fix disorder and misrule to support their intrusion, usurpation, and imposture; who esteem low cunning, concealment, and bitter calumny, superior to honesty, plain dealing, and fair reasoning; who prefer a silencing, inquisitorial spirit, to free discussion and friendly argument, together with all those pitiful beings, who, without any independence of mind of their own, will swallow such doctrines, and adhere to them. Such, my brother, are not to be moved from their errors, 'for they love darkness rather than light.'
>
> "But a higher necessity exists for publishing these documents; it is, a defence of TRUTH, which in your case, is SELF-DEFENCE. Upon this ground, your intruding upon the public, will be fully excused; but it is truly a subject of grief and pain of mind to expose those Masons who are ever ready to be called brothers whenever any office of profit or honour is to be obtained, who revile or praise the institution as best suits their own selfish purposes.
>
> "With me, you and every observing and unprejudiced brother, will notice with pity and concern, that the genuine spirit of Free-Masonry has, of late, severely suffered from false brethren; that its very foundations have been assailed by spurious pretenders, and an outrageous attempt made by usurpers to revolutionize its harmony; in sapping the vital supports of its organization, and setting at defiance all its valued rules of government.

"I would recommend to carefully observe dates on both sides of the question, as it will prove of great usefulness in the search after truth and I sincerely hope, may prove the means of instructing those who may be ignorant, if not too obstinately prejudiced; of animating the lukewarm friends of regularity; of reforming the irregular, and convincing them of the injustice they do the Craft, in censuring the only regular and legal body of Sublime Free-Masons which can exist, unless in correspondence with it; (a body which bas been established for more than forty years;) I say, in censuring them for doing their *duty*;—a duty which they owed to the God of all Truth, to the public, to their neighbours, and to themselves.

"Believing as I do, that the violation of fundamental principles, so long established and acted upon, and by the careful observance of which the institution has flourished for so many ages, will eventually overturn the fair fabric and bring ruin and confusion in its place, I would beg every brother to use his influence in guarding all the ancient Landmarks of the Order—it matters not of what degree; for if indulged in any one, the indulgence will soon creep into the others.

"You must not be surprised, if some brothers ridicule your work without ever reading it; some are so sensitive, that a breath alarms them; others so obstinate, that they will never examine."

After having extracted so largely from his friend's letter, the publisher will close with a few extracts from a pamphlet signed "*Truth and Justice*," and printed January 10th, 1810, by J. G. S. & Co. at Philadelphia.

This writer exposes many abuses and unmasonic acts in Joseph Cerneau's irregular bodies in New York city. He observes that honesty and good faith almost invariably lead just and upright men to think all other persons like themselves. But, alas, how sadly do they mistake! He warns and cautions all the fraternity not to be deluded into the irregular and spurious bodies, and recommends them previously to be well informed of the *regularity* of the body to which they would apply as well as of the *moral character* of the members who compose it.

He states that Joseph Cerneau upon his own individual authority, promulgated his R. C. Chapter, "Tripple Friendship" Oct. 28th, 1808, in New-York city, where in 1787, our Illustrious Brother Huet De Lachaille, had, with a proper authority, commenced to give the Sublime Degrees, and the brethren resident there had been recognized as correct by all the regular bodies of the same grade, Oct. 4th, 1804.

Joseph Cerneau, most probably soon saw, that the irregularity of his proceedings required some other authority than his own, and he drew up a petition, which he and two other brothers, (most probably of his own make,) signed and sent to the body in Barracoa, in the Island of Cuba, desiring constitutions for his spurious Chapter of Rose Croix.

This publication, (now thirteen years and more before the public, and uncontradicted,) states, "that the body at Barracoa, it is said, never acted on this strange petition. But that some time afterwards, Matthew Dupotet, and two other individuals, without any authority so to do, did fabricate and sign something which Joseph Cerneau and company call a patent. As this body at Barracoa was derivative [vi] from Jamaica, by the way of Cape Francois, it had no authority, even at the Cape, to establish other bodies; this pretended patent, therefore, could not authorize any other body, any more than one chartered Master-Mason's Lodge could charter another. Hence, Dupotet's power was no power at all. Nor was it conceived to grant any by Joseph Cerneau; for he thought it absolutely necessary to petition the illustrious body at Kilwinning, in Scotland, to either confirm Dupotet's authority, or to grant him an entirely new patent. On this occasion an attempt was made to interest a great personage in England to assist them in their irregularity. Their divers applications, however, remain to this day unanswered. He flattered himself that he could overturn in this way, the regular body of Rose Croix already established in New-York —wholly forgetting that when a Grand Lodge is once established in a state, or country, no new one can be established without its consent, unless by violating those principles which have been established for centuries, and are the very pivot upon which the whole institution revolves."

Joseph Cerneau did, in 1808, on the 10th day of the 4th month, at 11 o'clock, A. M. arbitrarily declare his Chapter of "Tripple Amitié" "to be without vigour and without function." (P. 5.)

As every creation of a new body procured J. Cerneau the sale of a new set of jewels, (he being a jeweller,) he, of his own authority, "*regularized brothers*," to use his own terms, as in the case of Torissant Mayday, who was expelled regularly from the Lodge at Cape Francois, in the Island of St. Domingo. He "*created brothers*" who were no Masons before, as in the case of John B. Subrannye, not to mention Entered-Apprentices that he advanced, to strengthen his party; so that by the year 1809, 21st February, he installed his new Rose Croix Chapter, Tripple Alliance, (pages 10–14.) For more information upon this subject, see De La Motta's Replication, in which all the dates of the public notices of his Scottish Heredon institutions were communicated.

Of J. C.'s masonic conduct in Havana de Cuba, we have many facts before us which would blacken any thing we have before communicated. His labours were concluded by his being expelled from the island by the governor, at the request of the fraternity who resided there. (P. 17.) The brotherhood will now be able to judge for themselves whether it is common in Free-Masonry for an arbitrary, avaricious individual to constitute himself Great Commander, make the bodies below him, and become both accuser and judge, in a country where all these bodies were years before regularly established.

"From these facts it plainly results, that all Joseph Cerneau's high councils and chapters, as he calls them, as well as all bodies emanating from, or chartered by him or them, or in any way deriving their authority from these usurpers, are unconstitutional, irregular, and spurious; and that all persons who have been, or may be admitted therein, are in an error, and can never present themselves to any regularly constituted body, without being previously reinstated." (P. 17, 18.)

"Magna est veritas et prevalebit."

Charleston, June, 1823.

Four Documents

'TO THE READER' is followed with:

Although these four documents are reprints, some of them have undergone alterations of a great importance. Besides M'Cosh added to the Report of the Grand Consistory many critical comments in footnotes. La Motta's Rejoinder ends with page 81. The next pages are transcribed below.

Pages 82–88

[82]

[The following attack was made upon the Editor as Secretary of the Sublime Grand Lodge of Perfection, and P. J. & Co. felt so unable to support their side of the contest against truth and legality, that they attempted to stop the press from inserting any more of his communications, by an interdiction of the officers of the Grand Lodge of South-Carolina.]

From the *Southern Patriot* of May 3, 1822.

To all whom it may concern, and the Craft in general.

THE subscriber has read, with extreme pain, various publications in the newspapers, and particularly one in Thursday evening's "Patriot," and Friday morning's "Courier," headed "*Lux E. Tenebris*," over the name of Joseph M'Cosh, Secretary.

The exclusive powers claimed in this last advertisement has compelled this public notice.

It is not proper to lay before the public, nor even the masonic family, in this way, the proceedings of the Sovereign Grand Consistory for the United States, sitting at N. York, as regards the improper acts and usurpation of authority by certain persons in this place, whilst her Grand Council for this State, duly and legally constituted, was existing and regularly working under charters thence derived. Pending the further deliberations, and until the final determination of the said Sovereign Grand Consistory at New-York, all correct masons may be satisfactorily informed, from the most full and indisputable documents, which are in possession of the subscriber, of the constitutionality and claim of the said Sovereign Grand Consistory to sole and exclusive sovereignty in the United States.

[83] A dissemination of such information may guard the unwary, and tend to prevent a reproduction of discord among the masonic family in this State.

P. JAVAIN,

Deputy Grand Inspector General, representing the Sovereign Grand Consistory of the United States, for the State of South-Carolina.*

*Like J. C. & Co. in New-York, from whom this illegal body emanated, they evince a total ignorance of the high degrees; here one styles, himself *"Deputy Grand Inspector General"*—most likely he obtained this title from some Old Certificate of a Brother made 25 or 30 years ago, for in 1786, the office was abolished in Europe, and in 1801 in this country. Also we lately saw that another styled himself *"President of the Sublime Lodge."* Now every Brother initiated regularly into the Sublime Degrees, well knows that there are no such offices in these Degrees. The reader will also observe from the expressions used, that their spurious mightinesses were attempting at New-York, something grand against a few Blue Masons. They seem to think lightly of their own names circulating (according to custom) in *Red Letters.* But "pending further deliberations and final determinations," we will follow truth wherever she may lead, nor shrink from the course she may pursue.

From the *Charleston Mercury* of May 6, 1822.

To all whom it may concern.

As silence might imply assent to the above notice of P. Javain, it seems proper for the accused, in self-defence, to inform "the Craft," that P. Javain, represents an illegal body of Masons in New-York, who have been regularly expelled as *imposters, usurpers* and *pretenders*, to a knowledge of degrees of which they are ignorant, and a power to confer such as they do know, contrary to the established rules of the order. Since February 1783, the degrees in question have been legally conferred in this city, by a power regularly emanating from Frederick of Prussia, who possessed [84] the sovereign power in Free-Masonry, from 1761, to 1st of May, 1786, when he delegated his high powers to a certain number of Grand Councils of Sov. Gr. Insp. Gen. who were to be initiated into a separate degree on that occasion, and were to continue *"for life,"* (except removed for improper conduct,) certain articles were established for their government and direction, called "the Grand Constitutions." By these they were empowered to meet whenever, and as often as they deemed fit. In all their patents and commissions were these remarkable words: "We authorize and empower you to establish, congregate and superintend and inspect Lodges, Chapters, &c. *agreeably to the Grand Constitutions!"* And by these Constitutions of 1st May, 1786, Deputy Inspectors General were restricted from acting.

In 1801, 31st May, a Supreme Council of Sov. Gr. Ins. Gen. was duly opened and established in this city, and its officers appointed " FOR LIFE; " four of whom are still living, and, agreeably to the *Grand Constitutions,* the Council cannot become extinct. Besides these four, there is in this country another Council of *seven* alive, who will succeed, if this Council should ever become extinct, but the last one of either Council possesses the power of renovating it at his pleasure.

P. Javain is the representative of a body created by one Joseph Cerneau, jeweller, who is first traced in this country, in "Longworth's Directory, 1809" with the letters G. I. G. P. S. G. C. attached to his name. By availing himself of the strong political divisions of the State of New-York at that time raging most furiously—a conduct directly opposite to every masonic principle; he strengthened himself so much as, by the spring of 1813, to burst from his secrecy, and publish to the world his famous "Tableau," by the very wording of which, he convinced every Mason initiated into these degrees, of his total ignorance of some of the highest which he pretended to communicate—nor has the angry representative of his expelled body yet learnt the titles of the degrees which he pretends to give, as plainly [85] appears by the wording of the above notice. After every exertion at an amicable adjustment had failed, the expulsions of Joseph Cerneau, *and all his abettors and followers,* was finally ratified 24th December, 1813, copies of which are left at the offices of the different newspapers, for the inspection of such as desire it.

The accused improve this opportunity to protest in the strongest terms possible, against dragging the concerns of the fraternity before the public, and should any contention arise among the Craft, they are blameless. P. Javain alone may thank himself for it. The accused resorted to every honourable expedient to avoid such a termination—and, but for P. Javain, all differences would have been amicably adjusted; yet he is only an *honorary* member of this body he is so strongly advocating on his individual responsibility.

"Ail correct Masons may be satisfactorily informed from the most full and indisputable documents which are in posssession [*sic*]" of the only regular body of Sublime Masons in South-Carolina, and which have been accumulating for these 40 years back, "of the constitutionality," and honest claims to sovereign authority, which invested the body who publish this reply to P. Javain's wanton attack. The unbiassed [*sic*] of the Masonic family are warmly invited to make the strictest investigation of all the circumstances connected with this subject, and they are asked, if any twenty or thirty Fellow-Crafts were to sign a charter to make Master Masons in some distant port, whether the Masons made under such Charter, would be legal; or whether they would not be denounced as impostors? But time will determine this question, and it is sincerely hoped, repair the breach that is now made in this fair fabric. No canting apology is made for the pain felt in this reply.

May the Grand Architect of the Universe, guide and direct all the Brotherhood, whether of high or low degree, in all their actions, and make them redound to his glory.

JOSEPH M'COSH, *Secretary.*

[86]

From the *Charleston Mercury* of May 7, 1822.

To all whom it may concern, and the Craft in General.

I HAVE already said that public journals are not the proper medium through which to make remarks respecting Masonic disputes, nor can they give either strength or credit to any *unmasonic* and *unauthorized* denunciations which they may convey to the public.

The only notice which it is necessary for me to take of the publication which appeared in yesterday's *Mercury*, over the name of Joseph M'Cosh, in reply to my Address *to the Members of the Craft*, in the Gazettes of this city, is again *earnestly* to invite *all Free Masons* of correct principles, to view the indisputable evidences in my possession, proving the constitutionality of the Sovereign Grand Consistory in New-York as above stated; which documents are opposed only by a *handbill*, the republication of which, I am authorized by a letter, bearing date first ult. to say, was not made with either the *knowledge* or the *approbation* of the *respectable* Brother whose name is used therein, to give a sanction to the proceedings of the persons associated with Joseph M'Cosh, which letter may also be seen on application to P. JAVAIN,

No. 187 King-street.*

*The "*Respectable Brother*" here alluded to was the Grand:Commander of the United States of America. The "*Representative*" has long been in the habit of writing and teazing this gentleman in his Official Capacity and thereby completely acknowledging him—and this very note of "*the 1st ultimo*" (I assert it from a gentleman who saw *the note*) was signed ****, "GRAND COMMANDER *of the United States.*"

> The "*indisputable documents*" are kept secret from others not of their kidney, and at the time of replying to the above, I did not know to what Peter Javain alluded. I have since understood their nature; two large trunks of papers were obtained from a widow lady, in rather a clandestine manner, containing correspondence, &c. by a person who had not the most distant right to them. These [87] papers have been palmed upon some persons, who did not look at *dates* and *outside directions*, and from them some shallow minds have been satisfied. *But this has not always been the case.* Observing Brothers have not been so easily duped, they have examined *both sides of the letters* shown them, and declare they were directed to "Col. John Mitchell, Gr. C. &c. &c. &c." [Some documents are on band upon this subject for which we have not room at present; they are of a piece with the rest of the history of this usurpation.]

[87]

From the Charleston Mercury of May 8, 1822.

To all the Masonic Family.

Brothers,

P. JAVAIN, No. 187 King-street, having completely admitted all the facts in my reply of the 6th inst. I sincerely hope this may be the last time I shall be obliged to wound your feelings in this public manner. In regard to his notice in the *Mercury* of yesterday morning, you all know that *truth* and *justice* will give "*strength* and credit to all *Masonic* and *authorized statements*."

To obtain the permission of an individual, to circulate what had been over *eight years* in circulation, seemed unnecessary, as the individual alluded to, repeatedly and most positively *refused* to take any part whatever in the subject at issue; and more especially as all the original letters relating thereto, in *the handwriting of the signers*, and the *sealed* expulsion itself, were carefully examined by myself and others before-hand; these documents were genuine.

How P. Javain's documents are "*indisputable*," which have been in continual dispute ever since they were made, is best known to him who has so long most carefully concealed them from the inspection of all those, who, from their knowledge of these degrees, are able to form an opinion of their genuineness. P. Javain's change of opinions [88] in speaking of the individual alluded to, is to be hailed as a presage of future good.

Finally, my Brothers, "*try all things, prove all things, and* HOLD FAST THAT WHICH IS GOOD." With respect,

JOSEPH M'COSH.*

*It has been a subject, Brethren, of serious regret to me, that a society so distinguished as is that of the Free Masons, for benevolence, charity and brotherly love, should be involved in such discord and diversity of opinion as could not be healed without an appeal to the public—that although we have endeavoured to produce a union of brethren so separated, our attempts have ail been frustrated—or this appeal would never have gone to the press.

I request every Brother to considerately and deliberately determine what motives may agitate his bosom at the time of his offering himself as a candidate for the higher degrees—are they *party feelings*? As a genuine Brother, discard them, I beseech you; go with pure motives, which ever way you go; and, upon convincing me that the other side is correct, I here publicly pledge my sacred honour, as a Man and a Mason, to peaceably and immediately *retrace my steps*, and *make every apology in my power, for the part I have taken.*

☞ The following observation, contained in Dr. Dalcho's Ahiman Rezon, p. 191, is "recommended to be adopted and used" by M. W. John S. Cogdell, G. M. and M. W. Thomas W. Bacot, P. G. M.: "Antiquity is dear to a Mason's heart. Innovation is treason, and saps the venerable fabric of the Order." *See Sanction to the second edition of the Ahiman Rezon.*

Pages 89–104 – The Appendix

[89]

APPENDIX,

CONTAINING A

HISTORY OF SOME OCCURRENCES

WHICH HAVE BEEN URGED AGAINST THE

Regular Lodge of Sublime Freemasons

In the City of Charleston;

BUT WHICH, IN REALITY, HAVE NO CONNEXION
WHATEVER WITH IT, AS THE FOLLOWING
PAGES WILL CLEARLY SHOW.

Page 89 of *Documents upon Sublime Free-Masonry*

[91]

APPENDIX, &c.

In the city of Charleston, whenever any one of the spurious usurpers speaks of the regular body of Sublime Freemasons, which was legally and publicly established A. D. 1783, he invariably calls it an "Association." Though this word carries no reproach in its common acceptation, as the Society is composed of nearly Seventy Brothers of correct habits and morals, all regularly initiated, properly acknowledged, and in full communion and correspondence with all regular Bodies of the same grade in all parts of the world, yet it rather shows a meanness and littleness of mind in the persons, who thus apply it. But *when dates are attended to*, it will clearly prove a desire to deceive, and to conceal facts, as well as a want of candour and veracity, which these impostors have never failed to exhibit; for the persons alluded to, were not (at the time they have chosen to speak of them) in any manner whatever connected with the regular Body of Sublime Masons. However, I will not prejudge the case, but proceed to state a concise history of transactions as they occurred; only premising that the threatening documents received by "*the eleven*," would of themselves make a large volume. [These documents are now in my possession and may be seen by any "Brother of correct principles."]

Early in the summer of the year 1821, several Blue Masons discovered, that many valuable Masonic papers were [92] scattered abroad in the hands of different persons. On reflection, they concluded that it would be an object of some importance to the cause of Freemasonry, which they had much at heart, to gather and unite them in one common collection. The attempt was made, and attended with almost complete success. Every Brother Master Mason, (none of lower degree being admitted) signed a solemn written agreement, "never to communicate to any person whatever, any information he might obtain from the manuscripts." (The original is before me, dated June 22, 1821.) To this instrument they invariably adhered—and so far was their number from increasing, though repeated intercessions were made for admission, that it actually decreased from, *twenty-eight* to ELEVEN, agreeably to a certain rule, which was adopted for their government. About the 20th of August, (for these usurpers did not affix any date,) a long string of "Resolutions" from some persons pretending to be S.P.R.S. evidently originating in false information of the meetings at the New-England Coffee House,[259] was communicated to "the eleven;" this was followed August 23d, 1821, by a huge folio letter of *seven pages*, large paper, and closely written, very officially communicated, and like the former, evidently founded in mistaken information, which to this day, they have obstinately refused to correct. This frightful communication accused "the eleven" of violating TRUTH, VIRTUE and JUSTICE. In a spirit of bitterness and domineering vengeance, they ungraciously assert that "the eleven" "*have violated every thing held dear and sacred* among Masons;" that their conduct "was *contrary to the principles of Justice and Morality, and calculated to destroy* ail the *social* and *moral virtues*." [93] They are several times, in this terrible letter, accused of "violating *truth*"—of "having forgotten the first principles of virtue, as well as their solemn obligations," and of "robbing "—aye, of "robbing!"—of "*striving to force from them by violence* (as was attempted with our D. G. M. of old) and by unmasonic means, what their sacred obligations bound them to preserve." They add: that "the eleven" "stand upon the brink of a precipice—another step and their fall is certain;" that if they do not give up every thing to these usurpers and acknowledge their fault "to save themselves from *certain destruction*," "they will find (when perhaps *too late*) that there is a *strength* and *power to punish* every offender." To avoid these empty threats, these *robbers*, these *liars*, these *assassins*, these *ruffians* (for these are the charming epithets which are implied in the above extracts from this uncharitable letter, "written," as they say, "in the spirit of" *their* "candour and" of *their* "brotherly love,") "these eleven" are finally informed "that they must unequivocally see their *error*, and abandon in the most *solemn manner* their unmasonic conduct, and thus prevent the steps which *must be pursued* against them, and the *consequences* which *must inevitably follow*." By this violent proceeding "the eleven" were deprived of using their own judgment, nor were they allowed to have any opinion of their own, or to reflect upon the best course to be pursued; but were at once held up as a "mark for the finger of scorn to point at;" and, as it were, already turned without the pale of the Masonic Family. The accusations it contained, were so *indefinitely* made that they could not be replied to, and the bitter threats which were strewed throughout the virulent mass of cowardly wrath and incivility [94], so overbearingly directed against eleven

259. See APPENDIX 1.4, Horatio Gates Street.

peaceful and quiet brothers of correct morals and domestic habits, aroused them to a consideration of the subject and taught them to examine for the cause of such uneasiness in these persons who pretended to such deference and demanded such respect.

These eleven individuals, respectable for their love of *order* and regularity, were at that time, entirely ignorant of the monstrous usurpation of authority and imposition, which was practised upon them by these spurious violators of all the rules and regularity of the order. They were, as other Brothers generally now are, wholly unacquainted with the History of Sublime Freemasonry, or of its establishment and progress in this country—nor were the means of obtaining this information then, so easily to be acquired; so uninstructed were they in the subject of dispute as not to know that there existed any connexion between this domineering body and Joseph Cerneau; or, in fact, that such a character as Joseph Cerneau was ever in existence: but perceiving that all the fundamental principles of Freemasonry were most grossly outraged in this last insulting communication, in which, "the eleven" were supposed to be entirely destitute of all the finer feelings of human nature—that a violent attempt was making to degrade, crush and expel them from all the privileges of an Institution which they so highly prized—they seriously engaged in an inquiry for the *truth* of the matter, for procuring which, they now felt the necessity of being in earnest.

Scarcely had they began the investigation, when they discovered that this threatening company was *spurious* and *illegal*—and that its secretary had acknowledged as much a [95] year or two previous, to ————. That it had recently stolen into existence, and had what it affected to call a Charter; but this pretended Charter was found to be signed by Joseph Cerneau & Co. who had been regularly expelled as "impostors and usurpers, Sept. 21st, 1813," for assuming and exercising powers and authority to which they had no right.

"The eleven" also learned that there still existed a regular body in this city, legally established A.D. 1783; that its authority emanated correctly from Frederick Wm: II. (more commonly called Frederick III.) of Prussia. To this latter and legal Body, they cheerfully surrendered all their papers, &c. &c. for inspection, and they applied to it to be regularly initiated.

Aug. 30th, 1821—they received another Communication from the Committee of the spurious—and as honest, upright Brothers, having no reasons for concealment, they openly informed the committee of impostors of their purpose. But as the vengeance of the intruders was about to fall heavily on one, whom the usurpers could seriously injure, and deprive of his living, "the eleven" withdrew their application and patiently waited the event of the storm that was gathering.

Sept. 10th, 1821, a chief of the spurious and illegal sent for one of "the eleven" and entreated him to use his best endeavours to heal the wounds which would be likely to ensue in the Masonic family, and begged him to use his influence with the Brothers at the New-England Coffee House to sign an application to his body, and they should be received. The Brother stating some objections to this plan, the Spurious Chief concluded his intercession with the following [96] pathetic appeal to his feelings: "Will you not do it," (that is, exert his influence to have "the eleven" apply to him;) "will you not do it for my sake—for the sake of Masonry will you not do it?" The Brother informed "the eleven" of the proposition which had been made to him, and the promise annexed to it.

Upon mature deliberation "the eleven" concluded, that after being received, it would be lawful for them to retire again, should the documents of the spurious, upon a careful inspection, be found illegal; and as it was then, and is still believed, that in ail disagreements *gentlemen can make propositions which gentlemen can receive without any derogation from principles of honour or urbanity*, "the eleven," on the 14th of September, 1821, consented, (to use the words of the application,) "for the sake of HARMONY, PEACE and GOOD-WILL, and an anxious desire of healing ail difficulties in the craft." Further, in their letter of application, these individuals, in reply to the repeated assertions in writing and in common conversation of the illegal pretenders, use these words: "as some false and malicious reports have been promulgated respecting our having formed an 'Association' for the purpose of receiving candidates and conferring on them said" [Sublime] " Degrees, we think it necessary here to state, that such reports are unfounded and without the least *shadow* of TRUTH, inasmuch as our number has *not increased* from the period of our first meeting." This letter was signed by "eleven" individuals—and they were all, who, *at that date*, had any right, title or claim to Masonic papers of any kind, or who in any way belonged to the meetings at the New-England Coffee House. This application was handed [97] "*unsealed*" [M'Cosh's foot-note: We challenge an investigation upon this point. They officially say it was "*sealed*"—which is positively denied.] to the Chief, as they call him, at whose earnest solicitation it had been made; nor did "the eleven" ask this as a gratuity; they proffered a handsome remuneration or fee at their reception.

Sept. 22d, 1821—This illegal body "Resolved, that the application was informal and could not be referred to a Committee." This resolution however held out the expectation that a modification of the letter would be acceptable, and in their conversations, they made great protestations of friendship, and told the pleasure it would give them to prevent any disturbance, and to quiet ail uneasy feelings whereupon "the eleven" being real friends to *order*, *peace*, and HARMONY, and firmly opposed to all *irregularity* and *misrule*, did, on the 25th of Sept. 1821, (the date of the official copy of their Secretary is incorrect,) agree to, and did sign another letter of application, worded just as P. J.[260] their "Representative" desired; he having first most solemnly pledged his sacred honour to prove the strict legality of his body, and the incorrectness of the other, (But, Brothers, this yet remains an unredeemed pledge, and, from the preceding documents of this book, it must ever remain unredeemed.) This letter was the same day handed to one who claimed to be a Chief among the Spurious, and while this application was in the possession of these pretended "Friends of Peace, sitting in the valley of Charleston;" you would, Brothers, have never imagined the perfidy of these usurpers! while this letter was in their hands unacted upon, an earnest attempt was made by them [98] to have a petition signed for the Grand Lodge of this State to expel these eleven Blue Masons from the Masonic Family. Here was deceit and treachery superior to that of Virgil's Sinon:—their object apparently was to gratify their ill-humoured spleen upon eleven peaceful Brothers, whose only crime was, that they dared to think for themselves, and who evidently showed an inclination to disbelieve such things as were not true, without any regard to the standing of the person who might utter them—certainly the effect was to injure them every way in their power, even after having solicited them to adopt the course they did. But probably to redeem the pledge of "*their regularity*" which they had so often and so positively given, was found to be impossible with Brothers, who they knew would *look on both sides of letters* that might be shown them;

260. Read Peter Javain.

and as the only alternative in a narrow and vindictive mind, the easiest way was to *crush* those whom in fair reasoning, they had no arguments to *convince*. But many whose signatures were applied for to this petition, had too much honour and nobleness of soul to lend their aid in support of these overbearing usurpers; hence the sorrowful paper with some signatures, was never presented to the Grand Lodge—and some of its signers have confessed that they were imposed upon, and asked pardon for ever having listened to the deceivers on a subject that would so deeply affect any Brother's welfare.

After the usurpers had held four or five meetings and admitted such as members of their "Friends of Peace," as would vote to reject the application, Nov. 9th 1821, this spurious body, (to use their own words,) "resolved to notify" ["the eleven"] "that their application was informal," [99] "and to inform them" how they might again apply. Perhaps the candid reader has already seen enough of their duplicity—but the author will only add one more instance, reserving several for a future occasion. Br.* * * * *, was every way entitled to be elected master of Lodge No. – but as he had shown some independence of mind in refusing to assent to all their plans—the spurious desired "to put him down;" to accomplish this, as they had made many Brothers believe that "the eleven" were monsters, they about this time, got a committee of his Lodge to wait upon their pretended mightinesses to examine papers, of the correctness of which they even now say they were incompetent to decide. The impostors *forged the name of this Brother*, upon a list with "the eleven," and made the blue committee believe he was guilty of—what? of thinking their pretended body usurpers. What the views or opinions of this respectable Brother, are, or have been, are entirely unknown to "the eleven," as he never was in any way associated with them in the subject of this history.

One of "the eleven," unconscious of the existence of any irregular body of Sublime Freemasons, had previously made an application to the usurpers, and they refused to notice his application, "as he was too young a Mason"—he having been only initiated during the last war; at the same time they had two who were younger, in their illegal body, and they have since admitted one young man who had not been raised to a Blue Master more than about three weeks when they received him. So much for the consistency of Impostors.

Nov. 11th 1821—"The eleven" met at the New-England Coffee House, and after reading the communications [100] of the spurious which have been alluded to, and these being under consideration, but more particularly the resolves in reply to the solicited applications and promised admission which had been made in the utmost good faith and in a respectful manner by "the eleven," it was "*Resolved*, That after waiting with much patience and anxiety from Sept. 14th 1821, to Nov. 10th 1821, during which time the illegal body had had seven or more meetings—during which time others had applied and been admitted by them, that the conduct of the pretenders must inevitably be considered as an equivocation, not compatible with their solicitations, nor consonant with the deportment of one Freemason to another; more particularly, 'the eleven' protest against their low artifice to obtain the names of the persons who had met at the New-England Coffee House, with a view to their expulsion,—therefore, unanimously resolved, never to have any thing further to do with these ungenerous usurpers."

A part of "the eleven" once more applied to the regular Supreme Council, which had been founded in 1783, (the Grand Commander having withdrawn from the Council during the present disturbance, from the nature of his vocation, and having desired to have no voice either directly or indirectly in the transactions which might ensue, desired not to be consulted in any respect about the business;) the Supreme Council correctly organized under the next officer, was in possession of all the requisite documents—and happily for the cause of Freemasonry, he, and the remaining members of the Council were not within the reach of the "tender mercies" of their revengeful charity.

[101] The legal Council proceeded to a consideration of the subject which by this time had obtained some adventitious importance: scarcely had they engaged in the discussion, when, like Virgil's harpies, the illegal body attempted to stop their progress by professing a great desire for harmony, and for healing all difficulties and removing every obstacle to a complete union of all parties, and about the last of Nov. 1821, begging the Council to defer all further consideration of the subject for a few days, and naming the coming Christmas (1821) as ample time to accomplish this project. This proposition was readily acceded to. But on the 9th January 1822, a further time of ten days or a fortnight was interceded for to complete their arrangements. As the object was important, this further delay was also granted. Saturday 9th Feb. 1822, all postponements agreed on having completely expired, the Supreme Council determined to be trifled with no longer, and proceeded to commence

the initiation of six of "the eleven," and at different meetings from that date until Christmas 1822 these six received S. P. R. S. with all the lower degrees.

The author now ingenuously appeals to the candid reader, whether in all this history of "the eleven," there was any threats or unmasonic conduct? If the spurious neglected to convince them of their errors, the fault was on the side of those who overflowing with *sensibility*, boasted so much greater light and knowledge; and "the eleven" confidently believe that when all their conduct is put together and impartially considered, that there will remain nothing uncivil, impolite, or wanting in the honourable conduct of gentlemen.

[102] To be particular he has necessarily been somewhat prolix, but he will hazard one observation more before he concludes—that, the repeated intercessions of the illegal, to have the initiation of "six" out of "the eleven" deferred so often, was completely acknowledging in strong terms the legality of the Council to which they applied.

The candid reader will easily discover that, this particular and minute statement of facts, *has no connexion whatever with the regular body* of sublime Freemasons into which a part of "the eleven" have been since initiated—nor can the candour or veracity of that brother be very great, who will hazard the assertion that it has any such connexion. Freemasonry rests on TRUTH, who violates that principle, sap the very base and foundation of the ancient institution. Should seventy worthy Brothers regularly initiated (many of whom are venerable for their age as well as their morals,) be reviled for the actions of six? —of six young men, who at the time of these so much boasted applications were quiet, uninitiated individuals? Shall usurpers in their spleen dictate to a legally constituted body whom it shall admit to membership? Each generous bosom answers—no.

As a vindication of the regular body who admitted such of "the eleven" as applied for initiation, and the *self-defence* of those admitted, have caused this appendix; the unprejudiced reader who will allow to others even a portion of the same honourable feelings which govern himself, will readily excuse in the preceding history any expression which may seem, at first sight, harsh and uncharitable—more particularly when he reflects that those who have [103] for several years broken through every established rule of the order and are expelled from it, are no longer entitled to claim an interchange of those endearing civilities, which are ever accorded in charity to a brother in error when Dot expelled. Nor can those who transgress expect that deference and respect which is due only to the regularly initiated whatever may be their standing in society. Though slighted, censured, *betrayed*, "the eleven" ever demeaned themselves quietly, modestly and with perfect good faith throughout the whole transaction; nor with anger do they view the gross violation of honour practised upon them but they pity and compassionate the deluded victims of one unacquainted with our language, and a stranger to our shores.

From honourable feeling for transgressors, and generous motives, this publication has been delayed until delay has been by some deemed a crime, and by a few others construed into an acquiescence in the authority of the usurpers. But never will they "while breath they draw," cease to reply and defend themselves, and the Regular Body with whom they have been incorporated. At the same time, they remember, (it cannot be easily forgotten) that these impostors once attempted to "gag" the press—I say *these impostors*, for it is believed that on this occasion all besides the impostors, were opposed to such a tyrannic proceeding; the time here alluded to, was about 10th May, 1822, when a notice was served upon the printers in whose papers these impostors had attacked the author, to prevent their publishing any reply in self-defence. Thank God my native state was not so far involved in the rudeness of the dark ages, as to listen to such cowardly despotism—as to [104] allow an attack in a public newspaper and forbid an answer to it. Generous men, my brothers, will never be governed by malice, deceit or arbitrary authority; and to preserve unsullied a good name and reputation, becomes to every gentleman, an object too sacred to suffer blight or mildew from despotic power to overcloud it, or to permit even the attempt to pass unanswered.

"May the blessing of Heaven rest upon us and all *regular* Freemasons." Amen.

P. S. Ail the Regular Bodies of Sublime Freemasons will, as is customary, be steadily supplied with the usual RED LISTS of the irregular and expelled; and they ere long may expect another publication upon this subject.

Note to Page 23. The word *"last"* in Br. De La Motta's expulsion, upon which the usurpers have built so much of their reply, is not in the original in his own handwriting, which is now before the Editor; but he did not conceive himself at liberty to correct the error of the printer.

FINIS.

3.5 Letter from PGM John Cogdell to 'The Grand Lodge of France', 21 November 1823

To the Most Worshipful Grand Lodge of France holding its Communications in Paris.[261]

Respected Brethren,

Although this Communication has become indispensible, it is nonetheless extremely painful because the occasions from there has occurred some interruption to that good order and charitable feeling – which the Craft have through all ages boasted themselves peculiarly distinguished for.

In the Course of the last Summer, a Pamphlet over the signature of Bro: Joseph McCosh and printed by Bro: C. C. Sebring at Charleston was circulated – and subsequently two letters, one purporting to have been printed in Charleston, the other at New York and circulated thro the Post Office.

The Pamphlet had induced an appeal on the Part of the Past Grand Master Bro. Thomas Wright Bacot and myself to the Grand Lodge against the conduct of the Brethren whose names you will find in the Printed Extracts from the Minutes of the Grand Lodge.

________But it is with pleasure I inform you, all the difficulties and all the differences have been masonically healed; superseding the necessity of further pursuing the appeal before the Grand Lodge, the same with all matters connected with it & the Pamphlet have been expunged from the Minutes, as you will perceive by the printed document which I have the honor now to transmit to your Most Worshipful Grand Lodge with a hope that your Body and your subordinate Lodges, may, by an extension of this information have all unfavorable Opinions & prejudices removed.

With the most sincere Wishes, for the happiness and prosperity of your Body & the Individuals composing the numerous Lodges under your Jurisdiction

I remain Dr Brethren

Yours fraternally

261. Grand Master Cogdell did not know that there was no Grand Lodge in France at that time but a Grand Orient. This letter was inserted in an original copy of the Proceedings of a Special Communication of the Grand Lodge of Ancient Free-Masons of South-Carolina held in Charleston on Friday Evening, the 31st of October, 5823, which I found at the Bibliothèque Nationale in Paris (FM^2 560).

John S. Cogdell
Grand Master
G. L. A. F. M.

South Carolina, Charleston

21st November 5823

3.6 Two Letters from Moses Holbrook to Joseph Gourgas in 1826[262]

[Private and confidential.]

Charleston, 31st May, 1826.

Most Ill. Brother:

Your esteemed favor of 18th instant is received and I hasten to return you my unfeigned thanks for it; the just and highly correct views of the different important objects of which it treats meet my cordial approbation and demand a speedy reply. With regard "to printing," your views are really Masonic. The only case in which I thought a reply ever suited, was at a time when everything was at stake. I was no higher than Rose ✝ and was presiding over the 14th Degree, when McCosh was openly attacked as Secretary—threatened with expulsion from Masonry in all the newspapers of the City. Mr. T. W. Bacot, an old and rich man—Postmaster—John G. Cogdell, naval officer of the port, and two or three lawyers of high standing, were on the Cerneau side of the question and openly advocating Cerneau's deputy in this City. Peter Javain—who put his name to the misstatement in all the city papers. We were said to be everything but honest men. I replied respectfully to the Craft through the same channel that the poison had been communicated. The statement of facts obliged them to make a second attempt with worse success, for the short reply which succeeded their second overture could not be answered. For these acts of *self-defence* I was arraigned before the Grand Lodge of the State, and after five meetings Mr. Cogdell and Mr. Bacot, my accusers, at the fifth meeting obtained a majority to try me and to punish me. Before the business proceeded any farther I set up for office, and I and my friends obtained it by a good majority, and so the business dropped forever, and Messrs. Bacot

262. *OB* X, 180–82 & 182–84.

and Cogdell offered terms for a treaty of peace and friendship, which were accepted—the treaty ratified by the Grand Lodge.

Peter Javain's attack and the statement of facts have set public opinion right in this vicinity. I believe no ordinary occasion should ever be used to reply and never to attack at any *time for the strong reasons you have given.*

The day after Col. Mitchell died Mr. T. Bacot sent a servant for all his Masonic papers, he being Grand Master at the time of the Gr. Lodge of the State. She imprudently gave him, she says, two large trunks full of papers. Peter Javain says the note (see the "documents") is a lie; it was only one big trunk full and a big basket full of papers. It was the vast correspondence formerly carried on by this Supreme Council, the minutes and the charters of the different Sublime Bodies; hence came the bulk of papers. With regard to the "auction," the Secretary of the 14th or 16th Degree died, and his things were sold, for rent due; among them a few things were seen belonging to the Sublime Lodge. His wife's father, Col. Rouse bought them in. Col. R. is not a Mason, but he kept them safely until the great fire 1818, when his house, being in immediate danger, was stripped of all the movables, but eventually saved. Col. R. has never seen any of these things since. I believe they, however, soon adorned P. Javain's Sublime Lodge room. I have by accident seen some pieces of the furniture that answer the description of some of the older members. I know of no other *auction* where any things were ever sold that belonged to the Sublime Body. Of the seals, a merchant named Porter was the keeper; he died; and his partner, named Cassin, administered upon his effects and estate, and soon after died, when Conly Cassin,[263] the other Cassin's nephew, administered upon his estate.

Conly Cassin, to obtain some cash immediately, gave the set of silver seals, which had come into his hands in the manner above mentioned, as a collateral pledge for the sixty or seventy dollars which he borrowed of Thos. W. Bacot—who continues to keep them to this day—the Supreme Council was not incorporated at that day and could not at that time come in for them—the Body had a much better set of seals—but stealing or detaining a set of seals from a body can certainly never destroy the body. Bro. Col. Mitchell, De la

263. Junior Grand Deacon of the AYM Grand Lodge in May 1817 and a Past Master of Lodge No. 13 in 1823 (*PRO* 1824, 24).

Motta and L. Harby Alexander died about this time—Doctr. Dalcho was at the Cape of Good Hope, Doct. Auld on Edisto Island, about 70 miles from the city, where he resides—so that you see that a concurrence of circumstances allowed Cerneau to make headway at the time he did. They were not able to obtain a set of manuscripts. Those belonging to Doctr. Dalcho, Doct. Auld and to the Body were in the hands of our late Brother De la Motta. They have been sold to a brother by Jacob De la Motta for a considerable sum of money—so the body lost these. Col. Mitchell's came into my hands and then to Doct. Auld's possession, and are now used by us. By the way, you have granted De la Motta his resignation from your S. Council. I think he would do better anywhere else than here. I have not full confidence in the man, and since be sold the property which was never his father's, and never pays nor never did pay anything to the support of the Order, and probably nothing for any of his Sublime Degrees, I cannot think him a useful member of the Society. The committee are drawing up a reply to your official communication, which ere long will be forwarded. Doct. Dalcho has laid aside the lancet and put on the canonical robe. He preaches in St. Michael's Church.

With haste, myself your friend,

M. HOLBROOK.

To J. J. J. Gourgas, Esq'r.

[Private and confidential.]

Charleston, August 18th, 1826.

M. Ill. Br∴

Your esteemed favor of 7 instant was duly received this morning. Without any feelings but those of gratitude and respect, I hasten to reply to it.

To give you a better idea of the proceedings of the Grand Lodge, which were very voluminous: J. T. [*sic*] Cogdell was Grand Master of the Grand Lodge of the State and the presiding officer of the spurious 32d of Cerneau in this City; T. W. Bacot was a Past Gr. Master of the Gr. L. and a past presiding officer of Cerneau's Body. These two ordered an extra call of the G. L. of the State, and read a long memorial about the pamphlet called "Documents upon Sublime Free-Masonry," of which I had the honor to forward a copy to yourself in 1823. It accused Joseph McCosh of editing, C. C. Sebring of printing, and Br. Moses Holbrook "of offering it to be openly sold to the community at a public bookstore, (perhaps from which pamphlet were read by him, (M. H.,) with the view deeply to injure them, the Gr. Master and Past Gr. Master, as *Masons* as well as citizens in a community among whom they were *born* and *reared* and have been thus far *respected*." There was the head and front of our offending. No copy of the "Documents" was ever offered for sale. A bookseller from N. Y. borrowed a copy in confidence over Sunday. He was so pleased with it that he showed it; hence came the trouble, and we were put upon trial for expulsion under this sweeping charge, no point of which was true. Five meetings of the Grand Lodge were held, and the result was that Bacot and Cogdell were left out of office in the Grand Lodge with their adherents. Jacob De La Motta allowed his father's trunk to be ransacked for the pamphlet which we published, and then "turned tail to" or opposed us. Of course we could not feel very cordial towards him, particularly when he sold everything he could find in his father's trunk, and then wanted to borrow to copy again to sell his copies. Dr. De La Motta moved from Savannah to Charleston in 1823, and on 26th May was admitted a member of our Sublime Lodge of Perfection, (14th.) We were anxious to get the papers out of his hands, and we concluded we had gained our point, for, unsolicited, he made the following motion on the same meeting, (26 May): "Whereas the MSS. of our Sub. Degr. have, through neglect or inadvertency, fallen into improper hands, therefore, to correct the evil and to confine the secrets of our Order to proper hands, *Resolved*, that it be obligatory hereafter on every member having degrees or manuscripts to deposit them in the archives of this Sub. Gr. Lodge." When he found that the members readily agreed to his resolution he amended his own motion by adding "subject to his removal when about leave the State, or to his inspection, as may be requisite." Within three days every member except De La Motta complied—he never did—for the next 11 eleven meetings he never came but once. On the 10th Aug., 1823, was the election of officers. I declined being a candidate for re-election, intending to assist in placing our worthy friend McDonald in the chair. After much conversation I was unanimously re-elected. McDonald would not run for it—(as I afterwards learnt,) because De La Motta expected he should have it ail hollow, and we would not run against him—De La M. had visited twice only—and wanted the 1st office—we admitted him a member without any fee through courtesy as one of your S. Council of 33d—old members of the S. L. were 2d & 3d officers. De La M. was elected Gr. Orator; "he objected to accept, saying that by attending to that duty it would interfere with the avocations of his profession—and that he resigned as a member of this S. Gr. Lodge, which we accepted"—he never offered to pay his arrears—"his professional avocations" are nothing worth mentioning. The Hebrew Lodge No. 9 have made him an honorary member of their Blue Lodge. You thus see "what situation he holds among the brethren of *the South*."

Dr. La M's interview with you was to obtain the "*big Tuilleur*" to copy from. I should be glad to hear something of that work. I have asked my friend, John Barker, S. G. I. G. of the 33d in this city, to call on you and converse about it.

I doubt whether Doct. Dalcho ever received your book or letter. I should not think it strange if among De La M. books it might be still found. In the "appendix" to the documents, page 95, in the paragraph beginning with "Aug. 30th, 1821," about the middle of it—"But as the vengeance of the intruders was now about to fall," &c., alluded to Doctor Dalcho; also page 100, the latter paragraph in the parenthesis, he is again spoken of. Isaac Auld, M. D., of Edisto, was then Lieutenant G. C., and acted. The Duke of Leinster is at the head of the 33d in Ireland. Thomas Fowler, Esq., Record Tower, Dublin, Ireland, is Lieut. G. C., and used to correspond here for near 20 yrs. I fear he is dead. His last letter to me was dated 28th May, 1825. However, I daily expect letters by the Decatur from Ireland. Should any information arise I will with pleasure communicate it to you. I am not able to give you the address of any other S. Council— not even of France. Several of our Sublime Free-Masons are now in Europe and will endeavour to obtain some information, but they can get but little.

On the 18th of next month, the Gen. Gr. Enct. of Templars meet in your City. With much exertion for 10 years part, I have raised the order to a high standing in this State. I have been placed at the head of the State Gr. Enct, for South Carolina, and by their partiality nominated as a candidate for one of the four first officers in that high Body. Now, Jo. Cerneau's men are very busy to counteract it. For the same reason I wish the friends to the regular Sublime might advocate it as far as is honorable and correct. Perhaps some friend of yours may have a vote and would not be biassed [*sic*] by such business. All the

Templars entitled to any high office in the Gen. G. Enct. from this State are our way of thinking and Sublime Masons.

With respect and esteem, I close, hoping soon to hear from you again.

Yours sincerely,

MOSES HOLBROOK

3.7 Mackey's Version (1861)[264]

But in 1820 Col. John Mitchell died,[265] leaving a widow in very destitute circumstances. Pressed by the urgent claims of poverty, she parted with the manuscript rituals of the higher degrees, which she found among the papers of her deceased husband, who was, at the time of his death, the Grand Commander of the Supreme Council, to thirteen Masons, no one of whom had proceeded beyond the Royal Arch of the York Rite. These brethren, thoughtless, we must charitably believe, at first, of the violation of Masonic honor which they were committing, united themselves in an association for the purpose of availing themselves of the instructions in Masonry which these manuscripts might afford. The spurious Consistory, hearing of these proceedings attempted to influence the "associators," as they were called, to what they supposed would be a better course, and, in 1821, sought to induce them to surrender the papers and to make application to the Consistory for regular initiation. To this they consented, but as several obstacles arose from constitutional difficulties, and as they were assured in the meantime that the Consistory was not regular, they determined to withdraw their application. The fact that Dr. Dalcho had, when the question was proposed to him, candidly acknowledged the illegality of the Consistory,[266] although he at the same time declared that he intended to take no part in the pending difficulty, caused him, involuntarily, to become mixed up with these troubles, for it was supposed by the Consistory that the influence and advice of Dr. Dalcho alone, kept the associators from surrendering the manuscripts and applying for admission into their body.

In consequence of this a long, and in many respects an unpleasant correspondence, took place between Messrs T. W. Bacot and Jno. S. Cogdell on the

264. Mackey 1861, 175–76.

265. Mackey had already written on page 174 'After the death of Col. Mitchell in 1820. . . .'

266. For the fourth time within a few lines Mackey terms the Charleston Grand Council a Consistory.

one part, and Dr. Dalcho on the other. Mortified at the estrangement of feeling which seemed on the point of being engendered by this Masonic dispute, between himself and two old friends, who were bound to him also by the close tie of membership in the Church of which he was the assistant Minister, Dr. Dalcho withdrew from the Supreme Council, having peremptorily refused to heal the associators. As soon as he had retired, Dr. Isaac Auld, the next officer of the Supreme Council, and who then constitutionally succeeded to the prerogatives of the Grand Commander, having no such delicate relations with Bros. Bacot and Cogdell, proceeded to legalize the associators, and, on the 9th of February, 1822, conferred on six of them the degree of Sublime Prince of the Royal Secret. This act does not, however, appear to have revived the ill feeling in the Grand Lodge. But in May, 1822, P. Javain, a leading member of the Cerneau Consistory, having denounced the new Consistory which had been formed by the Supreme Council, through the public Gazettes, a brief newspaper war took place between the two parties, which ended in the publication by Joseph McCosh, one of the "associators," in June, 1823, of a pamphlet of 140 pages,[267] with the following title: "Documents upon Sublime Freemasonry in the United States of America; being a collection of all the official documents which have appeared on both sides of the question, with Notes and an Appendix. By Joseph McCosh."

I have more than once attentively perused this work, and impartiality compels me to confess, that while the text contains a true history of the original differences between the Supreme Council at Charleston, and the irregular Consistory of Cerneau, entirely unobjectionable in its character, and principally consisting of the republication of old documents, yet the notes and appendix, which were the production of McCosh, are often couched in offensive language, well calculated to irritate the feelings of those whom he attacked. I have in my possession the copy which appears originally to have belonged to Brother Bacot. It is filled with marginal notes and comments in pen and pencil, which clearly show that an angry, and, of course, an unmasonic feeling existed between both parties.

Irritated at the language used in this pamphlet, and the accusations of perfidy and error with which they were charged, Brothers Bacot and Cogdell

267. *Recte*: 104 pages.

appealed to the Grand Lodge for protection. Here, however, the fraternal services of Dr. Dalcho were again called into requisition, and at a special Communication of the Grand Lodge, which was holden on the 31st of October, 1823, a solemn declaration was read, which had been obtained by the Grand Chaplain, and which was signed by Joseph McCosh, C. C. Sebring, and Moses Holbrook, the persons particularly named in the appeal of Brothers Cogdell and Bacot.

CHRONOLOGIES

The First Years of the Supreme Council for the United States of America

1801

—15 June. New members, Emanuel De La Motta,[268] Abraham Alexander and Thomas Bartholomew Bowen, likely elected on the same day.

—5 July.[269] The Grand Council of Princes of Jerusalem[270] issues a Warrant[271] signed by fifteen 'officers and Princes' – five of which, Mitchell, T. B. Bowen, La Motta, Abraham Alexander and Dalcho, added to their names 'Sovereign Grand Inspector General of the 33d'— to nine of his own members

> to open a Master Mason's Lodge and to form and constitute a Grand Elect Perfect and Sublime Lodge of Perfect Masons, to initiate Brethren into the Superior degrees as far as the Sublime degree of Perfection inclusive.

On the same day, it issued a Constitution in twelve articles[272] for that body.

—11 July. The 'Rules and Bye-Laws of the Sublime Grand Lodge of South Carolina', 26 articles, are 'Done and ratified in Open Lodge'.[273]

—23 Sept. Frederick Dalcho, 'Member of the Supreme Council of the 33d. Degree, and Grand Orator of the Sublime Lodge of Perfection', delivers

> an *Oration* … in the Sublime Grand Lodge, in Charleston, South Carolina, … before the members of that Lodge, the Symbolic Grand

268. Mitchell's and Dalcho's letter to La Motta, 23 August 1813 (Harris-Carter 1964, 119).

269. '5 July 1801 or twenty fourth day of Thamuz of the year 5561'. Both dates are equivalent in the Jewish and the Gregorian Calendars.

270. This Grand Council was opened in Charleston on 20 February 1788. Its Bye-Laws and Regulations were ratified in Charleston on 12 May 1788 (*OB* VIII, 731–33). They were printed in 1824 by C. C. Sebring in Charleston according to an endorsement by Grand Commander Holbrook (*OB* VII, 315). KW 56.

271. Dalcho's Register document 6, *OB* VIII, 721–22.

272. Dalcho's Register document 7, *OB* VIII, 722–24.

273. Dalcho's Register document 13, *OB* VIII, 733–38. No signatures. Endorsement made by Moses Holbrook when he sent it to Giles Fonda Yates in Schenectady, 4 October 1824 (*OB* VII, 315).

> Lodge of Ancient York Masons, and the Officers of the several Lodges in the City;

He dedicated it (among others) to 'Colonel John Mitchell, Sublime Grand Master [of the Sublime Grand Lodge of Perfection of South Carolina], and President of the Supreme Council of Masons in the United States'.[274] The Oration was printed in Charleston by T. B. Bowen.

—1 Nov. The Sublime Masons of Savannah, Georgia, invite Emanuel De La Motta, *as* a member of the Supreme Council in Charleston, to attend their meeting that evening.

—10 Nov. James Philip Puglia, Sovereign Prince of the Royal Secret & Inspector General, endorses in Charleston the patent delivered by John Mitchell to Frederick Dalcho on 24 May 1801 (Dalcho's Register document 4).

—25 Nov. James Philip Puglia, Sovereign Prince of the Royal Secret & Inspector General, endorses in Charleston the patent delivered by Barend Moses Spitzer to John Mitchell on 2 April 1795 (Dalcho's Register document 3).

1802

—21 Jan. The Grand Council of Princes of Jerusalem issues a Warrant[275] to sundry Brethren enabling them

> to establish a Lodge of Mark Masonry, to be known and distinguished by the name of the American Eagle Mark Lodge No. 1. And Whereas the Symbolical Grand Lodge of Ancient York Masons in this State does not acknowledge the extension of Masonry beyond the three first degrees,[276] whereby the Petitioners could not address their prayer to that body.

274. Dalcho 1801. Mentioned in Leblanc de Marconnay, Paris 1852, 10 & 23–24, and in the translation by Laffon de Ladébat, New Orleans 1853, 12 & 29, both with the wrong date 5802 instead of 5801.

275. Dalcho's Register document 8, *OB* VIII, 725–26. It is dated 'twenty-first day of the month called Shebat which answers to the twenty-first day of January ... of the Christian Æra 1802'. 21 January 1802 corresponds to 18 Shebat 5562. This is an example of the 'code cocktail' which I called the simplified Jewish code, likely invented by Grasse-Tilly (Bernheim 1986, 28–30).

276. An important remark.

> The Grand Council ... do deem it expedient to grant the prayers of the petitioners.[277]

The Warrant named the Reverend William Best[278] as Master, Emanuel De la Motta as Senior Warden and Isaac Auld as Junior Warden of that Lodge.

—1 Feb. Frederick Dalcho, De Grasse and others visit Lodge *La Candeur*.[279]

—16 Feb. John Mitchell certifies the copy of the patent he received from Barend Moses Spitzer on 2 April 1795.[280] De Grasse certifies the copy of the patent he received from Hyman Long, dated 12 December 1796.[281]

—21 Feb. Letters of Credence are delivered to Grasse-Tilly,[282] signed by seven Sovereign Inspectors General. They show Isaac Auld[283] and Israel de Lieben as new members of the Supreme Council. An undated list which stays in Grasse-Tilly's *Livre d'or* (Golden Book or Register) in the handwriting of Dalcho shows Auld and de Lieben as 6th and 7th members, and Grasse-Tilly and Delahogue as 8th and 9th members of the Supreme Council.[284]

— 15 March. De Grasse certifies the copy of the patent delivered to him on 21 February 1802.[285]

—18 March. Letters of Credence delivered to Pierre Dupont Delorme as Prince of the Royal Secret, signed by Grasse-Tilly and Delahogue,

277. This Warrant was returned and a new one issued on 27 February 1803 with De La Motta as Grand Overseer or Master, Dalcho as Senior Warden and Solomon Harby as Junior Warden (Mackey 1861, 498). A 'Mark Lodge' appears in the Charleston *Register* of the Grand Council of Princes of the Royal Secret in August 1821 with Horatio Gates Street as 'President'.

278. Then Senior Grand Warden of the AYM Grand Lodge and successor of Seth Paine who died of yellow fever in October 1801 (http://www.joycetice.com/families/painefreem.htm).

279. Lobingier 1931, 11.

280. Dalcho's Register document 3.

281. Dalcho's Register document 1, *OB* VIII, 711–13.

282. Dalcho's Register document 9, *OB* VIII, 726–27.

283. Auld was elected to the Supreme Council on 10 January 1802 according to a Memorandum made by Horatio Gates Street in 1822 (*OB* VII, 313).

284. Harris-Carter 1964, 94, with the wrong legend 'Page of the Register of Frederick Dalcho'. See Grasse-Tilly 2003, 112.

285. Dalcho's Register document 9, *OB* VIII, 726–27.

members of the Supreme Council of the 33rd degree at the Grand Orient of Cap Français.[286]

—20 & 23 March. Pierre Dupont Delorme certifies his patents dated 10 December 1797 and 18 March 1802.[287]

—9 May & 3 Aug.[288] Moses Clava Levy and Dr. James Moultrie are listed as 8th and 9th members of the Supreme Council in the *Annual Register* issued in Charleston in 1802.[289]

—10 Oct. 'At a meeting of Sovereign Grand Inspectors General in Supreme Council, of the 33d. degree,' a committee of three is appointed to make a *Report*, explanatory of the origin and nature of the Sublime Degrees of Masonry, and their establishment in South-Carolina. It is approved on 4 December by the Supreme Council.

1803

—1 Jan. The *Report* is dispatched under the title *Circular throughout the two Hemispheres* together with a separate Circular[290] signed by John Mitchell 'K.H.—P.R.S. Sovereign Grand Inspector General of the 33d, and Grand Commander in the United States of America'.

—21 March. Dalcho delivers a second Oration in Charleston. He is then 'Inspector General, and Grand Master of the Sublime Grand Lodge of South Carolina' and Worshipful Master of Lodge No. 8.[291] His *Oration* is printed in Charleston together with 'An Appendix[292] Containing an historical inquiry into the origin of the difference

286. Dalcho's Register document 10, *OB* VIII, 728–29.

287. Dalcho's Register documents 10 and 11 (both in French), *OB* VIII, 728–30. Document 11 is dated 10 December 1797 accompanied with a fantasy date in the Jewish chronology (10th day of the 10th month called Thebeth, year 5557 of the restoration), similar to that noticed above in note 275, at the Orient answering 18° 45' which is Port-au-Prince. It certifies that Pierre Dupont Delorme has been initiated 'Patriarch Noachite, Sovereign Knight of the Sun and of K.H. Deputy Grand Inspector General'. It was delivered and signed by Aveilhé. Grasse-Tilly, Delahogue, Dalcho and Auld likely added their signatures and respective titles when the copy of the patent was certified at Charleston by Dupont Delorme.

288. Both dates from the list made by Horatio Gates Street in 1822 (*OB* VII, 313).

289. Facsimile in Harris-Carter 1964, 315–16.

290. Facsimile in Harris-Carter 1964, 106, described as sent to the Grand Master of New Hampshire (*ibid.*, 101) accompanied with the wrong legend 'Mitchell Circular on Masonic Unity'.

291. Dalcho 1803, cover page and 44.

292. Dalcho mentioned the Appendix in his letter to La Motta, 23 August 1813 (Harris-Carter 1964, 118).

of Ancient and Modern Masons, usually so called; &c. &c.' In the 'Advertisement', page vi, Dalcho wrote:

> In the Circular Report of the Inspectors [the *Circular throughout the Two Hemispheres*], which is reprinted in the Appendix, some errors are corrected which escaped observation at the time it was published.

The reprint added several foot-notes to the *Circular*, one of which[293] includes the text of articles 9 to 12 of 'the Grand Constitution of the 33d. degree, or Supreme Council of Grand Inspectors General'. This was the first dated appearance in a printed work of part of that Constitution. The wording of the four articles is identical with the Dalcho's manuscript copy reproduced in Harris-Carter 1964, pp. 342–43.

1804

—29 July. The Supreme Council delivers a patent to Delahogue 'K.H. – P.R.S. Sovereign Grand Inspector General of the 33rd degree & Lieutenant Grand Commander in the French West Indies'. It is signed by Mitchell, Dalcho and La Motta; it authorizes Delahogue to establish, 'under the authority and protection of this Supreme Council, in the City of New Orleans in the Louisiana Territory, the several Lodges, Chapters and Councils … as far as the 18th [degree] inclusive, called the Chapter of Sovereign Princes of Heroden'.[294]

THE GRAND COUNCIL OF PRINCES OF THE ROYAL SECRET CHARLESTON 1815–1823

1815

—17 Aug. Creation of the Grand Council

—16 Oct. Chapter RX inaugurated

293. Pages 73–74 of the original Charleston edition, page 63 of the 1808 Dublin reprint.

294. Dalcho's Register document 14, *OB* VIII, 738–39. It is the last document of the Dalcho Register (communication from Ill. De Hoyos, 22 August 1998). The patent reads 'From the East … which answers to 32° 45' North Latitude', that is Charleston. According to the *City Gazette*, Dalcho was away from Charleston at that time (Harris 1959, 25). Also *TSJ* 1868, 18–19, and *Memoranda* Gourgas, *NMJ* 1876, 40.

1817

—26 Dec. Creation of the Grand Lodge of Ancient Free-Masons of South Carolina

1821

—17 May Death of Emanuel La Motta
—22 June Several Blue Masons gather – many valuable Masonic papers scattered abroad in the hands of different persons – twenty-eight sign an agreement never to communicate information obtain'd from the manuscripts
—17 Aug. Grand Council Meeting – Cogdell's list of thirteen – Books in their possession belonged to John Mitchell – Committee named
—18 Aug. Date of copy Rouse on book 2 of Mitchell's rituals
—20 Aug. Committee meets Street at the New England Coffee House – Street acknowledges that there was an association of persons of which he was the head, associated for the purpose of reading over the Degrees in Sublime Masonry of which they had obtained manuscript copies which belonged to the late Commander Mitchell
—21 Aug Three of the Eleven ask for Dalcho's advice
—23 Aug Two conversations Bacot Dalcho who spoke with Holbrook – Letter of seven pages
—27 Aug. Answer from Street – Three of the Eleven visit Bacot
—30 Aug. Committee's letter to Street
—10 Sept. Conversation of the 'Spurious Chef' with one of the Eleven
—14 Sept. McDonald's letter to the Gd Council – Consent of the Eleven
—21 Sept. Bacot's Report – McDonald's letter considered informal
—25 Sept. Second letter of application – Attempt to have them expelled?
—11 Nov. The Eleven meet at New England Coffee House
—28 Nov. The Association's compact – Report sent to Grand Consistory in New York
—last Nov. Delay until Xmas
—19 Dec. New York Report
—28 Dec. Several letters from Javain to New York, later one with Dalcho's suggestion

1822

—9 Jan. Request for further delay

—9 Feb. Dalcho refuses to open the Supreme Council – Auld & Moultrie charter a Council of Princes of Jerusalem –'at different meetings until Christmas 1822 six of the Eleven received SPRS with all the lower degrees'

—21 Feb. *Southern Patriot* – Sublime Grand Lodge, Documents La Motta

—26 Feb. Reading of New York's communication – Committee about the *Southern Patriot* and Sublime Grand Lodge's meeting

—28 Feb. Javain's letter with Dalcho's suggestion read in New York

—11 March Letter of Charleston to New York – Auld has formed a Lodge of Perfection

—26 March Letter from 11 March read in New York

—Spring Letter Rouse & Holbrook to Grand Commander Tompkins in New York brought by Jacob De La Motta with list of twenty-two members of the Grand Lodge of Perfection

—29 March Letter Javain to Dalcho

—1 April Answer Dalcho to Javain

—26 April Those persons who have been advertising in the newspapers are the same that have found the manuscripts of old Colonel Mitchell – Letters Javain to Dalcho

—3–8 May Charleston's newspapers – Letter signed * * * *, Grand Commander of the United States

—10 May Notice served upon the printers

—15 July Letter Holbrook to Gourgas

—15–17 Nov Street, Holbrook, McDonald and M'Cosh 33°

—24 Dec. Letter from New York – Delay

1823

—16 Jan. New Committee of the New York Consistory for Charleston

—19 Feb. Report of New York about Dalcho's proposal

—13 May Jacob De La Motta active member?

—June Date p. vii of M'Cosh's book

—14 July Javain's resignation letter read in New York

—15 Aug. Bacot receives M'Cosh's book

—22 Aug. Cogdell brings M'Cosh's book to the Grand Council – Petition to the Grand Lodge next Friday
—24–28 Aug. Javain's letters to New York with M'Cosh's book
—27 Aug. Opening of the Charleston Encampment – Holbrook M'Cosh
—3 Sept. Circular of the Encampment
—? 'I was arraigned before the Grand Lodge and after five meetings Mr. Cogdell and Mr. Bacot, my accusers, at the fifth meeting obtained a majority to try me and to punish me.' (Holbrook to Gourgas 31 May 1826)
—18 Oct. Demits Bacot and Cogdell
—28 Oct. Agreement M'Cosh, C. C. Sebring, Holbrook, Cogdell, Bacot
—31 Oct. Special Communication of Grand Lodge – Reading of two letters from Dalcho, one with the agreement, the other with his resignation – 'Messrs. Bacot and Cogdell offered terms for a treaty of peace and friendship, which were accepted' (Holbrook to Gourgas 31 May 1826)
—21 Nov. Letter Cogdell to the 'Grand Lodge of France'
—5 Dec. Grand Annual Communication of Grand Lodge – Letter from GM Cogdell
—19 Dec. Quarterly Communication – Resolution Sebring conc. Dalcho's resignation – Grand Master Cogdell reads his report
—20 Dec. Incorporation of Supreme Council (read in New York 10 April 1824)
—26 Dec. Adjourned Grand Lodge – Letters from Bacot and Javain withdrawing as members of the Grand Lodge

1824 and Afterwards

— Grand Lodge —295

Moses Holbrook
—19 Dec. 1823. Elected Corresponding Grand Secretary
—17 Dec. 1824–17 Dec. 1830. Elected Grand Treasurer

295. Quoted from the original Grand Lodge Proceedings except for the year 1833.

Alexander McDonald

—27 Dec. 1823 & 27 Dec. 1824. Appointed Senior Grand Deacon
—16 Dec 1825. Elected Junior Grand Warden
—15 Dec- 1826. Elected Senior Grand Warden
—14 Dec. 1827–14 Dec. 1833. Elected Corresponding Gd Secretary

> 'On 20 December 1833, Bro. A. McDonald, who had been elected Corresponding Grand Secretary, having refused to serve, an election was held to fill the vacancy'.[296]

Horatio Gates Street

—27 Dec. 1823–27 Dec. 1828. Appointed Senior Grand Deacon
—16 Dec. 1831 & 14 Dec. 1832. Elected Junior Grand Warden
—28 June 1833. 'The only transaction worthy of record that occurred at this Communication, was the resignation of Bro. H. G. Street, Junior Grand Warden, in consequence of his intended removal from the State, and the acceptance by the Grand Lodge of that resignation'.[297]

C. C. Sebring

—27 Dec. 1824–16 Dec. 1825 Appointed Grand Marshall
—27 Dec. 1826 C. C. Sebring attended as Grand Marshall for the last time, his brother Edward was appointed to that office in his place.[298]

Frederick Dalcho

—27 Dec. 1826, 1827, 1830, & 1831 Grand Lodge went in a procession to St. Michael's Church where prayers were offered up by the Most Rev. Past Grand Chaplain, Brother F. Dalcho.

T. W. Bacot

—After June 1824. T. W. Bacot attended most Gr. Lodge meetings in Charleston.

296. Mackey 1861,240.
297. Mackey 1861, 238.
298. C. C. Sebring certified the genuineness of Cross's 33d patent on 8 August 1851 in New York (Folger 1862, end of Document No. 85).

—30 March 1827. T. W. Bacot and McDonald became members of a committee of five concerned with the purchase of a lot and the building of a hall for Grand Lodge; however on 29 June, Bacot declined acting 'as it would be incompatible with the office he holds in the Masonic Hall Company' and Moses Holbrook 'was appointed to fill the vacancy'.

—27 Dec. 1827. T. W. Bacot installed Bro. F. Hunt as Grand Master.

—27 Dec. 1834. An eulogium was read for PGM T. W. Bacot who died on 2 October.

— GRAND COUNCIL —

—4 Dec. 1824. At a Special meeting of the Grand Council, a letter sent by Grand Commander Cerneau to Javain was read.[299] Cerneau had promised to Ill. Brother Lafayette and his son to let Javain know that both have been elevated to the 33d in his New York Supreme Council and added:

> he is instructed of the abominable Conduct of our ennemies in Charleston, he has requested me to write to you (to prevent he should fall in their snare) so that as soon as he should arrive in your City, you should present your self to him in your quality of Representative of our Sov^{n} Grand Council & Consistory ... he has even asked me a Letter of Introduction near our representative in order to not be exposed to be deceived by the others &.[300]

The Council moved that a committee consisting of T. W. Bacot and six others members be appointed 'in conjunction with the Chapter of R.·. +.·.' concerning the Ill.·. Brother Lafayette. T. W. Bacot attended the next meeting on 24 February 1825 and accepted to be a member of the committee to which John Cogdell's name was added.

—March 1825. We know what happened next through two extracts of the *Charleston Courier*[301]:

299. The letter was in French, the Council's Minutes reproduce its translation which I quote below.

300. Grand Consistory Minutes on 22 September 1824 (folio 121).

301. Transcribed in *TSJ* 1878, 10–11. The first extract was not reproduced either in Lobingier 1931, 140, or in Harris-Carter 1964, 158. Both quoted only the beginning of the second one up to the words 'for this purpose'. La Fayette arrived in South Carolina on 6 March. 'On the 16th he was waited on by deputations from South Carolina Encampment No. 1, of Knights Templar, of Charleston, and LaFayette Encampment, of Georgetown. He received the Knights in the Hall of St. Andrew's Society, where quarters had been furnished him by the City Council, and invited them

A delegation from the Council of Sublime Masons in this city holding in authority from the Sovereign Grand Consistory for the United States, &c., at New York, where the Illustrious Brother La Fayette lately received the highest Degree of Masonry, waited upon him on Tuesday last, when Brother T. W. Bacot, M. W. Past Gd. M., Past Prest. So. Re. S. & Insp. Gl. 33d Degree, acting as Chairman, addressed him as follows:

Most Illustrious Brother, we present ourselves before you as a deputation from the Council of Sublime Masons of this city, deriving its authority from the Sovereign Grand Consistory of Grand Inspectors General of the 33d Degree for the United States of America and its dependencies, holding its sitting in the Grand East of New York. We have it in charge from the body we represent to tender to you their heartfelt congratulations, and to offer you a most affectionate welcome: also, to show you that we feel proud to recognize as a brother one whom the world holds as a patriot and philanthropist. Our body feels peculiarly happy that when in New York you received the degree of Sublime Masonry from our parent Grand Consistory. We rejoice in everything that draws closer the ties which unite us to the companion-in-arms and the friend of our Washington, of whom Masonry is justly proud. We have only to express to you our sincerest wishes that the evening of your life may be as unclouded as its morn and meridian have been splendid and useful. Should it comport with your arrangements, it would be peculiarly grateful to us to receive a visit from you at such time as may best suit your convenience.

To which the most Illustrious Brother made a brief but affectionate reply, expressing particular gratification. at receiving this mark of respect from his Brethren, and assured the delegation of his pleasure in recognizing them as Brethren of the same Masonic Family, but regretted that his numerous engagements would leave him no time to meet them in council.

To the Enlightened of Every Degree:

The Supreme Council of the 33d Degree of the United States of America, located in Charleston, having passed a resolution on the 16th day of September, 1824, that on the arrival of their Illustrious Brother, General La Fayette, in this city, they would, as a mark of the

to au audience in his private room, where Dr. Moses Holbrook, the Grand Commander, and the other Templars, were introduced by the Rev. Cheever Felch, of the United States Navy. and was received (Mackey 1861, 197; Singleton 1898, 1374). On that occasion C. C. Sebring 'delivered an eloquent address of welcome' (Lobingier 1931, 152).

> respect they entertain for his virtues, and gratitude for his services to this country during the Revolutionary War, offer to confer on him the thirty-third, together with all the appendant degrees; but finding that his stay in this city would be too short to admit of it, they did not convene for this purpose; it is, therefore, not without astonishment and regret that they perceive, by an address published in the Courier of this morning, that a body of men in New York, who have been regularly expelled from ail intercourse with Sublime Masons throughout the world, and the expulsion widely published in both hemispheres, should have so far forgot the decency and respect they ought to entertain for so good and great a man, as to represent themselves to him as legal Sublime Masons. But however great an honor it may be to anybody to call the General a member, it cannot in this case alter facts. The General may have been imposed upon; but his presence cannot convert a spurious and illegal body into a regular and genuine one.
>
> A FRIEND TO TRUTH.

It seems hardly necessary to suggest that the second extract originated with Joseph M'Cosh whose style is recognizable.[302]

— *T*HE SUPREME COUNCIL —

—1822–1830. Few documents dated in this period show who were the Grand Commanders of the Supreme Council.

Frederick Dalcho

—13 Aug.–14 March 1830. On all documents reproduced in facsimile signed by Dalcho in this period, he always set after his name "Past Grand Commander in the U.S.A."[303]

Isaac Auld

He appears to have signed only two documents:

—9 Feb. 1822. Acting Grand Commander in the United States of America[304]

302. Which Mackey chose not to recognize: 'The visit of the spurious Consistory gave offence to many Masons, and public notice was taken of it in the newspapers in very harsh terms by some anonymous writer' (Mackey 1861, 198).

303. Harris-Carter 1964, 150, 178, 200 and 202

304. Harris-Carter 1964, 140 facsimile.

—15 Nov. 1822. Grand Commander of the United States of N. A.[305]

Moses Holbrook
—15 Nov. 1822. Lieut. Grand Commander in the U. S. A.[306]
—20 Dec. 1823, Lieut. Grand Commander.[307]
—24 June 1824. Grand Commander in the United States of America[308]
—13 Aug. 1824, Lieutenant Grand Commander in the United States of America[309]
—20 Oct. 1824. Grand Commander pro tempore[310]
—16 Feb. 1825. Lieutenant Grand Commander and Grand Commander pro tempore[311]
—May 1825. Lieut. Gr Commander in the U.S. of A.[312]
—21 Jan. 1827. Grand Commander in the S.J. of the U.S.A.[313]

BIBLIOGRAPHY

ABBREVIATIONS

KW Document number in Walgren 1994.

NMJ 1866 *Proceedings of the Supreme Council of Sovereign Grand Inspectors General ... for the Northern Masonic Jurisdiction* ... Volume VI. Boston: Press of the Freemasons Magazine.

NMJ 1876 *Proceedings of the Supreme Council of Sov∴ Gr∴ Inspectors General 33°, for the Northern Masonic Jurisdiction. Gourgas Body, 1813–1851. Raymond Body, 1851–1860. Van Rensselaer Body, 1860–1862.* Portland: Stephen Berry, Printer. 1876.

305. Harris-Carter 1964, 142 facsimile & *OB* VIII/745.
306. Harris-Carter 1964, 142 facsimile & *OB* VIII/745.
307. Harris-Carter 1964, 147.
308. Folger 1862 119 & Folger Document No. 85. On 17 November 1865 Grand Commander Pike declared this patent 'apocryphal' (*TSJ* 1878, 317) but admitted his mistake in 1890 (*OB* X, 295).
309. Harris-Carter 1964, 150.
310. Lobingier 1931, 141.
311. Harris-Carter 1964, 158.
312. Harris-Carter 1964, 160.
313. Harris-Carter 1964, 175. This seems to be the last official document signed by Holbrook before he departed in 1843 from Charleston for Florida where he died on 1 December 1844.

OB *Official Bulletin of the Supreme Council of the 33d Degree for the Southern Jurisdiction of the United States*. Volumes I to X were issued between May 1870 and June 1892.

PRO *Abstract of the Proceedings of the Grand Lodge of Ancient Free-Masons of South-Carolina*.

SCDF *Décisions du Suprême Conseil des Inspecteurs généraux du 33e et dernier degré du Rite ancien et accepté, pour la france, depuis L'année 1804. Jusques et Compris l'année 1815. Tome Ier. 1804 – 1812. Tome II.eme 1813 – 1815. [Tome III] Ecrits Originaux Des Archives du Suprême Conseil du 33e Dégré du rite Ancien et accepté – Pour La france – ou Collection des Pièces Sur les quelles ont été motivées ses Décisions Les plus Importantes.*

These three tomes include about 500 mostly manuscript documents. They belong to the archives of the Supreme Council, 33°, Southern Jurisdiction in Washington. Albert Pike was familiar with them (*see OB* VIII, 280 & Bernheim 2011, 217, note 132). My dear friend, Ill.∴ Arturo de Hoyos, 33°, copied them on a DVD and sent me a copy in 2008.

TSJ 1878 *Transactions of the Supreme Council of the 33d Degree ... for the Southern Jurisdiction of the United States of America—1857 to 1866. Reprinted*. Washington: Joseph L. Pearson. 1878.

Pamphlets, Books and Papers

1802. *Annual Register of the Brethren who compose the Sublime Grand Lodge of Perfection of South-Carolina, established at Charleston, Anno Lucis 5783....* Register for the year 5802. Charleston (South-Carolina). 23 pp. Printed by T. B. Bowen, No. 3, Broad-Street. (facsimile in Mackey 1898 & 1906, VII, 1821–1842 & Harris-Carter 1964, 305–16).

1809. *An Address in a Letter to the seceding Masons from the Grand Lodge of S. Carolina prepared by a select Committee for that purpose, appointed on the 24th of June, 5809. Unanimously approved of by, and published at the desire of the said Grand Lodge of South-Carolina*. Charleston. Printed by J. Hoff, No. 6, Broad-Street. 43 pp. + 1 p. Errata.

1809. *An Answer to the Address of the Committee of the Grand Lodge of South-Carolina, (not Ancient York Masons) from the Corresponding Committee of the Grand Lodge of South-Carolina Ancient York Masons. With a copious*

Appendix. 1809. Charleston. Printed by J. Hoff, No. 6, Broad-Street. 30 pp. + Appendix 40 pp.
1814. *An Abstract of the Proceedings, relative to the Union of Freemasons, in South-Carolina, And likewise of the Union of Free-Masons in England, Ireland, and Scotland, by which events, the Masonic Fraternity throughout the World, have been cemented into one Happy Family. Published by Order of the Right Worshipful Grand Lodge of South-Carolina*. Charleston: Printed by W. P. Young. 53 pp.
[1818]. *The Masonic Family Re-united. Proceedings of the Two Grand Lodges in South-Carolina, called The Grand Lodge of South-Carolina Ancient York Masons, and The Grand Lodge of South-Carolina, And of the Masonic Bodies under their respective Jurisdiction; for the purpose of uniting the mystic order into one harmonious body, under the jurisdiction of the Grand Lodge of Ancient Free-Masons of South Carolina, Completed in Charleston on the 26th December, A. L. 5817. Together with The Address of the M. W. Grand Master, and a Sermon, preached in St. Michael's Church by the M. R. The Grand Chaplain. Charleston*. Printed by A. E. Miller. 36 + 13 pp.
Baynard, Samuel Harrison, Jr. 1938. *History of the Supreme Council, 33°, Ancient and Accepted Rite of Freemasonry, Northern Masonic Jurisdiction of the United States of America and its Antecedents*. 2 vol. Boston, Massachusetts: Privately printed. Press of Grit Publishing Company, Williamsport, Pa.
Bernheim, Alain. 1984. 'Une découverte étonnante concernant les Constitutions de 1762'. *Renaissance Traditionnelle* 59: 161–73.
———1986. 'The Dating of Masonic Records'. *AQC* 99: 9–36.
———1986–1987, 'Le "Bicentenaire" des Grandes Constitutions de 1786: Essai sur les cinq textes de référence historique du Rite Écossais Ancien et Accepté'. *Renaissance Traditionnelle* 68: 241–303, 69: 29–80 & 70: 99–138.
———1996. 'Questions about Albany'. *Heredom* 4: 139–87.
———2007. 'Little-Known Documents about the Early Masonic Life of South-Carolina'. *Heredom* 15, 129–66.
———2010. 'Joseph Cerneau, His Masonic Bodies, and His Grand Consistory's Minute Book – Part I.' *Heredom* 18: 25–84.
———2011. *Le Rite en 33 grades*, Dervy, Paris, 695 pp.
Carson, Enoch T. 1889. *The History of Ancient and Accepted Scottish Rite Masonry in the United States*. (in Gould 1889, vol. IV, 611–99).

Coil, Henry Wilson & alia. 1961. *Coil's Masonic Encyclopedia.* New York: Macoy Publishing & Masonic Supply Company Incorporated.

Dadmun John W. & Newton John F (Compiled by). 1866. *History and By-Laws of Washington Lodge, Roxbury, Mass.* Boston: Press of Geo. C. Rand & Avery, 3 Cornhill.

Dalcho, Frederick. 1801. *An Oration delivered in the Sublime Grand Lodge in Charleston, South-Carolina, on the 23d of September, 5801, before the members of that Lodge, the Symbolic Grand Lodge of Ancient York Masons, and the Officers of the several Lodges in the City; and published at their request – by Brother Frederick Dalcho, member of the Supreme Council of the 33d. degree, and Grand Orator of the Sublime Lodge of Perfection.* Charleston: Printed by T. B. Bowen. No. 3 Broad-Street.

——— 1803. *An Oration delivered in the Sublime Grand Lodge of South-Carolina, in Charleston, on the 21st of March, A.L. 5807, A.D. 1803, Before the Members of that Lodge, the Symbolic Grand Lodge of Free and Accepted Masons, and a considerable number of visiting Brethren; And Published at their request, to which is added AN APPENDIX Containing an historical inquiry into the origin of the difference of Ancient and Modern Masons, usually so called; &c. &c. by Brother Frederick Dalcho, Inspector General, and Grand Master of the Sublime Grand Lodge of South-Carolina.* Charleston: Printed by T. B. Bowen, No. 3, Bedon's-Alley.

——— 1808. *Orations of the Illustrious Brother Frederick Dalcho Esq*r*. M.D., Reprinted By Permission of the Author under the Sanction of the Ill. the College of Knights of K.H. and the Original Chapter of Prince Masons of Ireland.* Dublin: Printed by John King Westmoreland St.

Daruty, J. Emile. 1879. *Recherches sur le Rite Ecossais Ancien Accepté.* Ile Maurice: General Steam Printing Company. Paris, chez le F∴ Panisset. – Reprint. 2002 Paris: Editions Télètes. Précédé d'un *Hommage à Jean-Émile Daruty* par Alain Bernheim.

de Hoyos, Arturo. 2007. *Scottish Rite Ritual Monitor & Guide.* The Supreme Council, 33°, Southern Jurisdiction. Washington, DC.

———2010. *Masonic Formulas and Rituals Transcribed by Albert Pike in 1854 and 1855.* The Scottish Rite Research Society. Washington, DC.

de Hoyos Arturo & Morris, Brent. 2008. *Committed to the Flames.* Lewis Masonic.

Desaussure, Henry-William. 1815. *The Grand Lodge of South-Carolina, vs. The Grand Lodge of South Carolina Ancient York Masons. Decree of the Honourable Judge Desaussaure, Chancellor in equity, South-Carolina District.* Charleston: Printed by Barnard Levy.

Directories Charleston. See Hagy.

Dorian, Max. 1977. *Un Bordelais Stephen Girard Premier Millionaire Américain.* Paris: Editions Albatros.

Escalle, Elisabeth & Gouyon Guillaume, Mariel. 1993. *Francs-Maçons des loges françaises "aux Amériques" 1770–1850. Contribution à l'étude de la société créole.* 865 pp. [No indication of a printer].

Folger, Robert. 1862. T*he Ancient and Accepted Scottish Rite in thirty-three Degrees … With an Appendix containing numerous documents….* 2nd édition 1881. New York: Published by the author.

Fox, William L. 1997. *Lodge of the Double-Headed Eagle.* Fayetteville: The University of Arkansas Press.

Gould, Robert Freke. 1882–1887. *The History of Freemasonry.* 3 vol. Edinburgh: T. C. & E. C. Jack, Grange Publishing Works.

———1889. *The History of Freemasonry … by Robert Freke Gould …, W. J. Hughan …, Rev. A. F. A. Woodford …, David Murray Lyon …, Enoch T. Carson …, Josiah H. Drummond …, T. S. Parvin … and others.* New York, Cincinnati, and Chicago: John C. Yorston & Co.

Gourdin, Theodore S. 1855. *Historical Sketch of the Order of Knights Templar.* 34 pp. Charleston, S. C. Walker & Evans, Book And Job Printers.[314]

Grasse-Tilly *(Livre d'or du comte de).* 2003. Facsimile ed. Transcription of the manuscript by Madame René Guilly. Many illustrations. Editions du Suprême Conseil de France. 458 pp.

Hagy, James W. 1996. *Charleston, South Carolina City Directories for the Years 1816, 1819, 1825, and 1829.* Clearfield Company, Baltimore, Maryland. Reprinted 2002.[315]

> 'The 1822 Directory was published by James R. Schenk with the title of *The Directory and Stranger's Guide for the City of Charleston. Also a Directory*

314. http://books.google.ch/books?id=dFNCAAAAYAAJ&printsec=frontcover&hl=fr&source=gbs_ge_summary_r&cad=0#v=onepage&q&f=false.

315. Parts of the 2002 reprint on the Web: http://books.google.ch/books?id=txpmjVltzJoC&printsec=frontcover&hl=fr&source=gbs_ge_summary_r&cad=0#v=onepage&q&f=false).

for Charleston Neck Between Boundary-Street and the Lines; Likewise for the Coloured Persons Within the City; and Another for Coloured Persons residing on the Neck for the Year 1822. To Which is Added an Almanac; The Tariff of Duties on All Goods Imported into the United States; and the Rates of Wharfage, Weighing, Storage, Dockage and Drayage, &c. (Charleston: Archibald E. Miller, 1822).' (Hagy 1996, 69).

Harris, Ray Baker. 1959. *Eleven Gentlemen from Charleston.* Washington D. C.

Harris-Carter 1964 [Harris, Ray Baker. Prepared for Publication by James D. Carter, 33°]. *History of The Supreme Council, 33° (Mother Council of the World) Ancient and Accepted Scottish Rite of Freemasonry Southern Jurisdiction, U.S.A. 1801–1861.* The Supreme Council, 33°: Washington, D. C.

Hewitt, Arthur Reginald. 1977. 'The Ancient and Accepted Rite. Another Francken Manuscript Rediscovered'. *Ars Quatuor Coronatorum* 89, 108–10.

Jackson, Brigadier A. C. F. 1980. *Rose Croix.* London: Lewis Masonic. – 1987. Revised and enlarged edition. London: Lewis Masonic.

———1984. 'The Authorship of the 1762 Constitutions of the Ancient and Accepted Rite'. *Ars Quatuor Coronatorum* 97, 176–91.

Jacobs, Abraham. *Rules & Statutes of the Sublime Degrees of Masonry.* Document No. 15 of Folger 1862–1881.

Jervey, Claire (Copied and Arranged by). 1906. I*nscriptions on the Tablets and Gravestones in St. Michael's Church and Churchyard, Charleston, S. C.* Columbia, S.C. The State Company Publishers.[316]

Kloss, Dr. Georg. 1852–1853. *Geschichte der Freimaurerei in Frankreich.* 2 vol. Darmstadt: G. Jonghaus. – 1971. Unveränderter Nachdruck. Graz: Akademische Druck-u. Verlagsanstalt.

Laffon-Ladébat, Charles. 1853. *Report on the Difficulties which exist between the Grand Lodge of the York Rite for the State of Louisiana and the Supreme Council of the Scotch Rite for the same State, and on the Pretentions of the several Supreme Councils existing in America and Irrefutable Proofs that the Scotch Rite, Ancient and Accepted, in 33 Degrees, originally belonged to the Grand Orient of France. Translated from the French, by Br∴ Laffon-Ladébat, a M∴M∴ of the York Rite and a Member of the Supr∴ Council of the Scotch Rite, Ancient and Accepted.* New Orleans: Br∴ J. Lamarre's Printing Office, Exchange Alley, 102, between Conti and Bienville sts.

316. http://archive.org/stream/inscriptionsonta00jerv#page/n7/mode/2up.

Le Bihan, Alain. 1967. *Loges et Chapitres de la Grande Loge et du Grand Orient de France (2e moitié du XVIIIe siècle)*. Paris: Biblliothèque nationale.

Leblanc de Marconnay, Hyacinthe. 1852. *Rapport sur des différends élevés entre la Gr.·. Loge du Rite d'York pour l'État de la Louisiane et le Suprême Conseil du Rite Ecossais pour le même Etat ... et preuves irrécusables que le Rite Écossais Ancien et Accepté en 33 degrés appartenait originairement au G.·. O.·. de France*. Paris: Imprimerie Saintin, Dentan, Pinard.

Lindsay, R. S. 1948. *Report on the Institutes, Statutes and General Regulations of 1763, found in the Golden Book of Dr. Charles Morison of Greenfield, Founder in 1846 of the Supreme Council for Scotland with Comments by the Grand Secretary General for Scotland on their bearings upon the history of the Ancient and Accepted Scottish Rite.*[317]

[Lobingier, Charles Sumner]. 1931. *The Supreme Council, 33°, Mother Council of the World. Ancient and Accepted Scottish Rite of Freemasonry, Southern Jurisdiction, U. S. A.* Louisville, Kentucky: The Standard Printing Co..

Lobingier's manuscript, History of the Supreme Council, was delivered to Grand Commander John H. Cowles on 31 December 1927. During the meeting of the Supreme Council, in June 1928, 'The Grand Commander asked the Council "to decide whether it will publish the entire manuscript or only that portion bearing upon our Supreme Council". The matter was referred to the Library Committee whose report was adopted to the effect "that the Grand Commander, together with Brother Witcover.... Brother Lobingier and Brother Boyden, be authorized to make condensation of the work and such changes as thought necessary"' (Lobingier 1931, Foreword of Grand Commander John H. Cowles and p. 765). Part of Lobingier's manuscript was printed in 1931 with the title The Supreme Council, 33° but without the name of the author, likely because of the 'changes thought necessary'. The 1004 pages of this remarkable book are accompanied with 4186 notes and references.[318]

L'Union Française N° 17. 1915. [collective work]. New York: [privately printed].

M'Cosh 1823. *Documents upon Sublime Free-Masonry in the United States of America being a collection of all the official documents which have appeared*

317. See the remarks of G. S. Draffen of Newington in *AQC* 92 (1980), 206.

318. The book was reprinted and copyrighted in two parts in 2003 and again in 2010 by Kessinger Publishing under the name *Supreme Council 33rd Degree Part 1 (Part 2) or Mother Council of the World of the Ancient and Accepted Scottish Rite of Freemasonry, Southern Jurisdiction, United States of America*, showing John H. Cowles as author [!]. However the 'Book description' says: 'It is the result of extensive research on the part of Charles S. Lobingier'.... Parts including the excellent 58 pages Index can be read on the Web.

on both sides of the question. With Notes and an Appendix. Charleston: C. C. Sebring [Reprinted].

The first five pages bear at the end '*Charleston, June*, 1823.', which constitutes its *terminus ad quo*. The fact that the book's last part is entitled 'Appendix', that Bacot wrote on the title-page of his own copy: 'This book was placed in my hands in the afternoon of the 15th August 1823–by a Brother'[319] and that John Cogdell brought it to a meeting of his Grand Council on 22 August suggests that it was likely printed two months later.

Mackey, Albert. 1861. *The History of Freemasonry in South Carolina, from its origin in the year 1736 to the present time....* 556 pp. Columbia, S.C.: South Carolina Power Press. 1936. – Reprinted for Solomon's Lodge No. 1, A.F.M. with a different pagination (584 pp.). Charleston, S.C.: Walker, Evans and Cogswell Co.

——— 1898 & 1906. *The History of Freemasonry... By Albert Gallatin Mackey, M.D., 33°* [.] *The History of the Symbolism of Freemasonry* [,] *The Ancient and Accepted Scottish Rite and The Royal Order of Scotland By William R. Singleton, 33° with an Addenda By William James Hughan.* 7 vol. 2'091 pp. Published by The Masonic History Company New York and London.

Posthumous publication, since Albert Mackey died 21 June 1881. William R. Singleton completed Mackey's unfinished monumental work and wrote, vol. V, p. 1305: 'The preceding chapters, ending on page 1302, were all written by him ... his publishers have complimented the present writer by selecting him to do, imperfectly as it will appear, what so able a writer as Dr. Mackey would have done, had his life been spared a little longer'. Before the Index (and a Pronouncing Dictionary by Charles T. McClenachan), volume VII ends with a 'Supplement to Dr. Mackey's Text' written by William James Hughan (pp. 2001–2013).

McClenachan, Charles T. 1888–1892. *History of the most ancient and honorable Fraternity of Free and Accepted Masons in New York from the earliest date.* 3 vol. New York: Published by the Grand Lodge.

Melchers, Theo A. W. (compiled by). 1882. *A Historical Sketch of South Carolina Commandery, No. 1, K. T. and the appendant orders, established in 1780, Located at Charleston....* Charleston, S.C.: Walker, Evans, & Cogswell, Printers, 3 Broad Street.[320] – 1900. Reprint.[321]

319. Harris-Carter 1964, 146.
320. http://books.google.ch/books?id=HGn-GgAACAAJ&hl=fr&source=gbs_navlinks_s.
321. http://www.clansinclairsc.org/SouthCarolinaCommanderyNo1Hist.htm.

Parvin, T. S. 1889. *The History of Knight Templar Masonry in the United States.* In Gould 1889, 549–607.

Pike, Albert. 1858. *Materials for the History of Freemasonry....* Unpublished manuscript fragments transcribed by Geo F. Moore, 33°, in *The New Age* between 1904 and 1909.

——— [anon. = Pike & de Ladébat] 1858. *Dissection of the* Manifesto *of Mr. James Foulhouze presented on the 24th day of July 1858, by Charles Bienvenu, Esq., To the Association of persons in New Orleans, that fancies itself a Supreme Council of the Ancient and Accepted Scottish Rite. – 1872.* Reprinted much shortened in *OB* II, part 1 (August 1872), 111–206, under the title 'A Historical Review'.

———1859. *The Statutes and Regulations, Institutes, Laws, and Grand Constitutions of the Ancient and Accepted Scottish Rite.* New York: Robt. Macoy, Publisher. 168 pp.[322]

———1872. *Ancient and Accepted Scottish Rite of Freemasonry.* New York: Masonic Publishing Company. A. M. 5632. – New Edition printed by J. J. Little & Co. 5664. 467 pp.

Pollard, Ralph J. 1945. *Freemasonry in Maine 1762 – 1945.*[323]

PROCEEDINGS

——— *of the Grand Lodge of New-Hampshire, from July 8, 5789, to June 8, 5841, inclusive.* Concord 1860.

——— *of the Grand Lodge of Pennsylvania, Free and Accepted Masons. 1730 to 1809.* Volume I.

———*of the Grand Lodge of Ancient Free-Masons of South-Carolina*:

1821. *Abstract of the Proceedings of the Grand Lodge of Ancient Free-Masons of South-Carolina, from the 18th of February, 5818 (being the first communication which was held after the union of the two late Grand Lodges) until St. John the Evangelist's Day, 5820, inclusive, embracing a term of three years. Published by order of the Grand Lodge.* Printed by A. E. Miller, 120, Broad-Street. 1821. 64 pp. [10 January 1818–27 December 1820. Rules &

322. This rare edition can be read on the Web: http://archive.org/details/cu31924030325017.
323. http://www.mainemasonrytoday.com/history/Books/Pollard/pollard_chap3.htm.

Regulations of the Grand Lodge of Ancient Free-Masons of South-Carolina. List of Lodges 1 to 52].

1823. *Abstract of the Proceedings of the Grand Lodge of Ancient Free-Masons of South-Carolina from the 31st Day of December, 5821, until St. John the Evangelist's Day, 5822, inclusive. Published by order of the Grand Lodge.* Printed by Brother A. E. Miller. No. 4, Broad-Street. 31 pp. [31 December 1821–27 December 1822. List of Lodges 1 to 51].

1823. *Proceedings of a Special Communication of the Grand Lodge of Ancient Free-Masons of SO. Ca. Held in Charleston on* Friday Evening, the 31st of October, 5823. Printed by Bro. C. C. Sebring, No. 44 Queen-street. 14 pp.

1824. *Abstract of the Proceedings of the Grand Lodge of Ancient Free-Masons of South-Carolina from* St. John the Evangelist's Day, 5822, until St. John the Evangelist's Day, 5823, inclusive. Published by order of the Grand Lodge. Printed by Bro. C. C. Sebring, No. 44 Queen-street. 47 +1 pp.[16 January–27 December 1823. Report of Lodges 1 to 54].

1825. *Abstract of the Proceedings of the Grand Lodge of Ancient Free-Masons of S. Carolina,* During the year 5824. Published by order of the Grand Lodge. Printed by Brother C. C. Sebring No. 44 Queen-street. 51+1 pp. [3 January–27 December 1824. Report of Lodges 1 to 53].

1826. *Abstract of the Proceedings of the Grand Lodge of Ancient Free-Masons of SO. CA.* During the year 1825. Published by order of the Grand Lodge. Printed by Brother C. C. Sebring No. 44 Queen-street. 56 pp. [4 March–27 December 1826. Report of Lodges 1 to 55. An Appendix includes the Minutes of 17 December 1825].

1827. *Abstract of the Proceedings of the Grand Lodge of Ancient Free-Masons of SO. CA.* During the year 5826. *Published by order of the Grand Lodge.* Printed by Brother C. C. Sebring No. 44 Queen-street. 32 pp. [4 March–27 December 1826. Report of Lodges 1 to 55].

1828. *Abstract of the Proceedings of the Grand Lodge of Ancient Free-Masons of S. Carolina,. During the year* 5827. Published by order of the Grand Lodge. Printed by Brother J. S. Burges, No. 44 Queen-street. 47 pp. [30 March–27 December 1827. Permanent Regulations. Report of Lodges 1 to 58].[324]

324. http://www.latinamericanstudies.org/freemasonry/Proceedings-SC-1827.pdf reproduces the title page and the Report of Lodges.

[anon.] *Recueil des Actes du Suprême Conseil de France.* 1832. Paris: Imprimerie de Sétier.

Reed, Parker McCobb. 1894. *History of Bath and Environs, Sagadahoc County, Maine. 1607–1894.* Portland, Me: Lakeside Press, Printers.

Sachse, Julius F. 1909. *Freemasonry in Pennsylvania.* Vol. 2. Lancaster: New Era Printing.

——— 1913. *Old Masonic Lodges of Pennsylvania.* 2 vol. Lancaster: New Era Printing.

——— 1915. *Ancient Documents relating to the A. and A. Scottish Rite in the archives of the R. W. Grand Lodge of Free and Accepted Masons of Pennsylvania.* Philadelphia: Grand Lodge F.&A.M. Pennsylvania.

Schultz, Edward T. 1884. *History of Freemasonry in Maryland....* Volume I. Baltimore: J. H. Medairy & Co.

——— 1889. *Which is the oldest Commandery of Knights Templar in the United States? A paper read before Maryland Commandery, No. 1, Masonic Knights Templar, Friday Evening, November 22nd, 1889. Printed by request of the Commandery.* 16 pp.[325]

——— 1891. *History of Commandery No. 1, Knights Templar, Stationed at Baltimore, State of Maryland, From 1790 to 1890.* Baltimore, John B. Kurtz. 328 pp.[326]

Singleton, William R. 1898. *The History of the Introduction and Progress of Freemasonry in the United States.* In Mackey 1898, Volume V, Chapter LII (pp. 1368–1383), 'The Introduction of Knight Templarism in America', can be read on the Web: http://www.freemason.com/library/hisma097.htm.

Speed, Frederick. 1890. *Knights Templar and Allied Orders.* Division XVI of Stillson & Hughan.

Stillson, Henry Leonard & Hughan, William James. 1890. *History of the Ancient and Honorable Fraternity of Free and Accepted Masons, and Concordant Orders.* Boston and New York, USA. The Fraternity Publishing Company.

The Medical Repository, Volume 3, New York 1806, 433sq.[327]

325. http://archive.org/stream/cu31924030372621#page/n23/mode/2up.

326. http://archive.org/details/cu31924030324309.

327. http://books.google.ch/books?id=dT9JAAAAYAAJ&printsec=frontcover&hl=fr&source=gbs_ge_summary_r&cad=0#v=onepage&q&f=false.

Includes 'A Case of Tetanus Communicated by Dr. Frederick Dalcho, Secretary to the Medical Society of South-Carolina, to Dr. Mitchill, April 10, 1805.' (pp. 1–4) in which Dalcho refers to 'my friend Dr. Auld' and 'my friend Dr. Moultrie'; and 'A case showing the Impropriety of taking the whole of the Virus out of a Vaccine Vesicle: Communicated by Dr. Frederick Dalcho', pp. 264–65.

Walgren, Kent. 1994. 'A Bibliography of Pre-1851 American Scottish Rite Imprints (non-Louisiana)'. *Heredom* 3: 55–119.

The Union of 1867

Arturo deHoyos, 33°, G∴C∴

One should never know too precisely whom one has married.

— *Nietzsche*

When we hear the two words *regular* and *irregular* used in a Masonic context today, we rely on our Grand Lodges to decide which designation is applied to a given body. Grand Lodges debate issues of recognition, and the lines are drawn and redrawn yearly. In the early 1800s, when Freemasonry was in a state of infancy, regularity was for the common Mason more nebulous than it is today, for Grand Lodges often ignored the so-called high grade systems. In 1802, when the first "Supreme Council of the 33d" at Charleston, South Carolina, announced its existence by issuing its now famous *Circular,*[1] the Grand Lodge of Scotland was overwhelmed by its multiplicity of degrees, and initially considered it to have been prepared in the "spirit of the Illuminati."

> A circular was this year received from the Grand Lodge of America [the Supreme Council]. The spirit of illumination which it breathed, and the supernumerary degrees, amounting to about fifty, which it authorized, were sufficient reasons for drawing down the contempt of Scottish Masons, whose honour it is to have preserved Free-Masonry for many centuries, in its original and simple

1. *Circular throughout the two Hemispheres* (Charleston, S.C., 1802).

> form; and whose pride it shall ever be to transmit, to the latest posterity, the principles and ceremonies of their Order unpolluted and unimpaired.[2]

When Emanual De La Motta, an agent of the Supreme Council, delivered a *Circular* to the Grand Lodge of New York it was returned "inasmuch as it related to degrees not known or acknowledged by the Grand Lodge."[3] Such attitudes made it possible for the so-called Cerneau Controversy to develop. *Cerneauism* refers to any claim to Scottish Rite authority derived in any way from Joseph Cerneau. Parties claiming authority from Cerneau are termed Cerneauists. Branded irregular by the Charleston Council, Cerneauism gained a foothold in much of the United States, remnants of which yet survive (e.g. The Supreme Council of Louisiana);[4] but today I will but briefly focus on its beginnings in what is now the Northern Masonic Jurisdiction, trace its several resurgences and its demise.

Pre-history of the Scottish Rite

Let's first briefly look at how the Scottish Rite likely came to be. It is believed that in 1732 an English lodge named *Loge L'Anglaise* was founded in Bordeaux, France. This lodge was later chartered by the English Modern Grand Lodge and still exists today. An early offshoot of *Loge L'Anglaise* was the *Loge la Français*, which is believed to have been French. The latter lodge had a penchant for the so-called *hauts grades*, then coming into vogue, and founded *Loge Parfaite Harmonie* in 1743. Étienne (Steven) Morin[5] was among the founders of *Loge Parfaite Harmonie*. The French strongholds of Freemasonry were, at

2. Alexander Lawrie, *The History of Freemasonry, Drawn from Authentic Sources of Information; with an Account of the Grand Lodge of Scotland, from its Institution in 1736 to the Present Time, Compiled from Records; and an Appendix of Original Papers* (Edinburgh, Scotland: 1804), 292. Lawrie's 1808 Dublin edition replaced "Grand Lodge of America" with "the Supreme Grand Council of America," and "spirit of illumination" with "spirit of the Illuminati." It has been suggested that David Brewster wrote *Lawrie's History*; see Henry W. Coil, *Coil's Masonic Encyclopedia* (New York: Macoy, 1961), 371.

3. Joseph M'Cosh [also McCosh], *Documents upon Sublime Free-Masonry in the United States of America* (Charleston, S.C.: [Cornelius C. Sebring?], 1823; reprint ed., n.d.), 62.

4. See *General Statutes Supreme Council of the Thirty-third Degree of the Ancient and Accepted Scotch Rite of Freemasonry State of Louisiana, Grand Orient of New Orleans* rev ed. (New Orleans: N.p., 1990).

5. For some years it was often assumed that Steven Morin was Jewish, however, recent discoveries indicate he was a self-styled "ancient catholic." See Alain Bernheim, "Estienne Morin New Information About his Birth," *Ars Quatuor Coronatorum* (hereafter cited as *AQC*), vol. 105 (1992), 255–56.

the time, in Bordeaux and Paris. A Parisian body, the "Council of Knights of the East," which soon changed its name to the "Council of the Emperors of the East and West," granted Morin a patent in 1761 (the first of its kind) to promulgate certain *hauts grades* in the New World.

Until recently it was believed that Morin was authorized to establish bodies of the twenty-five-degree rite (sometimes referred to as the "Rite of Perfection") which was, to a large measure, destined to become the parent of the Scottish Rite. As Bro. A.C.F. Jackson observes, however, the Rite of Perfection, properly refers only to the 1°–14° (Lodge of Perfection) of Morin's twenty-five degree rite. Indeed, recent research suggests that Morin was personally responsible for superimposing degrees atop the Lodge of Perfection, thereby creating the twenty-five degree rite which, Bro. Jackson suggests, might better be referred to as "Morin's Rite."[6] There is compelling evidence that, to bolster his authority, Morin forged and backdated the *Constitutions and Regulations of 1762,* a fraud which was not discovered for over two hundred-twenty years.[7]

About 1763 Morin introduced his system to Kingston, Jamaica, and empowered an enthusiastic Dutch Mason, Henry Andrew Francken, to establish bodies throughout the New World, including the United States. Francken soon sailed to New York, and in 1767 he began to confer the degrees. A brief extract from the minute book of the premiere American Lodge of Perfection relates the incident.

> About the 7th October 1767 Messers Pfister & Gamble were introduced at New York, to Mr. Henry Andrew Francken who a day or two after, by Authority invested in him, Initiated them in the 11 Degrees of Ancient Masonry, from the Secret Master being the 4th to the Perfection, which is the 14th and Known to be the utmost Limits of Symbolick Masonry.
>
> About a week after the above date Mr. Francken conferred on them the 2 first Degrees of Modern Masonry or Masonry Revived, and proposed to them that if they chose he would erect A Lodge of Perfection at Albany and appoint Wm. Gamble Master thereof (protempore) until Sr. William Johnson should have the refusal of it....[8]

6. A.C.F. Jackson, *Rose Croix. A History of the Ancient and Accepted Rite for England and Wales,* 2d ed. (London: A. Lewis, 1980, 1987).

7. A.C.F. Jackson, "The Authorship of the 1762 Constitutions of the Ancient and Accepted Rite," *AQC,* vol. 97 (1984), 176–91.

8. Cited in Samuel Harrison Baynard, Jr., *History of the Supreme Council, 33°* 2 vols. (Boston, 1938), vol. 1, 49–51. A facsimile reproduction appears in the 1906 *Proceedings of the Council of Deliberation for the State of New York.*

As a Lodge of Perfection this body could only confer the degrees from Secret Master through Perfection (4°–14°). The above named William Gamble, a draughtsman, is also remembered for the remarkable tracing boards he made for several of the *hauts grades* (reproduced in *Heredom* Vol 1), which curiously do not precisely correspond to the rituals Francken is known to have introduced to New York.[9] Fortunately, Francken also made several manuscript copies of Morin's Rite which permit us to study the rituals as he received them. The best of these copies, the *Francken Manuscript of 1783*, is owned by the Supreme Council, 33°, N.M.J.

On December 6, 1768, Francken appointed Moses Michael Hays (also *Hayes*), of Dutch parentage, a Deputy Inspector General for the West Indies and North America. The Hays patent granted authority to confer all of the degrees of Morin's Rite.

The following year Francken returned to Jamaica and by 1780 Hays emigrated to Newport, Rhode Island. In 1781 Hays traveled to Philadelphia where he met with eight Brethren whom he appointed Deputy Inspectors General over given states, with the exception of Samuel Myers who presided over the Leeward islands. Barend Moses Spitzer, a Deputy Inspector General, lived in Charleston from 1770 to 1781 and moved to Philadelphia where he was appointed Deputy for Georgia and, after traveling briefly abroad, returned to Charleston by 1788. On April 2, 1795, Spitzer appointed the Irish-born John Mitchell, then living in Charleston, a Deputy Inspector General.[10]

THE THIRTY-THIRD DEGREE

On May 24, 1801, Mitchell created the Reverend Frederick Dalcho (a Prussian, born in London) a Deputy Inspector General, and one week later "the Supreme Council of the 33d degree for the United States of America, was opened . . . agreeably to the Grand Constitutions"[11] with Mitchell and Dalcho

9. For example, the names of the angels on Gamble's 23° Knight of the Sun tracing board and the names of the steps on the mysterious ladder of the 24° Knight Kadosh differ than those used in Francken's rituals.

10. Josiah Drummond, "Ancient and Accepted Scottish Rite," in Henry Leonard Stillson and William James Hughan, *History of the Ancient and Honorable Fraternity of Free and Accepted Masons* (Boston: Fraternity Publishing, 1890, 1898, 1912), 795–828; Ray Baker Harris, *History of the Supreme Council, 33° 1801–1861* (Washington, DC: The Supreme Council, 1964), 32.

11. *Circular*, 5.

presiding. This body is often referred to as the Supreme Council at Charleston, and exists today as the Supreme Council, 33°, Southern Jurisdiction. As the premiere Supreme Council it is sometimes referred to as the "Mother Council of the World." In 1829 Moses Holbrook, then Sovereign Grand Commander of the Southern Jurisdiction, asked J. J. J. Gourgas about the origins of the Thirty-third Degree:

> I took the opportunity in mentioning it to Br. Dalcho, to ask how Mitchell got the 33rd. He replied that he could not ... recollect; but he [Mitchell] had signed some obligation in French for it. He thinks it came from some Prussian who was in Charleston, who was authorized to communicate it to him.[12]

It has been suggested that the "German or Prussian" may have been Henry Wilmans,[13] a Grand Inspector General who lived in Charleston from about 1788 to 1792, or perhaps Barend Spitzer,[14] but there is *no evidence* that either possessed the degree. Indeed, on August 23, 1813, Mitchell himself wrote "No person ever had the degree but Count De Grasse, & perhaps, but I am not sure, Mr. Delahogue,..."[15] the latter two having obtained it through Mitchell.

Although the enigma has yet to be conclusively solved, I am personally inclined to believe that Mitchell's Supreme Council at Charleston invented the Thirty-third Degree ritual. To but briefly touch the matter, I observe that the original Charleston Thirty-third Degree ritual, written in Dalcho's hand (but modified after 1804), includes what might be seen as "borrowings" from older rituals in his possession. These include the adorations[16] from Dalcho's 1801 copy of the "Grand Master Ecosé" Degree, while his 1801 "Prussian Knight" Degree includes a significant word and a gesture similar to one of the signs of Dalcho's Thirty-third Degree. The ritual text of Dalcho's Thirty-third Degree is followed by the original pattern for patents issued by the Supreme Council to its members. *As early as 1801–1802 these patents included the names of all the degrees held by the recipient, but the original pattern lists only the names of the degrees comprising Morin's Rite.*

12. Baynard, *History*, vol. 1, 89.

13. Baynard, *History*, 86–87.

14. Jean-Pierre Lassalle, "From the Constitutions and Regulations of 1762 to The Grand Constitutions of 1786" *Heredom*, vol. 2 (1993), 80–81.

15. Harris, *History*, 117.

16. The adorations in Dalcho's Thirty-third Degree were modified after 1804.

By comparison, Dalcho's 1801 patent[17] lists the degrees in an order which falls somewhere between the original pattern and the *Circular*, with which it is consistent through the Prince of Labanus Degree, but then follow the "Grand Master Ecosé Kt of St. Andrew, &c &c &c," "Chief of the Tabernacle," and "Prince of Mercy" Degrees; it then continues as in the *Circular*. Note that the "Grand Master Ecosé Kt of St. Andrew" is substituted for the "Prince of the Tabernacle," and that the former is listed as a detached degree in the *Circular*.[18] In view of this order given for the degrees, I suggest that when the Thirty-third Degree ritual was written the Charleston Supreme Council was as yet undecided which degrees would be interpolated into the rite.

The traditional authority of the Supreme Council, cited in the *Circular*, stems from the *Constitutions of 1786* (allegedly ratified by Frederick II, King of Prussia), which like Morin's *Constitutions and Regulations of 1762*, are of dubious origin and beyond the scope of this article.[19] The *Circular* also mentioned "an important discovery ... made in the year 5553, of a record in Syrian Characters, relating to the most remote antiquity....," adding, "Few of these characters were translated until the reign of our Illustrious and most Enlightened Brother, Frederick 2d King of Prussia...." This legend is from the Prussian Knight Degree which, as previously observed, shares a similar sign and word with the original Thirty-third Degree ritual. The Prussian Knight Degree also states that "The Grand Master General of the order, who is stiled, Knight Prince Commander, is the Most Illustrious Frederick of Brunswick, King of Prussia, whose ancestors have for 300 years, been the protectors of the said order...." Could the degree have inspired Frederick's alleged connection with the *1786 Constitutions*?

17. Harris, *History*, 330.

18. As in Dalcho's patent, the patents of Horatio Gates (Nov. 1822), John Fowler (Aug. 1824), James Kilvin (May 1825), and Perez Snell (May 1827) list the 29° as Kadosh, but they diverge by listing the 30° as Knight of St. Andrew. Although the names of each degree are unnumbered in these patents, they are listed in an order generally consistent with the *Circular* and/or the list given in M'Cosh, *Documents* (1823), and may reflect their contemporary numerical attributions.

19. For argument favoring the authenticity of the 1786 Constitutions, see Pike, *Grand Constitutions*, and Lassalle, "From the Constitutions and Regulations of 1762 to The Grand Constitutions of 1786" *Heredom*, vol. 2 (1993), 57.

ORIGIN OF THE SUPREME COUNCIL RITUALS

Where did the first Supreme Council get its rituals? If one follows the abbreviated genealogy of the *Circular* it appears that a lineal transmission from Morin to Mitchell may have provided the material, but I do not believe this was the case. However natural it may be to assume that the Supreme Council at Charleston depended on copies of Francken's rituals, a careful study of the surviving Dalcho rituals reveals that, textually, they often have more in common with the so-called *Jamaica Ritual*,[20] a circa 1790–1800 bound manuscript in the Supreme Council, 33°, S.J. archives. Like the *Francken Manuscript* the *Jamaica Ritual* includes a version of Morin's Rite, but it also has an additional appendix of three detached degrees listed in the *Circular* (Select Master of 27, Royal Arch, Grand Master Ecose) which are lacking in Francken's collection. A superscription preceding these degrees states: "The following three Degrees are not Included in those of Stephen Morins, [*sic*] but were first Introduced into the Island of Jamaica by Moses Cohen, from North America, as Deputy Inspector."[21]

I am not suggesting that the *Jamaica Ritual* itself was the *fons et origo* of the Dalcho rituals, but rather that the it belongs to a "family" of Morin ritual variants which shares similarities lacking from the *Francken Manuscript*. Possessing several of its own peculiarities, the Dalcho rituals are not a slavish copy of any English-language ritual of which I am aware, but were most likely translated directly from the French. This view is supported by an 1826 statement of Moses Holbrook: "Much of our Degrees is very badly done in English."[22] The following year Holbrook elaborated on the state of the rituals.

> [O]ur MSS [rituals] are a strange farrago of bad English, and Dr. De la Motta has sold the originals. They, our English MSS., were translated by different hands. Some did not understand English well who made our translations,

20. The *Jamaica Ritual* was first described in Eugene E. Hinman, Ray V. Denslow, and Charles C. Hunt, *A History of the Cryptic Rite* 2 vols. (Tacoma, Wash.: General Grand Council, R&SM, 1931), 99–101, but was "lost" in the archives of the Supreme Council, 33°, SJ, and simply labeled "Unmarked MS Book from Bx 31" until the author re-identified it in 1993. Note added in 2020: The Jamaica ritual was published in full in Arturo de Hoyos, *Freemasonry's Royal Secret* (Washington, DC: Scottish Rite Research Society, 2014).

21. Cohen was appointed Deputy Inspector General by Barend Spitzer in 1794, but had already conferred several degrees, including the detached degrees, on Abraham Jacobs in Jamaica in 1790.

22. Harris, *History*, 170.

> and some of them have the appearance of having been made by persons who understood no language grammatically.[23]

An example of "bad English" would include Dalcho's "28th Grand Knight of the Sun or Prince Adept," which is far inferior to the Francken and Jamaica versions.

It is believed that most of the "new degrees," i.e., those supplementing Morin's Rite, appeared after 1804 and, for reasons that are too extensive to treat here, their introduction became a point of contention between contending bodies.[24] In any case, the Charleston Council was the first Masonic body of its kind, agglomerating the twenty-five degrees of Morin's Rite with others invented or otherwise into a system of thirty-three degrees.

Antoine Bideaud's Irregular Act

In February 1802 the Charleston Council issued a patent to Alexandre Francois Auguste de Grasse Tilly (also known as Count de Grasse) certifying him Sovereign Grand Commander for life of a Supreme Council in the French West India Islands.[25] The following September Antoine Bideaud was granted a patent by the latter Supreme Council and became a member thereof. In August 1806 while traveling to Bordeaux, France, Bideaud passed through New York where he encountered John G. Tardy, John Baptiste Desdoity, John James Joseph Gourgas, Lewis de Saulles and Pierre A. DePeyrat, all members of *La Triple Union* Chapter, Rose Croix d'H-R-D-M of Kilwinning, one of the degrees of the Royal Order of Scotland. Unknown to its members, *La Triple Union* Chapter had been illegally chartered by Achille Huet de Lachelle in 1795, a Frenchman who fled to New York from Santo Domingo, West Indies.[26] But now, these Brethren were about to be imposed upon by Bideaud

23. Harris, *History*, 172.

24. For arguments concerning the degrees, see James Foulhouze, *Historical Inquiry into the Origin of the Ancient and Accepted Scotch Rite* (New Orleans: The True Delta, 1859), 179–83 and Anonymous [J. Lamarre, A. Pike, C. Laffon de Ladébat?], *Dissection of the Manifesto of Mr James Foulhouze* ([New Orleans]: N.p., 1858), 33.

25. Baynard, *History*, vol. 1, 92–93, 147.

26. [Albert Pike, ed.] *Grade, Mark Mason, Passed Master, and Royal Arch, Rite Ancien Maçonnerie D'York* (Supreme Council, 33°, 1879), 1–5; Baynard, *History*, vol. 1, 99, 153; Harold V.B. Voorhis, *The Royal Order of Scotland* (New York: Henry Emmerson, 1960), 17–19.

who saw the opportunity to make some quick money. J. J. J. Gourgas, one of the five, later wrote,

> This act of Bideaud's was completely irregular, unconstitutional. He had no right or power within any part of the United States of America, but then he was tempted and did succumb at the rate of five times $46, or $230. As to us, we were then new and raw in these matters, believing all was right....[27]

On August 6, 1806, these Brethren opened a Sovereign Grand Council and Consistory of Sublime Princes of the Royal Secret,[28] and two years three months later they initiated Daniel Decius Tompkins, Richard Riker, and Sampson Simson.

In October 1808 Abraham Jacobs organized a Council of Princes of Jerusalem and a Sublime Grand Lodge of Perfection in which members of Bideaud's Sovereign Grand Council and Consistory of Sublime Princes of the Royal Secret were active. Jacobs knew John Mitchell, Grand Commander of the Supreme Council at Charleston, as early as 1788, and was active in establishing bodies and conferring degrees (sometimes irregularly) for most of his life.[29] He also knew Emanuel De La Motta, another member of the Supreme Council, and had worked with him as early as 1801 in Georgia.[30] On November 11, 1808, Jacob's Council was visited by Joseph Cerneau and John Mulligan who announced themselves as an investigating committee from another Council of Princes of Jerusalem in the city.[31] Jacobs balked at the overtures and his group contacted the Supreme Council at Charleston concerning the matter.[32] Jacobs may have been aware of Cerneau's group when he organized his own, and, fearing that he had infringed on Cerneau's rights, several members of Jacob's group abandoned him and joined with Cerneau. Richard Riker, and other presiding officers, are said to have applied to Cerneau's group, "*as a body*, but their request as such could not be complied with."[33] Jacobs waited

27. Robert Freke Gould, ed., *A Library of Freemasonry* (Philadelphia: John C. Yorston Pub. Co., 1911), vol. 5, 300–301; Baynard, *History*, vol. 1, 153.

28. Lobingier, *History*, 60.

29. Baynard, *History*, vol. 1, 77–80.

30. See extracts from Jacobs' diary in Robert B. Folger, *The Ancient and Accepted Scottish Rite, in Thirty-three Degrees*, 2 vols. (New York: Published by the Author, 1862), vol. 2, 94.

31. Folger, vol. 2, 107.

32. Harris, *History*, 382.

33. Folger, vol. 2, 139.

in vain for relief from the Supreme Council. A likely reason for the failure to become directly involved was Article 6 of the *Constitution, Statutes, Regulations* (Dalcho version): "The power of the Supreme Council does not interfere with any degree below the 17th or Knight of the East and West. But every Council and Lodge of Perfect Masons are hereby required and directed, to acknowledge them in quality of Inspectors General...." The Supreme Council at Charleston would soon have reason to lament their lack of cooperation.

Beginnings of Cerneauism

In 1801, when the Charleston Council was founded, Joseph Cerneau, a native of France (born circa 1763), resided in Port Republicain (now Port-au-Prince), Santo Domingo, West Indies. On July 15, 1806, while living in Cuba, Cerneau received the Twenty-fifth Degree of Morin's Rite (Prince of the Royal Secret) from Antoine-Mathieu Dupotet. Dupotet received his patent from Germain Hacquet,[34] who received his from Pierre Le Barbier Duplessis, who obtained his from Augustin Prevost, who was appointed by Henry A. Francken. Cerneau's patent, however, included the following proviso:

> ... we create him our Deputy Inspector General, Deputy Grand Inspector, for the Northern part of the Island of Cuba ... we give him full and entire power to confer in the name of our aforesaid Grand Council, the highest Degrees of Masonry on a Kt: Prince Mason, one only each year....[35]

It is clear that Cerneau's authority was limited to the northern part of Cuba and that he could confer the Twenty-fifth Degree on but one Mason a year. Armed with his patent Cerneau traveled to New York in November 1806 where he set up business as a Jeweler and organized a Grand Consistory on October 28, 1807. This body, styled "The Grand Consistory for the United States of America, their Territories and Dependencies, of Supreme Chiefs of

34. Both Dupotet and Hacquet were listed as Honorary Members of Cerneau's 1813 Supreme Council as well as his Grand Consistory. See *List of the Grand Officers, Members, Honorary Members &c. of the Supreme Council of Grand Inspectors General, of the 33rd Degree, Regularly established according to the Ancient Constitutional Scottish Rite of Heredon, for the United States of America their Territories and dependencies, held in the city of New-York. Also of the Grand Consistory of Supreme Chiefs of Exalted Masonry, and the Constituted bodies of its Jurisdiction. Anno Lucis, 5813.* (New York: Hardcastle and Van Pelt, 1813), 4, 7.

35. Gould, *Library*, vol. 5, 302–3. Cerneau's original patent is in the archives of the Supreme Council, S.J. I appreciate S. Brent Morris and William L. Fox pointing this out to me.

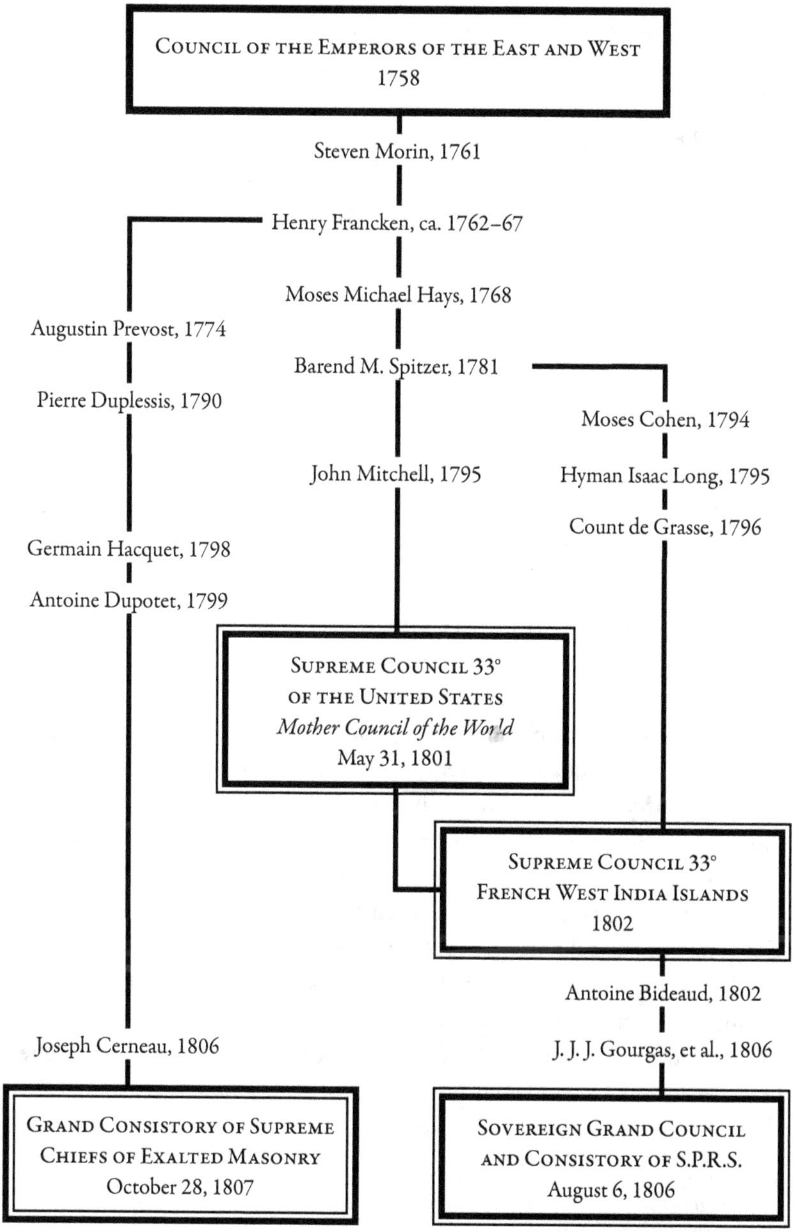
Council of the Emperors of the East and West
1758
Steven Morin, 1761
Henry Francken, ca. 1762–67
Moses Michael Hays, 1768
Augustin Prevost, 1774
Barend M. Spitzer, 1781
Pierre Duplessis, 1790
Moses Cohen, 1794
John Mitchell, 1795
Hyman Isaac Long, 1795
Count de Grasse, 1796
Germain Hacquet, 1798
Antoine Dupotet, 1799
Supreme Council 33°
of the United States
Mother Council of the World
May 31, 1801
Supreme Council 33°
French West India Islands
1802
Antoine Bideaud, 1802
Joseph Cerneau, 1806
J. J. J. Gourgas, et al., 1806
Grand Consistory of Supreme
Chiefs of Exalted Masonry
October 28, 1807
Sovereign Grand Council
and Consistory of S.P.R.S.
August 6, 1806

Figure 1. Genealogies of the Cerneau and Bideaud Grand Consistories.

Exalted Masonry, according to the Ancient Constitutional Rite of Heredon," claimed authority only over the twenty-five degrees of Morin's Rite. It has often been remarked that the organization of Cerneau's Grand Consistory exceeded both the limitations of his patent and the Constitutions of 1762. However, under the Articles in the "Collection of Constitutional Balustres" appended to the Constitutions of 1762, Cerneau may have believed himself justified in establishing the body.

> Whenever, in a State where there is neither a Grand Consistory nor a Grand Council of Sublime Princes of the Royal Secret, there are any Grand Inspectors General and Princes of the Royal Secret, the Grand Inspector General whose patent and recognition bear the oldest date, or, if there be no Inspectors General, then the oldest Prince of the Royal Secret, is invested with the administrative and dogmatic power of High Masonry, and takes accordingly the title of Sovereign.[36]

Although Cerneau may have been unaware of it, Bideaud's Grand Consistory was established a full year before his own.

Joseph Cerneau's Supreme Council, 1813–1832

By 1813 Cerneau was aware of the Supreme Council at Charleston and likely realized that his twenty-five degree system was no match for one of thirty-three. If he justified his creation of a Grand Consistory outside of Cuba he may have found it as easy to equate his Twenty-fifth Degree, Prince of the Royal Secret, with the Thirty-second Degree, Prince of the Royal Secret, of the Supreme Council at Charleston. Perhaps because the Inspector General of Morin's Rite was but a Twenty-fifth Degree Prince of the Royal Secret endowed with administrative powers, Cerneau believed that the Sovereign Grand Inspector General, 33°, was "a dignity granted as the reward of merit and experience."[37]

Cerneau roughly imitated the Charleston body and organized a "Supreme Council of Grand Inspectors General of the 33rd Degree," but it was curiously subordinate to, or equal with, his Grand Consistory.[38] The similarity in names, however, was not coincidental. Cerneau's *List of the Grand Officers, Members,*

36. See Albert Pike, *Grand Constitutions of Freemasonry* (reprint ed., Supreme Council, 33°, S.J., n.d.), 117–22.

37. *To the Glory of the Supreme Architect of the Universe....* (New York, 1814), p. 8. This document is sometimes called the "1814 Cerneau Response."

38. M'Cosh, *Documents*, 69.

Honorary Members &c. of the Supreme Council (1813) included a seal with a double-headed eagle clutching a sword, surrounded by the words "SUP... COUN... OF THE 33... FOR THE U... S... OF AM... DEUS MEUMQUE JUS." This was the identical name and virtually the identical seal which the Supreme Council at Charleston used eleven years earlier on its *Circular*.

Following its creation Cerneau's Supreme Council contacted the Supreme Council of France and was noted on its records, but a later investigation led them to believe that Cerneau was a fraud.[39] The Cerneauists also claimed they attempted to contact the Supreme Council at Charleston.

> Immediately on its installation the Grand Consistory gave notice to the supreme masonic bodies in Europe and the West-Indies, to whom it at the same time communicated *copies of the patents under which it was formed*. These were followed by the most ample recognition on the part of the Supreme Council of France, an act sufficient in itself to outweigh the cavils of all impostors.
>
> Having heard that a Council had existed at Charleston, South Carolina, which might yet be in activity, a circular, with copies of the Patent or Warrant, and a list of the members, was also transmitted thither and delivered.... No answer being received, another was dispatched, but with no better success. Your Committee here will just remark that if the council at Charleston was a regular body, and deemed us usurpers, it was their duty to take instant and effectual measures to arrest our progress. If we were regular, masonic courtesy, as well as their obligation, required them to acknowledge us without delay. They have done neither.
>
> This profound silence and neglect was of itself sufficient to satisfy the Grand Consistory that the Body at Charleston, if it ever had a lawful existence, was extinct.[40]

Perhaps Cerneau did contact Charleston, but if so, they had good reason not to respond by letter. Recall that as early as November 1808 Abraham Jacobs had contacted the Supreme Council at Charleston concerning Cerneau's activities. If Cerneau was now claiming to head a Supreme Council, it was a matter requiring personal investigation. Accordingly, in May 1813 De La Motta, the member of the Charleston Council who had worked with Jacobs in 1801, arrived in New York allegedly "not on any speculative, office-hunting or

39. Albert Pike, ed., *The Sup... Council for France and its Dependencies. In re JOSEPH CERNEAU* (Washington, DC: Supreme Council, 33°, S.J., 1886; reprint ed., Lafayette, La.: Michael Poll Pub., 1995).

40. *To the Glory of the Supreme Architect of the Universe....* (New York, 1814), p 10.

masonic errand, but in quest of health."[41] At that time there were five bodies claiming authority over high grade Masonry.

1. The (Bideaud) Sublime Grand Consistory of Sublime Princes of the Royal Secret, 30th, 31st and 32nd Degrees (organized in 1806).

2. The (Cerneau) Sovereign Grand Consistory of Sublime Princes of the Royal Secret of the Ancient and Constitutional Scottish Rite of Heredom (organized in 1807).

3. The (Jacobs) Council of Princes of Jerusalem, Concordia Crescimus (organized in 1808).

4. The (Jacobs) *Aurora Grata* Lodge of Perfection.

5. The (Cerneau) Supreme Council of Sovereign Grand Inspectors General of the Thirty-third Degree.[42]

The Jacobs bodies (nos. 3 and 4), which were in friendly relations with Charleston, were presumably chartered under authority of the *Constitutions and Regulations of 1762,* and were of no concern for De La Motta. According to the traditional view the Bideaud and Cerneau bodies were to receive equal consideration:

> De La Motta proceeded to carry out his instructions and applied to the officers of each of the several bodies, showing his credentials and authority and requesting that they exhibit theirs and allow him to inspect their records.
> In the Jacobs and Bideaud bodies he was afforded every assistance possible, and their books were opened to his inspection, while in the Cerneau bodies he was refused information and the right to inspect.[43]

This sequence contradicts De La Motta's personal account however, which states that he became aware of Cerneau's Grand Consistory and Supreme Council in July 1813, when he was given a copy of a tableau listing the officers of Cerneau's bodies.[44] But, as we have seen, members of Jacob's Council of Princes of Jerusalem had already contacted Charleston in November 1808,

41. M'Cosh, *Documents*, 40.
42. For details on these bodies, see Baynard, *History*, vol. 1, 153–65.
43. Baynard, *History*, vol. 1, 167.
44. M'Cosh, *Documents*, 40.

and it is likely that De La Motta was on a covert errand for the Supreme Council. On Aug. 5, 1813, *prior to meeting with Cerneau*, De La Motta organized and chartered the members of Bideaud's Consistory into "The Grand and Supreme Council of the Most Puissant Sovereigns, Grand Inspectors General of the Thirty-third Degree for the Northern District and Jurisdiction of the United States of America"[45] Daniel D. Tompkins was installed Sovereign Grand Commander and would serve until 1825.[46] This act was well within his powers, and was completely lawful.[47] De La Motta stated that, based on evidence provided to him by "well-informed gentlemen" (Jacobs' Council of Princes of Jerusalem?), he was already convinced of Cerneau's fraud.

> Maturely considering, and calmly perpending all the facts connected with the procedure of such detestable Masonic infractions ... and a full conviction that *Mr. Cerneau* was only a pretender to a degree he was not in possession of, and was assuming a title to which he had no claim; it became my absolute duty as a lawful Sovereign Grand Inspector General of the 33d degree, to detect and denounce any impostition practised on the Masonic world, by any individual. But being unfurnished with any masonic documents, I wrote on to the Council in Charleston, inclosing them one of *Mr. Cerneau's* celebrated tableau, requesting they would send me a copy of my Diploma, the original being deposited among papers which my family could not conveniently obtain.[48]

It was not until August 9, 1813, that De La Motta wrote to the Supreme Council at Charleston concerning Cerneau and requesting the copy of his patent.[49] It is thus clear that the members of the Bideaud Consistory were organized into a Supreme Council prior to seeing De La Motta's *bona fides*; this is consistent with the view they may have expected him. The Supreme Council received De La Motta's letter and request on August 21 and dispatched a copy of the patent two days later.

Cerneau's tableau directed "Communications to the Grand Consistory, &c. to be addressed to J. Cerneau, No. 118, William-Street." Accordingly to De La Motta's account, on September 14, 1813, he, and four officers of the newly formed Supreme Council (Peixotto, Gourgas, Riker, and Simson), visited

45. Baynard, *History*, vol. 1, 170–79.

46. Baynard, *History*, vol. 1, 170–79.

47. Note added 2020: Bideaud's creation of the Supreme Council was finally ratified by the Supreme Council of Charleston in 1815.

48. See M'Cosh, *Documents*, 40–3.

49. See Dalcho's reply to De La Motta; Lobingier, *History*, 89–90.

Cerneau at his residence on William Street. After inquiring of Cerneau if he was the person listed on the tableau and receiving an affirmative response, De La Motta announced himself in his "official capacity" and presented his credentials, inquiring whence Cerneau derived his authority. Cerneau may have recognized the other callers as members of the competing Jacob's bodies. If Richard Riker had previously and unsuccessfully applied to Cerneau for membership, he may have derived some satisfaction in causing Cerneau personal discomfort.

In spite of the tableau's invitation Cerneau responded that he was not permitted to comply with the request, stating that De La Motta would have to apply to the Grand Consistory. De La Motta replied that he could not acknowledge any body of Masons unless satisfied that they were legally constituted. As a Sovereign Grand Inspector General De La Motta's patent empowered him to "inspect all Lodges, Chapters, Councils, Colleges & Consistories of the Royal & Military Order of Ancient & Modern Free-Masonry, over the surface of the Two Hemispheres, agreeable to the Grand Constitutions."[50] Had Cerneau really received the Thirty-third Degree he should have been aware of this as well that, according to the *Grand Constitutions* (Article 11), he should not have conferred the highest degrees except in the presence of three Sovereign Grand Inspectors General. Cerneau's refusal to accommodate De La Motta as well as his failure to recognize the signs of the Thirty-third Degree reinforced De La Motta's belief that Cerneau was a fraud.

> ... he did however repeatedly and peremptorily refuse to let me have a sight of his patents, from which circumstances, and from his *not answering* certain signs thrown out to him, I was induced to suppose, and am still fully convinced, *Mr. Cerneau* knew nothing of the 33d degree, and, consequently, that he was imposing upon the credulity of respectable characters.[51]

De La Motta also reported on the unusual relationship between the Cerneau's Grand Consistory and Supreme Council:

> *Mr. Cerneau, as well as his society*, seems to be particularly anxious to blend together what they are accustomed to term *their Grand Consistory*, and *their Supreme Council of the 33d degree*. When I visited him on the 14th September, 5813, I was more than once obliged to specify very plainly, that I had not called

50. Harris, *History*, 119.
51. M'Cosh, *Documents*, 47–8.

> to make inquiries respecting a *Grand Consistory*, but what he had published and *just* acknowledged to me, viz. '*His Supreme Council of Sovereigns Grand Inspectors General of the 33d degree*,' &c. &c. &c. that point once settled, the succeeding could not suffer any difficulty, and must come in afterwards as a matter of course.[52]

Having received no relief from Cerneau, De La Motta called on DeWitt Clinton, Cerneau's "Deputy Grand Commander," who was also Grand Master for the State of New York. But prior to proceeding with this account, let us take a moment to briefly examine some remarkable parallels which existed between the principle officers of the two Supreme Councils in New York.

John James Joseph Gourgas, of the regular Supreme Council, and Joseph Cerneau were both immigrants: the former from French-speaking Geneva, Switzerland, the latter from France. Gourgas was a merchant; Cerneau, a jeweler. Both served as Masonic secretaries. Sampson Simson, of the regular Supreme Council, was elected Grand Treasurer of New York in 1812 and 1813, but was defeated by Cerneauist John W. Mulligan in 1814. The following year Mulligan was defeated by Simson. Cadwallader D. Colden, of the regular Supreme Council, and Cerneauist Richard Riker both practiced law and served as District Attorneys. Riker was elected Recorder of New York City, and Colden to the State Assembly, then as Mayor, then to Congress and to the State Senate. But the strongest parallels were between Daniel D. Tompkins and De Witt Clinton.

> Both graduated from Columbia and studied law. Clinton was elected to the United States Senate and Tompkins, to Congress. Clinton was appointed Mayor of New York City, Tompkins, a Justice of the State Supreme Court. Tompkins was elected Governor of New York and Clinton, Lieutenant Governor. Clinton succeeded Tompkins by election, and at the same time Tompkins was elected Vice President of the United States. Both were disappointed in their failure to attain the Presidency. Clinton was Grand Master of Masons in New York, and Tompkins succeeded him in that office.[53]

When De La Motta met with DeWitt Clinton the latter stated he was unaware of the Thirty-third Degree as a ritual, and supposed it was a title, or distinction, such as Grand Master of the State. Clinton further stated he

52. M'Cosh, *Documents*, 69.

53. Baynard, *History*, vol. 1, 182. Baynard credits William Homan (*Proceedings of the New York Council of Deliberation*, 1905) with these discoveries.

had never seen the patents of Cerneau's authority, but affiliated under the persuasions of Thomas Lownds (one the defectors from Jacobs body), Martin Hoffman, and John W. Mulligan. Although Clinton promised to make an investigation and contact De La Motta, he failed to do so.

De La Motta's dissatisfaction led him to report to the Supreme Council at Charleston, which responded by denouncing Cerneau "as an Impostor of the first Magnitude" in a circular dated September 21, 1813, in which they also presumed to expel him from "every Masonic Asylum within [their] Jurisdiction." The Supreme Council at Charleston also mandated that Cerneau's Masonic associates should renounce his system and "express their sorrow and abhorrence of such unlawful, nefarious conduct." Three months later, on Christmas Eve, the Supreme Council at Charleston prepared another circular, in which they denounced "Joseph Cerneau, and his abettors and followers," declaring them unworthy of

> Masonic Communication with any regular Free-Mason, whether of high or low degree, or wheresoever dispersed; and that each, and every of them, [was] [thereby] expelled from even every or any lawful Degree or Masonic Society, in which they may have been received or admitted[54]

until they should make amends with the Supreme Council at Charleston. This could hardly have pleased DeWitt Clinton, who was Grand Master of New York at the time. Ironically,

> all the members of the Charleston Supreme Council belonged to the Grand Lodge of South Carolina which, in the eyes of most American Grand Lodges, was considered irregular from 1809 to 1817.[55]

The Cerneauists responded by issuing their own circular reminding the Supreme Council at Charleston that only a Grand Lodge could expel members from the Craft degrees; it further accused Emanuel De La Motta of overstepping his jurisdiction. The Cerneauists would not be intimidated, and in 1816 they established a Council of Princes of the Royal Secret in Charleston.[56]

54. M'Cosh, *Documents*, 25. A photograph of the original appears in Baynard, *History*, vol. 1, 180.

55. Alain Bernheim, Introduction to James B. Scot, *Outline of the Rise and Progress of Freemasonry in Louisiana from its Organization to the Re-Organization of the Grand Lodge in 1850.* 1995 Reprint. Introduction and Index by Alain Bernheim (Lafayette, La.: Michael Poll Publishing, 1995), Introduction, 8.

56. Folger, vol. 1, 170–71.

Some have suggested that Cerneau obtained information about the Scottish Rite through surreptitious means. It is important to bear in mind that just prior to the organization of the Supreme Council at Charleston, there had been two Grand Lodges in South Carolina the Ancients and the Moderns. In 1808 they merged but divided again the following year. John Mitchell and Frederick Dalcho had belonged to the Ancients Grand Lodge before the 1808 union but retained membership in the new Grand Lodge of South Carolina after the split. When Mitchell died in 1816 Thomas W. Bacot, the Ancient Grand Master, reportedly sent a servant to Mitchell's widow requesting his Masonic papers. The widow, who may not have realized that her husband was no longer a member of Bacot's Grand Lodge, is said to have delivered "two large trunks full" to the servant.

Grand Master Bacot was a member of Cerneau's Grand Consistory. It is not known which rituals, if any, were obtained by Bacot for Cerneau; however, when a collection of the Charleston Council's rituals was discovered in 1938 among its several missing rituals were all those Cerneau would have needed to fill the gaps between Morin's Twenty-five Degree Rite and the Scottish Rite; that is, if these degrees existed at the time.

The degree structure of the *Circular* is more primitive than that outlined in the 1786 Constitutions and, for reasons I have already briefly explained, I do not believe that the Supreme Council at Charleston possessed rituals for all the degrees it claimed in 1801. Indeed, the *Prix des Initiations* (Price of Initiations) listed in Antoine Bideaud's 1803 Register includes the same primitive grade-structure as the *Circular*, and a circa 1804 French-language précis of the secret work, found with the Register, listing the then current members of the Supreme Council at Charleston, omits material relative to the 23°, 24°, 25° and 26° Degrees, while the 29° is listed as *Grand Elu, chev*ER *de Cadoch*, (Grand Elect, Knight Kadosh) and the 30°, 31° and 32° are given jointly as *Royal Secret ou chevalier de S*T *André g*D... *fidéle gardien du Trésore sacré* (Royal Secret or Knight of St. Andrew, Grand Faithful Guardian of the Sacred Treasure) as in the *Circular*.

Missing from the Charleston rituals, which are written in Dalcho's hand, are the 14°, 16°, 18°, 20°, 23°, 24°, 25°, 26°, 27°, 30°, 31° and 32°. Some evidence suggests that the later 29°, Knight of St. Andrew, listed by Joseph M'Cosh,

Documents upon Sublime Free-Masonry (1823),[57] was the "Grand Master Ecosé or, Scottish Elder Master and Knight of St. Andrew" Degree, which is in the Dalcho collection. Cerneau would have needed the 23°, 24°, 25°, 26°, 27°, 31° and 33°, and he likely had the Grand Master Ecosé Degree which was sometimes included as an appendix to collections of Morin's Rite, as it is in the *Jamaica Ritual*. However it happened, by 1822 Cerneau's patents listed the names of all the degrees in our current order, from the fourth through the Thirty-second Degree inclusive.[58]

In 1821 an unusual event occurred which is often overlooked. The Charleston Grand Commander, Frederick Dalcho, entertained the idea of establishing a line of demarcation with the Cerneau Grand Consistory, allotting them the area above Washington DC, and the following year he refused to call the Supreme Council together. This came about in part by events resulting from the death of Emanuel De La Motta in May, 1821. Following De La Motta's death several of his personal papers and rituals were somehow scattered about Charleston. A group of Masons known as "The Associators" or "The Eleven" was able to obtain most of them, and soon the Cerneauists desired the collection. Controversy ensued over the issue of regularity, and eventually the documents were returned to the Supreme Council at Charleston. Because of his then current position as Chaplain in the Grand Lodge of South Carolina, Rev. Dalcho was on friendly terms with Peter Javain, then Junior Grand Deacon and the Cerneau "Representative" who made overtures to "The Eleven."[59] In return for this favor "The Eleven" requested the Thirty-second Degree from the Supreme Council at Charleston, an act which would place Dalcho in a personal controversy with the Cerneauists something he wished to avoid. To avoid this Dalcho attempted a diplomatic maneuver a line of demarcation; but with his own Supreme Council unyielding to Cerneauism, he felt trapped and surrendered his active role as Grand Commander on February 9, 1822. In 1823 Joseph M'Cosh, one of "The Eleven,"[60] had become a member of the Supreme Council at Charleston and wrote about the matter.

57. M'Cosh, *Documents*, 19.
58. See the patent of Cerneauist Seth Driggs in Folger, vol. 2, 202–4.
59. M'Cosh, *Documents*, 97; Bernheim in Scot, Introduction, 8–9.
60. Lobingier, *History*, 125.

> [T]he Grand Commander having withdrawn from the Council during the present disturbance, from the nature of his vocation, and having desired no voice either directly or indirectly in the transactions which might ensue, desired not to be consulted in any respect about the business....[61]

On the day of Dalcho's retirement Issac Auld became "acting Grand Commander" of the Supreme Council at Charleston, and his first official act was to legitimize "The Eleven." Although Dalcho continued to sign patents and retained his membership, he again never assumed an *active* office in the Supreme Council.[62]

THE ANTI-MASONIC STORM

Daniel D. Tompkins served as Grand Commander of the Supreme Council, Northern Jurisdiction, from its founding in 1813 until 1825, when Sampson Simson assumed leadership. From 1813–1820 it appears that there was almost no activity in the Supreme Council, Northern Jurisdiction. In the latter year, however, Giles Fonda Yates succeeded in reawakening a Lodge of Perfection in Albany, where Francken had established the high degrees in 1767. Yates apparently rediscovered Francken's documents and revived the Lodge of Perfection in Albany without having been initiated into the degrees, but in 1824 John Barker, an agent of the Supreme Council at Charleston, was sent to "heal" him.[63] As of that date there had not yet been an officially established line of territorial jurisdiction, and the Supreme Council at Charleston acted as it thought fit. Further, it appears that the Supreme Council, Northern Jurisdiction, established in 1813, had failed to act as a Council. According to an 1825 letter of Moses Holbrook, Lieutenant Grand Commander of the Supreme Council at Charleston, to Yates the Supreme Council, Northern Jurisdiction, had not any meetings for ten years.[64]

In August 1824 the Cerneauists were honored when the Marquis de Lafayette accepted membership in their Grand Consistory and became a Thirty-third

61. M'Cosh, *Documents*, 100.

62. Lobingier, *History*, 125; Harris, *History*, 136–38.

63. "Address of M.P. Bro. Giles Fonda Yates," Albert G. Mackey and William R. Singleton, *The History of Freemasonry*, 7 vols. (New York and London: The Masonic History Co., 1898, 1907), vol. 7, 1863–1878; Lobingier, *History*, 142–47; Harris, *History*, 155.

64. Lobingier, *History*, 140–41; Harris, *History*, 156.

Degree Mason.[65] In spite of what later historians have written,[66] the authentication of letters written by Lafayette, just ten days prior to his death, indicate he was a proud Cerneauist.[67] As an honorary tribute in November 1824, the Cerneauists constituted "Lafayette Chapter of Rose Croix" in New York.

In September 1826 William Morgan disappeared and the anti-Masonic period was ushered in. This subject has been adequately treated elsewhere and is too extensive to treat in detail. Suffice it to say that the impact of the ensuing anti-Masonic storm was devastating. From its outset, exposures of the Craft degrees were common, and in 1829 the Reverend David Bernard published the first exposé of American Scottish Rite ritual,[68] which contained some authentic material from the Charleston body. To cite but one example, the Prince of Libanus Degree, Bernard, pp. 247–48, is a verbatim copy of the 1801 Dalcho ritual. Bernard later claimed he received the rituals from the hands of his friend, the Reverend Nathan N. Whiting, who was Deputy Grand Master of Delta Lodge of Perfection in Schenectady, New York. This was the body Yates revived in 1820. According to Bernard,

> And by this servant of God [N.N. Whiting], Mr. [Giles Fonda] Yates was gained, and though not willing to assume any responsibility in the matter, was willing to give up the manuscripts to Mr. Whiting to dispose of as he thought best. And my good brother Whiting thought best to loan them to me, and to me for publication.[69]

Bernard's book is not without its caveats, however, as he (or his printer) occasionally misread the manuscripts. To cite but two minor examples, Bernard prints "Gornel" for *Gomel* (p. 184), and "prosecution" for *perfection* (p. 191). In the higher degrees he strayed even further as his failure to obtain

65. Folger, vol. 1, 179, 219–20.

66. Harris, *History*, 158–59.

67. La Fayette's letter in Folger, vol. 1, 179, 219–20, was authenticated by Claude Gagne, 33°, Grand Archivist of the Supreme Council of France. See Michael R. Poll, *The Elimination of the French Influence in Louisiana Masonry* (Lafayette, La.: Michael Poll Pub., 1995, 1996), 7.

68. David Bernard, *Light on Masonry. A Collection of the Most Important Documents.* (Utica, NY: William Williams, 1829). An earlier publication, Mary Hanlon, *Revelations in Masonry, Made by a Late Member of the Craft. In Four Parts.* (New York, Printed for the Author, 1827), merely reproduced Richard Carlile's *exposé* published in the *Republican* XII (London, 1825).

69. David Bernard, *Reminiscences of Masonic Revelations* (Chicago: Ezra A. Cook, 1896), 25–31; *Proceedings of the United States anti-Masonic Convention* (September 1830), 2; Baynard, *History*, vol. 1, 217.

the "secret work" led him to rely on French sources which were sometimes incompatible with American workings (see *Heredom,* vol. 3, p. 98). A careful comparison of the different editions reveals that Bernard further confused things by altering key portions of text after the first edition was published.

On March 7, 1832, Sampson Simson resigned the Grand Commandership, which then passed to J. J. J. Gourgas. However, the effect of the anti-Masonic agitation was sufficient to stop regular activity in the Supreme Council, Northern Jurisdiction, and it remained dormant until 1842 or 1843 when Gourgas and Yates revived it. In spite of the fact that the Supreme Council was dormant, Gourgas, Yates and several other brethren met annually, occasionally conferring degrees on zealous Masons.[70] For his efforts in preserving the Scottish Rite during the Morgan episode Gourgas has been denominated the "Conservator" of the Rite in the Northern Jurisdiction.

The Hicks Council, 1827–1832

If the Gourgas Council suffered during the Morgan affair, the Cerneauists were more fortunate. On November 28, 1827, Cerneau, apparently for the first time, opened his Supreme Council rather than the Grand Consistory.[71] It should be recalled that in Cerneau's confusing arrangement the "Supreme Council" was subordinate to his Grand Consistory. Elias Hicks, who previously served as Grand Treasurer, passed over DeWitt Clinton and was elected Sovereign Grand Commander. Inexplicably, Hicks then proceeded to suspend and then dissolve Cerneau's Grand Consistory. Whether Cerneau approved of this or not, we only know that the following month he sailed back to France, and that but two months later DeWitt Clinton passed away.[72] Hicks called his body "The Supreme Council of the Most Potent Sovereign Grand Inspectors General of the Thirty-third and last degree of the Ancient and Accepted Scottish Rite, Supreme Chiefs of Exalted Masonry, for the United States of America, Her Territories and

70. Baynard, *History*, vol. 1, 237–8, 267.

71. William Sewall Gardner, *Freemason's Magazine* (November 1863), as cited by Baynard, *History*, 210–11.

72. Baynard, *History*, vol. 1, 206–12, 240. Folger incorrectly maintained that the Grand Consistory died as a result of the Morgan episode, although he published the 1832 Hicks-St. Laurent list of officers which gave November 28, 1827, as the "date of its dissolution" (Compare Folger, vol. 1, 200–1, vol. 2, 225).

Dependencies." This appears to have been the first time the title "Ancient and Accepted Scottish Rite"was used.

THE HICKS-ST. LAURENT "UNITED SUPREME COUNCIL," 1832–1846

On April 13, 1832, the Hicks Supreme Council merged with that of the so-called Marquis de Santa Rosa, Comte de St. Laurent, who allegedly exercised jurisdiction over South America, New Spain, the Canary Islands, and Puerto Rico.[73] This amalgamated body styled itself "The United Supreme Council for the Western Hemisphere, of the Puissant Sovereign Grand Inspectors General 33rd and last degree of the Ancient and Accepted Scottish Rite, Sublime Chiefs of Exalted Masonry."

It is important to recall that in 1832, under the pressures of anti-Masonry, the regular Supreme Council, Northern Jurisdiction, headed by J. J. J. Gourgas, ceased to function as such; and although its authority still resided with its members, the Supreme Council, for all practical purposes, slumbered during the storm. The Constitutions (Dalcho version, Article 5) required the presence of three Supreme Council members to lawfully enact business as such. In fact, the work of both regular Supreme Councils was curtailed. In February 1832 Moses Holbrook, Sovereign Grand Commander of the Supreme Council at Charleston, wrote to Gourgas:

> In our Supreme Council we have transacted no business of any importance for more than a year; if we had done anything I should have deemed it an important duty to have given you early information of the same.[74]

A letter from Gourgas reveals that his body was similarly affected.

> In 1832, fairly tired out and sick at the useless trouble I had undertaken for years, having been linked in these matters with men very respectable, to be sure, but most indifferent as to Masonic matters and proceedings, I stopped at once and entirely....[75]

The few active Masons in the northern United States with an interest in the Scottish Rite may have been drawn towards the Hicks-St. Laurent Council.

73. As Harold V.B. Voorhis observed in his *The Story of the Scottish Rite of Freemasonry,* rev. ed. (Richmond, Va.: Macoy, 1965, 1980), 5–8, very little is known about St. Laurent or his Supreme Council.

74. Baynard, *History*, vol. 1, 237.

75. Baynard, *History*, vol. 1, 237.

If nothing else Cerneauism preserved and perpetuated an interest in the high degrees during Masonry's most trying hour; however, the most significant contribution of this Supreme Council was its publication of the Latin Constitutions of 1786, which were later adopted by the Southern Jurisdiction as the law of the Rite. The Constitutions were published in connection with a Treaty that was signed in 1834 between the Hicks Council, the Supreme Council for France, and the Supreme Council for Brazil. In the opinion of many Masonic researchers, the Treaty was a sham which existed only on paper.[76] However this may be, the alleged Treaty upset several members of the Supreme Council, who, in consequence, took the Warrant of Lafayette Chapter of Rose Croix, and departed. The Hicks-St. Laurent Council then appears to have had a struggling existence until 1845, when a fire destroyed its Archives. The following year at a meeting with but four members present, the Hicks-St. Laurent Supreme Council voted to disperse its funds, *pro rata*, among the surviving members.[77] It is not known if this Supreme Council made any revisions to its rituals after Joseph Cerneau's departure.

The Gourgas-Yates Revival

In 1842, with Giles F. Yates as chief motivator, a Grand Council of Princes of Jerusalem and Lodge of Perfection were organized in Boston, Massachusetts and Portsmouth, New Hampshire.[78] The original authority for the Boston Grand Council was a patent issued by the Supreme Council at Charleston seventeen years earlier in 1825. Within two years Gourgas and Yates revived the Supreme Council, Northern Jurisdiction, with the assistance of such Brethren

76. The Latin version of the Grand Constitutions was allegedly first published in *Treaty of Masonic Union, Alliance and Confederation* (Paris: J.A. Boudon, 1836). It is reproduced in Folger, vol. 2 (Document No. 28), 238–95. Several arguments against the treaty and authenticity of the 1836 Paris version have been offered: 1) No authentic copy, with all the official signatures, has ever been discovered; 2) No earlier copy of the Latin Constitutions has been discovered; 3) The ratification of the treaty (signed December 6, 1836) could not have been transmitted from New York to Paris, for publication before the year's end, as there were no trans-Atlantic cables or Steam Ships in 1836; 4) Lafayette's name, ***but not his autograph***, was included on the Treaty (dated February 23, 1834), published two years after his death; 5) It is not mentioned in any of the proceedings or circulars of the Supreme Council of France at this time.

77. Folger, vol. 1, 226; Baynard, *History*, vol. 1, 245.

78. Baynard, *History*, vol. 1, 267–75. In conjunction with this the first new monitor of the Scottish Rite degrees (4°–16°) was published since the Morgan episode, i.e., *Sublime Freemasonry*, 2 vols. (Albany, NY: L.G. Hoffman, ca. 1842).

as Edward A. Raymond and Simon W. Robinson. Coincidental with this was the revival of the Supreme Council at Charleston.[79] In 1845, just after the revival of the Supreme Council, Northern Jurisdiction, petitions were received from Robert T. Crucefix, of England, for the Scottish Rite degrees, and in conjunction with this the Supreme Council for England and Wales was established.[80]

On August 25, 1851, Gourgas tendered his resignation and was succeeded by Giles F. Yates, who presided only ten days before resigning. Prior to his resignation, Yates delivered an eloquent lecture on the history of the Scottish Rite and his association with it.[81] Following this resignation Edward A. Raymond was installed Sovereign Grand Commander.

THE FIRST ATWOOD COUNCIL, 1849–1850

In 1826 James Cushman, the First Grand Lecturer of Virginia, and honorary member of the Supreme Council at Charleston, illegally conferred the Thirty-third Degree on Henry C. Atwood.[82] Both Cushman and Atwood were students of Jeremy Cross, the renowned Masonic lecturer. But this was not the first time Cushman had caused trouble. About 1822 or 1823 he declared a body of Richmond Knights Templar illegal, and, claiming the authority to create Knights and form Commanderies he required that the sum of $90.00 be paid to him for providing one. When he later tried the same maneuver in Winchester, Virginia, he was accused of invasion of jurisdiction.[83]

Henry C. Atwood was among those who left the Hicks-St. Laurent Council in 1834 on account of the alleged Treaty, and succeeded William F. Piatt as presiding officer of Lafayette Chapter of Rose Croix. With the prevailing

79. Harris, *History*, 224–31.

80. See A.C.F. Jackson, *Rose Croix: A History of the Ancient and Accepted Rite for England and Wales*, rev. ed. (London: A. Lewis, 1980, 1987); John Mandelberg, *Ancient and Accepted. A chronicle of the proceedings 1845–1945 of the Supreme Council established in England in 1845* (London: The Supreme Council, 33°, 1995).

81. This lecture is recorded in full in Robert Ingham Clegg, ed., *Mackey's History of Freemasonry*, rev. and enl. ed., 7 vols. (Chicago, New York, London: The Masonic History Co., 1921), vol. 6, 1889–1905.

82. A excellent synopsis of the events may be found in S. Brent Morris, *The Folger Manuscript. The Cryptanalysis and Interpretation of an American Masonic Document*. (Bloomington, Ill.: The Masonic Book Club, 1992).

83. Melvin M. Johnson, ed., *Gould's History of Freemasonry Throughout the World*, 6 vols. (New York: Charles Scribner's Sons, 1936), vol. 6, 337–37.

anti-Masonic sentiment in New York State the Grand Master had issued an edict in 1826 forbidding all public processions and displays; however, in 1836 Atwood and Piatt, both installed Masters, ignored the Grand Master's edict and participated in a successful St. John's Day parade. The predictable result was their expulsion from the Craft. Undeterred, Atwood organized his own "St. John's Grand Lodge," which remained active from 1837 to 1850, when it merged with the regular Grand Lodge and its past actions were regularized.[84]

In February 1828 Henry Atwood visited DeWitt Clinton just prior to the latter's death, and had him autograph his patent. Atwood later claimed the patent as authority for an alleged reorganization of the Cerneau Supreme Council in May 1849. As with the earlier Cerneau-Hicks Supreme Council, this body claimed to exercise authority over "the United States of America, her Territories and Dependencies."[85] It should be recalled that DeWitt Clinton was never Grand Commander of the Cerneau Supreme Council, but only of the Sovereign Grand Consistory.[86] If Atwood was on *terra firma*, why should he have to rely on a *post mortem* endorsement of Clinton to justify his position?

Following the 1850 reconciliation of Atwood's St. John's Grand Lodge with the Grand Lodge of New York, his status was elevated to a position enabling him to strengthen his Supreme Council. At that time Dr. Robert B. Folger, who attended a meeting prior to and concerning Atwood's St. John's

84. Johnson, ed., *Gould's History*, vol. 6, 57–8; Folger, vol. 1, 222–23; Edwood R. Cusick, "Atwood, Henry Clinton" in Henry W. Coil, et al., *Coil's Masonic Encyclopedia* (New York: Macoy, 1961), 80–81. This event recalls William Preston's "unlawful Masonic procession" on St. John's Day which resulted in his expulsion from the Craft. As a result Preston organized his Grand Lodge of England South of the River Trent, but was restored to the Modern Grand Lodge about ten years afterward. It is worth noting that Atwood is recognized today as a legitimate Past Grand Master in New York.

85. Gould, *Library*, vol. 5, 311. According to Baynard, *History*, vol. 1, 251, 265, Atwood's authority was limited to the State of New York, but this is likely confused with Atwood's second Supreme Council.

86. Of the Clinton's signing, Folger, vol. 1, 244, wrote, "It will also be recollected that Mr. Atwood, at this time, was Sovereign Grand Inspector General, Thirty-third degree, and held the power of the same, confirmed and countersigned by DeWitt Clinton, the M. Sovereign Grand Commander, which according to the Laws and Constitutions of the Order, gave him power for life, to establish, congregate, superintend and instruct Lodges, Chapters, Colleges, Consistories and Councils of the Royal and Military Order of Ancient and Modern Free Masonry, over the surface of the two hemispheres, &c." In ascribing these alleged powers to Atwood, Folger was merely parroting the words of Emanuel De La Motta, relative to his own Thirty-third Degree patent (See M'Cosh, *Documents*, 52). To the contrary, while De La Motta's patent, as an active member of the Supreme Council, granted him this power, Atwood's patent, of dubious authority, lacked this authoritative clause (See reproduction in Baynard, *History*, vol. 1, 248–49).

day march,[87] entered the scene, in his words, "attempting to build up the old Council on a better foundation."[88] In 1850 Atwood also published his monitor, *The Master Workman*.[89] Its contents suggest that there had been but little, if any, revision in the rituals.

THE CROSS COUNCIL, 1851–1852

In 1851 Dr. Folger persuaded Jeremy Cross, one of the most popular Masons in the United States and author of the *Hieroglyphic Monitor*, to join the Atwood Supreme Council and accept the Grand Commandership. Folger admitted that the reason they wanted Cross was because the old active Cerneau members had either died, or moved from the city, and that Cross also held an Honorary Thirty-third Degree from the Charleston Supreme Council.[90] According to Moses Holbrook, Grand Commander of the Supreme Council at Charleston in 1827, the only reason Jeremy Cross was given an honorary membership was because he and another Mason somehow came upon a bundle of rituals, including "a Grand 33d." In return for surrendering the rituals to the Supreme Council, they were constituted Honorary Members of the Charleston Supreme Council.[91] Curiously, Folger sought the authority of Jeremy Cross's Southern Jurisdiction patent while at the same time disavowing both the Charleston Supreme Council and the Constitutions of 1786, under which authority the patent was issued! The Cross body styled itself "The Supreme Council for the Northern Hemisphere."

According to Folger, Cross had received a complete set of rituals of the so-called "exalted degrees" from the hands of Joseph Cerneau and Thomas Lownds, and also a full set "up to the 32°" from the Consistory in Louisiana.[92] In another account Folger claims Cross had three sets of rituals, 1) the

87. Folger, vol. 1, 222–23.

88. Folger, vol. 1, 248.

89. Henry C. Atwood, *The Master Workman* (New York: Macoy, 1850). This work was republished as Robert Macoy, *The True Masonic Guide* (New York: Clark Austin & Co., 1852).

90. Folger, vol. 1, 248–49. Folger admitted he induced Cross to join on the pretense that the Scottish Rite would benefit the York Rite which it did not. When the Charleston Council learned of Cross's appointment it denied the authenticity of his Thirty-third Degree patent, but the original (in the archives of the Grand Lodge of New Hampshire) has been unquestionably verified.

91. Lobingier, 134.

92. Robert B. Folger, "Recollections of a Masonic Veteran," *New York Dispatch*, part 31, May 31, 1874.

Cerneau-Lownds set, 2) the Louisiana Consistory set, and 3) a set from the Supreme Council at Charleston, up to and including the ritual of the Thirty-third Degree.[93] If the information in the "Grand 33d" ritual was not authentic, there would have been no reason to grant Cross a Thirty-third Degree patent. Did Jeremy Cross retain a copy of the ritual? If we accept a June 1828 report of the Charleston Council, with one exception, "No copies of the 33d Degree have ever been given or allowed to be taken by any Inspector in either jurisdiction."[94] The exception alluded to involved the actions of a certain Bro. McFarlane and is briefly outlined below.

As mentioned earlier, when Grand Commander John Mitchell died in 1816, part of his documents fell into the hands of friends of Joseph Cerneau, while other ritual manuscripts, including the Thirty-third Degree, were obtained by Mitchell's son-in-law, Bro. William M. Dyre. A Bro. McFarlane, a friend of Bro. Dyre, reportedly stole the Thirty-third ritual and took it to Alabama, where he copied it. John G. Barker, an agent of the Charleston Council, obtained it from Bro. McFarlane, along with the copy, but Barker failed to return it to the Supreme Council.[95] After Barker received the ritual from McFarlane the Supreme Council at Charleston received reports that Barker was conferring degrees and collecting fees without authority, but the Supreme Council, perhaps hoping to obtain Mitchell's Thirty-third Degree ritual, apparently took no action. The ritual was only acquired from after Barker's death, from his widow. In connection with the reported set of Charleston rituals in Jeremy Cross's possession, Folger mentioned that both Cross and John Barker had a copy. If this is true perhaps Barker provided Cross with a copy of the Thirty-third Degree.

Cross's collection of rituals were likely used by his Supreme Council in a recension, because much of his 1853 Scottish Rite monitor is remarkably similar to the *Francken Manuscript*, which differs greatly from the earlier Webb-form monitors of his predecessors in both Northern Jurisdictions.[96]

93. Folger, vol. 1, 250; vol. 2, 353.
94. Harris, *History*, 190.
95. Harris, *History*, 186, 203.
96. Jeremy L. Cross, *The Supplement to the Templar's Chart: Containing the Following Thirty Ineffable Degrees....* (New York, 1853).

In 1852 Cross resigned from the Council, on account of his health, and retired to New Hampshire. During that year the Supreme Council corresponded with James Foulhouze, who had received his Thirty-third Degree from the Grand Orient of France in 1845.[97] Foulhouze was then acting Sovereign Grand Commander of the Supreme Council of Louisiana, which traced its authority back to the Marquis de Santangelo.[98] The Supreme Council of Louisiana would later make a Concordat with The Supreme Council at Charleston in 1855.

THE SECOND ATWOOD COUNCIL, 1852–1860

In July Foulhouze visited the Cross Supreme Council and installed new officers, including Henry C. Atwood as Grand Commander, and the Council was then known as "The Supreme Council of the Thirty-third Degree of and for the Free, Sovereign and Independent State of New York."[99] Foulhouze also convinced Atwood to adopt and practice his version of Scottish Rite craft degrees.[100] As a result of his infringements on the rights of the Grand Lodge of New York Atwood, and the members of his Council, were brought up on charges, tried and expelled from Freemasonry. In 1855 two members of his Supreme Council resigned, and another installation followed when the name "The Supreme Council for the Northern Masonic Jurisdiction of the Western Hemisphere" was adopted. At this time Hopkins Thompson was admitted into the Supreme Council.[101] Thomson would later become Sovereign Grand Commander of his own Council. From 1855 to 1860 Atwood's Council reportedly prospered, though in the latter year he moved to Connecticut "on account of ill health," where he died the following September.

The rituals of Atwood's second Supreme Council[102] borrowed liberally from Albert Pike's first revision of the Scottish Rite rituals, published in the

97. James Foulhouze, *Historical Inquiry into the Origin of the Ancient and Accepted Scotch Rite....* (New Orleans: The True Delta Job Office, 1859), 60–61.

98. See *General Statutes Supreme Council of the Thirty-third Degree of the Ancient and Accepted Scotch Rite of Freemasonry State of Louisiana, Grand Orient of New Orleans* rev ed. (New Orleans, 1990).

99. Folger, vol. 1, 251–2; Baynard, *History*, vol. 1, 266.

100. The rituals are given *in extenso* by Art deHoyos, "The Blue Degrees of Atwood's Cerneau Supreme Council" in *Collectanea*, vol. 15 (Grand College of Rites of the USA, 1994), part 2.

101. Folger, vol. 1, 254–6; Baynard, *History*, vol. 1, 256.

102. The rituals of Atwood's second Supreme Council were exposed in Jonathan Blanchard,

1857 *Magnum Opus*. Pike's *Magnum Opus* was the most extensive revision of the Scottish Rite degrees undertaken in the United States and served as the foundation for later revisions, but it failed to satisfy the needs of the Supreme Council at Charleston, and was not officially adopted. Scores of pages were deleted, large sections would have to be completely rewritten, and entire degrees, including the 27° Knight Commander of the Temple and 28° Knight of the Sun, were wholly discarded. Many of the deleted lectures were published in Pike's best known work, *Morals and Dogma*, which serves as Pike's commentary on the degrees.

Atwood's borrowing of Pike's material set a trend for the Northern Supreme Councils, regular and irregular alike, which continued to amalgamate texts, rather than rewrite the rituals from scratch. The Atwood Council also relied heavily on the rituals of Foulhouze's Supreme Council of Louisiana. In fact, the secret work in Atwood's Fourth through Thirtieth Degree rituals was lifted from Charles Laffon de Ladébat's English translation of the Foulhouze rituals,[103] while the full text of his Thirty-first and Thirty-second Degrees was purloined from a Pike-de Ladébat cooperative effort,[104] and his Thirty-third Degree ritual was only a slight abridgment of the Foulhouze ritual.[105]

THE HAYS COUNCIL, 1860–1863

A month after Atwood's death Edmund B. Hays presented the Supreme Council a letter of appointment, written in 1858 by Atwood, appointing him his

Scotch Rite Masonry Illustrated, 2 vols. (Chicago: Ezra A. Cook, 1887–8).

103. The secret work for the 4°–18° is found in Charles Laffon de Ladébat, *Ancient and Accepted Scotch Rite. Eighteenth Degree* (New Orleans, 1856), 67–127, 171–3, while that of the 19°–30° appears in Charles Laffon deLadébat, *Ancient and Accepted Scotch Rite. Thirtieth Degree* (New Orleans, 1856), 29–75, 135–7.

104. Albert Pike and Charles Laffon de Ladébat, *Ancient and Accepted Scottish Rite. Thirty-first and Thirty-Second Degrees* (New Orleans, 1858). Ironically, the Supreme Council of Louisiana adopted the Pike-de Ladébat rituals which it has since presumably copyrighted(!); see *Thirty-second Degree Ritual* (New Orleans: Supreme Council of Louisiana, 1949). The volume includes both the 31° and 32°.

105. Charles Laffon de Ladébat, *Thirty-Third and Last Degree of the Ancient and Accepted Scotch Rite: Sovereign Grand Inspector General* (New Orleans, 1857). This is the ritual which de Ladébat conferred on Albert Pike, and which, after a dispute with John Q.A. Fellows, Pike sought to eradicate. See Lobingier, 248; Harris, *History*, 254, 289; James D. Carter, *History of the Supreme Council, 33°... 1861–1891* (Washington, DC, 1967), 37–39.

successor to the Grand Commandership.[106] Hays was raised a Master Mason in 1847 in a Lodge chartered by Atwood's St. John's Grand Lodge. Nothing consequential seems to have occurred during Hays's administration, and no evidence of degree work has been discovered. There is no reason to believe that they made any modifications to Atwood's rituals.

THE RAYMOND COUNCIL, 1860–1863

The year 1860 also saw a strange event in the regular Supreme Council, Northern Jurisdiction, which historians have yet to fully understand. Edward Raymond reportedly

> conceived the idea that as the M.P. Grand Commander of the Supreme Council, *he* was the representative of Frederick the Great, and that his Masonic powers were absolute, that he could direct the Supreme Council as he chose, open or close it at his pleasure, and that the members were not his peers.[107]

Raymond, a Past Grand Master of Massachusetts,[108] concluded that unlike Craft Masonry, the Scottish Rite invested the supreme officer with unlimited powers within his jurisdiction. This was clearly contrary to the Constitutions of 1786 which specified that "*The Supreme Council* shall exercise all the Sovereign Masonic Power."[109] Then, with utter disregard for the Council, he proceeded to confer the Thirty-third Degree on persons without a vote of the Council and also refused to entertain motions. Ignoring the sessions of the Council, he accused his peers of insubordination and a conspiracy to usurp his authority; finally, he announced it was his "duty" to close the Council *sine die*, when he, and Simon W. Robinson, the Grand Treasurer General "abruptly left the room."[110]

With Raymond's departure a provisional Supreme Council continued to work with Killian H. Van Rensselaer as acting Grand Commander. Possible

106. Baynard, *History*, vol. 1, 349.

107. Gould, *Library*, vol. 5, 315.

108. Raymond served the constitutional limit of three years, from 1849–1851.

109. Article 12, Constitutions of 1786 (Gourgas copy, emphasis added), Baynard, *History*, vol. 1, 509. The Latin Constitutions, accepted by the Southern Jurisdiction, reads similarly, "each Supreme Council of Sovereign Grand Inspectors General... will of full right become legitimately endowed with all Masonic authority...." Pike, *Grand Constitutions*, 251–53.

110. Gould, *Library*, vol. 5, 315; Baynard, *History*, vol. 1, 324–27.

justification for the Van Rensselaer Council's "rebellion" was given in a speech made by Albert Pike two years earlier, in which he said

> There is always a right of *revolution*; and no doubt, if the rule of the Supreme Council at Charleston should become onerous and tyrannical, or inefficient, it may be shaken off . . . and new Supreme Councils established. The oath of allegiance always ceases to bind, when the reciprocal obligation of justice and protection is not kept.[111]

Raymond and Robinson visited Pike to obtain his opinion on the matter. In a written response Pike remarked that "there could be no doubt" that Raymond "had not been even formally deposed."[112] Pike advised Raymond to return to the Supreme Council, Northern Jurisdiction (which he had abandoned), summon the Active Members together and present a plan of reconciliation; however, rather than following Pike's advice Raymond organized another "Supreme Council" which, curiously, included two Thirty-second Degree Masons, William Field and Aaron B. Hughes.[113] This, of course, meant in that 1863 there were three competing Supreme Councils in the Northern United States:

1. The Hays-Cerneau body, with headquarters in New York City;
2. The Van Rensselaer body, with headquarters in Boston;
3. The Raymond body, with headquarters in Boston.[114]

In January 1862 Raymond preferred charges against Bros. Van Rensselaer and Charles W. Moore, whom he considered guilty of usurpation of authority; they were found guilty, *in absentia*, and expelled. As one good turn deserves another, four months later Grand Commander Van Rensselaer issued an Edict of Expulsion for Bros. Raymond and Robinson.[115] This state of affairs was distressing enough that Cerneau historian Robert B. Folger remarked, "the

111. *Lecture of Bro. . . Albert Pike, Delivered by Special Request, Before the M.W. Grand Lodge of Louisiana, at its Forty-sixth Annual Communication, Held in New Orleans, February, 1858. Published by Order of the Grand Lodge.* (New Orleans: Bulletin Book and Job Office, 1858), 62.

112. The Van Rensselaer Council, which also sought Pike's intervention, "deposed" Raymond from office on May 20, 1861. Lobingier, *The Supreme Council, 33°*, 81; Folger, vol. 1, 267.

113. Gould, *A Library*, vol. 5, 317.

114. Gould, *A Library*, vol. 5, 322. There was, in fact, a *fourth* Supreme Council in Connecticut, but its was of no consequence.

115. Both circulars are reproduced in Folger, vol. 2, 399–402.

contempt and bitter reproaches which such proceedings bring upon the Order, cannot be too greatly magnified or too severely condemned."[116]

The Raymond Council was not ritualistically inactive. Whereas the other Northern Supreme Councils were content to pass and copy manuscript rituals, in 1861 this Council proceeded to revise them for publication. In his defection Grand Commander Raymond must have brought a mass of the Boston Council's rituals with him, because in his revisions of ensuing years one clearly discovers ritualistic elements from both of these jurisdictions.

THE HAYS-RAYMOND COUNCIL, 1863–1866

In April 1862, at an emergent session of the Raymond Council, it was revealed that the Cerneau Hays Council made overtures for a merger. Anxious to strengthen their position, a consolidated Council was formed on April 15, 1863, which called itself the "Supreme Grand Council, Thirty-third and last degree of the Ancient and Accepted Scottish Rite for the United States of America, their Territories and Dependencies." Every member present took an oath of allegiance to the Council, over which Edmund B. Hays was elected to preside.

Like the Raymond Council before it this Supreme Council also worked on revising the rituals. In September 1863 Raymond and Charles T. McClenachan were appointed to review the rituals which was apparently done,[117] though less than a year later, on August 2, 1864, Raymond passed away.

In September 1865 a committee was appointed to visit the Supreme Council at Charleston in an effort to win recognition, and the following month the Hays-Raymond Council changed its name to the "Supreme Council for the Northern Jurisdiction of the United States of America." In doing so it limited its claim to but fifteen northern States, which is something the Charleston body would have no doubt demanded. In April 1866 Albert Pike, and a special Charleston committee investigating the northern Scottish Rite activity, concluded that "both the Van Rensselaer and the Raymond Supreme Councils were illegal, null and void; that the only surviving legal Sovereign Grand Inspectors of the 33d degree"[118] were the living active members of the

116. Folger, vol. 1, 273.

117. Irving E. Partridge, Jr., *The Rituals of the Supreme Council, 33°, for the Northern Masonic Jurisdiction U.S.A.* (Lexington, Mass.: Supreme Council, 33°, 1976), 13–15.

118. Partridge, *Rituals*, 327; Josiah H. Drummond, "Ancient and Accepted Scottish Rite of

Old Northern Supreme Council which Raymond had abandoned. In Pike's opinion Simon W. Robinson was Raymond's lawful successor, although at the same time he leveled harsh criticism for Robinson's involvement in the Hays-Raymond union of 1863. Pike maintained that the authority of the Raymond Council was suspended, but that Robinson could reorganize a legitimate Supreme Council if he could regain the old membership of the council he had abandoned. In the opinion of Northern Jurisdiction historian Samuel Baynard, however, Pike erred, and the authority rested with the Van Rensselaer Council.[119]

The Revived Raymond Council, 1866–1867

In December 1865 Hays resigned and Robinson was installed Grand Commander; and the following year, in an attempt to place his Council "within the pale of legitimacy, and secure fraternal relations with the Southern [Charleston] Council" the Hays-Raymond Council was dissolved.[120] Both the Hays-Raymond and the Van Rensselaer Councils had allowed their personal animosities to injure the Scottish Rite. "The demoralization of the Rite had become deplorable, the establishing of the bodies, and the conferring of degrees had degenerated into a farce, each trying to outdo and undo the other."[121]

On the advice of Albert Pike, in November 1866 Robinson summoned the living active members of his former Council to a meeting and, perhaps predictably, they ignored his summons.[122] With the dissolution of the Hays-Raymond Council, Robinson attempted to reorganize the Council he abandoned, notwithstanding the fact that Killian Van Rensselaer presumed to preside as its Sovereign Grand Commander. In spite of his efforts, Robinson could not reorganize the old Council, and this short-lived Revived Raymond Council (as it is now known) was in reality simply a reorganization of the Hays-Raymond Council. The New York Revived Raymond Council and the Boston

Freemasonry," in Henry Leonard Stillson and William James Hughan, eds., *History of the Ancient and Honorable Fraternity of Free and Accepted Masons and Concordant Orders*, rev. ed. (Boston: Fraternity Pub. Co., 1912), 825; Henry W. Coil, *Freemasonry Through Six Centuries*, 2 vols. (Richmond, Va.: Macoy, 1968), 371.

119. Baynard, *History*, vol. 1, 395–96.

120. Address of Simon W. Robinson, December 131866; Gould, *A Library*, vol. 5, 329–30.

121. Gould, *Library*, vol. 5, 336.

122. Baynard, *History*, vol. 1, 393–95.

Van Rensselaer Council having both failed to obtain recognition of the Southern Jurisdiction, determined to put an end to over half a century of hostility.

Whether it was the result of this Council, or one of its two immediate its predecessors, is not known, but between 1864 and 1866 the first authorized printed Scottish Rite rituals were produced in the Northern Jurisdiction. As alluded early, they were clearly an amalgamation of Albert Pike's *Magnum Opus* (1857) and the rituals of the Supreme Council, Northern Jurisdiction, periodically revised from its revival in 1843 to about 1860, when the official *Secret Directory of Manuscripts* (mss. ritual collection) was issued.

THE UNION OF 1867

Unfortunately, the architects of the Union of 1867 failed to keep a detailed record of the circumstances which resulted in this momentous union. In fact, the only extensive first-hand account in print is that of Josiah Drummond[123] who wrote that he, and five other members of the Boston Council, comprised a committee to receive "any propositions which may be made to [the Van Rensselaer Council] from any source within its jurisdictional limits" and to "adjust the differences which exist therein." An identically-worded resolution was adopted by the Revived Raymond Council one month later.[124] Just prior to meeting with the Van Rensselaer Council, Grand Commander Robinson resigned his office, and John L. Lewis succeeded him. In the chambers of the Boston Council, Grand Commander Van Rensselaer also resigned his office. The final terms of agreement, too long to relate here, were extremely fair and were adopted unanimously by both parties.[125] Josiah Drummond summarized the actions that led to the union.

> The committees, assisted by other brethren, met just before the annual session of the Boston Council in May, 1867. The general terms of union were soon tacitly agreed upon; but local, and possibly personal, interests caused much difficulty in arranging the details. In fact, more than once the negotiations were in danger of being broken off without result; at one time this danger was so imminent that several started to leave, with the idea that

123. Drummond, in Stillson and Hughan, *History*, 826–27.

124. George Adelbert Newbury and Louis Lenway Williams, *A History of The Supreme Council, 33° of the Ancient and Accepted Scottish Rite of Freemasonry for the Northern Masonic Jurisdiction of the United States of America* (Lexington, Mass.: Supreme Council, 1987), 144.

125. For the terms, see Gould, *Library*, vol. 5, 336–38.

> nothing could be done, when a brother invited all to break bread together, and insisted that all should accept the invitation. Before they returned to the committee room, everything had been arranged with mutual good will.
>
> The Treaty was signed by all the members of both committees and the two bodies at once proceeded to act upon it. It was ratified by each by unanimous vote and by the approval of all the Honorary members. The two councils came together as equals and all the acts of both were held to be valid, except the expulsions on account of former differences, and they were rescinded. . . .
>
> The Grand Commander was elected by concurrent vote of the two Councils, and the other officers designated, and when the preliminary arrangements had been completed, both Councils met as one body; the two Past Grand Commanders of the two Councils, Killian H. Van Rensselaer and John L. Lewis, conducted the Grand Commander-elect, Josiah H. Drummond, to the altar, where he took the oath of fealty in the presence of the Supreme Council, and then administered it to the brethren present, to the number of eighty. The officers, as already agreed upon, were then elected and installed: a constitution was adopted and the organization thereunder fully completed.
>
> Peace was thus established; the Supreme Council was everywhere recognized; it at once entered upon a career of unexampled prosperity; the old feuds were so completely buried that the members forgot who were "of the other party" in former times: active work was resumed: subordinate bodies furnished themselves with paraphernalia for *conferring* the degrees, and their mere "communication" almost ceased: bodies attained such proficiency in the work as to command the interest and attendance of more than their halls would accommodate; and the growth of the Rite exceeded the expectations of the most enthusiastic.[126]

The ritual adopted at the Union of 1867 was that of the Revived Raymond Council, printed in a new edition.[127] Perhaps surprisingly, it included the Atwood Thirty-third Degree ritual inherited from James Foulhouze and his Supreme Council of Louisiana.[128] This was likely used less than a year however, since Albert Pike completed his first revision of the Thirty-third Degree in

126. Drummond, in Stillson and Hughan, *History*, 827.

127. As an aside, this ritual is the *fons et origo* of the Prince Hall Scottish Rite rituals. The current (post-1946) ritual is an abridgment, with one interpolation: the second section of the Twentieth Degree includes a brief addition entitled "The Light of Patriotism," in which George Washington and Prince Hall discuss Freemasonry. *Book of the Scottish Rite 4°–32°* (United Supreme Council, Prince Hall Affiliation, [N.J. & S.J.], 1946, 1989).

128. The description of the decorations from the Union of 1867 Thirty-third Degree ritual is a verbatim match of the Atwood ritual, and differs greatly from the Dalcho ritual used by the Van Rensselaer Council. Compare Charles T. McClenachan, *The Book of the Ancient and Accept Scottish Rite of Freemasonry* (New York: Masonic Publishing & Manufacturing Co., 1867), 491–92 and Jonathan Blanchard, ed., *Scotch Rite Masonry Illustrated,* 2 vols. (Chicago: Ezra A. Cook, 1887–8), vol. 2, p. 460.

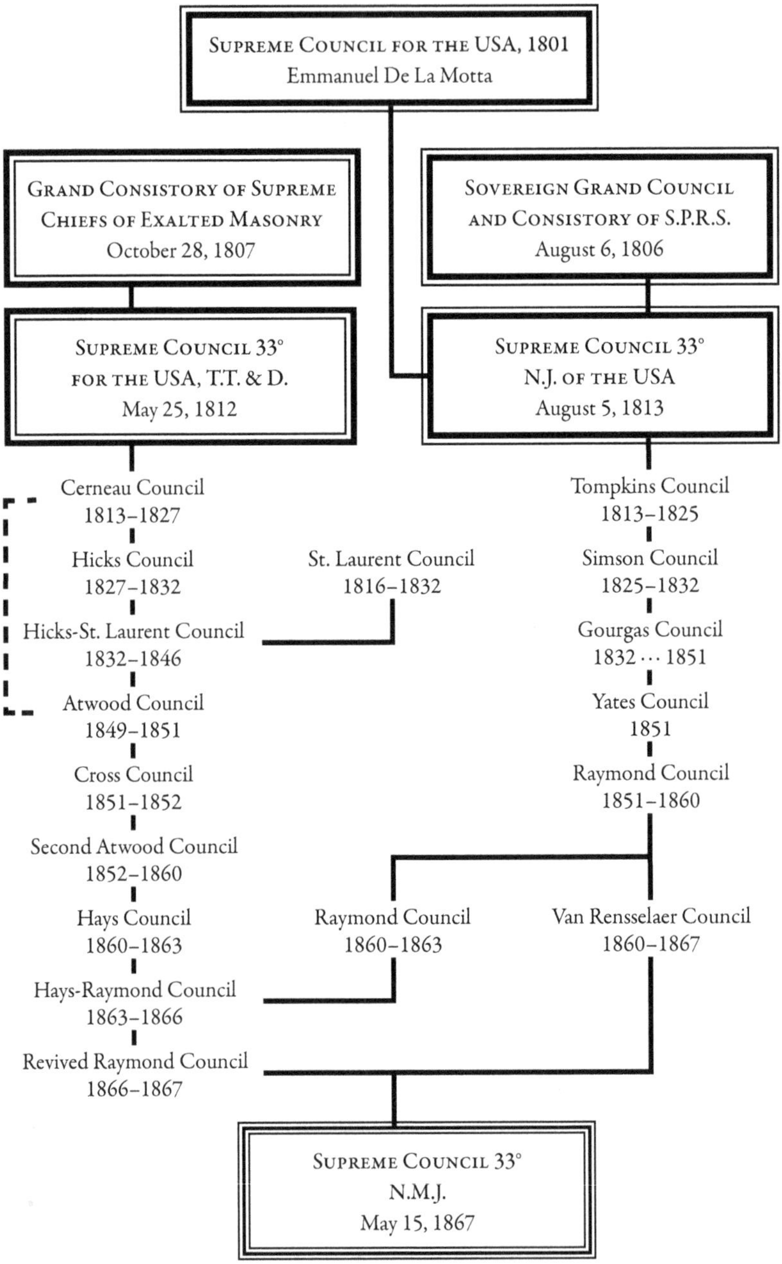

Figure 2. Genealogy of the Supreme Council 33° for the Northern Masonic Jurisdiction.

1868, and is known to have shared it with the Northern Jurisdiction.[129] Since the Union of 1867 all the rituals of the Northern Jurisdiction have been rewritten several times.[130] Today, many of their rituals do not even remotely resemble the Pike rituals used in the Southern Jurisdiction, they having adopted and introduced several modern historical and quasi-historical themes and features, including an Amerindian theme,[131] a post-Revolutionary War discussion between George Washington and Benedict Arnold,[132] and their popular World War II "Four Chaplains Degree."[133] Additionally, the Northern Jurisdiction adopts "Tentative Rituals" which remain in use for an indeterminate period. This frequent revision of ritual had its precedent in the constant ritual revisions of the Cerneau faction of the Northern Jurisdiction, and certainly, several of the current Northern Jurisdiction degrees yet contain the mixed elements introduced by former Cerneauists.

Finally, it remains only to be said that following the Union of 1867 peace and harmony reigned for five years in the Northern Jurisdiction until 1872, when an expelled member organized another so-called Cerneau Supreme Council; but that, Brethren, is another story.

EDITOR'S NOTE: *This was the* 1995 Scottish Rite Research Society Lecture, *delivered to the annual meeting of the society held on October 10, 1995.*

129. Ray Baker Harris, *Bibliography of the Writings of Albert Pike* (Washington, DC, 1957), 106. Newbury and Williams, *History*, 234, were apparently unaware of the Foulhouze ritual's brief use but refer to the subsequent revision of Pike's ritual.

130. "Chronological Development of the Rituals of the Northern Masonic Jurisdiction Since the Union of 1867," in Partridge, Jr., *Rituals*, 38; Newbury and Williams, *History*, 234, 271–73, 329–30.

131. *Twenty-fourth Degree. Prince of the Tabernacle.* (Lexington, Mass.: Supreme Council, 33°, 1986) [Tentative Ritual].

132. *Twentieth Degree. Master Ad Vitam.* (Boston, Mass.: Supreme Council, 33°, 1951).

133. *Twenty-third Degree. Chief of the Tabernacle.* (Lexington, Mass.: Supreme Council, 33°, 1988) [Tentative Ritual].

APPENDIX 1

JOSEPH CERNEAU'S PATENT, 1806

JOSEPH CERNEAU'S PATENT, 1806

Bibliothèque nationale de France, Paris, France
Source: gallica.bnf.fr, FM1 (307). Archives centrales.
Dossier concernant Joseph Cerneau. 1802–1822.

Translated by Josef Wäges, 32°

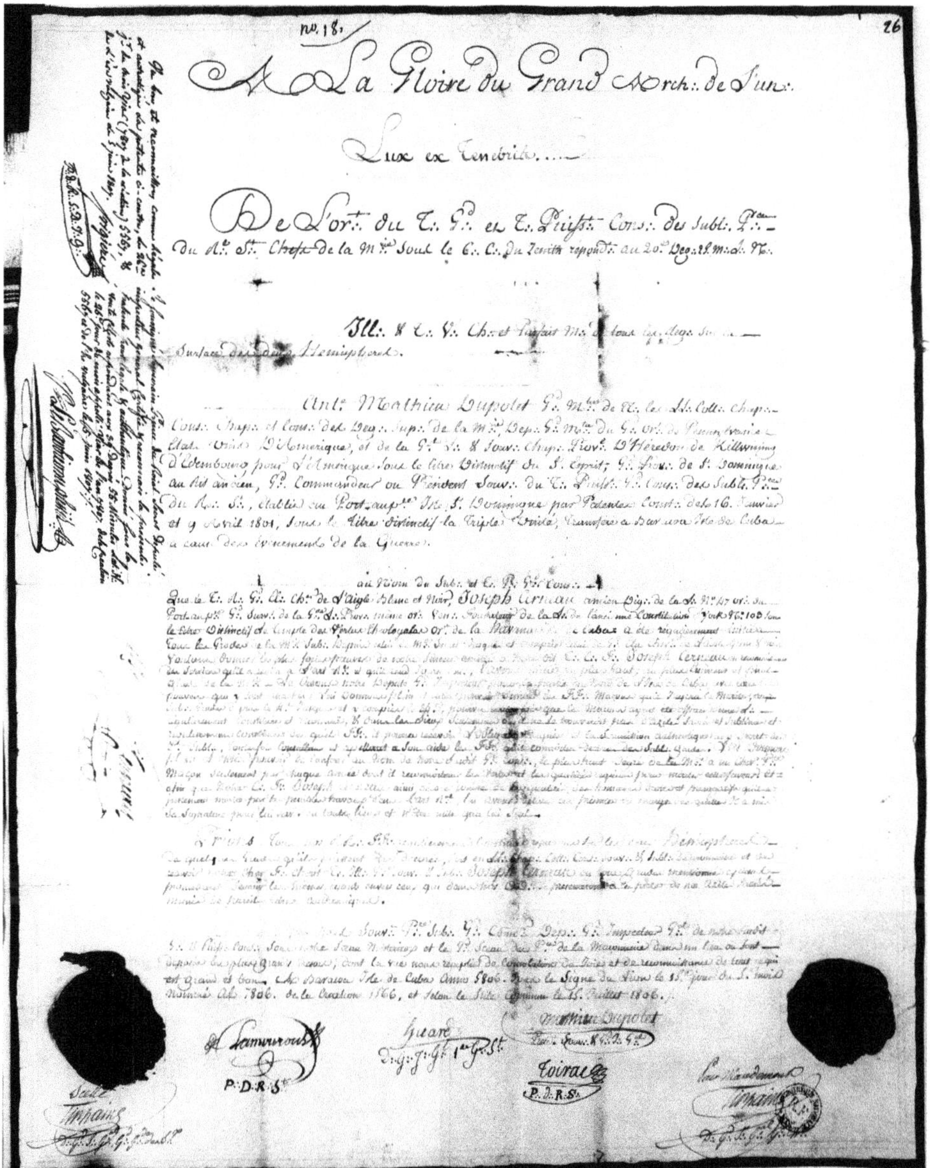
no. 18. 26

A La Gloire du Grand Arch.: de l'Un.:

Lux ex Tenebris....

De l'Or.: du T.: G.: et T.: Puiss.: Cons.: des Subl.: P.ces du R.: S.: Chefs de la M.rie Sous le C.: C.: du Zenith répondt.: au 20e Deg. 28 M.: de N.

Ill.: & T.: V.: Ch.: et Parfait M.: de tous les degs. sur la surface des deux Hemispheres.

Ant.e Mathieu Dupotet G.: M.: de ...

Au Nom du Subl.: et T.: P.: G.: Cons.:

Que le T.: ... Ch.r de l'Aigle Blanc et Noir, Joseph Cerneau ...

... Au Baracoa Isle de Cuba Anno 5806 ... et selon le Stile Commun le 15 Juillet 1806.

Mathieu Dupotet

P.D.R.S.

P.D.R.S.

Par Mandement

No. 18.

To The Glory of the Great Arch[itect] of the Un[iverse]

Lux ex tenebris....

At the O[rien]t of the M[ost] G[ran]d & M[ost] P[uissan]t Counc[i]l of the Subl[ime] P[rin]ces of the R[oya]l S[ecre]t Chiefs of M[ason]ry under the C[louded] C[anopy] of the Zenith at 20 Deg[rees] 25 M[inutes] N[orth] L[atitude]

To our Ill[ustrious] & M[ost] V[alorous] Kn[ights] and Perfect M[asons] of all the deg[rees] over the surface of the two Hemispheres:

Greetings.

{We} Ant[oin]e Mathieu Dupotet, G[ran]d M[as]ter of a[ll] the L[odges] Coll[eges] Chap[ters] Coun[cils] Ch[apters] and Coun[cils] of the Sup[erior] Deg[rees] of M[ason]ry, Dep[uty] G[ran]d M[aste]r of the G[ran]d Or[ien]t of Pennsylvania in the United States of America and of the G[ran]d L[odge] & Sov[ereign] Prov[inci]al Chap[ter] of Heredom of Kilwinning of Edinburgh for America under the distinctive title of the H[ol]y Spirit, G[ran]d Prov[incial] of S[ain]t Domingue in the Ancient Rite, G[ran]d Commander or Sov[ereign] President of the M[ost] Puiss[an]t G[ran]d Coun[cil] of the Subl[ime] P[rin]ces of the R[oyal] S[ecre]t, established at Port au P[rin]ce, Island of S[ain]t Domingue, by the Const[itutive] patents of January 16th and April 19th, 1801, under the distinctive title of The Triple Unity, transferred to Baracoa, Island of Cuba, due to events of war.

{Declaring,} in the name of the Sub[lime] and M[ost] P[uissant] G[ran]d Coun[cil], {we do certify and attest} That the M[ost] R[espectable] G[ran]d El[ect] Kn[igh]t of the White and Black Eagle, JOSEPH CERNEAU, Former Dig[nitary] of the L[odge] N.o 47, Or[ient] of Port au P[rin]ce, G[ran]d Ward[en] of the Prov[incial] G[ran]d L[odge] of the same Or[ient,] Wor[shipful] founder of the L[odge] N.o 103, Ancient York Constitution, under the distinctive title of The Temple of the Theological Virtues, Or[ien]t of Havana, Island of Cuba, being regularly initiated in all the Degrees of Sub[lime] M[ason]ry, from that of Secret M[aste]r up to and including that of G[ran]d Elect Kn[ight] of the White and Black Eagle; and wishing to give the strongest proofs of our sincere friendship for our said V[ery]

D[ear] B[rother] JOSEPH CERNEAU in recognition of the services he has rendered to the R[oya]l Art, and which he is rendering daily, we have initiated him in the highest, the most eminent & final Degree of M[ason]ry; we hereby create him our Deputy G[ran]d Inspector for the Northern part of the Island of Cuba, with all the powers that are attached thereto, giving him full and entire power to initiate into the Sub[lime] Degrees, from the 4.th up to and including the 24.th, B[rethren] Masons whom he may judge worthy, provided that these Masons have been officers of a L[odge] regularly constituted and recognized, and in places only where Sacred and Sublime Asylum, regularly constituted, may not be found, from which B[rethren] he will receive the obligation required and the authentic submission to the Decrees of the Subl[ime] P[rinces]; consulting, however, and calling to his aid the B[rethren] whom he shall know to be decorated with the Subl[ime] Degrees. We hereby grant him full and entire power to confer, only once each year, in the name of our aforesaid G[rand] Coun[cil], the highest Degrees of M[ason]ry upon a Kn[ight] P[rin]ce Mason in whom he shall recognize the virtues & qualities required to merit this favor; and so that our D[ear] B[rother] JOSEPH CERNEAU, thus decorated, may enjoy these qualities, honors, rights and prerogatives which he has justly merited by his arduous labors in the R[oya]l Art, we have delivered to him these presents, in the margin whereof he has placed his signature, to serve him in all places and to be useful to him alone.

We pray our R[especta]ble B[rethren], regularly constituted, spread over the two Hemispheres, with whatever Degree they may be decorated, whether in L[odge] Ch[apter] Col[lege] Sov[ereign] and Subl[ime] Coun[cil], to recognize and receive our D[ear] B[rother], the cherished M[ost] Ill[ustrious] Sov[ereign] & Subl[ime] P[rince] JOSEPH CERNEAU in all the Degrees mentioned above, promising to show the same consideration to all those who shall present themselves in our O[rients] at the doors of our Sacred asylum furnished with like authentic titles.

{Given} by us, Sov[ereig]n Sub[li]me P[rin]ce, G[ran]d Com[made]r, Dep[uty] G[ran]d Inspector G[ener]al of our aforesaid G[ran]d and Puiss[an]t Coun[cil] under our Mysterious Seal, and the G[ran]d Seal of the P[rin]ces of Masonry, in a place where are deposited the greatest of treasures, the sight whereof fills us with consolation, joy, and gratitude for all that is great and good. At Baracoa, Island of Cuba, anno 5806, under the sign of the Lion, the

15th day of the 5th month called Ab, 7806, of the Creation 5566, and according to the Common Style the 15th of July, 1806.

[Seal]

Sealed
Tiphane
D[eputy] G[ran]d
I[nspector] G[ener]al,
G[ran]d G[uar]d
of the S[eal]s

Lamouront
P[rince] o[f the]
R[oyal] S[ecre]t

Huard
D[eputy] G[rand]
I[nspector] G[eneral]
G[rand] J[unio]r W[arde]n

Mathieu Dupotet
Sov[erign] Pres[ident] &
G[ran]d I[nspector]
G[ener]al

Toirac
P[rince] o[f the]
R[oyal] S[ecret]

[Seal]

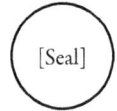

By Mandate
Tiphane
D[eputy] G[ran]d
I[nspector] G[ener]al
G[rand] S[ecretary]

[In the margin]
Seen and approved, and we hereby recognize the patent opposite as legal and authentic, this 26th d[a]y of the month Jiar (7807 of the creation) 5567, & of the vulgar era June 5th, 1807.

Frigiére
P[rince] o[f the] R[oyal] S[ecret] G[rand] I[nspector] G[eneral

I the undersigned, Sovereign Prince of the Royal Secret Deputy Inspector General, Certify & recognize this patent as legal and authentic. Done at the Celestial vault corresponding to 39 degrees 55 Minutes N[orth] Lat[itude] on the 26th of the month called Jiar in the year 7807, of Creation 5567 and of the vulgar era June 5th, 1807∴

P. Le Barbier Duplessis∴

Cerneau [ne varietur]

A COPY OF JOSEPH CERNEAU'S PATENT, 1806

Translated by Albert Pike, 33°, in
William R. Singleton, "The History of the A.·. A.·. Scottish Rite" in
Albert Gallatin Mackey, *The History of Freemasonry*
(New York: Masonic History Co., 1898), 7:1,853–55.
Refinements by Josef Wäges, 32°.

Archives of the Supreme Council, 33°, S.J., Washington, DC

This copy was made in the nineteenth century and for years it was thought to be the original patent.

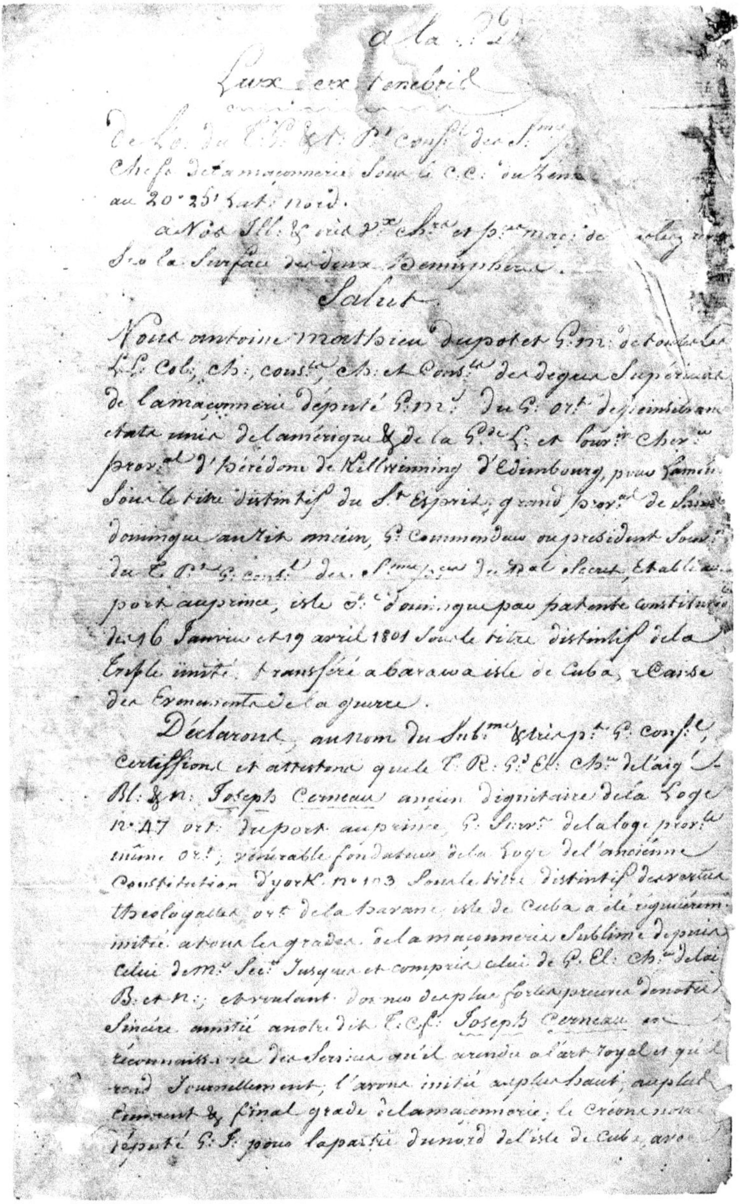

A la ∴ G∴

Lux ex tenebris

De la Lo∴ du C∴ P∴ & S∴ P∴ Consl∴ des Subl∴ Chefs de la maçonnerie Sous le C∴ C∴ du Zénit au 20° 25' Lat. nord.

A Nos Ill∴ & vid∴ P∴ Ch∴ et Ps∴ Maç∴ de ... répandus Sur la Surface des deux hemispheres.

Salut.

Nous antoine mathieu dupotet G∴ M∴ de toutes les LL∴ Col∴ ch∴, consr∴ et Consl∴ des degrés Supérieurs de la maçonnerie député G∴ M∴ du G∴ Ort∴ des Etats unis de l'amérique & de la G∴ L∴ et Cour∴ Ch∴ prov∴ d'Herédom de Killwinning d'Edimbourg, pour l'amérique Sous le titre distinctif du St Esprit, grand Provl de Saint domingue ancien, G∴ Commandeur ou président Souv∴ du C∴ P∴ G∴ Consl∴ des Subl∴ P∴ du Rl Secret, Etabli au port au prince, isle St Domingue par patente constitutive du 16 Janvier et 19 avril 1801 Sous le titre distinctif de la Triple unité transféré a havana isle de Cuba, a cause des Evenements de la guerre.

Déclarons, au nom du Subl∴ & très pt∴ G∴ Consl∴, certifions et attestons que le T∴ R∴ G∴ El∴ Ch∴ de l'aig∴ B∴ & N∴ Joseph Cerneau ancien dignitaire de la Loge N° 47 ort∴ du port au prince, G∴ Insp∴ de la loge provle même Or∴; vénérable fondateur de la Loge de l'ancienne Constitution d'york N° 103 Sous le titre distinctif des vertus theologales Ort∴ de la havane, isle de Cuba a été régulièrement initié a tous les grades de la maçonnerie Sublime depuis celui de Mtre Sec∴ Jusques et compris celui de P∴ El∴ Ch∴ de l'aig∴ B∴ et N∴; voulant donner des plus fortes preuves de notre Sincère amitié a notre dit T∴ C∴ f∴ Joseph Cerneau en reconnaissance des Services qu'il a rendu a l'art royal et qu'il rend journellement, l'avons initié au plus haut, au plus éminent & final grade de la maçonnerie, le créons nommons député G∴ I∴ pour la partie du nord de l'isle de Cuba, avec

[*folio 1, recto*]

[illegible] pouvoir qui y sont attachés, lui donnons plein &
pouvoir d'initier les ff∴ maçons qu'il jugera les
aux Sub.mes grades depuis le 4e jusques et y compris
pourvu toute fois que ces maçons ayent été officiers
Loge régulièrement constituée et reconnue et dans les
[illegible] uniquement où il ne se trouverait pas d'asiles Sacrés
et Sublimes, et régulièrement constitués, desquels g∴ g∴ il
pourra recevoir l'obligation requise et la soumission
authentiques aux décrets des g∴ ces Sub.mes; toutes fois consultant
et appellant à son aide les ff∴ qu'il connaitra décorés des
Sublimes grades; lui donnons plein et entier pouvoir de conférer
au nom de notre susdit g∴ C∴ le plus haute degré de la m∴ne
à un ch∴ prince maçon, seulement par chaque année, dont il
reconnaitra les vertus, & les qualités requises pour mériter cette
faveur; et afin que notre C. f∴ Joseph Cerneau, ainsi décoré,
jouisse en ces qualités, des honneurs, droits et prérogatives
qu'il a justement mérités par ses pénibles travaux
dans l'art royal, lui avons délivré ces présentes, en marge
desquelles il a mis sa signature pour lui servir [illegible]
lieux et n'être utile qu'à lui seul.

Prions tous nos R.bles ff∴ régulièrement constitués
épandus sur les deux hémisphères de quelque grade qu'ils
puissent être décorés; soit en Loge, ch∴ Col∴ Conseil Souverain
Sublimes, de reconnaitre et recevoir [illegible] g∴ C∴ Berie, C∴ Ill.
P.ce Souv∴ & Sublime Joseph Cerneau, en tous les grades
mentionnés ci dessus; promettant d'avoir les mêmes
égards envers ceux qui, dans nos orients, se présenteront
à la porte de nos asiles Sacrés munis de pareils titres
authentiques.

Donné par nous S∴ P.ces Sub.mes g∴ C∴ P∴ I∴ g.al de notre
susdit g.d et p.t Cons.el, sous notre [illegible] mystérieux et le
g.d sceau des p.ces de la maçonnerie, dans un Lieu où sont déposés
les plus grands trésors, dont la vue nous remplit de
Consolation, de joie et de reconnaissance de tout ce qui
est grand & bon.

A Baracoa isle de Cuba anno 5806, sous le signe du
[illegible] le 13e jour du 5e mois nommé A. L. 7806, de la
[illegible] 5560, & selon le stile commun le 15e Juillet 1806.

[*folio 1, verso*]

Signé mathieu dupotet présid[en]t
G:al.
pour Copie conform, Signé Mathieu
Président S: G: I: G:al.
Je certiffie ce qui est transmis ci dessus et de l'autre
part conforme a mon régistre Tiphaine
S: P: R: S: D: I: G:al G: comm.

[*folio 2, recto; folio 2, verso—blank*]

To The G[lory] O[f the Great Architect of the Universe]

Lux ex Tenebris.

From the Orient of the Very Great and Very Puissant Council of the Sublime Princes [of the Royal Secret], Chiefs of Masonry, under the C: C: of the Zenith [which responds] to the 20° 25' N: Lat:

To our Ill: and Very Valiant Knights and Princes, Masons of all the Degrees, over the surface of the two Hemispheres:

Health!

We, Antoine Mathieu Dupotet, G[rand] M[aster] of all the L[odges], Colleges, Chapters, Councils, Chapters and Consistories, of the higher degrees of Masonry, Deputy Grand Master of the Grand Orient of Pennsylvania, in the United States of America ; and of the Grand Lodge and Sovereign Provincial Grand Chapter of Heredom of Kilwinning, of Edinburgh, for America, under the distinctive title of the Holy Ghost, Grand Provincial of San Domingo in the Ancient Rite, Grand Commander or Sovereign President of the Th: Puissant Grand Council of the Sublime Princes of the Royal Secret, established at Port au Prince, Island of San Domingo, by constitutive patent of 16 January and 19 April, 1801, under the distinctive title of The Triple Unity; transferred to Baracoa, Island of Cuba, on account of the events of war,

Declaring, in the name of the Sublime and Th: Puissant Grand Council, do certify and attest, that the Very Resp: Gr: Elect Knight of the White and Black Eagle, *Joseph Cerneau*, Ancient Dignitary of the Lodge No. 47, Orient of Port au Prince, Grand Warden of the Provincial Lodge, same Orient, Venerable founder of the Lodge of the Ancient Constitution of York, No. 103, under the distinctive title of The Theological Virtues, Orient of the Habana, Island of Cuba, has | been regularly initiated in all the Degrees of the Sublime Masonry, from that of Secret Master to and including that of Grand Elect Knight of the White and Black Eagle ; and wishing to give the strongest proofs of our sincere friendship for our said Very Dear Bro: *Joseph Cerneau*, in recognition of the services which he has rendered to the Royal Art, and which he is rendering daily, we have initiated him in the highest, in the most eminent and final Degree of Masonry ; we create him our Deputy Grand Inspector, for the Northern part of the Island of Cuba, with all the powers that are attached thereto, giving him full and entire power to initiate the Bros: Masons, whom he may judge [worthy ?], to promote them to the Sublime Degrees, from the 4th up to and including the 24th ; provided, however, that these Masons shall have been officers of a Lodge regularly constituted and recognized, and in places only where there may not be found Sacred and Sublime and regularly constituted Asyla; from which Bros: he will receive the obligation required and the authentic submission to the Decrees of the Sublime Princes ; consulting, however, and calling to his aid the BB: whom he shall know to be decorated with the Sublime Degrees ; we give him full and entire power to confer in the name of our aforesaid Grand Council the highest Degrees of Masonry on a Kt: Prince Mason, one only each year, whose virtues he shall recognize, and the qualities required to deserve this favor ; and to the end that our dear Bro: *Joseph Cerneau*, so decorated, may enjoy, in this quality, the honours, rights, and prerogatives which he has justly deserved, by his arduous labors in the Royal Art, we have delivered to him these presents, in the margin whereof he has placed his signature, that it may avail him everywhere, and be useful to him alone.

We pray our Resp: BB: regularly constituted, spread over the two Hemispheres, with whatever Degree they may be decorated, whether in Lodge, Ch:, Col:, Sovereign Council . . . Sublime, to recognize and receive our dear Bro:, the Very Illustrious Sov: and Subl: Prince, Joseph Cerneau, in all the Degrees above mentioned; promising to pay the same attention to those who in our Orients shall present themselves at the doors of our Sacred Asyla furnished with like authentic titles.

Given by us, S: Sublime Princes, G: C: G: I: G:al: of our aforesaid Grand and Perfect Council, under our Mysterious Seal, and the Grand Seal of the Princes of Masonry, in a place where are deposited the greatest treasures, the sight whereof fills us with consolation, joy, and gratitude for all that is great and good.

At Baracoa, Island of Cuba, anno 5806, under the sign of the Lion, the 15th day of the 5th month called Ab, 7806, of the Creation 5566, and according to the Common Style the 15th July, 1806. |

Signed, Mathieu Dupotet, *President, Soverign G:*[al]

A true copy, Signed, Mathieu Dupotet,
President, S: G: I: G'al·

I certify that what is transmitted above and the other portions are conformable to my Register.

Tiphaine,
S: P: R: S:, D: I: G'al: G: Comm:

The foregoing translation of the ancient copy in French has been correctly and faithfully made by me.

March 20, 1882. Albert Pike.

APPENDIX 2

DOCUMENTS UPON SUBLIME FREE-MASONRY, 1823

Joseph M'Cosh. *Documents Upon Sublime Free-masonry.*
Charleston, SC: [C. C. Sebring]: [1823].
From the Archives of the Supreme Council, 33°, SJ, USA.

Note that the publication date on the title page has been cut out, a small rectangle of paper has been pasted over the hole, and the date "1823" pencilled in. All known copies had the printer's name cut out after publication. The printer, C. C. Sebring, was a member of the Supreme Council at Charleston who removed his name to avoid possible lawsuits and/or Masonic charges. The handwriting on the title page ("J. B. of Alexandria now at Charleston") and p. 104 ("Candor") is that of Dr. Moses Holbrook, Sovereign Grand Commander, SJ (1826–44).

To the M. W. Gr. Lodge of the District of Columbia — Washington City from its friend J. B. of Alexandria now at Charleston

DOCUMENTS

UPON

SUBLIME FREE-MASONRY

IN THE

United States of America.

BEING

A COLLECTION OF ALL THE OFFICIAL DOCUMENTS WHICH HAVE APPEARED ON BOTH SIDES OF THE QUESTION.

With

NOTES, AND AN APPENDIX.

By JOSEPH M'COSH. Esq.—Merchant Charleston S. C

Si quid novisti rectius istis,
Candidus imperti; si non, his utere mecum.

1823

TO THE READER.

DEAR BROTHER,

Hearing much conversation upon the Sublime Degrees of Free-Masonry, and finding two parties in existence, one of which must be totally wrong, I have made it an object to embrace every opportunity of conversing with the well informed in these degrees, to obtain that information of which I was in pursuit. During the search, I have accumulated a vast bulk of letters, pamphlets, &c. upon the subject; and believing that a selection of them laid before the public might be of essential service to the craft, in their search after the truth, I wrote a note to a friend more than a year since, for his opinion upon the subject. His advice was, "to defer it for the present, as there was a hope that mattters would be all made up." I complied; but as the parties are now to appearance no nearer being reconciled, I have again written him, and I copy a portion of his answer below:

"DEAR SIR AND BROTHER,

"Your proposal to publish the papers you mention, containing a complete view of the subject in dispute, by inserting all the documents which have been published by both parties, partially meets my approbation. I beg you would not publish them all: better save such as I have marked for some future occasion; for they will be too voluminous.

"The scarcity of the documents not marked, their want of durability in their present form, and the difficulty for any person to obtain them all at one time, and having a full view of the subject at once before him, will, in my opinion, authorize you to unite them in one volume; thus arranged, their usefulness must be apparent to every *rational* brother. But you must not calculate to please all; you cannot convince those of their error, who blindly follow *names* in opposition to *truth;* who endeavour to subvert the real principles of our most ancient institution; who, destitute of all nobleness of soul, will circulate falsehoods and substitute obstinacy in the place of benevolence; who show a disposition to overturn all the foundations of Free-Masonry, and, in their stead, fix disorder and misrule to support their intrusion, usurpation, and imposture; who esteem low cunning, concealment, and bitter calumny, superior to honesty, plain dealing, and fair reasoning; who prefer a silencing, inquisitorial spirit, to free discussion and friendly argument; together with all those pitiful beings, who, without any independence of mind of their own, will swallow such doctrines, and adhere to them. Such, my brother, are not to be moved from their errors, 'for they love darkness rather than light.'

"But a higher necessity exists for publishing these documents; it is, a defence of TRUTH, which, in your case, is SELF-DEFENCE. Upon this ground, your intruding upon the public, will be fully excused; but it is truly a subject of grief and pain of mind to expose those Masons who are ever ready to be called brothers whenever any office of profit or honour is to be obtained, who revile or praise the institution as best suits their own selfish purposes.

"With me, you and every observing and unprejudiced brother, will notice with pity and concern, that the genuine spirit of Free-Masonry has, of late, severely suffered from false brethren; that its very foundations have been assailed by spurious pretenders, and an outrageous attempt made by usurpers to revolutionize its ancient precepts, by destroying the venerable principles of its harmony; in sapping the vital supports of its organization, and setting at defiance all its valued rules of government.

"I would recommend to carefully observe *dates* on both sides of the question, as it will prove of great usefulness in the search after truth; and I sincerely hope, may prove the means of instructing those who may be ignorant, if not too obstinately prejudiced; of animating the lukewarm friends of regularity; of reforming the irregular, and convincing them of the injustice they do the Craft, in censuring the only regular and legal body of Sublime Free-Masons which can exist, unless in correspondence with it; (a body which has been established for more than forty years;) I say, in censuring them for doing their *duty;*—a duty which they owed to the God of all Truth, to the public, to their neighbours, and to themselves.

"Believing as I do, that the violation of fundamental principles, so long established and acted upon, and by the careful observance of which the institution has flourished for so many ages, will eventually overturn the fair fabric and bring ruin and confusion in its place, I would beg every brother to use his influence in guarding all the ancient Landmarks of the Order—it matters not of what degree; for if indulged in any one, the indulgence will soon creep into the others.

"You must not be surprised, if some brothers ridicule your

work without ever reading it; some are so *sensitive*, that a breath alarms them; others so obstinate, that they will never examine."

After having extracted so largely from his friend's letter, the publisher will close with a few extracts from a pamphlet signed "*Truth and Justice*," and printed January 10th, 1810, by J. G. S. & Co. at Philadelphia.

This writer exposes many abuses and unmasonic acts in Joseph Cerneau's irregular bodies in New-York city. He observes that honesty and good faith almost invariably lead just and upright men to think all other persons like themselves. But, alas, how sadly do they mistake! He warns and cautions all the fraternity not to be deluded into the irregular and spurious bodies, and recommends them previously to be well informed of the *regularity* of the body to which they would apply as well as of the *moral character* of the members who compose it.

He states that Joseph Cerneau upon his own individual authority, promulgated his R. C. Chapter, "Tripple Friendship" Oct. 28th, 1808, in New-York city, where in 1787, our Illustrious Brother Huet De Lachaille, had, with a proper authority, commenced to give the Sublime Degrees, and the brethren resident there had been recognized as correct by all the regular bodies of the same grade, Oct. 4th, 1804.

Joseph Cerneau, most probably soon saw, that the irregularity of his proceedings required some other authority than his own, and he drew up a petition, which he and two other brothers, (most probably of his own make,) signed and sent to the body in Barracoa, in the Island of Cuba, desiring constitutions for his spurious Chapter of Rose Croix.

This publication, (now thirteen years and more before the public, and uncontradicted,) states, "that the body at Barracoa, it is said, never acted on this strange petition. But that some time afterwards, Matthew Dupotet, and two other individuals, without any authority so to do, did fabricate and sign something which Joseph Cerneau and company call a patent. As this body at Barracoa was derivative from Jamaica, by the way of Cape Francois, it had no authority, even at the Cape, to establish other bodies; this pretended patent, therefore, could not authorize any other body, any more than one chartered Master-Mason's Lodge could charter another. Hence, Dupotet's power was no power at all. Nor was it conceived to grant any by Joseph Cerneau; for he thought it absolutely necessary to petition the illustrious body at Kilwinning, in Scotland, to either confirm Dupotet's authority, or to grant him an entirely new patent. On this occasion an attempt was made to interest a great personage in England to assist them in their irregularity. Their divers applications, however, remain to this day unanswered. He flattered himself that he could overturn in this way, the regular body of Rose Croix already established in New-York—wholly forgetting that when a Grand Lodge is once established in a state, or country, no new one can be established without its consent, unless by violating those principles which have been established for centuries, and are the very pivot upon which the whole institution revolves."

Joseph Cerneau did, in 1808, on the 10th day of the 4th month, at 11 o'clock, A. M. arbitrarily declare his Chapter of "Tripple Amitiè" "to be without vigour and without function." (P. 5.)

As every creation of a new body procured J. Cerneau the sale of a new set of jewels, (he being a jeweller,) he, of his own authority, "*regularized brothers*," to use his own terms, as in the case of Torissant Mayday, who was expelled regularly from the Lodge at Cape Francois, in the Island of St. Domingo. He "*created brothers*" who were no Masons before, as in the case of John B. Subrannye, not to mention Entered-Apprentices that he advanced, to strengthen his party; so that by the year 1809, 21st February, he installed his new Rose Croix Chapter, Tripple Alliance, (pages 10—14.) For more information upon this subject, see De La Motta's Replication, in which all the dates of the *public* notices of his Scottish Heredon institutions were communicated.

Of J. C.'s masonic conduct in Havana de Cuba, we have many facts before us which would blacken any thing we have before communicated. His labours were concluded by his being expelled from the island by the governor, at the request of the fraternity who resided there. (P. 17.) The brotherhood will now be able to judge for themselves whether it is common in Free-Masonry for an arbitrary, avaricious individual to constitute himself Great Commander, make the bodies below him, and become both accuser and judge, in a country where all these bodies were years before regularly established.

"From these facts it plainly results, that all Joseph Cerneau's high councils and chapters, as he calls them, as well as all bodies emanating from, or chartered by him or them, or in any way deriving their authority from these usurpers, are *unconstitutional*, *irregular*, and *spurious;* and that all persons who have been, or may be admitted therein, are in an error, and can never present themselves to any regularly constituted body, without being previously reinstated." (P. 17, 18.)

"Magna est veritas et prevalebit."

Charleston, *June*, 1823.

[The following Report was immediately put in circulation, agreeably to the intention of it; it was also published more than twenty years ago, in "Dalcho's Orations," which have passed through several editions in Europe; so that it has been extensively known.]

CIRCULAR

THROUGHOUT THE TWO HEMISPHERES.

UNIVERSI TERRARUM ORBIS ARCHITECTONIS PER GLORIAM INGENTIS.

Deus Meumque Jus.

ORDO AB CHAO.

From the East of the Grand and Supreme Council of the Most Puissant Sovereigns, Grand Inspectors General, under the Celestial Canopy of the Zenith, which answers to the 32d degree, 45 minutes N. L.

To our Illustrious, Most Valiant and Sublime Princes of the Royal Secret, Knights of K—H, Illustrious Princes and Knights, Grand, Ineffable, and Sublime, Free and Accepted Masons of all degrees, ancient and modern, over the surface of the two hemispheres.

To all those to whom these letters shall come:

Health, Stability, and Power.

At a meeting of Sovereign Grand Inspectors General in Supreme Council of the thirty-third degree, duly and lawfully established and congregated, held at the Grand Council Chamber, on the 14th day of the 7th month, called

Tisri, 5563, Anno Lucis, 5802, and of the Christian era, the 10th day of October, 1802.

Union, Contentment, and Wisdom.

The Grand Commander informed the Inspectors, that they were convened for the purpose of taking into consideration, the propriety of addressing circular letters to the different Symbolic Grand Lodges, and Sublime Grand Lodges and Councils throughout the two hemispheres; explanatory of the origin and nature of the Sublime Degrees of Masonry, and their establishment in South-Carolina.

When a resolution to that effect was immediately adopted, and a committee, consisting of the illustrious brethren, Dr. Frederick Dalcho, Dr. Isaac Auld, and Emanuel De La Motta, Esq. Grand Inspectors General, was appointed to draft and submit such letter to the Council at their next meeting.

At a meeting of the Sovereign Grand Inspectors General in Supreme Council of the thirty-third degree, &c. &c. &c. on the 10th day of the 8th month, called Chisleu, 5563, A. L. 5802, and of the Christian era, this 4th day of December, 1802.

The Committee to whom was referred the foregoing resolve, respectfully submitted to the Council, the following

REPORT.

To trace the progress of Masonry from its earliest period, and to fix precisely, the dates of the establishment of each of the degrees, is involved in much difficulty. As Symbolic Masons, we date our origin from the creation of the world, when the Almighty Builder, the Grand Architect of the Universe, established those immutable laws, which gave rise to the Sciences. Mutual wants and necessities impelled our primordial brethren to seek for mutual assistance. Diversity of talents, genius, and pursuits, rendered them, in some measure, dependant on each other, and thus society was formed, and, as a natural consequence, men of the same habits and dispositions associated more intimately together, which gave rise to institutions connected with their design, and suited to their geniuses; these led to the exclusion of those whose talents, habits, or circumstances, either disqualified them from participating in the knowledge of the others, or rendered them dangerous or unprofitable to the welfare of their general interests.

As civilization began to extend through the world, and the minds of men became enlarged from the contemplation of the works of nature, the arts and sciences were cultivated by the most ingenious of the people. The contemplation of the planetary system, as the work of an Almighty Artist, and the attributes of their God, gave rise to Religion and the Science of Astronomy. The measurement of land and the division and marking of their property, gave rise to Geometry, and these, collectively, to the Mystic order; and *watch words*, *signs*, and *tokens*, were established to designate the initiated or admitted.

It is, perhaps, impossible to fix precisely the time, when the first degrees were established in the form in which they are now given, as most of the ancient records of the craft were lost or destroyed in England, in the wars of the Danes and Saxons. Much of the history of Masonry in the early ages, is so mixed with fable and enveloped with the rust of time, that little satisfaction can be obtained; but as we approach nearer to our own times, we have authentic records for our government.

The peculiar manner in which the three first, or blue, degrees are given, as well as the matter of them, clearly evince them to be merely symbols of the superior or sublime degrees. They were formed as the test of the character and capacity of the initiated, before they should be admitted to the knowledge of the more important mysteries.

In the third degree we are informed that, in consequence of the death of H. A. the Master's word was lost, and that a new one, which was not known before the building of the Temple, was substituted in its place. If Masonry, as is generally believed, and as many of our ancient records import, took its rise from the creation, and flourished in the first ages of man, they were in possession of a secret word, of which the Masons under Solomon had no knowledge. Here, then, was an innovation of one of the fundamental principles of the craft, and a removal of one of the ancient Landmarks; this, however, we are unwilling to allow. It is well known to the Blue Master, that King Solomon and his royal visiter were in possession of the real and pristine word, but of which, he must remain ignorant, unless initiated into the sublime degrees. The authenticity of this mystic word, as known to us, and for which our much respected Master died, is proven to the most sceptic mind, from the sacred pages of holy writ, and the Jewish history from the earliest period of time. Dr. Priestley, in his Letters to the Jews, has the following remarkable passage, when speaking of the miracles of Christ—"and it has since been said by your writers, that he performed his miracles by means of some ineffable name of God, which he stole out of the Temple." Notwithstanding the Symbolic Masons profess their societies to have originated in the first ages of the world, and date from the creation, yet in their degrees, nothing is taught them but occurrences which took place at the building of the first Temple, (an inconsiderable period of about seven years,) 2992 years after the creation. The history of their order previously to that period, and the extensive and important improvements in the art, both before and since, they are unacquainted with.

Many of the Lectures of the sublime degrees contain an epitome of the arts and sciences, and in their history many valuable and important facts are recorded, obtained from authentic archives in the possession of our society, and which, from the manner of their communication, can never be mutilated or corrupted. This is an object of the first magnitude in a society whose principles and practices should be invariable. Much variety and irregularity has unfortunately crept into the blue degrees, in consequence of the want of masonic knowledge in many of those who preside over their meetings, and it is particularly so with those who are unacquainted with the Hebrew language, in which all the words and pass words are given. So essentially necessary is it for a man of science to preside over a Lodge, that much injury may arise from the smallest deviation in the ceremony of initiation, or in the lectures of instruction. We read in the Book of Judges, that the transposition of a single point over the *Sheen*, in consequence of a national defect among the Ephraimites, designated the cowans, and led to the slaughter of forty-two thousand. The sublime figure of the Divinity formed in the Fellow-Craft's degree, can be elegantly illustrated only by those who possess some knowledge of the Talmud. Most of the words in the sublime degrees are derived from the Chaldean, Hebrew, and Latin languages.

The various translations which the symbolic degrees have undergone since their first establishment, from one language to another, and that, oftentimes, by men illiterate even in their mother tongue, is another cause of the variety which we lament. Not so the superior degrees; they appear in that sublime dress which their founders gave them; originating in science and embellished by genius. Many of the sublime degrees are founded on the polite arts, and unfold a mass of information of the first importance to Masons.

Although many of the sublime degrees are, in fact, a continuation of the blue degrees, yet there is no interference between the two bodies. Throughout the continent of Europe, and the West Indies, where they are very generally known, they are acknowledged and encouraged. The sublime Masons never initiate any into the blue degrees, without a legal warrant obtained for that purpose from a Symbolic Grand Lodge; but they communicate the secrets of the Chair to such applicants who have not already received them, previous to their initiation into the Sublime Lodge, but they are, at the same time, informed, that it does not give them rank as Past-Masters in the Grand Lodge.

The Sublime Grand Lodge, sometimes called the Ineffable Lodge, or the Lodge of Perfection, extends from the fourth to the fourteenth degree inclusive, which last, is the degree of Perfection. The sixteenth degree is the Grand

Council of Princes of Jerusalem, who hold jurisdiction over the fifteenth degree, called Knights of the East, and also over the Sublime Grand Lodge, and is to them, what a Symbolic Grand Lodge is to the subordinate Lodges. Without a warrant and Constitution regularly issued by them, or by a higher Council or Inspector, they are deemed irregular and are punished accordingly. All the degrees above the sixteenth, are under the jurisdiction of the Supreme Council of Grand Inspectors General, who are Sovereigns of Masonry. When it is necessary to establish the Sublime degrees, in a country where they are unknown, a brother of the twenty-ninth degree, which is called K—H, is appointed Deputy Inspector General over the district. He selects from among the Craft such brethren as he believes will do honour to the society, and communicates the Sublime degrees to as many as is necessary for the first organization of the Lodge, when they elect their own officers, and govern themselves by the constitution and warrant which is furnished them. The jurisdiction of a Lodge of Perfection, is twenty-five leagues.

It is well known that about 27,000 Masons accompanied the Christian Princes in the Crusades, to recover the Holy Land from the Infidels. While in Palestine, they discovered several important Masonic manuscripts, among the descendants of the ancient Jews, which enriched our archives with authentic written records, and on which, some of our degrees are founded.

In the years 5304 and 5311, some very extraordinary discoveries were made, and occurrences took place, which renders the Masonic History of that period, of the highest importance. A period dear to the Mason's heart, who is zealous in the cause of his Order, his Country and his God

Another very important discovery was made in the year 5553, of a record in Syrian characters, relating to the most remote antiquity, and from which it would appear that the world is many thousand years older than given by the Mosaic account; an opinion entertained by many of the learned. Few of these characters were translated until the reign of our Illustrious and most Enlightened

Brother, Frederick II. King of Prussia, whose well known zeal for the craft, was the cause of much improvement in the society, over which he condescended to preside.

As society improved, and as discoveries of old records were made, the number of our degrees were increased, until, in progress of time, the system became complete.

From such of our records as are authentic, we are informed of the establishment of the Sublime and Ineffable degrees of Masonry in Scotland, France and Prussia, immediately after the Crusades. But from some circumstances, which to us are unknown, after the year 4658, they fell into neglect until the year 5744, when a Nobleman from Scotland, visited France, and re-established the Lodge of Perfection in Bordeaux.

In 5761, the Lodges and councils of the superior degrees being extended throughout the continent of Europe, His Majesty the King of Prussia, as Grand Commander of the order of Prince of the Royal Secret, was acknowledged by all the Craft as the head of the Sublime and Ineffable degrees of Masonry, throughout the two hemispheres. His Royal Highness Charles, Hereditary Prince of the Swedes, Goths and Vandals, Duke of Sudermania, Heir of Norway, &c. &c. &c. was, and still continues the Grand Commander and protector of the Sublime Masons in Sweden; and his Royal Highness Louis of Bourbon, Prince of the Blood, Duke de Chartres, &c. &c. &c. and the Cardinal, Prince and Bishop of Rouen, were at the head of those degrees in France.

On the 25th of October 5762, the Grand Masonic Constitutions were finally ratified in Berlin, and proclaimed for the government of all the Lodges of Sublime and Perfect Masons, Chapters, Councils, Colleges and Consistories of the Royal and Military art of Free-Masonry, over the surface of the two hemispheres. There are secret Constitutions, which have existed from time immemorial, and are alluded to, in these instruments.

In the same year the Constitutions were transmitted to our illustrious Brother Stephen Morin, who had been appointed* on the 27th of August, 5761, Inspector General over all Lodges, &c. &c. &c. in the new world, by the Grand Consistory of Princes of the Royal Secret convened in Paris, at which presided the King of Prussia's deputy, "Chaillon de Johnville, substitute general of the order, Right Worshipful Master of the first Lodge in France, called St. Anthony's, Chief of the Eminent degrees, Commander and Sublime Prince of the Royal Secret, &c. &c. &c."

The following Illustrious Brethren were also present:

"The Brother Prince of Rouen, Master of the Grand Intelligence Lodge, and Sovereign Prince of Masonry, &c.

"La Corne, substitute of the Grand Master, Right Worshipful Master of the Trinity Lodge, Grand Elect, Perfect, Knight and Prince of Masons, &c.

"Maximilian de St. Simon, Senior Grand Warden, Grand, Elect, Perfect, Knight and Prince of Masons, &c.

"Savalette de Buchelay, Grand Keeper of the Seals, Grand, Elect, Perfect, Knight and Prince of Masons, &c.

"Duke de Choiseuil, Right Worshipful Master of the Lodge of the Children of Glory, Grand, Elect, Perfect, Master, Knight and Prince of Masons, &c.

"Topin, Grand Ambassador from his Serene Highness, Grand, Elect, Perfect, Master, Knight and Prince of Masons, &c.

"Boucher de Lenoncour, Right Worshipful Master of the Lodge of Virtue, Grand, Elect, Perfect, Master, Knight and Prince of Masons, &c.

"Brest de la Chausee, Right Worshipful Master of the Exactitude Lodge, Grand, Elect, Perfect, Master, Knight and Prince of Masons, &c. The Seals of the Order were affixed and the Patent countersigned by

"Daubertain, Grand, Elect, Perfect, Master, Knight and Prince of Masons, Right Worshipful Master of the Lodge of St. Alphonso, Grand Secretary of the Grand Lodge and Sublime Council of Princes of Masons, &c."

* A copy of his commission is in the archives of the Supreme Council at full length. *Editor.*

When Brother Morin arrived in St. Domingo, he, agreeably to his patent, appointed a Deputy Inspector General for North-America. This high honour was conferred on Brother M. M. Hayes, with the power of appointing others, where necessary. Brother Morin also appointed Brother Frankin, Deputy Inspector General for Jamaica and the British Leeward Islands, and Brother Colonel Provost, for the Windward Islands and the British Army.

Brother Hayes appointed Brother Isaac Da Costa, Deputy Inspector General, for the State of South-Carolina, who, in the year 5783, established the Sublime Grand Lodge of Perfection in Charleston. After Brother Da Costa's death, Brother Joseph Myers was appointed Deputy Inspector General for this State, by Brother Hayes, who, also, had previously appointed Brother Colonel Solomon Bush, Deputy Inspector General for the State of Pennsylvania, and Brother Barend M. Spitzer to the same rank for Georgia, which was confirmed by a convention of Inspectors when convened in Philadelphia, on the 15th of June, 5781.

On the 1st of May, 5786, the Grand Constitution of the thirty-third degree, called the Supreme Council of Sovereign Grand Inspectors General, was finally ratified by his Majesty the King of Prussia, who as Grand Commander of the order of Prince of the Royal Secret, possessed the Sovereign Masonic power over all the Craft. In the new Constitution this high Power was conferred on a Supreme Council of nine Brethren in each nation, who possess all the Masonic prerogatives in their own district, that his Majesty individually possessed; *and are Sovereigns of Masonry.*

On the 20th of February, 5788, the Grand Council of Princes of Jesuralem was opened in this city, at which were present, Brother J. Myers, D. I. G. for South-Carolina, Brother B. M. Spitzer, D. I. G. for Georgia, and Brother A. Forst, D. I. G. for Virginia. Soon after the opening of the Council, a Letter was addressed to His Royal Highness the Duke of Orleans, on the subject, requesting certain records from the archives of the society in

France, which, in his answer through Col. Shee, his Secretary, he very politely promised to transmit; but which, the commencement of the French revolution, most unfortunately prevented.

On the 2d of August, 5795, Brother Colonel John Mitchell, late Deputy Quarter Master General in the Armies of the United States, was made a Deputy Inspector General for this State, by Brother Spitzer, who acted in consequence of Brother Myer's removal out of the country. Brother Mitchell was restricted from acting until after Brother Spitzer's death, which took place in the succeeding year.

As many Brethren of eminent degrees, had arrived from foreign parts, Consistories of Princes of the Royal Secret, were occasionally held, for initiations, and other purposes.

On the 31st of May, 5801, the Supreme Council of the thirty-third degree for the United States of America, was opened with the high honours of Masonry, by Brothers John Mitchell and Frederick Dalcho, Sovereign Grand Inspectors General, and in the course of the present year, the whole number of Grand Inspectors General was completed, agreeably to the Grand Constitutions.

On the 21st of January, 5802, a warrant of Constitution passed the Seal of the Grand Council of Princes of Jerusalem, for the establishment of a Master Mark Mason's Lodge in this city.

On the 21st of February, 5802, our Illustrious Brother, Count Alexandre Francois Auguste Degrasse, Deputy Inspector General, was appointed by the Supreme Council, a Grand Inspector General, and Grand Commander of the French West-Indies; and our Illustrious Brother Jean Baptiste Marie De La Hougue, Deputy Inspector General was also received as an Inspector General, and appointed Lieutenant Grand Commander of the same Islands.

On the 4th of December, 5802, a warrant of Constitution passed the seal of the Grand Council of Princes of Jerusalem, for the establishment of a Sublime Grand Lodge in Savannah, Georgia.

The names of the Masonic Degrees are as follows, viz.

1st degree, called	Entered-Apprentice.	Given in the Symbolic Lodge.
2	Fellow-Craft.	
3	Master Mason.	
4	Secret Master.	Given in the Sublime Grand Lodge.
5	Perfect Master.	
6	Intimate Secretary.	
7	Provost and Judge.	
8	Intendant of the Building.	
9	Elected Knights of 9.	
10	Illustrious Elected of 15.	
11	Sublime Knight Elected.	
12	Grand Master Architect.	
13	Royal Arch.	
14	Perfection.	
15	Knight of the East.	Given by the Princes of Jerusalem, which is a Governing Council.
16	Prince of Jerusalem.	
17	Knight of the East and West.	Given by the Council of Grand Inspectors, who are Sovereigns of Masonry.
18	Sovereign Prince of Rose Croix de Heredon.	
19	Grand Pontiff.	
20	Grand Master of all Symbolic Lodges.	
21	Patriarch Noachite, or Chevalier Prussien.	
22	Prince of Libanus.	
23	Chief of the Tabernacle.	
24	Prince of the Tabernacle.	
25	Prince of Mercy.	
26	Knight of the Brazen Serpent.	
27	Commander of the Temple.	
28	Knight of the Sun.	
29	Knight of St. Andrew.	
30	K—H.	
31	Grand Inq. Commander.	
32	Sublime Prince of the Royal Secret, Prince of Masons.	
33	Sovereign Grand Inspectors General. Officers appointed for life.	

Besides those degrees, which are in regular succession, most of the Inspectors are in possession of a number of detached degrees, given in different parts of the world, and which, they generally communicate, free of expense, to those brethren, who are high enough to understand them.

Such as Select Masons of 27 and the Royal Arch, as given under the Constitution of Dublin. Six degrees of Maconnerie D'Adoption, Compagnon Ecossois, Le Maitre Ecossois and Le Grand Maitre Ecossois, &c. &c. making in the aggregate 52 degrees.

The Committee respectfully submit to the consideration of the Council, the above report on the principles and establishment of the Sublime degrees in South-Carolina, extracted from the archives of the Society. They cannot however conclude, without expressing their ardent wishes for the prosperity and dignity of the Institutions over which this Supreme Council preside; and they flatter themselves that if any unfavourable impressions have existed among their brethren of the Blue degrees, from the want of a knowledge of the principles and practices, of Sublime Masonry, it will be done away, and that harmony and affection, will be the happy cement of the universal society of Free and Accepted Masons. That as all aim at the improvement of the general condition of mankind by the practice of virtue, and the exercise of benevolence, so they sincerely wish, that any little differences which may have arisen, in unimportant ceremonies of *Ancient* and *Modern*, may be reconciled, and give way to the original principles of the order, those great bulwarks of society, universal benevolence and brotherly love, and that the extensive fraternity of Free-Masons throughout the two Hemispheres, may form but one band of Brotherhood. "Behold how good, and how pleasant it is for Brethren to dwell together in unity."

They respectfully salute your Supreme Council, by the *Sacred Numbers.*

Charleston, South-Carolina, the 10th day of the 8th Month, called Chisleu, 5553, A. L. 5802, and of the Christian era, this 4th day of December, 1802.

FREDERICK DALCHO,

K—H, P. R. S., Sovereign Grand Inspector General of the 33d, and Lieutenant Grand Commander in the United States of America.

ISAAC AULD,
K—H, P. R. S., Sovereign Grand Inspector General of the 33d.

E. DE LA MOTTA,
K—H, P. R. S., Sovereign Grand Inspector General of the 33d, and Illustrious Treasurer General of the H. Empire.

The above report was taken into consideration, and the Council was pleased to express the highest approbation of the same.

Whereupon, *Resolved*, that the foregoing report be printed and transmitted to all the Sublime and Symbolic Grand Lodges, throughout the two Hemispheres.

JN. MITCHELL,
K—H, P. R. S., Sovereign Grand Inspector General of the 33d, and Grand Commander in the United States of America.

True Extract from the deliberations of the Council.

ABM. ALEXANDER,
[SEAL.] K—H, P. R. S., Sovereign Grand Inspector General of the 33d, and Illustrious Secretary General of the H. Empire.

Deus Meumque Jus.

[That the following expulsion was promptly circulated, will be seen by the reply which follows it.]

UNIVERSI TERRARUM ORBIS ARCHITECTONIS PER GLORIAM INGENTIS.

Deus Meumque Jus.

ORDO AB CHAO.

IN *the name*, and at *the special request* of the Grand and Supreme Council of the most Puissant Sovereigns, Grand Inspectors General of the thirty-third degree, duly and lawfully constituted, under the celestial canopy of the Zenith which answers to the thirty-second degree, forty-five minutes north latitude.

To our Illustrious, most Valiant and Sublime Princes of the Royal Secret, Knights of K—H, Illustrious Princes and Knights, Grand, Ineffable, and Sublime, Free and Accepted Masons of all degrees, ancient and modern, over the surface of the Two Hemispheres.

TO ALL THOSE TO WHOM THESE LETTERS SHALL COME:

Union, Contentment and Wisdom.

BE IT KNOWN AND REMEMBERED, That whereas a certain individual of the name of JOSEPH CERNEAU, a Frenchman, born at Villeblerin, aged 50, and a jeweller by trade, residing at present, No. 118 William-street, in the city of New-York; did, some time this last spring, publish certain printed pamphlets, by the French, called Tableaux, signed and sealed, wherein he styles himself as "*Most Potent, Sovereign Grand Commander of the thirty-third Degree for the United States of America, their Territories and Dependencies, &c. &c. &c.*" *And whereas* the *only lawful body* of the kind in the United States of America, was legally established on the 31st May, 5801, at the city of Charleston, South-Carolina, and which is recognized all over the world: I, therefore, the undersigned, Grand Inspector General of the 33d, Grand Dignitary officer of the aforesaid Supreme Council of the 33d degree in Charleston, South-Carolina, do hereby, *in their name*, and *at their special request*, *declare*, and *certify*, that having previously taken such measures as were expedient in all such cases: *having also ascertained that he is not of, nor knows any thing at all about the thirty-third Degree;* and that having received no satisfaction whatsoever from the said *Joseph Cerneau*, for his assuming a Degree, Title, and Powers, to which he has not the smallest claim or right whatever; in consequence thereof, and being in duty bound to stop, crush and publish all such characters, so as to prevent their doing any further mischief, and continue to delude and impose upon otherwise worthy Brethren *unacquainted* with the Superior Degrees of Free-Masonry:

Be it known and remembered, therefore, that by, and in virtue of my High Powers, Rights and Prerogatives, as a *lawful* Grand Inspector General of the 33d Degree, in the United States of America, I do hereby publish and declare to the whole world, as well in my own name, as in that, and at the special request of my Supreme Council, in Charleston, South-Carolina, the aforesaid *Joseph Cerneau*, a Frenchman by birth, and a jeweller by trade, &c. &c. &c. *as an Impostor of the first magnitude, and whom we have expelled from every Masonic Asylum within our Jurisdiction;* and further, that whatever Masonic works or proceedings he may have performed, or put his hands to, ever since his arrival in this country from the West-Indies, are also, hereby declared as unlawful, void, and *totally vitiated by his last barefaced imposture, and highly anti-masonic conduct.*

That all those symbolic Brethren, and others who have been raised by him and his associates, in what *he* or *they* have been accustomed to call his or their *Sovereign Chap-*

ter of R. C. Grand Council of the 33d, are hereby declared irregular and unlawful, and that unless they shall each of them, individually, come forward, express their sorrow and abhorrence of such unlawful, nefarious conduct, and submit themselves, according to the exact tenor of the laws, they shall also be published over the two Hemispheres, and declared, each of them, individually, as impostors, and accomplices in his unlawful deeds.

BE IT KNOWN AND REMEMBERED, also, That being determined to stop, and crush at once and for ever, all such impositions as have been practised and persisted in for so many years by Joseph Cerneau and others, from foreign countries, particularly the West-Indies, I hereby, and in my own official capacity, declare, to whomsoever it may concern, that the *Sovereign Grand Consistory of the 30th, 31st and 32d Degrees*, originally established in this city, on the 6th day of August, 5806, by the *thrice Illustrious Brethren, John Gabriel Tardy, John Baptist Desdoity, Moses Levy, Madura Piexotto, and John James Joseph Gourgas*, all of them R. C. Eco, K—H, S. P. R. S., Deputies Grand Inspectors General and Grand Masters under the old System, &c. &c. &c. and others, has been rigorously inspected, and their proceedings approved of by me; in consequence whereof, I hereby declare, acknowledge, and recognize them, as well in my own name, as in that of my aforesaid Grand and Supreme Council of the 33d Degree, at Charleston, South-Carolina, as being the *only* lawful body in New-York, *which can exist* for the *Northern District* of the United States of America, &c. &c.

IN TESTIMONY WHEREOF, I, the aforesaid and undersigned, Emanuel De La Motta, K—H, S. P. R. S., Sovereign Grand Inspector General of the 33d Degree, and Illustrious Treasurer General of the Holy Empire in the United States of America, &c. &c. &c. have delivered the present, under my hand and Grand Seal of S. Ps. of the R. S.; and also of the Stamp of the 33d, at this Grand East of New-York City, by the 40th degree 42 minutes north latitude, the 26th day of the 6th month, called Elul

Ao. Mi. 5573, Ao. Ls. 5813, and of the Christian era, this 21st day of September, 1813.

Deus Meumque Jus.

E. DE LA MOTTA,

(Signed, sealed, and stamped on the original.)

K—H, S. P. R. S., Sovereign Grand Inspector General of the 33d, and Illustrious Treasurer General of the Holy Empire in the United States of America.

Deus Meumque Jus.

In the *name* and in *behalf* of the Supreme Grand Council of Sovereign Grand Inspectors General of the 33d Degree, holding its sittings in Charleston, South-Carolina: We do hereby approve of, and confirm, *all* and *every* of the foregoing declaration and proceedings of our Illustrious Brother, E. De La Motta, the Illustrious Treasurer General of the H. E. against a certain *Joseph Cerneau*, who has assumed to himself the profession of Principles and Degrees of which he is ignorant, and has arrogated to himself powers and privileges which never have been lawfully committed to him; and we do therefore, declare and publish, that the aforesaid *Joseph Cerneau, and his abbettors and followers*, are unworthy of Masonic Communion with any regular Free-Masons, whether of high or low degree, or wheresoever dispersed; and that each, and every of them, are hereby expelled from even every or any lawful Degree or Masonic Society, in which they may have been received or admitted, until they shall make their peace with our aforesaid Grand Council, upon such terms as our aforesaid Illustrious Treasurer General of the H. E. shall recommend and adopt for that purpose.

Given under our hands and seals of the Grand Council of Princes of the Royal Secret, and of the Supreme Council of the 33d Degree for the United

States of America, and dated this 24th day of December, 5813.

JN. MITCHELL,

(Signed, and stamped with two seals on the original.)

K—H, P. R. S., Sovereign Grand Inspector General of the 33d, and Grand Commander in the United States of America.

FREDERICK DALCHO,

K—H, P. R. S., Sovereign Grand Inspector General of the 33d, and Lieutenant Grand Commander in the United States of America.

Issued by me this thirty-first day of January, 5814.

(Signed) E. DE LA MOTTA,

K—H, S. P R. S., Sovereign Grand Inspector General of the 33d degree, Illustrious Treasurer General of the H. E. in the United States of America, &c. &c. &c.

Approved by

ISAAC AULD, M. D.

K—H, S. P. R. S., Sovereign Grand Inspector General of the 33d Degree.

JAMES MOULTRIE, M. D.

K—H, S. P. R. S., Sovereign Grand Inspector General of the 33d Degree.

[Before introducing the following reply of the usurpers, we would premise that the subject at issue was whether "*Joseph Cerneau, his abettors and followers*," had any legal right to the privileges for the assumption of which they were expelled, or whether they had not? It was not of Mr. De La Motta or of his "*malice*," but of their own *title* to the prerogatives which they had usurped, of their own *correctness* and *regularity*, that they should have written. Observe, reader, how studiously the subject is avoided through the whole performance. Suppose Mr. De La Motta to have been all they would make him—does that make their bodies legal? No. He, in his Replication, has handsomely vindicated himself and clearly exposed their barefaced falsehoods. It must clearly prove their want of all authority more strongly than any thing that could be said by Mr. De La Motta, at least, to every one who considers the subject. The truth is, they could not answer him, and they adopted the following pettifogging manner:]

TO THE GLORY OF THE SUPREME ARCHITECT OF THE UNIVERSE.

Ordo ab Chao.

*At the Orient of the most powerful Sovereign Grand Consistory of Grand Inspectors General of the 33d degree, and Princes of the Royal Secret, Supreme Chiefs of Exalted Masonry of the Ancient Scottish rite of Heredon, for the United States of America, under the celestial canopy, at the central point, answering to 40 degrees, 41 minutes, north latitude.**

HEALTH. STABILITY. POWER.

Extract from the minutes of the Grand Consistory, at its session the 28th day of the 12th month, A. L. 5813.†

THE Committee appointed at the last Session to take into consideration the printed circular then communicated, made their report, which is as follows:

* Every Brother initiated into 33d Degree will at once detect the imposture of J. C.'s body, and be completely satisfied, that he is entirely ignorant of it; and this same consummate ignorance is continued throughout the whole pamphlet.

† From this expression the reader is left to determine whether they use the civil Calender of the Hebrews or the Romans; whether he must understand them to mean December, February or August. But it is as accurate as the rest of the pamphlet.

To the most potent Sovereign Grand Consistory of the United States of America, its Territories and Dependencies, sitting at New-York:

The Report of the Committee to whom was referred a printed paper purporting to be issued under the signatures of E. Dela Motta, John Mitchell and Frederick Dalcho.

Your Committee in undertaking the charge committed to them, have felt that this production derives its only title to the consideration of the Gr. Consist. from the manner in which it has been published and distributed.*

Had it been only communicated to those who, regularly clothed with the exalted degrees, were furnished with the means to detect its absurdity, the dignity of the Gr. Consist would have been properly vindicated in consigning it without notice to merited contempt. But the means which have been used to disseminate it will not permit the Gr. Consist. to be passive, nor to withhold from the Masonic world, the proof that it is but a malicious calumny, in every respect anti-masonic, and published with no other view than the gratification of private malice.

To this effect your committee submit their reflections on this extraordinary proceeding, on the degrees and power arrogated by E. Dela Motta, a native of St. Croix, in the West-Indies, and on the authority of his two chiefs, pretending to act in the name of a Supr. Council at Charleston.

From these it will appear to what extent Dela Motta has relied on the want of information and on the credulity of those to whom his missive has been sent.†

It purports to be the act of an individual in virtue of his own powers; yet affecting to proceed at the special request of a collective body to which he belongs, and must be either his act or theirs. If his own, in virtue of exclusive authority in him, there could be no necessity, or even propriety, in using the name of the Body. If its previous

* The manner of its publication prevented their deluding many a brother.

† The expulsion was sent to every sublime body regularly established *per orbem terrarum*.

sanction were requisite, why is not that act promulgated with the regular attestations in support of its authenticity? Wherever a derivative authority is claimed, it can never be allowed unless accompanied by a constituent act in its perfect form. But an approbatory decree is subjoined. Of whom? Of the body? No. Two other representatives; without credentials, start up to approve in the name of a Council, the proceedings of Dela Motta; and, so barren is it of members, that it cannot supply a Chancellor or Secretary, or Keeper of the Seals, to attest an important document, directed to all the masonic bodies of the universe. The reason must be obvious. It appears from the very instruments—no such council ever made such request—no such council in fact exists.*

On the 21st September, 1813, at New-York, (the designated latitude of which, does not reflect much credit on the geographical attainments of this Sovereign Grand Inspector General,) this denunciation is made. Had it been previously authorised, a confirmation would be nugatory. Yet, on the 24th December following, two persons, acting as individuals, but in the name of a Council, give their approbation; and by this very instrument, subscribed by them as Sovereign Grand Commander and his Lieutenant,† exclude themselves from deliberating or deciding on ulterior measures, leaving these to the absolute and arbitrary will of their Treasurer and *inferior officer*, whose *future* acts, just or unjust, lawful or unlawful, they adopt and sanction in advance. Can any Mason, or any man, believe that so preposterous an act, can proceed from men having the slightest knowledge of the principles of our order, or of common sense?

* They speak very boldly about that, of which they are unacquainted, through their own obstinacy or negligence. In a communication dated Aug. 1821, from the Secretary of the spurious body which J. Cerneau's representative has intruded into Charleston, S. C. very officially handed to some private gentlemen, are these words: "Our late Illustrious Brother Colonel John Mitchell, Sovereign Grand Inspector General."

† Look at the signatures.

Amply as other circumstances have proved to the Gr. Consist. that if there ever was a Council at Charleston, it has long ceased to exist, no more decisive evidence could be wanted than these absurd contrivances of its pretended members. If there were such a body, would it not be seen vindicating to the Masonic world its prerogatives and jurisdiction, against the usurpation of which it complained, by one of its most solemn acts, authenticated in the amplest form?*

Nor will the authority of Dela Motta and his coadjutors, appear in a more favorable light from the matter, than from the form, of this daring calumny.

After some confused recitals, it declares, First, that Joseph Cerneau is an impostor, expelled by Dela Motta from every Masonic Asylum. Secondly, that his proceedings and masonic works, since his arrival from the West-Indies, are unlawful, void, and totally *vitiated.* Thirdly, it declares the reason why they are so, that is, "by his last bare-faced imposture, and highly anti-masonic conduct." Now the only specific imposture and conduct alledged, and which is called the last, and of course must be the first also, is the publication of the Tableaux or list of the members of this Gr. Consist. This then is the highly anti-masonic conduct by which he declares the previous proceedings to be *vitiated,* admitting thereby that they were regular before. This absurdity cannot escape the notice of the most careless. Can the publication of a list of persons, composing a collective body, vitiate its acts? Even supposing such a measure improper, it cannot annul antecedent regular transactions.

Yet this is the only reason offered to cover the malignity which has prompted this atrocious libel on a valuable and zealous Mason, an industrious artizan, the father of a family, a meritorious and peaceful citizen.

But the malice of this production is not more apparent

* The very pamphlet under consideration is proof then that they did right in vindicating their prerogatives and jurisdiction in the manner they did.

than its arrogance and injustice. Betraying the greatest ignorance of the masonic system in the United States, it usurps jurisdiction over the three degrees of what is usually denominated ancient masonry.

It is well known that the three first degrees are under the exclusive superintendance of Independent Grand Lodges. Admitting that Dela Motta is in fact a Gr. Inspec. Gen. (which your Committee have the most satisfactory reasons to disbelieve) he has gone beyond the line of his duties and his powers to interfere with that jurisdiction.*

Your Committee on the point refer the consistory to the communication, giving notice of its establishment, to the Grand Lodge of the state of New-York, in which they expressly recognize its supremacy over Master-Masons.

The Sovereign Grand Commander Cerneau, is punished and condemned according to the "Old System." *Castigat audit que dolos*, with some improvements of this Modern Rhadamanthus, for he will *hear* nothing. Next the associates or members of the consistory are threatened with the same fate unless they submit; and this summons to answer, kept secret for more than three months, is for the first time promulgated with the decree of this threefold Council of single men, expelling them in mass "from every or any lawful degree or Masonic Society."

Did not the daring malignity of this pretended denunciation, sustain the indignation it excites, its ludicrous inconsistency would put all gravity at defiance.†

As to the declaration in favour of a Sov. Gr. Const. said to be formed the 6th August, 1806, it is only necessary to

* Remember how J. C.'s body of usurpers proceeded in Charleston, S. C. in the summer of 1821; they strained every nerve to have certain brothers who had never been initiated into the sublime degrees, expelled by the Grand Lodge of South-Carolina. J. C.'s representative carried a petition for signatures to several highly respectable brothers, with a view to have the Grand Lodge assist in supporting his disorder and misrule. Also see De La Motta's Replication, page 10, for a further explanation.

† "Projecit ampullas, et sesquipedalia verba." Horace. Bombast will never prove *legality* or *regularity* for J. C.

remark, that those who have any knowledge of our degrees, of Dela Motta, and of some of the persons he names, must allow that it is *utterly impossible* that they ought to be what they profess.*

It is well known that that body never pretended to any power previous to the notice of its formation on the 7th March, 1809, long after this was established and its formation publicly announced.† So well aware were the persons who composed that Consist. of its defects and of the regularity of this, that after many efforts to sustain it and much expense, borne in no equitable proportion, by many who were deluded to enter it, they suffered it to sink at once into an inactivity and oblivion.‡

Some individuals, who had assisted in its irregular proceedings, convinced of their error, applied for and received the degrees depending on this Gr. Consistory.§

Others, tenacious of their pride, but convinced of our correctness, applied for admission collectively; a proposition obviously inadmissible, which was at once rejected, and which could only have proceeded from persons ignorant of our laws and institutions, or disposed to sanction the violation of the obligations they impose.||

Your committee might securely rely on the observations they have made on this defamatory paper, to establish its total irregularity; but it is in such direct violation of the

* The conclusion of this sentence is unintelligible to common grammarians.

† In this case, orderly, regular brothers will inquire by what *authority* a Masonic body holds its meetings and admits members; the *youngest* Lodge in this city is equally entitled to respectability as the *oldest*, and their doings are as regular.

‡ As a comment upon this falsehood, I would just inform the brotherhood that J. C.'s friends paid some nothing, some $10, or so. But Mr. Gourdaine was obliged to pay 50 or $60, but ever after declined being concerned with such avaricious persons.

§ We should suppose that they would have kept this matter quiet, if they had remembered that an *installed* officer went over to them with the charter, and he constitutes "*some individuals.*"

|| It seems somewhat inconsistent for J. C. & Co. to talk of *laws* that they have steadily broken, and of *obligations*, when they violated every one they ever regularly received.

fundamental laws and institutions of exalted masonry, that they cannot refrain from showing that by these, that point is put beyond the reach of doubt.

The Gr. Consist. is vested with the sole power of administration and legislation, including that of granting constitutions, in all the degrees which appertain to exalted Masonry. The establishment of a Gr. Consistory absolutely supercedes the individual authority of the Gr. Inspectors General, in the regulation and government of the order.*

As to this degree of Grand Inspector General, in rank the 33d, the laws and regulations direct the manner in which the members on whom it is conferred shall be selected. It is a dignity granted as the reward of merit and experience. Those who are invested with it do not possess the arbitrary and irresponsible power which some who pretend to act under "*secret constitutions*" imagine they are authorised to exercise.*

Before your Committee dismiss this disgusting mass of absurdity and wickedness, which certainly discovers no characteristic of the Christian morality of our order, they beg leave to draw the attention of the Consistory to the insinuation contained in the words "having received no satisfaction, &c." which leave it to be inferred that our Sovereign Grand Commander was bound to give such satisfaction. Dela Motta has not pretended to alledge† that any regular application (which ought to have preceded an accusation for neglect or refusal) was made to brother

* Look at J. C.'s representative in Charleston, S. C.—see how he considers it in his notice in the Charleston Mercury of 6th May, 1822. But if the individual authority of the Inspectors is taken away by the 33d degree, how came J. C. to act under it, as he says he did? The 33d degree was formed May 1st, 1786, and went into operation in Europe upon the death of Frederick III. August 17th, of the same year, and in the United States it was regularly established 31st of May, 1801. We have in these two paragraphs, then, a complete acknowledgment of their *illegality* and *usurpation*.

† See De La Motta's Replication, p. 9—13, then the reader can form his opinion of the veracity of the statements in this document.

Cerneau: But the multiplied abuses existing in this country by means of persons falsely pretending to possess the Exalted degrees, early attracted the notice of the Gr. Consist. and connected with various insidious attempts to take advantage of the deficiency of our Sovn. Grand Commander in the English language, and of the unsuspicious confidence of his character, produced a determination to have all applications referred to the Grand Consist. Of this Dela Motta was apprized, he was told if he wished to inspect our documents, he should by applying to the Grand Consistory have all the satisfaction he required, provided he proved his right to it. Had he pursued this course, his conduct would have been conformable to that of a person clothed with lawful powers. This refusal indicates that he was not willing to examine too closely, into our powers, nor to submit his claims to that investigation which the Consistory might deem it their duty to make.

After this ample exposure of an Instrument which can inflict disgrace on none but its authors and abettors, your committee might safely conclude their labours: but they prefer submitting on this occasion some of the circumstances attending the establishment and progress of the Grand Consistory, which will also reflect some more light on the pretended Council at Charleston, which, in a spirit of appropriation your committee have no doubt is in strict conformity with the fact, Dela Motta emphatically calls his.

Immediately on its installation the Grand Consistory gave notice to the supreme masonic bodies in Europe and the West-Indies, to whom it at the same time communicated *copies of the patents under which it was formed.* These were followed by the most ample recognition on the part of the Supreme Grand Council of France, an act sufficient in itself to outweigh the cavils of all impostors.*

* Some clouds and doubt rest upon this, unless we suppose German Hacquet and company to be another like set of impostors; for in a communication for January, 1823, from the regular Gr. Orient of France for the 33d degree, no mention whatever is made of J. Cerneau, or any of his company of intruders.

Having heard that a Council had existed at Charleston, South-Carolina, which might yet be in activity, a circular, with copies of the Patent or Warrant, and a list of the members, was also transmitted thither and delivered to the person whose name appears as Grand Commander to the act approving Dela Motta's denunciation. No answer being received, another was dispatched, but with no better success. Your Committee here will just remark that if the Council at Charleston was a regular body, and deemed us usurpers, it was their duty to take instant and effectual measures to arrest our progress. If we were regular, masonic courtesy, as well as their obligation, required them to acknowledge us without delay. They have done neither.*

This profound silence and neglect was of itself sufficient to satisfy the Grand Consistory that the Body at Charleston, if it ever had a lawful existence, was extinct.

The subsequent transactions of the Grand Consistory were warranted by the high constitutions under which it acts; and were required by the abuses produced in various parts of the United States, by impostors who made a shameful traffic of their pretended degrees.†

Its inherent power is the fullest warrant for the extent of its jurisdiction, recognized as at least co-extensive with the limits of the nation where it is established.‡

The public papers throughout the United States bear testimony to the publicity which it has given to all the acts of which it concerned the dispersed members of the higher orders to be apprised. Years have since elapsed, and till now no one has had the hardihood to impeach its proceedings. It has persevered peacefully and successful-

* No communications were ever received by the Council of the 33d in this city But they immediately, as they learnt there was a body of usurpers in New-York, (a distance of 900 miles from this city,) did take the necessary steps, as this pamphlet proves.

† This paragraph, if applied to J. C. would be too true for the credit of the craft.

‡ What is here said would be true, if spoken of the Council of 33d in Charleston.

ly towards its ultimate objects, the correction of abuses, and the establishment, on a firm foundation, of the degrees under its peculiar care.*

Men distinguished in the annals of our order have received from it constitutions for the establishment of exalted bodies, in various parts of the United States.†

And does this pretended Council of Charleston, after years of torpid indifference, expect now to rival the vital energies of this Consistory? If two or three members, the fragments of its dissevered frame (and of their title to be thus considered there is no proof) do now reside at Charleston, it is obvious they have made no efforts to raise it from the dust. They have not a sufficient number for any deliberation, or official purpose, according to the established laws of the order. How futile must be their expectations, that, after so many years of peaceful slumber, three individuals could overturn, or even shake, a body regularly formed, respectable as well on account of its labours as of the individuals who compose it, and recognized by competent authority, whose testimony must outweigh the attempts of ten thousand such detractors.

The Consistory, if called upon by a body competent to decide, might view with triumph the opportunity such an occasion would present to disclose all the evidence which they possess to confound their calumniators.‡

After this ample statement, your Committee are of opinion that the Grand Consistory should submit to the good sense of all who may be called on to judge, the decision between it and its accusers. With respect to any future attack, either from the same or any other quarter,

* A New-York newspaper can hardly be called "*the public papers throughout the United States;*" and for "*years have elapsed,*" read "*eighteen months.*"

† However distinguished they may be, their distinction becomes sullied the moment they encourage irregularity, disorder, and misrule, nor will any name or standing shelter such from merited reproach.

‡ It seems none "competent to decide" has ever given them an opportunity to disclose, for they have never yet communicated any evidence.

your Committee deem it most dignified and proper for the Consistory to oppose the invitation for all who feel interested in their concerns to apply directly to it for information.

Your Committee advise that the Consistory should on no other similar occasion give any other answer than that it is willing to submit its acts to the investigation of all whom it may concern to make it in a regular and constitutional manner.

But your Committee cannot hesitate to advise that the Consistory owe to themselves and the interests of masonry in general, to denounce to the masonic world this proceeding of Dela Motta and his associates.

All which is respectfully submitted.

New-York, 28th February, A. L. 5814.

(Signed,)

JOHN W. MULLIGAN.
JONA. SCHIEFFELIN.
E. HICKS.
JOS. BOUCHAUD.
MARTIN HOFFMAN.
A. RAINETAUX.
FRANCIS DUBUAR.

WHEREUPON, Resolved unanimously, That this Grand Consistory approve and adopt the said report, that it be entered at length on the minutes of this session, and the original be deposited among the Archives of the Grand Consistory.

Resolved, That the conduct of Emanuel Dela Motta and his associates, in framing and publishing their said act against our sovereign Grand Commander, and the members of this Grand Consistory, be and it is hereby denounced to the Masonic world as irregular, anti-masonic and scandalous.

Resolved, That this Grand Consistory does not recognize the said Emanuel Dela Motta and his associates as legally possessing the degrees or powers which they claim, nor as worthy of admission into any regular assembly of exalted Masons. And that their pretended acts are void and insignificant.*

Resolved, That it be and hereby is enjoined on all the masonic bodies under our jurisdiction to govern themselves by the tenor of these proceedings.

Resolved, That copies, authenticated in due form, of the said report, and of the resolutions taken thereon at this meeting, be transmitted with all possible dispatch to the different bodies corresponding with the Grand Consistory in the two hemispheres; to the Grand Councils of P. R. S. and other bodies under its jurisdiction. To the most Worshipful the Grand Lodge of the State of New-York, and the other most Worshipful Grand Lodges of the U. States, and elsewhere under the canopy of heaven; and to such other bodies as the sovereign Grand Commander shall direct.

A true copy from the Minutes.

By order of the Grand Consistory.

A. RAINETAUX,
R. C. K. H. S. P. R. S.
Grand Secretary.

Sealed and Stamped by

(L. S.) J. SCHIEFFELIN, (L. S.)
R. C. K. H. S. P. R. S.
Gr. Insp. Gen. 33d. deg.
Gr. Keeper of the Seals.

* Whether they consider the regular body legal or not, they have never failed to teaze every one of the old members in Charleston to visit them and to join them; but their success has been small; a hard-drinking stranger served them as tyler until he was drowned, and now a Welshman does the same duty for them; these men were both gladly received to the highest degree into which they had been initiated in the regular body.

UNIVERSI TERRARUM ORBIS ARCHITECTONIS PER GLORIAM INGENTIS.

Deus Meumque Jus.

ORDO AB CHAO.

In *the name*, of the Grand and Supreme Council of the most Puissant Sovereigns, Grand Inspectors General of the thirty-third degree, duly and lawfully constituted in the United States of America, under the celestial canopy of the Zenith, which answers to the thirty-second degree, forty-five minutes north latitude.

To our Illustrious, most Valiant and Sublime Princes of the Royal Secret, Knights of K—H, Illustrious Princes and Knights, Grand, Ineffable, and Sublime, Free and Accepted Masons of all degrees, ancient and modern, over the surface of the Two Hemispheres.

TO ALL THOSE TO WHOM THESE LETTERS SHALL COME:

Union, Contentment and Wisdom.

Imperious necessity has again imposed on me the unpleasant task of appearing before the masonic world in a conspicuous point of view. Existing circumstances, at this period, have led me to wish, not to obtrude myself into the attention of the reflecting, liberal, and unbiassed mason; but the duty I owe myself, my friends, and those masonic bodies to which I am connected, compels me, unwillingly, to step forward to refute the obloquy and unmerited opprobrium thrown out against me in a certain pamphlet industriously circulated, and said to emanate from a certain society of gentlemen, entitling themselves—"*The most powerful Grand Consistory of Grand Inspectors General of the thirty-third degree, and Princes of the Royal Secret, Supreme Chiefs of Exalted Masonry of the ancient Scottish Rite of Heredon, for the United States of America, under the celestial canopy, at the central point, answering to* 40 *degrees,* 41 *minutes, north latitude.*" Deeming the language both indecorous and anti-masonic in its personality, I have laid aside every consideration which might have had a tendency to retard this publication; nor should I have waited to this late hour to present this replication, were it not for the following reasons: absence from the city—confined by long and severe indisposition to a sick chamber—abstracted from the world, consequently unacquainted with various occurrences, a copy of the pamphlet alluded to having never come to my hands until within a very few weeks. The charges exhibited against me in that pamphlet I hope to prove to the impartial and uninfluenced mind to be a complete calumny. My attentive readers will have the goodness to bear with patience the recital of some circumstances which I pledge myself shall be in strict conformity with truth, with documents, and incontestable evidence, to prove the correctness of my assertions, and to establish beyond the reach of just refutation the circular issued on the 31st January, 5814. In the early part of May, 5813, I arrived here, not on any *speculative, office-hunting*, or *masonic errand*, but in quest of health. Some time in July a certain pamphlet or tableau, signed, sealed and stamped, was placed in my hands, entitled—"*List of the Grand Officers, Members, Honorary Members, &c. of the Supreme Council of Grand Inspectors General of the thirty-third degree, regularly established according to the ancient constitutional Scottish Rite of Heredon, for the U. States of America, their territories and dependencies, held in the city of New-York. Also, the Grand Consistory of Supreme Chiefs of Exalted Masonry, and the Constituted Bodies of its jurisdiction. Anno Lucis* 5813—*New-York: Printed by Hardcastle and Van Pelt, No.* 86 *Nassau-st.* 1813." On the very front of which I perceived the name of Mr. *Joseph Cerneau*, in the glaring character of "*Most*

Potent Sovereign Grand Commander." Convinced that he must either have been egregiously imposed upon, or that he was imposing on some respectable characters in the community, from a number of names which I understood to be very *respectable* in the city, *many* of them dignified with titles which that degree does not recognise, I was led to make some inquiry respecting *this Mr. Joseph Cerneau* and his pretensions to certain titles; when I received the following information from well-informed gentlemen: 1st. That this Mr. *Cerneau* had first made his appearance in Longworth's Directory for the year 1809, as "*G. I. G. P.* "*S. G. C.*" (meaning I suppose) "*Grand Inspector Gene-*"*ral, Potent Sovereign Grand Commander* (of his) *most Potent Sovereign Grand Council of Sublime Princes of the Royal Secret, Supreme Chiefs of High Masonry,*" *&c.*

2d. By an advertisement in the newspapers, 5th of September, 1811, his new created body is styled "*The Grand Consistory of P. P. of Supreme Chiefs, of exalted Masonry,*" *&c.*

3d. In another advertisement communicated through the vehicle of a newspaper, 1st February, 1812, he caused his said association to appear under the *new* and *improved* title of "*Grand Consistory for the United States of America, their territories and dependencies, of Supreme Chiefs of Exalted Masonry, according to the ancient constitutional Scottish Rite of Heredon, held at New-York.*"

4th. His *two* Sovereign Chapters of *Rose Croix*, the *Triple Amitiè* announced in the first instance, I expect must have been closed as legally as it had been opened, so as to make room for another of a better description under the denomination of the *Triple Alliance*, which to this day *decorates* Longworth's Directory; both of which, his initiating, together with all his other proceedings in this 18th degree, the Rose Croix, *is precisely as lawful* as it would be for *onè* or *more* Royal Arch Masons, in the very place where regular Chapters of Royal Arch Masons should have for years been lawfully established; to come forward and introduce into that sublime degree, Symbolic Brethren, even the profane, then, with their help, establish, consecrate, instal; and finally publish themselves as having *a lawfully constituted Chapter of Royal Arch Masons*. I call upon all worthy companions to pronounce what would be the natural consequence of such irregular, unwarranted, and unlawful antimasonic proceedings.

5th. *Mr. Cerneau* and *his Society* under the denomination of *Grand Consistory for the United States of America, their territories and dependencies, &c.* under date of the 25th day of the 5th month, Anno Lucis 5812, came out with a grand decree, *famous* for its presumptuous ignorance, and which in itself is a masonic enormity: therein they style the kind of masonry to which they have devoted themselves, namely; the *exalted*, the *sublime*, the *philanthropic*, or *philosophic masonry, &c. &c. &c.* considering and *feelingly* complaining of the great abuses existing in this country by means of an improper choice and conduct on the part of the Deputies Inspectors General, &c. *Mr. Cerneau's exalted, sublime, philanthropic*, or *philosophic*, and *Grand Association, &c.* declare by the third resolve of their aforesaid Grand Decree, that no Sublime Masons, Deputies Inspectors General within the sphere of *Mr. Cerneau's Society, Grand Jurisdiction*, "can or shall be admitted or acknowledged in their degrees, after the period of the 30th November, 1812, being the day of St. Andrew of Scotland, unless he can prove his having had no knowledge of *Mr. Cerneau's Society*, advertisement and appeal in the newspapers dated 30 November, 1811. The *aforesaid Grand Society* reserving to itself in such cases the faculty of pronouncing upon the merit of claims." So that every Sublime Mason of any degree whatever, descending in a direct and lawful line from our Illustrious, well-beloved, and of far famed memory, Brother *Stephen Morin*, who may not see fit to advance and range himself quietly under the banners of this Most Potent Sovereign Grand Masonic character, before the expiration of a specified time, will of course be deemed and declared *Irregular*, as opportunity and circumstances may offer. By whom? by *Mr. Cerneau and his Sovereign Grand Association*, and therefore each and every one of the *lawful Deputies Inspectors Generals* within the United states of America, who have been appointed to their office, some of them perhaps twenty years or more before *Mr. Cerneau* came over to this country, and who have grown gray in the faithful performance of their duties, are now to come submissively to *Mr. Cerneau* and his *Grand Association*, with their silver locks bleached in the performance of the hardest labours of judicious and correct masonry, to be approved of, rejected, or restricted in their powers.

6thly. Mr. Cerneau crowned the whole of his anti-masonic career, in the spring of 1813, by means of his *celebrated* tableaux or pamphlets, therein *publishing* to the Masonic World, *His Supreme Council of Sovereigns, Grand Inspectors General of the 33d degree, himself, of course*, as the Chief or *Most Potent Sovereign Grand Commander of the 33d degree for the United States of America, their Territories and Dependencies*, &c. which has already been denounced by us, over the two Hemispheres, as the most flagrant and monstrous Masonic imposition that ever was, or ever can be practised on the Royal Order.

Maturely considering, and calmly perpending all the facts connected with the procedure of such detestable Masonic infractions; and from the above stated circumstances, and a full conviction that *Mr. Cerneau* was only a pretender to a degree that he was not in possession of, and was assuming a title to which he had no claim; it became my absolute duty as a *lawful* Sovereign Grand Inspector General of the 33d degree, to detect and denounce any imposition practised on the Masonic world, by any individual. But being unfurnished with any Masonic documents, I wrote on to the council in Charleston, inclosing them one of *Mr. Cerneau's* celebrated tableaux, requesting they would send me a copy of my Diploma, the original being deposited among papers which my family could not conveniently obtain. Having received their answer, and a

Diploma, with strong injunctions to prosecute and expose to view the unexampled conduct of *Mr. Cerneau*, on the 14th September, 1813, I took with me *four* respectable brethren of the city, *two* of them native citizens, and *two* foreigners, well versed in the French and English languages, who were witnesses to the conversation which took place between *Mr. Joseph Cerneau* and myself, to which I beg leave to refer the reader as follows:

Conversation with *Mr. Joseph Cerneau*, transcribed from the original.

"Let it be known and remembered, that at the Grand East of New-York, on the 19th day of the 6th month, called Elul, A. M. 5573, of the restoration 2343 and of the Christian era the 14th day of September, 1813.

"I, the undersigned, Emanuel De La Motta, K—H; S. P. R. S.; Sovereign Grand Inspector General of the 33d degree; Illustrious Treasurer General of the Holy Empire in the United States of America, &c. &c. &c. being at my own request, accompanied by the Thrice Puissant Brethren, Moses Levy Maduro Peixotto, John James Joseph Gourgas, K—H; S. P. R. S.; Deputies Inspectors General; Richard Riker, and Sampson Simson, K—H; S. P. R. S., do hereby declare that I waited on Mr. Joseph Cerneau, at No. 118 William Street; that I inquired of him, if he was a Mr. *Joseph Cerneau, Past Master, M. P. Sov. G. Commander*, designated as such in a certain pamphlet or tableau entitled '*List of the Grand Officers, members, honorary members, &c. of the Supreme Council of Grand Inspectors General, of the 33d degree, regularly established according to the ancient constitutional Scottish Rite of Heredon, for the United States of America, their territories and dependencies, held in the city of New-York—also of the Grand Consistory of Supreme Chiefs of Exalted Masonry, and the constituted bodies of its Jurisdiction. Anno Lucis* 5813, *New-York, printed by Hardcastle and Van Pelt, No.* 86, *Nassau Street*, 1813.' To which he replied in the affirmative. I then announced myself in my official capacity, showing him at the same time my credentials, stating that I called as a friend and as a gentleman, to ascertain whence he derived his powers in establishing *'a Grand Council of the 33d degree in this city,'* and from whom he 'had received that degree; requesting, at the same time, a sight of his patent and other papers relating thereto. His answer was—He could not comply with my request: that I, Emanuel De La Motta, must apply to the *'Grand Council of the 33d degree in this city,'* of which he, Mr. Cerneau, called himself the *head;* that he had made a promise to his aforesaid Grand Council to answer no questions on that subject, but referred me to that body for an answer, although he had no doubt of Mr. De La Motta being the character whom he represented himself to be, and therefore acknowledged him in his official capacity. My reply was, That I could not acknowledge any body of masons, unless I was satisfied they were legally constituted. Upon his refusing to admit me to a sight of his credentials, applying to him as a gentleman and a friend, I then demanded them of him in my official capacity, as an object of right; and that I should not leave the city of New-York until I had made a thorough investigation of the business, which I felt myself compelled to do by his refusal; more especially as I was particularly requested by the Supreme Council of the 33d, at Charleston, South Carolina, to investigate his proceedings, and those of what he called *his* Grand Council of the 33d at this city of New-York, he still persisting to refer me to *'his Grand Council.'* I then informed him I should leave the city on Monday in the ensuing week; that in the meanwhile he might reflect on the subject, and gave him my address and place of residence.

"Given under my hand and seal at the Grand East of New-York, under the above specified date."

Signed on the original.

(L. S.) E. DE LA MOTTA, (STAMP.)

K—H; S. P. R. S.;

Sovereign Grand Inspector General of the 33d, and Illustrious Treasurer General of the Holy Empire, in the United States of America.

Attest,

R. RIKER,
K—H; S. P. R. S.;
SAMPSON SIMSON,
K—H; S. P. R. S.;
M. L. M. PEIXOTTO,
K—H; S. P. R. S.
Dep. Insp. Gen.
J. J. J. GOURGAS,
K—H; S. P. R. S.
Dep. Insp. Gen.

Another Extract.

"Be it known and herewith recorded, that when on the 14th day of September, instant, 1813, I, the undersigned Emanuel De La Motta, &c. &c. &c. accompanied at my own request, (as before specified,) called on Mr. Joseph Cerneau at No. 118, William-Street, the two following circumstances took place, which I think it highly important to specify particularly, that they may be remembered, and serve hereafter as the case may require. 1. That in the presence of the aforesaid most illustrious and Puissant Brethren, I did ascertain the positive fact, that the said Joseph Cerneau was not of the 33d degree, nor did he even appear to me to possess any knowledge of that degree whatever; or of a certain finger ring which was shown to him, with which he went to the window and returned without comment or ceremony, *but not until he had taken care to examine it with a great deal of attention.* 2d. That during the conversation I had with him respecting what he called *his Grand Council of the 33d degree*, he, the said Joseph Cerneau, mentioned positively, that he had been recognized by *France*. In testimony whereof I the undersigned, &c. &c. &c. herewith attach my name at the Grand East of New-York, on the 26th day of the 6th month called Elul, A. M. 5573, of the Restoration 2343 and of the Christian era the 21st day of September, 1813."

Signed on the Original.

(L. S.) E. DE LA MOTTA, (STAMP.)

K—H; S. P. R. S.;

Sovereign Grand Inspector General of the 33d, and Illustrious Treasurer General of the Holy Empire in the United States of America.

Attest,

R. RIKER,
K—H; S. P. R. S.;
SAMPSON SIMSON,
K—H; S. P. R. S.;
M. L. M. PEIXOTTO,
K—H; S. P. R. S.;
Dep. Insp. Gen.
J. J. J. GOURGAS,
K—H; S. P. R. S.;
Dep. Insp. Gen.

I do now appeal to my readers, without, I trust, incurring the imputation of presumption, whether my conduct appeared antimasonic, irregular, malicious, *and scandalous*, as was so lavishly pronounced in a resolve, signed by the subtile, and respectable coadjutors of this manifestly pretended Inspector General. What motives could have actuated me in applying for a view of *Mr. Cerneau's* papers, when I did not wish them placed into my hands, but merely required to overlook them? He could not be apprehensive of my mutilating them, or depriving him of such *valuable documents*, being surrounded by gentlemen, who would not have permitted such an act, had I even been so inclined. Having acknowledged and recognized the Supreme Council of the 33d degree in Charleston, and myself as their representative; with what colour, and under what lawful pretence, could he refuse me full and entire satisfaction of what I had a right to expect, as appertaining to my Masonic standing; he did however repeatedly and peremptorily refuse to let me have a sight of his patents, from which circumstance, and from his *not answering* certain signs thrown out to him, I was induced to suppose, and am still fully convinced, *Mr. Cerneau* knew nothing of the 33d degree, and, consequently, that he was imposing upon the credulity of respectable characters. But still wishing to act the friendly and brotherly part towards *Mr. Cerneau*, I requested him to reflect on our conversation, and that I should be happy to hear from him previous to my leaving the city, since which period I have neither seen nor heard from *Mr. Cerneau*, but through the medium of *his most powerful Grand Consistory of Grand Inspectors General of the 33d degree, &c. &c. &c. &c.* by an (to use their own language) "*inconsistent, calumniating and ludicrous*" pamphlet published in February last. Stilll anxious to do no act which might be unfavourably construed, I waited the next day on *his Deputy Grand Commander*, when the following was the conversation which took place between us.

Conversation with *Mr. De Witt Clinton*, transcribed from the original:

"Be it known and remembered, that at the Grand East of New-York, on the 20th day of the 6th month called Elul, A. M. 5573, of the Restoration 2343, and of the Christian era the 15th day of September, 1813,

"I, the undersigned, Emanuel De La Motta, K—H; S. P. R. S.; Sovereign Grand Inspector General of the 33d degree, Illustrious Treasurer General of the Holy Empire in the United States of America, &c. &c. &c. do hereby declare, that having called on Illustrious Brother Sampson Simson, K—H; S. P. R. S., to accompany me to Mr. De Witt Clinton, we therefore waited on him and communicated, that the respect which I entertained of him as a Gentleman and as Grand Master for the State of New-York, had induced me to deviate from the line of my duty as an Inspector General, at the same time presenting him my credentials; on reading which, he appeared to be satisfied as to my official character, and on presenting him with a certain pamphlet or tableau, entitled '*List of the Grand officers, Members, Honorary Members, &c. of the Supreme Council of Grand Inspectors General of the 33d degree, regularly established according to the ancient Constitutional Scottish Rite of Heredon, for the United States of America, their Territories and Dependencies, held in the city of New-York, also of the Grand Consistory of Supreme Chiefs of Exalted Masonry, and the Constituted Bodies of its Jurisdiction. Anno Lucis* 5813. *New-York, printed by Hardcastle and Van Pelt, No.* 86, *Nassau Street*, 1813, he declared that it was a *collusion*, and acknowledged he had signed the said pamphlet, together with others, at the special request of *Mr. Thomas Lownds*, who had brought them to him for that special purpose. I asked him if he had seen *Mr. Cerneau's* Patent, and from whom he had received the 33d degree, and had derived his powers for establishing a Grand Council of the 33d. Mr. Clinton replied he had never seen any of his patents or papers relating thereto, but had depended on the gentlemen that called on him, to wit, *Messrs. Martin Hoffman* and *John W. Mulligan*, and at their particular request had some degrees communicated to him by this *Mr. Cerneau*, and observed he conceived it rather *a distinction* as Grand Master of the State. On my asking if *Mr. Cerneau* had conferred the 33d degree on him, Mr. Clinton replied, it was impossible for him to say, as he did not recollect, and had as little knowledge of it as his child; on which I, Emanuel De La Motta, informed Mr. Clinton that I should be compelled to publish *Mr. Cerneau* as an impostor, as I was convinced he had not the powers he had assumed, but through delicacy and respect for him, Mr. Clinton, that I would not take any steps against *Joseph Cerneau* till he had first seen him on the subject. When Mr. Clinton solicited me to suspend any proceedings against the said *Cerneau* till he should see some gentlemen on the subject. He then inquired my place of residence, and on being informed, replied I should hear from him. Given under my hand and seal, at the

Grand East of New-York, under the above specified date."

Signed on the Original.

(L. S.) E. DE LA MOTTA, (STAMP.)
K—H; S. P. R. S.;

Sovereign Grand Inspector General of the 33d, and Illustrious Treasurer General of the Holy Empire in the United States of America.

Witness,

SAMPSON SIMSON,
K—H; S. P. R. S.

On the day previous to my leaving the city, Mr. Dewitt Clinton called upon me at my place of residence, and mentioned that it had not been in his power to see his friends on the subject, inquiring what stay I should make in Philadelphia. I replied, three or four weeks. He then observed, that in that time he would see his friends, and wished me to suspend all further proceedings until I heard from him through the medium of Mr. Sampson Simson; but not hearing either from *Mr. Cerneau* or *Mr. Dewitt Clinton*, and urged by my council to know what had been done, I transmitted them the circular which I intended to issue, requesting their sanction to it, which I received some time afterwards; the original is in my possession for the investigation of any of the brethren.

And now I shall endeavour, in a very circumspect manner, to answer the several parts of this elaborate and declamatory pamphlet, said to be issued by and under the authority of *Mr. Joseph Cerneau's most powerful Sovereign Grand Consistory of Grand Inspectors General of the 33d degree, &c. &c. &c.* Must it not appear very extraordinary, that in their tableaux those gentlemen should call themselves the *Supreme Council of Grand Inspectors General of the 33d degree, &c. &c. &c.* and a few months afterwards, in their pamphlet, style themselves *the most powerful Sovereign Grand Consistory of Grand Inspectors General of the 33d degree, &c. &c. &c.?* Does it not appear very inconsistent to every judicious mind?

Does it not explicate their total ignorance of that degree, or even the principles on which it is predicated?

To review the most conspicuous paragraphs in the pamphlet now under consideration, and that demand replication, it will become necessary that I quote them as published, which will expose in more glaring colours the absurd and incongruous proceedings that mark the conduct of Mr. Cerneau and his adherents.

"Had it been only communicated to those who, regularly clothed with the exalted degrees, were furnished with the means to detect its absurdity, the dignity of the Gr. Consist. would have been properly vindicated in consigning it without notice to merited contempt; but the means which have been used to disseminate it will not permit the G. Consist. to be passive, nor to withhold from the masonic world the proof that it is but a malicious calumny, in every respect antimasonic, and published with no other view than the gratification of private malice."

To whom should it have been sent, if not to masons of every degree, so as to put them on their guard against the gross impositions so long practised with impunity by *Mr. Cerneau?* And further, was not *this consistory*, or *council*, or *whatever other denomination* they may be pleased to give to it, informed at the time by *their most Potent Sovereign Grand Commander and his Deputy*, of my positive determination to issue my solemn protest against such antimasonic proceedings? As to what relates to malicious calumny, how can any one bestow such an epithet, from the friendly and brotherly manner I proceeded with *Mr. Cerneau*, to which, had he answered by exhibiting to me his papers, or had *Mr. Dewitt Clinton* fulfilled his promise to procure a view of those papers, which, if on examination had been found genuine or correct, would have prevented this unpleasant altercation. It was not a contention between *Mr. Cerneau* and myself for the *Grand Commandership;* it was not a competition with *Mr. Cerneau* for his crown of straw, attempting at the same time to wrest it from his brows to decorate my own; but imperious duty as a *law-*

ful Sovereign Grand Inspector General of the 33d degree, necessitated me either to bring by friendly means *Mr. Cerneau* to a due sense of his antimasonic proceedings, so long persisted in, or to exhibit him to the public view of the fraternity. I beg leave to insert here the following articles from the Grand Constitutions of the 33d degree, as ratified at Berlin on the 1st of May, 5786.

Article 9th. "No Deputy Inspector can use his patent in any country, where a Supreme Council of Inspectors General is established, *unless it shall be signed by the said Council!*"

Article 10th. "No Deputy Inspector heretofore appointed, or who may hereafter be appointed, by virtue of this constitution, shall have power to grant patents, nor to give the degree of K—H, or the higher degrees."

Article 11th. "The degree of K—H, and the degree of Prince of the Royal Secret, are never to be given, but in the presence of *three* Sovereign Grand Inspectors General."

Article 12th. "The Supreme Council shall exercise all the sovereign masonic power, of which his august majesty, Frederick II, King of Prussia, is now possessed, in recalling the patents of Deputy Inspectors for improper unmasonic conduct," &c. &c. &c.

And the patent of every *lawful* Sovereign Grand Inspector General of the 33d degree, contains the following paragraph: "And we hereby authorize and empower our said illustrious brother, to establish, congregate, superintend, and inspect, all Lodges, Chapters, Councils, Colleges and Consistories of the Royal and Military Order of Ancient and Modern Free-Masonry, over the surface of the two hemispheres, *agreeably to the grand constitutions,*" &c. &c. &c.

From the latter clause in my patent, it became a bounden duty to interest myself in exposing *Mr. Cerneau's* impositions, for so many years practised with impunity, on the masonic world. It must appear evident, also, that I had no other alternative in pursuing the line of conduct towards Mr. C. after his contempt of my repeated requests. Does it not seem, therefore, self-evident to a mind the least given to reflection, that the epithet bestowed on me of "*the gratification of private malice*," is completely ungenerous, and considered unfounded on the broad basis of correct principles?

"To this effect your committee submit their reflections on this extraordinary proceeding, on the degrees and powers arrogated by E. De La Motta, a native of St. Croix, in the West Indies, and on the authority of his two chiefs, pretending to act in the name of a Supr. Council at Charleston."

As to the degrees and powers arrogated by me—who are they—pretending to be acquainted and *lawfully* vested with the sublime degrees of masonry, that are not also furnished with *legal private registers duly signed and sealed*, by means of which they may easily see and know what the several constitutions of the order truly and really are, and learn, also, that the Supreme Council of the 33d at Charleston, South-Carolina, was legally established on the 31st day of May, 5801, and that at that time I was *lawfully* initiated in *council*, and appointed the *third* grand officer for life? Are those sublime masons also unacquainted that our illustrious brother *Comte Alexandre François Auguste De Grasse Tilly*, a Deputy Inspector General, *was initiated by the Supreme Council at Charleston*, on the 21st February, 5802, a Sovereign Grand Inspector General of the 33d degree, and *appointed Grand Commander ad vitam, for the French West-India Islands?* And that our illustrious brother *Jean Baptiste Marie De La Hogue*, a Deputy Inspector General, *was also initiated* a Sovereign Grand Inspector General of the 33d degree, and *appointed Lieutenant Grand Commander ad vitam*, for the same islands? To those who wish for still further proofs, I beg leave to refer them to the *circular* issued under date of 4th December, 5802, by the Supreme Council of the 33d at Charleston, South-Carolina. Regular sublime masons must be acquainted, likewise, by means of their private registers, that on the 19th day of April, 5802, our illustrious brother the *Reverend Doctor Frederick Dalcho*, Lieutenant Grand Commander in the United States of America, was appointed representative of the Supreme Council of the 33d established at Cape François by illustrious brother Comte De Grasse, for the United States of America, and, consequently, that he is the *only* lawful organ of that body in this country.

How palpable must it not appear to the enlightened, the extreme ignorance shown of that degree by this committee acting for and sanctioned by *Mr. Cerneau's Society*, otherwise called *Most Powerful Sovereign Grand Consistory of Grand Inspectors General of the 33d degree*, &c. &c. &c.? In making such advancement, are they uninformed that a Supreme Council of the 33d once *constitutionally* established, whilst a single member remains, is considered in existence; or that a *lawful* Sovereign Grand Inspector General of the 33d once appointed *is so for life*, unless an improper act or acts of his should vitiate his powers, which, in such a case, the withdrawing of his patents would be the consequence attending his conduct, and the same made known to the fraternity? Has this been my case? No; the contrary will appear by the sanction of the Supreme Council of the 33d at Charleston on my circular issued on the 31st day of January last.

"It purports to be the act of an individual in virtue of his own powers; yet affecting to proceed at the special request of a collective body to which he belongs, and must be either his act or theirs. If his own, in virtue of exclusive authority in him, there could be no necessity, or even propriety, in using the name of the body. If its previous sanction were requisite, why is not that act promulgated with the regular attestations in support of its authenticity? Wherever a derivative authority is claimed, it can never be allowed, unless accompanied by a constituent act in its perfect form. But an approbatory decree is subjoined. Of whom? Of the body? No. Two other representatives, without credentials, start up to approve, in the name of a Council, the proceedings of De La Motta; and so barren is it of members, that it cannot supply a Chancellor or Secretary, or Keeper of the Seals, to attest an important document, directed to all the masonic bodies of the universe. The reason must be obvious. It appears from the very instruments—no such council ever made such request—no such council, in fact, exists."

The whole tenor of this clause, as appears in the report of the committee of *this aforesaid society*, is generally refuted in the preceding pages; in addition to which I do aver, that the form of my circular, with its sanction, was perfectly correct and consistent with the 33d degree, which to those who have *lawfully* received that degree, is a fact well known.

"On the 21st September, 1813, at New-York, (the designated latitude of which does not reflect much credit on the geographical attainments of this Sovereign Grand Inspector General,) this denunciation is made. Had it been previously authorized, a confirmation would be nugatory. Yet, on the 24th December following, two persons, acting as individuals, but in the name of a Council, give their approbation; and by this very instrument, subscribed by them as Sovereign Grand Commander and his Lieutenant, exclude themselves from deliberating or deciding on ulterior measures, leaving these to the absolute and arbitrary will of their Treasurer and *inferior officer*, whose *future* acts, just or unjust, lawful or unlawful, they adopt and sanction in advance. Can any mason, or any man, believe that so preposterous an act can proceed from men having the slightest knowledge of the principles of our order, or of common sense?"

How futile an effort to cavil at geographical knowledge! How imbecile their observations must appear relative to the latitude of New-York! How irrelevant to the subject! Of what consequence was it whether the latitude of New-York was placed in 40d. 41m. or 40. 23? May it not have proceeded from a typographical error? But this conduct reminds me of what I have often witnessed at the bar in a court of justice practised by *petty attorneys* when employed in a lame case; to catch at every little faux pas, or inadvertency of the adverse party, to make the best of a bad cace; it may also be assimilated to a vulgar *adage*—"a drowning man will catch at a straw."

On the 14th of September, 5813, as appears from the attested conversations, I called on *Mr. Cerneau*, and on the next day, the 15th, on *Mr. Dewitt Clinton*, and on the 21st, I left the city, apprising *Mr. Clinton* I should remain in Philadelphia for some time; from neither of the gentlemen having received any information, I was compelled, in the early part of December, to transmit my circular to the Supreme Council of the 33d in Charleston, for their decision; and after its return to me with their approbation and act, I retained it until the 31st January, 5814, before it was promulgated. Will not my forbearance in publishing this circular appear to the candid and impartial mind, as a willingness to act consistently or in conformity to the disposition and advice of my council, observing strictly the most regular and circumspect conduct?

"Amply as other circumstances have proved to the Gr. Consist. that if there ever was a Council at Charleston, it has long ceased to exist, no more decisive evidence could be wanted than these absurd contrivances of its pretended members. If there were such a body, would it not be seen vindicating to the masonic world its prerogatives and jurisdiction, against the usurpation of which it complained, by one of its most solemn acts, authenticated in the amplest form?"

In answer to this, it will be sufficient to refer the reader to the act of the Supreme Council of the 33d at Charleston, on my circular.

"Nor will the authority of De La Motta and his coadjutors appear in a more favourable light from the matter, than from the form, of this daring calumny."

Who have I calumniated? Have I attempted to traduce the character of *Mr. Cerneau* and *his adherents*? Could it be deemed a calumny to hold up to masonic view, a character who had imposed and was imposing on a number of persons, a grade he was not and is not entitled to? What authority could delegate to *Mr. Cerneau the powers to assume the title of Most Potent Sovereign Grand Commander of the 33d degree for the United States of America, their Territories and Dependencies?* If they did, how could they constitutionally give such a power to any person not lawfully admitted into the 33d degree, and who in fact is perfectly and totally unacquainted with that degree? As to any powers *whatsoever* issuing from *any foreign jurisdiction*, however supreme it might be, a moment's reflection will prove its invalidity. As well might the Grand Lodge for the state of New-York, or any other, grant a warrant for the purpose of enforcing supremacy in the symbolic degrees, in any of the European kingdoms. In such a case, the legal authority there would no doubt take the necessary steps to stop such unwarrantable proceedings against their own natural and constitutional rights.

"After some confused recitals, it declares, First, That Joseph Cerneau is an impostor, expelled by De La Motta from every masonic asylum. Secondly, That his proceedings and masonic works, since his arrival from the West Indies, are unlawful, void, and totally *vitiated*. Thirdly, It declares the reason why they are so, that is, 'by his last bare-faced imposture, and highly antimasonic conduct.' Now, the only specific imposture and conduct alleged, and which is called the last, and, of course, must be the first also, is the publication of the Tableaux, or list of the members of this Gr. Consist. This, then, is the highly antimasonic conduct by which he declares the previous proceedings to be *vitiated*, admitting thereby that they were regular before. This absurdity cannot escape the notice of the most careless. Can the publication of a list of persons, composing a collective body, vitiate its acts? Even supposing such a measure improper, it cannot annul antecedent regular transactions."

The expulsion of *Mr. Joseph Cerneau* was the natural consequence of his impositions, and of his well-fixed determination to persist therein. I beg leave to submit the following *quære* to every mason, particularly the blue or symbolic brethren. In the event that *three* fellow-crafts, who have been regularly entered and passed in a regularly constituted Lodge, should, by some unlawful means, obtain an insight into the third degree, and should apply and obtain a warrant from the Grand Lodge, and under that sanction should initiate persons, and after a lapse of time their nefarious conduct should be brought to light; whether such characters would not be expelled from every masonic institution, their acts deemed void and of no effect, and persons so initiated by them, pronounced clandestinely made; and would they not be compelled to go over the same ground in a regularly constituted Lodge; and should it so occur, that one or more of them persist in their refusal to apply to the regularly constituted authority, whether they would not share the same fate with their master and wardens? *Thus stands the case of Mr. Cerneau and his adherents.* Further, what *Mr. Cerneau's gentlemen* pretend to deem of minor consideration, the "*publication of their celebrated* tableau or pamphlet," is of the *highest importance;* and I will prove incontestably to the most uninformed mind the impositions practised; and which stamps *Mr. Cerneau* as a masonic impostor; and, if established, as I have no doubt I shall be able to do to the full conviction of every unprejudiced brother, must and will *vitiate all Mr. Cerneau's former acts,* even in the supposition of their being correct, *which I by no means do admit.*

1st. On the first blush of this tableau or pamphlet, *Mr. Cerneau* publishes to the masonic world his being of the 33d degree; the impossibility of *Mr. Cerneau's* obtaining this supreme degree *under its several restrictions,* known to every one *lawfully* initiated therein, formed the groundwork of my inquiries; fully satisfied of the impracticability of *Mr. Cerneau* being possessed of that degree by intuition, or inspiration; and its communication by letter was as impossible as obtaining the three first degrees of masonry through that channel.

2dly. Mr. Cerneau's assuming the title of *Most Potent Sovereign Grand Commander of the 33d degree for the whole of the United States of America, their Territories and Dependencies*, could be but an assumption, for no masonic institution, however supreme, and wherever situated, could *lawfully* invest him with *such a power;* it must, therefore, be a self-evident truth—the man who assumes a character he is not entitled to, is decidedly an impostor.

3dly. By what patent right did *Mr. Cerneau* arrogate to himself the title of Sovereign Grand Inspector of the 33d degree? Where is his authority for establishing a Supreme Council of the 33d? He has none—he has shown none—nor can he refer to any.

4thly. Another proof of his total ignorance of this degree, which is manifested in his *celebrated* tableaux, is his appointments of offices or places of dignity, and the incorrect number composing his council; this, together with the subsequent conversations which took place with *Mr. Cerneau* and *Mr. Dewitt Clinton,* fully established *Mr. Cerneau* as a masonic impostor.

The 33d degree was established on the first day of May, 5786. The occasion of it I will state. By the constitutions of Sublime Prince of the Royal Secret, which were ratified on the 25th of October, 5762, the King of Prussia was proclaimed as the chief of the eminent degrees, with the rank of *Sovereign Grand Inspector General,* and *Grand Commander;* the higher councils and chapters could not be opened without his presence, or that of his substitute, whom he must appoint; all the transactions of the consistory of the 32d degree required his sanction, or that of his substitute, to establish their legality; and many other prerogatives were attached to his masonic rank; no provision, however, had been made in the constitution for the appointment of his successor; and as it was an office of the highest importance, the utmost caution was necessary to prevent an improper person from obtaining it. The king, being conscious of this, established the 33d degree. *Nine* brethren in *each* nation, form the *Supreme Council* of Sovereign Grand Inspectors General of the 33d degree, who, after his decease, possess all his masonic prerogatives over the craft. Their appointment is *ad vitam*. They are the executive body of the masonic fraternity, and their approval is now necessary to the acts of the consistory, before they can become laws; and from their decision there can be no appeal.

After this full explanation, it will be rather difficult to understand the following farrago of nonsense—*I allude* to the report of the committee of *Mr. Cerneau's Grand Society*, page 8.

"*As to this degree of Grand Inspector General, in rank the 33d, the laws and regulations direct the manner in which the members on whom it is conferred, shall be selected. It is a dignity granted as the reward of merit and experience. Those who are invested with it do not possess the arbitrary and irresponsible power which some who pretend to act under 'secret constitutions,'* imagine they are authorized to exercise."

Does it not put "*all gravity at defiance*" (reverting to the gentlemen's words) to perceive *thinking* men assuming to write with *as much erudite consequence*, as is manifested in the above paragraph? They speak of *laws, regulations of the 33d degree*, and "*secret constitutions*," exactly as if they had them in *their possession*, when it has repeatedly been clearly proved that *their leader, Mr. Joseph Cerneau*, from whom, of course, they must have derived *all* their knowledge and information, is nothing else but a *pretender* and masonic impostor of the 33d degree.

"Yet this is the only reason offered to cover the malignity, which has prompted this atrocious libel on a valuable and zealous mason, an industrious artisan, the father of a family, a meritorious and peaceful citizen."

How must the shafts of calumny recoil to the bosom of those who so liberally darted them at me! Have I traduced *Mr. Cerneau's* character as not being a peaceful citizen?

Have I accused him of *mixing alloy with his work?* Have I charged him with not attending to his *business faithfully as a jeweller?* Can any expression of mine be construed to have a tendency to injure *Mr. Cerneau* in the opinion of *his friends?* I could have no enmity to *Mr. Cerneau*, as I knew not the *gentleman*, never having seen him but once in my life, nor did I ever hear his name mentioned until his *celebrated* tableau or pamphlet fell into my hands, of which I deemed it my duty to investigate the validity, and trace the *gentleman's* masonic conduct. Can this committee of *Mr. Cerneau's society* allude to my wishing to injure *Mr. Cerneau* by preventing him from selling *masonic jewels*, as charged against him by a certain pamphlet purporting to be published at Philadelphia in the year 1810?

Had *Mr. Cerneau* confined his high dignities to his friends in the city of New-York alone, and had he not possessed the *effrontery* to publish this pamphlet or tableau, blazing to the masonic world his elevated situation, he might with impunity within his circle of friends and supporters, have called himself *the Emperor of Emperors; the King of Kings; the most Potent and Powerful Commander of Commanders;* and even the *Grand Saviour and Protector of all the Masonic Institutions for the whole of the United States of America, their Territories and Dependencies.* He might have sat securely adorned with a crown of straw on his head, issuing his aërial mandates, and encircled by his august dignitaries.

"But the malice of this production is not more apparent than its arrogance and injustice. Betraying the greatest ignorance of the masonic system in the United States, it usurps jurisdiction over the three degrees of what is usually denominated ancient masonry.

"It is well known that the three first degrees are under the exclusive superintendence of independent Grand Lodges. Admitting that De La Motta is in fact a Gr. Inspec. Gen. (which your Committee have the most satisfactory reasons to disbelieve,) he has gone beyond the line of his duties and his powers to interfere with that jurisdiction.

"Your Committee on the point refer the consistory to the communication, giving notice of its establishment to the Grand Lodge of the state of New-York, in which they expressly recognise its supremacy over Master-Masons."

The charges of malice, arrogance, and injustice, as exhibited in this clause, is as little established on the principles of correctness as *Mr. Cerneau's Grand Commandership.* In what point have I exhibited any malice? Was it in bringing to light the impositions of an individual? Was it an act of injustice to hold up this individual to the Masonic Brotherhood of every degree to prevent his further impositions? Wherein have I exercised a power to which I am not legally authorised? Is not every Mason compelled to expose an impostor in masonry? Have I in any one solitary instance interfered with the jurisdiction of the Grand Lodge, or any of its subordinate Lodges? Am I censurable because I directed one of my circulars to the Grand Lodge for the State of New-York, which they thought proper to return to me, mentioning "*inasmuch as it related to degrees not known or acknowledged by the said Grand Lodge?*" My duty compelled me to give them the information and put them on their guard as well as every other *lawful* Masonic Body over the surface of the two Hemispheres. *They chose to take no other notice of it. I have nothing further to say*, except, that although sublime masons have not in this country initiated into the blue or symbolic degrees, yet their councils possess the indefeasible right of granting warrants for that purpose. It is common on the continent of Europe, and may be the case here, should circumstances render the exercise of this power necessary. The legality of this right is derived from the highest Masonic authority in the world, (*however ready Mr. Cerneau and his gentlemen have been to relinquish it at once and in toto, which is another strong corroborative proof of their irregularity, or else they never could lawfully alienate their rights as sublime masons,*) as can be demonstrated to the perfect satisfaction of every Masonic, judicial or legislative body.

Throughout the continent of Europe, England, Ireland, and the West Indies, every sublime mason is recognised *as a lawful Past Master;* in England, and in many of the States of America, the Grand Officers must be royal arch masons: In Dublin, the Grand Master must be a Prince of Jerusalem. The Sovereign Grand Inspectors General of the 33d degree have not as yet insisted on it in this country, merely because these degrees are *here but little known* and *less understood,* also because they wished to have no interference with the symbolic degrees; but they are, at the same time, fully convinced, that the sublime masons are as lawfully made Past Masters, under as regular and authentic warrants and constitutions, as his Royal Highness the Prince Regent, who is Grand Master of England.

"Did not the daring malignity of this pretended denunciation, sustain the indignation it excites, its ludicrous inconsistency would put all gravity at defiance."

The whole of this clause is already replied to generally in the preceding pages. The risibility of the gentlemen composing this committee of *Mr. Cerneau's Society* may be excited at the "ludicrous inconsistency" of my circular, as they term it, but how would their feelings be lacerated should circumstances occur, which would cause them to visit a city where regularly constituted bodies of sublime masons are established; and they should announce themselves in the high grades of masonry, be refused admittance, and told they were spuriously made, which, under existing circumstances, would be the case? How then would *their rejoicing be turned into mourning!*

"As to the declaration in favour of a Sov. Gr. Const. said to be formed on the 6th August, 1806, it is only necessary to remark, that those who have any knowledge of our degrees, of De La Motta, and of some of the persons he names, must allow that it is *utterly impossible* that they ought to be what they profess.

"It is well known that that body never pretended to any power previous to the notice of its formation on the 7th March, 1809, long after this was established, and its formation publicly announced. So well aware were the persons who composed that Const. of its defects, and of the regularity of this, that after many efforts to sustain it, and much expense, borne in no equitable proportion, by many who were deluded to enter it, they suffered it to sink at once into an inactivity and oblivion.

"Some individuals who had assisted in its irregular proceedings, convinced of their error, applied for and received the degrees depending on this Gr. Consistory."

In August, 5806, there were resident in this city the following illustrious brethren *lawful* Sublime Princes of the Royal Secret and *Inspectors* 32d degree, *John Gabriel Tardy; John Baptist Desdoity; John James Joseph Gourgas; Pierre Adrien Du Peyrat; Lewis De Saulles;* they formed and established a Sovereign Grand Consistory of Sublime Princes of the Royal Secret 30th, 31st, and 32d degrees. On the third day of November, 5808, the Gr. Council of Princes of Jerusalem was *lawfully* opened in this city, by and in the presence of the Thrice Puissant and most Illustrious Brethren *John Gabriel Tardy; John Baptist Desdoity; John James Joseph Gourgas; Moses Levy; Maduro Peixotto;* R. C. Scott. K—H; S. P. R. S. *Inspectors.* Aided and assisted by *nine* Knights of the Sun, and *nine* Princes of Jerusalem. On the sixth day of November, 5808, a warrant of constitutions passed the seal of the aforesaid Grand Council of Princes of Jerusalem, for the establishment in this City of a Sublime Grand Lodge of Grand Elect, Perfect and Sublime Masons, under the specific appellation of, *Aurora Grata.*

Due notice of which was immediately given in the public prints, and in the succeeding month of March, the Sovereign Grand Consistory of the 30th, 31st, and 32d degrees were induced to publish themselves as having been in existence *"for some time back,"* in order to evince to *Mr. Cerneau, his Grand Association*, and the Masonic

World in general, that their establishment had existed for a considerable time.

Does it not excite the indignation of every enlightened mason, on a cursory perusal of the above paragraph? Can *the gentlemen composing this committee of Mr. Cerneau's Association* mean to impeach my character, or that of the gentlemen alluded to? *They dare not.* Or is it in consequence of our being Israelites? If so, it is another strong corroborative proof, not only of their total want of information of the Sublime Degrees, but in fact of the *whole system* of masonry. What are the first principles requisite to qualify a candidate for admission into the first degree? Is it not the belief in the existence of a Supreme Being? Does not a Hebrew manifest such faith? Is not every thing whatever relative to religion and politics, prohibited in our Lodges? Does it require more than that a man should possess that belief, and enjoy a good moral character, to entitle him to the benefit of masonry? Is there a path where the foot of civilized man has traversed, that masonic institutions are not established, and its benefits extended to all the believers in a Supreme Deity, without its being confined to any particular sect? Let us take a view of the three first degrees. Is it not evident to every Symbolic Mason, that there are no distinctions as to religious or political principles? It is as evident to the Royal Arch Mason that a Hebrew has the same privilege extended to him, as a companion of any other persuasion. If, then, the principles of Masonry are predicated upon such grounds, is it presumable that the more Sublime degrees could shut its doors against the admission of any person of morality, virtue and religion. Admitting *for a moment that Mr. Cerneau and his Society* should be in possession of the High degrees, I call upon them to produce, if they can, one single instance in any one degree of masonry, which disfranchises a Hebrew from enjoying every privilege granted to any other sect. Were I at liberty fully to explain myself, it being impossible to say into whose hands this may fall I would lead them through each degree, *particularly* the *Rose Croix* and the *Royal Secret*, and point out whether a Hebrew is not as much entitled as a Christian Brother, or any other of whatever persuasion, to the Royal Arch, the Perfection, the Chief of the Tabernacle, the Prince of the Tabernacle, the Prince of Mercy, the Knight of the Brazen Serpent, and *many more*, both under and above. If they are the least acquainted with the Constitutions of the Royal Secret, as ratified at *Berlin* on the 25th day of October, 5762, and in the supposition that their copy is *genuine* and *duly certified by lawful authority*, I refer them to the very first article of that constitution, to the emblems on our Diplomas, and to the sacred engagements of *a Rose Croix of Heredon*, and of *a Royal Secret* for a confirmation of what I do rigidly maintain. I leave the candid reader to determine whether the *insinuations* of the gentlemen of the Committee, are bottomed on the broad basis of correct principles.

Those acts of some "individuals," as alluded to in the elaborate pamphlet, when investigated, will be found to be the proceedings of one individual, who may be *noted* by his having repaid kindness, by going over to *Mr. Cerneau's Grand Society*, and refusing afterwards to give up and return the warrant then in his possession, as Grand Master of the Sublime Grand Lodge of Perfection the *Aurora Grata*.

"The Grand Consist. is vested with the sole power of administration and legislation, including that of granting constitutions, in all the degrees which appertain to exalted masonry. The establishment of a Gr. Consistory absolutely supersedes the individual authority of the Grand Inspectors General, in the regulation and government of the order.

"As to this degree of Grand Inspector General, in rank the 33d, the laws and regulations direct the manner in which the members on whom it is conferred shall be selected. It is a dignity granted as the reward of merit and experience. Those who are invested with it do not possess the arbitrary and irresponsible power which some who pretend to act under '*secret constitutions*' imagine they are authorized to exercise."

In allusion to this clause, the *gentlemen composing the Committee of Mr. Cerneau's Society*, have made a jumble of different points under different heads. 1*st*. They have blended the Supreme Council of the 33d degree with the Sovereign Grand Consistory of the 30th, 31st, and 32d degrees; by calling *the Council a Consistory*, and *the Consistory a Council;* 2dly. They have commingled together three distinct bodies under one general head, to wit, *Inspectors* whose powers are limited *solely* to inspect. *Deputies Inspectors General*, who have the power to inspect generally, and to constitute as far as K—H, inclusively, and finally, *Sovereign Grand Inspectors General of the 33d degree*, who are authorized and empowered to *establish*, *congregate*, *superintend*, and *inspect* all and every degree, agreeably to the Grand Constitutions; the *extreme ignorance* of the gentlemen of the committee, respecting all these points, is sufficiently palpable without any further comment.

In reference to the "*secret constitutions*," I do affirm, that they have existed from *time immemorial;* that special mention is made of them in the Constitutions of Sublime Prince of the Royal Secret, as ratified at *Berlin* on the 25th day of October, 5762; further, that they are *unchangeable*, and are the very bases and old landmarks of every other Constitution (in the whole Masonic System) framed since, or which time and circumstance may require hereafter. Every Mason of whatever degree, is subject to them, whether he is acquainted with them or not, although I must acknowledge that as well as the 33d degree, they are not to be met with in *every hand*, as *Mr. Cerneau's Association* have clearly proved and exhibited strong evidences of their want of knowledge in that exalted grade. Innumerable instances can be made apparent in their publication and declaration, of being possessed of a degree which they never did receive.

"Before your Committee dismiss this disgusting mass of absurdity and wickedness, which certainly discovers no characteristic of the Christian morality of our order, they beg leave to draw the attention of the Consistory to the insinuation contained in the words 'having received no satisfaction,' &c. which leave it to be inferred that our Sovereign Grand Commander was bound to give such satisfaction. De La Motta has not pretended to allege that any regular application (which ought to have preceded an accusation for neglect or refusal) was made to Brother Cerneau: But the multiplied abuses existing in this country by mean of persons falsely pretending to possess the exalted degrees, early attracted the notice of the Gr. Consist. and connected with various insidious attempts to take advantage of the deficiency of our Sovn. Gr. Commander in the English language, and of the unsuspicious confidence of his character, produced a determination to have all applications referred to the Grand Consistory. Of this De La Motta was apprised; he was told if he wished to inspect our documents, he should, by applying to the Gr. Consistory, have all the satisfaction he required, provided he proved his right to it. Had he pursued this course, his conduct would have been conformable to that of a person clothed with lawful powers. This refusal indicates that he was not willing to examine too closely into our powers, nor submit his claims to that investigation which the Consistory might deem it their duty to make."

As to what relates to the obligations of *Mr. Cerneau*, to give me satisfaction, I submit to the candid reader to determine if *Mr. Cerneau* knew his duty in the high grade to which he has pretended, whether he was not bound to render me, *as Representative of the Supreme Head in this country*, a full and ample view of his patents, and proceedings since his arrival in these states; particularly after having placed into his hands *my credentials*, and his *acknowledging* the *legality* of the same, and *also* of the Supreme Council of the 33d at Charleston, South-Carolina, to which I beg leave to refer the reader to the before recited attested conversations. I call on the Brethren Symbolic, as well as Sublime, to say if it is not customary among us to exchange views of certificates, patents, &c. &c. which *Mr. Cerneau* peremptorily refused.

Mr. Cerneau, as well as his society, seems to be particularly anxious to blend together what they are accustomed to term *their Grand Consistory*, and *their Supreme Council of the 33d degree.* When I visited him on the 14th September, 5813, I was more than once obliged to specify very plainly, that I had not called to make inquiries respecting *a Grand Consistory*, but what he had published and *just* acknowledged to me, viz. "*His Supreme Council of Sovereigns Grand Inspectors General of the 33d degree*," *&c. &c. &c.* that point once settled, the succeeding could not suffer any difficulty, and must come in afterwards as a matter of course. Upon *Mr. Cerneau's* repeated refusal to exhibit his papers, and referring me to "*his Supreme Council of the 33d Degree*," what were my observations to him? Show me *the powers* you have *for establishing a Supreme Council of the 33d*, and I will readily meet your council. I beg leave to submit the following *quære* to my Symbolic Brethren. Should any master mason apply to visit a lodge which he had never visited before, would he suffer himself to be examined by a committee before he had a view of their warrant, or would he enter that lodge before he had the *proof* of its being *legally* constituted?

As to what relates to my taking an advantage of *Mr. Cerneau's* want of information in the language of the country—how little do I merit the charge; when previous to my visiting him, I prevailed on two illustrious brethren, well versed in the French and English languages, to accompany me in order to explain to *Mr. Cerneau*, should he be at a loss to understand, the purport of my visit. The accompanying brethren did very readily repeat in French, such parts of the conversation as we supposed he did not understand. In the attempt to explain to him in

French what I observed, *Mr Cerneau* declared that he *fully* understood every syllable I uttered.

As *"to the multiplied abuses and impositions existing and practised in this country, by means of persons falsely pretending to possess the exalted degrees,"* so feelingly complained of by *this committee of Mr. Cerneau's society,* I think it is hardly possible to meet any where, whether in this or any other country, over the surface of the two hemispheres, with *a character* that can stand *more pre-eminent* in all those charges than *Mr. Cerneau.*

"Immediately on its installation the Grand Consistory gave notice to the supreme masonic bodies in Europe and the West Indies, to whom it, at the same time, communicated *copies of the patents under which it was formed* These were followed by the most ample recognition on the part of the Supreme Grand Council of France, an act sufficient in itself to outweigh the cavils of all impostors."

As to the correctness of all they boasted of, *"most ample recognition by the Supreme Council of France,"* we know that *Mr. Cerneau and his society* first came out with *their pretended* Supreme Council of Sovereign Grand Inspectors General of the 33d degree, *only* in May, 1813, and yet the report of the committee sanctioned and published by *Mr. Cerneau's association* asserted they are recognised. How can that be possible? How, under the difficulties attending a navigation on account of war, could all this be effected, between May and the 14th September, 1813, or even between May, 1813, and February, 1814. It is also rather surprising that they should not positively state all the different *supreme* bodies over the surface of the two hemispheres, who have thought proper to acknowledge them; but on the contrary they should bring forward the *solitary* instance of their recognition by the Supreme Council of France. Have you, for instance, been acknowledged by *Heredon*, or by any one of the supreme bodies, in *England, Scotland, Ireland, Prussia, Sweden, Denmark, Russia, Germany, Italy, Switzerland,* or even *Asia?* I believe you can show no such recognitions, and I can assure you that the *Supreme Council of the 33d, at Charleston, South-Carolina,* will continue to take such special good care to follow you up into every quarter of the globe, where masonic institutions are established; that it ever will be impossible for you to obtain any thing whatever from, or even be admitted or acknowledged any where among, *lawful* sublime masons, *should you persist in your obstinacy.*

"Having heard that a Council had existed at Charleston, South-Carolina, which might yet be in activity, a circular with copies of the Patent or Warrant, and a list of the members, was also transmitted thither and delivered to the person whose name appears as Grand Commander to the act approving De La Motta's denunciation. No answer being received, another was despatched, but with no better success. Your Committee here will just remark, that if the Council at Charleston was a regular body, and deemed us usurpers, it was their duty to take instant and effectual measures to arrest our progress. If we were regular, masonic courtesy, as well as their obligation, required them to acknowledge us without delay. They have done neither.

"This profound silence and neglect was of itself sufficient to satisfy the Grand Consistory that the Body at Charleston, if it ever had a lawful existence, was extinct."

If the Supreme Council of the 33d, at Charleston, South-Carolina, did receive the *two* communications above alluded to, why did they not answer them? 1st. *Mr. Cerneau* arriving in this country, provided with *foreign patents* and *powers;* what was the *very first step* for him to insure their legality in this country? To send and have them recognized and endorsed by the Supreme Council of the 33d, at Charleston, South-Carolina.

2dly. What was he next bound to do, if his wish was to act lawfully? To ask of Charleston the permission to form and establish here, a lawful body of *Sublime Princes of the Royal Secret,* (in case there was none already formed,) which would no doubt have been granted to him or any other brother acting *agreeably to the Grand Constitu-*

tions. But they never would have rescinded their supreme rights into the hands of *Mr. Cerneau* or any other person.

Supposing *Mr. Cerneau* had so far acted constitutionally, what would have been the manner for him to proceed on the lawful establishment of *a Consistory* of Sublime Princes of the Royal Secret? To have had nothing to do with symbolic brethren, but call to his assistance a competent number of already *lawfully* raised brethren of (at least) *a certain* degree, then with their advice, counsel and information proceed on together to the aforesaid establishment of a *lawful* consistory. When all had been *regularly* accomplished and approved of by the *Supreme head* at Charleston, South-Carolina; then write and require the recognition of all other bodies of the same kind over the surface of the two hemispheres.

Was this the conduct of *Mr. Joseph Cerneau?*

No, it was not—If he had patents or powers of *any description,* they have been issued and sent to him from *a Foreign Jurisdiction;* say, by a few *French emigrants,* Brethren from St. Domingo, who had taken refuge in the small port of *Baracoa,* island of Cuba, who probably knew as much of our language and localities as he himself did on his first arrival here. *I assert* that none of his patents or powers ever made their appearance or ever were endorsed by the Supreme Council of the 33d, at Charleston, South-Carolina, or *any* Inspector General *lawfully* authorized by them. I further affirm that *Mr. Cerneau's* name has never appeared on our registers, and other lawful documents, more particularly, *as a sublime Mason, vested with the sole control of the High Orders of Masonry in the United States of America, their Territories and Dependencies.*

What was *Mr. Cerneau's* conduct then?

He first commenced to work in the dark; and when he and his friends arrived at the point they thought themselves sufficiently *strong* and *respectable,* then they published themselves as *a Grand Consistory,* without *assuming,* however, the *supremacy* over all the States of America, their Territories and Dependencies, they then, and not until then, wrote and sent *copies* (agreeably to their pamphlet,) of their *high deeds* all over the world, and, as they say, also, to Charleston. Under such circumstances was it probable, or could they so far blindly flatter themselves, that they would receive from Charleston their recognition? Had they seriously reflected a moment, they might certainly have foreseen, what has at last occurred; all they could get by it was that their councils would be set down *in red characters.* Finding the Supreme Council of the 33d at Charleston, South-Carolina, did not recognise them, *Mr. Cerneau* and *his friends* declared them *extinct*, and proclaimed *themselves* as the *Supreme head* of masonry for the *whole* of the United States of America, their Territories and Dependencies—and no doubt in time, pursuing fast upon the *lawful* road they were and are travelling on, they will also declare *as extinct*, all the other Supreme Bodies over the surface of the two hemispheres, who do not think proper to acknowledge *their Grand Association.*

I will now propose to my *Symbolic* Brethren, a case *nearly* the same with that under consideration of *Mr. Joseph Cerneau* and *his Grand Association.* Admit for a moment that *a Master Mason* should delude a number of Brethren of the *first* and *second* degrees by informing and convincing them that he is a Master Mason, and fully persuades them he has the *right* and *power* to raise to the Sublime Degree of a Master Mason any individual, they consent, and he thus initiates them into the *third* degree. Now, he observes, we are all very *lawful* and very good Master Masons, let us form and establish a Master Mason's Lodge—they all consent—it is accomplished;—he then says further, we must be acknowledged or recognised—but it is requisite we send copies of what *we shall deem* sufficient of our proceedings to all the *Symbolic Grand Lodges* in the world. *One* of them, *very far distant*, not fully informed, and wherein this Master Mason has luckily *some good friends*, recognises *their* lodge; *but* the Grand Lodge under whose jurisdiction he is placed, discovering the absurdity of their whole business, &c. &c. &c. for the present, and for good reasons, takes no particular notice of it: this emboldens this *worthy* mason and his *coadjutors* to progress; some time after *he* and *his* party declare that *very* Grand Lodge under whose jurisdiction they are situated, *as being extinct*, and all its further acts as "*insignificant*, and invalid"—and why? Because *he* and *his advocates* conceive themselves *respectable* and sufficiently strong to make such a declaration; and because they were not at the time honoured with an answer. They declare and *publish* themselves for ever *as being* the *real*, *true* and *lawful Grand Lodge* of Master Masons, which has, as they conceive, by right, taken the place of the one by them *declared extinct.* What ought to be and what would be the consequence of *such* a masonic enormity? More especially after friendly and brotherly means had *repeatedly* been resorted to without success?

To return to *Mr. Joseph Cerneau* and *his Grand Association*, I believe what follows to be *as exact* a history of his transactions as can possibly be given or depended on in *such obscure* dealings.

We will for a moment suppose that *Mr. Cerneau* was, at his arrival from the Havana in this city of New-York, *a regular Sublime Prince of the Royal Secret*, even *a lawful Deputy Inspector General, old system; suppose* also that he wrote after his arrival here for powers, &c. &c. &c. that those powers were actually sent to him *signed* by 3—5—7—9—or even more *legal* Illustrious Brethren collected in some corner of the world, for him to do every thing that *might* be performed; such full powers coming forth from *a Foreign Jurisdiction* (which by the by I have great doubts whether it has ever been *known* or acknowledged by any other) could not be *lawful* unless restricted by this *absolute* and well understood *proviso*, that *Mr. Cerneau* should act and comport himself in all things whatsoever to the old landmarks, and in conformity with all the Rules, Regulations and Constitutions of all and every the several degrees of Masonry. *Uuder such a supposition*, which was the lawful road to be pursued by *Mr. Cerneau?* Arriving in a foreign country of which he little knew, if at all, the localities and language; as a good and faithful brother he would have made very special inquiries respecting those degrees, and the Brethren belonging thereto, by means of which he would have found, that in this *city* of *New-York* there existed the *Triple Union;* a *lawful* Sovereign Chapter of *Rose Croix*, working in the ancient form: also a number of the most respectable Brethren belonging to all the sublime degrees, in particular *five lawful* Sublime Princes of the Royal Secret and *Inspectors:* that *in Philadelphia* there was *an ancient*, regular Sovereign Chapter of *Rose Croix* and *three lawful* Deputies Inspectors General, *old system—in Baltimore* and *Norfolk* Sovereign Chapters of *Rose Croix—in Charleston*, South-Carolina, the *Grand* and *Supreme Council* of the most Puissant Sovereign Grand Inspectors General of the 33d degree; the Sovereign Grand Consistory of Sublime Princes of the Royal Secret—30th, 31st, and 32d degrees for the *Southern* District of the United States of America; *a Grand metropolitan Lodge and Sovereign Grand Chapter of Rose Croix of Heredon—a Grand Council of Princes of Jerusalem—a Sublime Grand Lodge of Perfection*, and in Savannah *also* a Sublime Grand Lodge of Perfection—and throughout the United States of America, *a host* of *lawful* Deputies Inspectors General 32d degree, who had laboured in the faithful performance of their duties. He should then have communicated with *a competent* number of these Brethren, and after consultation, had he and they felt inclined to proceed—there was *no other lawful* line of conduct to be pursued but that which I have already pointed out; besides on information he would have found that in the *very* city of New-York, there were a number of Illustrious Brethren *at least* equally *if not more so* entitled to form and be at the *head* of such an establishment, as himself. Is this what you have done *Mr. Cerneau?* I appeal to *you*, your friends and supporters, as ingenuous men to answer the question in *truth*. For if you and your children are genuine lawful Brethren, *you* and *they* must *love* the truth with all *your* hearts; *Masonry* being supported by nothing but the *unveiled, plain, unsophisticated* Truth!

Mr. Cerneau, was this the line of conduct pursued by you, and your *abettors?* No, Sir, as I have proved before, you have *no* Patents or Powers endorsed or in any form signed and recognised by the Supreme Council of the 33d degree at Charleston, South-Carolina, or by any Illustrious Brother lawfully authorized by them; you have called none to your assistance, nor consulted with *any one equal or superior to yourself* as to degrees or *information*, although you had them in numbers and every way *most respectable within call;* you have had to do with none but Symbolic Masons, and to acknowledge at this day, *all* the masonic establishments you *pretend* to, you must, without any kind of scruple or ceremony, have leapt over the *most sacred engagements, landmarks*, rules, laws, regulations, constitutions, &c. &c. &c. So that you must have *initiated all your* Royal Arch Masons; *your* Grand Elect Perfect and Sublime Masons; *your* Princes of Jerusalem; *your* Sovereign Princes of the *Rose Croix; your* K—H; *all your* Sublime Princes of the Royal Secret; *your* Deputy Inspectors General; and *all your pretended* Sovereigns Grand Inspectors General of the 33d degree. In fact you, *Mr. Cerneau, per se*, and in the *very* face of a whole *host* of *lawful* Most Illustrious Brethren of *all* degrees, and *lawful high* bodies of every description, have *initiated, healed, consecrated, formed, established*, and *installed all* and *every* degree of masonry from the 4th up to *your very pretended* 33d degree, *inclusively*. Can there exist *a single worthy mason* who can approve *such* conduct, or even think that *such absurdities* ever could be sanctioned by, and *such* powers be *lawfully* vested in any individual?

"Men distinguished in the annals of our order have received from it, constitutions for the establishment of exalted bodies, in various parts of the United States."

It is true that the *original* intent of the Superior degrees were designed *only* for the *select few;* and to prove the *excellent* election of *Mr. Cerneau* and *his Society* of *a Deputy Inspector* for the State of Rhode Island, and of *a President* for *their* Grand Council of Sublime Princes of the Royal Secret, sitting at Newport, Rhode Island; I beg leave to submit the following two letters *verbatim* (without comment,) received from those *exalted* gentlemen, whom, under the *fostering* care of *Mr. Joseph Cerneau* and *his* Grand Association, have *devoted* themselves to the *profound* study of *their highly exalted, sublime, philosophic* and *philanthropic masonry,* according to the ancient *Scottish* Rite of Heredon, &c. &c. &c.

COPY.

"E De La Motta Esq.

Newport R. I.
Feb. 5th, 1814.

"Sir,

"Your circular under date of the 31st ult. I received per mail last evening, the contents of which in every point of view merits the contempt of every mason or man of common sense. If any controversy or misunderstanding had taken place between your self-styled Royal Highness, Illustrious General of the Holy Empire and the Grand Consistory of the United States, it was your duty to pointedly address them, and if our interference had been deemed necessary we ought to have been addressed in a manner becoming a Mason and a gentleman. The consistory from which we had the honour of receiving our charter and which we now work under, we were previous to our application to them convinced were regularly and legally established and acknowledged in different parts of the world, our authority we do not mean to conceal but enjoy every privilege granted us and defend the dignity attached thereto to the last extremity, your threats to expose the gentlemen composing the said Grand Consistory particularly the Hon. Dewitt Clinton I doubt not will take such notice of it as it requires, in which he will be supported by his worthy companions. In a short time we shall call a meeting of our members and jointly reply to your contemptuous letter, in the mean time we shall address Mr. Joseph Cerneau and enclose him one of your letters for his inspection and direction. Let me respectfully caution your High and mighty illustrious Grand Inspector General, and Royal Treasurer of the United States not to harbour an idea of advertising my name as he threatens, for the moment I see it, I will advertise you as a scoundrell through the world, and individually prosecute you to the extremity of the law, in which I assure you I shall be followed by each of my worthy companions. If you have any further communications to make, let them be couched in proper language and in the like manner they will be replied to; and if you wish letters post paid, you will please set the example by paying the postage of any further letters you write.

Your Obt. Hble Servant,

(*Signed* on the original)

STEPHEN DEBLOIS."

COPY.

"E. De La Motta Esq.

Newport, Feb. 6th, 1814.

"Sir,

"Having received a circular, destitute of every Masonic Principle, addressed to me with your name annexed to the same, I feel it a duty I owe myself as well as the Council to which I have the honour to belong to reply to it. Now, Sir, be it known to you and all concerned, that the Dep. Gd. Council in Newport, R. I. obtained from the Grand Consistory in New-York, whereof Joseph Cerneau is Gd. Commander, Dewitt Clinton Dep. Gd. Commander, &c. &c. &c. a charter for the establishment of the same, I, Sir, had the honour to be one of the number who was appointed to visit New-York for attainment of the same and was appointed Dep. Gd. Inspector for the State of Rhode Island. While, there, Sir, I saw their charter from both France and Great Britain. Now, Sir, I wish you to understand that in addressing the Members of the Council to which I have the honour to belong, you do not address Boys, fools or *Drunckards;* they are men, Sir, who never will subscribe to the sentence that Joseph Cerneau, Dewitt Clinton and others are Impostors, &c. consequently, base villains, because Mr. E. De La Motta sees fit from some motive or other, to say they are. No, Sir, you have mistaken the ground. You, Sir, are bound by every Masonic, by every manly principle, to proove beyond the powers of refutation, that they are the base characters you have represented them to be; then Sir, and not untill then, would I exert every power which I possess to have a fair and candid examination of the subject in the Council to which I belong; this Sir you have not done—I have wrote to New-York and have no doubt but Joseph Cerneau Esq. Hon. Dewitt Clinton and others who compose the Gd. Consistory will take such steps, as will bring their accusers to a sence of Justice. But, Sir, you say we have been basely imposed on, for which imposition unless we acknowedge our sorrow to you, we shall be published, here Mr. E. De La Motta let me caution you to tread lightly and pause before you do that which you may wish to recall when too late, for I pledge you my word as a Mason, that whoever shall dare to publish an Individual belonging to the Council in Newport, that I will retaliate the indignity and hold him or them up to the world as a scoundrel and base Impostor —and if his or their character shall merit notice he or they shall be called to account. But, Sir, I wish to be understood that we are ready at all times to correspond with any legal *Masonic Body* in a *Masonic* manner but we are not to be the dupes of any men or set of men. I am Sir, a friend to legal *Masonic Institution.*

Signed on the original,

JOHN A. SHAW."

An advertisement appeared in the newspapers some time last winter, under the sanction of *Mr. Cerneau's Grand Association*, respecting the establishment of *a Grand Encampment* of Knight Templars, Knights of Malta, &c. &c. for this state. It is another proof of their *total want* of *reflection* or *information*, being in the most pointed and positive *opposition* with the *sacred engagements* of K—H. To perceive names mentioned in *their celebrated* Tableau, as possessing the grade of K—H, *designated* as Grand Officers in that Grand Encampment; a thing so incompatible with the degree of K—H, that *every true* and *lawful* brother arriving at that degree must *shudder* at *their improper* conduct; a circumstance in its own self, *sufficient* to cause *their expulsion* from those high degrees. Does this conduct among their many others not evidence their total ignorance of the *Higher* Orders of Masonry?

And now I shall *fully* abandon the *gentlemen* of the *committee* to all the "vital energies," (page 12, of their elaborate pamphlet,) and their "Most Powerful Sovereign Grand Consistory of Grand Inspectors General of the 33d degree, and Princes of the Royal Secret, Supreme Chiefs of Exalted Masonry of the Ancient Scottish Rite of Heredon, for the United States of America, under the celestial canopy, at the central point, answering to 40 degrees 41 minutes north latitude. Or their *alias cidevant* Supreme Council of Grand Inspectors General of the 33d degree, regularly established according to the Ancient Constitutional Scottish Rite of Heredon, for the United States of America, their Territories and Dependencies, held in the city of New-York; also the Grand Consistory of Supreme Chiefs of Exalted Masonry, and the constituted bodies of its jurisdiction, Anno Lucies 5813."

Having independently replied, as amply as the situation of my health would permit, to their *elaborate, gentlemanly*, and *declamatory* pamphlet issued in February last; I beg leave to submit to the candid reader *unequivocally* to say, who is most entitled to the very elegant epithets *so liberally* bestowed in said pamphlet, such as "malicious calumny; antimasonic; the gratification of private malice; arrogance; pretension; daring calumny; absurdity; atrocious libel; injustice; the greatest ignorance; Modern Rhadamanthus; daring malignity; pretended denunciation; disgusting mass of absurdity and wickedness"! ! ! whether the *accused* or *accusers* stand most entitled to them? My greatest fault has been to endeavour to *rend* the *veil* that obscured the vision of the deluded; and to *mutilate* the *mantle of imposition* in which *Mr. Joseph Cerneau* had enveloped himself.

I take also my final leave of you, my deluded brethren. Permit me to exhort you to reflect, and ere it is too late, to relinquish the untenable ground you have taken, and abandon the false standard you have enrolled under.

Done and delivered under my hand and stamp of the 33d degree at the grand East of New-York city, by the 40th degree 41 minutes north latitude, the 20th day of the sixth month called Elul, A. M. 5574, of the Restoration, 2344, A. L. 5814, and of the Christian Era the 5th day of September, 1814.

E. DE LA MOTTA,
R. C.; K—H; S. P. R. S.; Sovereign Grand Inspector General of the 33d degree; Illustrious Treasurer General of the Holy Empire in the United States of America, &c. &c. &c.

(SEAL)

By command,

JACOB DE LA MOTTA,
R. C.; K—H; S. P. R. S.

Deus Meumque Jus.

[The following attack was made upon the Editor as Secretary of the Sublime Grand Lodge of Perfection, and P. J. & Co. felt so unable to support their side of the contest against truth and legality, that they attempted to stop the press from inserting any more of his communications, by an interdiction of the officers of the Grand Lodge of South-Carolina.]

From the Southern Patriot of May 3, 1822.

To all whom it may concern, and the Craft in general.

THE subscriber has read, with extreme pain, various publications in the newspapers, and particularly one in Thursday evening's "Patriot," and Friday morning's "Courier," headed "*Lux E. Tenebris*," over the name of Joseph M'Cosh, Secretary.

The exclusive powers claimed in this last advertisement has compelled this public notice.

It is not proper to lay before the public, nor even the masonic family, in this way, the proceedings of the Sovereign Grand Consistory for the United States, sitting at N. York, as regards the improper acts and usurpation of authority by certain persons in this place, whilst her Grand Council for this State, duly and legally constituted, was existing and regularly working under charters thence derived. Pending the further deliberations, and until the final determination of the said Sovereign Grand Consistory at New-York, all correct masons may be satisfactorily informed, from the most full and indisputable documents, which are in possession of the subscriber, of the constitutionality and claim of the said Sovereign Grand Consistory to sole and exclusive sovereignty in the United States.

A dissemination of such information may guard the unwary, and tend to prevent a reproduction of discord among the masonic family in this state.

P. JAVAIN,

Deputy Grand Inspector General, representing the Sovereign Grand Consistory of the United States, for the State of South-Carolina.*

From the Charleston Mercury of May 6, 1822.

To all whom it may concern.

As silence might imply assent to the above notice of P. Javain, it seems proper for the accused, in self-defence, to inform "the Craft," that P. Javain, represents an illegal body of Masons in New-York, who have been regularly expelled as *impostors, usurpers* and *pretenders*, to a knowledge of degrees of which they are ignorant, and a power to confer such as they do know, contrary to the established rules of the order. Since February 1783, the degrees in question have been legally conferred in this city, by a power regularly emanating from Frederick of Prussia, who pos-

* Like J. C. & Co. in New-York, from whom this illegal body emanated, they evince a total ignorance of the high degrees; here one styles himself "*Deputy Grand Inspector General*"—most likely he obtained this title from some Old Certificate of a Brother made 25 or 30 years ago, for in 1786, the office was abolished in Europe, and in 1801 in this country. Also we lately saw that another styled himself "*President of the Sublime Lodge.*" Now every Brother initiated regularly into the Sublime Degrees, well knows that there are no such offices in these Degrees. The reader will also observe from the expressions used, that their spurious mightinesses were attempting at New-York, something grand against a few Blue Masons. They seem to think lightly of their own names circulating (according to custom) in *Red Letters*. But "pending further deliberations and final determinations," we will follow truth where-ever she may lead, nor shrink from the course she may pursue.

sessed the sovereign power in Free-Masonry, from 1761, to 1st of May, 1786, when he delegated his high powers to a certain number of Grand Councils of Sov. Gr. Insp. Gen. who were to be initiated into a separate degree on that occasion, and were to continue "*for life*," (except removed for improper conduct,) certain articles were established for their government and direction, called "the Grand Constitutions." By these they were empowered to meet whenever, and as often as they deemed fit. In all their patents and commissions were these remarkable words: "We authorize and empower you to establish, congregate and superintend and inspect Lodges, Chapters, &c. *agreeably to the Grand Constitutions!*" And by these Constitutions of 1st May, 1786, Deputy Inspectors General were restricted from acting.

In 1801, 31st May, a Supreme Council of Sov. Gr. Ins. Gen. was duly opened and established in this city, and its officers appointed "FOR LIFE;" four of whom are still living, and, agreeably to the Grand Constitutions, the Council cannot become extinct. Besides these four, there is in this country another Council of *seven* alive, who will succeed, if this Council should ever become extinct, but the last one of either Council possesses the power of renovating it at his pleasure.

P. Javain is the repesentative of a body created by one Joseph Cerneau, jeweller, who is first traced in this country, in "Longworth's Directory, 1809" with the letters G. I. G. P. S. G. C. attached to his name. By availing himself of the strong political divisions of the state of New-York at that time raging most furiously—a conduct directly opposite to every masonic principle; he strengthened himself so much as, by the spring of 1813, to burst from his secrecy, and publish to the world his famous "Tableau," by the very wording of which, he convinced every Mason initiated into these degrees, of his total ignorance of some of the highest which he pretended to communicate—nor has the angry representative of his expelled body yet learnt the titles of the degrees which he pretends to give, as plainly appears by the wording of the above notice. After every exertion at an amicable adjustment had failed, the expulsions of Joseph Cerneau, *and all his abettors and followers*, was finally ratified 24th December, 1813, copies of which are left at the offices of the different newspapers, for the inspection of such as desire it.

The accused improve this opportunity to protest in the strongest terms possible, against dragging the concerns of the fraternity before the public, and should any contention arise among the Craft, they are blameless. P. Javain alone may thank himself for it. The accused resorted to every honourable expedient to avoid such a termination—and, but for P. Javain, all differences would have been amicably adjusted; yet he is only an *honorary* member of this bődy he is so strongly advocating on his individual responsibility.

"All correct Masons may be satisfactorily informed from the most full and indisputable documents which are in possession" of the only regular body of Sublime Masons in South-Carolina, and which have been accumulating for these 40 years back, "of the constitutionality," and honest claims to sovereign authority, which invested the body who publish this reply to P. Javain's wanton attack. The unbiassed of the Masonic family are warmly invited to make the strictest investigation of all the circumstances connected with this subject, and they are asked, if any twenty or thirty Fellow-Crafts were to sign a Charter to make Master Masons in some distant port, whether the Masons made under such Charter, would be legal; or whether they would not be denounced as impostors? But time will determine this question, and it is sincerely hoped, repair the breach that is now made in this fair fabric. No canting apology is made for the pain felt in this reply.

May the Grand Architect of the Universe, guide and direct all the Brotherhood, whether of high or low degree, in all their actions, and make them redound to his glory.

JOSEPH M'COSH, *Secretary*.

From the Charleston Mercury of May 7, 1822.

To all whom it may concern, and the Craft in General.

I HAVE already said that public journals are not the proper medium through which to make remarks respecting Masonic disputes, nor can they give either strength or credit to any *unmasonic* and *unauthorized* denunciations which they may convey to the public.

The only notice which it is necessary for me to take of the publication which appeared in yesterday's *Mercury*, over the name of Joseph M'Cosh, in reply to my Address *to the Members of the Craft*, in the Gazettes of this city, is again *earnestly* to invite *all Free Masons* of correct principles, to view the indisputable evidences in my possession, proving the constitutionality of the Sovereign Grand Consistory in New-York as above stated; which documents are opposed only by a *handbill*, the republication of which, I am authorized by a letter, bearing date first ult. to say, was not made with either the *knowledge* or the *approbation* of the *respectable* Brother whose name is used therein, to give a sanction to the proceedings of the persons associated with Joseph M'Cosh, which letter may also be seen on application to

P. JAVAIN,
No. 187 King-street.*

* The "*Respectable Brother*" here alluded to was the Grand Commander of the United States of America. The "*Representative*" has long been in the habit of writing and teazing this gentleman in his Official Capacity and thereby completely acknowledging him—and this very note of "*the 1st ultimo*" (I assert it from a gentleman who saw *the note*) was signed ****, "GRAND COMMANDER *of the United States*."

The "*indisputable documents*" are kept secret from others not of their kidney, and at the time of replying to the above, I did not know to what Peter Javain alluded. I have since understood their nature; two large trunks of papers were obtained from a widow lady, in rather a clandestine manner, containing correspondence, &c. by a person who had not the most distant right to them. These

From the Charleston Mercury of May 8, 1822.

To all the Masonic Family.

BROTHERS,

P. JAVAIN, No. 187 King-street, having completely admitted all the facts in my reply of the 6th inst. I sincerely hope this may be the last time I shall be obliged to wound your feelings in this public manner. In regard to his notice in the *Mercury* of yesterday morning, you all know that *truth* and *justice* will give "*strength* and credit to all *Masonic* and *authorized statements.*"

To obtain the permission of an individual, to circulate what had been over *eight years* in circulation, seemed unnecessary, as the individual alluded to, repeatedly and most positively *refused* to take any part whatever in the subject at issue; and more especially as all the original letters relating thereto, in *the handwriting of the signers*, and the *sealed* expulsion itself, were carefully examined by myself and others before-hand; these documents were genuine.

How P. Javain's documents are "*indisputable*," which have been in continual dispute ever since they were made, is best known to him who has so long most carefully concealed them from the inspection of all those, who, from their knowledge of these degrees, are able to form an opinion of their genuineness. P. Javain's change of opinions

papers have been palmed upon some persons, who did not look at *dates* and *outside directions*, and from them some shallow minds have been satisfied. *But this has not always been the case.* Observing Brothers have not been so easily duped, they have examined *both sides of the letters* shown them, and declare they were directed to "Col. John Mitchell, Gr. C. &c. &c. &c." [Some documents are on hand upon this subject for which we have not room at present; they are of a piece with the rest of the history of this usurpation.]

in speaking of the individual alluded to, is to be hailed as a presage of future good.

Finally, my Brothers, "*try all things, prove all things, and* HOLD FAST THAT WHICH IS GOOD." With respect,

JOSEPH M'COSH.*

* It has been a subject, Brethren, of serious regret to me, that a society so distinguished as is that of the Free Masons, for benevolence, charity and brotherly love, should be involved in such discord and diversity of opinion as could not be healed without an appeal to the public—that although we have endeavoured to produce a union of brethren so separated, our attempts have all been frustrated—or this appeal would never have gone to the press.

I request every Brother to considerately and deliberately determine what motives may agitate his bosom at the time of his offering himself as a candidate for the higher degrees—are they *party feelings?* As a genuine Brother, discard them, I beseech you; go with pure motives, which ever way you go; and, upon convincing me that the other side is correct, I here publicly pledge my sacred honour, as a Man and a Mason, to peaceably and immediately *retrace my steps*, and *make every apology in my power, for the part I have taken.*

☞ The following observation, contained in Dr. Dalcho's Ahiman Rezon, p. 191, is "recommended to be adopted and used" by M. W. John S. Cogdell, G. M. and M. W. Thomas W. Bacot, P. G. M.: "ANTIQUITY IS DEAR TO A MASON'S HEART. INNOVATION IS TREASON, AND SAPS THE VENERABLE FABRIC OF THE ORDER." *See Sanction to the second edition of the Ahiman Rezon.*

APPENDIX,

CONTAINING A

HISTORY OF SOME OCCURRENCES

WHICH HAVE BEEN URGED AGAINST THE

Regular Lodge of Sublime Freemasons

In the City of Charleston;

BUT WHICH, IN REALITY, HAVE NO CONNEXION
WHATEVER WITH IT, AS THE FOLLOWING
PAGES WILL CLEARLY SHOW.

**

APPENDIX, &c.

IN the city of Charleston, whenever any one of the spurious usurpers speaks of the regular body of Sublime Free-masons, which was legally and publicly established A. D. 1783, he invariably calls it an "*Association.*" Though this word carries no reproach in its common acceptation, as the Society is composed of nearly Seventy Brothers of correct habits and morals, all regularly initiated, properly acknowledged, and in full communion and correspondence with all *regular* Bodies of the same grade in all parts of the world, yet it rather shows a meanness and littleness of mind in the persons, who thus apply it. But *when dates are attended to*, it will clearly prove a desire to deceive, and to conceal facts, as well as a want of candour and veracity, which these impostors have never failed to exhibit; for the persons alluded to, were not (*at the time they have chosen to speak of them*) in any manner whatever connected with the regular Body of Sublime Masons. However, I will not prejudge the case, but proceed to state a concise history of transactions as they occurred; only premising that the threatening documents received by "*the eleven,*" would of themselves make a large volume. [These documents are now in my possession and may be seen by any "Brother of correct principles."]

Early in the summer of the year 1821, several Blue Masons discovered, that many valuable Masonic papers were scattered abroad in the hands of different persons. On reflection, they concluded that it would be an object of some importance to the cause of Freemasonry, which they had much at heart, to gather and unite them in one common collection. The attempt was made, and attended with almost complete success. Every Brother Master Mason, (none of lower degree being admitted) signed a solemn written agreement, "never to communicate to any person whatever, any information he might obtain from the manuscripts." (The original is before me, dated June 22, 1821.) To this instrument they invariably adhered—and so far was their number from increasing, though repeated intercessions were made for admission, that it actually decreased from *twenty-eight* to ELEVEN, agreeably to a certain rule, which was adopted for their government. About the 20th of August, (for these usurpers did not affix any date,) a long string of "Resolutions" from some persons pretending to be S. P. R. S. evidently originating in false information of the meetings at the New-England Coffee House, was communicated to "the eleven;" this was followed August 23d, 1821, by a huge folio letter of *seven pages*, large paper, and closely written, very officially communicated, and like the former, evidently founded in mistaken information, which to this day, they have obstinately refused to correct. This frightful communication accused "the eleven" of violating TRUTH, VIRTUE and JUSTICE. In a spirit of bitterness and domineering vengeance, they ungraciously assert that "the eleven" "*have violated every thing held dear and sacred* among Masons;" that their conduct "was *contrary to the principles of Justice and Morality, and calculated to destroy* all the *social* and *moral virtues.*"

They are several times, in this terrible letter, accused of "violating *truth*"—of "having forgotten the first principles of virtue, as well as their solemn obligations," and of "robbing"—aye, of "robbing!"—of "*striving to force from them by violence* (as was attempted with our D. G. M. of old) and by unmasonic means, what their sacred obligations bound them to preserve." They add: that "the eleven" "stand upon the brink of a precipice—another step and their fall is certain;" that if they do not give up every thing to these usurpers and acknowledge their fault "to save themselves from *certain destruction*," "they will find (when perhaps *too late*) that there is a *strength* and *power to punish* every offender." To avoid these empty threats, these *robbers*, these *liars*, these *assassins*, these *ruffians*, (for these are the charming epithets which are implied in the above extracts from this uncharitable letter, "written," as they say, "in the spirit of" *their* "candour and" of *their* "brotherly love,") "these eleven" are finally informed "that they must unequivocally see their *error*, and abandon in the most *solemn manner* their unmasonic conduct, and thus prevent the steps which *must be pursued* against them, and the *consequences* which *must inevitably follow*." By this violent proceeding "the eleven" were deprived of using their own judgment, nor were they allowed to have any opinion of their own, or to reflect upon the best course to be pursued; but were at once held up as a "mark for the finger of scorn to point at;" and, as it were, already turned without the pale of the Masonic Family. The accusations it contained, were so *indefinitely* made that they could not be replied to, and the bitter threats which were strewed throughout the virulent mass of cowardly wrath and incivility, so overbearingly directed against eleven peaceful and quiet brothers of correct morals and domestic habits, aroused them to a consideration of the subject and taught them to examine for the cause of such uneasiness in these persons who pretended to such deference and demanded such respect.

These eleven individuals, respectable for their love of *order* and regularity, were at that time, entirely ignorant of the monstrous usurpation of authority and imposition, which was practised upon them by these spurious violators of all the rules and regularity of the order. They were, as other Brothers generally now are, wholly unacquainted with the History of Sublime Freemasonry, or of its establishment and progress in this country—nor were the means of obtaining this information then, so easily to be acquired; so uninstructed were they in the subject of dispute as not to know that there existed any connexion between this domineering body and Joseph Cerneau; or, in fact, that such a character as Joseph Cerneau was ever in existence: but perceiving that all the fundamental principles of Freemasonry were most grossly outraged in this last insulting communication, in which, "the eleven" were supposed to be entirely destitute of all the finer feelings of human nature—that a violent attempt was making to degrade, crush and expel them from all the privileges of an Institution which they so highly prized—they seriously engaged in an inquiry for the *truth* of the matter, for procuring which, they now felt the necessity of being in earnest.

Scarcely had they began the investigation, when they discovered that this threatening company was *spurious* and *illegal*—and that its secretary had acknowledged as much a year or two previous, to ———. That it had recently stolen into existence, and had what it affected to call a Charter; but this pretended Charter was found to be signed by Joseph Cerneau & Co. who had been regularly expelled as "impostors and usurpers, Sept. 21st, 1813," for assuming and exercising powers and authority to which they had no right.

"The eleven" also learned that there still existed a regular body in this city, legally established A. D. 1783; that its authority emanated correctly from Frederick Wm. II. (more commonly called Frederick III.) of Prussia. To this latter and legal Body, they cheerfully surrendered all their papers, &c. &c. for inspection, and they applied to it to be regularly initiated.

Aug. 30th, 1821—they received another Communication from the Committee of the spurious—and as honest, upright Brothers, having no reasons for concealment, they openly informed the committee of impostors of their purpose. But as the vengeance of the intruders was now about to fall heavily on one, whom the usurpers could seriously injure, and deprive of his living, "the eleven" withdrew their application and patiently waited the event of the storm that was gathering.

Sept. 10th, 1821, a chief of the spurious and illegal sent for one of "the eleven" and entreated him to use his best endeavours to heal the wounds which would be likely to ensue in the Masonic family, and begged him to use his influence with the Brothers at the New-England Coffee House to sign an application to his body, and they should be received. The Brother stating some objections to this plan, the Spurious Chief concluded his intercession with the following pathetic appeal to his feelings: "Will you not do it," (that is, exert his influence to have "the eleven" apply to him;) "will you not do it for my sake—for the sake of Masonry will you not do it?" The Brother informed "the eleven" of the proposition which had been made to him, and the promise annexed to it.

Upon mature deliberation "the eleven" concluded, that after being received, it would be lawful for them to retire again, should the documents of the spurious, upon a careful inspection, be found illegal; and as it was then, and is still believed, that in all disagreements *gentlemen can make propositions which gentlemen can receive without any derogation from principles of honour or urbanity*, "the eleven," on the 14th of September, 1821, consented, (to use the words of the application,) "for the sake of HARMONY, PEACE and GOOD-WILL, and an anxious desire of healing all difficulties in the craft." Further, in their letter of application, these individuals, in reply to the repeated assertions in writing and in common conversation of the illegal pretenders, use these words; "as some false and malicious reports have been promulgated respecting our having formed an 'Association' for the purpose of receiving candidates and conferring on them said" [Sublime] "Degrees, we think it necessary here to state, that such reports are unfounded and without the least *shadow* of TRUTH, inasmuch as our number has *not increased* from the period of our first meeting." This letter was signed by "eleven" individuals—and they were all, who, *at that date*, had any right, title or claim to Masonic papers of any kind, or who in any way belonged to the meetings at the New-England Coffee House. This application was handed *"unsealed"** to the Chief, as they call him, at whose earnest solicitation it had been made; nor did "the eleven" ask this as a gratuity; they proffered a handsome remuneration or fee at their reception.

Sept. 22d, 1821—This illegal body "Resolved, that the application was informal and could not be referred to a Committee." This resolution however held out the expectation that a modification of the letter would be acceptable, and in their conversations, they made great protestations of friendship, and told the pleasure it would give them to prevent any disturbance, and to quiet all uneasy feelings—whereupon "the eleven" being real friends to *order*, *peace*, and HARMONY, and firmly opposed to all *irregularity* and *misrule*, did, on the 25th of Sept. 1821, (the date of the official copy of their Secretary is incorrect,) agree to, and did sign another letter of application, worded just as P. J. their "Representative" desired; he having first most solemnly pledged his sacred honour to prove the strict legality of his body, and the incorrectness of the other. (But, Brothers, this yet remains an unredeemed pledge, and, from the preceding documents of this book, it must ever remain unredeemed.) This letter was the same day handed to one who claimed to be a Chief among the Spurious, and while this application was in the possession of these pretended "Friends of Peace, sitting in the valley of Charleston;" you would, Brothers, have never imagined the perfidy of these usurpers! while this letter was in their hands unacted upon, an earnest attempt was made by them

* We challenge an investigation upon this point. They officially say it was *"sealed,"*—which is positively denied.

to have a petition signed for the Grand Lodge of this State to expel these eleven Blue Masons from the Masonic Family. Here was deceit and treachery superior to that of Virgil's Sinon:—their object apparently was to gratify their ill-humoured spleen upon eleven peaceful Brothers, whose only crime was, that they dared to think for themselves, and who evidently showed an inclination to disbelieve such things as were not true, without any regard to the standing of the person who might utter them—certainly the effect was to injure them every way in their power, even after having solicited them to adopt the course they did. But probably to redeem the pledge of "*their regularity*" which they had so often and so positively given, was found to be impossible with Brothers, who they knew would *look on both sides of letters* that might be shown them; and as the only alternative in a narrow and vindictive mind, the easiest way was to *crush* those whom in fair reasoning, they had no arguments to *convince*. But many whose signatures were applied for to this petition, had too much honour and nobleness of soul to lend their aid in support of these overbearing usurpers; hence the sorrowful paper with some signatures, was never presented to the Grand Lodge—and some of its signers have confessed that they were imposed upon, and asked pardon for ever having listened to the deceivers on a subject that would so deeply affect any Brother's welfare.

After the usurpers had held four or five meetings and admitted such as members of their "Friends of Peace," as would vote to reject the application, Nov. 9th 1821, this spurious body, (to use their own words,) "resolved to notify" ["the eleven"] "that their application was informal," "and to inform them" how they might again apply. Perhaps the candid reader has already seen enough of their duplicity—but the author will only add one more instance, reserving several for a future occasion. Br. *****, was every way entitled to be elected master of Lodge No. —— but as he had shown some independence of mind in refusing to assent to all their plans—the spurious desired "to put him down;" to accomplish this, as they had made many Brothers believe that "the eleven" were monsters, they about this time, got a committee of his Lodge to wait upon their pretended mightinesses to examine papers, of the correctness of which they even now say they were incompetent to decide. The impostors *forged the name of this Brother*, upon a list with "the eleven." and made the blue committee believe he was guilty of—what? of thinking their pretended body usurpers. What the views or opinions of this respectable Brother, are, or have been, are entirely unknown to "the eleven," as he never was in any way associated with them in the subject of this history.

One of "the eleven," unconscious of the existence of any irregular body of Sublime Freemasons, had previously made an application to the usurpers, and they refused to notice his application, "as he was too young a Mason"—he having been only initiated during the last war; at the same time they had two who were younger, in their illegal body, and they have since admitted one young man who had not been raised to a Blue Master more than about three weeks when they received him. So much for the consistency of Impostors.

Nov. 11th 1821—"The eleven" met at the New-England Coffee House, and after reading the communications of the spurious which have been alluded to, and these being under consideration, but more particularly the resolves in reply to the solicited applications and promised admission which had been made in the utmost good faith and in a respectful manner by "the eleven," it was "*Resolved*, That after waiting with much patience and anxiety from Sept. 14th 1821, to Nov. 10th 1821, during which time the illegal body had had seven or more metings—during which time others had applied and been admitted by them, that the conduct of the pretenders must inevitably be considered as an equivocation, not compatible with their solicitations, nor consonant with the deportment of one Freemason to another; more particularly, 'the eleven' protest against their low artifice to obtain the names of the persons who had met at the New-England Coffee House, with a view to their expulsion,—therefore, unanimously resolved, never to have any thing further to do with these ungenerous usurpers."

A part of "the eleven" once more applied to the regular Supreme Council, which had been founded in 1783, (the Grand Commander having withdrawn from the Council during the present disturbance, from the nature of his vocation, and having desired to have no voice either directly or indirectly in the transactions which might ensue, desired not to be consulted in any respect about the business;) the Supreme Council correctly organized under the next officer, was in possession of all the requisite documents—and happily for the cause of Freemasonry, he, and the remaining members of the Council were not within the reach of the "tender mercies" of their revengeful charity.

The legal Council proceeded to a consideration of the subject which by this time had obtained some adventitious importance: scarcely had they engaged in the discussion, when, like Virgil's harpies, the illegal body attempted to stop their progress by professing a great desire for harmony, and for healing all difficulties and removing every obstacle to a complete union of all parties, and about the last of Nov. 1821, begging the Council to defer all further consideration of the subject for a few days, and naming the coming Christmas (1821) as ample time to accomplish this project. This proposition was readily acceded to. But on the 9th January 1822, a further time of ten days or a fortnight was interceded for to complete their arrangements. As the object was important, this further delay was also granted. Saturday 9th Feb. 1822, all postponements agreed on having completely expired, the Supreme Council determined to be trifled with no longer, and proceeded to commence the initiation of six of "the eleven," and at different meetings from that date until Christmas 1822—these six received S. P. R. S. with all the lower degrees.

The author now ingenuously appeals to the candid reader, whether in all this history of "the eleven," there was any threats or unmasonic conduct? If the spurious neglected to convince them of their errors, the fault was on the side of those who overflowing with *sensibility*, boasted so much greater light and knowledge; and "the eleven" confidently believe that when all their conduct is put together and impartially considered, that there will remain nothing uncivil, impolite, or wanting in the honourable conduct of gentlemen.

To be particular he has necessarily been somewhat prolix, but he will hazard one observation more before he concludes—that, the repeated intercessions of the illegal, to have the initiation of "six" out of "the eleven" deferred so often, was completely acknowledging in strong terms the legality of the Council to which they applied.

The candid reader will easily discover, that, this particular and minute statement of facts, *has no connexion whatever with the regular body* of Sublime Freemasons into which a part of "the eleven" have been since initiated—nor can the candour or veracity of that brother be very great, who will hazard the assertion that it has any such connexion. Freemasonry rests on TRUTH, who violates that principle, saps the very base and foundation of the ancient institution. Should seventy worthy Brothers regularly initiated (many of whom are venerable for their age as well as their morals,) be reviled for the actions of six?—of six young men, who at the time of these so much boasted applications were quiet, uninitiated individuals? Shall usurpers in their spleen dictate to a legally constituted body whom it shall admit to membership? Each generous bosom answers—no.

As a vindication of the regular body who admitted such of "the eleven" as applied for initiation, and the *self-defence* of those admitted, have caused this appendix; the unprejudiced reader who will allow to others even a portion of the same honourable feelings which govern himself, will readily excuse in the preceding history any expression which may seem, at first sight, harsh and uncharitable —more particularly when he reflects that those who have for several years broken through every established rule of the order and are expelled from it, are no longer entitled to claim an interchange of those endearing civilities, which are ever accorded in charity to a brother in error when not expelled. Nor can those who transgress expect that deference and respect which is due only to the regularly initiated whatever may be their standing in society. Though slighted, censured, *betrayed*, "the eleven" ever demeaned themselves quietly, modestly and with perfect good faith throughout the whole transaction; nor with anger do they view the gross violation of honour practised upon them—but they pity and compassionate the deluded victims of one unacquainted with our language, and a stranger to our shores.

From honourable feeling for transgressors, and generous motives, this publication has been delayed until delay has been by some deemed a crime, and by a few others construed into an acquiescence in the authority of the usurpers. But never will they "while breath they draw," cease to reply and defend themselves, and the Regular Body with whom they have been incorporated. At the same time, they remember, (it cannot be easily forgotten) that these impostors once attempted to "gag" the press—I say *these impostors*, for it is believed that on this occasion all besides the impostors, were opposed to such a tyrannic proceeding; the time here alluded to, was about 10th May, 1822, when a notice was served upon the printers in whose papers, these impostors had attacked the author, to prevent their publishing any reply in self-defence. Thank God my native state was not so far involved in the rudeness of the dark ages, as to listen to such cowardly despotism—as to allow an attack in a public newspaper and forbid an answer to it. Generous men, my brothers, will never be governed by malice, deceit or arbitrary authority; and to preserve unsullied a good name and reputation, becomes to every gentleman, an object too sacred to suffer blight or mildew from despotic power to overcloud it, or to permit even the attempt to pass unanswered.

"May the blessing of Heaven rest upon us and all *regular* Freemasons." Amen.

P. S. All the Regular Bodies of Sublime Freemasons will, as is customary, be steadily supplied with the usual RED LISTS of the irregular and expelled; and they ere long may expect another publication upon this subject.

Note to Page 23. The word "*last*" in Br. De La Motta's expulsion, upon which the usurpers have built so much of their reply, is not in the original in his own handwriting, which is now before the Editor; but he did not conceive himself at liberty to correct the error of the printer.

FINIS.

M W Brother
This Pamphlet will explain
the strange letter of J. S. Cogdell
read before your Most Wpful body
27th Dec last — I have obtained
it expressly for the information
of your Gr Lodge — Much of the Appendix is to me enigmatical — but
it was felt — and Brs Cogdell & Bacot u
dared to go into court where every a
llusion should be substantiated — but the
dared not to do it — as appears by this pa
mphlet sent you —
Candor —

INDEX

Prepared by S. Brent Morris, PhD, 33°, G∴C∴

D

G

H

I

J

ARTURO DE HOYOS, 33°, G∴C∴

Grand Archivist & Grand Historian, Supreme Council, 33°, S.J.
SRRS Fellow & Dual Mackey Scholar
Past Master McAllen Lodge No. 1110, Texas
Member Quatuor Coronati Lodge No. 2076, E.C.
Fellow of the Philalethes Society
Fellow, Texas Lodge of Research
Grand Abbot, Society of Blue Friars

S. BRENT MORRIS, PH.D., 33°, G∴C∴

Managing Editor, *Scottish Rite Journal,* & Editor, *Herecom*

SRRS Fellow & Mackey Scholar

Past Master Patmos-Solomon's Lodge No. 70, Maryland

Past Master Quatuor Coronati Lodge No. 2076, E.C.

Fellow of the Philalethes Society

Fellow, Texas Lodge of Research

Past Grand Abbot, Society of Blue Friars

Colophon

Layout and design by S. Brent Morris, 33°, G∴C∴

Composed in InDesign CS5 using Garamond Premier Pro
and Academy Engraved

Cover and half-title page design by Steve Adams, 32°, K.C.C.H
EsotericEditions.com

Back cover design by Jeffrey Barnes

Related Titles from Westphalia Press

Ancient Mysteries and Modern Masonry: The Collected Writings of Jewel P. Lightfoot, Edited by Billy J. Hamilton Jr.

Jewel P. Lightfoot. Former Attorney General of the State of Texas. Past Grand Master of the Masonic Grand Lodge of Texas. From humble beginnings in rural Arkansas, he worked to become an educated man who excelled in law and Freemasonry. He was a gentleman of his time, well-known as a scholar, public speaker, and Masonic philosopher.

Essay on The Mysteries and the True Object of The Brotherhood of Freemasons
by Jason Williams

This isn't a reprint of a classic. It's a new rendition with new life breathed into it, to be enjoyed both by the layperson trying to understand the Craft and Masonic scholars taking a deeper dive into the fraternity's golden years—when the concepts of liberty and equality were still fresh.

Female Emancipation and Masonic Membership: An Essential Collection
By Guillermo De Los Reyes Heredia

Female Emancipation and Masonic Membership: An Essential Combination is a collection of essays on Freemasonry and gender that promotes a transatlantic discussion of the study of the history of women and Freemasonry and their contribution in different countries.

Freemasonry, Heir to the Enlightenment
by Cécile Révauger

Modern Freemasonry may have mythical roots in Solomon's time but is really the heir to the Enlightenment. Ever since the early eighteenth century freemasons have endeavored to convey the values of the Enlightenment in the cultural, political and religious fields, in Europe, the American colonies and the emerging United States.

Freemasonry: A French View
by Roger Dachez and Alain Bauer

Perhaps one should speak not of Freemasonry but of Freemasonries in the plural. In each country Masonic historiography has developed uniqueness. Two of the best known French Masonic scholars present their own view of the worldwide evolution and challenging mysteries of the fraternity over the centuries.

Worlds of Print: The Moral Imagination of an Informed Citizenry, 1734 to 1839
by John Slifko

John Slifko argues that freemasonry was representative and played an important role in a larger cultural transformation of literacy and helped articulate the moral imagination of an informed democratic citizenry via fast emerging worlds of print.

Why Thirty-Three?: Searching for Masonic Origins
by S. Brent Morris, PhD

What "high degrees" were in the United States before 1830? What were the activities of the Order of the Royal Secret, the precursor of the Scottish Rite? A complex organization with a lengthy pedigree like Freemasonry has many basic foundational questions waiting to be answered, and that's what this book does: answers questions.

The Great Transformation: Scottish Freemasonry 1725-1810
by Dr. Mark C. Wallace

This book examines Scottish Freemasonry in its wider British and European contexts between the years 1725 and 1810. The Enlightenment effectively crafted the modern mason and propelled Freemasonry into a new era marked by growing membership and the creation of the Grand Lodge of Scotland.

Getting the Third Degree: Fraternalism, Freemasonry and History
Edited by Guillermo De Los Reyes and Paul Rich

As this engaging collection demonstrates, the doors being opened on the subject range from art history to political science to anthropology, as well as gender studies, sociology and more. The organizations discussed may insist on secrecy, but the research into them belies that.

The Great Transformation: Scottish Freemasonry 1725-1810
by Dr. Mark C. Wallace

This book examines Scottish Freemasonry in its wider British and European contexts between the years 1725 and 1810. The Enlightenment effectively crafted the modern mason and propelled Freemasonry into a new era marked by growing membership and the creation of the Grand Lodge of Scotland.

Getting the Third Degree: Fraternalism, Freemasonry and History
Edited by Guillermo De Los Reyes and Paul Rich

As this engaging collection demonstrates, the doors being opened on the subject range from art history to political science to anthropology, as well as gender studies, sociology and more. The organizations discussed may insist on secrecy, but the research into them belies that.

Freemasonry: A French View
by Roger Dachez and Alain Bauer

Perhaps one should speak not of Freemasonry but of Freemasonries in the plural. In each country Masonic historiography has developed uniqueness. Two of the best known French Masonic scholars present their own view of the worldwide evolution and challenging mysteries of the fraternity over the centuries.

Worlds of Print: The Moral Imagination of an Informed Citizenry, 1734 to 1839
by John Slifko

John Slifko argues that freemasonry was representative and played an important role in a larger cultural transformation of literacy and helped articulate the moral imagination of an informed democratic citizenry via fast emerging worlds of print.

Why Thirty-Three?: Searching for Masonic Origins
by S. Brent Morris, PhD

What "high degrees" were in the United States before 1830? What were the activities of the Order of the Royal Secret, the precursor of the Scottish Rite? A complex organization with a lengthy pedigree like Freemasonry has many basic foundational questions waiting to be answered, and that's what this book does: answers questions.

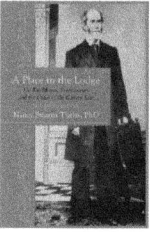

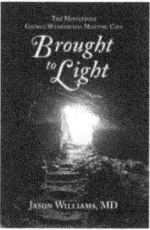

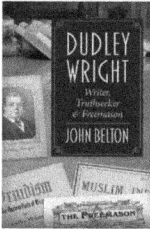

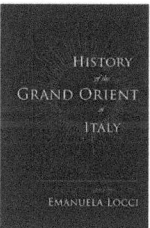

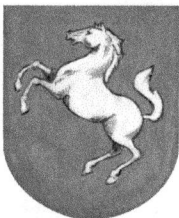

www.ingramcontent.com/pod-product-compliance
Lightning Source LLC
Chambersburg PA
CBHW071959260326
41914CB00004B/862
9781633919433